'Subtle is the Lord . . .'

Albert Einstein 1896.
Aus einem Gruppenbilde der Maturitäts-
klasse der "Gewerbeschule" Aarau.

Albert Einstein in 1896.
(Einstein Archive)

'Subtle is the Lord...'

The Science and the Life of Albert Einstein

ABRAHAM PAIS
Rockefeller University

OXFORD UNIVERSITY PRESS
Oxford   New York   Toronto   Melbourne

Oxford University Press

Oxford London Glasgow
New York Toronto Melbourne Auckland
Delhi Bombay Calcutta Madras Karachi
Kuala Lumpur Singapore Hong Kong Tokyo
Nairobi Dar es Salaam Cape Town

and associate companies in
Beirut Berlin Ibadan Mexico City Nicosia

© Oxford University Press 1982
First published by Oxford University Press, Oxford and New York, 1982
First issued as an Oxford University Press paperback, 1983

Library of Congress Cataloging in Publication Data
Pais, Abraham, 1918–
Subtle is the Lord—
Bibliography: p. Includes index.
1. Einstein, Albert, 1879–1955. 2. Physicists—
Biography. 3. Physics—History. I. Title.
QC16.E5P26 530′.092′4 [B] 82-2273
ISBN 0-19-853907-X AACR2
ISBN 0-19-520438-7 (US pbk.)

British Library Cataloguing in Publication Data
Pais, Abraham
Subtle is the Lord—the science and the life of
Albert Einstein.
1. Einstein, Albert 2. Physicists—Biography
I. Title
530′.092′4 QC16.E5
ISBN 0-19-853907-X
ISBN 0-19-285138-1 (UK pbk.)

Printing (last digit): 987654321

Printed in the United States of America

To Sara, Joshua, and Daniel

'Science without religion is lame, religion without science is blind.' So Einstein once wrote to explain his personal creed: 'A religious person is devout in the sense that he has no doubt of the significance of those super-personal objects and goals which neither require nor are capable of rational foundation.' His was not a life of prayer and worship. Yet he lived by a deep faith—a faith not capable of rational foundation—that there are laws of Nature to be discovered. His lifelong pursuit was to discover them. His realism and his optimism are illuminated by his remark: 'Subtle is the Lord, but malicious He is not' ('Raffiniert ist der Herrgott aber boshaft ist er nicht.'). When asked by a colleague what he meant by that, he replied: 'Nature hides her secret because of her essential loftiness, but not by means of ruse' ('Die Natur verbirgt ihr Geheimnis durch die Erhabenheit ihres Wesens, aber nicht durch List.').

To the Reader

Turn to the table of contents, follow the entries in italics, and you will find an almost entirely nonscientific biography of Einstein. Turn to the first chapter and you will find a nontechnical tour through this book, some personal reminiscences, and an attempt at a general assessment.

The principal aim of this work is to present a scientific biography of Albert Einstein. I shall attempt to sketch the concepts of the physical world as they were when Einstein became a physicist, how he changed them, and what scientific inheritance he left. This book is an essay in open history, open because Einstein's oeuvre left us with unresolved questions of principle. The search for their answers is a central quest of physics today. Some issues cannot be discussed without entering into mathematical details, but I have tried to hold these to a minimum by directing the reader to standard texts wherever possible.

Science, more than anything else, was Einstein's life, his devotion, his refuge, and his source of detachment. In order to understand the man, it is necessary to follow his scientific ways of thinking and doing. But that is not sufficient. He was also a highly gifted stylist of the German language, a lover of music, a student of philosophy. He was deeply concerned about the human condition. (In his later years, he used to refer to his daily reading of *The New York Times* as his adrenaline treatment.) He was a husband, a father, a stepfather. He was a Jew. And he is a legend. All these elements are touched on in this story; follow the entries in italics.

Were I asked for a one-sentence biography of Einstein, I would say, 'He was the freest man I have ever known.' Had I to compose a one-sentence scientific biography of him, I would write, "Better than anyone before or after him, he knew how to invent invariance principles and make use of statistical fluctuations.' Were I permitted to use one illustration, I would offer the following drawing:

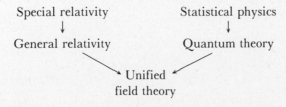

Special relativity   Statistical physics
↓   ↓
General relativity   Quantum theory

Unified
field theory

with the caption, 'The science and the life of Albert Einstein.' This picture with its entries and its arrows represents my most concise summary of Einstein's greatness, his vision, and his frailty. This book is largely an attempt to explain this cryptic description of the skeletal drawing. Toward the end of the book, the drawing will return.

The generosity, wisdom, knowledge, and criticism of many have been invaluable to me in preparing this work. To all of them I express my deep gratitude. No one helped me more than Helen Dukas, more familiar than anyone else at this time with Einstein's life, trusted guide through the Einstein Archives in Princeton. Dear Helen, thank you; it was wonderful. I have benefited importantly from discussions with Res Jost, Sam Treiman, and George Uhlenbeck, each of whom read nearly the whole manuscript, made many suggestions for improvement, and gave me much encouragement. I also gratefully record discussions on particular subjects: with Valentin Bargmann, Banesh Hoffmann, and Ernst Straus on Einstein's life, on general relativity, and on unified field theory; with Robert Dicke, Peter Havas, Malcolm Perry, Dennis Sciama, and John Stachel on relativity; with Armand Borel on Poincaré; with Eddie Cohen, Mark Kac, and Martin Klein on statistical physics; with Anne Kox on Lorentz; and with Harold Cherniss and Felix Gilbert on topics ranging from Greek atomism to the Weimar Republic. Special thanks go to Beat Glaus from the ETH and Günther Rasche from the University of Zürich for helping me find my way in archives in Zürich. To all of them as well as to those numerous others who answered questions and inspired with comments: thank you again.

This book was completed at The Institute for Advanced Study in Princeton. I thank Harry Woolf for his hospitality and for support from the Director's Fund. I am greatly beholden to the Alfred P. Sloan Foundation for an important grant that helped me in many phases of preparation. For permission to quote from unpublished material, I express my deep appreciation to the Einstein Estate, the Pauli Estate, the Rijksarchief in the Hague (Lorentz correspondence), and the Boerhaave Museum in Leiden (Ehrenfest correspondence). I also thank the K. Vetenskapsakademiens Nobel Kommittéer in Stockholm, and in particular Bengt Nagel, for making available to me the documentation regarding Einstein's Nobel Prize.

I had the great good fortune of my dear wife Sara's counsel and support.

I have left the text of this Preface as it was written before the death of Helen Dukas on February 10, 1982.

On references

Each chapter has its own set of references, which are marked in the text by a square bracket containing a letter and a number. The following abbreviations have been used for entries that occur frequently:

AdP: *Annalen der Physik* (Leipzig).

  EB: *Albert Einstein–Michele Besso Correspondance 1903–1955* (P. Speziali, Ed.). Hermann, Paris, 1972.

PAW: *Sitzungsberichte*, Preussische Akademie der Wissenschaften.

  Se: Carl Seelig, *Albert Einstein*. Europa Verlag, Zürich, 1960.

Contents
(Entries in italics are almost entirely biographical)

'Subtle is the Lord . . . '

I

INTRODUCTORY

1

Purpose and Plan

It must have been around 1950. I was accompanying Einstein on a walk from The Institute for Advanced Study to his home, when he suddenly stopped, turned to me, and asked me if I really believed that the moon exists only if I look at it. The nature of our conversation was not particularly metaphysical. Rather, we were discussing the quantum theory, in particular what is doable and knowable in the sense of physical observation. The twentieth century physicist does not, of course, claim to have the definitive answer to this question. He does know, however, that the answer given by his nineteenth century ancestors will no longer do. They were almost exactly right, to be sure, as far as conditions of everyday life are concerned, but their answer cannot be extrapolated to things moving nearly as fast as light, or to things that are as small as atoms, or—in some respects—to things that are as heavy as stars. We now know better than before that what man can do under the best of circumstances depends on a careful specification of what those circumstances are. That, in very broad terms, is the lesson of the theory of relativity, which Einstein created, and of quantum mechanics, which he eventually accepted as (in his words) the most successful theory of our period but which, he believed, was none the less only provisional in character.

We walked on and continued talking about the moon and the meaning of the expression *to exist* as it refers to inanimate objects. When we reached 112 Mercer Street, I wished him a pleasant lunch, then returned to the Institute. As had been the case on many earlier occasions, I had enjoyed the walk and felt better because of the discussion even though it had ended inconclusively. I was used to that by then, and as I walked back I wondered once again about the question, Why does this man, who contributed so incomparably much to the creation of modern physics, remain so attached to the nineteenth century view of causality?

To make that question more precise, it is necessary to understand Einstein's credo in regard not just to quantum physics but to all of physics. That much I believe I know, and will endeavor to explain in what follows. However, in order to answer the question, one needs to know not only his beliefs but also how they came to be adopted. My conversations with Einstein taught me little about that. The issue was not purposely shunned; it simply was never raised. Only many years after Einstein's death did I see the beginnings of an answer when I realized that, nearly a decade before the discovery of modern quantum mechanics, he had been the first to understand that the nineteenth century ideal of causality was about to become a grave issue in quantum physics. However, while I know more now about the evolution of his thinking than I did when I walked with him, I would not go so far as to say that I now understand why he chose to believe what he did believe. When Einstein was fifty years old, he wrote in the introduction to the biography by his son-in-law Rudolph Kayser, 'What has perhaps been over-looked is the irrational, the inconsistent, the droll, even the insane, which nature, inexhaustibly operative, implants in an individual, seemingly for her own amusement. But these things are singled out only in the crucible of one's own mind.' Perhaps this statement is too optimistic about the reach of self-knowledge. Certainly it is a warning, and a fair one, to any biographer not to overdo answering every question he may legitimately raise.

I should briefly explain how it happened that I went on that walk with Einstein and why we came to talk about the moon. I was born in 1918 in Amsterdam. In 1941 I received my PhD with Léon Rosenfeld in Utrecht. Some time thereafter I went into hiding in Amsterdam. Eventually I was caught and sent to the Gestapo prison there. Those who were not executed were released shortly before VE Day. Immediately after the war I applied for a postdoctoral fellowship at the Niels Bohr Institute in Copenhagen and at The Institute for Advanced Study in Princeton where I hoped to work with Pauli. I was accepted at both places and first went to Copenhagen for one year. Soon thereafter, I worked with Bohr for a period of several months. The following lines from my account of that experience are relevant to the present subject: 'I must admit that in the early stages of the collaboration I did not follow Bohr's line of thinking a good deal of the time and was in fact often quite bewildered. I failed to see the relevance of such remarks as that Schroedinger was completely shocked in 1927 when he was told of the probability interpretation of quantum mechanics or a reference to some objection by Einstein in 1928, which apparently had no bearing whatever on the subject at hand. But it did not take very long before the fog started to lift. I began to grasp not only the thread of Bohr's arguments but also their purpose. Just as in many sports a player goes through warming-up exercises before entering the arena, so Bohr would relive the struggles which it took before the content of quantum mechanics was understood and accepted. I can say that in Bohr's mind this struggle started all over every single day. This, I am convinced, was Bohr's inexhaustible source of identity. Einstein appeared forever as his leading spiritual partner—even after the latter's death he would argue with him as if Einstein were still alive' [P1].

In September 1946 I went to Princeton. The first thing I learned was that, in the meantime, Pauli had gone to Zürich. Bohr also came to Princeton that same month. Both of us attended the Princeton Bicentennial Meetings. I missed my first opportunity to catch a glimpse of Einstein as he walked next to President Truman in the academic parade. However, shortly thereafter, Bohr introduced me to Einstein, who greeted a rather awed young man in a very friendly way. The conversation on that occasion soon turned to the quantum theory. I listened as the two of them argued. I recall no details but remember distinctly my first impressions: they liked and respected each other. With a fair amount of passion, they were talking past each other. And, as had been the case with my first discussions with Bohr, I did not understand what Einstein was talking about.

Not long thereafter, I encountered Einstein in front of the Institute and told him that I had not followed his argument with Bohr and asked if I could come to his office some time for further enlightenment. He invited me to walk home with him. So began a series of discussions that continued until shortly before his death.* I would visit with him in his office or accompany him (often together with Kurt Gödel) on his lunchtime walk home. Less often I would visit him there. In all, I saw him about once every few weeks. We always spoke in German, the language best suited to grasp both the nuances of what he had in mind and the flavor of his personality. Only once did he visit my apartment. The occasion was a meeting of the Institute faculty for the purpose of drafting a statement of our position in the 1954 Oppenheimer affair.

Einstein's company was comfortable and comforting to those who knew him. Of course, he well knew that he was a legendary figure in the eyes of the world. He accepted this as a fact of life. There was nothing in his personality to promote his mythical stature; nor did he relish it. Privately he would express annoyance if he felt that his position was being misused. I recall the case of Professor X, who had been quoted by the newspapers as having found solutions to Einstein's generalized equations of gravitation. Einstein said to me, 'Der Mann ist ein Narr,' the man is a fool, and added that, in his opinion, X could calculate but could not think. X had visited Einstein to discuss this work, and Einstein, always courteous, had said to him that his, X's, results would be important if true. Einstein was chagrined to have been quoted in the papers without this last provision. He said that he would keep silent on the matter but would not receive X again. According to Einstein, the whole thing started because X, in his enthusiasm, had repeated Einstein's opinion to some colleagues who saw the value of it as publicity for their university.

To those physicists who could follow his scientific thought and who knew him personally, the legendary aspect was never in the foreground— yet it was never wholly absent. I remember an occasion in 1947 when I was giving a talk at the Institute about the newly discovered π and μ mesons. Einstein walked in just after I had begun. I remember being speechless for the brief moment necessary to overcome a sense of the unreal. I recall a similar moment during a symposium** held

---

*My stay at the Institute had lost much of its attraction because Pauli was no longer there. As I was contemplating returning to Europe, Robert Oppenheimer informed me that he had been approached for the directorship of the Institute. He asked me to join him in building up physics there. I accepted. A year later, I was appointed to a five-year membership and in 1950 to a professorship at the Institute, where I remained until 1963.

**The speakers were J. R. Oppenheimer, I. I. Rabi, E. P. Wigner, H. P. Robertson, S. M. Clemence, and H. Weyl.

in Princeton on March 19, 1949, on the occasion of Einstein's seventieth birthday. Most of us were in our seats when Einstein entered the hall. Again there was this brief hush before we stood to greet him.

Nor do I believe that such reactions were typical only of those who were much younger than he. There were a few occasions when Pauli and I were both with him. Pauli, not known for an excess of awe, was just slightly different in Einstein's company. One could perceive his sense of reverence. Bohr, too, was affected in a similar way, differences in scientific outlook notwithstanding.

Whenever I met Einstein, our conversations might range far and wide but invariably the discussion would turn to physics. Such discussions would touch only occasionally on matters of past history. We talked mainly about the present and the future. When relativity was the issue, he would often talk of his efforts to unify gravitation and electromagnetism and of his hopes for the next steps. His faith rarely wavered in the path he had chosen. Only once did he express a reservation to me when he said, in essence, 'I am not sure that differential geometry is the framework for further progress, but, if it is, then I believe I am on the right track.' (This remark must have been made some time during his last few years.)

The main topic of discussion, however, was quantum physics. Einstein never ceased to ponder the meaning of the quantum theory. Time and time again, the argument would turn to quantum mechanics and its interpretation. He was explicit in his opinion that the most commonly held views on this subject could not be the last word, but he also had more subtle ways of expressing his dissent. For example, he would never refer to a wave function as *die Wellenfunktion* but would always use mathematical terminology: *die Psifunktion*. I was never able to arouse much interest in him about the new particles which appeared on the scene in the late 1940s and especially in the early 1950s. It was apparent that he felt that the time was not ripe to worry about such things and that these particles would eventually appear as solutions to the equations of a unified theory. In some sense, he may well prove to be right.

The most interesting thing I learned from these conversations was how Einstein thought and, to some extent, who he was. Since I never became his co-worker, the discussions were not confined to any particular problem. Yet we talked physics, often touching on topics of a technical nature. We did not talk much about statistical physics, an area to which he had contributed so much but which no longer was the center of his interests. If the special and the general theory of relativity came up only occasionally, that was because at that time the main issues appeared to have been settled. Recall that the renewed surge of interest in general relativity began just after his death. However, I do remember him talking about Lorentz, the one father figure in his life; once we also talked about Poincaré. If we argued so often about the quantum theory, that was more his choice than mine. It had not taken long before I grasped the essence of the Einstein–Bohr dialogue: complementarity versus objective reality. It became clear to me from listening to them both that the advent of quantum mechanics in 1925 represented a far greater break with the past than had been the case with the coming of special relativity in 1905 or of general relativity in 1915. That had not been obvious to me earlier, as I belong to the generation which was exposed to 'ready-made' quantum mechanics. I came to understand how wrong I was in accepting a rather wide-spread belief that Einstein simply did not care anymore about the quantum theory. On the contrary, he wanted nothing more than to find a unified field theory which not only would join together gravitational and electromagnetic forces but also would provide the basis for a new interpretation of quantum phenomena. About relativity he spoke with detachment, about the quantum theory with passion. The quantum was his demon. I learned only much later that Einstein had once said to his friend Otto Stern, 'I have thought a hundred times as much about the quantum problems as I have about general relativity theory' [J1]. From my own experiences I can only add that this statement does not surprise me.

We talked of things other than physics: politics, the bomb, the Jewish destiny, and also of less weighty matters. One day I told Einstein a Jewish joke. Since he relished that, I began to save good ones I heard for a next occasion. As I told these stories, his face would change. Suddenly he would look much younger, almost like a naughty schoolboy. When the punch line came, he would let go with contented laughter, a memory I particularly cherish.

An unconcern with the past is a privilege of youth. In all the years I knew Einstein, I never read any of his papers, on the simple grounds that I already knew what to a physicist was memorable in them and did not need to know what had been superseded. Now it is obvious to me that I might have been able to ask him some very interesting questions had I been less blessed with ignorance. I might then have learned some interesting facts, but at a price. My discussions with Einstein never were historical interviews. They concerned live physics. I am glad it never was otherwise.

I did read Einstein's papers as the years went by, and my interest in him as an historical figure grew. Thus it came about that I learned to follow his science and his life from the end to the beginnings. I gradually became aware of the most difficult task in studying past science: to forget temporarily what came afterward. The study of his papers, discussions with others who knew him, access to the Einstein Archives, personal reminiscences—these are the ingredients which led to this book. Without disrespect or lack of gratitude, I have found the study of the scientific papers to be incomparably more important than anything else.

In the preface, I promised a tour through this book. The tour starts here. For ease I introduce the notation, to be used only in this and in the next chapter, of referring to, for example, Chapter 3 as (3) and to Chapter 5, Section (c), as (5c). To repeat, symbols such as [J1] indicate references to be found at the end of the chapter.

I shall begin by indicating how the personal biography is woven into the narrative. The early period, from Einstein's birth in 1879 to the beginning of his academic career as Privatdozent in Bern in February 1908, is discussed in (3), which contains a sketch of his childhood, his school years (contrary to popular belief he earned high marks in elementary as well as high school), his brief religious phase, his student days, his initial difficulties in finding a job, and most of the period he spent at the patent office in Bern, a period that witnesses the death of his father, his marriage to Mileva Marić, and the birth of his first son. In (10a) we follow him from the time he began as a Privatdozent in Bern to the end, in March 1911, of his associate professorship at the University of Zürich. In that period his second son was born. The next phase (11a) is his time as full professor in Prague (March 1911 to August 1912). In (12a) we follow him back to Zürich as a professor at the Federal Institute of Technology (ETH) (August 1912 to April 1914). The circumstances surrounding his move from Zürich to Berlin, his separation from Mileva and the two boys, and his reaction to the events of the First World War, are described in (14a). The story of the Berlin days is continued in (16) which ends with Einstein's permanent departure from Europe. This period includes years of illness, which did not noticeably affect his productivity; his divorce from Mileva and marriage to his cousin Elsa; and the death in his home in Berlin, of his mother (16a). Following this, (16b) and (16c) are devoted to the abrupt emergence in 1919 of Einstein (whose genius had already been fully recognized for some time by his scientific peers) as a charismatic world figure and to my views on the causes of this striking phenomenon. Next, (16d), devoted to Einstein's hectic years in Berlin in the 1920s, his early involvements with the Jewish destiny, his continued interest in pacifism, and his connection with the League of Nations, ends with his final departure from Germany in December 1932. The Belgian interlude and the early years in Princeton are described in (25b), the final years of his life in (26) to (28). The book ends with a detailed Einstein chronology (32).

Before starting on a similar tour of the scientific part, I interject a few remarks on Einstein and politics and on Einstein as a philosopher and humanist.

Whenever I think of Einstein and politics, I recall my encounter with him in the late evening of Sunday, April 11, 1954. That morning, a column by the Alsop brothers had appeared in the New York *Herald Tribune,* entitled 'Next McCarthy target: the leading physicists,' which began by stating that the junior senator from Wisconsin was getting ready to play his ace in the hole. I knew that the Oppenheimer case was about to break. That evening I was working in my office at the Institute when the phone rang and a Washington operator asked to speak to Dr Oppenheimer. I replied that Oppenheimer was out of town. (In fact, he was in Washington.) The operator asked for Dr Einstein. I told her that Einstein was not at the office and that his home number was unlisted. The operator told me next that her party wished to speak to me. The director of the Washington

Bureau of the Associated Press came on the line and told me that the Oppenheimer case would be all over the papers on Tuesday morning. He was eager for a statement by Einstein as soon as possible. I realized that pandemonium on Mercer Street the next morning might be avoided by a brief statement that evening and so said that I would talk it over with Einstein and would call back in any event. I drove to Mercer Street and rang the bell; Helen Dukas, Einstein's secretary, let me in. I apologized for appearing at such a late hour and said it would be good if I could talk briefly with the professor, who meanwhile had appeared at the top of the stairs dressed in his bathrobe and asked, 'Was ist los?' What is going on? He came down and so did his stepdaughter Margot. After I told him the reason for my call, Einstein burst out laughing. I was a bit taken aback and asked him what was so funny. He said that the problem was simple. All Oppenheimer needed to do, he said, was go to Washington, tell the officials that they were fools, and then go home. On further discussion, we decided that a brief statement was called for. We drew it up, and Einstein read it over the phone to the AP director in Washington. The next day Helen Dukas was preparing lunch when she saw cars in front of the house and cameras being unloaded. In her apron (she told me) she ran out of the house to warn Einstein, who was on his way home. When he arrived at the front door, he declined to talk to reporters.

Was Einstein's initial response correct? Of course it was, even though his suggestion would not and could not be followed. I remember once attending a seminar by Bertrand de Jouvenel in which he singled out the main characteristic of a political problem: it has no answer, only a compromise. Nothing was more alien to Einstein than to settle any issue by compromise, in his life or in his science. He often spoke out on political problems, always steering to their answer. Such statements have often been called naive.* In my view, Einstein was not only not naive but highly aware of the nature of man's sorrows and his follies. His utterances on political matters did not always address the immediately practicable, and I do not think that on the whole they were very influential. However, he knowingly and gladly paid the price of sanity.

As another comment on political matters, I should like to relate a story I was told in 1979 by Israel's President Navon. After the death of the then Israeli president, Weizman, in November 1952, Ben Gurion and his cabinet decided to offer the presidency to Einstein. Abba Eban was instructed to transmit the offer from Washington (27). Shortly thereafter, in a private conversation, Ben Gurion asked Navon (who at that time was his personal secretary), 'What are we going to do if he accepts?'

Einstein often lent his name to pacifist statements, doing so for the first time in 1914 (14a). In 1916 he gave an interview to the Berlin paper *Die Vossische Zeitung* about the work on Mach by his pacifist friend Friedrich Adler, then in jail

---

*Oppenheimer's description, 'There was always with him a wonderful purity at once childlike and profoundly stubborn' [O1] shows the writer's talent for almost understanding everything.

for having shot and killed Karl Stürgkh, the prime minister of Austria [E1]. After the death of Leo Arons, a physicist Einstein admired for his political courage but whom he did not know personally, he wrote an obituary in *Sozialistische Monatshefte* [E2]. After the assassination in 1922 of his acquaintance Walther Rathenau, foreign minister of the Weimar republic and a physicist by education, Einstein wrote of him in *Neue Rundschau:* 'It is no art to be an idealist if one lives in cloud-cuckoo land. He, however, was an idealist even though he lived on earth and knew its smell better than almost anyone else' [E3]. In 1923 Einstein became a cofounder of the Association of Friends of the New Russia. Together with Lorentz, Marie Curie, Henry Bergson, and others, he worked for a time as a member of the League of Nations' Committee for Intellectual Cooperation (16d). Among those he proposed or endorsed for the Nobel peace prize (31) were Masaryk; Herbert Runham Brown, honorary secretary of War Resisters International; Carl von Ossietzky, at the time in a German concentration camp; and the organization Youth Aliyah. He spoke out about the plight of the Jews and helped. Numerous are the affidavits he signed in order to bring Jews from Europe to the United States.

Pacifism and supranationalism were Einstein's two principal political ideals. In the 1920s he supported universal disarmament and a United Europe (16d). After the Second World War, he especially championed the concept of world government, and the peaceful—and only peaceful—uses of atomic energy (27). That pacifism and disarmament were out of place in the years 1933 to 1945 was both deeply regrettable and obvious to him (25b). In 1939 he sent his sensible letter to President Roosevelt on the military implications of nuclear fission. In 1943 he signed a contract with the U.S. Navy Bureau of Ordnance as occasional consultant (his fee was $25 per day).* Perhaps his most memorable contribution of that period is his saying, 'I am in the Navy, but I was not required to get a Navy haircut.' [B1]. He never forgave the Germans (27).**

Einstein's political orientation, which for simplicity may be called leftist, derived from his sense of justice, not from an approval of method or a sharing of philosophy. 'In Lenin I honor a man who devoted all his strength and sacrificed his person to the realization of social justice. I do not consider his method to be proper,' he wrote in 1929 [E4] and, shortly thereafter, 'Outside Russia, Lenin and Engels are of course not valued as scientific thinkers and no one might be interested to refute them as such. The same might also be the case in Russia, but there one cannot dare to say so' [E5]. Much documentation related to Einstein's interests in and involvements with political matters is found in the book *Einstein on Peace* [N1]).

Einstein was a lover of wisdom. But was he a philosopher? The answer to that

---

*The account of Einstein's consultancy given in [G1] is inaccurate.

**Einstein's cousin Lina Einstein died in Auschwitz. His cousin Bertha Dreyfus died in Theresienstadt.

question is no less a matter of taste than of fact. I would say that at his best he was not, but I would not argue strenuously against the opposite view. It is as certain that Einstein's interest in philosophy was genuine as it is that he did not consider himself a philosopher.

He studied philosophical writings throughout his life, beginning in his high school days, when he first read Kant (3). In 1943 Einstein, Gödel, Bertrand Russell, and Pauli gathered at Einstein's home to discuss philosophy of science about half a dozen times [R1]. 'Science without epistemology is—in so far as it is thinkable at all—primitive and muddled,' he wrote in his later years, warning at the same time of the dangers to the scientist of adhering too strongly to any one epistemological system. 'He [the scientist] must appear to the systematic epistemologist as a type of unscrupulous opportunist: he appears as *realist* in so far as he seeks to describe a world independent of the acts of perception; an *idealist* in so far as he looks upon the concepts and theories as the free inventions of the human spirit (not logically derivable from what is empirically given); as *positivist* in so far as he considers his concepts and theories justified *only* to the extent to which they furnish a logical representation of relations among sensory experiences. He may even appear as a *Platonist* or *Pythagorean* in so far as he considers the viewpoint of logical simplicity as an indispensable and effective tool of his research' [E6].

Elements of all these 'isms' are clearly discernible in Einstein's thinking. In the last thirty years of his life, he ceased to be an 'unscrupulous opportunist', however, when, much to his detriment, he became a philosopher by freezing himself into realism or, as he preferred to call it, objective reality. That part of his evolution will be described in detail in (25). There can be as little doubt that philosophy stretched his personality as that his philosophical knowledge played no direct role in his major creative efforts. Further remarks by Einstein on philosophical issues will be deferred until (16e), except for his comments on Newton.

The men whom Einstein at one time or another acknowledged as his precursors were Newton, Maxwell, Mach, Planck, and Lorentz. As he told me more than once, without Lorentz he would never have been able to make the discovery of special relativity. Of his veneration for Planck, I shall write in (18a); of the influence of Mach* in (15e); and of his views of Maxwell in (16e). I now turn to Newton but first digress briefly.

Einstein's deep emotional urge not to let anything interfere with his thinking dates back to his childhood and lends an unusual quality of detachment to his personal life. It was not that he was aloof or a loner, incapable of personal attachments. He was also capable of deep anger, as his attitude toward Germany during

---

*I should note that I do not quite share Isaiah Berlin's opinion [B2] that Mach was one of Einstein's philosophical mentors and that Einstein first accepted, then rejected Mach's phenomenalism. Einstein's great admiration for Mach came entirely from the reading of the latter's book on mechanics, in which the relativity of all motion is a guiding principle. On the other hand, Einstein considered Mach to be 'un déplorable philosophe' [E7], if only because to Mach the reality of atoms remained forever anathema.

and after the Nazi period attests. When he spoke or wrote of justice and liberty for others, called the Jews his brothers, or grieved for the heroes of the Warsaw ghetto, he did so as a man of feeling at least as much as a man of thought. That, having thus spoken and thus felt, he would want to return to the purity and safety of the world of ideas is not an entirely uncommon desire. Truly remarkable, however, was his gift to effect the return to that world without emotional effort. He had no need to push the everyday world away from him. He just stepped out of it whenever he wished. It is therefore not surprising either that (as he wrote shortly before his death) he twice failed rather disgracefully in marriage or that in his life there is an absence of figures with whom he identified—with the exception, perhaps, of Newton.

It seems to me that, when in midlife Einstein wrote of 'The wonderful events which the great Newton experienced in his young days. . . Nature to him was an open book. . . . In one person he combined the experimenter, the theorist, the mechanic, and, not least, the artist in exposition. . . . He stands before us strong, certain, and alone: his joy in creation and his minute precision are evident in every word and every figure . . .' [E8], he described his own ideals, the desire for fulfillment not just as a theorist but also as an experimental physicist. (In the second respect, he, of course, never matched Newton.) Earlier he had written that Newton 'deserves our deep veneration' for his achievements, and that Newton's own awareness of the weaknesses of his own theories 'has always excited my reverent admiration' [E9] (these weaknesses included the action of forces at a distance, which, Newton noted, was not to be taken as an ultimate explanation).

'Fortunate Newton, happy childhood of Science!' [E8]. When Einstein wrote these opening words in the introduction to a new printing of Newton's *Opticks*, he had especially in mind that Newton's famous dictum 'hypotheses non fingo,' I frame no hypotheses, expressed a scientific style of the past. Elsewhere Einstein was quite explicit on this issue:

> We now know that science cannot grow out of empiricism alone, that in the constructions of science we need to use free invention which only *a posteriori* can be confronted with experience as to its usefulness. This fact could elude earlier generations, to whom theoretical creation seemed to grow inductively out of empiricism without the creative influence of a free construction of concepts. The more primitive the status of science is the more readily can the scientist live under the illusion that he is a pure empiricist. In the nineteenth century, many still believed that Newton's fundamental rule 'hypotheses non fingo' should underlie all healthy natural science. [E10]

Einstein again expressed his view that the scientific method had moved on in words only he could have written:

> Newton, forgive me; you found the only way which in your age was just about possible for a man with the highest powers of thought and creativity. The concepts which you created are guiding our thinking in physics even today,

although we now know that they will have to be replaced by others farther removed from the sphere of immediate experience, if we aim at a profounder understanding of relationships. [E11]

However, in one respect Einstein forever continued to side with Newton and to quote his authority. That was in the matter of causality. On the occasion of the bicentenary of Newton's death, Einstein wrote to the secretary of the Royal Society, 'All who share humbly in pondering over the secrets of physical events are with you in spirit, and join in the admiration and love that bind us to Newton', then went on to comment on the evolution of physics since Newton's day and concluded as follows:

It is only in the quantum theory that Newton's differential method becomes inadequate, and indeed strict causality fails us. But the last word has not yet been said. May the spirit of Newton's method give us the power to restore unison between physical reality and the profoundest characteristic of Newton's teaching—strict causality. [E12]

What is strict Newtonian causality? As an example, if I give you the precise position *and* velocity of a particle at a given instant, and if you know all the forces acting on it, then you can predict from Newton's laws the precise position and velocity of that particle at a later time. Quantum theory implies, however, that I am unable to give you that information about position *and* velocity with ideal precision, even if I have the most perfect instrumentation at my disposal. That is the problem I discussed with Einstein in our conversation about the existence of the moon, a body so heavy that the limitations on the precision of information on position *and* velocity I can give you are so insignificant that, to all astronomical intents and purposes, you can neglect the indeterminacy in the information you obtained from me and continue to talk of the lunar orbit.

It is quite otherwise for things like atoms. In the hydrogen atom, the electron does not move in an orbit in the same sense as the moon moves around the earth, for, if it did, the hydrogen atom would be as flat as a little pancake whereas actually it is a little sphere. As a matter of principle, there is no way back to Newtonian causality. Of course, this recognition never diminished Newton's stature. Einstein's hope for a return to that old causality is an impossible dream. Of course, this opinion, held by modern physicists, has not prevented them from recognizing Einstein as by far the most important scientific figure of this century. His special relativity includes the completion of the work of Maxwell and Lorentz. His general relativity includes the completion of Newton's theory of gravitation and incorporates Mach's vision of the relativity of all motion. In all these respects, Einstein's oeuvre represents the crowning of the work of his precursors, adding to and revising the foundations of their theories. In this sense he is a transitional figure, perfecting the past and changing the stream of future events. At the same time he is a pioneer, as first Planck, then he, then Bohr founded a new physics without precursors—the quantum theory.

Einstein deserves to be given the same compliment he gave Newton: he, too, was an artist in exposition. His talent for the German language was second only to his gift for science. I refer not so much to his proclivity for composing charming little rhymes as to the quality of his prose. He was a master of nuances, which are hard to maintain in translation. The student of Einstein should read him in German. It is fitting that several of his important papers, such as his scientific credo in the *Journal of the Franklin Institute* of 1936, and his autobiographical sketch in the Schilpp book [E6], should appear side by side in the original German and in English translation. He wrote all his scientific papers in German, whether or not they eventually appeared in that language. Not only his mastery of language but also his perceptiveness of people is evident in his writings in memory of colleagues and friends: of Schwarzschild and Smoluchowski, of Marie Curie and Emmy Noether, of Michelson and Thomas Edison, of Lorentz, Nernst, Langevin, and Planck, of Walther Rathenau, and, most movingly, of Paul Ehrenfest. These portraits serve as the best foil for the opinion that Einstein was a naive man.

In languages other than German, he was less at ease.* On his first visit to Paris, in 1922, he lectured in French[K1]. He spoke in German, however, when addressing audiences on his first visits to England and the United States, but became fluent in English in later years.

Music was his love. He cared neither for twentieth century composers nor for many of the nineteenth century ones. He loved Schubert but was not attracted to the heavily dramatic parts of Beethoven. He was not particularly fond of Brahms and disliked Wagner. His favorite composers were earlier ones—Mozart, Bach, Vivaldi, Corelli, Scarlatti. I never heard him play the violin, but most of those who did attest to his musicality and the ease with which he sight-read scores. About his predilections in the visual arts, I quote from a letter by Margot Einstein to Meyer Schapiro:

> In visual art, he preferred, of course, the old masters. They seemed to him more 'convincing' (he used this word!) than the masters of our time. But sometimes he surprised me by looking at the *early* period of Picasso (1905, 1906). . . . Words like *cubism, abstract painting* . . . did not mean anything to him. . . . Giotto moved him deeply . . . also Fra Angelico . . . Piero della Francesca. . . . He loved the small Italian towns. . . . He loved cities like Florence, Siena (Sienese paintings), Pisa, Bologna, Padua and admired the architecture. . . . If it comes to Rembrandt, yes, he admired him and felt him deeply. [E13]**

*During the 1920s, Einstein once said to a young friend, 'I like neither new clothes nor new kinds of food. I would rather not learn new languages' [S1].

**I have no clear picture of Einstein's habits and preferences in regard to literature. I do not know how complete or representative is the following randomly ordered list of authors he liked: Heine, Anatole France, Balzac, Dostoyevski (*The Brothers Karamazov*), Musil, Dickens, Lagerlof, Tolstoi (folk stories), Kazantzakis, Brecht (*Galilei*), Broch (*The Death of Virgil*), Gandhi (autobiography), Gorki, Hersey (*A Bell for Adano*), van Loon (*Life and Times of Rembrandt*), Reik (*Listening with the Third Ear*).

As a conclusion to this introductory sketch of Einstein the man, I should like to elaborate the statement made in the Preface that Einstein was the freest man I have known. By that I mean that, more than anyone else I have encountered, he was the master of his own destiny. If he had a God it was the God of Spinoza. Einstein was not a revolutionary, as the overthrow of authority was never his prime motivation. He was not a rebel, since any authority but the one of reason seemed too ridiculous to him to waste effort fighting against (one can hardly call his opposition to Nazism a rebellious attitude). He had the freedom to ask scientific questions, the genius to so often ask the right ones. He had no choice but to accept the answer. His deep sense of destiny led him farther than anyone before him. It was his faith in himself which made him persevere. Fame may on occasion have flattered him, but it never deflected him. He was fearless of time and, to an uncommon degree, fearless of death. I cannot find tragedy in his later attitude to the quantum theory or in his lack of success in finding a unified field theory, especially since some of the questions he asked remain a challenge to this day (2b)—and since I never read tragedy in his face. An occasional touch of sadness in him never engulfed his sense of humor.

I now turn to a tour of Einstein's science.

Einstein never cared much for teaching courses. No one was ever awarded a PhD degree working with him, but he was always fond of discussing physics problems, whether with colleagues his age or with people much younger. All his major papers are his own, yet in the course of his life he often collaborated with others. A survey of these collaborative efforts, involving more than thirty colleagues or assistants, is found in (29). From his student days until well into his forties, he would seek opportunities to do experiments. As a student he hoped to measure the drift of the aether through which (as he then believed) the earth was moving (6d). While at the patent office, he tinkered with a device to measure small voltage differences (3, 29). In Berlin he conducted experiments on rotation induced by magnetization (14b), measured the diameter of membrane capillaries (29), and was involved with patents for refrigerating devices and for a hearing aid (29). But, of course, theoretical physics was his main devotion.

There is no better way to begin this brief survey of his theoretical work than with a first look at what he did in 1905. In that year Einstein produced six papers:

1. The light-quantum and the photoelectric effect, completed March 17 (19c), (19e). This paper, which led to his Nobel prize in physics, was produced before he wrote his PhD thesis.
2. A new determination of molecular dimensions, completed April 30. This was his doctoral thesis, which was to become his paper most often quoted in modern literature (5c).

3. Brownian motion, received* May 11. This was a direct outgrowth of his thesis work (5d).
4. The first paper on special relativity, received* June 30.
5. The second paper on special relativity, containing the $E = mc^2$ relation, received* September 27.
6. A second paper on Brownian motion, received* December 19.

There is little if anything in his earlier published work that hints at this extraordinary creative outburst. By his own account, the first two papers he ever wrote, dating from 1901 and 1902 and dealing with the hypothesis of a universal law of force between molecules, were worthless (4a). Then followed three papers of mixed quality (4c, 4d) on the foundations of statistical mechanics. The last of these, written in 1904, contains a first reference to the quantum theory. None of these first five papers left much of a mark on physics, but I believe they were very important warming-up exercises in Einstein's own development. Then came a year of silence, followed by the outpouring of papers in 1905. I do not know what his trains of thought were during 1904. His personal life changed in two respects: his position at the patent office was converted from temporary to permanent status. And his first son was born. Whether these events helped to promote the emergence of Einstein's genius I cannot tell, though I believe that the arrival of the son may have been a profound experience. Nor do I know a general and complete characterization of what genius is, except that it is more than an extreme form of talent and that the criteria for genius are not objective. I note with relief that the case for Einstein as a genius will cause even less of an argument than the case for Picasso and much less of an argument than the case for Woody Allen, and I do hereby declare that—in my opinion—Einstein was a genius.

Einstein's work before 1905 as well as papers 2, 3, and 6 of that year resulted from his interest in two central early twentieth-century problems, the subjects of Part II of this book.

The first problem: molecular reality. How can one prove (or disprove) that atoms and molecules are real things? If they are real, then how can one determine their size and count their number? In (5a), there is an introductory sketch of the nineteenth century status of this question. During that period the chemist, member of the youngest branch of science, argued the question in one context, the physicist in another, and each paid little attention to what the other was saying. By about 1900 many, though not all, leading chemists and physicists believed that molecules were real. A few among the believers already knew that the atom did not deserve its name, which means 'uncuttable.' Roughly a decade later, the issue of molecular reality was settled beyond dispute, since in the intervening years the many methods for counting these hypothetical particles all gave the same result, to within small errors. The very diversity of these methods and the very sameness of the

*By the editors of *Annalen der Physik*.

answers gave the molecular picture the compelling strength of a unifying principle. Three of these methods are found in Einstein's work of 1905. In March he counted molecules in his light-quantum paper (19c). In April he made a count with the help of the flow properties of a solution of sugar molecules in water (5c). In May he gave a third count in the course of explaining the long-known phenomenon of Brownian motion of small clumps of matter suspended in solution (5d). The confluence of all these answers is the result of important late nineteenth-century developments in experimental physics. Einstein's March method could be worked out only because of a breakthrough in far-infrared spectroscopy (19a). The April and May methods were a consequence of the discovery by Dr Pfeffer of a method for making rigid membranes (5c). Einstein's later work (1911) on the blueness of the sky and on critical opalescence yielded still other counting methods (5e).

The second problem: the molecular basis of statistical physics. If atoms and molecules are real things, then how does one express such macroscopic concepts as pressure, temperature, and entropy in terms of the motion of these submicroscopic particles? The great masters of the nineteenth century—Maxwell, Boltzmann, Kelvin, van der Waals, and others did not, of course, sit and wait for the molecular hypothesis to be proved before broaching problem number two. The most difficult of their tasks was the derivation of the second law of thermodynamics. What is the molecular basis for the property that the entropy of an isolated system strives toward a maximum as the system moves toward equilibrium? A survey of the contributions to this problem by Einstein's predecessors as well as by Einstein himself is presented in (4). In those early days, Einstein was not the only one to underestimate the mathematical care that this very complex problem rightfully deserves. When Einstein did this work, his knowledge of the fundamental contributions by Boltzmann was fragmentary, his ignorance of Gibbs' papers complete. This does not make any easier the task of ascertaining the merits of his contributions.

To Einstein, the second problem was of deeper interest than the first. As he said later, Brownian motion was important as a method for counting particles, but far more important because it enables us to demonstrate the reality of those motions we call heat, simply by looking into a microscope. On the whole, Einstein's work on the second law has proved to be of less lasting value than his investigations on the verification of the molecular hypothesis. Indeed, in 1911 he wrote that he would probably not have published his papers of 1903 and 1904 had he been aware of Gibbs' work.

Nevertheless, Einstein's preoccupation with the fundamental questions of statistical mechanics was extremely vital since it led to his most important contributions to the quantum theory. It is no accident that the term *Boltzmann's principle,* coined by Einstein, appears for the first time in his March 1905 paper on the light-quantum. In fact the light-quantum postulate itself grew out of a statistical argument concerning the equilibrium properties of radiation (19c). It should also be remembered that the main applications of his first work (1904) on energy fluctuations (4c) are in the quantum domain. His analysis of these fluctuations in blackbody radiation led him to become the first to state, in 1909, long before the discovery of quantum mechanics, that the theory of the future ought to be based on a dual description in terms of particles and waves (21a). Another link between statistical mechanics and the quantum theory was forged by his study of the Brownian motion of molecules in a bath of electromagnetic radiation. This investigation led him to the momentum properties of light-quanta (21c). His new derivation, in 1916, of Planck's blackbody radiation law also has a statistical basis (21b). In the course of this last work, he observed a lack of Newtonian causality in the process called spontaneous emission. His discomfort about causality originated from that discovery (21d).

Einstein's active involvement with statistical physics began in 1902 and lasted until 1925, when he made his last major contribution to physics: his treatment of the quantum statistics of molecules (23). Again and for the last time, he applied fluctuation phenomena with such mastery that they led him to the very threshold of wave mechanics (24b). The links between the contributions of Einstein, de Broglie, and Schroedinger, discussed in (24), make clear that wave mechanics has its roots in statistical mechanics—unlike matrix mechanics, where the connections between the work of Bohr, Heisenberg, and Dirac followed in the first instance from studies of the dynamics of atoms (18c).

Long periods of gestation are a marked characteristic in Einstein's scientific development. His preoccupation with quantum problems, which began shortly after Planck's discovery of the blackbody radiation law late in 1900, bore its first fruit in March 1905. Questions that lie at the root of the special theory of relativity dawned on him as early as 1895 (6d); the theory saw the light in June 1905. He began to think of general relativity in 1907 (9); that theory reached its first level of completion in November 1915 (14c). His interest in unified field theory dates back at least to 1918 (17a). He made the first of his own proposals for a theory of this kind in 1925 (17d). As far as the relativity theories are concerned, these gestation periods had a climactic ending. There was no more than about five weeks between his understanding of the correct interpretation of the measurement of time and the completion of his first special relativity paper (7a). Similarly, after years of trial and error, he did all the work on his ultimate formulation of general relativity in approximately two months (14c).

I focus next on special relativity. One version of its history could be very brief: in June, 1905, Einstein published a paper on the electrodynamics of moving bodies. It consists of ten sections. After the first five sections, the theory lies before us in finished form. The rest, to this day, consists of the application of the principles stated in those first five sections.

My actual account of that history is somewhat more elaborate. It begins with brief remarks on the nineteenth century concept of the aether (6a), that quaint, hypothetical medium which was introduced for the purpose of explaining the transmission of light waves and which was abolished by Einstein. The question has often been asked whether or not Einstein disposed of the aether because he was familiar with the Michelson–Morley experiment, which, with great accuracy, had demonstrated the absence of an anticipated drift of the aether as the earth moved through it without obstruction (6a). The answer is that Einstein undoubtedly knew of the Michelson–Morley result (6d) but that probably it played only an indirect role in the evolution of his thinking (7a). From 1907 on, Einstein often emphasized the fundamental importance of the work by Michelson and Morley, but continued to be remarkably reticent about any direct influence of that experiment on his own development. An understanding of that attitude lies beyond the edge of history. In (8) I shall dare to speculate on this subject.

Two major figures, Lorentz and Poincaré, take their place next to Einstein in the history of special relativity. Lorentz, founder of the theory of electrons, codiscoverer of the Lorentz contraction (as Poincaré named it), interpreter of the Zeeman effect, acknowledged by Einstein as his precursor, wrote down the Lorentz transformations (so named by Poincaré) in 1904. In 1905, Einstein, at that time aware only of Lorentz's writings up to 1895, rediscovered these transformations. In 1898, Poincaré, one of the greatest mathematicians of his day and a consummate mathematical physicist, had written that we have no direct intuition of the simultaneity of events occurring in two different places, a remark almost certainly known to Einstein before 1905 (6b). In 1905 Einstein and Poincaré stated independently and almost simultaneously (within a matter of weeks) the group properties of the Lorentz transformations and the addition theorem of velocities. Yet, both Lorentz and Poincaré missed discovering special relativity; they were too deeply steeped in considerations of dynamics. Only Einstein saw the crucial new point: the dynamic aether must be abandoned in favor of a new kinematics based on two new postulates (7). Only he saw that the Lorentz transformations, and hence the Lorentz–Fitzgerald contraction, can be derived from kinematic arguments. Lorentz acknowledged this and developed a firm grasp of special relativity, but even after 1905 never quite gave up either the aether or his reservations concerning the velocity of light as an ultimate velocity (8). In all his life (he died in 1912), Poincaré never understood the basis of special relativity (8).

Special relativity brought clarity to old physics and created new physics, in particular Einstein's derivation (also in 1905) of the relation $E = mc^2$ (7b). It was some years before the first main experimental confirmation of the new theory, the energy-mass-velocity relation for fast electrons, was achieved (7e). After 1905 Einstein paid only occasional attention to other implications (7d), mainly because from 1907 he was after bigger game: general relativity.

The history of the discovery of general relativity is more complicated. It is a tale of a tortuous path. No amount of simplification will enable me to match the minihistory of special relativity given earlier. In the quantum theory, Planck started before Einstein. In special relativity, Lorentz inspired him. In general relativity, he starts the long road alone. His progress is no longer marked by that light touch and deceptive ease so typical of all his work published in 1905. The first steps are made in 1907, as he discovers a simple version of the equivalence principle and understands that matter will bend light and that the spectral lines reaching us from the sun should show a tiny shift toward the red relative to the same spectral lines produced on earth (9). During the next three and a half years, his attention focuses on that crisis phenomenon, the quantum theory, rather than on the less urgent problems of relativity (10). His serious concentration on general relativity begins after his arrival in Prague in 1911, where he teaches himself a great deal with the help of a model theory. He gives a calculation of the bending of light by the sun. His result is imperfect, since at that time he still believes that space is flat (11). In the summer of 1912, at the time of his return to Zürich, he makes a fundamental discovery: space is not flat; the geometry of the world is not Euclidean. It is Riemannian. Ably helped by an old friend, the mathematician Marcel Grossmann, he establishes the first links between geometry and gravity. With his habitual optimism he believes he has solved the fifty-year-old problem (13) of finding a field theory of gravitation. Not until late in 1915 does he fully realize how flawed his theory actually is. At that very same time, Hilbert starts his important work on gravitation (14d). After a few months of extremely intense work, Einstein presents the final revised version of his theory on November 25, 1915 (14c).

One week earlier he had obtained two extraordinary results. Fulfilling an aspiration he had had since 1907, he found the correct explanation of the long-known precession of the perihelion of the planet Mercury. That was the high point in his scientific life. He was so excited that for three days he could not work. In addition he found that his earlier result on the bending of light was too small by a factor of 2. Einstein was canonized in 1919 when this second prediction also proved to be correct (16b).

After 1915 Einstein continued to examine problems in general relativity. He was the first to give a theory of gravitational waves (15d). He was also the founder of general relativistic cosmology, the modern theory of the universe at large (15e). Hubble's discovery that the universe is expanding was made in Einstein's lifetime. Radio galaxies, quasars, neutron stars, and, perhaps, black holes were found after his death. These post-Einsteinian observational developments in astronomy largely account for the great resurgence of interest in general relativity in more recent times. A sketchy account of the developments in general relativity after 1915 up to the present appears in (15).

I return to earlier days. After 1915 Einstein's activities in the domain of relativity became progressively less concerned with the applications of general relativity than with the search for generalization of that theory. During the early years following the discovery of general relativity, the aim of that search appeared to be highly plausible: according to general relativity the very existence of the gravitational field is inalienably woven into the geometry of the physical world. There was nothing equally compelling about the existence of the electromagnetic field, at that time the only field other than that of gravity known to exist (17a). Riemannian geometry does not geometrize electromagnetism. Should not one therefore try to invent a more general geometry in which electromagnetism would be just as fundamental as gravitation? If the special theory of relativity had unified electricity and magnetism and if the general theory had geometrized gravitation, should not one try next to unify and geometrize electromagnetism and gravity? After he experimentally unified electricity and magnetism, had not Michael Faraday tried to observe whether gravity could induce electric currents by letting pieces of metal drop from the top of the lecture room in the Royal Institution to a cushion on the floor? Had he not written, 'If the hope should prove well-founded, how great and mighty and sublime in its hitherto unchangeable character is the force I am trying to deal with, and how large may be the new domain of knowledge that may be opened to the mind of man'? And when his experiment showed no effect, had he not written, 'They do not shake my strong feeling of the existence of a relation between gravity and electricity, though they give no proof that such a relation exists'? [W1] Thoughts and visions such as these led Einstein to his program for a unified field theory. Its purpose was neither to incorporate the unexplained nor to resolve any paradox. It was purely a quest for harmony.

On his road to general relativity, Einstein had found the nineteenth century geometry of Riemann waiting for him. In 1915 the more general geometries which he and others would soon be looking for did not yet exist. They had to be invented. It should be stressed that the unification program was not the only spur to the search for new geometries. In 1916, mathematicians, acknowledging the stimulus of general relativity, began the very same pursuit for their own reasons. Thus Einstein's work was the direct cause of the development of a new branch of mathematics, the theory of connections (17c).

During the 1920s and 1930s, it became evident that there exist forces other than those due to gravitation and electromagnetism. Einstein chose to ignore those new forces although they were not and are not any less fundamental than the two which have been known about longer. He continued the old search for a unification of gravitation and electromagnetism, following one path, failing, trying a new one. He would study worlds having more than the familiar four dimensions of space and time (17b) or new world geometries in four dimensions (17d). It was to no avail.

In recent years, the quest for the unification of all forces has become a central theme in physics (17e). The methods are new. There has been distinct progress (2b). But Einstein's dream, the joining of gravitation to other forces, has so far not been realized.

In concluding this tour, I return to Einstein's contributions to the quantum theory. I must add that, late in 1906, Einstein became the founder of the quantum theory of the solid state by giving the essentially correct explanation of the anomalous behavior of hard solids, such as diamond, for example, at low temperatures (20). It is also necessary to enlarge on the remark made previously concerning the statistical origins of the light-quantum hypothesis. Einstein's paper of March 1905 contains not one but two postulates. First, the light-quantum was conceived of as a parcel of energy as far as the properties of pure radiation (no coupling to matter) are concerned. Second, Einstein made the assumption—he called it the heuristic principle—that also in its coupling to matter (that is, in emission and absorption), light is created or annihilated in similar discrete parcels of energy (19c). That, I believe, was Einstein's one revolutionary contribution to physics (2). It upset all existing ideas about the interaction between light and matter. I shall describe in detail the various causes for the widespread disbelief in the heuristic principle (19f), a resistance which did not weaken after other contributions of Einstein were recognized as outstanding or even after the predictions for the photoelectric effect, made on the grounds of the heuristic principle, turned out to be highly successful (19e).

The light-quantum, a parcel of energy, slowly evolved into the photon, a parcel of energy and momentum (21), a fundamental particle with zero mass and unit spin. Never was a proposal for a new fundamental particle resisted more strongly than this one for the photon (18b). No one resisted the photon longer than Bohr (22). All resistance came to an end when experiments on the scattering of light by electrons (the Compton effect) proved that Einstein was right (21f, 22).

Quantum mechanics was born within a few months of the settling of the photon issue. In (25) I describe in detail Einstein's response to this new development. His initial belief that quantum mechanics contained logical inconsistencies (25a) did not last long. Thereafter, he became convinced that quantum mechanics is an incomplete description of nature (25c). Nevertheless, he acknowledged that the nonrelativistic version of quantum mechanics did constitute a major advance. His proposal of a Nobel prize for Schroedinger and Heisenberg is but one expression of that opinion (31).

However, Einstein never had a good word for the relativity version of quantum mechanics known as quantum field theory. Its successes did not impress him. Once, in 1912, he said of the quantum theory that the more successful it is, the sillier it looks (20). When speaking of successful physical theories, he would, in his later years, quote the example of the old gravitation theory (26). Had Newton not been successful for more than two centuries? And had his theory not turned out to be incomplete?

Einstein himself never gave up the search for a theory that would incorporate quantum phenomena but would nevertheless satisfy his craving for causality. His vision of a future interplay of relativity and quantum theory in a unified field theory is the subject of the last scientific chapter of this book (26), in which I return to the picture drawn in the preface.

Finally, I may be permitted to summarize my own views. Newtonian causality is gone for good. The synthesis of relativity and the quantum theory is incomplete (2). In the absence of this synthesis, any assessment of Einstein's vision must be part of open history.

The tour ends here. General comments on relativity and quantum theory come next, followed by a sketch of Einstein's early years. Then the physics begins.

References

B1. S. Brunauer, *J. Wash. Acad. Sci.* **69,** 108, (1979).
B2. I. Berlin. *Personal Impressions,* pp. 145, 150. Viking, New York, 1980.
E1. A. Einstein, *Die Vossische Zeitung,* May 23, 1916.
E2. ——, *Sozialistische Monatshefte,* 1919, p. 1055.
E3. ——, *Neue Rundschau* **33,** 815 (1922).
E4. ——, statement prepared for the *Liga für Menschenrechte*, January 6, 1929.
E5. ——, letter to K. R. Leistner, September 8, 1932.
E6. —— in *Albert Einstein: Philosopher-Scientist* (P. A. Schilpp, Ed.), p. 684. Tudor, New York, 1949.
E7. ——, *Bull. Soc. Fran. Phil.* **22,** 97 (1923).
E8. —— in I. Newton, *Opticks,* p. vii. McGraw-Hill, New York, 1931.
E9. ——, *Naturw.* **15,** 273 (1927). English trans. in *Smithsonian Report for 1927,* p. 201.
E10. —— in *Emanuel Libman Anniversary Volumes,* Vol. 1, p. 363. International, New York, 1932.
E11. ——, [E6], p. 31.
E12. ——, *Nature* **119,** 467, (1927); *Science* **65,** 347 (1927).
E13. Margot Einstein, letter to M. Schapiro, December 1978.
G1. G. Gamow, *My World Line,* p. 148. Viking, New York, 1970.
J1. R. Jost, letter to A. Pais, August 17, 1977.
K1. A. Kastler, *Technion-Informations,* No. 11, December 1978.
N1. O. Nathan and H. Norden, *Einstein on Peace,* Schocken, New York, 1968.
O1. J. R. Oppenheimer in *Einstein, a Centennial Volume* (A. P. French, Ed.), p. 44. Harvard University Press, 1979.
P1. A. Pais in *Niels Bohr* (S. Rozental, Ed.), p. 215. Interscience, New York, 1967.
R1. B. Russell, [N1], p. xv.
S1. E. Salaman, *Encounter,* April 1979, p. 19.
W1. L. P. Williams, *Michael Faraday,* pp. 468–9. Basic Books, New York, 1965.

2

Relativity Theory
and Quantum Theory

Einstein's life ended . . . with a demand on us for synthesis.

W. Pauli [P1]

2a. Orderly Transitions and Revolutionary Periods

In all the history of physics, there has never been a period of transition as abrupt, as unanticipated, and over as wide a front as the decade 1895 to 1905. In rapid succession the experimental discoveries of X-rays (1895), the Zeeman effect (1896), radioactivity (1896), the electron (1897), and the extension of infrared spectroscopy into the 3 μm to 60 μm region opened new vistas. The birth of quantum theory (1900) and relativity theory (1905) marked the beginning of an era in which the very foundations of physical theory were found to be in need of revision. Two men led the way toward the new theoretical concepts: Max Karl Ernst Ludwig Planck, professor at the University of Berlin, possessed—perhaps obsessed—by the search for the universal function of frequency and temperature, known to exist since 1859, when Gustav Robert Kirchhoff formulated his fundamental law of blackbody radiation (19a)*; and Albert Einstein, technical expert at the Swiss patent office in Bern, working in an isolation which deserves to be called splendid (3).

In many superficial ways, these two men were quite unlike each other. Their backgrounds, circumstances, temperaments, and scientific styles differed profoundly. Yet there were deep similarities. In the course of addressing Planck on the occasion of Planck's sixtieth birthday, Einstein said:

> The longing to behold . . . preestablished harmony** is the source of the inexhaustible persistence and patience with which we see Planck devoting himself to the most general problems of our science without letting himself be deflected by goals which are more profitable and easier to achieve. I have often heard that colleagues would like to attribute this attitude to exceptional will-power

*In this chapter, I use for the last time parenthetical notations when referring to a chapter or a section thereof. Thus, (19a) means Chapter 19, Section a.

**An expression of Leibniz's which Einstein considered particularly apt.

and discipline; I believe entirely wrongly so. The emotional state which enables such achievements is similar to that of the religious person or the person in love; the daily pursuit does not originate from a design or program but from a direct need [E1].

This overriding urge for harmony directed Einstein's scientific life as much as it did Planck's. The two men admired each other greatly.

The main purpose of this chapter is to make some introductory comments on Einstein's attitude to the quantum and relativity theories. To this end, it will be helpful to recall a distinction which he liked to make between two kinds of physical theories [E2]. Most theories, he said, are constructive, they interpret complex phenomena in terms of relatively simple propositions. An example is the kinetic theory of gases, in which the mechanical, thermal, and diffusional properties of gases are reduced to molecular interactions and motions. 'The merit of constructive theories is their comprehensiveness, adaptability, and clarity.' Then there are the theories of principle, which use the analytic rather than the synthetic method: 'Their starting points are not hypothetical constituents but empirically observed general properties of phenomena.' An example is the impossibility of a perpetuum mobile in thermodynamics. '[The merit of] theories of principle [is] their logical perfection and the security of their foundation.' Then Einstein went on to say, 'The theory of relativity is a theory of principle.' These lines were written in 1919, when relativity had already become 'like a house with two separate stories': the special and the general theory. (Of course, the special theory by itself is a theory of principle as well.)

Thus, toward the end of the decade 1895–1905 a new theory of principle had emerged: special relativity. What was the status of quantum theory at that time? It was neither a theory of principle nor a constructive theory. In fact, it was not a theory at all. Planck's and Einstein's first results on blackbody radiation proved that there was something wrong with the foundations of classical physics, but old foundations were not at once replaced by new ones—as had been the case with the special theory of relativity from its very inception (7). Peter Debye recalled that, soon after its publication, Planck's work was discussed in Aachen, where Debye was then studying with Arnold Sommerfeld. Planck's law fitted the data well, 'but we did not know whether the quanta were something fundamentally new or not' [B1].

The discovery of the quantum theory in 1900 (19a) and of special relativity in 1905 (7) have in common that neither was celebrated by press releases, dancing in the streets, or immediate proclamations of the dawn of a new era. There all resemblance ends. The assimilation of special relativity was a relatively fast and easy process. It is true that great men like Hendrik Antoon Lorentz and Henri Poincaré had difficulty recognizing that this was a new theory of kinematic principle rather than a constructive dynamic theory (8) and that the theory caused the inevitable confusion in philosophical circles, as witness, for example, the little book on the subject by Henry Bergson written as late as 1922 [B2]. Nevertheless, senior men like Planck, as well as a new generation of theorists, readily recognized special relativity to be fully specified by the two principles stated by Einstein in his 1905 paper (7a). All the rest was application of these theoretical principles. When special relativity appeared, it was at once 'all there.' There never was an 'old' theory of relativity.

By contrast, the 'old' quantum theory, developed in the years from 1900 to 1925, progressed by unprincipled—but tasteful—invention and application of ad hoc rules rather than by a systematic investigation of the implications of a set of axioms. This is not to say that relativity developed in a 'better' or 'healthier' way than did quantum physics, but rather to stress the deep-seated differences between the evolution of the two. Nor should one underestimate the tremendous, highly concrete, and lasting contributions of the conquistadores, Einstein among them, who created the old quantum theory. The following four equations illustrate better than any long dissertation what they achieved:

$$\rho(\nu, T) = \frac{8\pi h\nu^3}{c^3} \frac{1}{\exp(h\nu/kT) - 1},$$ (2.1)

Planck's formula for the spectral density ρ of blackbody radiation in thermal equilibrium as a function of frequency ν and temperature T (h = Planck's constant, k = Boltzmann's constant, c = velocity of light), the oldest equation in the quantum theory of radiation. It is remarkable that the old quantum theory would originate from the analysis of a problem as complex as blackbody radiation. From 1859 until 1926, this problem remained at the frontier of theoretical physics, first in thermodynamics, then in electromagnetism, then in the old quantum theory, and finally in quantum statistics;

$$E = h\nu - P,$$ (2.2)

Einstein's 1905 equation for the energy E of photoelectrons liberated from a metallic surface irradiated by light of frequency ν (19e), the oldest equation in the quantum theory of the interaction between radiation and matter;

$$c_\nu = 3R \left(\frac{h\nu}{kT} \right)^2 \frac{\exp(h\nu/kT)}{[\exp(h\nu/kT) - 1]^2},$$ (2.3)

Einstein's 1906 equation for the specific heat c_ν of one gram-atom of an idealized crystalline solid, in which all lattice points vibrate harmonically with a unique frequency ν around their equilibrium positions (R is the gas constant) (20), the oldest equation in the quantum theory of the solid state; and

$$\text{Rydberg's constant} = \frac{2\pi^2 e^4 m}{h^3 c},$$ (2.4)

the equation given in 1913 by Niels Bohr, the oldest equation in the quantum theory of atomic structure. Long before anyone knew what the principles of the quantum theory were, the successes of equations like these made it evident that such a theory had to exist. Every one of these successes was a slap in the face of hallowed classical concepts. New inner frontiers, unexpected contraventions of accepted knowledge, appeared in several places: the equipartition theorem of classical statistical mechanics could not be true in general (19b); electrons appeared to be revolving in closed orbits without emitting radiation.

The old quantum theory spans a twenty-five-year period of revolution in physics, a revolution in the sense that existing order kept being overthrown. Relativity theory, on the other hand, whether of the special or the general kind, never was revolutionary in that sense. Its coming was not disruptive, but instead marked an extension of order to new domains, moving the outer frontiers of knowledge still farther out.

This state of affairs is best illustrated by a simple example. According to special relativity, the physical sum $\sigma(v_1,v_2)$ of two velocities v_1 and v_2 with a common direction is given by

$$\sigma(v_1,\ v_2) = \frac{v_1 + v_2}{1 + \dfrac{v_1 v_2}{c^2}} \tag{2.5}$$

a result obtained independently by Poincaré and Einstein in 1905. This equation contains the limit law, $\sigma(v_1,c) = c$, as a case of extreme novelty. It also makes clear that for any velocities, however small, the classical answer, $\sigma(v_1,v_2) = v_1 + v_2$, is no longer rigorously true. But since c is of the order of one billion miles per hour, the equation also says that the classical answer can continue to be trusted for all velocities to which it was applied in early times. That is the correspondence principle of relativity, which is as old as relativity itself. The ancestors, from Galileo via Newton to Maxwell, could continue to rest in peace and glory.

It was quite otherwise with quantum theory. To be sure, after the discovery of the specific heat expression, it was at once evident that Eq. 2.3 yields the long-known Dulong–Petit value of 6 calories/mole (20a) at high temperature. Nor did it take long (only five years) before the connection between Planck's quantum formula (Eq. 2.1) and the classical 'Rayleigh–Einstein–Jeans limit' ($h\nu \ll kT$) was established (19b). These two results indicated that the classical statistical law of equipartition would survive in the correspondence limit of (loosely speaking) high temperature. But there was (and is) no correspondence limit for Eqs. 2.2 and 2.4. Before 1925, nothing was proved from first principles. Only after the discoveries of quantum mechanics, quantum statistics, and quantum field theory did Eqs. 2.1 to 2.4 acquire a theoretical foundation.

The main virtue of Eq. 2.5 is that it simultaneously answers two questions: where does the new begin? where does the old fit in? The presence of the new indicates a clear break with the past. The immediate recognizability of the old shows that this break is what I shall call an orderly transition. On the other hand, a revolution in science occurs if at first *only* the new presents itself. From that moment until the old fits in again (it is a rule, not a law, that this always happens in physics), we have a period of revolution. Thus the births of the relativities were orderly transitions, the days of the old quantum theory were a revolutionary period. I stress that this distinction is meant to apply to the historical process of discovery, not to the content of one or another physical theory. (I would not argue against calling the abandonment of the aether and the rejection of absolute simultaneity in 1905 and the rejection of Newton's absolute space in 1915 amazing, astounding, audacious, bold, brave . . . or revolutionary steps.)

No one appreciated the marked differences between the evolution of relativity and quantum theory earlier and better than Einstein, the only man who had been instrumental in creating both. Nor, of course, was anyone better qualified than he to pronounce on the structure of scientific revolutions. After all, he had been to the barricades. Let us see what he had to say about this subject.

Early in 1905 he wrote a letter to a friend in which he announced his forthcoming papers on the quantum theory and on special relativity. He called the first paper 'very revolutionary.' About the second one he only remarked that 'its kinematic part will interest you' [E3].

In a report of a lecture on relativity that Einstein gave in London on June 13, 1921, we read, 'He [Einstein] deprecated the idea that the new principle was revolutionary. It was, he told his audience, the direct outcome and, in a sense, the natural completion of the work of Faraday, Maxwell, and Lorentz. Moreover there was nothing specially, certainly nothing intentionally, philosophical about it. . . .' [N1].

In the fall of 1919, in the course of a discussion with a student, Einstein handed her a cable which had informed him that the bending of light by the sun was in agreement with his general relativistic prediction. The student asked what he would have said if there had been no confirmation. Einstein replied, 'Da könnt' mir halt der liebe Gott leid tun. Die Theorie stimmt doch.' Then I would have to pity the dear Lord. The theory is correct anyway [R1]. (This statement is not at variance with the fact that Einstein was actually quite excited when he first heard the news of the bending of light (16b).)

These three stories characterize Einstein's lifelong attitude to the relativity theories: they were orderly transitions in which, as he experienced it, he played the role of the instrument of the Lord, Who, he deeply believed, was subtle but not malicious.

Regarding Einstein's judgment of his own role in quantum physics, there is first of all his description of his 1905 paper 'On a heuristic point of view concerning the generation and transformation of light' as very revolutionary (19c). Next we have his own summary: 'What I found in the quantum domain are only occasional insights or fragments which were produced in the course of fruitless struggles with the grand problem. I am ashamed* to receive at this time such a great honor for this' [E4]. Those words he spoke on June 28, 1929, the day he received

---

*I have translated *Ich bin beschämt* as *I am ashamed* rather than as *I am embarrassed* because I believe that the first alternative more accurately reflects Einstein's mood.

the Planck medal from Planck's own hands. By then the revolutionary period of the old quantum theory—which coincided exactly with the years of Einstein's highest creativity!—had made way for nonrelativistic quantum mechanics (and the beginning of its relativistic extension), a theory which by 1929 was recognized by nearly everyone as a new theory of principle.

Einstein dissented. To him, who considered relativity theory no revolution at all, the quantum theory was still in a state of revolution and—as he saw it—remained so for the rest of his life; according to him the old did not yet fit in properly. That is the briefest characterization of Einstein's scientific philosophy. He was more deeply committed to orderly transition than to revolution. He could be radical but never was a rebel.

In the same speech in 1929, he also said, 'I admire to the highest degree the achievements of the younger generation of physicists which goes by the name quantum mechanics and believe in the deep level of truth of that theory; but I believe that the restriction to statistical laws will be a passing one.' The parting of ways had begun. Einstein had started his solitary search for a theory of principle that would maintain classical causality in an orderly way and from which quantum mechanics should be derivable as a constructive theory.

Far more fascinating to me than the substance of Einstein's critique of quantum mechanics—to be discussed in detail in (26)—is the question of motivation. What drove Einstein to this search which he himself called 'quite bizarre as seen from the outside' [E5]? Why would he continue 'to sing my solitary little old song' [E6] for the rest of his life? As I shall discuss in (27), the answer has to do with a grand design which Einstein conceived early, before the discovery of quantum mechanics, for a synthetic physical theory. It was to be a theory of particles and fields in which general relativity and quantum theory would be synthesized. This he failed to achieve.

So to date have we all.

The phenomena to be explained by a theory of principle have become enormously richer since the days when Einstein made the first beginnings with his program. Theoretical progress has been very impressive, but an all-embracing theory does not exist. The need for a new synthesis is felt more keenly as the phenomena grow more complex.

Therefore any assessment of Einstein's visions can be made only from a vantage point that is necessarily tentative. It may be useful to record ever so briefly what this vantage point appears to be to at least one physicist. This is done in the following 'time capsule,' which is dedicated to generations of physicists yet unborn.*

2b. A Time Capsule

When Einstein and others embarked on their programs of unification, three particles (in the modern sense) were known to exist, the electron, the proton, and the

---

*The following section is meant to provide a brief record without any attempt at further explanation or reference to literature. It can be skipped without loss of continuity.

photon, and there were two fundamental interactions, electromagnetism and gravitation. At present the number of particles runs into the hundreds. A further reduction to more fundamental units appears inevitable. It is now believed that there are at least four fundamental interactions. The unification of all four types of forces—gravitational, electromagnetic, weak, and strong—is an active topic of current exploration. It has not been achieved as yet.

Relativistic quantum field theories (in the sense of special relativity) are the principal tools for these explorations. Our confidence in the general field theoretical approach rests first and foremost on the tremendous success of quantum electrodynamics (QED). One number, the g factor of the electron, may illustrate both the current level of predictability of this theory and the level of experimental precision which has been reached:

$$\tfrac{1}{2}(g - 2) = \begin{cases} 1\ 159\ 652\ 460\ (127)\ (75) \times 10^{-12}\ \text{predicted by pure QED*} \\ 1\ 159\ 652\ 200\ (40) \times 10^{-12}\ \quad\quad\ \text{observed} \end{cases}$$

It has nevertheless become evident that this branch of field theory will merge with the theory of other fields.

'If we could have presented Einstein with a synthesis of his general relativity and the quantum theory, then the discussion with him would have been considerably easier' [P1]. To date, this synthesis is beset with conceptual and technical difficulties. The existence of singularities associated with gravitational collapse is considered by some an indication for the incompleteness of the general relativistic equations. It is not known whether or not these singularities are smoothed out by quantum effects.

There is hope that gravitational waves will be observed in this century (15d).

The ultimate unification of weak and electromagnetic interactions has probably not yet been achieved, but a solid beach-head appears to have been established in terms of local non-Abelian gauge theories with spontaneous symmetry breakdown. As a result, it is now widely believed that weak interactions are mediated by massive vector mesons. Current expectations are that such mesons will be observed within the decade.

It is widely believed that strong interactions are also mediated by local non-Abelian gauge fields. Their symmetry is supposed to be unbroken so that the corresponding vector mesons are massless. The dynamics of these 'non-Abelian photons' are supposed to prohibit their creation as single free particles. The technical exploration of this theory is in its early stages.

Promising steps have been made toward grand unification, the union of weak, electromagnetic, and strong interactions in one compact, non-Abelian gauge

---

*In this prediction (which does not include small contributions from muons and hadrons), the best value of the fine-structure constant α has been used as an input: α^{-1} = 137.035 963 (15). The principal source of uncertainty in the predicted value of $(g - 2)$ stems from the experimental uncertainties of α, leading to the error (127). The error (75) is mainly due to uncertainties in the eighth order calculation [K1].

group. In most grand unified theories the proton is unstable. News about the proton's fate is eagerly awaited at this time.

Superunification, the union of all four forces, is the major goal. Some believe that it is near and that supergravity will provide the answer. Others are not so sure.

All modern work on unification may be said to represent a program of geometrization that resembles Einstein's earlier attempts, although the manifold subject to geometrization is larger than he anticipated and the quantum framework of the program would not have been to his liking.

In the search for the correct field theory, model theories have been examined which reveal quite novel possibilities for the existence of extended structures (solitons, instantons, monopoles). In the course of these investigations, topological methods have entered this area of physics. More generally, it has become clear in the past decade that quantum field theory is much richer in structure than was appreciated earlier. The renormalizability of non-Abelian gauge fields with spontaneous symmetry breakdown, asymptotic freedom, and supersymmetry are cases in point.

The proliferation of new particles has led to attempts at a somewhat simplifed underlying description. According to the current picture, the basic constituents of matter are: two classes of spin-½ particles, the leptons and the quarks; a variety of spin-1 gauge bosons, some massless, some massive; and (more tentatively) some fundamental spin-zero particles. The only gauge boson observed so far is the photon. To date, three kinds of charged leptons have been detected. The quarks are hypothetical constituents of the observed hadrons. To date, at least five species of quarks have been identified. The dynamics of the strong interactions are supposed to prohibit the creation of quarks as isolated, free particles. This prohibition, confinement, has not as yet been implemented theoretically in a convincing way. No criterion is known which enables one to state how many species of leptons and of quarks should exist.

Weak, electromagnetic, and strong interactions have distinct intrinsic symmetry properties, but this hierarchy of symmetries is not well understood theoretically. Perhaps the most puzzling are the small effects of noninvariance under space reflection and the even smaller effects of noninvariance under time reversal. It adds to the puzzlement that the latter phenomenon has been observed so far only in a single instance, namely, in the $K° - \overline{K}°$ system. (These phenomena were first observed after Einstein's death. I have often wondered what might have been his reactions to these discoveries, given his 'conviction that pure mathematical construction enables us to discover the concepts and the laws connecting them' [E7].)

It is not known why electric charge is quantized, but it is plausible that this will be easily explicable in the framework of a future gauge theory.

In summary, physicists today are hard at work to meet Einstein's demands for synthesis, using methods of which he probably would be critical. Since about 1970, there has been much more promise for progress than in the two or three decades before. Yet the theoretical structures now under investigation are not as simple and economical as one would wish. The evidence is overwhelming that the theory of particles and fields is still incomplete. Despite much progress, Einstein's earlier complaint remains valid to this day: 'The theories which have gradually been associated with what has been observed have led to an unbearable accumulation of independent assumptions' [E8]. At the same time, no experimental evidence or internal contradiction exists to indicate that the postulates of general relativity, of special relativity, or of quantum mechanics are in mutual conflict or in need of revision or refinement. We are therefore in no position to affirm or deny that these postulates will forever remain unmodified.

I conclude this time capsule with a comment by Einstein on the meaning of the occurrence of dimensionless constants (such as the fine-structure constant or the electron–proton mass ratio) in the laws of physics, a subject about which he knew nothing, we know nothing: 'In a sensible theory there are no [dimensionless] numbers whose values are determinable only empirically. I can, of course, not prove that . . . dimensionless constants in the laws of nature, which from a purely logical point of view can just as well have other values, should not exist. To me in my 'Gottvertrauen' [faith in God] this seems evident, but there might well be few who have the same opinion' [E9].

References

B1. U. Benz, *Arnold Sommerfeld*, p. 74. Wissenschaftliche Verlags Gesellschaft, Stuttgart, 1975.

B2. H. Bergson, *Durée et Simultanéité: A Propos de la Théorie d'Einstein*. Alcan, Paris, 1922.

E1. A. Einstein, *Ansprachen in der Deutschen Physikalischen Gesellschaft*, p. 29. Müller, Karlsruhe, 1918.

E2. ———, *The London Times*, November 28, 1919.

E3. ———, letter to C. Habicht, undated, most probably written in March 1905.

E4. ———, *Forschungen und Fortschritte* **5**, 248 (1929).

E5. ———, letter to L. de Broglie, February 8, 1954.

E6. ———, letter to N. Bohr, April 4, 1949.

E7. ———, *On the Method of Theoretical Physics*. Oxford University Press, Oxford, 1933. Reprinted in *Philos. Sci.* **1**, 162, (1934).

E8. ———, *Lettres à Maurice Solovine*, p. 130. Gauthier-Villars, Paris, 1956.

E9. ———, letters to I. Rosenthal-Schneider, October 13, 1945, and March 24, 1950. Reprinted in [R1], pp. 36, 41.

K1. T. Kinoshita and W. B. Lindquist, *Phys. Rev. Lett.* **47**, 1573 (1981).

N1. *Nature* **107**, 504 (1921).

P1. W. Pauli, *Neue Züricher Zeitung*, January 12, 1958. Reprinted in W. Pauli *Collected Scientific Papers*, Vol. 2, p. 1362. Interscience, New York, 1964.

R1. I. Rosenthal-Schneider, *Reality and Scientific Truth*, p. 74. Wayne State University Press, 1980.

3

Portrait of the Physicist
as a Young Man

Apart . . . 4. Away from others in action or function; separately,
independently, individually.

Oxford English Dictionary

It is not known whether Hermann Einstein became a partner in the featherbed
enterprise of Israel and Levi before or after August 8, 1876. Certain it is that by
then he, his mother, and all his brothers and sisters, had been living for some time
in Ulm, in the kingdom of Württemberg. On that eighth of August, Hermann
married Pauline Koch in the synagogue in Cannstatt. The young couple settled
in Ulm, first on the Münsterplatz, then, at the turn of 1878–9, on the Bahnhofstrasse. On a sunny Friday in the following March their first child was born, a
citizen of the new German empire, which Württemberg had joined in 1871. On
the following day Hermann went to register the birth of his son. In translation the
birth certificate reads, 'No. 224. Ulm, March 15, 1879. Today, the merchant Hermann Einstein, residing in Ulm, Bahnhofstrasse 135, of the Israelitic faith, personally known, appeared before the undersigned registrar, and stated that a child
of the male sex, who has received the name Albert, was born in Ulm, in his residence, to his wife Pauline Einstein, née Koch, of the Israelitic faith, on March
14 of the year 1879, at 11:30 a.m. Read, confirmed, and signed: Hermann Einstein. The Registrar, Hartman.' In 1944 the house on the Bahnhofstrasse was
destroyed during an air attack. The birth certificate can still be found in the Ulm
archives.

Albert was the first of Hermann and Pauline's two children. On November 18,
1881, their daughter, Maria, was born. There may never have been a human
being to whom Einstein felt closer than his sister Maja (as she was always called).
The choice of nonancestral names for both children illustrates the assimilationist
disposition in the Einstein family, a trend widespread among German Jews in the
nineteenth century. Albert was named (if one may call it that) after his grandfather Abraham,* but it is not known how the name Maria was chosen. 'A liberal

---

*Helen Dukas, private communication.

spirit, nondogmatic in regard to religion, prevailed in the family. Both parents had themselves been raised that way. Religious matters and precepts were not discussed' [M1]. Albert's father was proud of the fact that Jewish rites were not practised in his home [R1].

Maja's biographical essay about her brother, completed in 1924, is the main source of family recollections about Albert's earliest years. It informs us of the mother's fright at the time of Albert's birth because of the unusually large and angular back of the baby's head (that uncommon shape of the skull was to be permanent); of a grandmother's first reaction upon seeing the newest member of the family: 'Viel zu dick! Viel zu dick!' (much too heavy!); and of early apprehensions that the child might be backward because of the unusually long time before it could speak [M2]. These fears were unfounded. According to one of Einstein's own earliest childhood memories, 'when he was between two and three, he formed the ambition to speak in whole sentences. He would try each sentence out on himself by saying it softly. Then, when it seemed all right, he would say it out loud' [S1]. He was very quiet as a young child, preferring to play by himself. But there was early passion, too. On occasion, he would throw a tantrum. 'At such moments his face would turn pale, the tip of his nose would become white, and he would lose control of himself' [M2]. On several such occasions, dear little Albert threw things at his sister. These tantrums ceased when he was about seven.

The relationship between the parents was an harmonious and very loving one, with the mother having the stronger personality. She was a talented pianist who brought music into the home so the children's musical education started early. Maja learned to play the piano. Albert took violin instruction from about the time he was six until he was thirteen. The violin was to become his beloved instrument, although playing remained a burdensome duty to him through most of these early years, in which he took lessons from Herr Schmied [R2]. He taught himself to play the piano a bit and grew especially fond of improvising on that instrument.

Hermann Einstein, an unruffled, kind-hearted, and rather passive man, loved by all acquaintances [R3], was fond of literature and in the evenings would read Schiller and Heine aloud to his family [R4]. (Throughout Albert's life, Heine remained one of his most beloved authors.) In his high school years, Hermann had shown evidence of mathematical talent, but his hopes for university study were not realized because the family could not afford it.

Hermann's venture into the featherbed business was not very successful. Shortly after Albert's birth, Hermann's enterprising and energetic younger brother Jakob, an engineer, proposed that together they start a small gas and water installation business in Munich. Hermann agreed to take care of the business end and also to invest a substantial part of his and Pauline's funds in the enterprise. In 1880 Hermann and his family moved to Munich, where they registered on June 21. The modest undertaking opened on October 11 and had a promising beginning, but Jakob had greater ambitions. A few years later, he proposed starting an electrotechnical factory to produce dynamos, arc lamps, and electrical measuring equipment for municipal electric power stations and lighting systems. He also suggested that the brothers jointly buy a house in Sendling, a suburb of Munich. These plans were realized in 1885 with financial support from the family, especially Pauline's father. The firm was officially registered on May 6, 1885.

Albert and Maja loved their new home on the Adelreiterstrasse with its large garden shaded by big trees. It appears that business also went well in the beginning. In a book entitled *Versorgung von Städten mit elektrischem Strom*, we find four pages devoted to the 'Elektrotechnische Fabrik J. Einstein und Co. in München' from which we learn that the brothers had supplied power stations in München-Schwabing as well as in Varèse and Susa in Italy [U1].

Thus Einstein spent his earliest years in a warm and stable milieu that was also stimulating. In his late sixties he singled out one particular experience from that period: 'I experienced a miracle . . . as a child of four or five when my father showed me a compass' [E1]. It excited the boy so much that 'he trembled and grew cold' [R5]. 'There had to be something behind objects that lay deeply hidden . . .the development of [our] world of thought is in a certain sense a flight away from the miraculous' [E1]. Such private experiences contributed far more to Einstein's growth than formal schooling.

At the age of five, he received his first instruction at home. This episode came to an abrupt end when Einstein had a tantrum and threw a chair at the woman who taught him. At about age six he entered public school, the Volksschule. He was a reliable, persistent, and slow-working pupil who solved his mathematical problems with self-assurance though not without computational errors. He did very well. In August 1886, Pauline wrote to her mother: 'Yesterday Albert received his grades, he was again number one, his report card was brilliant' [E1a]. But Albert remained a quiet child who did not care to play with his schoolmates. His private games demanded patience and tenacity. Building a house of cards was one of his favorites.

In October 1888 Albert moved from the Volksschule to the Luitpold Gymnasium, which was to be his school till he was fifteen. In all these years he earned either the highest or the next-highest mark in mathematics and in Latin [H1]. But on the whole, he disliked those school years; authoritarian teachers, servile students, rote learning—none of these agreed with him. Further, 'he had a natural antipathy for . . . gymnastics and sports. . . . He easily became dizzy and tired' [R6]. He felt isolated and made few friends at school.

There was no lack of extracurricular stimuli, however. Uncle Jakob would pose mathematical problems and after he had solved them 'the boy experienced a deep feeling of happiness' [M3]. From the time Albert was ten until he turned fifteen, Max Talmud, a regular visitor to the family home, contributed importantly to his education. Talmud, a medical student with little money, came for dinner at the Einstein's every Thursday night. He gave Einstein popular books on science to read and, later, the writings of Kant. The two would spend hours discussing science and philosophy.* 'In all these years I never saw him reading any light lit-

*After Talmud moved to the United States, he changed his name to Talmey. A book he wrote contains recollections of his early acquaintance with Einstein [T1].

erature. Nor did I ever see him in the company of schoolmates or other boys of his age,' Talmud recalled later [T2]. In those years, 'his only diversion was music, he already played Mozart and Beethoven sonatas, accompanied by his mother' [M4]. Einstein also continued to study mathematics on his own. At the age of twelve he experienced a second miracle: he was given a small book on Euclidean geometry [H2], which he later referred to as the holy geometry book. 'The clarity and certainty of its contents made an indescribable impression on me' [E1]. From age twelve to age sixteen, he studied differential and integral calculus by himself.

Bavarian law required that all children of school age receive religious education. At the Volksschule, only instruction in Catholicism was provided. Einstein was taught the elements of Judaism at home by a distant relative [M5]. When he went to the Luitpold Gymnasium, this instruction continued at school. As a result of this inculcation, Einstein went through an intense religious phase when he was about eleven years old. His feelings were of such ardor that he followed religious precepts in detail. For example, he ate no pork [M6]. Later, in his Berlin days, he told a close friend that during this period he had composed several songs in honor of God, which he sang enthusiastically to himself on his way to school [S2]. This interlude came to an abrupt end a year later as a result of his exposure to science. He did not become bar mitzvah. He never mastered Hebrew. When he was fifty, Einstein wrote to Oberlehrer Heinrich Friedmann, his religion teacher at the Gymnasium, 'I often read the Bible, but its original text has remained inaccessible to me' [E2].

There is another story of the Munich days that Einstein himself would occasionally tell with some glee. At the Gymnasium a teacher once said to him that he, the teacher, would be much happier if the boy were not in his class. Einstein replied that he had done nothing wrong. The teacher answered, 'Yes, that is true. But you sit there in the back row and smile, and that violates the feeling of respect which a teacher needs from his class' [S1, S2].

The preceding collection of stories about Einstein the young boy demonstrates the remarkable extent to which his most characteristic personal traits were native rather than acquired. The infant who at first was slow to speak, then becomes number one at school (the widespread belief that he was a poor pupil is unfounded) turned into the man whose every scientific triumph was preceded by a long period of quiet gestation. The boy who sat in the classroom and smiled became the old man who—as described in Chapter 1—laughed because he thought the authorities handling the Oppenheimer case were fools. In his later years, his pacifist convictions would lead him to speak out forcefully against arbitrary authority. However, in his personal and scientific conduct, he was not a rebel, one who resists authority, nor—except once*—a revolutionary, one who

---

*Einstein's one truly revolutionary contribution is his light-quantum paper of 1905. It is significant that he never believed that the physical meaning of the light-quantum hypothesis had been fully understood. These are matters to which I shall return in later chapters.

aims to overthrow authority. Rather, he was so free that any form of authority but the one of reason seemed irresistibly funny to him. On another issue, his brief religious ardor left no trace, just as in his later years he would often wax highly enthusiastic about a scientific idea, then drop it as of no consequence. About his religious phase, Einstein himself later wrote, 'It is clear to me that [this] lost religious paradise of youth was a first attempt to liberate myself from the "only-personal"' [E3], an urge that stayed with him all his life. In his sixties, he once commented that he had sold himself body and soul to science, being in flight from the 'I' and the 'we' to the 'it' [E4]. Yet he did not seek distance between himself and other people. The detachment lay within and enabled him to walk through life immersed in thought. What is so uncommon about this man is that at the same time he was neither out of touch with the world nor aloof.

Another and most important characteristic of Einstein is already evident in the child quietly at play by itself: his 'apartness.' We also see this in the greater importance of private experience than of formal schooling and will see it again in his student days, when self-study takes precedence over class attendance, and in his days at the patent office in Bern when he does his most creative work almost without personal contact with the physics community. It is also manifested in his relations to other human beings and to authority. Apartness was to serve him well in his single-handed and single-minded pursuits, most notably on his road from the special to the general theory of relativity. This quality is also strongly in evidence during the second half of his life, when he maintained a profoundly skeptical attitude toward quantum mechanics. Finally, apartness became a practical necessity to him, in order to protect his cherished privacy from a world hungry for legend and charisma.

Let us return to the Munich days. Hermann's business, successful initially, began to stagnate. Signor Garrone, the Italian representative, suggested moving the factory to Italy, where prospects appeared much better. Jakob was all for it; his enthusiasm carried Hermann along. In June 1894, the factory in Sendling was liquidated, the house sold, and the family moved to Milan. All except Albert, who was to stay behind to finish school. The new factory, 'Einstein and Garrone,' was established in Pavia. Some time in 1895, Hermann and his family moved from Milan to Pavia, where they settled at Via Foscolo 11 [S3].

Alone in Munich, Albert was depressed and nervous [M4]. He missed his family and disliked school. Since he was now sixteen years old, the prospect of military service began to weigh on him.* Without consulting his parents, he decided to join them in Italy. With the help of a certificate from his family doctor attesting to

---

*By law, a boy could leave Germany only before the age of seventeen without having to return for military service. Einstein's revulsion against military service started when, as a very young boy, he and his parents watched a military parade. The movements of men without any apparent will of their own frightened the boy. His parents had to promise him that he would never become a soldier [R4].

understand.

nervous disorders, he obtained a release from the Gymnasium and in the early spring of 1895 traveled to Pavia. He promised his parents, who were upset by his sudden arrival, that he would prepare himself by self-study for the admission examination at the ETH in Zürich and also informed them that he planned to give up his German citizenship [F1]. A new, freer life and independent work transformed the quiet boy into a communicative young man. The Italian landscape and the arts made a lasting impression on him [M7].

In October 1895 Einstein went to Zürich to take the ETH examination. He failed, although he did well in mathematics and the sciences.* Following a suggestion to obtain the Matura, the high school diploma that would entitle him to enroll at the ETH, he next went to the cantonal school in Aarau, in the German-speaking part of Switzerland, where he boarded with the Winteler family. For Jost Winteler, one of his teachers and a scholar in his own right, Einstein developed great respect, for Frau Winteler a deep affection. He got along well with their seven children and was treated as part of the family.

For the first time in his life he enjoyed school. Shortly before his death he wrote, 'This school has left an indelible impression on me because of its liberal spirit and the unaffected thoughtfulness of the teachers, who in no way relied on external authority' [E5]. The frontispiece photograph, taken in Aarau, shows Einstein as a confident-looking, if not cocky, young man without a trace of the timidity of the earlier years. A classmate later remembered his energetic and assured stride, the touch of mockery in his face, and his 'undaunted ways of expressing his personal opinion, whether it offended or not' [S4]. He may always have been sure of himself. Now it showed.

A brief essay by Einstein, entitled 'Mes Projets d'Avenir,' has survived from his Aarau schooldays (reproduced on pp. 42–43). Written in less-than-perfect French in about 1895, it conveys his sense of purpose. In translation, it reads

My plans for the future

A happy man is too content with the present to think much about the future. Young people, on the other hand, like to occupy themselves with bold plans. Furthermore, it is natural for a serious young man to gain as precise an idea as possible about his desired aims.

If I were to have the good fortune to pass my examinations, I would go to [the ETH in] Zürich. I would stay there for four years in order to study mathematics and physics. I imagine myself becoming a teacher in those branches of the natural sciences, choosing the theoretical part of them.

Here are the reasons which led me to this plan. Above all, it is [my] disposition for abstract and mathematical thought, [my] lack of imagination and practical ability. My desires have also inspired in me the same resolve. That is quite natural; one always likes to do the things for which one has ability. Then there is also a certain independence in the scientific profession which I like a great deal. [E5]

*He was examined in political and literary history, German, French, biology, mathematics, descriptive geometry, chemistry, physics, and drawing and also had to write an essay.

In 1896 Einstein's status changed from that of German high school pupil in Aarau to that of stateless student at the ETH. Upon payment of three mark, he received a document, issued in Ulm on January 28, 1896, which stated that he was no longer a German (more precisely, a Württemberger) citizen. In the fall he successfully passed the Matura with the following grades (maximum = 6): German 5, Italian 5, history 6, geography 4, algebra 6, geometry 6, descriptive geometry 6, physics 6, chemistry 5, natural history 5, drawing (art) 4, drawing (technical) 4. On October 29 he registered as a resident of Zürich and became a student at the ETH. Upon satisfactory completion of the four-year curriculum, he would qualify as a Fachlehrer, a specialized teacher, in mathematics and physics at a high school. Throughout his student years, from 1896 to 1900, Einstein lived on an allowance of one hundred Swiss francs per month, of which he saved twenty each month to pay for his Swiss naturalization papers.*

At this time, however, his family was in financial trouble. Hermann and Jakob's factory in Pavia failed and had to be liquidated in 1896. Most of the family funds poured into the enterprise were lost. Jakob found employment with a large firm. Hermann decided once more to start an independent factory, in Milan this time. Albert warned his father in vain against this new venture and also visited an uncle in Germany to urge him to refrain from further financial support. His advice was not followed. The Einsteins moved back to Milan and began anew. Two years later Hermann again had to give up. At that time, Albert wrote to Maja, 'The misfortune of my poor parents, who for so many years have not had a happy moment, weighs most heavily on me. It also hurts me deeply that I as a grown-up must be a passive witness . . . without being able to do even the smallest thing about it. I am nothing but a burden to my relatives. . . . It would surely be better if I did not live at all. Only the thought . . . that year after year I do not allow myself a pleasure, a diversion, keeps me going and must protect me often from despair' [M8]. This melancholy mood passed when his father found new work, again related to the installation of electrical power stations.

Einstein's student days did have their pleasant moments. He would allow himself an occasional evening at a concert or a theatre or at a Kaffeehaus to talk with friends. He spent happy hours with the distinguished historian Alfred Stern and his family, and with the family of Marcel Grossmann, a fellow student and friend. His acquaintance in Zürich with Michele Angelo Besso grew into a life-long friendship. Then and later he could savor the blessings of friendship and the beauty of music and literature. But, already as a young man, nothing could distract him from his destiny, which with poetic precision he put in focus at the age of eighteen: 'Strenuous labor and the contemplation of God's nature are the angels which, reconciling, fortifying, and yet mercilessly severe, will guide me through the tumult of life' [E6].

*In the *Tagesblatt der Stadt Zürich* of 1895, one finds the following typical advertisements: small furnished room SF 20/month; two daily hot meals in a boarding house SF 1.40/day without wine; a better room with board SF 70/month. (I thank Res Jost for finding this out for me.) Thus Einstein's allowance was modest but not meager.

Albert Einstein

Mes projets d'avenir.

Un homme heureux est trop con-
tent de la présence (du présent) pour penser beaucoup
à l'avenir. Mais de l'autre côté ce sont
surtout les jeunes gens qui aiment s'occu-
per de hardis projets. Du reste c'est aussi
une chose naturelle pour un jeune
homme sérieux, qu'il se fasse une
idée aussi précise que possible du but
de ses désirs.

Si j'avais le bonheur de
passer heureusement mes examens,
j'irai à l'école polytechnique de
Zurich. J'y resterais quatre ans pour
étudier les mathématiques et la physique.
Je m'imagine (de) devenir professeur dans
ces branches de la science de la nature (naturelles),
en choisissant la partie théorétique
de ces sciences.

Einstein's essay written in Aarau, for which he received the grade 3 to 4 (out of 6).
Courtesy Staatsarchiv Kanton Aargau.

Voici les ~~choses~~ raisons ~~causes~~ qui m'ont

porté à ce projet. ~~Et~~ surtout la disposition

individuelle pour les pensées abstraites et

mathématiques, le manque ~~de la~~ phantaisie

et du talent pratique. Ce sont aussi mes

désirs qui ~~me présentent le même but,~~
m'ont inspiré la même ~~profession~~ résolution.
me conduisaient à la même ~~profession.~~

C'est tout naturel, on aime ~~toujours~~ faire
les
~~les~~ choses, pour lesquelles on a ~~le~~ du talent.

~~Puis ... est aussi ... ...~~

de la profession ~~qui~~ scientifique qui me

plaît beaucoup.

3 — 4.

'Most of the time I worked in the physical laboratory, fascinated by the direct contact with observation,' Einstein later wrote about his years at the ETH [E7]. However, his experimental projects were not received with enthusiasm by his professor, Heinrich Friedrich Weber. In particular, Einstein was not allowed to conduct an experiment on the earth's movement against the aether [R8].* At one point Weber is supposed to have said to Einstein: 'You are a smart boy, Einstein, a very smart boy. But you have one great fault: you do not let yourself be told anything' [S5]. Einstein's fascination with experiment must have been dampened. It is recorded in the Protokollbuch of the mathematics-physics section of the ETH that he received a strong warning *(Verweis)* because he neglected his laboratory work.

Einstein, in turn, was not impressed with Weber's physics courses. He 'did not care much for [Weber's] introduction to theoretical physics because he was disappointed not to learn anything new about Maxwell theory. . . . As a typical representative of classical physics, [Weber] simply ignored everything which came after Helmholtz [S6]. He followed some other courses with intense interest, however.** On several later occasions, he singled out Adolf Hurwitz and Hermann Minkowski as excellent mathematics teachers [R9, E6].† But on the whole Einstein did not excel in regular course attendance. He relied far more on self-study. As a student he read the works of Kirchhoff, Hertz, and Helmholtz; learned Maxwell theory from the first edition of *Einführung in die Maxwellsche Theorie der Elektrizität* by August Föppl, which had come out in 1894 [F1]; read Mach's book on mechanics, 'a book which, with its critical attitudes toward basic concepts and basic laws, made a deep and lasting impression on me' [S8]; and studied papers by Lorentz and by Boltzmann.‡ Among other subjects which drew his attention was the work of Darwin [R9].

'In all there were only two examinations; for the rest one could do what one wanted . . . a freedom which I thoroughly enjoyed . . . up to a few months before the examination' [E9]. These few-month periods were made easy for Einstein because Marcel Grossmann made available his lecture notes, beautifully written, meticulously organized.§ Nevertheless, these times of working under orders imposed by others were an ordeal to him. It took him a year after his final examination to fully regain his taste for physics [E9]. His final grades were 5 each for theoretical physics, experimental physics, and astronomy; 5.5 for the theory of

*See Section 6d.

**For a complete list of Einstein's four-year curriculum, see [S7].

†It is of interest for Einstein's later work on general relativity that he also attended some of Geiser's lectures on differential geometry [K1, R10]. I discuss Geiser's influence in Section 12b.

‡I have not found any evidence for the correspondence between Boltzmann and Einstein referred to in [M9] and [S9].

§These lecture notes are now in the historical collection of the library in Zürich.

functions; 4.5 for an essay on heat conductivity (out of a maximum of 6). And so, in August 1900, Einstein became qualified as a Fachlehrer, together with three other students, who each immediately obtained positions as assistants at the ETH [S5]. A fifth student, Mileva Marič, did not pass.* Einstein himself was jobless.

It was a disappointment for him. He never quite forgave Weber for holding out an assistantship and then letting the matter drop.** In September he wrote to Hurwitz, asking if he could be considered for a vacant assistantship [E11]. A few days later, he wrote again, 'I note with great joy that there is a prospect of obtaining the position' [E12]. Nothing came of this, however. And so as the year ended, he was still without work.

However, there were some satisfactions. In December 1900 he finished his first scientific paper, dealing with intermolecular forces, and submitted it from Zürich to the *Annalen der Physik* [E13]. On February 21, 1901, he was granted the Swiss citizenship for which he had saved so long.† For the rest of his life, he remained a citizen of Switzerland, 'the most beautiful corner on earth I know' [S10].

Early in 1901 Einstein again tried to find a university position. 'I have been with my parents [in Milan] for three weeks to seek from here a position as an assistant at a university. I would have found one long ago if Weber had not played a dishonest game with me' [E14].‡ In March 1901 he sent a reprint of his first paper to Friedrich Wilhelm Ostwald in Leipzig, along with a letter in which he inquired 'whether you perhaps might have use for a mathematical physicist who is familiar with absolute measurements' [E15]. In April he wrote to Heike Kamerlingh Onnes asking for a position in Leiden [E16]. Perhaps he never received replies. Certainly his applications were unsuccessful. He was discouraged, as we know from a letter from his father to Ostwald§: 'My son is deeply unhappy with his current state of unemployment. Day by day the feeling grows in him that his career is off the track . . . the awareness weighs on him that he is a burden to us, people of small means' [E17]. Hermann asked Ostwald to at least send a few words of encouragement about his son's paper. Nine years later, Einstein and Ostwald would both be in Geneva to receive honorary doctorates. The year after that Ostwald would be the first to propose Einstein for the Nobel prize.¶

*Mileva made a second try in July 1901 and failed again.

**After Weber's death in 1912, Einstein wrote to a friend, in a way quite uncommon for him, 'Weber's death is good for the ETH' [E10].

†He had formally applied for citizenship on October 19, 1899. On January 10, 1900, his father made the required declaration that he had no objections to this application [F2]. On March 13, 1901, he was declared unfit for the army (Untauglich A) because of flat feet and varicose veins.

‡' . . . wenn Weber nicht ein falsches Spiel gegen mich spielte.'

§The letters from the Einsteins to Ostwald have been reproduced in [K2].

¶See Chapter 30.

Finally Einstein found a temporary job. Starting May 19, 1901, he became a substitute teacher for two months at a high school in Winterthur. He wrote to Winteler that he had never expected to derive such pleasure from teaching. 'After having taught for five or six hours in the morning, I am still quite fresh and work in the afternoon either in the library on my further education or at home on interesting problems. . . . I have given up the ambition to get to a university since I saw that also under the present circumstances I maintain the strength and desire to make scientific efforts' [E18].* To Grossmann he wrote, also from Winterthur, that he was at work on kinetic gas theory and that he was pondering the movement of matter relative to the aether [E19].

After Winterthur, another temporary position came his way. He was appointed for one year, to begin in September 1901, at a private school in Schaffhausen [F3]. Once again there was enough time for physics. Here is Einstein writing in December 1901: 'Since September 15, 1901, I am a teacher at a private school in Schaffhausen. During the first two months of my activities at that school, I wrote my doctoral dissertation on a topic in the kinetic theory of gases. A month ago I handed in this thesis at the University of Zürich'** [E20]. This work was not accepted as a thesis, however.† This setback was the last one in Einstein's career. It came at about the time that he left Schaffhausen for Bern, where he was to spend the most creative years of his life.

The first initiative for the move to Bern had already been taken some time in 1900, when Marcel Grossmann had spoken to his family about Einstein's employment difficulties. This led Marcel's father to recommend Einstein to Friedrich Haller, the director of the federal patent office in Bern. Einstein was deeply grateful for this recommendation.‡ There the matter rested until December 11, 1901, when a vacancy at the patent office was advertised in the *Schweizerische Bundesblatt*. Einstein at once sent a letter of application [E20]. At some point he was interviewed by Haller. Perhaps he received some assurances of a position at that time. In any event, he resigned his job at Schaffhausen and settled in Bern in February 1902, before he had any appointment there. At first his means of support were a small allowance from his family and fees from tutoring in mathematics and physics. One of his students described him as follows: 'about five feet ten, broad-shouldered, slightly stooped, a pale brown skin, a sensuous mouth, black moustache, nose slightly aquiline, radiant brown eyes, a pleasant voice, speaking

*In this same letter, Einstein also reported that he had met one of the leading German physicists. I have been unable to find out who that was.

**At that time, the ETH did not yet grant the PhD degree.

†I have been unable to find a response from Zürich concerning Einstein's proposed thesis. This kinetic theory paper was later published [E21]. Earlier in the year, Einstein had contemplated submitting an extended version of his first paper, on intermolecular forces, as a PhD thesis [E14].

‡He expressed his gratitude in a letter to Marcel Grossmann dated April 14, 1901, [E14] (not 1902, as is stated in [S11]).

French correctly but with a light accent' [F4]. It was at this time that he met Maurice Solovine, 'der gute Solo,' who came to be tutored and became a friend for life. Einstein, Solovine, and another friend, Konrad Habicht, met regularly to discuss philosophy, physics, and literature, from Plato to Dickens. They solemnly constituted themselves as founders and sole members of the 'Akademie Olympia,' dined together, typically on sausage, cheese, fruit, and tea, and generally had a wonderful time.*

Meanwhile, Einstein's appointment by the Swiss federal council came through. As of June 16, 1902, he was technical expert third class at the patent office at an annual salary of SF 3500—on a trial basis.

Before settling in Bern, Einstein already had plans to marry a fellow student from the ETH with whom he had often discussed science in Zürich. She was Mileva Marič (or Marity), born in 1875 in Titel (South Hungary), of Greek Catholic background. Einstein's parents were strongly opposed to the marriage; 'perhaps they had wished to pursue other plans' [M10]. In 1902 there was temporary friction between Einstein and his mother, who neither then nor later liked Mileva [E23]. It was altogether a hard year for Pauline. Her husband's series of misfortunes had undermined his robust health. A brief and fatal heart disease felled him. Einstein came from Bern to Milan to be with his father, who on his death-bed finally consented to his son's marriage. When the end was near, Hermann asked everyone to leave so that he could die alone. It was a moment his son never recalled without feelings of guilt**. Hermann Einstein died on October 10, 1902, and was buried in Milan

Albert and Mileva married on January 6, 1903. There was a small party that evening. Afterward, when the couple arrived at their lodgings, Einstein had to wake up the landlord. He had forgotten his keys [M10]. Much later, Einstein recalled the inner resistance with which he had entered the marriage [E24]. On May 14, 1904, their son Hans Albert was born, through whom the family line continues to this day.

Einstein did well at the patent office. He took his work seriously and often found it interesting. There was always enough time and energy left for his own physics. In 1903 and 1904 he published papers on the foundations of statistical mechanics. On September 16, 1904, his provisional appointment was made permanent. Further promotion, wrote Haller, 'should wait until he has fully mastered machine technology; he studied physics' [F5].

No one before or since has widened the horizons of physics in so short a time as Einstein did in 1905. His work of that year will of course be discussed at length

---

*In his late sixties, Einstein remembered the days 'when we ran our happy "Academy," which after all was less childish than those respectable ones which I got to know later from close in' [E22]. The best description of the Akademie is the one by Solovine, who records that the members also read Spinoza, Hume, Mach, Poincaré, Sophocles, Racine, and Cervantes [S12].

**Helen Dukas, private communication.

in later chapters.* Here I note only that in March he completed a paper which was to earn him the Nobel prize and that in April he finished an article which finally gained him the PhD degree from the University of Zürich [E25].

On April 1, 1906, Einstein was promoted to technical expert second class with a salary raise to SF 4500. He now knew enough technology and, writes Haller, 'belongs among the most esteemed experts at the office' [F6]. At the end of 1906, he finished a fundamental paper on specific heats. He also found time to write book reviews for the *Annalen der Physik* [K3]. At the end of 1907 Einstein made the first important strides toward the general theory of relativity (see Chapter 9).

Here the sketch of the young man's life ends. Einstein's days in Bern are not yet over, but a new phase is about to begin: his academic career (see further Section 10a).

At the end of his life, Einstein wrote that the greatest thing Marcel Grossman did for him was to recommend him to the patent office with the help of the elder Grossman [E26]. That no doubt is true. Einstein's funds may have been limited, his marriage may not have been perfect. But, for the man who preferred to think in apartness, the Bern days were the closest he would ever come to paradise on earth.

An Addendum on Einstein Biographies

In preparing this chapter, I have striven to rely as much as possible on original documents. The Einstein Archives in Princeton and Helen Dukas's guidance were, of course, of prime importance. I also derived great benefit from the *Wissenschaftschistorische Sammlung* of the ETH Library in Zürich, where Dr. B. Glaus gave me much help. In addition, I have made grateful use of the following biographies.

1. *Albert Einstein, Beitrag für sein Lebensbild* by Maja Einstein; in manuscript form. Completed in Florence on February 15, 1924. The original manuscript is in the hands of the Besso family; a copy is present in the Princeton Archives. Cited in the references to this chapter as M.
2. *Albert Einstein, a Biographical Portrait* by Anton Reiser, the pen name for Rudolf Kayser; A. and C. Boni, New York, 1930. Cited below as R. In 1931, Einstein wrote about this book: 'The book by Reiser is, in my opinion, the best biography which has been written about me. It comes from the pen of a man who knows me well personally' [E8]. (Kayser, a connoisseur of the German language, was for many years the chief editor of the influential *Neue Rundschau*, a Berlin monthly; he was also the author of numerous books and a teacher. In 1924 he married Einstein's stepdaughter Ilse.)

*For the doctoral thesis and Brownian motion, see Chapter 5. For special relativity, see Chapters 6 through 8. For the light-quantum hypothesis, see Chapter 19.

3. A. Einstein, Autobiographisches, in *Albert Einstein: Philosopher-Scientist* (P. Schilpp, Ed.); Tudor, New York, 1949. Cited below as E. The closest Einstein ever came to writing an autobiography. Indispensable.

4. C. Seelig, *Albert Einstein;* Europa Verlag, Zürich, 1960. Quoted below as Se. The material is based in part on an extensive correspondence between the author and A. Einstein, Margot Einstein, and Helen Dukas. This biography is a much-expanded version of an earlier book by C. Seelig, *Albert Einstein;* Europa Verlag, Zürich, 1954. (The English translation of this last book is not recommended.)

5. B. Hoffmann in collaboration with II. Dukas, *Albert Einstein, Creator and Rebel;* Viking, New York, 1972.

6. *Albert Einstein in Bern* by M. Flückiger; Paul Haupt Verlag, Bern, 1974. Cited below as F. Contains a number of reproductions of rare documents pertaining to Einstein's younger days. The text contains numerous inaccuracies.

7. Philipp Frank, *Albert Einstein, sein Leben und seine Zeit;* Vieweg, Braunschweig, 1979. This German version is superior to the English edition, *Einstein, His Life and Time,* Knopf, New York, 1947, since large parts of the German edition do not appear in the English one. The German edition also contains an introduction by Einstein in which he mentions that he encouraged Frank to write this book.

8. H. E. Specker, Ed. *Einstein und Ulm;* Kohlhammer, Stuttgart, 1979. Contains details about Einstein's ancestry, including a family tree.

9. C. Kirsten and H. J. Treder, Ed., *Albert Einstein in Berlin 1913–1933;* Akademie Verlag, Berlin, 1979. An annotated collection of documents from the archives of the Prussian Academy of Sciences. Splendid.

References

E1. E, p. 8.

E1a. Pauline Einstein, letter to Jette Koch, August 1, 1886.

E2. A. Einstein, letter to H. Friedmann, March 18, 1929.

E3. E, p. 4.

E4. A. Einstein, letter to Hermann Broch, September 2, 1945.

E5. ——, *Mes Projets d'Avenir;* the original is in the Staatsarchiv Kanton Aargau.

E6. ——, letter to Rosa Winteler, June 3, 1897.

E7. E, p. 14.

E8. A. Einstein, letter to E. F. Magnin, February 25, 1931.

E9. E, p. 16.

E10. A. Einstein, letter to H. Zangger, summer 1912.

E11. ——, letter to A. Hurwitz, September 23, 1900.

E12. ——, letter to A. Hurwitz, September 26, 1900.

E13. ——, *AdP* **4**, 513, (1901).

E14. ——, letter to M. Grossman, April 14, 1901.

E15. ——, letter to W. Ostwald, March 19, 1901.

E16. ——, letter to H. Kamerlingh Onnes, April 17, 1901.

E17. H. Einstein, letter to W. Ostwald, April 13, 1901.

E18. A. Einstein, letter to J. Winteler, undated, 1901.

E19. ——, letter to M. Grossman, undated, 1901.

E20. ——, letter to the Eidgenössisches Amt für geistiges Eigentum, December 18, 1901; reproduced in F, p. 55.

E21. ———, *AdP* **9,** 417 (1902).

E22. ——, letter to M. Solovine, November 25, 1948.

E23. Pauline Einstein, letter to R. Winteler, February 20, 1902.

E24. A. Einstein, letter to C. Seelig, May 5, 1952.

E25. ——, *Eine neue Bestimmung der Moleküldimensionen.* Buchdruckerei K. J. Wyss, Bern, 1905.

E26. ———, in *Helle Zeit, Dunkle Zeit*, p. 12. C. Seelig Ed. Europa Verlag, Zürich, 1956.

F1. A. Föppl, *Einführung in die Maxwellsche Theorie der Elektrizität.* Teubner, Leipzig, 1894.

F2. F, pp. 43–44.

F3. F, p. 34.

F4. F, p. 11.

F5. F, p. 67.

F6. F, p. 65.

H1. Ph. Hausel, *Münchner Merkur*, March 14, 1979.

H2. E. Heis and T. J. Eschweiler, *Lehrbuch der Geometrie zum Gebrauch an hoheren Lehranstalten.* Du-Mont and Schauberg, Cologne, 1867.

K1. L. Kollros, *Helv. Phys. Acta Suppl.* **4,** 271 (1956).

K2. H. Körber, *Forschungen und Fortschritte* **38,** 74 (1974).

K3. M. J. Klein and A. Needell, *Isis* **68,** 601 (1977).

M1. M, p. 12.

M2. M, pp. 9–10.

M3. M, p. 14.

M4. M, p. 15.

M5. M, pp. 11–12.

M6. M, p. 13.

M7. M, p. 16.

M8. M, p. 18.

M9. M, p. 20.

M10. M, p. 23.

R1. R, p. 28.

R2. R, p. 31.

R3. R, p. 24.

R4. R, p. 26.

R5. R, p. 25.

R6. R, p. 33.

R7. R, p. 54.

R8. R, p. 52.

R9. R, p. 48.

R10. R, p. 49.

S1. E. G. Straus, lecture given at Yeshiva University, September 18, 1979.
S2. Se, p. 15.
S3. E. Sanesi, *Physis* **18,** 174 (1976).
S4. Se, pp. 21–22.
S5. Se, p. 48.
S6. Se, p. 47.
S7. Se, pp. 38–40.
S8 Se, p. 54.
S9. Se, p. 43.
S10. Se, p. 415.
S11. Se, p. 85.
S12. M. Solovine, Ed., *Albert Einstein, Lettres à Maurice Solovine,* introduction. Gauthier Villars, Paris, 1956.
T1. M. Talmey, *The Relativity Theory Simplified and the Formative Years of Its Inventor.* Falcon Press, New York, 1932.
T2. [T1], pp. 164–5.
U1. F. Uppenborn, Ed., *Die Versorgung von Städten mit elektrischem Strom,* p. 63. Springer, Berlin, 1891.

II
STATISTICAL PHYSICS

4

Entropy and Probability

4a. Einstein's Contributions at a Glance

Einstein's activities related to thermodynamics, statistical mechanics, and kinetic theory begin with his very first paper, completed at the end of 1900, and span a quarter of a century, during which time he wrote close to forty articles bearing in varying degree on these subjects. The first of the vintage years was 1905, when he developed theoretically three independent methods for finding Avogadro's number.

In an autobiographical sketch published in 1949, Einstein's comments on his contributions to statistical physics are relatively brief. The main message is contained in the following phrases: 'Unacquainted with the investigations of Boltzmann and Gibbs which had appeared earlier and which in fact had dealt exhaustively with the subject, I developed statistical mechanics and the molecular-kinetic theory of thermodynamics based on it. My main purpose for doing this was to find facts which would attest to the existence of atoms of definite size' [E1]. Here he is referring to his three papers published* in the period 1902–4, in which he made 'a rediscovery of all essential elements of statistical mechanics' [B1]. At that time, his knowledge of the writings of Ludwig Boltzmann was fragmentary and he was not at all aware of the treatise by Josiah Willard Gibbs [G1]. In 1910, Einstein wrote that had he known of Gibbs's book, he would not have published his own papers on the foundations of statistical mechanics except for a few comments [E2]. The influential review on the conceptual basis of statistical mechanics completed in that same year by his friends and admirers Paul Ehrenfest and Tatiana Ehrenfest-Affanasjewa refers to these Einstein articles only in passing, in an appendix [E3]. It is true that Einstein's papers of 1902–4 did not add much that was new to the statistical foundations of the second law of thermodynamics. It is also true that, as Einstein himself pointed out [E4], these papers are no prerequisite for the understanding of his work of 1905 on the reality of molecules. Nevertheless, this early work was of great importance for his own further scientific development. In particular, it contains the germ of the theory of fluctuations which he was to apply with unmatched skill from 1905 until 1925.

It would be entirely beside the mark, however, to consider Einstein's main con-

---

*In 1901, he had sent the first of these papers to Zürich in the hope that it might be accepted as his doctoral thesis; see Chapter 3.

tributions to statistical physics and kinetic theory as neither more nor less than extremely ingenious and important applications of principles discovered independently by him but initially developed by others. Take, for example, his treatment of Brownian motion. It bristles with new ideas: particles in suspension behave like molecules in solution; there is a relation between diffusion and viscosity, the first fluctuation–dissipation theorem ever noted; the mean square displacement of the particles can be related to the diffusion coefficient. The final conclusion,* that Avogadro's number can essentially be determined from observations with an ordinary microscope, never fails to cause a moment of astonishment even if one has read the paper before and therefore knows the punch line. After 1905, Einstein would occasionally mention in conversation that 'it is puzzling that Boltzmann did not himself draw this most perspicuous consequence [i.e., the explanation of Brownian motion], since Boltzmann had laid the foundations for the whole subject' [S1]. However, it is hard to imagine the embattled Boltzmann evincing the serious yet playful spirit with which Einstein handled the problem of molecular reality.

Even more profoundly novel are Einstein's applications of statistical ideas to quantum physics. In his first paper on this subject, the light-quantum hypothesis is arrived at by a statistical argument. This work was completed two months before his paper on Brownian motion. After 1905, Einstein did occasionally return to classical statistical physics, but in those later years all his main work on statistical problems was in the domain of the quantum theory. In fact, a stronger statement can be made: all of Einstein's principal contributions to the quantum theory are statistical in origin. They include his work on specific heats, on particle–wave duality, on the particle nature of the light-quantum, on spontaneous and induced radiative processes, and on a new derivation of the blackbody radiation formula. His last encounter with statistics occurred as an aside—as he put it [S2]—late in 1924 and early in 1925, when he was already working hard on unified field theory. The three papers produced at that time brought him to the very threshold of wave mechanics.

Since Einstein's papers on statistical physics cover so much ground, it may be helpful to preface a more detailed discussion of their main points with a brief chronology.

1901–2. Thermodynamics of liquid surfaces [E5] and of electrolysis [E6]. In these papers, Einstein was looking for experimental support for a hypothesis concerning molecular forces. Making an analogy with gravitation, he conjectured that the potential between two molecules of species i and j is of the form $c_i c_j \phi(r)$, where the c's are characteristic for the species and $\phi(r)$ is a universal function of distance. In a further analogy with gravitation, he assumed that each c_i is of the form Σc_α, where c_α is a number characteristic for the αth atom in the molecule of kind i. He was able to relate the c's to the specific volume and to the surface tension and its

---

*This reasoning will be discussed in detail in Chapter 5.

temperature derivative. Using known data, he could check his hypothesis, which, he found, actually worked fairly well for a limited range of carbon compounds (with molecular weights mainly of the order of 100) but not for lighter molecules, such as water.

Einstein's hypothesis is, of course, incorrect. As is now well known, even in the simplest semiphenomenological models (such as the Lennard–Jones potential), the intermolecular forces not only have a characteristic strength constant but also depend on the molecular size. This first paper by Einstein is of interest only in that it shows how from the start he was groping for universal principles, in the present case for a relation between molecular forces and gravitation. 'It should be noted,' he remarked, 'that the constants c increase in general but not always with increasing weight; however, this increase is not linear. Therefore the question if and how our forces are related to gravitational forces must for the time being be kept completely open' [E5]. The purpose of his second paper [E6] was likewise to obtain information on his conjectured force law. Here, no comparison data were available. The paper concludes with an apology by Einstein for not being in a position to contribute personally to the experimental clarification of his theoretical ideas.

That Einstein was quite taken with the concept of a universal molecular force is seen from a letter to Grossmann in 1901. 'I am certain now that my theory of the attractive forces . . . can be extended to gases . . . Then the decision about the question of the close relation of molecular forces with the Newtonian forces acting at a distance will come a big step nearer' [E7]. Then follows a lyrical passage. 'It is a wonderful feeling to recognize the unifying features of a complex of phenomena which present themselves as quite unconnected to the direct experience of the senses.'

In December 1907, Einstein wrote to Stark: 'I am sending you . . . all my publications except for my worthless first two papers [E8]. And so we meet for the first time a trait typical of Einstein throughout his life. He could be very enthusiastic about his own ideas and then, when necessary, drop them some time later, without any pain, as being of no consequence.

I have dwelt at disproportionate length on these first two papers simply because by doing so I shall have no need to return to them. Two final comments about them: (1) one thermodynamic relation contained in the first paper did survive;* and (2) in 1911 Einstein briefly returned one more time to the molecular theory of liquid surface phenomena.**

---

*Let l be the heat capacity at constant pressure p of a liquid held in a container, ω the liquid surface, and σ the surface tension. Einstein derived the relation [E5]

$$\frac{\partial l}{\partial \omega} = -T \, (\partial^2 \sigma / \partial T^2)_{p,\omega}$$

This result is discussed by Schottky [S3].

**In a short note on the Eötvös relation between surface tension, specific volume, and temperature [E9].

1902-4.   The three studies on the foundations of statistical mechanics. The first paper deals with the definitions of temperature and entropy for thermal equilibrium conditions and with the equipartition theorem [E10], the second one with irreversibility [E11], the third one with fluctuations and new ways to determine the magnitude of the Boltzmann constant [E12]. Einstein published a brief comment on these papers in 1911 [E2].

March 1905.   Introduction of the light-quantum hypothesis with the help of an argument based on Boltzmann statistics [E13]. The first correct application of equipartition to radiation.

April 1905.   Completion of the PhD thesis on a new determination of molecular dimensions [E14]. A correction to this paper was published in 1911 [E15] and a minor comment in 1920 [E16].

1905-8.   Several papers on Brownian motion. The first and most important dates from May 1905 [E17]. A sequel in 1906 includes the discussion of rotatory Brownian motion [E18]. A brief comment on the interpretation of mean velocity was published in 1907 [E19] and a semipopular account of the whole subject in 1908 [E20].

1906.   Quantum theory of specific heats of solids [E21]. With this paper, solid state quantum theory begins.

1907.   Voltage fluctuations in a condensor as a means of measuring Boltzmann's constant [E22]. Relativistic transformation of thermodynamic quantities [E23].*

1909.   Two papers containing details of the energy fluctuations of electromagnetic radiation around thermal equilibrium and the first statement in history of particle-wave duality, arrived at by the interpretation of these fluctuation formulae. Discussion of the Brownian motion exhibited by a mirror moving uniformly through a radiation field [E24, E25].

1910.   Statistical aspects of the motion of resonator in a radiation field [E26, E27]; a further comment in 1915 [E28]. The theory of critical opalescence [E29].

1911.   Two additional comments on the specific heat paper of 1906 [E21]: an attempt to relate the specific heat of solids to their elastic properties [E30] and an attempt to refine his assumption, made earlier for reasons of simplicity, that lattice vibrations can be treated as approximately monochromatic [E31].

1912-13.   The thermodynamics of photochemical processes [E32, E33].

1914.   An abortive attempt to explain anomalies in the specific heat of gases [E34].

1916-17.   Three overlapping but nonidentical papers dealing with spontaneous and induced radiative processes (*A* and *B* coefficients), a new derivation of the blackbody radiation law, and the Brownian motion of a molecular gas in equilibrium with radiation, from which the momentum properties of a light-quantum are deduced [E35, E36, E37].

1924.   A qualitative discussion of thermal conductivity in gases for the case

---

*This last topic is not yet ripe for historic assessment [L1].

where the mean free path of the molecules is small compared with the linear dimensions of the container [E38]. At that time it was believed by some that the motion of foils in a radiometer was somehow induced by radiation pressure. Einstein's paper, which complements earlier work by Knudsen, was a contribution toward the elimination of this incorrect idea.

1924–5. Three papers on the quantum theory of a molecular gas; discovery of the condensation phenomenon named after Einstein and also after Bose; Einstein's last application of fluctuation theory, which leads him to particle–wave duality for matter by a route independent of the one taken earlier by de Broglie [E39, E40, E41].

Reviews. In 1911 Einstein summarized the status of the specific heat problem before the first Solvay conference [E42]. In 1915 he wrote a semipopular review on kinetic problems [E43].

This concludes the introductory summary of Einstein's work on statistical physics and related subjects. I shall, of course, return in more detail to the main topics mentioned in this chronology. Sections 4c and 4d deal with the 1902–4 papers and with Einstein's subsequent involvement with Boltzmann's principle. Chapter 5, which opens with introductory remarks on the highly complex subject of molecular reality in the nineteenth century, is devoted mainly to Einstein's doctoral thesis, Brownian motion, and critical opalescence. All the principal papers mentioned above that belong to the area of quantum physics will be discussed in Chapters 19 to 24.

At the beginning of this section, I remarked that Einstein devoted some but not much attention to his contributions to statistical physics when, at age seventy, he looked back on his work. At that time, he had much more to say about his relativity theories and devoted more space to his critique of quantum mechanics than to all the work summarized above [E1]. It is an additional purpose of the foregoing chronology to make clear that in doing so he did not fully convey the breadth of his life's work.

Einstein's position regarding questions of principle in statistical mechanics is best explained by first reviewing briefly the contributions of Maxwell and, especially, of Boltzmann. Gibbs will not enter into this review because he did not influence Einstein and also because, as Lorentz noted in Einstein's presence, the Einstein and Gibbs approaches are different [L2]. Einstein did not disagree. Indeed, in responding to Lorentz's remark, he observed, '[My] point of view is characterized by the fact that one introduces the probability of a specific state in a phenomenological manner. In that way one has the advantage of not interposing any particular theory, for example, any statistical mechanics' [E44]. His critical attitude to Boltzmann's approach, implied by this statement, will be discussed in Section 4d. One of the aims of this chapter is to explain what Einstein had in mind with his phenomenological approach.

In concluding this introduction, I note that the period of Einstein's activities

concerning the foundations of statistical mechanics preceded the appearance of the
first papers in which it was noted that all was not well with Boltzmann's ergodic
hypothesis. In what follows, I shall therefore have no occasion to make reference
to ergodic theory.

4b. Maxwell and Boltzmann*

Boltzmann's grave, in the Central Cemetery in Vienna, is marked by a monument
on which the formula

$$S = k \log W \tag{4.1}$$

is carved. 'It is immaterial that Boltzmann never wrote down the equation in this
form. This was first done by Planck. . . . The constant k was also first introduced
by Planck and not by Boltzmann' [S4]. Indeed, k is a twentieth century symbol
which was used for the first time in the formula

$$\rho(\nu, T) = \frac{8\pi h\nu^3}{c^3} \frac{1}{\exp(h\nu/kT) - 1} \tag{4.2}$$

proposed on December 14, 1900, by Planck [P1] for the thermal equilibrium distribution of blackbody radiation.** The quantity $\rho(\nu, T)\,d\nu$ is the radiative energy
per unit volume in the frequency interval ν to $\nu + d\nu$ at temperature T. Equation
4.1, or rather (and better)

$$S = k \ln W + \text{constant} \tag{4.3}$$

is also found for the first time in a paper by Planck, one completed a few weeks
later [P3]. Lorentz referred to k as *Planck's constant* as late as 1911 [L3]. Nor
was he the only one to do so at that time [J1].

The essence of Eq. 4.3, the insight that the second law of thermodynamics can
be understood only in terms of a connection between entropy and probability, is
one of the great advances of the nineteenth century.† It appears that Maxwell was

---

*In writing this section, M. Klein's studies of the work of Maxwell and Boltzmann have served me
as an indispensable guide.

**Planck's discovery will be treated in Chapter 19. An equation equivalent to Eq. 4.2 but in which
h and k do not yet occur explicitly had been proposed by Planck on the preceding October 19 [P2].

†Recall that the period of discovery of the first law of thermodynamics (the impossibility of a perpetuum mobile of the first kind) is approximately 1830 to 1850. Many scientists, from engineers to
physiologists, made this discovery independently [K1]. The law of conservation of energy for purely
mechanical systems is, of course, much older. The second law was discovered in 1850 [C1] by Rudolf
Julius Emmanuel Clausius while he was pondering the work of Sadi Carnot. In its original form
(Clausius's principle), the second law said in essence that heat cannot go from a colder to a warmer
body without some other accompanying change. The term *entropy* was also introduced by Clausius,
in 1865, at which time he stated the two laws as follows: 'The energy of the world is constant, its
entropy strives toward a maximum,' and commented that 'the second law of thermodynamics is much
harder for the mind to grasp than the first' [C2].

the first to state that the second law is statistical in nature.* In a letter about his 'demons,' probably written early in 1868, he discussed their naming, their characteristics, and their purpose:

'1. Who gave them this name? Thompson.**
2. What were they by nature? Very small *but* lively beings incapable of doing work but able to open and shut valves which move without friction or inertia.
3. What was their chief end? To show that the 2nd Law of Thermodynamics was only a statistical certainty . . .' [M2].

Boltzmann had already begun his attempts to derive the second law when Maxwell wrote these lines, but he did not yet understand its statistical character. The stated purpose of Boltzmann's first paper on the subject (1866) was 'to give a completely general proof of the second law of the theory of heat, as well as to discover the theorem in mechanics that corresponds to it' [B2].† He made a fresh start when he returned to the problem in 1871–2: 'The problems of the mechanical theory of heat are . . . problems in the theory of probability' [B3]. His new proof was based on the so called kinetic method [E3, K3]. In the first of two papers, he dealt with the equilibrium relation between entropy, heat, and temperature [B4]. The sequel, published in 1872 [B3], is one of his most important papers. It contains the Boltzmann equation. It also contains the H theorem: there exists a quantity, later called H, defined in terms of the velocity distribution, with the property that $dH/dt \leq 0$ so that, up to a negative multiplicative constant, H can be identified with the entropy. Both mechanical and probabilistic arguments are used in the derivation of this theorem. (In that same period, Boltzmann also did important work on the equipartition theorem and in 1876 gave the derivation of the 'law' of Dulong and Petit. The discussion of equipartition and of specific heats will be deferred to Chapter 20.)

At that time, Boltzmann still did not have it entirely straight, however. He believed that he had shown that the second law is absolute, that H can never increase. He made the final step as the result of his reflections‡ on a remark by Johann Joseph Loschmidt [L4] which in modern terms can be phrased as follows. Consider a large number of particles moving according to fully specified initial conditions and subject to the standard time-reversal invariant Newtonian laws.

---

*Maxwell's views on the second law are discussed in more detail by Klein [K2].

**This is William Thomson, later Baron Kelvin of Largs. In December 1867, Maxwell had written a letter to Peter Guthrie Tait in which he introduced 'a finite being who knows the path and velocities of all the molecules by simple inspection' [M1]. Tait had shown this letter to Thomson, who invented the name *demon* for Maxwell's finite being.

†A quite similar attempt was made by Clausius in 1871 [C3]. This led to a priority argument between Boltzmann and Clausius—to the amusement of Maxwell [K2].

‡For the influence of Loschmidt's ideas on Boltzmann, see especially [K3].

Suppose that H decreases in the course of time. Then for a second system, which differs from the first one only in that the initial conditions are time-reversed, H must increase in the course of time. Thus, the law of increase of entropy cannot be an absolute law. Boltzmann immediately recognized the importance of this observation [B5] and in a major paper, published in 1877 [B6], finally arrived at the modern view: in the approach to equilibrium the increase in entropy is not the actual but the most probable course of events. Just as Loschmidt's remark guided Boltzmann, so, twenty years later, did Boltzmann play a similar role for Planck, who at that time was trying to derive the equilibrium distribution for blackbody radiation under the assumption that the increase in entropy is an absolute law. In the course of a polemic between these two men, Boltzmann became the first to prove the property of time-reversal in electromagnetic theory: the Maxwell equations are invariant under the joint inversion of the directions of time and of the magnetic field, the electric field being left unaltered [B7]. More generally, we owe to Boltzmann the first precise statement that for a time-reversal invariant dynamics, macroscopic irreversibility is due to the fact that in the overwhelming majority of cases a physical system evolves from an initial state to a final state which is almost never less probable.* Boltzmann was also the first to state explicitly that this interpretation might need reconsideration in the presence of time-asymmetric dynamic forces.**

I turn next to Boltzmann's definition of the concept of thermodynamic probability. Actually, one finds two such definitions in his writings. The first one dates from 1868 [B9]: Consider a system of N structureless particles with fixed total energy. The evolution in time of this system can be represented as an orbit on a surface of constant energy in the $6N$-dimensional phase space (later called the Γ space [E3]). To a state $S_i (i = 1, 2, \ldots)$ of the system corresponds a point on the orbit. The state S_i shall be specified up to a small latitude, and thus the corresponding point is specified up to a small neighborhood. Observe the system for a long time τ during which it is in S_i for a period τ_i. Then τ_i / τ (in the limit $\tau \to \infty$) is defined to be the probability of the system being in the state S_i. This we shall call Boltzmann's *first* definition of probability.

I alluded earlier to Einstein's critical attitude toward some of Boltzmann's ideas. That has nothing to do with the first definition of probability. In fact, that very definition was Einstein's own favorite one. He independently reintroduced it him-

---

*See [P4] for a quantum mechanical version of the H theorem.

**See [B8]. The most important initial condition in our physical world is the selection of the Friedmann universe—in which, it seems, we live—as the one realized solution of the time-reversal invariant gravitational equations. It has been speculated that this particular choice of actualized universe is one indication of the incompleteness of our present physical laws, that the actual physical laws are not all time-symmetric, that the time-reversal violation observed in the neutral K-particle system is only a first manifestation of this asymmetry, and that the conventional view on the statistical arrow of time may indeed need revision. For a discussion of all these topics, see the review by Penrose [P5].

self in 1903 [E11], evidently unaware of Boltzmann's paper of 1868. (Lorentz later called this definition the time ensemble of Einstein [L3], perhaps not the most felicitous of names.) Rather, Einstein had reservations about the second definition of probability, which Boltzmann gave in the paper of 1877 [B6]. In that paper, Boltzmann introduced for the first time a new tool, the so-called statistical method, in which there is no need to deal explicitly with collision mechanisms and collision frequencies (as there is in the kinetic method). His new reasoning only holds close to equilibrium [B10]. He applied the method only to an ideal gas [B11]. For that case, he not only gave his second definition of probability but also showed how that probability can be computed explicitly by means of counting 'complexions.'

In preparation for some comments on Einstein's objections (Section 4d) as well as for a later discussion of the differences between classical and quantum statistics (Chapter 23), it is necessary to recall some elementary facts about this counting procedure.*

Suppose I show someone two identical balls lying on a table and then ask this person to close his eyes and a few moments later to open them again. I then ask whether or not I have meanwhile switched the two balls around. He cannot tell, since the balls are identical. Yet I know the answer. If I have switched the balls, then I have been able to follow the continuous motion which brought the balls from the initial to the final configuration. This simple example illustrates Boltzmann's first axiom of classical mechanics, which says, in essence, that identical particles which cannot come infinitely close to each other can be distinguished by their initial conditions and by the continuity of their motion. This assumption, Boltzmann stressed, 'gives us the sole possibility of recognizing the same material point at different times' [B13]. As Erwin Schroedinger emphasized, 'Nobody before Boltzmann held it necessary to define what one means by [the term] the same material point' [S5]. Thus we may speak classically of a gas with energy E consisting of N identical, distinguishable molecules.

Consider next (following Boltzmann) the specific case of an ideal gas *model* in which the energies of the individual particles can take on only discrete values $\epsilon_1, \epsilon_2, \ldots$ Let there be n_i particles with energy ϵ_i so that

$$N = \sum_i n_i \quad , \quad E = \sum_i \epsilon_i n_i \quad . \tag{4.4}$$

Since the gas is ideal, the particles are uncorrelated and therefore have no *a priori* preference for any particular region in one-particle phase space (μ space), i.e., they are statistically independent. Moreover, they are distinguishable in the sense

---

*See Lorentz [L3] for the equivalence of this method with the microcanonical ensemble of Gibbs. Also, the notion of ensemble has its roots in Boltzmann's work [B12], as was stressed by Gibbs in the preface of his book on statistical mechanics [G1].

just described. Therefore, the number of microstates (or complexions, as Boltzmann called them) corresponding to the partition Eq. 4.4 is given by

$$w = \frac{N!}{\prod_i n_i!} \tag{4.5}$$

Boltzmann took w to be proportional to the probability of the distribution specified by $(n_1, n_2, \dots)$. This will be called his *second* definition of probability.

For later purposes I need to mention a further development, one not due to Boltzmann. The number of microstates w is now called a fine-grained probability. For the purpose of analyzing general macroscopic properties of systems, it is very important to use a contracted description, which leads to the so-called coarse-grained probability,* a concept that goes back to Gibbs. The procedure is as follows. Divide μ space into cells $\omega_1, \omega_2, \dots$ such that a particle in ω_A has the *mean* energy E_A. Partition the N particles such that there are N_A particles in ω_A:

$$N = \sum_A N_A \tag{4.6}$$

$$E = \sum_A E_A N_A \tag{4.7}$$

The set (N_A, E_A) defines a coarse-grained state. For the special case of the ideal gas model, it follows from Eq. 4.5 that the volume W in Γ space corresponding to the partition of Eqs. 4.6 and 4.7 is given by

$$W = N! \prod_A \frac{\omega_A^{N_A}}{N_A!} \tag{4.8}$$

where W is the so-called coarse-grained probability. The state of equilibrium corresponds to the maximum W_{max} of W considered as a function of N_A and subject to the constraints imposed by Eqs. 4.6 and 4.7. Thus the Maxwell–Boltzmann distribution follows** from the extremal conditions

$$\sum_A \delta N_A (\ln \omega_A - \ln N_A - \lambda + \beta E_A) = 0 \tag{4.9}$$

The entropy in equilibrium, S_{eq}, is given by (see Eq. 4.3)

$$S_{eq} = k \ln W_{max} + \text{constant} \tag{4.10}$$

and $\beta^{-1} = kT$ follows from $\partial S_{eq}/\partial E = T^{-1}$.

---

*The names *fine-grained* and *coarse-grained density* (feine und grobe Dichte) were introduced by the Ehrenfests [E45].

**For the *classical* ideal gas, one can get the Maxwell–Boltzmann distribution directly from Eqs. 4.4 and 4.5; that is just what Boltzmann himself did.

Einstein's precursors have now been sufficiently introduced. I conclude this section with three final comments.

The first definition of probability, in terms of time spent, is the natural one, directly linked to observation. For example, the most probable state is the state in which the system persists for the longest time. The second definition (either for w or for W) is not directly linked to observation; it is more like a declaration. It has the advantage, however, that one can more readily compute with it. Logic demands, of course, that these two definitions be equivalent, that 'time spent' be proportional to 'volume in Γ space.' This is the profound and not yet fully solved problem of ergodic theory.* Boltzmann was well aware of the need to show this equivalence. Einstein's physical intuition made him comfortable with the first but not with the second definition.

Second, why did Boltzmann himself not introduce the symbol k?** After all, his 1877 paper [B6] contains a section entitled 'The Relation of the Entropy to the Quantity Which I Have Called Partition Probability,' that quantity being essentially $\ln W$. Moreover, in that section he noted that $\ln W$ 'is identical with the entropy up to a constant factor and an additive constant.' He was also quite familiar with Eq. 4.9, with its two Lagrange multipliers [B14]. I can imagine that he did not write down Eq. 4.3 because he was more concerned with understanding the second law of thermodynamics than with the applications of an equation such as Eq. 4.3 to practical calculations. I hope that this question will be discussed some day by someone more at home with Boltzmann's work than I am.

Finally, Eq. 4.3 is evidently more general than Eq. 4.10. Boltzmann was aware of this: '[$\ln W$] also has a meaning for an irreversible body† and also steadily increases during [such a process]' [B6]. The first one to make use of Eq. 4.3 in its broader sense was Einstein. It was also Einstein who, in 1905, in his paper on the light-quantum hypothesis [E13], gave that equation its only fitting name: Boltzmann's principle.

4c. Preludes to 1905

Boltzmann's qualities as an outstanding lecturer are not reflected in his scientific papers, which are sometimes unduly long, occasionally obscure, and often dense. Their main conclusions are sometimes tucked away among lengthy calculations. Also (and especially in regard to the theoretical interpretation of the second law), Boltzmann would change his point of view from one paper to the next without

---

*For introductions to this problem, see, e.g., [U1] and [V1].

**As to what might have been, in 1860 Maxwell could have been the first to introduce k when he derived his velocity distribution, in which the Boltzmann factor makes its first appearance. Maxwell wrote this factor as $\exp(-v^2/\alpha^2)$, where v = velocity, showed that α^2 is proportional to the average of v^2, and knew full well that this average is proportional to T.

†Obviously, he must have meant *process* instead of *body*.

advance warning to the reader.* Maxwell said of his writings: 'By the study of Boltzmann I have been unable to understand him. He could not understand me on account of my shortness, and his length was and is an equal stumbling block to me' [M3]. Einstein once said to a student of his: 'Boltzmann's work is not easy to read. There are great physicists who have not understood it' [S6].** That statement was made around 1910, when he was a professor at the University of Zürich. By then he must have read Boltzmann's major memoir of 1877 on the statistical mechanical derivation of the second law, since he referred to that paper (for the first time!) in 1909 [E47]. However, it is very doubtful whether in the years from 1901 to 1904, when he did his own work on this subject, Einstein knew either this paper or the one of 1868, in which Boltzmann had introduced his first definition of probability.

It must have been difficult for Einstein to get hold of scientific journals. Recall that the first of his three papers on the foundations of statistical mechanics was completed while he was still a teacher at Schaffhausen.† His move to Bern does not seem to have improved his access to the literature very much [E48]. It is also unclear whether he had read Maxwell's papers on kinetic theory at that time. Certainly, he did not know English then, since he did not start to study that language until about 1909 [S7] and his knowledge of it was still rudimentary when he came to the United States.‡

Yet Einstein was acquainted with some of Maxwell's and Boltzmann's achievements. As he put it in his first paper on statistical physics [E10]: 'Maxwell's and Boltzmann's theories have already come close to the goal' of deriving the laws of thermal equilibrium and the second law from the equations of mechanics and the theory of probability. However, he remarked, this goal had not yet been achieved and the purpose of his own paper was 'to fill the gap' left by these men. From the single reference in Einstein's paper, it is clear how much he could have learned about their work. This reference is to Boltzmann's lectures on gas theory [B15], a two-volume work which contains much original research and which was certainly not intended by Boltzmann to be a synopsis of his earlier work. The book is largely based on the kinetic method (the Boltzmann equation); by comparison, the comments on the statistical method are quite brief. The counting formula of complexions is mentioned [B6]; however, said Boltzmann, 'I must content myself to indicate [this method] only in passing,' and he then concluded this topic with a reference to his 1877 paper. Also, it seems possible to me that Einstein knew of

---

*See especially Klein's memoir [K3] for a discussion of Boltzmann's style.

**The encyclopedia article by the Ehrenfests contains several such qualifying phrases as 'The aim of the . . . investigations by Boltzmann seems to be . . .' [E46].

†See Chapter 3.

‡Helen Dukas, private communication. However, it may be that Einstein did see one of the German translations of Maxwell's *Theory of Heat,* dating from the 1870s.

Maxwell's work on kinetic theory only to the extent that it was discussed by Boltzmann in those same volumes. Thus Einstein did not know the true gaps in the arguments of Maxwell and, especially, of Boltzmann; nor did he accidentally fill them. The reading of Einstein's paper [E10] is not facilitated by the absence of an explicit statement as to what, in his opinion, the gaps actually were. This paper is devoted exclusively to thermal equilibrium. The statistical interpretation of temperature, entropy, and the equipartition theorem are discussed. The tool used is essentially (in modern terms) the canonical ensemble. The paper is competent and neither very interesting nor, by Einstein's own admission [E2], very well written.

Einstein believed that in his next paper, completed in 1903 [E11], he gave a proof of the second law for irreversible processes. At this stage, he of course needed some definition for the thermodynamic probability W, and it is here that he independently introduced Boltzmann's first definition in terms of the time spent in the appropriate interval in Γ space. His proof is logically correct but rests on an erroneous assumption: 'We will have to assume that more probable distributions will always follow less probable ones, that is, that W *always* [my italics] increases until the distribution becomes constant and W has reached a maximum' [E49]. Three days after he sent this paper to the *Annalen der Physik*, he wrote to Besso, 'Now [this work] is completely clear and simple so that I am completely satisfied with it' [E50]. He had been studying Boltzmann's book since 1901 [E51]. The book does refer to the Loschmidt objection, but, in typical Boltzmann fashion, in a somewhat tucked-away place [B16]. Einstein must have missed it; at any rate, it is obvious that in 1903 he was unaware of the main subtlety in the proof of the second law: the overwhelming probability, rather than the certainty, of entropy increase.

It was not until 1910 that, for the first time, Einstein's 'derivation' was criticized in the literature. At that time, Paul Hertz pointed out that 'if one assumes, as Einstein did, that more probable distributions follow less probable ones, then one introduces thereby a special assumption which is not evident and which is thoroughly in need of proof' [H1]. This is a remarkable comment. Hertz does not say, 'Your assumption is wrong.' Rather, he asks for its proof. Here we have but one example of the fact that, at the end of the first decade of the twentieth century, Boltzmann's ideas had not yet been assimilated by many of those who were active at the frontiers of statistical physics. A larger audience acquired some degree of familiarity with Boltzmann's work only after its exegesis by the Ehrenfests, published in 1911 [E3].

Einstein's reply to Hertz, also written in 1910 [E2] is remarkable as well. He agrees with Hertz's objection and adds, 'Already then [i.e., in 1903] my derivation did not satisfy me, so that shortly thereafter I gave a second derivation.' The latter is contained in the only paper Einstein completed in 1904 [E12].* It is indeed a

---

*For other discussions of Einstein's 1902–4 papers, see [K4] and [K5].

different derivation, in that use is made of the canonical ensemble, yet it contains once again the assumption Hertz had criticized.

It is interesting but not all that surprising that in 1903 and 1904 Einstein, in his isolation, had missed the point about time reversal. After all, the great Boltzmann had done the same thirty years earlier. However, the exchange between Einstein and Hertz took place in 1910, when Einstein was a professor at Zürich (and taught the kinetic theory of heat during the summer semester of that year [S8]). By that time, he had read Boltzmann's work of 1877 (as mentioned earlier), in which it was stated that the entropy does not always, but rather *almost* always, increase. A month before replying to Hertz, he had phrased the second law quite properly in another paper.* One can only conclude that Einstein did not pay much attention when he replied to Hertz.

As a postscript to the issue of the second law, it is fitting to recall the first personal exchange between Einstein and Ehrenfest, which took place in Prague in February 1912. The Einsteins had come to the train to meet the Ehrenfests. After the first greetings, 'their conversation turned at once to physics, as they plunged into a discussion of the ergodic hypothesis' [K6].

What was the harvest of Einstein's scientific efforts up to this point? Five papers. The first two, dealing with his quest for a universal molecular force, are justly forgotten.** One main ambition of the next three, to establish a dynamic basis for the thermodynamic laws, did not entirely come to fulfillment either. Nothing indicates Einstein's flowering in 1905, which begins with his very next paper. Nothing yet. However, there is one aspect (not yet mentioned) of his brief 1904 paper which does give the first intimations of things to come. In the years 1902 to 1904, Einstein may not have grasped the awesome problems—still a subject of active research—which have to be coped with in giving the second law a foundation which stands the tests of requisite mathematical rigor. Yet these early struggles of his played an important role in his development. They led him to ask, in 1904, What is the meaning of the Boltzmann constant? How can this constant be measured? His pursuit of these questions led to lasting contributions to statistical physics and to his most important discovery in quantum theory.

In the opening paragraphs of Einstein's paper of 1904 [E12], reference is made to Eq. 4.3: 'An expression for the entropy of a system . . . which was found by Boltzmann for ideal gases and assumed by Planck in his theory of radiation. . . .' Here, for the first time, Planck appears in Einstein's writings, and we also catch a first brief glimpse of Einstein's subsequent concern with the quantum theory in

---

*'The irreversibility of physical phenomena is only apparent . . . [a] system *probably* [my italics] goes to states of greater probability when it happens to be in a state of relatively small probability' [E29].

**See Section 4a.

the context of statistical considerations. It seems that he had already been brooding for some time about the mysterious formula Eq. 4.2. Much later he wrote, 'Already soon after 1900, i.e., shortly after Planck's trailblazing work, it became clear to me that neither mechanics nor thermodynamics could (except in limiting cases) claim exact validity' [E52].

His statement that thermodynamics is not exact refers, of course, to the phenomena of fluctuations. Einstein turned to fluctuations for the first time in 1904, when he considered a system with variable energy E in thermal equilibrium with a very large second system at temperature T. The equilibrium energy $\langle E \rangle$ of the first system is given by

$$\langle E \rangle = \frac{\int_0^\infty E e^{-\beta E} \omega(E) dE}{\int_0^\infty e^{-\beta E} \omega(E) dE}, \qquad \beta = \frac{1}{kT} \qquad (4.11)$$

where $\omega(E)$ is the density of states with energy E. In 1904 Einstein deduced a formula for the mean square energy fluctuation

$$\langle \epsilon^2 \rangle \equiv \langle (E - \langle E \rangle)^2 \rangle = \langle E^2 \rangle - \langle E \rangle^2 \qquad (4.12)$$

of the first system. Differentiating Eq. 4.11 with respect to β, he obtained

$$\langle \epsilon^2 \rangle = - \frac{\partial \langle E \rangle}{\partial \beta} = kT^2 \frac{\partial \langle E \rangle}{\partial T} \qquad (4.13)$$

The quantity $\langle \epsilon^2 \rangle$ (Einstein noted) is a measure for the thermal stability of the system. The larger the fluctuations, the smaller the system's degree of stability. 'Thus the absolute constant* [k] determines the thermal stability of the system. [Equation 4.13] is of interest since it does not contain any quantities which remind one of the assumptions on which the theory is based' [E12].

Next, Einstein introduced a criterion for fluctuations to be large:

$$\xi \equiv \frac{\langle \epsilon^2 \rangle}{\langle E \rangle^2} \approx 1 \qquad (4.14)$$

This relation is not satisfied by a classical ideal gas under normal conditions, since then $\langle E \rangle = nkT/2$ (n is the number of particles) so that $\xi = O(n^{-1})$, independent of the volume. He went on to note that ξ can be of order unity only for one kind of system: blackbody radiation. In that case, $\langle E \rangle = aVT^4$, by the Stefan–Boltzmann law (V is volume, a is a constant), and hence $\xi = 4k/aVT^3$. The temperature T is proportional to the inverse of λ_{max}, the wavelength at which the spectral distribution reaches its maximum. He therefore concluded that volume dependence is important: for fixed T, ξ can become large if λ_{max}^3/V is large, i.e.,

---

*Einstein used a symbol other than k.

if V is small.* Thus he believed that radiation is 'the only kind of physical system . . . of which we can suspect that it exhibits an energy fluctuation.'

This subject deserves two comments. First, the conclusion is incorrect. Consider the radiation to be composed of n modes. Then $\langle E \rangle = aVT^4 = nkT$, so that again $\xi = 0(n^{-1})$. In the classical theory (which, of course, Einstein was using in 1904), fluctuations are therefore not all that different for radiation and for an ideal gas. Second, the reasoning was most important for Einstein's work in 1905, since it drew his attention to the volume dependence of thermodynamic quantities, a dependence which played a crucial role in his formulation of the light-quantum hypothesis, which appeared in his very next paper.

Nevertheless, in 1904 Einstein had already taken a bold new step (of which he was aware): he had applied statistical reasonings to radiation.** In 1905 he was to do this again. In 1909, Eq. 4.13 would again be his starting point, and it would lead him to the realization of the particle–wave duality of electromagnetic radiation. In 1925, a formula closely related to Eq. 4.13 would make it clear to him that a similar duality has to exist for matter. These topics will be discussed in detail in Part VI of this book. For now, two last comments on Eq. 4.13. When Einstein first derived it, he did not know that Gibbs had done so before him [G2]. And it is his most important and only memorable result prior to 1905.

In May 1905, Einstein was again busy with fluctuations, though in a different style, when he did his work on Brownian motion, to be discussed in Chapter 5. The remainder of the present chapter is devoted to a discussion of Einstein's general views on statistical physics, in 1905 and in the years following.

4d. Einstein and Boltzmann's Principle

I have already stressed that all of Einstein's main contributions to the quantum theory are statistical in origin. Correspondingly, most of his more important comments on the principles of statistical mechanics are found in his papers on quantum physics. His light-quantum paper of 1905 [E13] is a prime example. Two-and-a-half of its seventeen pages deal with the photoelectric effect—nine with statistical and thermodynamic questions. This paper, in which the term *Boltzmann's principle* appears in the literature for the first time, contains a critique of Boltzmann's statistical method.

During the years 1905 to 1920, Einstein stated more than once his displeasure with the handling of probability by others. In 1905 he wrote, 'The word *probability* is used in a sense that does not conform to its definition as given in the theory of probability. In particular, "cases of equal probability" are often hypothetically defined in instances where the theoretical pictures used are sufficiently definite to

*For $\xi = 1$, $V^{1/3} \approx 0.4/T$ and $\lambda_{max} \approx 0.3/T$. Einstein found this near-coincidence pleasing.

**Rayleigh had done so before him (see Section 19b), but I do not believe that Einstein knew that in 1904.

give a deduction rather than a hypothetical assertion' [E13]. Since Einstein had by then already reinvented Boltzmann's first definition, it appears safe to assume that he was referring to the counting of complexions. Not only did he regard that definition as artificial. More than that, he believed that one could dispense with such countings altogether: 'In this way, [I] hope to eliminate a logical difficulty which still hampers the implementation of Boltzmann's principle' [E13]. In order to illustrate what he had in mind, he gave a new derivation of a well-known formula for the change of entropy S of an ideal gas when, at constant temperature T, the volume changes reversibly from V_0 to V:

$$S(V,T) - S(V_0,T) = \frac{R}{N} \ln \left(\frac{V}{V_0} \right)^n \qquad (4.15)$$

where n is the number of molecules in the gas, R is the gas constant, and N is Avogadro's number. As we shall see later, this equation played a crucial role in Einstein's discovery of the light-quantum. (To avoid any confusion, I remind the reader that this relation has nothing to do with any subtleties of statistical mechanics, since it is a consequence of the second law of thermodynamics for reversible processes and of the ideal gas law.*) Einstein derived Eq. 4.15 by the following reasoning. Boltzmann's principle (Eq. 4.3), which he wrote in the form

$$S = \frac{R}{N} \ln W + \text{constant} \qquad (4.17)$$

(it took until 1909 before Einstein would write k instead of R/N) implies that a reversible change from a state 'a' to a state 'b' satisfies

$$S^a - S^b = \frac{R}{N} \ln \frac{W^a}{W^b} \qquad (4.18)$$

Let the system consist of subsystems $1, 2, \ldots$, which do not interact and therefore are statistically independent. Then

---

*For an infinitesimal reversible change, the second law can be written (p = pressure)

$$T dS = c_V dT + [(\partial U/\partial V) + p] dV \qquad (4.16)$$

where c_V, the specific heat at constant volume, S, and U, the internal energy, all are in general functions of V and T. From

$$\frac{\partial(\partial S/\partial V)}{\partial T} = \frac{\partial(\partial S/\partial T)}{\partial V}$$

and from Eq. 4.16 it follows that

$$\frac{\partial p}{\partial T} - \frac{(p + \partial U/\partial V)}{T} = 0$$

For a classical ideal gas, this last relation reduces to $\partial U/\partial V = 0$ since in this case $NpV = nRT$. In turn, $\partial U/\partial V = 0$ implies that c_V is a function of T only. (Actually, for an ideal gas, c_V does not depend on T either, but we do not need that here.) Hence $T dS(V,T) = c_V(T) dT + nRT dV/NV$. For a finite reversible change, this yields Eq. 4.15 by integration with respect to the volume.

$$W = W_1 W_2 \ldots \tag{4.19}$$

$$S^a - S^b = \frac{R}{N} \ln \frac{W_1^a}{W_1^b} \cdot \frac{W_2^a}{W_2^b} \ldots$$

For the case of an ideal gas, the subsystems may be taken to be the individual molecules. Let the gas in the states a and b have volume and temperature (V, T) and (V_0, T), respectively. Einstein next unveils his own definition of probability: 'For this probability [W^a / W^b], which is a "statistical probability," one *obviously* [my italics] finds the value

$$\frac{W^a}{W^b} = \left(\frac{V}{V_0} \right)^n, \tag{4.20}$$

Equations 4.17 and 4.20 again give Eq. 4.15.

Equation 4.20 can of course also be derived from Boltzmann's formula Eq. 4.8, since each factor ω_A can be chosen proportional to V (for all A). Therefore Eq. 4.8 can be written $W = V^N$ times a complexion-counting factor which is the same for states a and b. Einstein was therefore quite right in saying that Eq. 4.15 (and, therefore, the ideal gas law which follows from Eqs. 4.15 and 4.16) can be derived without counting complexions. 'I shall show in a separate paper [he announced] that, in considerations about thermal properties, the so-called statistical probability is completely adequate' [E13]. This statement was too optimistic. Equation 4.8 yields much stronger results than Eq. 4.15. No physicist will deny that the probability for finding n statistically independent particles in the subvolume V of V_0 is 'obviously' equal to $(V/V_0)^n$. The counting of complexions gives more information, however, to wit, the Maxwell–Boltzmann distribution. No wonder that the promised paper never appeared.

Einstein did not cease criticizing the notion of complexion, however. Here he is in 1910: 'Usually W is put equal to the number of complexions. . . . In order to calculate W, one needs a *complete* (molecular-mechanical) theory of the system under consideration. Therefore it is dubious whether the Boltzmann principle has any meaning without a *complete* molecular-mechanical theory or some other theory which describes the elementary processes. [Eq. 4.3] seems without content, from a phenomenological point of view, without giving in addition such an *Elementartheorie*' [E29].

My best understanding of this statement is that, in 1910, it was not clear to him how the complexion method was to be extended from an ideal to a real gas. It is true that there are no simple and explicit counting formulas like Eqs. 4.5 and 4.8 if intermolecular forces are present. However, as a matter of principle the case of a real gas can be dealt with by using Gibbs's coarse-grained microcanonical ensemble, a procedure with which Einstein apparently was not yet familiar.

After 1910, critical remarks on the statistical method are no longer found in Einstein's papers. His subsequent views on this subject are best illustrated by his comments on Boltzmann and Gibbs in later years. Of Boltzmann he wrote in

1915: 'His discussion [of the second law] is rather lengthy and subtle. But the effort of thinking [about it] is richly rewarded by the importance and the beauty of the subject' [E43]. Of Gibbs he wrote in 1918: '[His] book is . . . a masterpiece, even though it is hard to read and the main points are found between the lines' [E54]. A year before his death, Einstein paid Gibbs the highest compliment. When asked who were the greatest men, the most powerful thinkers he had known, he replied, 'Lorentz,' and added, 'I never met Willard Gibbs; perhaps, had I done so, I might have placed him beside Lorentz' [D1].

At the end of Section 4a, I mentioned that Einstein preferred to think of probability in a phenomenological way, without recourse to statistical mechanics. The final item of this chapter is an explanation of what he meant by that. To begin with, it needs to be stressed that Boltzmann's principle was as sacred to Einstein as the law of conservation of energy [E54]. However, his misgivings about the way others dealt with the probability concept led him to a different way, uniquely his own, of looking at the relation between S and W. His proposal was not to reason from the microscopic to the macroscopic but rather to turn this reasoning around. That is to say, where Boltzmann made an Ansatz about probability in order to arrive at an expression for the entropy, Einstein suggested the use of phenomenological information about entropy in order to deduce what the probability had to be.

In order to illustrate this kind of reasoning, which he used to great advantage, I shall give one example which, typically, is found in one of his important papers on quantum physics. It concerns the fluctuation equation 4.13, which had been derived independently by Gibbs and by Einstein, using in essence the same method. In 1909, Einstein gave a new derivation, this one all his own [E24]. Consider a large system with volume V in equilibrium at temperature T. Divide V into a small subvolume V_0 and a remaining volume V_1, where $V = V_0 + V_1$, $V_0 \ll V_1$. The fixed total energy is likewise divided, $E = E_0 + E_1$. Assume* that the entropy is also additive:

$$S = S_0 + S_1 \tag{4.21}$$

Suppose that E_0, E_1 deviate by amounts ΔE_0, ΔE_1 from their respective equilibrium values. Then

$$\Delta S = \left[\frac{\partial S_0}{\partial E_0}\right] \Delta E_0 + \left[\frac{\partial S_1}{\partial E_1}\right] \Delta E_1 + \frac{1}{2}\left[\frac{\partial^2 S_0}{\partial E_0^2}\right](\Delta E_0)^2$$
$$+ \frac{1}{2}\left[\frac{\partial^2 S_1}{\partial E_1^2}\right](\Delta E_1)^2 + \cdots \tag{4.22}$$

*This assumption was briefly challenged at a later time; see Section 21a.

where the expressions in brackets refer to equilibrium values. The first-order terms cancel since $\Delta E_0 = -\Delta E_1$ (energy conservation) and $[\partial S_0/\partial E_0] = [\partial S_1/\partial E_1]$ (equilibrium). Furthermore, $[\partial^2 S_0/\partial E_0^2] = -1/c_0 T^2$ and $[\partial^2 S_1/\partial E_1^2] = -1/c_1 T^2$, where c_0, c_1 are the respective heat capacities at constant volume and $c_1 \gg c_0$ since $V_1 \gg V_0$. Thus Eq. 4.22 becomes

$$\Delta S = \Delta S_0 = -\frac{(\Delta E_0)^2}{2 c_0 T^2} \tag{4.23}$$

Next Einstein applied the relation $S_0 = k \ln W_0$ to the subsystem and reinterpreted this equation to mean that W_0 is the probability for the subsystem to have the entropy S_0 (at a given time). Hence,

$$W_0 = \overline{W}_0 e^{\Delta S/k} \tag{4.24}$$

where $\overline{W}_0$ is the equilibrium value of W_0. Equations 4.22 and 4.24 show that W_0 is Gaussian in ΔE_0. Denote (as before) the mean square deviation of this distribution by $\langle \epsilon^2 \rangle$. Then $\langle \epsilon^2 \rangle = kc_0 T^2$, which is again Eq. 4.13.

As we now know, although it was not at once clear then, in the early part of the twentieth century, physicists concerned with the foundations of statistical mechanics were simultaneously faced with two tasks. Up until 1913, the days of the Bohr atom, all evidence for quantum phenomena came either from blackbody radiation or from specific heats. In either case, statistical considerations play a key role. Thus the struggle for a better understanding of the principles of classical statistical mechanics was accompanied by the slowly growing realization that quantum effects demand a new mechanics and, therefore, a new statistical mechanics. The difficulties encountered in separating the two questions are seen nowhere better than in a comment Einstein made in 1909. Once again complaining about the complexions, he observed, 'Neither Herr Boltzmann nor Herr Planck has given a definition of W' [E24]. Boltzmann, the classical physicist, was gone when these words were written. Planck, the first quantum physicist, had ushered in theoretical physics of the twentieth century with a new counting of complexions which had absolutely no logical foundation whatsoever—but which gave him the answer he was looking for.* Neither Einstein, deeply respectful and at the same time critical of both men, nor anyone else in 1909 could have foreseen how odd it would appear, late in the twentieth century, to see the efforts of Boltzmann and Planck lumped together in one phrase.

In summary, Einstein's work on statistical mechanics prior to 1905 is memorable first because of his derivation of the energy fluctuation formula and second because of his interest in the volume dependence of thermodynamic quantities,

---

*Planck's counting is discussed in Section 19a.

which became so important in his discovery of the light-quantum. He reinvented Boltzmann's first definition of probability in terms of 'time spent.' His critical position in regard to Boltzmann's second definition may have led him to replace the 'Boltzmann logic,' $W \to S$, by the 'Einstein logic,' $S \to W$. Out of his concern with the foundations of statistical mechanics grew his vastly more important applications to the theoretical determination of the Boltzmann constant. These applications are the main topic of the next chapter, where we meet Einstein in the year of his emergence, 1905. One of the reasons for his explosive creativity in that year may well be the liberation he experienced in moving away from the highly mathematical foundation questions which did not quite suit his scientific temperament.

References

B1. M. Born in *Albert Einstein: Philosopher-Scientist* (P. Schilpp, Ed.), p. 46. Tudor, New York, 1949.

B2. L. Boltzmann, *Wiener Ber.* **53**, 195 (1866). Reprinted in *Wissenschaftliche Abhandlungen von Ludwig Boltzmann* (F. Hasenöhrl, Ed.), Vol. 1, p. 9. Chelsea, New York, 1968. (These collected works are referred to below as *WA*.)

B3. ——, *Wiener Ber.* **66**, 275 (1872); *WA*, Vol. 1, p. 316.

B4. ——, *Wiener Ber.* **63**, 712 (1871); *WA*, Vol. 1, p. 288.

B5. ——, *Wiener Ber.* **75**, 62 (1877); *WA*, Vol. 2, p. 112 (esp. Sec. 2).

B6. ——, *Wiener Ber.* **76**, 373 (1877); *QA*, Vol. 2, p. 164.

B7. ——, *PAW*, 1897, p. 660; *WA*, Vol. 3, p. 615.

B8. ——, *WA*, Vol. 2, p. 118, footnote 2.

B9. ——, *Wiener Ber.* **58**, 517 (1868); *WA*, Vol. 1, p. 49 and Sec. III. See also L. Boltzmann, *Nature* **51**, 413 (1895); *WA*, Vol. 3, p. 535.

B10. ——, *WA*, Vol. 2, p. 218.

B11. ——, *WA*, Vol. 2, pp. 166, 223.

B12. ——, *Wiener Ber.* **63**, 679 (1871); *WA*, Vol. 1, pp. 259, (esp. p. 277); *Crelles J.* **100**, 201 (1887); *WA*, Vol. 3, p. 258.

B13. ——, *Vorlesungen über die Principe der Mechanik,* Vol. 1, p. 9. Barth, Leipzig, 1897. Reprinted by Wissenschaftliche Buchges, Darmstadt, 1974.

B14. ——, *Wiener Ber.* **72**, 427 (1875); *WA*, Vol. 2, p. 1, Eq. 13.

B15. ——, *Vorlesungen über Gastheorie.* Barth, Leipzig, 1896, 1898. Translated as *Lectures on Gas Theory* (S. G. Brush, Tran.). University of California Press, Berkeley, 1964.

B16. ——, [B15], Vol. 1, Sec. 6.

C1. R. Clausius, *AdP* **79**, 368, 500 (1850).

C2. ——, *AdP* **125**, 353 (1865), esp. p. 400.

C3. ——, *AdP* **142**, 433 (1871).

D1. V. A. Douglas, *J. Roy. Astr. Soc. Can.* **50**, 99 (1956).

E1. A. Einstein, [B1], p. 46.

E2. ——, *AdP* **34**, 175 (1911).

E3. P. and T. Ehrenfest, *Enz. d. Math. Wiss.*, Vol. 4, Part 2, Sec. 28. Teubner,

Leipzig, 1911. Translated as *The Conceptual Foundations of the Statistical Approach in Mechanics* (M. J. Moravcsik, Tran.). Cornell University Press, Ithaca, N.Y., 1959.

E4.   A. Einstein, *AdP* **17,** 541 (1905), footnote on p. 551.

E5.   ——, *AdP* **4,** 513 (1901).

E6.   ——, *AdP* **8,** 798 (1902).

E7.   ——, letter to M. Grossmann, April 14, 1901.

E8.   ——, letter to J. Stark, December 7, 1907. Reprinted in A. Hermann, *Sudhoffs Archiv.* **50,** 267 (1966).

E9.   ——, *AdP* **34,** 165 (1911).

E10. ——, *AdP* **9,** 417 (1902).

E11. ——, *AdP* **11,** 170 (1903).

E12. ——, *AdP* **14,** 354 (1904).

E13. ——, *AdP* **17,** 132 (1905).

E14. ——, *Eine neue Bestimmung der Moleküldimensionen.* K. J. Wyss, Bern, 1905. Apart from a short addendum identical with *AdP* **19,** 289 (1906).

E15. ——, *AdP* **34,** 591 (1911).

E16. ——, *Kolloidzeitschr* **27,** 137 (1920).

E17. ——, *AdP* **17,** 549 (1905).

E18. ——, *AdP* **19,** 371 (1906).

E19. ——, *Z. Elektrochem.* **13,** 41 (1907).

E20. ——, *Z. Elektrochem.* **14,** 235 (1908).

E21. ——, *AdP* **22,** 180, 800 (1907).

E22. ——, *AdP* **22,** 569 (1907).

E23. ——, *Jahrb. Rad. Elektr.* **4,** 411 (1907), Secs. 15, 16.

E24. ——, *Phys. Zeitschr.* **10,** 185 (1909).

E25. ——, *Phys. Zeitschr.* **10,** 817 (1909).

E26. —— and L. Hopf, *AdP* **33,** 1096 (1910).

E27. —— and ——, *AdP* **33,** 1105 (1910).

E28. ——, *AdP* **47,** 879 (1915).

E29. ——, *AdP* **33,** 1275 (1910).

E30. ——, *AdP* **34,** 170, 590 (1911).

E31. ——, *AdP* **35,** 679 (1911).

E32. ——, *AdP* **37,** 832 (1912); **38,** 881 (1912).

E33. ——, *J. de Phys.* **3,** 277 (1913).

E34. —— and O. Stern, *AdP* **40,** 551 (1914).

E35. ——, *Verh. Deutsch. Phys. Ges.* **18,** 318 (1916).

E36. ——, *Mitt. Phys. Ges. Zürich* **16,** 47 (1916).

E37. ——, *Phys. Zeitschr.* **18,** 121 (1917).

E38. ——, *Z. Phys.* **27,** 392 (1924).

E39. ——, *PAW,* 1924, p. 261.

E40. ——, *PAW,* 1925, p. 3.

E41. ——, *PAW,* 1925, p. 18.

E42. ——, in *Proceedings of the First Solvay Conference* (P. Langevin and M. de Broglie, Eds.), p. 407. Gauthier-Villars, Paris, 1911.

E43. ——, in *Kultur der Gegenwart* (E. Lecher, Ed.). Teubner, Leipzig, 1915 (2nd ed., 1925).

E44. ——, [E42], p. 441.

E45. [E3], Sec. 23.
E46. [E3], Sec. 11.
E47. A. Einstein, [E24], p. 187.
E48. ——, letter to M. Besso, March 17, 1903. *EB*, p. 13.
E49. ——, [E11], p. 184.
E50. ——, letter to M. Besso, January 1903. *EB*, p. 3.
E51. ——, letter to M. Grossmann, 1901, undated.
E52. ——, [B1], p. 52.
E53. ——, [E42], p. 436.
E54. ——, letter to M. Besso, June 23, 1918. *EB*, p. 126.
G1. J. W. Gibbs, *Elementary Principles of Statistical Mechanics.* Yale University Press, New Haven, Conn., 1902.
G2. ——, [G1], Chap. 7.
H1. P. Hertz, *AdP* **33,** 537 (1910), esp. p. 552.
J1. See, e.g., S. Jahn, *Jahrb. Rad. Elektr.* **6,** 229 (1909), esp. p. 236.
K1. T. S. Kuhn in *Critical Problems in the History of Science* (M. Clagett, Ed.), p. 321. University of Wisconsin Press, Madison, 1962.
K2. M. Klein, *Am. Scientist* **58,** 84 (1970).
K3. ——, in *The Boltzmann Equation* (E. G. D. Cohen and W. Thirring, Eds.), p. 53. Springer Verlag, New York, 1973.
K4. ——, *Science* **157,** 509 (1967).
K5. ——, in *Proceedings of the Jerusalem Einstein Centennial Symposium,* March 1979.
K6. ——, *Paul Ehrenfest,* Vol. 1, p. 176. North Holland, Amsterdam, 1970.
L1. P. T. Landsberg, *Phys. Rev. Lett.* **45,** 149 (1980).
L2. H. A. Lorentz, [E42], p. 441.
L3. ——, *Entropie en Waarschynlykheid,* p. 39. Brill, Leiden, 1923. Translated as *Lectures on Theoretical Physics* (L. Silberstein and A. Trivelli, Trans.), Vol. II, p. 175. Macmillan, London, 1927.
L4. J. Loschmidt, *Wiener Ber.* **73,** 128 (1876), see esp. p. 139; **75,** 67 (1877).
M1. J. C. Maxwell, letter to P. G. Tait, December 11, 1867. Reprinted in C. G. Knott, *Life and Scientific Work of P. G. Tait,* p. 213. Cambridge University Press, Cambridge, 1911.
M2. ——, letter to P. G. Tait, undated; Knott, p. 214.
M3. ——, letter to P. G. Tait, August 1873; Knott, p. 114.
P1. M. Planck, *Verh. Deutsch. Phys. Ges.* **2,** 237 (1900).
P2. ——, *Verh. Deutsch. Phys. Ges.* **2,** 202 (1900).
P3. ——, *AdP* **4,** 553 (1901).
P4. W. Pauli, *Collected Scientific Papers* (R. Kronig and V. Weisskopf, Eds.), Vol. 1, p. 549. Interscience, New York, 1964.
P5. R. Penrose in *General Relativity* (S. W. Hawking and W. Israel, Eds.), p. 581. Cambridge University Press, Cambridge, 1979.
S1. A. Sommerfeld, *Phys. Zeitschr.* **18,** 533 (1917).
S2. E. Salaman, *Encounter,* April 1979, p. 19.
S3. W. Schottky, *Thermodynamik,* p. 116. Springer, Berlin, 1929.
S4. A. Sommerfeld, *Thermodynamics and Statistical Mechanics,* p. 213. Academic Press, New York, 1956.
S5. E. Schroedinger in E. Broda, *Ludwig Boltzmann,* p. 65. Deuticke, Vienna, 1955.

S6. Se, p. 176.

S7. Se, p. 198.

S8. Se, p. 169.

U1. G. E. Uhlenbeck and G. W. Ford, *Lectures in Statistical Mechanics,* Chap. I. American Mathematical Society, Providence, 1963.

V1. V. I. Arnold and A. Avez, *Problèmes Ergodiques de la Mécanique Classique,* Gauthier-Villars, Paris, 1967.

5

The Reality of Molecules

5a. About the Nineteenth Century, Briefly

1. Chemistry. In 1771 work was completed on the first edition of the *Encyclopedia Britannica,* 'a Dictionary of Arts and Sciences compiled upon a new plan ... by a Society of Gentlemen in Scotland.' The entry *atom,* written by William Smellie, a man renowned for his devotion to scholarship and whisky [K1], reads as follows. '*Atom.* In philosophy, a particle of matter, so minute as to admit no division. Atoms are the *minima naturae* |smallest bodies| and are conceived as the first principles or component parts of all physical magnitude.' Democritus might have disagreed, since his atoms were not necessarily minute. Epicurus might have objected that the atom has structure—though it cannot be divided into smaller parts by physical means. Both men might have found the definition incomplete since it did not mention that atoms—as they believed—exist in an infinite variety of sizes and shapes, any one variety being forever incapable of transforming itself into any other. They might have wondered why no reference was made to the $\pi\rho\acute{\omega}\tau\eta$ $\ddot{\upsilon}\lambda\eta$, the prime matter of which all atoms are made. It is likely, however, that an imaginary dialogue between the Greek and the late eighteenth century philosophers might rapidly have led to a common understanding that in the two thousand years which separated them very little had changed regarding the understanding of the basic structure of matter.

The period of rapid change began in 1808, when John Dalton commenced the publication of his *New System of Chemical Philosophy* [D1]. This event marks the birth of modern chemistry, according to which all modes of matter are reducible to a finite number of atomic species (eighteen elements were known at that time). Dalton's early assessment (in 1810) of the youngest of the sciences sounds very modern: 'I should apprehend there are a considerable number of what may be properly called *elementary* principles, which can never be metamorphosed, one into another, by any power we can control. We ought, however, to avail ourselves of every means to reduce the number of bodies or principles of this appearance as much as possible; and after all we may not know what elements are absolutely indecomposable, and what are refractory, because we do not know the proper means for their reduction. We have already observed that all *atoms of the same kind,* whether simple or compound, must necessarily be conceived to be alike in shape, weight, and every other particular' [B1]. Note that Dalton's compound atom is what we call a molecule. Great confusion reigned through most of the nineteenth century regarding such terminology, one man's molecule being another man's atom. The need for a common language developed, but slowly. Fifty years later, at the first international scientific conference ever held, the 1860 Karlsruhe congress of chemists,* the steering committee still considered it necessary to put at the top of the agenda of points to be discussed the question, 'Shall a difference be made between the expressions *molecule* and *atom,* such that a molecule be named the smallest particle of bodies which can enter into chemical reactions and which may be compared to each other in regard to physical properties—atoms being the smallest particles of those bodies which are contained in molecules?,' [M1]. More interesting than the question itself is the fact that, even in 1860, no consensus was reached.

Especially illuminating for an understanding of science in the nineteenth century are the topics discussed by young August Kekulé von Stradonitz (who by then had already discovered that carbon atoms are tetravalent) in the course of his opening address to the Karlsruhe conference. '[He] spoke on the difference between the physical molecule and the chemical molecule, and the distinction between these and the atom. The physical molecule, refers, he said, to the particle of gas, liquid, or solid in question. The chemical molecule is the smallest particle of a body which enters or leaves a chemical reaction. These are not indivisible. Atoms are particles not further divisible' [M1]. Both physics and chemistry could have profited if more attention had been paid to the comment by Stanislao Cannizzaro, in the discussion following Kekulé's paper, that the distinction between physical and chemical molecules has no experimental basis and is therefore unnecessary. Indeed, perhaps the most remarkable fact about the nineteenth century debates on atoms and molecules is the large extent to which chemists and physicists spoke at cross purposes when they did not actually ignore each other. This is not to say that there existed one common view among chemists, another among physicists. Rather, in either camp there were many and often strongly diverging opinions which need not be spelled out in detail here. It should suffice to give a few illustrative examples and to note in particular the central themes. The principal point of debate among chemists was whether atoms were real objects or only mnemonic devices for coding chemical regularities and laws. The main issues for the physicists centered around the kinetic theory of gases; in particular, around the meaning of the second law of thermodynamics.

An early illustration of the dichotomies between the chemists and the physicists is provided by Dalton's opinion about the work of Joseph Louis Gay-Lussac. Dalton's chemistry was based on his law of multiple proportions: if there exists

*The meeting was held September 3–5, 1860. There were 127 chemists in attendance. Participants came from Austria, Belgium, France, Germany, Great Britain, Italy, Mexico, Poland, Russia, Spain, Sweden, and Switzerland.

more than one compound of two elements, then the ratios of the amounts of weight of one element which bind with the same amounts of the other are simple integers. As said, the publication of Dalton's major opus began in 1808. In 1809, Gay-Lussac published his law of combining volumes: the proportions by volume in which gases combine are simple integers. Gay-Lussac mentioned that his results were in harmony with Dalton's atomic theory [G1]. Dalton, on the other hand, did not believe Gay-Lussac: 'His notion of measures is analogous to mine of atoms; and if it could be proved that all elastic fluids have the same number of atoms in the same volume, of numbers that are as 1, 2, 3, 4, etc., the two hypotheses would be the same, except that mine is universal and his applies only to elastic fluids. Gay-Lussac could not but see that a similar hypothesis had been entertained by me and abandoned as untenable' [D2]. (Elastic fluids are now better known as gases.) Also, Dalton did not accept the hypothesis put forward in 1811 by Amedeo Avogadro, that for fixed temperature and pressure equal volumes of gases contain equal numbers of molecules [A1].* Nor was Dalton's position one held only by a single person for a brief time. By all accounts the high point of the Karlsruhe congress was the address by Cannizzaro, in which it was still necessary for the speaker to emphasize the importance of Avogadro's principle for chemical considerations.** That conference did not at once succeed in bringing chemists closer together. 'It is possible that the older men were offended by the impetuous behavior and imposing manner of the younger scientists' [M2]. However, it was recalled by Dmitri Ivanovich Mendeleev thirty years later that 'the law of Avogadro received by means of the congress a wider development, and soon afterwards conquered all minds' [M3].

The law of Avogadro is the oldest of those physical-chemical laws that rest on the explicit assumption that molecules are real things. The tardiness with which this law came to be accepted by the chemists clearly indicates their widespread resistance to the idea of molecular reality. For details of the atomic debate among chemists, I refer the reader to recent excellent monographs [B1, N1]. Here I mention only some revealing remarks by Alexander Williamson, himself a convinced atomist. In his presidential address of 1869 to the London Chemical Society, he said, 'It sometimes happens that chemists of high authority refer publicly to the atomic theory as something they would be glad to dispense with, and which they are ashamed of using. They seem to look upon it as something distinct from the general facts of chemistry, and something which the science would gain by throwing off entirely. . . . On the one hand, all chemists use the atomic theory, and . . . on the other hand, a considerable number view it with mistrust, some with positive dislike. If the theory really is as uncertain and unnecessary as they imagine it to

---

*The reason for Dalton's opposition was that he did not realize (as Avogadro did) that the smallest particles of a gaseous element are not necessarily atoms but may be molecules.

**The views of this remarkable man are most easily accessible in the English translation, published in 1961, of an article he wrote in 1858 [C1].

be, let its defects be laid bare and examined. Let them be remedied if possible, or let the theory be rejected, and some other theory be used in its stead, if its defects are really as irremediable and as grave as is implied by the sneers of its detractors' [W1].

As a final comment on chemistry in the nineteenth century, mention should be made of another regularity bearing on the atomicity of matter and discovered in that period. In an anonymous paper written in 1815, William Prout, a practising physician in London with a great interest in chemistry, claimed to have shown that the specific gravities of atomic species can be expressed as integral multiples of a fundamental unit [P1]. In an addendum written the next year, and also published anonymously [P2], he noted that this fundamental unit may be identified with the specific gravity of hydrogen: 'We may almost consider the πρώτη ὕλη of the ancients to be realized in hydrogen.' Yet Prout did not consider his hypothesis as a hint for the reality of atoms: 'The light in which I have always been accustomed to consider it [the atomic theory] has been very analogous to that in which I believe most botanists now consider the Linnean system; namely, as a conventional artifice, exceedingly convenient for many purposes but which does not represent nature' [B2].

2. Kinetic Theory. The insight that gases are composed of discrete particles dates back at least to the eighteenth century. Daniel Bernoulli may have been the first to state that gas pressure is caused by the collisions of particles with the walls within which they are contained [B3]. The nineteenth century masters of kinetic theory were atomists—by definition, one might say. In Clausius's paper of 1857, 'On the Kind of Motion We Call Heat' [C2], the distinction between solids, liquids, and gases is related to different types of molecular motion. In 1873, Maxwell said, 'Though in the course of ages catastrophes have occurred and may yet occur in the heavens, though ancient systems may be dissolved and new systems evolved out of their ruins, the molecules [i.e., atoms!] out of which these systems [the earth and the whole solar system] are built—the foundation stones of the material universe—remain unbroken and unworn. They continue this day as they were created—perfect in number and measure and weight ...' [M4].*

Boltzmann was less emphatic and in fact reticent at times, but he could hardly have developed his theory of the second law had he not believed in the particulate structure of matter. His assertion that entropy increases almost always, rather than always, was indeed very hard to swallow for those who did not believe in molecular reality. Planck, then an outspoken skeptic, saw this clearly when in 1883 he wrote, 'The consistent implementation of the second law [i.e., to Planck, increase of entropy as an absolute law] ... is incompatible with the assumption of finite atoms. One may anticipate that in the course of the further development of the theory a battle between these two hypotheses will develop which will cost

---

*Faraday had reservations. In 1844 he wrote, 'The atomic doctrine ... is at best an assumption of the truth of which we can assert nothing, whatever we may say or think of its probability' [W2].

one of them its life' [P3]. This is the battle which Ostwald joined in 1895 when he addressed a meeting of the Deutsche Gesellschaft für Naturforscher und Ärzte: 'The proposition that all natural phenomena can ultimately be reduced to mechanical ones cannot even be taken as a useful working hypothesis: it is simply a mistake. This mistake is most clearly revealed by the following fact. All the equations of mechanics have the property that they admit of sign inversion in the temporal quantities. That is to say, theoretically perfectly mechanical processes can develop equally well forward and backward [in time]. Thus, in a purely mechanical world there could not be a before and an after as we have in our world: the tree could become a shoot and a seed again, the butterfly turn back into a caterpillar, and the old man into a child. No explanation is given by the mechanistic doctrine for the fact that this does not happen, nor can it be given because of the fundamental property of the mechanical equations. The actual irreversibility of natural phenomena thus proves the existence of processes that cannot be described by mechanical equations; and with this the verdict on scientific materialism is settled' [O1]. It was in essence a replay of the argument given by Loschmidt twenty years earlier.

Such were the utterances with which Boltzmann, also present at that meeting, had to cope. We are fortunate to have an eye-witness report of the ensuing discussion from a young physicist who attended the conference, Arnold Sommerfeld. 'The paper on "Energetik" was given by Helm* from Dresden; behind him stood Wilhelm Ostwald, behind both the philosophy of Ernst Mach, who was not present. The opponent was Boltzmann, seconded by Felix Klein. Both externally and internally, the battle between Boltzmann and Ostwald resembled the battle of the bull with the supple fighter. However, this time the bull was victorious over the torero in spite of the latter's artful combat. The arguments of Boltzmann carried the day. We, the young mathematicians of that time, were all on the side of Boltzmann; it was entirely obvious to us that one could not possibly deduce the equations of motion for even a single mass point—let alone for a system with many degrees of freedom—from the single energy equation . . .' [S1]. As regards the position of Ernst Mach, it was anti-atomistic but of a far more sober variety than Ostwald's: 'It would not become physical science [said Mach] to see in its self-created, changeable, economical tools, molecules and atoms, realities behind phenomena . . . the atom must remain a tool . . . like the function of mathematics' [M5].

Long before these learned *fin de siècle* discourses took place, in fact long before the laws of thermodynamics were formulated, theoretical attempts had begun to estimate the dimensions of molecules. As early as 1816 Thomas Young noted that 'the diameter or distance of the particles of water is between the two thousand and

---

*The physicist Georg Helm was an ardent supporter of Ostwald's 'Energetik,' according to which molecules and atoms are but mathematical fictions and energy, in its many forms, the prime physical reality.

the ten thousand millionth of an inch' [Y1].* In 1866 Loschmidt calculated the diameter of an air molecule and concluded that 'in the domain of atoms and molecules the appropriate measure of length is the millionth of the millimeter' [L1]. Four years later Kelvin, who regarded it 'as an established fact of science that a gas consists of moving molecules,' found that 'the diameter of the gaseous molecule cannot be less than 2.10^{-9} of a centimeter' [T1]. In 1873 Maxwell stated that the diameter of a hydrogen molecule is about 6.10^{-8} cm [M6]. In that same year Johannes Diderik van der Waals reported similar results in his doctoral thesis [W3]. By 1890 the spread in these values, and those obtained by others [B4], had narrowed considerably. A review of the results up to the late 1880s placed the radii of hydrogen and air molecules between 1 and 2.10^{-8} cm [R2], a remarkably sensible range. Some of the physicists just mentioned used methods that enabled them to also determine Avogadro's number N, the number of molecules per mole. For example, Loschmidt's calculations of 1866 imply that $N \approx 0.5 \times 10^{23}$ [L1], and Maxwell found $N \approx 4 \times 10^{23}$ [M6]. The present best value [D3] is

$$N \approx 6.02 \times 10^{23} \tag{5.1}$$

Toward the end of the nineteenth century, the spread in the various determinations of N was roughly 10^{22} to 10^{24}, an admirable achievement in view of the crudeness—stressed by all who worked on the subject—of the models and methods used.

This is not the place to deal with the sometimes obscure and often wonderful physics contained in these papers, in which the authors strike out into unexplored territory. However, an exception should be made for the work of Loschmidt [L1] since it contains a characteristic element which—as we shall soon see—recurs in the Einstein papers of 1905 on molecular radii and Avogadro's number: the use of two simultaneous equations in which two unknowns, N, and the molecular diameter d, are expressed in terms of physically known quantities.

The first of the equations used by Loschmidt is the relation between d, the mean free path λ, and the number n of molecules per unit volume of a hard-sphere gas: $\lambda n \pi d^2 =$ a calculable constant.** The second relation concerns the quantity $n \pi d^3 / 6$, the fraction of the unit volume occupied by the molecules. Assume that in the liquid phase these particles are closely packed. Then $n \pi d^3 / 6 = \rho_{gas} / 1.17$ ρ_{liquid}, where the ρ's are the densities in the respective phases and the geometric factor 1.17 is Loschmidt's estimate for the ratio of the volume occupied by the molecules in the liquid phase and their proper volume. Thus we have two equa-

---

*Young arrived at this estimate by a rather obscure argument relating the surface tension to the range of the molecular forces and then equating this range with the molecular diameter. Rayleigh, along with many others, had trouble understanding Young's reasoning [R1].

**This relation was derived by Clausius and Maxwell. The constant is equal to $1/\sqrt{2}$ if one uses the Maxwell velocity distribution of identical molecules. Loschmidt used Clausius's value of ¾, which follows if all the gas molecules are assumed to have the same speed. References to refinements of Loschmidt's calculations are found in [T2].

tions for n (hence for N) and d. (Loschmidt applied his reasoning to air, for which λ was known experimentally. However, in order to estimate the densities of liquid oxygen and nitrogen, he had to use indirect theoretical estimates.)

It is not surprising that, on the whole, molecular reality met with less early resistance in physics than it did in chemistry. As is exemplified by Loschmidt's 1866 calculation, physicists could already *do* things with molecules at a time when chemists could, for most purposes, take them to be real or leave them as coding devices. However, it became increasingly difficult in chemical circles to deny the reality of molecules after 1874, the year in which Jacobus Henricus van 't Hoff and Joseph Achille Le Bel independently explained the isomerism of certain organic substances in terms of stereochemical properties of carbon compounds. Even then skeptics did not yield at once (van 't Hoff himself was initially quite cautious on the issue, [N2]). But by the 1880s, the power of a truly molecular picture was widely recognized.

In order to complete this survey of topics bearing on molecular reality prior to the time Einstein got involved, it is necessary to add two further remarks.

3. The End of Indivisibility.   Until the very last years of the nineteenth century, most if not all physicists who believed in the reality of atoms shared Maxwell's view that these particles remain unbroken and unworn. 'They are ... the only material things which still remain in the precise condition in which they first began to exist,' he wrote in his book *Theory of Heat* [M7], which contains the finest expression of his atomic credo.* It is true that many of these same physicists (Maxwell among them) were convinced that something had to rattle inside the atom in order to explain atomic spectra. Therefore, while there was a need for a picture of the atom as a body with structure, this did not mean (so it seemed) that one could take the atom apart. However, in 1899, two years after his discovery of the electron, Joseph John Thomson announced that the atom had been split: 'Electrification [that is, ionization] essentially involves the splitting of the atom, a part of the mass of the atom getting free and becoming detached from the original atom' [T3]. By that time it was becoming increasingly clear that radioactive phenomena (first discovered in 1896) also had to be explained in terms of a divisible atom. 'Atoms [of radioactive elements], indivisible from the chemical point of view, are here divisible,' Marie Curie wrote in 1900 [C3]. She added that the explanation of radioactivity in terms of the expulsion of subatomic particles 'seriously undermines the principles of chemistry.' In 1902 Ernest Rutherford and Frederick Soddy proposed their transformation theory, according to which radioactive bodies contain unstable atoms, a fixed fraction of which decay per unit time. Forty years later, a witness to this event characterized the mood of those early times: 'It must be difficult if not impossible for the young physicist or chemist to realize how

---

*To Maxwell, electrolytic dissociation was not at variance with the indivisibility of atoms—but that is another story.

extremely bold [the transformation theory] was and how unacceptable to the atomists of the time' [R3].

Thus, at the turn of the century, the classical atomists, those who believed both in atoms and in their indivisibility, were under fire from two sides. There was a rapidly dwindling minority of conservatives, led by the influential Ostwald and Mach, who did not believe in atoms at all. At the same time a new breed arose, people such as J. J. Thomson, the Curies, and Rutherford, all convinced of the reality of atoms and all—though not always without trepidation, as in the case of Marie Curie—aware of the fact that chemistry was not the last chapter in particle physics. For them, the ancient speculations about atoms had become reality and the old dream of transmutation had become inevitable.

4. The End of Invisibility.   If there was one issue on which there was agreement between physicists and chemists, atomists or not, it was that atoms, if they exist at all, are too small to be seen. Perhaps no one expressed this view more eloquently than van der Waals in the closing lines of his 1873 doctoral thesis, where he expressed the hope that his work might contribute to bringing closer the time when 'the motion of the planets and the music of the spheres will be forgotten for a while in admiration of the delicate and artful web formed by the orbits of those invisible atoms' [W3].

Direct images of atoms were at last produced in the 1950s with the field ion microscope [M8]. In a broad sense of the word, particles smaller than atoms were 'seen' much earlier, of course. At the turn of the century, alpha particles were perceived as scintillations on zinc sulfide screens, electrons as tracks in a cloud chamber. In an 1828 paper entitled, in part, 'A Brief Account of Microscopical Observations Made in the Months of June, July and August, 1827, on the Particles Contained in the Pollen of Plants' [B5], the botanist Robert Brown reported seeing the random motion of various kinds of particles sufficiently fine to be suspended in water. He examined fragments of pollen particles, 'dust or soot deposited on all bodies in such quantity, especially in London,' particles from pulverized rock, including a fragment from the Sphinx, and others. Today, we say that Brown saw the action of the water molecules pushing against the suspended objects. But that way of phrasing what we see in Brownian motion is as dependent on theoretical analysis as is the statement that a certain cloud chamber track can be identified as an electron.

In the case of Brownian motion, this analysis was given by Einstein, who thereby became the first to make molecules visible. As a last preparatory step toward Einstein's analysis, I must touch briefly on what was known about dilute solutions in the late nineteenth century.

5b. The Pots of Pfeffer and the Laws of van 't Hoff

In the mid-1880s, van 't Hoff, then professor of chemistry, mineralogy, and geology at the University of Amsterdam, discovered in the course of his studies of chemical equilibrium in solutions 'that there is a fundamental analogy, nay almost an identity, with gases, more especially in their physical aspect, if only in solutions we consider the so-called osmotic pressure. . . . We are not here dealing with a fanciful analogy, but with one which is fundamental' [H1]. The experimental basis for these discoveries was provided by the measurements on osmosis through rigid membranes performed a decade earlier by Wilhelm Pfeffer, then an extraordinarius in Bonn [P4].

Let us first recall what van 't Hoff meant by *the* osmotic pressure. Consider a vessel filled with fluid, the solvent. A subvolume V of the fluid is enclosed by a membrane that is fully permeable with respect to the solvent. Another species of molecules, the solute, is inserted in V. If the membrane is fully impermeable to the solute, solvent will stream into V until equilibrium is reached. In equilibrium, the pressure on the membrane is *an* osmotic pressure. If the membrane has some degree of elasticity, then this pressure will cause the membrane to dilate. For the special case where the membrane is rigid and unyielding, the pressure exerted on it is *the* osmotic pressure to which van 't Hoff referred and which we shall always have in mind in what follows. (This pressure can be sizable; for example, a 1% sugar solution exerts a pressure of ⅔ atm.)

It is one of the great merits of Pfeffer, renowned also for his work in botany and plant physiology, that he was the first to prepare such rigid membranes. He did this by placing unglazed, porous, porcelain pots filled with an aqueous solution of $K_3Fe(CN)_6$ in a bath filled with copper sulfate. The resulting precipitate of $Cu_2Fe(CN)_6$ in the pores of the porcelain pots constituted the rigid membrane. Pfeffer performed elaborate measurements with his new tool. His results led him to suspect that 'evidently there had to exist some connection between osmotic [pressure] on the one hand and the size and number of molecules on the other' [C4]. The connection conjectured by Pfeffer was found by Einstein and reported in his doctoral thesis, with the help of the laws found by van 't Hoff. In turn, van 't Hoff's purely phenomenological discovery was based exclusively on the analysis of data obtained by Pfeffer.

Van 't Hoff's laws apply to ideal solutions, 'solutions which are diluted to such an extent that they are comparable to ideal gases' [H1].* For such ideal solutions, his laws can be phrased as follows (it is assumed that no electrolytic dissociation takes place):

1. In equilibrium, one has

$$pV = R'T \qquad (5.2)$$

independent of the nature of the solvent. In this analog of the Boyle–Gay-Lussac law, p is the osmotic pressure, V the volume enclosed by the rigid membrane, T the temperature, and R' a constant.

---

*Van 't Hoff noted that a negligible heat of dilution is a practical criterion for solutions to be ideal.

2. The extension of Avogadro's law: equal volumes of solutions at the same p and T contain the same number of solute molecules. This number is equal to the number of gas molecules at the same (gas) pressure p and the same T. Hence, for one gram-mole

$$R' = R \qquad (5.3)$$

where R is the gas constant. Thus, after van 't Hoff, the liquid phase offered a new way of measuring the gas constant and, consequently, new possibilities for the determination of Avogadro's number.

'The fact that the dissolved molecules of a diluted solution exert on a semi-permeable membrane—in spite of the presence of the solvent—exactly the same pressure as if they alone were present, and that in the ideal gas state—this fact is so startling that attempts have repeatedly been made to find a kinetic interpretation that was as lucid as possible', Ehrenfest wrote in 1915 [E1]. Einstein briefly discussed the statistical derivation of van 't Hoff's laws in 1905 [E2]; more important, however, are the applications he made of these laws.

In 1901, van 't Hoff became the first to receive the Nobel prize for chemistry. The presentation speech delivered on that occasion illustrates vividly that, at the beginning of the twentieth century, molecular reality had become widely accepted among chemists as well as physicists: 'He proved that gas pressure and osmotic pressure are identical, and thereby that the molecules themselves in the gaseous phase and in solutions are also identical. As a result of this, the concept of the molecule in chemistry was found to be definite and universally valid to a degree hitherto undreamed of' [N3].

5c. The Doctoral Thesis

In his PhD thesis, Einstein described a new theoretical method for determining molecular radii and Avogadro's number. From a comparison of his final equations with data on sugar solutions in water, he found that

$$N = 2.1 \times 10^{23} \qquad (5.4)$$

The printed version of his thesis [E3] carries the dedication 'to my friend Marcel Grossman' and gives April 30, 1905, as the completion date. Einstein did not submit his dissertation to the dean of the philosophical faculty, Section II, at the University of Zürich until July 20 [E4]. This delay may have had its technical reasons. More important, probably, was the fact that, between April and July, Einstein was rather busy with other things: during those months he completed his first papers on Brownian motion and on the special theory of relativity. The thesis was rapidly accepted. On July 24* the dean forwarded to the faculty for their

---

*Einstein later recalled that, after having been told that the manuscript was too short, he added one sentence, whereupon it was accepted [S2]. I have found no trace of such a communication, nor is it clear to me when this exchange could have taken place.

approval the favorable reports by Kleiner and by Burkhardt, who had been asked by Kleiner to check the most important parts of the calculations. The faculty approved (Burkhardt had failed to note a rather important mistake in Einstein's calculations—but that comes later). Einstein was now Herr Doktor.

It is not sufficiently realized that Einstein's thesis is one of his most fundamental papers. Histories and biographies invariably refer to 1905 as the miraculous year because of his articles on relativity, the light-quantum, and Brownian motion. In my opinion, the thesis is on a par with the Brownian motion article. In fact, in some—not all—respects, his results on Brownian motion are by-products of his thesis work. This goes a long way toward explaining why the paper on Brownian motion was received by the *Annalen der Physik* on May 11, 1905, only eleven days after the thesis had been completed.

Three weeks after the thesis was accepted, this same journal received a copy (without dedication) for publication. It was published [E5] only after Einstein supplied a brief addendum in January 1906 (I shall refer to this paper as the 1906 paper). As a result of these various delays, the thesis appeared as a paper in the *Annalen der Physik* only after the Brownian motion article had come out in the same journal. This may have helped create the impression in some quarters (see, for example, [L2]) that the relation between diffusion and viscosity—a very important equation due to Einstein and Sutherland—was first obtained in Einstein's paper on Brownian motion. Actually, it first appeared in his thesis.

In the appendix to the 1906 paper, Einstein gave a new and (as turned out later) improved value for N:

$$N = 4.15 \times 10^{23} \tag{5.5}$$

The large difference between this value and his value of eight months earlier was entirely due to the availability of better data on sugar solutions.

Quite apart from the fundamental nature of some results obtained in the thesis, there is another reason why this paper is of uncommon interest: it has had more widespread practical applications than any other paper Einstein ever wrote.

The patterns of scientific reference as traced through the study of citations are, as with Montaigne's description of the human mind, *merveilleux et ondoyant*. The history of Einstein's influence on later works, as expressed by the frequency of citations of his papers, offers several striking examples. Of the eleven scientific articles published by any author before 1912 and cited most frequently between 1961 and 1975, four are by Einstein. Among these four, the thesis (or, rather, the 1906 paper) ranks first; then follows a sequel to it (to which I return later in this section), written in 1911. The Brownian motion paper ranks third, the paper on critical opalescence fourth. At the top of the list of Einstein's scientific articles cited most heavily during the years 1970 to 1974 is the 1906 paper. It was quoted four times as often as Einstein's first survey article of 1916 on general relativity and eight times as often as his 1905 paper on the light-quantum [C5].

Of course, relative citation frequencies are no measure of relative importance. Who has not aspired to write a paper so fundamental that very soon it is known to everyone and cited by no one? It is nevertheless obvious that there must be valid reasons for the popularity of Einstein's thesis. These are indeed not hard to find: the thesis, dealing with bulk rheological properties of particle suspensions, contains results which have an extraordinarily wide range of applications. They are relevant to the construction industry (the motion of sand particles in cement mixes [R4]), to the dairy industry (the motion of casein micelles in cow's milk [D4]), and to ecology (the motion of aerosol particles in clouds [Y2]), to mention but a few scattered examples. Einstein might have enjoyed hearing this, since he was quite fond of applying physics to practical situations.

Let us consider Einstein's Doktorarbeit in some detail. His first step is hydrodynamic. Consider the stationary flow of an incompressible, homogeneous fluid. If effects of acceleration are neglected, then the motion of the fluid is described by the Navier–Stokes equations:

$$\vec{\nabla}p = \eta\,\Delta\vec{v} \qquad \text{div } \vec{v} = 0 \tag{5.6}$$

where $\vec{v}$ is the velocity, p the hydrostatic pressure, and η the viscosity. Next, insert a large number of identical, rigid, spherical particles in the fluid. The radius of the solute particles is taken to be large compared with the radius of the solvent molecules so that the solvent can still be treated as a continuum. The solution is supposed to be dilute; the total volume of the particles is much smaller than the volume of the liquid. Assume further that (1) the overall motion of the system is still Navier–Stokes, (2) the inertia of the solute particles in translation and their rotational motion can be neglected, (3) there are no external forces, (4) the motion of any one of the little spheres is not affected by the presence of any other little sphere, (5) the particles move under the influence of hydrodynamic stresses at their surface only, and (6) the boundary condition of the flow velocity v is taken to be $v = 0$ on the surface of the spheres. Then, Einstein showed, the flow can still be described by Eq. 5.6 provided η is replaced by a new 'effective viscosity' η^*, given by

$$\eta^* = \eta\,(1 + \varphi) \tag{5.7}$$

where φ is the fraction of the unit volume occupied by the (uniformly distributed) spheres. Let the hard spheres represent molecules (which do not dissociate). Then

$$\varphi = \frac{N\rho}{m}\frac{4\pi}{3}\,a^3 \tag{5.8}$$

where N is Avogadro's number, a the molecular radius, m the molecular weight of the solute, and ρ the amount of mass of the solute per unit volume. Einstein had available to him values for η^*/η for dilute solutions of sugar in water, and φ

and m were also known. Thus Eqs. 5.7 and 5.8 represent one relation between the two unknowns N and a.

The next thing that Einstein of course did (in the spirit of Loschmidt*) was find a second connection between N and a. To this end, he used a reasoning which is partly thermodynamic, partly dynamic. This argument is sketched in his thesis and repeated in mòre detail in his first paper on Brownian motion [E2]. It is extremely ingenious.

Cónsider first an ideal gas and a time-independent force K acting on its molecules in the negative x direction. The force exerted per unit volume equals $K\rho N/m$. In thermal equilibrium, the balance between this force and the gas pressure p is given by

$$\frac{K\rho N}{m} = \frac{\partial p}{\partial x} = \frac{RT}{m}\frac{\partial \rho}{\partial x} \qquad (5.9)$$

where R is the gas constant. Now, Einstein reasoned, according to van 't Hoff's law, Eq. 5.9 should also hold for dilute solutions as long as the time-independent force K acts only on the solute molecules.

Let K impart a velocity v (relative to the solvent) to the molecules of the solute. If the mean free path of the solvent molecules is much less than the diameter of the solute molecules, then (also in view of the boundary condition $v = 0$ on the surface of the solute particles) we have the well-known Stokes relation

$$K = 6\pi\eta a v \qquad (5.10)$$

so that, under the influence of K, $K\rho N/6\pi\eta am$ solute molecules pass in the negative x direction per unit area per second. The resulting concentration gradient leads to a diffusion in the x direction of $DN/m \cdot (\partial\rho/\partial x)$ particles/cm²/sec, where, by definition, D is the diffusion coefficient. Dynamic equilibrium demands that the magnitude of the diffusion current equal the magnitude of the current induced by K:

$$\frac{\rho K}{6\pi\eta a} = D\frac{\partial \rho}{\partial x} \qquad (5.11)$$

Then, from the thermal equilibrium condition (Eq. 5.9) and the dynamic equilibrium condition (Eq. 5.11)

$$D = \frac{RT}{N} \cdot \frac{1}{6\pi\eta a} \qquad (5.12)$$

Observe that the force K has canceled out in Eq. 5.12. The trick was therefore to use K only as an intermediary quantity to relate the diffusion coefficient to the

*See Section 5a. The only nineteenth century method for finding N and a that Einstein discussed in his 1915 review article on kinetic theory [E6] was the one by Loschmidt.

viscosity in the Stokes regime. Equation 5.12 is the second relation for the two unknowns N and a.

By a quite remarkable coincidence, Eq. 5.12 was discovered in Australia at practically the same time Einstein did his thesis work. In March 1905 William Sutherland submitted a paper that contained the identical result, arrived at by the method just described [S2a]. Thus, Eq. 5.12 should properly be called the Sutherland–Einstein relation.

Note that the derivation of Eq. 5.12 is essentially independent of any details regarding the motion of the solute particles. Therein lies the strength of the argument that, as a theme with variations, recurs a number of times in Einstein's later work: a 'systematic force,' a drag force of the Stokesian type (that is, proportional to the velocity) balances with a random, or fluctuating, force. In the present case, as well as for Brownian motion, the fluctuating force is the one generated by the thermal molecular motions in the environment, the fluctuations leading to a net diffusion. Later, in 1909 and again in 1917, Einstein was to use the balance between a Stokesian force and a fluctuating force generated by electromagnetic radiation.

As to the contents of Einstein's thesis, all was quiet for the five years following its publication. Then a Mr. Bacelin, a pupil of Jean Baptiste Perrin's, informed Einstein of measurements which gave a value for η^* that was too high to be compatible with Eq. 5.7. As we shall see in the next section, by this time Perrin had a very good idea how big N had to be. Therefore, η^* could now be computed (knowing a from other sources) and the result could be compared with experiment! Upon hearing this news, Einstein set one of his own pupils to work, who discovered that there was an elementary but nontrivial mistake in the derivation of Eq. 5.7. The correct result is [E7]

$$\frac{\eta^*}{\eta} = 1 + \frac{5\varphi}{2} \qquad (5.13)$$

With the same data that Einstein had used earlier to obtain Eq. 5.5, the new value for N is

$$N = 6.6 \times 10^{23} \qquad (5.14)$$

a far better result, on which I shall comment further in the next section.

In conclusion, it is now known that Einstein's Eq. 5.13 is valid only for values of $\varphi \lesssim 0.02$.* Theoretical studies of corrections $0(\varphi^2)$ to the rhs of Eq. 5.13 were made as late as 1977. Effects that give rise to φ^2 terms are two-particle correlations [B6] and also a phenomenon not yet discussed in the thesis: the Brownian motion of the solute particles [B7].

---

*See the reviews by Rutgers, which contain detailed comparisons of theory with experiment, as well as a long list of proposals to modify Eq. 5.13 [R5].

5d. Eleven Days Later: Brownian Motion*

1. Another Bit of Nineteenth Century History.   During the nineteenth century, it had become clear from experiments performed in various laboratories that Brownian motions increase with decreasing size and density of the suspended particles (10^{-3} mm is a typical particle radius above which these motions are hardly observable) and with decreasing viscosity and increasing temperature of the host liquid. Another important outcome of this early research was that it narrowed down the number of possible explanations of this phenomenon, beginning with Brown's own conclusion that it had nothing to do with small things that are alive. Further investigations eliminated such causes as temperature gradients, mechanical disturbances, capillary actions, irradiation of the liquid (as long as the resulting temperature increase can be neglected), and the presence of convection currents within the liquid. As can be expected, not all of these conclusions were at once generally accepted without controversy.

In the 1860s, the view emerged that the cause of the phenomenon was to be found in the internal motions of the fluid. From then on, it did not take long before the more specific suggestion was made that the zigzag motions of the suspended particles were due to collisions with the molecules of the fluid. At least three physicists proposed this independently: Giovanni Cantoni from Pavia and the two Belgian Jesuits Joseph Delsaulx and Ignace Carbonelle. Of course, this was a matter of speculation rather than proof. 'Io penso che il moto di danza delle particelle solide . . . possa attribuirsi alle differenti velocità che esser devono . . . sia in coteste particelli solide, sia nelle molecole del liquido che le urtano da ogni banda,' wrote Cantoni [C6].** '[Les] mouvements browniens . . . seraient, dans ma manière de considérer le phénomène, le résultat des mouvements moléculaires calorifiques du liquide ambiant,' wrote Delsaulx [D5].†

However, these proposals soon met with strong opposition, led by the Swiss botanist Carl von Naegeli and by William Ramsey. Their counterargument was based on the incorrect assumption that every single zig or zag in the path of a suspended particle should be due to a single collision with an individual molecule. Even though experiments were not very quantitative at that time, it was not difficult to realize that this assumption led to absurdities. Nevertheless, the expla-

---

*Einstein's papers on Brownian motion as well as the 1906 paper have been collected in a handy little book by Fürth [F1, F2]. A useful though not complete set of references to nineteenth century experimental work and theoretical speculation can be found in a paper by Smoluchowski [S3]; see also [B8] and [N4].

**I believe that the dancing motion of the solid particles . . . can be attributed to the different velocities which ought to be ascribed . . . either to the said solid particles, or to the molecules of the liquid which hit [these solid particles] from all directions.

†In my way of considering the phenomenon, the Brownian motions should be the consequence of the molecular heat motions of the ambient liquid.

nation in terms of molecular collisions was not entirely abandoned. Take, for example, the case of Louis Georges Gouy, who did some of the best nineteenth century experiments on Brownian motion. He agreed with the remark by Naegeli and Ramsey, but conjectured that the molecules in liquids travel in organized bunches so that an individual kick imparted to a suspended particle would be due to the simultaneous action of a large number of molecules.

Gouy was also the first to note that it was not easy to comprehend Brownian motion from a thermodynamic point of view. It seemed possible to him—at least in principle—that one could construct a perpetuum mobile of the second kind driven by those ceaseless movements (It should be mentioned that the explicit disproof of this statement is delicate. The best paper on this question is by Leo Szilard [S4].). This led Gouy to express the belief that Carnot's principle (the second law of thermodynamics) might not apply to domains with linear dimensions of the order of one micrometer [G2].

Poincaré—often called on at the turn of the century to pronounce on the status of physics—brought these ideas to the attention of large audiences. In his opening address to the 1900 International Congress of Physics in Paris, he remarked, after referring to Gouy's ideas on Brownian motion, 'One would believe seeing Maxwell's demon at work' [P5]. In a lecture entitled 'The Crises of Mathematical Physics,' given before the Congress of Arts and Science in St. Louis in 1904, he put Carnot's principle at the head of his list of endangered general laws: '[Brown] first thought that [Brownian motion] was a vital phenomenon, but soon he saw that inanimate bodies dance with no less ardor than the others; then he turned the matter over to the physicists. . . . We see under our eyes now motion transformed into heat by friction, now heat changed inversely into motion. This is the contrary of Carnot's principle' [P6].

2. The Overdetermination of N.   In 1905, Einstein was blissfully unaware of the detailed history of Brownian motion. At that time, he knew neither Poincaré's work on relativity nor the latter's dicta 'On the Motion Required by the Molecular Kinetic Theory of Heat of Particles Suspended in Fluids at Rest,' as Einstein entitled his first paper on Brownian motion [E2]. In referring to fluids at rest, he clearly had in mind the fluids in motion dealt with in his previous paper, finished eleven days earlier. The absence of the term *Brownian motion* in this title is explained in the second sentence of the paper: 'It is possible that the motions discussed here are identical with the so-called Brownian molecular motion; the references accessible to me on the latter subject are so imprecise, however, that I could not form an opinion about this.'

This paper, received by the *Annalen der Physik* on May 11, 1905, marks the third occasion in less than two months on which Einstein makes a fundamental discovery bearing on the determination of Avogadro's number. The three methods are quite distinct. The first one (submitted to the *Annalen* on March 18, 1905), in which use is made of the long-wavelength limit of the blackbody radiation law, gave him $N = 6.17 \times 10^{23}$ (!).* The second one makes use of the incompressible flow of solutions and gave him $N = 2.1 \times 10^{23}$, as we saw in the previous section. The third one, on Brownian motion, gave him a formula but not yet a number. 'May some researcher soon succeed in deciding the question raised here, which is important for the theory of heat,' he wrote at the end of this paper.** Even though he did not know the literature, he was right in surmising that the appropriate data were not yet available. It would soon be otherwise. Incidentally, neither in his thesis nor in his Brownian motion paper does Einstein mention that in 1905 he had made not just one but several proposals for determining N. If sparseness of references to the work of others is typical of his writings, so it is with references to his own work. He never was a man to waste much time on footnotes.

Einstein was still not done with the invention of new ways for obtaining Avogadro's number. Later in the year, in December, he finished his second paper on Brownian motion, which contains two further methods for finding N [E8]. In 1907 he noted that measurements of voltage fluctuations give another means for determining N [E9]. In 1910 he gave yet another method, critical opalescence [E10]. He must have realized that the ubiquity of N would once and for all settle the problem of molecular reality, as indeed it did.

It was indicated earlier that, as the nineteenth century drew to an end, the acceptance of the reality of atoms and molecules was widespread, though there were still some pockets of resistance. Nevertheless, it is correct to say that the debate on molecular reality came to a close only as a result of developments in the first decade of the twentieth century. This was not just because of Einstein's first paper on Brownian motion or of any single good determination of N. Rather, the issue was settled once and for all because of the extraordinary agreement in the values of N obtained by many different methods. Matters were clinched not by a determination but by an overdetermination of N. From subjects as diverse as radioactivity, Brownian motion, and the blue in the sky, it was possible to state, by 1909, that a dozen independent ways of measuring N yielded results all of which lay between 6 and 9×10^{23}. In concluding his 1909 memoir on the subject, Perrin [P7, P8] had every reason to state, 'I think it is impossible that a mind free from all preconception can reflect upon the extreme diversity of the phenomena which thus converge to the same result without experiencing a strong impression, and I think that it will henceforth be difficult to defend by rational arguments a hostile attitude to molecular hypotheses' [P8].†

3. *Einstein's First Paper on Brownian Motion.* Enlarging on an earlier comment, I shall explain next in what sense this first paper on Brownian motion is

*See Section 19b.

**I heed Einstein's remark [E2] that his molecular-kinetic derivation of van 't Hoff's law, also contained in this article, is not essential to an understanding of the rest of his arguments.

†For the status of our knowledge about N in 1980, see [D3].

a scholium to the doctoral thesis. To this end, I return to the relation between the diffusion coefficient D and the viscosity η discussed previously

$$D = \frac{RT}{N} \frac{1}{6\pi\eta a} \qquad (5.12)$$

where a is the radius of the hard-sphere molecules dissolved in the liquid. Recall the following main points that went into the derivation of Eq. 5.12:

1. The applicability of van 't Hoff's laws (Eqs. 5.2 and 5.3)
2. The validity of Stokes's law (Eq. 5.10)
3. The mechanism of diffusion in the x direction, described by the equation (not explicitly used in the foregoing)

$$D \frac{\partial^2 n}{\partial x^2} = \frac{\partial n}{\partial t} \qquad (5.15)$$

where $n(x, t)$ is the number of particles per unit volume around x at time t.

The essence of Einstein's attack on Brownian motion is his observation that, as far as these three facts are concerned, what is good for solutions is good for suspensions:

1. Van 't Hoff's laws should hold not only for dilute solutions but also for dilute suspensions: 'One does not see why for a number of suspended bodies the same osmotic pressure should not hold as for the same number of dissolved molecules' [E2].
2. Without making an explicit point of it, Einstein assumes that Stokes's law holds. Recall that this implies that the liquid is treated as a continuous medium. (It also implies that the suspended particles all have the same radius.)
3. Brownian motion is described as a diffusion process subject to Eq. 5.15. (For simplicity, Einstein treats the motion as a one-dimensional problem.)

Now then, consider the fundamental solution of Eq. 5.15 corresponding to a situation in which at time $t = 0$ all particles are at the origin:

$$n(x,t) = \frac{n}{\sqrt{4\pi D t}} \exp\left(-\frac{x^2}{4Dt}\right) \qquad (5.16)$$

where $n = \int n(x)dx$. Then, the mean square displacement $\langle x^2 \rangle$ from the origin is given by

$$\langle x^2 \rangle = \frac{1}{n} \int x^2 n(x,t)\, dx = 2Dt \qquad (5.17)$$

From Eqs. 5.12 and 5.17

$$\langle x^2 \rangle = \frac{RT}{3\pi N a \eta} t \qquad (5.18)$$

In this, Einstein's fundamental equation for Brownian motion, $\langle x^2 \rangle$, t, a, η are measurable; therefore N can be determined. As mentioned earlier, one never ceases to experience surprise at this result, which seems, as it were, to come out of nowhere: prepare a set of small spheres which are nevertheless huge compared with simple molecules, use a stopwatch and a microscope, and find Avogadro's number.

As Einstein emphasized, it is not necessary to assume that all particles are at the origin at $t = 0$. That is to say, since the particles are assumed to move independently, one can consider $n(x,t)\,dx$ to mean the number of particles displaced by an amount between x and $x + dx$ in t seconds. He gave an example: for water at 17°C, $a \approx 0.001$ mm, $N \approx 6 \times 10^{23}$, one has $\langle x^2 \rangle^{1/2} \approx 6$ μm if $t = 1$ minute.

Equation 5.18 is the first instance of a fluctuation–dissipation relation: a mean square fluctuation is connected with a dissipative mechanism phenomenologically described by the viscosity parameter.

Einstein's paper immediately drew widespread attention. In September 1906 he received a letter from Wilhelm Conrad Roentgen asking him for a reprint of the papers on relativity. In the same letter Roentgen also expressed great interest in Einstein's work on Brownian motion, asked him for his opinion on Gouy's ideas and added, 'It is probably difficult to establish harmony between [Brownian motion] and the second law of thermodynamics' [R6]. It is hard to imagine that Einstein would not have replied to such a distinguished colleague. Unfortunately, Einstein's answer (if there was one) has not been located.

4. Diffusion as a Markovian Process. All the main physics of the first Einstein paper on Brownian motion is contained in Eq. 5.18. However, this same paper contains another novelty, again simple, again profound, having to do with the *interpretation* of Eq. 5.15. This equation dates from the nineteenth century and was derived and applied in the context of continuum theories. In 1905 Einstein, motivated by his reflections on Brownian motion, gave a new derivation of the diffusion equation.

As was already done in the derivation of Eq. 5.12, assume (Einstein said) that the suspended particles move independently of each other. Assume further that we can define a time interval τ that is small compared with the time interval of observation (t in Eq. 5.18) while at the same time τ is so large that the motion of a particle during one interval τ does not depend on its history prior to the commencement of that interval. Let $\phi(\Delta)\,d\Delta$ be the probability that a particle is displaced, in an interval τ, by an amount between Δ and $\Delta + d\Delta$. The probability ϕ is normalized and symmetric:

$$\int_{-\infty}^{\infty} \phi(\Delta)\,d\Delta = 1 \qquad \phi(\Delta) = \phi(-\Delta) \tag{5.19}$$

Since the particles move independently, we can relate $n(x,t + \tau)dx$ to the distribution at time t by

$$n(x,t + \tau)dx = dx \int_{-\infty}^{\infty} n(x + \Delta,t)\,\phi(\Delta)d\Delta \qquad (5.20)$$

Develop the lhs to first order in τ, the rhs to second order in Δ, and use Eq. 5.19. Then we recover Eq. 5.15, where D is now *defined* as the second moment of the probability distribution ϕ:

$$D = \frac{1}{2\tau} \int_{-\infty}^{\infty} \Delta^2 \phi(\Delta)d\Delta \qquad (5.21)$$

All information on the dynamics of collision is contained in the explicit form of $\phi(\Delta)$. The great virtue of Eq. 5.18 is therefore that it is independent of all details of the collision phenomena except for the very general conditions that went into the derivation of Eq. 5.21.

Today we would say that, in 1905, Einstein treated diffusion as a Markovian process (so named after Andrei Andreievich Markov, who introduced the so-called Markov chains in 1906), thereby establishing a link between the random walk of a single particle and the diffusion of many particles.

5. *The Later Papers.* I give next a brief review of the main points contained in Einstein's later papers on Brownian motion.

1) December 1905 [E8]. Having been informed by colleagues that the considerations of the preceding paper indeed fit, as to order of magnitude, with the experimental knowledge on Brownian motion, Einstein entitles his new paper 'On the Theory of Brownian Motion.' He gives two new applications of his earlier ideas: the vertical distribution of a suspension under the influence of gravitation and the Brownian rotational motion for the case of a rotating solid sphere. Correspondingly, he finds two new equations from which N can be determined. He also notes that Eq. 5.18 cannot hold for small values of t since that equation implies that the mean velocity, $\langle x^2 \rangle^{1/2}/t$, becomes infinite as $t \rightarrow 0$. 'The reason for this is that we . . . implicitly assumed that, during the time t, the phenomenon is independent of [what happened] in earlier times. This assumption applies less well as t gets smaller.'*

2) December 1906 [E9]. A brief discussion of 'a phenomenon in the domain of electricity which is akin to Brownian motion': the (temperature-dependent) mean square fluctuations in the potential between condensor plates.

3) January 1907 [E11]. Einstein raises and answers the following question. Since the suspension is assumed to obey van 't Hoff's law, it follows from the equipartition theorem that $\langle v^2 \rangle$, the mean square of the *instantaneous* particle velocity, equals $3RT/mN$ (m is the mass of the suspended particle). Thus, $\langle v^2 \rangle$

---

*The general solution for all t was given independently by Ornstein [O2] and Fürth [F3].

is larger by many orders of magnitude than $\langle x^2 \rangle /t^2$, the squared average velocity computed from Eq. 5.18 for reasonable values of t. Is this paradoxical? It is not, since one can estimate that the instantaneous velocity changes magnitude and direction in periods of about 10^{-7} s; $\langle v^2 \rangle$ is therefore unobservable in Brownian motion experiments. Here is also the answer to the Naegeli–Ramsey objection.

4) 1908.   At the suggestion of the physical chemist Richard Lorenz, Einstein writes an elementary exposé of the theory of Brownian motion [E12].

This completes the account of Einstein's contributions to Brownian motion in the classical domain. Applications to the quantum theory will be discussed in Part VI. I conclude with a few scattered comments on the subsequent history of classical Brownian motion.

Einstein's relation (Eq. 5.18) is now commonly derived with the help of the Langevin equation (derived by Paul Langevin in 1908 [L3]). The first review article on Brownian motion appeared in 1909 [J1]. In later years, the subject branched out in many directions, including the behavior for small values of t, the non-Stokesian case, and the presence of external forces [W4]. Brownian motion was still a subject of active research in the 1970s [B9].

The rapid experimental confirmation of Einstein's theory by a new generation of experiments, in particular the key role of Jean Perrin and his school, has been described by Nye [N1]. Perrin's own account in his book *Les Atomes* [P9], first published in 1913 (and also available in English translation [P10]), remains as refreshing as ever.* This work contains not only an account of the determination of N from Brownian motion but also a summary of all methods for determining N which had been put to the test at that time. It is remarkable that the method proposed by Einstein in his thesis is missing. I mentioned earlier that a communication by a pupil of Perrin had led Einstein to discover a mistake in his thesis. Perrin must have known about this, since Einstein wrote to him shortly afterward to thank him for this information and to inform him of the correct result [E13]. Einstein's very decent value for N (Eq. 5.14) was published in 1911. Its absence in Perrin's book indicates that Einstein's doctoral thesis was not widely appreciated in the early years. This is also evident from a brief note published by Einstein in 1920 [E14] for the sole purpose of drawing attention to his erratum published in 1911 [E7] 'which till now seems to have escaped the attention of all who work in this field.'

'I had believed it to be impossible to investigate Brownian motion so precisely,' Einstein wrote to Perrin from Zürich late in 1909 [E15]. This letter also shows that, by that time, Einstein's preoccupation had moved to the quantum theory. He asked Perrin if any significance should be attached to the 15 per cent difference between the values of N obtained from Planck's blackbody radiation law and from

---

*Perrin's collected papers are also strongly recommended [P11].

Brownian motion. This difference seemed to him to be 'disquieting, since one must say that the theoretical foundation of Planck's formula is fictitious.'

The foregoing account of Einstein's work on Brownian motion emphasizes its role in securing general acceptance of the reality of molecules. That, however, was not the only thing nor, in Einstein's own opinion, the most important thing that his theory of Brownian motion did for the development of physics. In 1915, he wrote about this work:

> [It] is of great importance since it permits an exact computation of N. . . . The great significance as a matter of principle is, however, . . . that one sees directly under the microscope part of the heat energy in the form of mechanical energy. [E6]

and in 1917:

> Because of the understanding of the essence of Brownian motion, suddenly all doubts vanished about the correctness of Boltzmann's interpretation of the thermodynamic laws. [E16]

5e. Einstein and Smoluchowski; Critical Opalescence

If Marian Ritter von Smolan-Smoluchowski had been only an outstanding theoretical physicist and not a fine experimentalist as well, he would probably have been the first to publish a quantitative theory of Brownian motion.

Smoluchowski, born to a Polish family, spent his early years in Vienna, where he also received his university education. After finishing his studies in 1894, he worked in several laboratories abroad, then returned to Vienna, where he became Privatdozent. In 1900 he became professor of theoretical physics in Lemberg (now Lvov), where he stayed until 1913. In that period he did his major work. In 1913 he took over the directorship of the Institute for Experimental Physics at the Jagiellonian University in Cracow. There he died in 1917, the victim of a dysentery epidemic.*

It is quite remarkable how often Smoluchowski and Einstein simultaneously and independently pursued similar if not identical problems. In 1904 Einstein worked on energy fluctuations [E17], Smoluchowski on particle number fluctuations [S5] of an ideal gas. Einstein completed his first paper on Brownian motion in May 1905; Smoluchowski his in July 1906 [S3]. Later on, we shall encounter a further such example. Let us first stay with Brownian motion, however.

Unlike Einstein, Smoluchowski was fully conversant with the nineteenth cen-

---

*For a detailed account of the life and work of Smoluchowski, the reader is referred to the biography by Teske [T4], in which the Einstein–Smoluchowski correspondence referred to hereafter is reproduced. My understanding of Smoluchowski's contributions was much helped by my reading of an unpublished manuscript by Mark Kac.

tury studies on Brownian motion, not least because he had remained in touch with Felix Exner, a comrade from student days who had done very good experimental work on the subject. Indeed, Smoluchowski's paper of 1906 contains a critique of all explanations of the phenomenon prior to Einstein's. Like Einstein (but prior to him) Smoluchowski also refuted the Naegeli–Ramsey objection, pointing out that what we see in Brownian motion is actually the average motion resulting from about 10^{20} collisions per second with the molecules of the ambient liquid. He also countered another objection: 'Naegeli believes that [the effect of the collisions] should in the average cancel each other. . . . This is the same conceptual error as when a gambler would believe that he could never lose a larger amount than a single stake.' Smoluchowski followed up this illustrative comment by computing the probability of some fixed gain (including sign!) after a prescribed number of tosses of a coin.

Smoluchowski began his 1906 paper [S3] by referring to Einstein's two articles of 1905: 'The findings [of those papers] agree completely with some results which I had . . . obtained several years ago and which I consider since then as an important argument for the kinetic nature of this phenomenon.' Then why had he not published earlier? 'Although it has not been possible for me till now to undertake an experimental test of the consequences of this point of view, something I originally intended to do, I have decided to publish these considerations. . . .' In support of this decision, he stated that his kinetic method seemed more direct, simpler, and therefore more convincing than Einstein's, in which collision kinetics plays no explicit role. Whether or not one agrees with this judgment of relative merits (I do not) depends to some extent on familiarity with one or the other method. In any case, Smoluchowski's paper is an outstanding contribution to physics, even though the priority of Einstein is beyond question (as Smoluchowski himself pointed out [S6]).

Smoluchowski treats the suspended particles as hard spheres with a constant instantaneous velocity given by the equipartition value. He starts out with the Knudsen case (the mean free path is *large* compared with the radius a), uses the kinematics of hard-sphere collisions, calculates the average change in direction per collision between the suspended particle and a molecule of the liquid, and therefrom finds an expression for $\langle x^2 \rangle$ (different from Eq. 5.18 of course). He must have treated the Knudsen case first since it is kinetically much easier than the Stokesian case, for which the free path is *small* compared with a. For the latter case, he arrived at Eq. 5.18 for $\langle x^2 \rangle$ but with an extra factor 27/64 on the rhs. This incorrect factor was dropped by Smoluchowski in his later papers.

Six letters between Einstein and Smoluchowski have survived. All show cordiality and great mutual respect. The correspondence begins with a note in 1908 by Einstein informing Smoluchowski that he has sent Smoluchowski some reprints and requesting some reprints of Smoluchowski's work [E18]. The next communication, in November 1911, is again by Einstein and deals with a new subject to which both men had been drawn: critical opalescence.

It had been known since the 1870s [A2] that the scattering of light passing through a gas increases strongly in a neighborhood $O(1°C)$ of the critical point. In 1908 Smoluchowski became the first to ascribe this phenomenon to large density fluctuations [S7]. He derived the following equation for the mean square particle number fluctuations $\overline{\delta^2}$:

$$\overline{\delta^2} = \frac{RT}{NV(-\partial p/\partial V)_T} \qquad (5.22)$$

valid up to terms $O((\partial^3 p/\partial V^3)_T)$. For an ideal gas, $\overline{\delta^2} \sim 1/N$, but near the critical point, where $(\partial p/\partial V)_T = (\partial^2 p/\partial V^2)_T = 0$, the rhs of Eq. 5.22 blows up. 'These agglomerations and rarefactions must give rise to corresponding local density fluctuations of the index of refraction from its mean value and thus the coarsegrainedness of the substance must reveal itself by Tyndall's phenomenon, with a very pronounced maximal value at the critical point. In this way, the critical opalescence explains itself very simply as the result of a phenomenon the existence of which cannot be denied by anybody accepting the principles of kinetic theory' [S8].

Thus, Smoluchowski had seen not only the true cause of critical opalescence but also the connection of this phenomenon with the blueness of the midday sky and the redness at sunset. Already in 1869 John Tyndall had explained the blue color of the sky in terms of the scattering of light by dust particles or droplets, the 'Tyndall phenomenon' [T5]. Rayleigh, who worked on this problem off and on for nearly half a century, had concluded that the inhomogeneities needed to explain this phenomenon were the air molecules themselves. Smoluchowski believed that the link between critical opalescence and Rayleigh scattering was a *qualitative* one. He did not produce a detailed scattering calculation: 'A precise calculation . . . would necessitate far-reaching modifications of Rayleigh's calculations' [S7].

Along comes Einstein in 1910 and computes the scattering in a weakly inhomogeneous nonabsorptive medium and finds [E10] (for monochromatic polarized light)

$$r = \frac{RT}{9N} \frac{(n^2 - 1)^2(n^2 + 2)^2}{-v(\partial p/\partial v)_T} \left(\frac{2\pi}{\lambda}\right)^4 \frac{\Phi}{(4\pi\Delta)^2} \cos^2\vartheta \qquad (5.23)$$

where r is the ratio of the scattered to the primary intensity, n the index of refraction, v the specific volume, λ the incident wavelength, Φ the irradiated gas volume, Δ the distance of observation, and ϑ the scattering angle. For an ideal gas ($n \approx 1$),

$$r = \frac{RT}{N} \frac{(n^2 - 1)^2}{p} \left(\frac{2\pi}{\lambda}\right)^4 \frac{\Phi}{(4\pi\Delta)^2} \cos^2\vartheta \qquad (5.24)$$

'[Equation 5.24] can also be obtained by summing the radiations off the individual molecules as long as these are taken to be randomly distributed'. Thus Einstein found that the link between critical opalescence and Rayleigh scattering is *quantitative* and, once again, obtained (for the last time) new methods for measuring Avogadro's number. As we read in Perrin's *Les Atomes,* these measurements were made shortly afterward.

Smoluchowski was delighted. In a paper published in 1911, he spoke of Einstein's contribution as 'a significant advance' [S9]. However, he had not quite understood Einstein's argument. In an appendix to his 1911 paper Smoluchowski mentioned that the blue of the sky is due to two factors: scattering off molecules and scattering that results from density fluctuations. Einstein objected by letter [E19]. There is one and only one cause for scattering. 'Reileigh [sic] treats a special case of our problem, and the agreement between his final formula and my own is no accident.' Shortly thereafter, Smoluchowski replied; 'You are completely right' [S10].

Smoluchowski's last contribution to this problem was experimental: he wanted to reproduce the blue of the sky in a terrestrial experiment. Preliminary results looked promising [S11], and he announced that more detailed experiments were in progress. He did not live to complete them.*

After Smoluchowski's death, Sommerfeld [S12] and Einstein [E16] wrote obituaries in praise of a good man and a great scientist. Einstein called him an ingenious man of research and a noble and subtle human being.

Finally:

Einstein's paper on critical opalescence and the blue of the sky was written in October 1910. It was submitted from Zürich, where he was an associate professor at the university. It was his last major paper on classical statistical physics. In March 1911 he moved to Prague—to become a full professor for the first time—and began his main attack on general relativity.

Ostwald conceded in 1908. Referring to the experiments on Brownian motion and those on the electron, he stated that their results 'entitle even the cautious scientist to speak of an experimental proof for the atomistic constitution of space-filled matter' [O3].

Mach died in 1916, unconvinced.**

Perrin received the Nobel prize in 1926 for his work on Brownian motion. *Les Atomes,* one of the finest books on physics written in the twentieth century, contains a postmortem, in the classical French style, to the struggles with the reality of molecules:

---

*For references to later experimental work on critical opalescence, see, e.g., [C7]. The problems of the modern theory of critical opalescence are reviewed in [M9].

**Stefan Meyer recalled Mach's reaction upon being shown, in Vienna, the scintillations produced by alpha particles: 'Now I believe in atoms' [M10]. Mach's text on optics, written after he left Vienna, shows that this belief did not last, however [M11].

La théorie atomique a triomphé. Nombreux encore naguère, ses adversaires enfin conquis renoncent l'un après l'autre aux défiances qui longtemps furent légitimes et sans doute utiles.**

References

A1. A. Avogadro, *J. de Phys.* **73,** 58 (1811); *Alembic Reprints,* No. 4. Livingstone, Edinburgh, 1961.

A2. M. Avenarius, *Ann. Phys. Chem.* **151,** 306 (1874).

B1. Quoted in *The Atomic Debates* (W. H. Brock, Ed.), p. 8. Leicester University Press, Leicester, 1967.

B2. Quoted by W. H. Brock and M. Knight, *Isis* **56,** 5 (1965).

B3. D. Bernoulli, *Hydrodynamica.* Dulsecker, Strassbourg, 1738. German translation by K. Flierl, published by Forschungsinstitut für die Gesch. d. Naturw. und Technik, Series C, No. 1a, 1965.

B4. S. G. Brush, *The Kind of Motion We Call Heat,* Vol. 1, Chap. 1. North Holland, Amsterdam, 1976.

B5. R. Brown, *Phil. Mag.* **4,** 161 (1828); see also, *Phil. Mag.* **6,** 161 (1829).

B6. G. K. Batchelor and J. T. Green, *J. Fluid Mech.* **56,** 401 (1972).

B7. ——, *J. Fluid Mech.* **83,** 97 (1977).

B8. S. G. Brush, [B4], Vol. 2, Chap. 15.

B9. G. K. Batchelor, *J. Fluid Mech.* **74,** 1 (1976).

C1. S. Cannizzaro, Alembic Reprints, No. 18, Livingstone, Edinburgh, 1961.

C2. R. Clausius, *AdP* **10,** 353 (1857).

C3. M. Curie, *Rev. Scientifique* **14,** 65 (1900).

C4. E. Cohen, *Naturw.* **3,** 118 (1915).

C5. T. Cawkell and E. Garfield, in *Einstein, the First Hundred Years* (M. Goldsmith, A. McKay, and J. Woudhuysen, Eds.), p. 31. Pergamon Press, London, 1980.

C6. G. Cantoni, *N. Cimento* **27,** 156 (1867).

C7. B. Chu and J. S. Lin, *J. Chem. Phys.* **53,** 4454 (1970).

D1. J. Dalton, *New System of Chemical Philosophy.* Bickerstaff, London, Vol. 1, Part 1: 1808; Vol. 1, Part 2: 1810; Vol. 2: 1827.

D2. ——, [D1], Vol. 1, Part 2, Appendix.

D3. R. D. Deslattes, *Ann. Rev. Phys. Chem.* **31,** 435 (1980).

D4. R. K. Dewan and V. A. Bloomfield, *J. Dairy Sci.* **56,** 66 (1973).

D5. J. Delsaulx, quoted in T. Svedberg, *Die Existenz der Moleküle,* p. 91. Akademisches Verlag, Leipzig, 1912.

E1. P. Ehrenfest, *Collected Scientific Papers* (M. J. Klein, Ed.), p. 364. North Holland, Amsterdam, 1959.

E2. A. Einstein, *AdP* **17,** 549 (1905).

E3. ——, *Eine neue Bestimmung der Moleküldimensionen.* Wyss, Bern, 1905.

E4. ——, letter to the Dekan der II. Sektion der philosophischen Fakultät der Universität Zürich, July 20, 1905.

**The atomic theory has triumphed. Until recently still numerous, its adversaries, at last overcome, now renounce one after another their misgivings, which were, for so long, both legitimate and undeniably useful.

E5. ——, *AdP* **19**, 289 (1906).

E6. ——, in *Kultur der Gegenwart* (E. Lecher, Ed.). Teubner, Leipzig, 1915 (2nd edn., 1925).

E7. ——, *AdP* **34**, 591 (1911).

E8. ——, *AdP* **19**, 371 (1906).

E9. ——, *AdP* **22**, 569 (1907).

E10. ——, *AdP* **33**, 1275 (1910).

E11. ——, *Z. Elektrochem.* **13**, 41 (1907).

E12. ——, *Z. Elektrochem.* **14**, 235 (1908).

E13. ——, letter to J. Perrin, January 12, 1911.

E14. ——, *Kolloidzeitschr* **27**, 137 (1920).

E15. ——, letter to J. Perrin, November 11, 1909.

E16. ——, *Naturw.* **5**, 737 (1917).

E17. ——, *AdP* **14**, 354 (1904).

E18. ——, letter to M. v. Smoluchowski, June 11, 1908.

E19. ——, letter to M. v. Smoluchowski, November 27, 1911.

F1. R. Fürth, Ed., *Untersuchungen über die Theorie der Brownschen Bewegung.* Akademische Verlags Gesellschaft, Leipzig, 1922.

F2. ——, *Investigations on the Brownian Movement* (A. D. Cowper, Tran.). Methuen, London, 1926.

F3. ——, *Z. Phys.* **2**, 244 (1922).

G1. J. L. Gay-Lussac, *Mém. Soc. d'Arceuil* **2**, 207 (1809); Alembic Reprint, No. 4, Livingstone, Edinburgh, 1961.

G2. L. G. Gouy, *J. de Phys.* **7**, 561 (1888).

H1. J. H. van 't Hoff, *Arch Néerl des Sci Exactes et Nat.* **20**, 239 (1886); Alembic Reprint, No. 19, Livingstone, Edinburgh, 1961.

J1. S. Jahn, *Jahrb. Rad. Elektr.* **6**, 229 (1909).

K1. H. Kogan, *The Great Encyclopedia Britannica.* University of Chicago Press, Chicago, 1958.

L1. J. Loschmidt, *Wiener Ber.* **52**, 395 (1866).

L2. C. Lanczos, *The Einstein Decade,* p. 140. Academic Press, New York, 1974.

L3. P. Langevin, *C. R. Ac. Sci. Paris* **146**, 530 (1908).

M1. Cf. C. de Milt, *Chymia* **1**, 153 (1948).

M2. E. von Meyer, *J. Prakt. Chem.* **83**, 182 (1911).

M3. D. Mendeleev, *The principles of chemistry,* Vol. 1, p. 315. Translated from the 5th Russian edn. by G. Kamensky. Greenaway, London, 1891.

M4. J. C. Maxwell, *Collected Works,* Vol. 2, pp. 376–7. Dover, New York.

M5. E. Mach, *Popular Scientific Lectures,* p. 207. Open Court, Chicago, 1910.

M6. J. C. Maxwell, [M4], Vol. 2, p. 361.

M7. ——, *Theory of Heat,* Chap. 22. Longmans, Green and Co., London, 1872. Reprinted by Greenwood Press, Westport, Conn.

M8. E. W. Müller, *Phys. Rev.* **102**, 624 (1956); *J. Appl. Phys.* **27**, 474 (1956); **28**, 1 (1957); Sci. Amer., June 1957, p. 113.

M9. A. Münster, *Handbuch der Physik* (S. Flügge, Ed.), Vol. 13, p. 71. Springer, Berlin, 1962.

M10. S. Meyer, *Wiener Ber.* **159**, 1 (1950).

M11. E. Mach, *The Principles of Physical Optics,* preface. Methuen, London, 1926.

N1. M. J. Nye, *Molecular Reality,* Elsevier, New York, 1972.

N2.   ——, [N1], p. 4.
N3.   *Nobel Lectures in Chemistry,* p. 3. Elsevier, New York, 1966.
N4.   M. J. Nye, [N1], pp. 9–13 and 21–9.
O1.   W. Ostwald, *Verh. Ges. Deutsch. Naturf. Ärzte* **1,** 155 (1895); French translation: *Rev. Gén. Sci.* **6,** 956 (1895).
O2.   L. S. Ornstein, *Versl. K. Ak. Amsterdam* **26,** 1005 (1917); *Proc. K. Ak. Amsterdam* **21,** 96 (1919).
O3.   W. Ostwald, *Grundriss der Physikalischen Chemie,* introduction. Grossbothen, 1908.
P1.   W. Prout, *Ann. Phil.* **6,** 321 (1815).
P2.   ——, *Ann. Phil.* **7,** 111 (1816); Alembic Reprints, No. 20. Gurney and Jackson, London, 1932.
P3.   M. Planck, *AdP* **19,** 358 (1883).
P4.   W. Pfeffer, *Osmotische Untersuchungen.* Engelmann, Leipzig, 1877.
P5.   H. Poincaré in *Rapports du Congrès International de Physique* (C. Guillaume and L. Poincaré, Eds.), Vol. 1, p. 27. Gauthier-Villars, Paris, 1900.
P6.   H. Poincaré in *The Foundations of Science,* p. 305. Scientific Press, New York, 1913.
P7.   J. Perrin, *Ann. Chim. Phys.* **18,** 1 (1909).
P8.   ——, *Brownian Movement and Molecular Reality* (F. Soddy, Tran.). Taylor and Francis, London, 1910.
P9.   ——, *Les Atomes,* 4th edn. Librairie Alcan, Paris, 1914.
P10.   ——, *Atoms* (D. L. Hammick, Tran.). Van Nostrand, New York, 1916.
P11.   ——, *Oeuvres Scientifiques,* CNRS, Paris, 1950.
R1.   Lord Rayleigh, *Phil. Mag.* **30,** 456 (1890).
R2.   A. W. Rücker, *J. Chem. Soc.* (London) **53,** 222 (1888).
R3.   H. R. Robinson, *Proc. Phys. Soc.* (London) **55,** 161 (1943).
R4.   M. Reiner, *Deformation, Strain and Flow.* Lewis, London, 1949.
R5.   R. Rutgers, *Rheol. Acta* **2,** 202, 305 (1965).
R6.   W. C. Roentgen, letter to A. Einstein, September 18, 1906.
S1.   A. Sommerfeld, *Wiener Chem. Zeitung* **47,** 25 (1944).
S2.   Se, p. 112.
S2a.   W. Sutherland, *Phil. Mag.* **9,** 781 (1905).
S3.   M. von Smoluchowski, *AdP* **21,** 756 (1906).
S4.   L. Szilard, *Z. Phys.* **53,** 840 (1929). Reprinted in *The Collected Works of Leo Szilard* (B. T. Feld and G. W. Szilard, Eds.), p. 103. MIT Press, Cambridge, Mass., 1972.
S5.   M. von Smoluchowski, *Boltzmann Festschrift,* p. 627. Barth, Leipzig, 1904.
S6.   ——, letter to J. Perrin, undated; quoted in [T4], p. 161.
S7.   ——, *AdP* **25,** 205 (1908).
S8.   ——, *Phil. Mag.* **23,** 165 (1912).
S9.   ——, *Bull. Ac. Sci. Cracovie, Classe Sci. Math. Nat.,* 1911, p. 493.
S10.   ——, letter to A. Einstein, December 12, 1911.
S11.   ——, *Bull. Ac. Sci. Cracovie, Classe Sci. Math. Nat.* 1916, p. 218.
S12.   A. Sommerfeld, *Phys. Zeitschr.* **18,** 534 (1917).
T1.   W. Thomson, *Nature* **1,** 551 (1870).
T2.   C. Truesdell, *Arch. Hist. Ex. Sci.* **15,** 1 (1976).

T3. J. J. Thomson, *Phil. Mag.* **48,** 565 (1899).

T4. A. Teske, *Marian Smoluchowski, Leben und Werk.* Polish Academy of Sciences, Warsaw, 1977.

T5. J. Tyndall, *Phil. Mag.* **37,** 384 (1869); **38,** 156 (1869).

W1. A. W. Williamson, *J. Chem. Soc.* (London) **22,** 328 (1869).

W2. Quoted by L. P. Williams, *Contemp. Phys.* **2,** 93 (1960).

W3. J. D. van der Waals, *Over de Continuiteit van den Gas–en Vloeistoftoestand.* Syth-off, Leiden, 1873.

W4. N. Wax (Ed.), *Selected Papers on Noise and Stochastic Processes.* Dover, New York, 1954.

Y1. T. Young, *Miscellaneous Works.* Murray, London, 1855. Reprinted by Johnson Reprint, New York, 1972, Vol. 9, p. 461.

Y2. Y. I. Yalamov, L. Y. Vasiljeva, and E. R. Schukin, *J. Coll. Interface Sci.* **62,** 503 (1977).

III
RELATIVITY, THE SPECIAL THEORY

6

'Subtle is the Lord...'

6a. The Michelson–Morley Experiment

Maxwell's article *Ether,* written for the ninth edition of the *Encyclopedia Britannica* [M1], begins with an enumeration of the 'high metaphysical . . . [and] mundane uses to be fulfilled by aethers' and with the barely veiled criticism that, even for scientific purposes only, 'all space had been filled three or four times over with aethers.' This contribution by Maxwell is an important document for numerous reasons. To mention but three, it shows us that, like his contemporaries, Maxwell was deeply convinced of the reality of some sort of aether: 'There can be no doubt that the interplanetary and interstellar spaces are not empty but are occupied by a material substance or body, which is certainly the largest, and probably the most uniform, body of which we have any knowledge'; it tells us of an unsuccessful attempt by Maxwell himself to perform a terrestrial optical experiment aimed at detecting the influence of an aether drag on the earth's motion; and it informs us of his opinion that effects of the second order in v/c (v = velocity of the earth relative to the aether, c = velocity of light) are too small to be detectable. This last comment was prompted by his observation that 'all methods . . . by which it is practicable to determine the velocity of light from terrestrial experiments depend on the measurement of the time required for the double journey from one station to the other and back again,' leading to an effect at most of $O((v/c)^2) = O(10^{-8})$.

However, Maxwell still hoped that first-order effects might be astronomically observable. The example he gave was the determination of the velocity of light from the eclipses of Jupiter's satellites when Jupiter is seen from the earth at nearly opposite points of the ecliptic. If one defines the aether* in the sense of Maxwell, or, which is the same thing, in the sense of Augustin Jean Fresnel—a medium in a state of absolute rest relative to the fixed stars, in which light is propagated and through which the earth moves as if it were transparent to it—then one readily sees that the Jupiter effect, if it exists at all, is of first order in the velocity of the solar system relative to this aether.

---

*For a review of aether theories and aether models, see especially [L1] and [S1]. Some speak of aether, others of ether. I prefer the former. In quotations I follow the predilections of the original authors, however.

Maxwell requested and received data on the Jovian system from David Peck Todd, Director of the Nautical Almanac Office in Washington, D.C. On March 19, 1879, Maxwell sent a letter of thanks in which he referred Todd to his encyclopedia article and in particular reiterated his remark on the second-order nature of terrestrial experiments. This letter (not reproduced in his collected papers) was written when Maxwell had less than eight months to live and Einstein was five days old. After Maxwell's death, the letter was forwarded to the secretary of the Royal Society, who saw to its publication in the January 29, 1880, issue of Nature [M2].

A year and a half later, in August 1881, there appeared an article in an issue of the *American Journal of Science,* authored by Albert A. (for Abraham) Michelson, Master, U.S. Navy [M3]. Michelson, then on leave from the Navy and doing post-graduate work in Helmholtz's laboratory in Berlin, had read Maxwell's 1879 letter. Being already an acknowledged expert on measurements of the velocity of light (he had by then published three papers on the subject [L2]), he had concluded that Maxwell had underrated the accuracy with which terrestrial experiments could be performed. The instrument he designed in Berlin in order to measure Maxwell's second-order effect is known as the Michelson interferometer. In order not to be bothered by urban vibrations, Michelson performed his experiments at the astrophysical observatory in nearby Potsdam. The method he used was to compare the times it takes for light to travel the same distance either parallel or transversely to the earth's motion relative to the aether. In his arrangement a stationary aether would yield a time difference corresponding to about an extra $1/25$ of a wavelength of yellow light traveling in the parallel direction, an effect that can be detected by letting the transverse and parallel beams interfere. For easily accessible details of the experiment I refer the reader to textbooks* and state only Michelson's conclusion: there was no evidence for an aether wind. 'The result of the hypothesis of a stationary aether is thus shown to be incorrect, and the necessary conclusion follows that the hypothesis is erroneous,' [M3].

Early in 1887 Michelson wrote to Rayleigh** that he was 'discouraged at the slight attention the work received' [M4], a statement which perhaps was justified if one counts the number of those who took note, but not if one considers their eminence. Kelvin and Rayleigh, both of whom Michelson had met at Johns Hopkins University in 1884 [S3] certainly paid attention. So did Lorentz, who found an error in Michelson's theory of the experiment [L3] and who was dubious about the interpretation of the results [L4]. Lorentz's misgivings and Rayleigh's urgings contributed to Michelson's decision—he was now at the Case School of Applied Science in Cleveland—to repeat his experiment, this time in collaboration with Edward Williams Morley, a chemist from next-door Western Reserve University.

*See, e.g., [P1].

**For details of the Michelson–Rayleigh correspondence, see especially [S2] and [H1].

Proceeding along the same general lines used in the Potsdam experiments, they built a new interferometer. Great care was taken to minimize perturbative influences. In August 1887, Michelson wrote to Rayleigh that again a null effect had been found [M5]. The paper on the Michelson–Morley experiment came out the following November [M6]. Understandably, the negative outcome of this experiment was initially a disappointment, not only to its authors, but also to Kelvin, Rayleigh, and Lorentz.

However, more important, the experimental result was accepted. There had to be a flaw in the theory. In 1892 Lorentz queried Rayleigh: 'Can there be some point in the theory of Mr Michelson's experiment which had as yet been overlooked?' [L5]. In a lecture before the Royal Institution on April 27, 1900, Kelvin referred to the experiment as 'carried out with most searching care to secure a trustworthy result' and characterized its outcome as a nineteenth century cloud over the dynamic theory of light [K1]. In 1904 he wrote in the preface to his Baltimore lectures: 'Michelson and Morley have by their great experimental work on the motion of the ether relatively to the earth raised the one and only serious objection against our dynamical explanations. . . .' [K2].

In later years, Michelson repeated this experiment several times, for the last time in 1929 [M7]. Others did likewise, notably Dayton Clarence Miller, at one time a junior colleague of Michelson's at Case. In 1904, Morley and Miller were the first to do a hilltop experiment: 'Some have thought that [the Michelson–Morley] experiment only proves that the ether in a certain basement room is carried along with it. We desire therefore to place the apparatus on a hill to see if an effect can there be detected' [M8].* Articles in 1933 [M9] and 1955 [S4] give many technical and historical details of these experiments. No one has done more to unearth their history than Robert S. Shankland, whose papers are quoted extensively in this section. For the present purposes, there is no need to discuss these later developments, except for one interlude which directly involved Einstein.

On April 2, 1921, Einstein arrived for the first time in the United States, for a two-month visit. In May, he gave four lectures on relativity theory at Princeton University [E1]. While he was there, word reached Princeton that Miller had found a nonzero aether drift during preliminary experiments performed (on April 8–21 [S4]) at Mount Wilson observatory. Upon hearing this rumor, Einstein commented: 'Raffiniert ist der Herr Gott, aber boshaft ist er nicht,' Subtle is the Lord, but malicious He is not. Nevertheless, on May 25, 1921, shortly before his departure from the United States, Einstein paid a visit to Miller in Cleveland, where they talked matters over [S5].

There are two postscripts to this story. One concerns transitory events. On April 28, 1925, Miller read a paper before the National Academy of Sciences in Washington, D.C., in which he reported that an aether drift had definitely been estab-

---

*Michelson had pointed out earlier that perhaps the aether might be trapped in the basements in which he had done his experiments [M4].

lished [M10]. Later that year, he made the same claim in his retiring address in Kansas City as president of the American Physical Society [M11]. The outcome of all this was that Miller received a thousand dollar prize for his Kansas City paper from the American Association for the Advancement of Science [L6]—presumably in part an expression of the resistance to relativity which could still be found in some quarters [B1]—while Einstein got flooded with telegrams and letters asking him to comment. The latter's reactions to the commotion are best seen from a remark he made in passing in a letter to Besso: 'I have not for a moment taken [Miller's results] seriously' [E2].* As to present times, quantum field theory has drastically changed our perceptions of the vacuum, but that has nothing to do with the aether of the nineteenth century and earlier, which is gone for good.**

The second postscript to the Miller episode concerns a lasting event. Oswald Veblen, a professor of mathematics at Princeton, had overheard Einstein's comment about the subtlety of the Lord. In 1930 Veblen wrote to Einstein, asking his permission to have this statement chiseled in the stone frame of the fireplace in the common room of Fine Hall, the newly constructed mathematics building at the university [V1]. Einstein consented.† The mathematics department has since moved to new quarters, but the inscription in stone has remained in its original place, Room 202 in what once was Fine Hall.

Let us now move back to the times when Einstein was still virtually unknown and ask how Michelson reacted to Einstein's special theory of relativity and what influence the Michelson–Morley experiment had on Einstein's formulation of that theory in 1905.

The answer to the first question is simple. Michelson, a genius in instrumentation and experimentation, never felt comfortable with the special theory. He was the first American scientist to receive a Nobel prize, in 1907. The absence of any mention of the aether wind experiments in his citation¶ is not surprising. Relativity was young; even fifteen years later, relativity was not mentioned in Einstein's citation. It is more interesting that Michelson himself did not mention these experiments in his acceptance speech [N1]—not quite like Einstein, who responded to the award given him in 1922 for the photoelectric effect by delivering a lecture on relativity [E4]. Truly revealing, however, is Michelson's verdict on relativity given in 1927 in his book *Studies in Optics* [M12]. He noted that the

---

*In 1927 Einstein remarked that the positive effect found by Miller could be caused by tiny temperature differences in the experimental equipment [E2a].

**In 1951 Dirac briefly considered a return to the aether [D1].

†In his reply to Veblen, Einstein gave the following interpretation of his statement. 'Die Natur verbirgt ihr Geheimnis durch die Erhabenheit ihres Wesens, aber nicht durch List,' Nature hides its secret because of its essential loftiness, but not by means of ruse [E3]. In June 1966 Helen Dukas prepared a memorandum about this course of events [D2].

¶The citation reads 'For his optical precision instruments and the spectroscopical and metrological investigations carried out with their aid' [N1].

theory of relativity 'must be accorded a generous acceptance' and gave a clear exposé of Lorentz transformations and their consequences for the Michelson–Morley experiment and for the experiment of Armand Hippolyte Louis Fizeau on the velocity of light in streaming water. Then follows his summation: 'The existence of an ether appears to be inconsistent with the theory. . . . But without a medium how can the propagation of light waves be explained? . . . How explain the constancy of propagation, the fundamental assumption (at least of the restricted theory) if there be no medium?'

This is the lament not of a single individual but of an era, though it was an era largely gone when Michelson's book came out. Michelson's writings are the perfect illustration of the two main themes to be developed in this and the next two chapters. The first one is that in the early days it was easier to understand the mathematics of special relativity than the physics. The second one is that it was not a simple matter to assimilate a new kinematics as a lasting substitute for the old aether dynamics.

Let us turn to the influence of the Michelson–Morley experiment on Einstein's initial relativity paper [E5]. The importance of this question goes far beyond the minor issue of whether Einstein should have added a footnote at some place or other. Rather, its answer will help us to gain essential insights into Einstein's thinking and will prepare us for a subsequent discussion of the basic differences in the approaches of Einstein, Lorentz, and Poincaré.

Michelson is mentioned neither in the first nor in any of Einstein's later research papers on special relativity. One also looks in vain for his name in Einstein's autobiographical sketch of 1949 [E6], in which the author describes his scientific evolution and mentions a number of scientists who did influence him. None of this should be construed to mean that Einstein at any time underrated the importance of the experiment. In 1907 Einstein was the first to write a review article on relativity [E7], the first paper in which he went to the trouble of giving a number of detailed references. Michelson and Morley are mentioned in that review, in a semipopular article Einstein wrote in 1915 [E8], again in the Princeton lectures of 1921 [E1], and in the book *The Meaning of Relativity* [E9] (which grew out of the Princeton lectures), where Einstein called the Michelson–Morley experiment the most important one of all the null experiments on the aether drift.

However, neither in the research papers nor in these four reviews does Einstein ever make clear whether before 1905 he knew of the Michelson–Morley experiment. Correspondence is of no help either. I have come across only one letter, written in 1923, by Michelson to Einstein [M13] and none by Einstein to Michelson. In that letter, Michelson, then head of the physics department at the University of Chicago, offers Einstein a professorship at Chicago. No scientific matters are mentioned. The two men finally met in Pasadena. There was great warmth and respect between them, as Helen Dukas (who was with the Einsteins in California) told me. On January 15, 1931, at a dinner given in Einstein's honor at the Atheneum of Cal Tech, Einstein publicly addressed Michelson in person for the first and last time: 'I have come among men who for many years have been true comrades with me in my labors. You, my honored Dr Michelson, began with this work when I was only a little youngster, hardly three feet high. It was you who led the physicists into new paths, and through your marvelous experimental work paved the way for the development of the theory of relativity. You uncovered an insidious effect in the ether theory of light, as it then existed, and stimulated the ideas of H. A. Lorentz and FitzGerald out of which the special theory of relativity developed' [E10]. One would think that Einstein might have associated himself explicitly with Lorentz and FitzGerald had he believed that the occasion warranted it. He was worldly enough to know that this would be considered an additional compliment to Michelson rather than a lack of modesty.

Michelson was very ill at the time of that festive dinner and died four months later. On July 17, 1931, Einstein, back in Berlin, gave a speech in Michelson's memory before the Physikalische Gesellschaft of Berlin [E11]. The talk ended with a fine anecdote. In Pasadena, Einstein had asked Michelson why he had spent so much effort on high-precision measurements of the light velocity. Michelson had replied, 'Weil es mir Spass macht,' Because I think it is fun. Einstein's main remark about the Michelson–Morley experiment was, 'Its negative outcome has much increased the faith in the validity of the general theory of relativity.' Even on this most natural of occasions, one does not find an acknowledgement of a direct influence of Michelson's work on his own development.

Nevertheless, the answers to both questions—did Einstein know of Michelson's work before 1905? did it influence his creation of the special theory of relativity?—are, yes, unquestionably. We know this from discussions between Shankland and Einstein in the 1950s and from an address entitled 'How I Created the Relativity Theory' given by Einstein on December 14, 1922, at Kyoto University (and referred to in what follows as the Kyoto address). Let us first note two statements made by Einstein to Shankland, recorded by Shankland soon after they were made, and published by him some time later [S6], as well as part of a letter which Einstein wrote to Shankland [S7].*

a) Discussion on February 4, 1950. 'When I asked him how he had learned of the Michelson–Morley experiment, he told me that he had become aware of it through the writings of H. A. Lorentz, but *only after 1905* [S. 's italics] had it come to his attention! "Otherwise," he said, "I would have mentioned it in my paper." He continued to say that experimental results which had influenced him most were the observations on stellar aberration and Fizeau's measurements on the speed of light in moving water. "They were enough," he said' [S6].

b) Discussion on October 24, 1952. 'I asked Professor Einstein when he had first heard of Michelson and his experiment. He replied, "This is not so easy, I

*This letter, written at Shankland's request, was read before the Cleveland Physics Society on the occasion of the centenary of Michelson's birth.

am not sure when I first heard of the Michelson experiment. I was not conscious that it had influenced me directly during the seven years that relativity had been my life. I guess I just took it for granted that it was true." However, Einstein said that in the years 1905–1909, he thought a great deal about Michelson's result, in his discussion with Lorentz and others in his thinking about general relativity. He then realized (so he told me) that he had also been conscious of Michelson's result before 1905 partly through his reading of the papers of Lorentz and more because he had simply assumed this result of Michelson to be true' [S6].

c) December 1952, letter by Einstein to Shankland. 'The influence of the crucial Michelson–Morley experiment upon my own efforts has been rather indirect. I learned of it through H. A. Lorentz's decisive investigation of the electrodynamics of moving bodies (1895) with which I was acquainted before developing the special theory of relativity. Lorentz's basic assumption of an ether at rest seemed to me not convincing in itself and also for the reason that it was leading to an interpretation of the Michelson–Morley experiment which seemed to me artificial' [S7].

What do we learn from these three statements?

First, that memory is fallible. (Einstein was not well in the years 1950–2 and already knew that he did not have much longer to live.) There is an evident inconsistency between Einstein's words of February 1950 and his two later statements. It seems sensible to attach more value to the later comments, made upon further reflection, and therefore to conclude that Einstein did know of Michelson and Morley before 1905. One also infers that oral history is a profession which should be pursued with care and caution.

Second, there is Einstein's opinion that aberration and the Fizeau experiment were enough for him. *This is the most crucial statement Einstein ever made on the origins of the special theory of relativity.* It shows that the principal argument which ultimately led him to the special theory was not so much the need to resolve the conflict between the Michelson–Morley result and the version of aether theory prevalent in the late nineteenth century but rather, *independent of the Michelson Morley experiment,* the rejection of this nineteenth century edifice as inherently unconvincing and artificial.

In order to appreciate how radically Einstein departed from the ancestral views on these issues, it is necessary to compare his position with the 'decisive investigation' published by Lorentz in 1895 [L4]. In Section 64 of that paper, we find the following statement, italicized by its author: *'According to our theory the motion of the earth will never have any first-order* [in v/c] *influence whatever on experiments with terrestrial light sources.'* By Einstein's own account, he knew this 1895 memoir in which Lorentz discussed, among other things, both the aberration of light and the Fizeau experiment. Let us briefly recall what was at stake. Because of the velocity v of the earth, a star which would be at the zenith if the earth were at rest is actually seen under an angle α with the vertical, where

$$tg\alpha = \frac{v}{c} \tag{6.1}$$

The concept of an aether at absolute rest, introduced in 1818 by Fresnel in his celebrated letter to Dominique François Jean Arago [F1], served the express purpose of explaining this aberration effect (which would be zero if the aether moved along with the earth). As to the Fizeau effect, Fresnel had predicted that if a liquid is moving through a tube with a velocity v relative to the aether and if a light beam traverses the tube in the same direction, then the net light velocity c' in the laboratory is given by

$$c' = \frac{c}{n} + v\left(1 - \frac{1}{n^2}\right) \tag{6.2}$$

where n is the refractive index of the liquid (assumed a nondispersive medium). Fresnel derived this result from the assumption that light imparts elastic vibrations to the aether it traverses. According to him, the presence of the factor $1 - 1/n^2$ (now known as Fresnel's drag coefficient) expresses the fact that light cannot acquire the full additional velocity v since it is partially held back by the aether in the tube. In 1851 Fizeau had sent light from a terrestrial source into a tube filled with a moving fluid and had found reasonable experimental agreement with Eq. 6.2 [F2].

Lorentz discussed both effects from the point of view of electromagnetic theory and gave a dynamic derivation of the Fresnel drag in terms of the polarization induced in a medium by incident electromagnetic waves.* Throughout this paper of 1895, the Fresnel aether is postulated explicitly. In rejecting these explanations of aberration and the Fizeau experiment, Einstein therefore chose to take leave of a first-order *terra firma* which had been established by the practitioners, limited in number but highly eminent and influential, of electromagnetic theory. I shall leave for the next chapter a discussion of his reasons for doing so. Note, however, that it was easy to take the Michelson–Morley experiments for granted (as Einstein repeatedly said he did) once a new look at the first-order effects had led to the new logic of the special theory of relativity. Note also that this experiment was discussed at length in Lorentz's paper of 1895 and that Einstein was familiar with this paper before 1905!

Finally, there is the Kyoto address. It was given in German and translated into Japanese by Jun Ishiwara** [I1]. Part of the Japanese text was retranslated into English [O1]. I quote a few lines from this English rendering:

> As a student I got acquainted with the unaccountable result of the Michelson experiment and then realized intuitively that it might be our incorrect thinking

---

*For a calculation along these lines, see the book by Panofsky and Phillips [P2].

**From 1912 to 1914, Ishiwara studied physics in Germany and in Switzerland. He knew Einstein personally from those days. He also translated a number of Einstein's papers into Japanese.

to take account of the motion of the earth relative to the aether, if we recognized the experimental result as a fact. In effect, this is the first route that led me to what is now called the special principles of relativity. . . . I had just a chance to read Lorentz's 1895 monograph, in which he had succeeded in giving a comprehensive solution to problems of electrodynamics within the first approximation, in other words, as far as the quantities of higher order than the square of the velocity of a moving body to that of light were neglected. In this connection I took into consideration Fizeau's experiment. . . .

In his first paper on relativity, Einstein mentions 'the failed attempts to detect a motion of the earth relative to the "light-medium" ' without specifying what attempts he had in mind.* Neither Michelson nor Fizeau is mentioned, though he knew of both. Einstein's discontent with earlier explanations of first-order effects may have made the mystery of Michelson and Morley's second-order null effect less central to him. Yet this 'unaccountable result' did affect his thinking and thus a new question arises: Why, on the whole, was Einstein so reticent to acknowledge the influence of Michelson on him? I shall return to this question in Chapter 8.

6b. The Precursors

1. What Einstein Knew. Historical accounts of electromagnetism in the late nineteenth century almost invariably cite a single phrase written by that excellent experimental and theoretical physicist, Heinrich Rudolf Hertz: 'Maxwell's theory is Maxwell's system of equations.'** By itself, this is a witty, eminently quotable, and meaningless comment on the best that the physics of that period had to offer. The post-Maxwell, pre-Einstein attitude which eventually became preponderant was that electrodynamics is Maxwell's equations plus a specification of the charge and current densities contained in these equations plus a conjecture on the nature of the aether.

Maxwell's own theory placed the field concept in a central position. It did not abolish the aether, but it did greatly simplify it. No longer was 'space filled three or four times over with ethers,' as Maxwell had complained [M1]. Rather, 'many workers and many thinkers have helped to build up the nineteenth century school of *plenum*, one ether for light, heat, electricity, magnetism', as Kelvin wrote in 1893 [K3]. However, there still were many nineteenth century candidates for this one aether, some but not all predating Maxwell's theory. There were the aethers of Fresnel, Cauchy, Stokes, Neumann, MacCullagh, Kelvin, Planck, and probably others, distinguished by such properties as degree of homogeneity and com-

---

*In a thoughtful article on Einstein and the Michelson–Morley experiment, Holton [H2] raised the possibility that Einstein might have had in mind other null effects known by then, such as the absence of double refraction [B2, R1] and the Trouton–Noble experiment [T1].

**See the second volume of Hertz's collected works [H3], which is also available in English translation [H4].

pressibility, and the extent to which the earth dragged the aether along. This explains largely (though not fully) why there was such a variety of post-Maxwellian Maxwell theories, the theories of Hertz, Lorentz, Larmor, Wiechert, Cohn, and probably others.

Hertz was, of course, aware of these options [M14]. After all, he had to choose his own aether (the one he selected is dragged along by the earth). Indeed, his dictum referred to earlier reads more fully: 'Maxwell's theory is Maxwell's system of equations. Every theory which leads to the same system of equations, and therefore comprises the same possible phenomena, I would consider as being a form or special case of Maxwell's theory.'

The most important question for all these authors of aethers and makers of Maxwell theories was to find a dynamic understanding of the aberration of light, of Fresnel drag, and, later, of the Michelson–Morley experiment. In a broad sense, all these men were precursors of Einstein, who showed that theirs was a task both impossible and unnecessary. Einstein's theory is, of course, not just a Maxwell theory in the sense of Hertz. Rather, Einstein's resolution of the difficulties besetting the electrodynamics of moving bodies is cast in an all-embracing framework of a new kinematics. Going beyond Lorentz and Poincaré, he based his theory on the first of the two major re-analyses of the problem of measurement which mark the break between the nineteenth and the twentieth centuries (the other one being quantum mechanics).

It is not the purpose of this section on precursors to give a detailed discussion of the intelligent struggles by all those men named above. Instead I shall mainly concentrate on Lorentz and Poincaré, the precursors of the new kinematics. A final comparison of the contributions of Einstein, Lorentz, and Poincaré will be deferred until Chapter 8. Nor shall I discuss Lorentz's finest contribution, his atomistic interpretation of the Maxwell equations in terms of charges and currents carried by fundamental particles (which he called charged particles in 1892, ions in 1895, and, finally, electrons in 1899), even though this work represents such a major advance in the development of electrodynamics. Rather, I shall confine myself largely to the evolution and the interpretation of the Lorentz transformation:

$$x' = \gamma(x - vt) \qquad y' = y \qquad z' = z \qquad t' = \gamma(t - vx/c^2) \qquad (6.3)$$
$$\gamma = (1 - v^2/c^2)^{-1/2} \qquad (6.4)$$

which relates one set of space–time coordinate systems (x',y',z',t') to another, (x,y,z,t), moving with constant velocity v relative to the first. (For the purpose of this section, it suffices to consider only relative motion in the x direction.)

The main characters who will make their appearance in what follows are: Voigt, the first to write down Lorentz transformations; FitzGerald, the first to propose the contraction hypothesis; Lorentz himself; Larmor, the first to relate the contraction hypothesis to Lorentz transformations; and Poincaré. It should also be mentioned that before 1900 others had begun to sense that the aether as a material medium might perhaps be dispensed with. Thus Paul Drude wrote in 1900: 'The conception of an ether absolutely at rest is the most simple and the most natural— at least if the ether is conceived to be not a substance but merely space endowed with certain physical properties' [D3]; and Emil Cohn in 1901, 'Such a medium fills every element of our space; it may be a definite ponderable system or also the vacuum' [C1].

Of the many papers on the subject treated in this section, the following in particular have been of great help to me: Tetu Hirosige on the aether problem [H5], McCormmach on Hertz [M14], Bork [B3] and Brush [B4] on FitzGerald, and Miller [M15] on Poincaré.

As to Einstein himself, in his first relativity paper he mentions only three physicists by name: Maxwell, Hertz, and Lorentz. As he repeatedly pointed out elsewhere, in 1905 he knew Lorentz's work only up to 1895. It follows—as we shall see—that in 1905 Einstein did not know of Lorentz transformations. He invented them himself. Nor did he know at that time those papers by Poincaré which deal in technical detail with relativity issues.

2. *Voigt.*   It was noted in 1887 [V2] by Woldemar Voigt that equations of the type

$$\Box \phi = 0 \tag{6.5}$$

$$\Box \equiv \frac{\partial^2}{\partial x^2} + \frac{\partial^2}{\partial y^2} + \frac{\partial^2}{\partial z^2} - \frac{\partial^2}{c^2 \, \partial t^2} \tag{6.6}$$

retain their form if one goes over to the new space–time variables

$$x' = x - vt \qquad y' = y/\gamma \qquad z' = z/\gamma \qquad t' = t - vx/c^2 \tag{6.7}$$

These are the Lorentz transformations (Eq. 6.3) up to a scale factor. Voigt announced this result in a theoretical paper devoted to the Doppler principle. As an application of Eq. 6.7, he gave a derivation of the Doppler shift, but only for the long-familiar longitudinal effect of order v/c. His new method has remained standard procedure to this day: he made use of the invariance of the phase of a propagating plane light wave under Eq. 6.7 [P3]. Since the Doppler shift is a purely kinematic effect (in the relativistic sense), it is irrelevant that Voigt's argument is set in the dynamic framework of the long-forgotten elastic theory of light propagation, according to which light is propagated as a result of oscillations in an elastic incompressible medium.

Lorentz was familiar with some of Voigt's work. In 1887 or 1888, the two men corresponded—about the Michelson–Morley experiment [V3]. However, for a long time Lorentz seems not to have been aware of the Voigt transformation (Eq. 6.7). Indeed, Lorentz's Columbia University lectures, given in 1906 and published in book form in 1909, contain the following comment: 'In a paper . . . published in 1887 . . . and which to my regret has escaped my notice all these years, Voigt has applied to equations of the form [of Eq. 6.5] a transformation equivalent to [Eq. 6.3]. The idea of the transformations [Eq. 6.3] . . . might therefore have been borrowed from Voigt and the proof that it does not alter the form of the equations for the *free* ether is contained in his paper' [L7]. (Although these lines were written after Einstein's work of 1905, they still contain a reference to the aether. So does the second edition of Lorentz's book, published in 1915. I shall have more to say on this subject in Chapter 8.)

At a physics meeting in 1908, Minkowski drew attention to Voigt's 1887 paper [M16]. Voigt was present. His response was laconic: ' . . . already then [in 1887] some results were found which later were obtained from the electromagnetic theory' [V4].

3. FitzGerald. The collected papers of the Irish physicist George Francis FitzGerald, edited by his friend Joseph Larmor [L8], show that FitzGerald belonged to that small and select group of physicists who participated very early in the further development of Maxwell's theory. (In 1899, he was awarded a Royal Medal for his work in optics and electrodynamics by the Royal Society, of which he was a member.) However, this handsome volume does not contain the very brief paper for which Fitzgerald is best remembered, the one dealing with the hypothesis of the contraction of moving bodies. This paper appeared in 1889 in the American journal *Science* [F3] under the title 'The Ether and the Earth's Atmosphere.' It reads, in full:

> I have read with much interest Messrs. Michelson and Morley's wonderfully delicate experiment attempting to decide the important question as to how far the ether is carried along by the earth. Their result seems opposed to other experiments showing that the ether in the air can be carried along only to an inappreciable extent. I would suggest that almost the only hypothesis that can reconcile this opposition is that the length of material bodies changes, according as they are moving through the ether or across it, by an amount depending on the square of the ratio of their velocities to that of light. We know that electric forces are affected by the motion of the electrified bodies relative to the ether, and it seems a not improbable supposition that the molecular forces are affected by the motion, and that the size of a body alters consequently. It would be very important if secular experiments on electrical attractions between permanently electrified bodies, such as in a very delicate quadrant electrometer, were instituted in some of the equatorial parts of the earth to observe whether there is any diurnal and annual variation of attraction—diurnal due to the rotation of the earth being added and subtracted from its orbital velocity, and annual similarly for its orbital velocity and the motion of the solar system.

Here for the first time appears the proposal of what now is called the Fitz-Gerald–Lorentz contraction. The formulation is qualitative and distinctly prerelativistic. Consider the statement ' . . . the length of material bodies changes, according as they are moving through the aether. . . .' First of all, there is (of course) still an aether. Second, the change of length is considered (if I may borrow a later phrase of Einstein's) to be objectively real; it is an absolute change, not a change relative to an observer at rest. Consider next the statement about the molecular forces being affected by the motion. The author clearly has in mind a *dynamic* contraction mechanism which presses the molecules together in their motion through the aether.

FitzGerald's hypothesis was referred to several times in lectures (later published) by Oliver Joseph Lodge [B3]. Larmor, too, properly credited FitzGerald in the introduction to the latter's collected works: 'He [F.] was the first to suggest . . . that motion through the aether affects the dimensions of solid molecular aggregations' [L9]. Elsewhere in that same book, we find FitzGerald himself mentioning the contraction hypothesis, in 1900. In that year, Larmor's essay *Aether and Matter* [L10] had come out. In a review of this book, FitzGerald wrote that in the analysis of the Michelson–Morley experiment 'he [Larmor] has to assume that the length of a body depends on whether it is moving lengthwise or sideways through the ether' [L11], without referring, however, to his own suggestion made more than ten years earlier!

FitzGerald's curious silence may perhaps be explained in part by what he once wrote to his friend Oliver Heaviside: 'As I am not in the least sensitive to having made mistakes, I rush out with all sorts of crude notions in hope that they may set others thinking and lead to some advance' [F4]. Perhaps he was also held back by an awareness of those qualities of his which were described by Heaviside soon after FitzGerald's death: 'He had, undoubtedly, the quickest and most original brain of anybody. That was a great distinction; but it was, I think, a misfortune as regards his scientific fame. He saw too many openings. His brain was too fertile and inventive. I think it would have been better for him if he had been a little stupid—I mean not so quick and versatile but more plodding. He would have been better appreciated, save by a few' [O2].

Lorentz was one of those few who appreciated FitzGerald the way he was.

4. Lorentz. The first paper by Lorentz relevant to the present discussion is the one of 1886—that is, prior to the Michelson–Morley experiment—in which he criticized Michelson's theoretical analysis of the 1881 Potsdam experiment [L3]. The main purpose of Lorentz's paper was to examine how well Fresnel's stationary aether fitted the facts. He therefore reexamined the aberration and Fizeau effects and noted in particular another achievement (not yet mentioned) of Michelson and Morley: their repetition of the Fizeau experiment with much greater accuracy, which bore out Fresnel's prediction for the drag coefficient in a much more quantitative way than was known before [M17]. Since at that time Lorentz had a right to be dubious about the precision of the Potsdam experiment, he concluded that there was no particular source for worry: 'It seems doubtful in my opinion that the hypothesis of Fresnel has been refuted by experiment' [L3].

We move to 1892, the year in which Lorentz publishes his first paper on his atomistic electromagnetic theory [L12]. The Michelson–Morley experiment has meanwhile been performed, and Lorentz is now deeply concerned (as was noted before): 'This experiment has been puzzling me for a long time, and in the end I have been able to think of only one means of reconciling it with Fresnel's theory.

It consists in the supposition that the line joining two points of a solid body, if at first parallel to the direction of the earth's motion, does not keep the same length when it is subsequently turned through 90°' [L13]. If this length be l in the latter position, then, Lorentz notes, Fresnel's aether hypothesis can be maintained if the length in the former position l' were

$$l' = l\left(1 - \frac{v^2}{2c^2}\right) \tag{6.8}$$

Today we call Eq. 6.8 the FitzGerald–Lorentz contraction up to second order in v/c. In order to interpret this result, Lorentz assumed that molecular forces, like electromagnetic forces, 'act by means of an intervention of the aether' and that a contraction effect $O(v^2/c^2)$ cannot be excluded on any known experimental grounds.

These conclusions agree in remarkable detail with FitzGerald's earlier proposal: save the aether by its dynamic intervention on the action of molecular forces. In 1892, Lorentz was still unaware of FitzGerald's earlier paper, however.

The fall of 1894. Lorentz writes to FitzGerald, telling him that he has learned of the latter's hypothesis via an 1893 paper by Lodge, informing FitzGerald that he had arrived at the same idea in his own paper of 1892, and asking him where he has published his ideas so that he can refer to them [L14]. A few days later, FitzGerald replies: His paper was sent to *Science*, 'but I do not know if they ever published it. . . . I am pretty sure that your publication is prior to any of my printed publications'(!) [F5]. He also expresses his delight at hearing that Lorentz agrees with him, 'for I have been rather laughed at for my view over here.'

From that time on, Lorentz used practically every occasion to point out that he and FitzGerald had independently arrived at the contraction idea. In his memoir of 1895, he wrote of 'a hypothesis . . . which has also been arrived at by Mr FitzGerald, as I found out later' [L15]. This paper also marks the beginning of Lorentz's road toward the Lorentz transformations, our next subject.

In the paper of 1895, Lorentz proved the following 'theorem of corresponding states.' Consider a distribution of nonmagnetic substances described in a coordinate system $\vec{x},t$ at rest relative to the aether. Denote by $\vec{E}$, $\vec{H}$, $\vec{D}$, the electric, magnetic, and electric displacement fields, respectively. $\vec{D} = \vec{E} + \vec{P}$; $\vec{P}$ is the electric polarization. Consider a second coordinate system $\vec{x}',t'$ moving with velocity v relative to the $(\vec{x},t)$ system. Then to first order in v/c, there is a corresponding state in the second system in which $\vec{E}'$, $\vec{H}'$, $\vec{P}'$ are the same functions of $\vec{x}',t'$ as $\vec{E}$, $\vec{H}$, $\vec{P}$ are of $\vec{x},t$, where

$$\vec{x}' = \vec{x} - vt \tag{6.9}$$
$$t' = t - \vec{vx}/c^2 \tag{6.10}$$
$$\vec{E}' = \vec{E} + \vec{v} \times \vec{H}/c \tag{6.11}$$
$$\vec{H}' = \vec{H} - \vec{v} \times \vec{E}/c \tag{6.12}$$
$$\vec{P}' = \vec{P}$$

Like Voigt before him, Lorentz regarded the transformations (Eqs. 6.9 and 6.10) only as a convenient mathematical tool for proving a physical theorem, in his case that to $O(v/c)$ terrestrial optical experiments are independent of the motion of the earth, a result already mentioned in Section 6a. Equation 6.9 was obviously familiar to Lorentz, but the novel Eq. 6.10 led him to introduce significant new terminology. He proposed to call t the *general time* and t' the *local time* [L16]. Although he did not say so explicitly, it is evident that to him there was, so to speak, only one true time: t. At this stage, Lorentz's explanation for the absence of any evidence for a stationary aether was hybrid in character: to first order he had derived the null effects from electrodynamics; to second order he had to introduce his ad hoc hypothesis expressed by Eq. 6.8.

One last remark on the 1895 paper. It contains another novelty, the *assumption* that an 'ion' with charge e and velocity v is subject to a force $\vec{K}$:

$$\vec{K} = e(\vec{E} + \vec{v} \times \vec{H}/c) \qquad (6.13)$$

the Lorentz force (Lorentz called it the *electrische Kraft* [L17]).

As has been noted repeatedly, in 1905 Einstein knew of Lorentz's work only up to 1895. Thus Einstein was aware of no more and no less than the following: Lorentz's concern about the Michelson–Morley experiment, his 'first-order Lorentz transformation,' Eqs. 6.9 and 6.10, his proof of the first-order theorem for optical phenomena, his need to supplement this proof with the contraction hypothesis, and, finally, his new postulate of the Lorentz force, Eq. 6.13.

As a conclusion to the contributions of Lorentz prior to 1905, the following three papers need to be mentioned.

1898. Lorentz discusses the status of his work in a lecture given in Düsseldorf [L18]. It is essentially a summary of what he had written in 1895.

1899. He gives a 'simplified version' of his earlier theory [L19]. Five years later, he characterized this work as follows. 'It would be more satisfactory if it were possible to show, by means of certain fundamental assumptions, and without neglecting terms of one order of magnitude or another, that many electromagnetic actions are entirely independent of the motion of the system. Some years ago [in 1899] I had already sought to frame a theory of this kind' [L20]. In 1899 he wrote down the transformations

$$x' = \epsilon\gamma(x - vt) \qquad (6.14)$$
$$y' = \epsilon y, \ z' = \epsilon z \qquad (6.15)$$
$$t' = \epsilon\gamma(t - vx/c^2) \qquad (6.16)$$

which are the Lorentz transformations (Eq. 6.3) up to a scale factor ϵ. He noted among other things that 'the dilatations determined by [Eqs. 6.14 and 6.15] are precisely those which I had to assume in order to explain the experiment of Mr Michelson'! Thus the reduction of the FitzGerald–Lorentz contraction to a consequence of Lorentz transformations* is a product of the nineteenth century. Lorentz referred to t' defined by Eq. 6.16 as a modified local time. Concerning the scale factor ϵ, he remarked that it had to have a well-defined value which one can determine only 'by a deeper knowledge of the phenomena.' Note that it is, of course, not necessary for the interpretation of the Michelson–Morley experiment to know what ϵ is. (As for all optical phenomena in free space, one may allow not only for Lorentz invariance but also for scale invariance, in fact, for conformal invariance.) In 1899 Lorentz did not examine whether his theorem of corresponding states could be adapted to the transformations represented by Eqs. 6.14–6.16.

1904.   Lorentz finally writes down the transformations (Eqs. 6.3–6.4) [L20]. He fixes ϵ to be equal to unity from a discussion of the transformation properties of the equation of motion of an electron in an external field. This time he attempts to prove a theorem of corresponding states (that is, Lorentz covariance) for the inhomogeneous Maxwell–Lorentz equations. He makes an error in the transformation equations for velocities ([L20], Eq. 8). As a result, he does not obtain the covariance beyond the first order in v/c (compare Eqs. 2 and 9 in [L20]).

I shall return to this 1904 paper in the next chapter. However, as far as the history of relativistic kinematics is concerned, the story of Lorentz as precursor to Einstein is herewith complete.

5. *Larmor.*   Larmor's prize-winning essay *Aether and Matter* [L10] was completed in 1898 and came out in 1900. It contains not only the exact transformations (Eqs. 6.3 and 6.4) but also the proof that one arrives at the FitzGerald–Lorentz contraction with the help of these transformations [L21]. Larmor was aware of Lorentz's paper of 1895 and quoted it at length, but he could not have known the 1899 paper.

It is true that Larmor's reasonings are often obscured by his speculations (of no interest here) about dynamic interrelations between aether and matter. However, there is no doubt that he gave the Lorentz transformations and the resulting contraction argument before Lorentz independently did the same. It is a curious fact that neither in the correspondence between Larmor and Lorentz** nor in Lorentz's papers is there any mention of this contribution by Larmor.

The first time I became aware of Larmor's work was in the early 1950s, when Adriaan Fokker told me that it was known in Leiden that Larmor had the Lorentz transformations before Lorentz. Alas, I never asked Fokker (an ex-student of Lorentz's) what Lorentz himself had to say on that subject.

6. *Poincaré.*   In 1898 there appeared an utterly remarkable article by Poincaré entitled 'La Mesure du Temps' [P5].† In this paper, the author notes that '*we have no direct intuition about the equality of two time intervals.* People who

---

*For the simple mathematics of this reduction, see standard textbooks, e.g., [P4].

**This correspondence is deposited in the Ryksarchief in the Hague. I am grateful to A. Kox for information related to this correspondence.

†This essay is available in English as Chapter 2 in *The Value of Science* [P6].

believe they have this intuition are the dupes of an illusion' (the italics are Poin-caré's). He further remarks, 'It is difficult to separate the qualitative problems of simultaneity from the quantitative problem of the measurement of time; either one uses a chronometer, or one takes into account a transmission velocity such as the one of light, since one cannot measure such a velocity without *measuring* a time.' After discussing the inadequacies of earlier definitions of simultaneity, Poincaré concludes, 'The simultaneity of two events or the order of their succession, as well as the equality of two time intervals, must be defined in such a way that the state-ments of the natural laws be as simple as possible. In other words, all rules and definitions are but the result of an unconscious opportunism.' These lines read like the general program for what would be given concrete shape seven years later. Other comments in this paper indicate that Poincaré wrote this article in response to several other recent publications on the often-debated question of the measure-ment of time intervals. The new element which Poincaré injected into these dis-cussions was his questioning of the objective meaning of simultaneity.

In 1898 Poincaré did not mention any of the problems in electrodynamics. He did so on two subsequent occasions, in 1900 and in 1904. The style is again pro-grammatic. In these works, the aether questions are central. 'Does the aether really exist?' he asked in his opening address to the Paris Congress of 1900 [P7].* 'One knows where our belief in the aether stems from. When light is on its way to us from a far star . . . it is no longer on the star and not yet on the earth. It is necessary that it is somewhere, sustained, so to say, by some material support.' He remarked that in the Fizeau experiment 'one believes one can touch the aether with one's fingers.' Turning to theoretical ideas, he noted that the Lorentz theory 'is the most satisfactory one we have.'** However, he considered it a drawback that the independence of optical phenomena from the motion of the earth should have separate explanations in first and in second order. 'One must find one and the same explanation for one and for the other, and everything leads us to antic-ipate that this explanation will be valid for higher-order terms as well and that the cancellation of the [velocity-dependent] terms will be rigorous and absolute.' His reference to cancellations would seem to indicate that he was thinking about a conspiracy of dynamic effects.

In 1904 he returned to the same topics, once again in a programmatic way, in his address to the International Congress of Arts and Science at St. Louis [P9].† 'What is the aether, how are its molecules arrayed, do they attract or repel each other?' He expressed his unease with the idea of an absolute velocity: 'If we suc-ceed in measuring something we will always have the freedom to say that it is not

---

*This address is available in English as Chapters 9 and 10 in *Science and Hypothesis* [P8].

**During the period 1895 to 1900, Poincaré considered it a flaw of the theory that it did not satisfy momentum conservation in the Newtonian sense, that is, conservation of momentum for matter only. He withdrew this objection soon afterward.

†This address is available in English as Chapters 7 to 9 in *The Value of Science* [P6].

the absolute velocity, and if it is not the velocity relative to the aether, it can always be the velocity relative to a new unknown fluid with which we would fill space.' He gently chides Lorentz for his accumulation of hypotheses, and then he goes beyond Lorentz in treating local time as a *physical* concept. He considers two observers in uniform relative motion who wish to synchronize their clocks by means of light signals. 'Clocks regulated in this way will not mark the true time, rather they mark what one may call the *local time*.' All phenomena seen by one observer are retarded relative to the other, but they all are retarded equally (Poincaré points out) and 'as demanded by the relativity principle [the observer] cannot know whether he is at rest or in absolute motion.' Poincaré is getting close. But then he falters: 'Unfortunately [this reasoning] is not sufficient and *complementary hypotheses are necessary* [my italics]; one must assume that bodies in motion suffer a uniform contraction in their direction of motion.' The reference to complementary hypotheses makes clear that relativity theory had not yet been discovered.

Poincaré concluded this lecture with another of his marvelous visions: 'Perhaps we must construct a new mechanics, of which we can only catch a glimpse, . . . in which the velocity of light would become an unpassable limit.' But, he added, 'I hasten to say that we are not yet there and that nothing yet proves that [the old principles] will not emerge victoriously and intact from this struggle.'

The account of Einstein's precursors ends here, on a note of indecision. Lorentz transformations had been written down. Simultaneity had been questioned. The velocity of light as a limiting velocity had been conjectured. But prior to 1905 there was no relativity theory. Let us now turn to what Poincaré did next, not as a precursor to Einstein but essentially simultaneously with him.

6c. Poincaré in 1905

All three papers just mentioned are qualitative in character. Poincaré, one of the very few true leaders in mathematics and mathematical physics of his day, knew, of course, the electromagnetic theory in all its finesses. He had published a book on optics in 1889 [P10] and one on electromagnetic theory in 1901 [P11]. In 1895 he had written a series of papers on Maxwellian theories [P12]. From 1897 to 1900 he wrote several articles on the theory of Lorentz [P13]. All this work culminated in his two papers completed in 1905. Both bear the same title: 'Sur la Dynamique de l'Électron.' The occurrence of the term *dynamics* is most significant. So is the following sequence of dates:

June 5, 1905. Poincaré communicates the first of these two papers to the Académie des Sciences in Paris [P14].

June 30, 1905. Einstein's first paper on relativity is received by the *Annalen der Physik*.

July, 1905. Poincaré completes his second paper, which appears in 1906 [P15].

The first of the Poincaré papers is in essence a summary of the second, much longer one. The content of his articles is partly kinematic, partly dynamic. Here I shall discuss only their kinematic part, leaving the remainder until the next chapter.

The June paper begins with the remark that neither the aberration of light and related phenomena nor the work of Michelson reveals any evidence for an absolute motion of the earth. 'It seems that this impossibility of demonstrating absolute motion is a general law of nature.' Next Poincaré refers to the contraction hypothesis and to Lorentz's paper of 1904 [L20] in which—as he has it—Lorentz had succeeded in modifying the hypothesis 'in such a way as to bring it in accordance with the *complete* impossibility of determining absolute motion.' This statement is not quite correct, since (as was mentioned earlier) Lorentz had not succeeded in proving the covariance of the inhomogeneous Maxwell–Lorentz equations. Poincaré was to return to this point in July. However, in June he already had the correct transformation properties of the velocities, the point Lorentz had missed. 'I have been led to modify and complete [Lorentz's analysis] in certain points of detail.'

Poincaré then turns to the transformations (Eqs. 6.14–6.16), 'which I shall name after Lorentz,' and continues, 'The ensemble of all these transformations, together with the ensemble of all spatial rotations must form a group; but in order for this to be so it is necessary that* $\epsilon = 1$; one is thus led to assume that $\epsilon = 1$, a result which Lorentz had obtained in another way.'

The final topic discussed in this paper concerns gravitation. Following Lorentz's dynamic picture, Poincaré reasons in a more general and abstract way that all forces should transform in the same way under Lorentz transformations. He concludes that therefore Newton's laws need modification and that there should exist gravitational waves which propagate with the velocity of light! Finally, he points out that the resulting corrections to Newton's law must be $O(v^2/c^2)$ and that the precision of astronomical data does not seem to rule out effects of this order.

The July paper of Poincaré gives many more details. Its Section 1, entitled 'Lorentz Transformation,' contains the complete proof of covariance of electrodynamics. 'It is here that I must point out for the first time a difference with Lorentz' [P16]. Section 4 contains a discussion of 'a continuous group which we shall call the Lorentz group.' Poincaré explains his argument for $\epsilon = 1$: starting from Eqs. 6.14–6.16, consider the inverse of these transformations, that is, replace v by $-v$. Clearly,

$$\epsilon(v)\epsilon(-v) = 1 \qquad (6.17)$$

Moreover, from a rotation of 180° around the y axis it follows that

$$\epsilon(v) = \epsilon(-v) \qquad (6.18)$$

---

*I use the notation of Eqs. 6.14–6.16; Poincaré used the symbol l instead of ϵ.

so that

$$\epsilon(v) = 1 \tag{6.19}$$

Once it is settled that $\epsilon = 1$, the Lorentz transformations have the property that

$$x^2 + y^2 + z^2 - c^2t^2 \text{ remains unaltered.} \tag{6.20}$$

In showing the group property of Lorentz transformations, Poincaré remarked that the 'product' of two transformations (Eq. 6.3), one with velocity v_1, the other with v_2, results in another Lorentz transformation with velocity v given by

$$v = \frac{v_1 + v_2}{1 + v_1 v_2 / c^2} \tag{6.21}$$

He did, of course, not know that a few weeks earlier someone else had independently noted the group properties of Lorentz transformations and had derived Eqs. 6.19–6.21 by an almost identical argument.

I shall return later to the efforts by Lorentz in 1904 and by Poincaré in 1905 to give a theory of the electron. However, I believe I have presented at this point all the evidence that bears on the role of Lorentz and of Poincaré in the development of relativity theory. I shall now let their case rest until the discussion of Einstein's first two papers on the subject has been completed. Thereafter an attempt will be made to compare the contributions of all three men.

As a last step preparatory to the account of Einstein's discovery of relativity, I should like to mention what little we know about his thoughts on the subject prior to 1905.

6d. Einstein before 1905

Einstein's curiosity in electromagnetic theory goes back at least to his Pavia days of 1895, which followed his escape from the hated high school in Munich. The following brief and rather disconnected remarks bear on his interest in electrodynamics during the decade preceding his creation of the special theory of relativity.

1. *The Pavia Essay.** In 1895 Einstein sent a manuscript entitled *Über die Untersuchung des Ätherzustandes im magnetischen Felde* (On the Examination of the State of the Aether in a Magnetic Field) to his uncle Caesar Koch in Belgium. This paper—which Einstein never published—was accompanied by a covering letter in which he wrote: '[The manuscript] deals with a very special theme and is . . . rather naive and incomplete, as can be expected from a young fellow.'

---

*In 1950, Einstein dated this manuscript to be from 1894 or 1895. It was sent to Caesar Koch in 1895, since in its covering letter Einstein tells of his intent to go to the ETH and adds, 'In the next letter I shall write you what may come of this.' Both the essay and its covering letter were reproduced in a paper by Mehra [M18].

In the opening lines of the essay, he asks the reader's forbearance: 'Since I completely lacked the material for penetrating deeper into the subject, I beg that this circumstance will not be interpreted as superficiality.'

The main questions raised in the essay are, How does a magnetic field, generated when a current is turned on, affect the surrounding aether? How, in turn, does this magnetic field affect the current itself? Evidently Einstein believed in an aether at that time. He regarded it as an elastic medium and wondered in particular how 'the three components of elasticity act on the velocity of an aether wave' which is generated when the current is turned on. He came to the following main conclusion. 'Above all, it ought to be [experimentally] shown that there exists a passive resistance to the electric current's ability for generating a magnetic field; [this resistance] is proportional to the length of the wire and independent of the cross section and the material of the conductor.' Thus, the young Einstein discovered independently the qualitative properties of self-induction (a term he did not use). It seems clear that he was not yet familiar with earlier work on this phenomenon. In his paper he mentions 'the wonderful experiments of Hertz.' I do not know how he became aware of Hertz's work. At any rate, it is evident that at that time he already knew that light is an electromagnetic phenomenon but did not yet know Maxwell's papers.

2. *The Aarau Question.* In his final autobiographical note [E12], Einstein wrote, 'During that year [sometime between October 1895 and the early fall of 1896] in Aarau the question came to me: If one runs after a light wave with [a velocity equal to the] light velocity, then one would encounter a time-independent wavefield. However, something like that does not seem to exist! This was the first juvenile thought experiment which has to do with the special theory of relativity' (and he added, 'Invention is not the product of logical thought, even though the final product is tied to a logical structure.'). Also, in his more extensive autobiographical notes, published in 1949, Einstein remarked that 'after ten years of reflection such a principle [special relativity] resulted from [this] paradox upon which I had already hit at the age of sixteen' [E6].

3. *The ETH Student.* Since Rudolf Kayser, Einstein's son-in-law and biographer, was himself not a physicist, it is hard to believe that the following lines from the biography could have come from anyone but Einstein himself. 'He encountered at once, in his second year of college [1897–8], the problem of light, ether and the earth's movement. This problem never left him. He wanted to construct an apparatus which would accurately measure the earth's movement against the ether. That his intention was that of other important theorists, Einstein did not yet know. He was at that time unacquainted with the positive contributions, of some years back, of the great Dutch physicist Hendrik Lorentz, and with the subsequently famous attempt of Michelson. He wanted to proceed quite empirically, to suit his scientific feeling of the time, and believed that an apparatus such as he sought would lead him to the solution of the problem, whose far-reaching perspectives he already sensed. But there was no chance to build this apparatus.

The skepticism of his teachers was too great, the spirit of enterprise too small. Albert had thus to turn aside from his plan, but not to give it up forever. He still expected to approach the major questions of physics by observation and experiment' [R2].

As to electromagnetic theory, Einstein was not offered a course on this subject in his ETH days. As noted in Chapter 3, he learned this theory from Föppl's textbook.

4. *The Winterthur Letter.*   A letter by Einstein to Grossmann, written in 1901 from Winterthur, informs us that aether drift experiments were still on Einstein's mind: 'A new and considerably simpler method for investigating the motion of matter relative to the light-aether has occurred to me. If the merciless fates would just once give me the necessary quiet for its execution!' [E13]. Since there are no preliminaries to this statement, one gains the impression that Grossmann knew something about a previous method which Einstein must have had in mind when they were together at the ETH.

This letter also shows that Einstein still believed in an aether as late as 1901.

5. *The Bern Lecture.*   On the evening of December 5, 1903, Albert Einstein, technical expert third class with provisional appointment, held a lecture in the conference room of the Hotel Storchen in Bern before the Naturforschende Gesellschaft Bern. He had been elected to membership of this society on May 2, 1903. The subject of his December lecture was 'Theorie der elektromagnetischen Wellen' [F6]. It would obviously be extraordinarily interesting to know what Einstein said that evening. However, to the best of my knowledge, no record of his talk exists.

6. *The Kyoto Address.*   Finally I quote another part of the translation from German to Japanese to English of the Kyoto address that Einstein gave in 1922. Before doing so, I should point out that I do not know what times are referred to in the statements 'I then thought . . .' and 'In those days . . .'.

'I then thought I would want to prove experimentally to myself in any way the flow of the aether to the earth, that is to say, the motion of the earth. In those days when this problem arose in my mind, I had no doubt as to the existence of the aether and the motion of the earth in it. Meanwhile I had a plan to try to test it by means of measuring the difference of heats which were to appear in a thermocouple according as the direction along or against which the light from a single source was made to reflect by suitable mirrors, as I presupposed there should be a difference between the energies of reflected lights in the opposite directions. This idea was similar to the one in the Michelson experiment, but I had not carried out the experiment yet to obtain any definite result' [O1].

7. *Summary.*   In the same lecture Einstein remarked, 'It is never easy to talk about how I got to the theory of relativity because there would be various concealed complexities to motivate human thinking and because they worked with different weights' [O1]. Even with this admonition in mind, it would seem that the following is a fair summary of Einstein's work and thoughts on electrodynamics prior to 1905.

Einstein's first important creative act dates from his high school days, when he independently discovered self-induction, a contribution which should, of course, not be associated with his name. At least twice he had an idea for a new experimental method to measure the aether drift. He intended to perform these experiments himself but did not succeed in doing so, either because his teachers would not let him [R2] or because he did not have enough free time [E13]. He believed in an aether at least until 1901 [E13]. Sometime during 1895 or 1896, the thought struck him that light cannot be transformed to rest [E12]. He knew of the Michelson–Morley experiment which, however, was not as crucial to his formulation of special relativity as were the first-order effects, the aberration of light, and the Fresnel drag [S6, O1]. He knew the 1895 paper of Lorentz in which the Michelson–Morley experiment is discussed at length. He did not know the Lorentz transformations. He did not know any of those writings by Poincaré which deal with physics in technical detail.

It is virtually certain, however, that prior to 1905 Einstein was aware of the 1900 Paris address by Poincaré and that he had also read Poincaré's remark of 1898 concerning the lack of intuition about the equality of two time intervals. Before 1905 Einstein, together with his friends of the Akademie Olympia, did indeed read some of Poincaré's general essays on science: 'In Bern I had regular philosophical reading and discussion evenings, together with K. Habicht and Solovine, during which we were mainly concerned with Hume. . . . The reading of Hume, along with Poincaré and Mach, had some influence on my development' [E14].

The four collections of Poincaré essays—*La Science et l'Hypothèse, La Valeur de la Science, Science et Méthode,* and *Dernières Pensées*—first appeared in 1902, 1905, 1908, and 1913, respectively. All three programmatic papers by Poincaré mentioned in Section 6b are contained in one or another of these volumes. His 1898 article, in which he questioned the naive use of simultaneity, and his St. Louis address of 1904 are found in *La Valeur de la Science,* his Paris address of 1900 in *La Science et l'Hypothèse.* This last book, the only one of the four to appear before 1905, is the one Einstein and his friends read in Bern. I therefore believe that, prior to his own first paper on relativity, Einstein knew the Paris address in which Poincaré suggested that the lack of any evidence for motion relative to the aether should hold generally to all orders in v/c and that 'the cancellation of the [velocity-dependent] terms will be rigorous and absolute.' But there is more. In *La Science et l'Hypothèse,* there is a chapter on classical mechanics in which Poincaré writes, 'There is no absolute time; to say that two durations are equal is an assertion which has by itself no meaning and which can acquire one only by convention. . . . Not only have we no direct intuition of the equality of two durations, but we have not even direct intuition of the simultaneity of two events occurring in different places; this I have explained in an article entitled "La Mesure du Temps".' I stress that Einstein and his friends did much more than just browse through Poincaré's writings. Solovine has left us a detailed list of books which the Akademie members read together. Of these, he singles out one and only one, *La Science et l'Hypothèse,* for the following comment: '[This] book profoundly impressed us and kept us breathless for weeks on end' [E15]!

I must say more about Einstein and Poincaré and shall do so in Chapter 8 after having discussed Einstein's creation of special relativity in the next chapter.

References

B1. Cf. W. L. Bryan (Ed.), *A Debate on the Theory of Relativity.* Open Court, Chicago, 1927.

B2. D. B. Brace, *Phil. Mag.* **7,** 317 (1904).

B3. A. M. Bork, *Isis* **57,** 199 (1966).

B4. S. G. Brush, *Isis* **58,** 230 (1967).

C1. E. Cohn, *Goett. Nachr.,* 1901, p. 74.

D1. P. A. M. Dirac, *Nature* **168,** 906 (1951); **169,** 702 (1951).

D2. H. Dukas, memorandum to V. Hobson, secretary to Professor J. R. Oppenheimer, June 21, 1966.

D3. P. Drude, *The Theory of Optics* (C. R. Mann and R. A. Millikan, Trans.), p. 457. Dover, New York, 1959.

E1. A. Einstein, *The Meaning of Relativity* (E. P. Adams Tran.). Princeton University Press, Princeton, N.J., 1921.

E2. ——, letter to M. Besso, December 23, 1925; *EB*, p. 215.

E2a. ——, *Forschungen und Fortschritte* **3,** 36 (1927).

E3. ——, letter to O. Veblen, April 30, 1930.

E4. ——, *Grundgedanken und Probleme der Relativitätstheorie.* Imprimerie Royale, Stockholm, 1923. English translation in [N1], p. 482.

E5. ——, *AdP* **17,** 891 (1905).

E6. —— in *Albert Einstein: Philosopher–Scientist* (P. A. Schilpp, Ed.). Tudor, New York, 1949.

E7. ——, *Jahrb. Rad. Elektr.* **4,** 411 (1907).

E8. ——, in *Kultur der Gegenwart* (E. Lecher, Ed.), Vol. 3, Sec. 3. Teubner, Leipzig, 1915.

E9. ——, *The Meaning of Relativity* (5th edn.). Princeton University Press, Princeton, N.J., 1955.

E10. ——, *Science* **73,** 375 (1931).

E11. ——, *Z. Angew. Chemie* **44,** 685 (1931).

E12. —— in *Helle Zeit, Dunkle Zeit* (C. Seelig, Ed.). Europa Verlag, Zürich, 1956.

E13. ——, letter to M. Grossmann, 1901, undated.

E14. ——, letter to M. Besso, March 6, 1952; *EB*, p. 464.

E15. ——, *Lettres à Maurice Solovine,* p. VIII. Gauthier-Villars, Paris 1956.

F1. A. Fresnel, letter to F. Arago, September 1818. Reprinted in *Oeuvres d'Augustin Fresnel,* Vol. 2, p. 627. Imprimerie Royale, Paris, 1868.

F2. A. Fizeau, *C. R. Ac. Sci. Paris* **33,** 349 (1851).

F3. G. F. FitzGerald, *Science* **13,** 390 (1889).

F4. ——, letter to O. Heaviside, quoted in A. M. Bork, *Dictionary of Scientific Biography,* Vol. 5, p. 15. Scribner's, New York, 1972.

F5. ——, letter to H. A. Lorentz, November 10, 1894. Reprinted in [B4].

F6. M. Flückiger, *Albert Einstein in Bern*, pp. 71–6. Paul Haupt Verlag, Bern, 1974.

H1. J. N. Howard, *Isis* **58,** 88 (1967).

H2. G. Holton, *Isis* **60,** 133 (1969).

H3. H. Hertz, *Gesammelte Werke* (2nd edn.), Vol. 2, p. 23. Barth, Leipzig, 1894.

H4. H. Hertz, *Electric Waves* (D. E. Jones, Tran.), p. 21. Dover, New York, 1962.

H5. T. Hirosige, *Hist. St. Phys. Sci.* **7,** 3 (1976).

I1. J. Ishiwara, *Einstein Kōen-Roku*, Tokyo-Tosho, Tokyo, 1977.

K1. Kelvin, *Baltimore Lectures,* Appendix B. Clay, London, 1904.

K2. ——, [K1], p. vi.

K3. ——, [H4], p. xv.

L1. H. A. Lorentz, *Lectures on Theoretical Physics,* Vol. 1, p. 3. McMillan, London, 1927.

L2. D. M. Livingston, *The Master of Light,* Chap. 3. Scribner's, New York, 1973.

L3. H. A. Lorentz, *Arch. Néerl.* **21,** 103 (1886). Reprinted in H. A. Lorentz, *Collected Papers,* Vol. 4, p. 153. Nyhoff, the Hague, 1936.

L4. ——, *Versuch Einer Theorie der Electrischen und Optischen Erscheinungen in Bewegten Körpern,* Collected Papers, Vol. 5, p. 1. Brill, Leiden, 1895.

L5. ——, letter to Lord Rayleigh, August 18, 1892. Reprinted in [S2].

L6. B. E. Livingston, *Science* **63,** 105 (1926).

L7. H. A. Lorentz, *The Theory of Electrons,* Sec. 169. Teubner, Leipzig, 1909.

L8. J. Larmor (Ed.), *The Scientific Writings of the Late George Francis FitzGerald.* Longmans Green, London, 1902.

L9. ——, [L8], p. lviii.

L10. ——, *Aether and Matter.* Cambridge University Press, Cambridge, 1900.

L11. ——, [L8], p. 514.

L12. H. A. Lorentz, *Arch. Néerl.* **25,** 363 (1892); Collected Papers, Vol. 2, p. 164.

L13. ——, *Versl. K. Ak. Amsterdam* **1,** 74 (1892); Collected Papers, Vol. 4, p. 219.

L14. ——, letter to G. F. FitzGerald, November 10, 1894. Reprinted in [B4].

L15. ——, [L4], Sec. 89.

L16. ——, [L4], Sec. 31.

L17. ——, [L4], Sec. 12.

L18. ——, *Verh. Ges. Deutsch. Naturf. Ärzte* **70,** 56 (1898); Collected Papers, Vol. 7, p. 101.

L19. ——, *Versl. K. Ak. Amsterdam* **10,** 793 (1902); Collected Papers, Vol. 5, p. 139.

L20. ——, *Proc. K. Ak. Amsterdam* **6,** 809 (1904); Collected Papers, Vol. 5, p. 172.

L21. J. Larmor, [L10], Chap. 11.

M1. J. C. Maxwell, *Encyclopedia Britannica,* 9th edn., Vol. 8, 1878. Reprinted in *The Scientific Papers of James Clerk Maxwell,* Vol. 2, p. 763. Dover, New York.

M2. ——, *Nature* **21,** 315 (1880).

M3. A. A. Michelson, *Am. J. Sci.* **22,** 120 (1881).

M4. ——, letter to Lord Rayleigh, March 6, 1887. Reprinted in [S2].

M5. ——, letter to Lord Rayleigh, August 17, 1887. Reprinted in [S2].

M6. —— and E. W. Morley, *Am. J. Sci.* **34,** 333 (1887).

M7. ——, F. G. Pease, and F. Pearson, *Nature* **123,** 88 (1929); *J. Opt. Soc.* **18,** 181 (1929).

M8. E. W. Morley and D. C. Miller, *Phil. Mag,* **9,** 680 (1905).

M9. D. C. Miller, *Rev. Mod. Phys.* **5,** 203 (1933).

M10. ——, *Proc. Nat. Ac. Sci.* **11,** 306 (1925); *Science* **61,** 617 (1925).

M11. ——, *Science* **63,** 433 (1926).

M12. A. A. Michelson, *Studies in Optics,* Chap. 14. University of Chicago Press, Chicago, 1927.

M13. ——, letter to A. Einstein, December 5, 1923.

M14. R. McCormmach in *Dictionary of Scientific Biography,* Vol. 6, p. 340. Scribner's, New York, 1972.

M15. A. I. Miller, *Arch. Hist. Ex. Sci.* **10,** 207 (1973).

M16. H. Minkowski, *Phys. Zeitschr.* **9,** 762 (1908).

M17. A. A. Michelson and E. W. Morley, *Am. J. Sci.* **31,** 377 (1886).

M18. J. Mehra, *Phys. Blätt.* **27,** 385 (1971); University of Texas at Austin, Report CPT-82, 1971.

N1. *Nobel Lectures in Physics 1901–1921,* pp. 159ff. Elsevier, New York, 1967.

O1. T. Ogawa, *Jap. St. Hist. Sci.* **18,** 73 (1979).

O2. O. Heaviside, letter quoted in [L8], p. xxvi.

P1. W. K. H. Panofsky and M. Phillips, *Classical Electricity and Magnetism,* Addison-Wesley, Reading, Mass., 1955.

P2. ——, [P1], p. 174.

P3. ——, [P1], p. 347.

P4. ——, [P1], Chap. 15.

P5. H. Poincaré, *Rev. Métaphys. Morale* **6,** 1 (1898).

P6. ——, *The Value of Science.* Reprinted in *The Foundations of Science* (G. R. Halsted, Tran.). Science Press, New York, 1913.

P7. ——, *Report of the International Physics Congress* (C. Guillaume and L. Poincaré, Eds.), Vol. 1, p. 1. Gauthier-Villars, Paris, 1900.

P8. ——, *Science and Hypothesis.* Dover, New York, 1952.

P9. ——, *Bull. Sci. Math.* **28,** 302 (1904).

P10. ——, *Theorie Mathématique de la Lumière.* Carré, Paris, 1889.

P11. ——, *Électricité et Optique.* Carré and Naud, Paris, 1901.

P12. ——, *Oeuvres,* Vol. 9, pp. 369–426. Gauthier-Villars, Paris, 1954.

P13. ——, *Oeuvres,* Vol. 9. pp. 427–88.

P14. ——, *C. R. Ac. Sci. Paris* **140,** 1504 (1905); *Oeuvres,* Vol. 9, p. 489.

P15. ——, *Rend. Circ. Mat. Palermo* **21,** 129 (1906); *Oeuvres,* Vol. 9, p. 494.

P16. ——, *Oeuvres,* Vol. 9, p. 500.

R1. Rayleigh, *Phil. Mag.* **4,** 678 (1902).

R2. A. Reiser, *Albert Einstein,* p. 52. Boni, New York, 1930.

S1. L. S. Swenson, *The Ethereal Aether,* p. 194. University of Texas Press, Austin, 1972.

S2. R. S. Shankland, *Isis* **58,** 86 (1967).

S3. ——, *Am. J. Phys.* **32,** 16 (1964).

S4. ——, S. W. McCuskey, F. C. Leone, and G. Kuerti, *Rev. Mod. Phys.* **27,** 167 (1955).

S5. R. S. Shankland, Biography Quarterly, Vol. 2, No. 3. University of Hawaii Press, Honolulu, 1979.

S6. ——, *Am. J. Phys.* **31,** 47 (1962); **41,** 895 (1973).

S7. ——, *Am. J. Phys.* **32,** 16 (1964).

T1. F. T. Trouton and H. R. Noble, *Phil. Trans. Roy. Soc.* **A202,** 165 (1903).

V1. O. Veblen, letter to A. Einstein, April 17, 1930.

V2. W. Voigt, *Goett. Nachr.,* 1887, p. 41.

V3. W. Voigt, *AdP* **35,** 370, see footnote on p. 390 (1888).

V4. W. Voigt, *Phys. Zeitschr.* **9,** 762 (1908).

7

The New Kinematics

7a. June 1905: Special Relativity Defined, Lorentz Transformations Derived

1. Relativity's Aesthetic Origins. Without a carrying medium, light can as little be seen as sound can be heard. Such was the sensible prejudice of nineteenth century physics. The better light was understood, the more circumscribed became the properties of its medium, the aether. The best of all possible aethers, it appeared, was one which blows through man and his planet as they speed through this absolutely immobile medium. When light turned out to be a transverse wave phenomenon, the aether had to be declared quasi-rigid.

The special theory of relativity divested the aether of its principal mechanical property, absolute rest, and thereby made the aether redundant. As Einstein put it in the introduction to his June 1905 paper (referred to in this chapter as the June paper), 'the introduction of a "light-aether" will prove to be superfluous since, according to the view to be developed [here], neither will a "space in absolute rest" endowed with special properties be introduced nor will a velocity vector be associated with a point of empty space in which electromagnetic processes take place' [E1].* Special relativity represents the abandonment of mechanical pictures as an aid to the interpretation of electromagnetism. The one preferred coordinate system in absolute rest is forsaken. Its place is taken by an infinite set of preferred coordinate systems, the inertial frames. By definition, any two of these are in uniform motion with respect to each other. The preference for uniformity of relative motion makes this version of relativity a special one.

In the spring of 1905, even before the completion of the relativity paper, Einstein had written to his friend Conrad Habicht, 'The fourth work [i.e., E1, the fourth paper Einstein published in 1905] is available only in draft form and is an electrodynamics of moving bodies in which use is made of a modification of the tenets about space and time; the purely kinematic part of this work will surely interest you' [E2]. Small wonder that Einstein would draw his friend's attention to the kinematic part. In its entirety, the June paper consists of an introduction, five sections on kinematics followed by five sections on electrodynamics, no references, and one acknowledgment. The kinematic part contains the complete first principles of the special relativity theory.

*For an English translation of this paper, see [S1].

As indicated in Chapter 6, special relativity was born after a decade of gestation. However, the crucial kinematic insights which underlie this theory dawned on its author not more than five or six weeks before the actual completion of the paper under discussion. We know this from the talk given by Einstein in Kyoto, in December 1922, which also reveals that this climactic period was preceded by a year of struggle which had led him nowhere. I quote once again from the Kyoto address [O1]:

'I took into consideration Fizeau's experiment, and then attempted to deal with the problems on the assumption that Lorentz's equations concerning the electron should hold as well in the case of our system of coordinates being defined on the moving bodies as defined in vacuo. At any rate, at that time I felt certain of the truth of the Maxwell–Lorentz equations in electrodynamics. All the more, it showed to us the relations of the so-called invariance of the velocity of light that those equations should hold also in the moving frame of reference. This invariance of the velocity of light was, however, in conflict with the rule of addition of velocities we knew of well in mechanics.

'I felt a great difficulty to resolve the question why the two cases were in conflict with each other. I had wasted time almost a year in fruitless considerations, with a hope of some modification of Lorentz's idea, and at the same time I could not but realize that it was a puzzle not easy to solve at all.

'Unexpectedly a friend of mine in Bern then helped me. That was a very beautiful day when I visited him and began to talk with him as follows:

' "I have recently had a question which was difficult for me to understand. So I came here today to bring with me a battle on the question." Trying a lot of discussions with him, I could suddenly comprehend the matter. Next day I visited him again and said to him without greeting: "Thank you. I've completely solved the problem." My solution was really for the very concept of time, that is, that time is not absolutely defined but there is an inseparable connection between time and the signal velocity. With this conception, the foregoing extraordinary difficulty could be thoroughly solved. Five weeks after my recognition of this, the present theory of special relativity was completed.'

The friend in Bern was Besso, close to Einstein since the student days in Zürich, colleague at the patent office since 1904. Thus the Kyoto address makes clear what was the substance of the 'loyal assistance of my friend M. Besso,' to which Einstein devoted the acknowledgment in his June paper. As to the completion of the work in five weeks, since the paper was received by the Annalen der Physik on June 30, Einstein's total concentration on relativity followed immediately upon the relief of his having finished three major projects in statistical physics: the paper on the light-quantum, his thesis, and the paper on Brownian motion, completed on March 17, April 30, and around May 10, respectively.

In 1905 Einstein's belief in 'the truth of the Maxwell–Lorentz equations' was not unqualified, as we shall see later. It was strong enough, however, for him to perceive the conflict between the constancy of the velocity of light (in the vacuum) and the relativity principle of classical mechanics. This principle, already long known by then, states that all mechanical laws should be the same in any two coordinate systems (x,y,z,t) and (x',y',z',t') related by*

$$x' = x - vt \qquad y' = y \qquad z' = z \qquad t' = t \qquad (7.1)$$

Since 1909 these transformations have been called Galilean transformations.** (Recall that in 1905 there existed as yet no evidence against the general validity of Galilean invariance in pure mechanics.) The conflict arises if one attempts to elevate Galilean invariance to a universal principle. An aether at absolute rest hardly fits this scheme of things. Some physicists believed therefore that the very foundations of electrodynamics should be revised.† Einstein opted for the alternative: 'The phenomena of electrodynamics and mechanics possess no properties corresponding to the idea of absolute rest' [E1]. In the June paper, he gave two concrete reasons for this view: first, the absence of experimental evidence for an aether drift and second, the existence of 'asymmetries which do not appear to be inherent in the phenomena.' As an example of such an asymmetry, he considered a system consisting of a magnet and a conductor. If the magnet moves in the presence of a resting conductor, then an electric field is generated which induces a current in the conductor. If, on the other hand, the conductor moves in the presence of the resting magnet, then an electromotive force (proportional to $\vec{v} \times \vec{H}$) is generated, which again causes a current. Transcribed rather freely, one might say that Einstein cared for neither the logical disconnectedness of electricity and magnetism nor the asymmetry between the two coordinate systems just described.

I argued in Chapter 6 that Einstein rejected the nineteenth century explanations of the first-order aether drift effects as unconvincing and artificial and that the second-order Michelson–Morley paradox was to some extent secondary to him. Add to this his remark that 'Maxwell's electrodynamics—as usually understood at the present time—when applied to moving bodies, leads to asymmetries which are not inherent in the phenomena' and one has the motivation for the June paper: Einstein was driven to the special theory of relativity mostly by aesthetic arguments, that is, arguments of simplicity. This same magnificent obsession would stay with him for the rest of his life. It was to lead him to his greatest achievement, general relativity, and to his noble failure, unified field theory.

2. The Two Postulates. The new theory is based in its entirety on two postulates¶ [E1]:

---

*As in the previous chapter, I shall, for simplicity, consider relative motions in the x direction only.

**This term was introduced by Philipp Frank [F1].

†For details, see Section 3 of Pauli's encyclopedia article, in German [P1], or in its English translation [P2].

¶I do not copy Einstein verbatim. The term *inertial frame* gained currency only some time later, as did the terms *Galilean invariance* and *Lorentz invariance*, which I freely use from now on.

1. The laws of physics take the same form in all inertial frames.
2. In any given inertial frame, the velocity of light c is the same whether the light be emitted by a body at rest or by a body in uniform motion.

FitzGerald and Lorentz had already seen that the explanation of the Michelson–Morley experiment demanded the introduction of a new postulate, the contraction hypothesis. Their belief that this contraction is a dynamic effect (molecular forces in a rod in uniform motion differ from the forces in a rod at rest) was corrected by Einstein: the contraction of rods is a necessary consequence of his two postulates and is for the very first time given its proper observational meaning in the June paper.

What is so captivating about the Einstein of 1905 is the apparent ease and the *fraîcheur* with which he introduces new ideas. If free radiation consists of light-quanta, then the emission and absorption of light should also go by discrete steps; if van't Hoff's law holds for solutions, then it should also hold for suspensions; if the velocity of light does not seem to depend on the velocity of the emitter, then why not make that into a postulate? Steps like these were the result of very hard thinking, yet the final product has that quality of greatness of looking easy if not obvious.

The big question was, of course, the compatibility of the two postulates, about which Einstein had the following to say in his review article of 1907 [E3]: 'Surprisingly, it turned out that it was only necessary to formulate the concept of time sufficiently precisely to overcome the first-mentioned difficulty [i e , the Michelson–Morley result, which Einstein did mention for the first time in this 1907 paper]. All that was needed was the insight that an auxiliary quantity introduced by H. A. Lorentz and denoted by him as "local time" can be defined as "time", pure and simple.'

There are as many times as there are inertial frames. That is the gist of the June paper's kinematic sections, which rank among the highest achievements of science, in content as well as in style. If only for enjoyment, these sections ought to be read by all scientists, whether or not they are familiar with relativity. It also seems to me that this kinematics, including the addition of velocity theorem, could and should be taught in high schools as the simplest example of the ways in which modern physics goes beyond everyday intuition.* (If only I could make a similar recommendation for the case of quantum theory. . . .)

I briefly recapitulate the content of the new kinematics.** In a given inertial frame an observer A measures his position $\vec{x}_A$ relative to the origin by means of rigid rods, using (as Einstein states explicitly) 'the methods of Euclidean geometry.' A second observer B does likewise for $\vec{x}_B$. Then A's clock at $\vec{x}_A$ is synchronized with B's clock at $\vec{x}_B$ by means of light signals. If A's clock is synchronous with

---

*See, for example, the excellent popular yet rigorous account by Born [B1].

**More details are found in standard texts, e.g., [M1] and [P3].

B's, and B's with that of a third observer C, then A's is synchronous with C's. Synchronicity is therefore fully defined within any one inertial frame. Because of the second postulate, the use of light signals remains a valid tool for the comparison of the A and B clocks even if, after initial synchronization in the common inertial frame, B and his clock start moving with uniform velocity relative to A, that is, if B joins another inertial frame.

[Remark. In an unpublished manuscript,† written in 1921, Einstein spells out three additional assumptions which are made in this reasoning: (1) Homogeneity: the properties of rods and clocks depend neither on their position nor on the time at which they move, but only on the way in which they move. (2) Isotropy: the properties of rods and clocks are independent of direction. (3) These properties are also independent of their history.]

The time of an event is defined as the reading of a clock coincident with the event and at rest relative to it. Events which are simultaneous in one inertial frame are not simultaneous in another. Einstein's example: two identical rods R_1 and R_2 are coincident in a given inertial frame in which two observers O_1 and O_2 have synchronized their respective clocks. Observer O_1 stays with R_1 in this frame, O_2 moves with R_2 into another inertial frame. Three durations are measured: O_1 measures the time t_1 for a light ray to move from one end of R_1 to the other and back, and O_2 does the same for R_2, finding a time t_2. Observer O_1 also measures the duration t_1' for light to move from one end of R_2 to the other and back. Then $t_1 = t_2$, in accordance with the first postulate, but $t_1 \neq t_1'$: 'We see that we cannot attach *absolute* meaning to the concept of simultaneity.'

The two postulates of special relativity have physical content *only* if the experimental prescriptions for measuring position and time (and, therefore, for velocity) are added. The postulates *together* with these prescriptions fully specify Einstein's theory of special relativity.

3. *From the Postulates to the Lorentz Transformations.*   Let us continue with the example of the two rods. Physics would be incomplete if the inequality $t_1 \neq t_1'$ could not be sharpened into a specific relation between these two durations. Einstein obtained this relation by deriving the Lorentz transformation from his postulates. In essence, his argument runs as follows. Consider two inertial frames, (x,y,z,t) and (x',y',z',t'), the second moving with a velocity v in the x direction relative to the first. At $t = t' = 0$, the two frames coincide. At that moment a spherical light wave is emitted from the joint origin. t seconds later the wave is spread over the sphere

$$x^2 + y^2 + z^2 = c^2 t^2 \tag{7.2}$$

The compatibility of the two postulates demands that the wave be equivalently spread over

$$(x')^2 + (y')^2 + (z')^2 = c^2(t')^2 \tag{7.3}$$

†This is the Morgan manuscript, the origins of which are described in Chapter 9.

The relations between the two sets of coordinates implied by these two equations are assumed to be linear, in accordance with the homogeneity of space and time. Then simple arithmetic yields

$$x' = \epsilon\gamma(x - vt) \qquad y' = \epsilon y \qquad z' = \epsilon z \qquad t' = \epsilon\gamma(t - vx/c^2), \quad (7.4)$$
$$\gamma = (1 - v^2/c^2)^{-1/2} \qquad (7.5)$$

where ϵ is an arbitrary scale factor depending on v only. Since the product of this transformation and its inverse should yield the identity, one has

$$\epsilon(v)\epsilon(-v) = 1 \qquad (7.6)$$

Symmetry demands that the transformations on y and z should not change if $v \rightarrow -v$, and hence

$$\epsilon(v) = \epsilon(-v) \qquad (7.7)$$

Thus $\epsilon(v) = 1$ (since $\epsilon(0) = 1$) and

$$x' = \gamma(x - vt) \qquad y' = y \qquad z' = z \qquad t' = \gamma(t - vx/c^2) \quad (7.8)$$

In Chapter 6, we encountered Eqs. 7.4–7.8 in the discussion of papers by Lorentz and Poincaré. The derivation of the Lorentz transformations (Eq. 7.8) from first principles occurs for the first time in Einstein's paper, however.*

Einstein also pointed out that transformations of the type shown in Eq. 7.8 form a group, 'wie dies sein muss,' as it should be**: two successive transformations with velocities v_1, v_2 in the same direction result in a new transformation of the form of Eq. 7.8 with a velocity v given by

$$v = \frac{v_1 + v_2}{1 + v_1 v_2/c^2} \qquad (7.9)$$

Twenty years later, Einstein heard something about the Lorentz group that greatly surprised him. It happened while he was in Leiden. In October 1925 George Eugene Uhlenbeck and Samuel Goudsmit had discovered the spin of the electron [U1] and thereby explained the occurrence of the alkali doublets, but for a brief period it appeared that the magnitude of the doublet splitting did not come out correctly. Then Llewellyn Thomas supplied the missing factor, 2, now known as the Thomas factor [T1]. Uhlenbeck told me that he did not understand a word of Thomas's work when it first came out. 'I remember that, when I first heard about it, it seemed unbelievable that a relativistic effect could give a factor of 2 instead of something of order v/c. . . . Even the cognoscenti of the relativity theory (Einstein included!) were quite surprised' [U2]. At the heart of the Thomas precession lies the fact that a Lorentz transformation with velocity $\vec{v}_1$ followed by a second one with a velocity $\vec{v}_2$ in a different direction does not lead to the same

*See [R1] for interesting comments on the roles of postulates and observations in the special theory of relativity.

**He did not expand on this cryptic statement.

inertial frame as one single Lorentz transformation with the velocity $\vec{v}_1 + \vec{v}_2$ [K1]. (It took Pauli a few weeks before he grasped Thomas's point.*)

4. Applications.   In his June paper, Einstein put his postulates to use in ways which are now standard textbook material. No derivations will therefore be given in what follows next. (For Einstein's own derivations, see [S1].)

a) From the postulates to the Lorentz transformations, as already discussed.

b) From the Lorentz transformations to the FitzGerald–Lorentz contraction of rods and the dilation of time:

$$\gamma l = l_0 \qquad t = \gamma t_0 \qquad\qquad (7.10)$$

where l_0 and t_0 are, respectively, a length and a duration in the rest frame. The kinematic origins of these relations were not at once generally understood. In 1911 Einstein still had to explain: 'The question whether the Lorentz contraction does or does not exist is confusing. It does not "really" exist in so far as it does not exist for an observer who moves [with the rod]; it "really" exists, however, in the sense that it can as a matter of principle be demonstrated by a resting observer' [E4].

c) The addition of velocities, already mentioned.

d) The relativistic expression of the aberration from the zenith:

$$tg\alpha = \gamma \frac{v}{c} \qquad\qquad (7.11)$$

e) The transformation law for light frequencies:

$$\nu' = \gamma\nu(1 - v \cos \phi/c) \qquad\qquad (7.12)$$

where ϕ is the angle between a monochromatic light ray with frequency ν and the x direction. Thus Einstein is the discoverer of the transverse Doppler effect: ν' differs from ν even if the motion of the light source is perpendicular to the direction of observation. In 1907 he published a brief note about the experimental detectability of the transverse effect [E5].

f) *Not* found in the June paper is a derivation of the Fresnel formula**

$$c' = \frac{c}{n} + v(1 - 1/n^2) \qquad\qquad (7.13)$$

---

*See the correspondence between Pauli, Bohr, and Kramers between February 26 and March 12, 1926 [P4].

**See Section 6a for the meaning of the various symbols. For comments by Einstein on the drag in dispersive media, see [E5a].

which is an immediate consequence of Eq. 7.9: let $v_1 = c/n$, $v_2 = v$ and expand to the first order in $v_1 v_2 / c^2$. I find the absence of this derivation in the June paper more remarkable than the absence of any mention of Michelson and Morley. The labor involved is not excessive, the Fizeau experiment had been very important for Einstein's thinking, and a successful aether-free derivation might have pleased even a man like Einstein, who was not given to counting feathers in his cap. The honor of the first derivation (in 1907) goes to Max von Laue, who pointed out that 'according to the relativity principle, light is *completely* dragged along by the body [i.e., the streaming fluid], but just because of that its velocity relative to an observer who does not participate in the motion of the body does not equal the vector sum of its velocity relative to the body and [the velocity] of the body relative to the observer' [L1]. As was noted in Chapter 6, for small v/c it is possible to derive Eq. 7.13 by means of a dynamic calculation that does not explicitly involve relativity [P5]. The kinematic derivation just given does not mean that such a calculation is incorrect, but rather that it is not necessary. Lorentz invariance suffices to obtain the desired result.

g) Einstein rather casually mentioned that if two synchronous clocks C_1 and C_2 are at the same initial position and if C_2 leaves A and moves along a closed orbit, then, upon return to A, C_2 will run slow relative to C_1. He called this result a theorem and cannot be held responsible for the misnomer *clock paradox*, which is of later vintage. However, as Einstein himself explained some time later [E6], the logic of special relativity does not suffice for the explanation of this phenomenon (which has since so often been observed in the laboratory) since frames other than inertial ones come into play.

h) Covariance of the electrodynamic equations. Using a horrible but not uncommon notation in which each component of the electric and magnetic field has its own name,* Einstein proved the Lorentz covariance of the Maxwell–Lorentz equations, first for the source-free case, then for the case with sources. He also discussed the equations of motion of an electrically charged particle with charge e and mass m in an external electromagnetic field. In a frame $(\dot{x},t)$ in which the particle is instantaneously at rest, these equations are

$$m \frac{d^2 \vec{x}}{dt^2} = e\vec{E} \tag{7.14}$$

Applying the transformations (Eq. 7.8), he found that in a frame with velocity v in the x direction:

$$m\gamma^3 \frac{d^2 x'}{d(t')^2} = K'_{x'} \qquad m\gamma \frac{d^2 y'}{d(t')^2} = K'_{y} \qquad m\gamma \frac{d^2 z'}{d(t')^2} = K'_{z} \tag{7.15}$$

$$\vec{K}' = e(\vec{E}' + \vec{v} \times \vec{H}'/c) \tag{7.16}$$

*Hertz, Planck, and Poincaré did likewise. Lorentz used three-vector language.

and thus obtained what he called a 'new manner of expression' for the Lorentz force: whereas in 1895 Lorentz [L2] had introduced Eq. 7.16 as a new assumption (see Eq. 6.13), Einstein obtained this force kinematically from the purely electric force acting on a charged particle that is instantaneously at rest. He also gave an expression for the kinetic energy W of the particle for the case where accelerations are small and therefore no energy is given off in the form of radiation. In that case,

$$W = \int K'_{x'} dx' = m \int_0^v \gamma^3 v \, dv = mc^2(\gamma - 1) \qquad (7.17)$$

a relation which led him to comment: 'When $v = c$, W becomes infinite. Velocities greater than light have ... no possibilities of existence.' (During 1907 Einstein had a correspondence with W. Wien on this question.)

[Remark. This conclusion is perhaps not quite correct. The precise statement is: If a particle moves with a velocity smaller (larger) than c in one inertial frame, then it moves with a velocity smaller (larger) than c in all inertial frames. (The relative velocity of inertial frames is $\le c$ by definition.) Thus c is a velocity barrier in two respects. According to Eq. 7.9, c is the upper (lower) limit for a particle moving with sublight (superlight) velocity. Several physicists have speculated about the weird properties of 'tachyons,' the name coined by Gerald Feinberg [F2] for hypothetical superlight-velocity particles.* Tachyons can appear in our cosy sub-c world only if they are produced in pairs. Tachyon physics is therefore necessarily a topic in quantum field theory. The quantum theory of free tachyons has been developed to some extent [F2]. The theoretical description of interactions involving tachyons is thus far an open problem.]

5. *Relativity Theory and Quantum Theory.* The June paper also contains the transformation law for the energy E of a light beam:

$$E' = \gamma E(1 - v \cos \phi/c) \qquad (7.18)$$

(where ϕ is defined as in Eq. 7.12) as well as the following comment by Einstein on the similarities between Eqs. 7.12 and 7.18: 'It is remarkable that the energy and the frequency of a light complex vary with the state of motion of the observer in accordance with the same law.'

Three months earlier, Einstein had completed a paper which contains the relation

$$E = h\nu \qquad (7.19)$$

between the energy and the frequency of a light-quantum [E7]. It is therefore of interest that Einstein would call the similarities in transformation properties of E

---

*See, e.g., [B2] and [F2] also for references to earlier literature.

and ν remarkable without referring to his own quantum relation between the energy and the frequency of light, which must have been fresh in his mind. Remarkable though this silence may be, it is not inexplicable. As I have already intimated, Einstein's belief in the validity of the Maxwell–Lorentz electrodynamics was strong but not unqualified. As he put it in his light-quantum paper, 'The wave theory of light which operates with continuous functions of space variables has proved itself an excellent tool for the description of purely optical phenomena. . . . [However] it is conceivable that [this] theory may lead to conflicts with experiment when one applies it to the phenomena of the generation and conversion of light' [E7]. He considered the Maxwell–Lorentz theory of the *free* electromagnetic field to be so good that 'it will probably never be replaced by another theory'; but he had his doubts about this theory where the interaction of light and matter was concerned. Also, he rightly regarded his own quantum hypotheses of 1905 more of a new phenomenological description than a new theory, in sharp contrast to his relativity theory, which he rightly regarded as a true theory with clearly defined first principles. Thus it is not surprising that he would derive Eqs. 7.12 and 7.18 separately, without appeal to Eq. 7.19.

Not just in 1905 but throughout his life Einstein considered quantum theory as a preliminary to a true theory and relativity as the royal road toward such a theory. But that is a subject that will have to wait until Chapter 26.

6. *'I Could Have Said That More Simply.'*   In the fall of 1943 Einstein received a visit from Julian Boyd, then the librarian of the Princeton University library. The purpose of Boyd's call was to ask Einstein to give the manuscript of the June paper to the Book and Authors War Bond Committee as a contribution to the sale of war bonds. Einstein replied that he had discarded the original manuscript after its publication but added that he was prepared to write out a copy of its text in his own hand. This offer was gladly accepted. Einstein completed this task on November 21, 1943. Under the auspices of the committee, this manuscript was auctioned at a sale in Kansas City on February 3, 1944, sponsored by the Kansas City Women's City Club and the Women's Division of the Kansas City War Finance Committee. The winning bid of six and a half million dollars was made by the Kansas City Life Insurance Company. On that same occasion, an original incomplete manuscript by Einstein and Valentin Bargmann, entitled 'Das Bi-Vektor Feld,' was auctioned for five million dollars.* Soon after these events both manuscripts were given to the Library of Congress [B3].

Helen Dukas told me how the copy of the June paper was produced. She would sit next to Einstein and dictate the text to him. At one point, Einstein lay down his pen, turned to Helen and asked her whether he had really said what she had just dictated to him. When assured that he had, Einstein said, 'Das hätte ich einfacher sagen können.'

---

*This paper was published in English in 1944 [E8].

7b. September 1905: About $E = mc^2$

'The mass of a body is a measure of its energy content,' Einstein, technical expert third class at the patent office in Bern, concluded in September 1905 [E9]. 'The law of conservation of mass is a special case of the law of conservation of energy,' Einstein, technical expert second class, wrote in May 1906 [E10]. 'In regard to inertia, a mass m is equivalent to an energy content ... mc^2. This result is of extraordinary importance since [it implies that] the inertial mass and the energy of a physical system appear as equivalent things,' he stated in 1907 [E11]. For special cases the equivalence of mass and energy had been known for about twenty-five years.* The novelty of 1905 was the generality of this connection.

Einstein's proof of 1905** for the relation

$$E = mc^2 \tag{7.20}$$

runs as follows. Consider a body with energy E_i at rest in a given inertial frame. The body next emits plane waves of light with energy $L/2$ in a direction making an angle ϕ with the x axis and an equal quantity of light in the opposite direction. After these emissions the body has an energy E_f, so that $\Delta E = E_i - E_f = L$. Consider this same situation as seen from an inertial frame moving with a velocity v in the x direction. According to Eq. 7.18, $\Delta E' = E_i' - E_f' = \gamma L$ independently of ϕ. Thus

$$\Delta E' - \Delta E = L(\gamma - 1) \tag{7.21}$$

or, to second order,

$$\Delta E' - \Delta E = \frac{1}{2}\left(\frac{L}{c^2}\right)v^2 \tag{7.22}$$

Now, Einstein said, note that Eq. 7.21 for the energy differential is identical in structure to Eq. 7.17 for the kinetic energy differential of a particle, so that 'if a body gives off the energy L in the form of radiation, its mass diminishes by L/c^2. The fact that the energy withdrawn from the body becomes energy of radiation evidently makes no difference.'

This brief paper of September 1905 ends with the remark that bodies 'whose energy content is variable to a high degree, for example, radium salts,' may perhaps be used to test this prediction. But Einstein was not quite sure. In the fall of 1905 he wrote to Habicht, 'The line of thought is amusing and fascinating, but

---

*See Section 7e on electromagnetic mass. Also before September 1905, Fritz Hasenöhrl had discovered that the kinetic energy of a cavity increases when it is filled with radiation, in such a way that the mass of the system appears to increase [H1].

**He gave two proofs in later years. In 1934 he gave the Gibbs lecture in Pittsburgh and deduced Eq. 7.20 from the validity in all inertial frames of energy and momentum conservation for a system of point particles [E12]. In 1946 he gave an elementary derivation in which the equations for the aberration of light and the radiation pressure are assumed given [E13].

I cannot know whether the dear Lord doesn't laugh about this and has played a trick on me' (. . . mich an der Nase herumgeführt hat) [E14]. In his 1907 review he considered it 'of course out of the question' to reach the experimental precision necessary for using radium as a test [E15]. In another review, written in 1910, he remarked that 'for the moment there is no hope whatsoever' for the experimental verification of the mass–energy equivalence [E16].

In all these instances, Einstein had in mind the loss of weight resulting from radioactive transformations. The first to remark that the energy–mass relation bears on binding energy was Planck. In 1907 he estimated the mass equivalent of the molecular binding energy for a mole of water [P6]. This amount (about 10^{-8} g) was of course too small to be observed—but at least it could be calculated. A quarter of a century had to pass before a similar estimate could be made for nuclear binding energy. Even that question did not exist until 1911, the year the nuclear model of the atom was published. Two years later, Paul Langevin had an idea: 'It seems to me that the inertial mass of the internal energy [of nuclei] is evidenced by the existence of certain deviations from the law of Prout' [L3]. That was also the year in which J. J. Thomson achieved the first isotope separation. Langevin's interesting thought did not take account of the influence of isotopic mixing and therefore overrated nuclear binding effects. Next came the confusion that the nucleus was supposed to consist of protons and electrons—no one had the right constituents yet. Still, Pauli was correct in surmising—we are now in 1921—that 'perhaps the law of the inertia of energy will be tested *at some future time* [my italics] by observations on the stability of nuclei' [P7]. In 1930 it was written in the bible of nuclear physics of the day that one can deduce from the binding energy of the alpha particle that a free proton weighs 6.7 MeV more than a proton bound in a helium nucleus [R2]. What else could one say in terms of a proton–electron model of the nucleus?

Nuclear binding energy and its relation to $E = mc^2$ came into its own in the 1930s. In 1937 it was possible to calculate the velocity of light from nuclear reactions in which the masses of the initial and final products and also the energy release in the reaction were known. The resulting value for c was accurate to within less than one half of one per cent [B4]. When in 1939 Einstein sent his well-known letter to President Roosevelt, it is just barely imaginable that he might have recalled what he wrote in 1907: 'It is possible that radioactive processes may become known in which a considerably larger percentage of the mass of the initial atom is converted into radiations of various kinds than is the case for radium' [E15].

7c. Early Responses

Maja Einstein's biographical sketch gives a clear picture of her brother's mood shortly after the acceptance of his June paper by the *Annalen der Physik*: 'The young scholar imagined that his publication in the renowned and much-read journal would draw immediate attention. He expected sharp opposition and the severest criticism. But he was very disappointed. His publication was followed by an icy silence. The next few issues of the journal did not mention his paper at all. The professional circles took an attitude of wait and see. Some time after the appearance of the paper, Albert Einstein received a letter from Berlin. It was sent by the well-known Professor Planck, who asked for clarification of some points which were obscure to him. After the long wait this was the first sign that his paper had been at all read. The joy of the young scientist was especially great because the recognition of his activities came from one of the greatest physicists of that time' [M2]. Maja also mentioned that some time thereafter letters began to arrive addressed to 'Professor Einstein at the University of Bern.'

The rapidity with which special relativity became a topic of discussion and research is largely due to Planck's early interest. In his scientific autobiography, Planck gave his reasons for being so strongly drawn to Einstein's theory: 'For me its appeal lay in the fact that I could strive toward deducing absolute, invariant features following from its theorems' [P7a]. The search for the absolute—forever Planck's main purpose in science—had found a new focus. 'Like the quantum of action in the quantum theory, so the velocity of light is the absolute, central point of the theory of relativity.' During the winter semester of 1905–6, Planck presented Einstein's theory in the physics colloquium in Berlin. This lecture was attended by his assistant von Laue. As a result von Laue became another early convert to relativity, published in 1907 the pretty note [L1] on the Fizeau experiment, did more good work on the special theory, and became the author of the first monograph on special relativity [L4]. Planck also discussed some implications of the 'Relativtheorie' in a scientific meeting held in September 1906 [P8]. The first PhD thesis on relativity was completed under his direction [M3].

The first paper bearing on relativity but published by someone other than Einstein was by Planck [P6], as best I know. Among his new results I mention the first occasion on which the momentum–velocity relation

$$\vec{p} = \gamma m \vec{v} \tag{7.23}$$

the transformation laws

$$p'_x = \gamma \left(p_x - \frac{vE}{c^2} \right) \qquad p'_y = p_y$$

$$p'_z = p_z \qquad E' = \gamma \left(E - \frac{vp_x}{c^2} \right) \tag{7.24}$$

and the variational principle

$$\delta \int L dt = 0 \tag{7.25}$$

$$L = \gamma mc^2 \tag{7.26}$$

of relativistic point mechanics were written down. Planck derived Eq. 7.23 from the action of an electromagnetic field on a charged point particle, rewriting Eqs.

7.15, 7.16 as $d(m\gamma\dot{\vec{x}}')/dt' = \vec{K}'$. The straightforward derivation of Eq. 7.23 via the energy–momentum conservation laws of mechanics was not found until 1909 [L5].

Among other early papers on relativity, I mention one by Ehrenfest in 1907 [E17], in which is asked for the first time the important question: How does one apply Lorentz transformations to a rigid body?

Planck was also the first to apply relativity to the quantum theory. He noted that the action is an invariant, not only for point mechanics, (where it equals the quantity $\int L dt$ in Eq. 7.25), but in general. From this he deduced that his constant h is a relativistic invariant. 'It is evident that because of this theorem the significance of the principle of least action is extended in a new direction' [P9]—a conclusion Einstein might have drawn from his Eqs. 7.13, 7.18, and 7.19.

Not only the theoreticians took early note of the relativity theory. As early as 1906, there was already interest from experimentalists in the validity of the relation

$$E = \gamma mc^2 \tag{7.27}$$

between the total energy and the velocity of a beta ray, as will be discussed in Section 7e.

The publication of the 1905 papers on special relativity marked the beginning of the end of Einstein's splendid isolation at the patent office. From 1906 on, visitors would come to Bern to discuss the theory with him. Von Laue was one of the first (perhaps the very first) to do so. 'The young man who met me made such an unexpected impression on me that I could not believe he could be the father of the relativity theory,' von Laue later recalled [S2].* Other young men came as well. From Würzburg Johann Jakob Laub wrote to Einstein, asking if he could work with him for three months [L6]; the ensuing stay of Laub in Bern led to Einstein's first papers published jointly with a collaborator [E18, E19]. Rudolf Ladenburg, who became a close friend of Einstein in the Princeton years, came from Breslau (now Wrocław). Yet in these early years the relativists were few in number. In July 1907 Planck wrote to Einstein, 'As long as the advocates of the relativity principle form such a modest-sized crowd, it is doubly important for them to agree with one another' [P10].

Then, in 1908, came the 'space and time' lecture of Herman Minkowski. In 1902, Minkowski, at one time Einstein's teacher in Zürich, had moved to the University of Goettingen. There, on November 5, 1907, he gave a colloquium about relativity in which he identified Lorentz transformations with pseudorotations for which

$$x_1^2 + x_2^2 + x_3^2 + x_4^2 \text{ is invariant,} \qquad x_4 = ict \tag{7.28}$$

---

*Von Laue had been on an alpine trip before coming to Bern. Einstein delivered himself of the opinion, 'I don't understand how one can walk around up there' [S3].

where x_1, x_2, x_3 denote the spatial variables. The most important remarks made in this colloquium were that the electromagnetic potentials as well as the charge–current densities are vectors with respect to the Lorentz group, while the electromagnetic field strengths form a second-rank tensor (or a Traktor, as Minkowski then called it). Soon thereafter Minkowski published a detailed paper [M5] in which for the first time the Maxwell–Lorentz equations are presented in their modern tensor form, the equations of point mechanics are given a similar treatment, and the inadequacy of the Newtonian gravitation theory from the relativistic point of view is discussed. Terms such as *spacelike vector, timelike vector, light cone,* and *world line* stem from this paper.

Thus began the enormous formal simplification of special relativity. Initially, Einstein was not impressed and regarded the transcriptions of his theory into tensor form as 'überflüssige Gelehrsamkeit,' (superfluous learnedness).* However, in 1912 he adopted tensor methods and in 1916 acknowledged his indebtedness to Minkowski for having greatly facilitated the transition from special to general relativity [E20].

Minkowski's semitechnical report on these matters, the 'space and time' lecture given in Cologne in 1908, began with these words:** 'The views of space and time which I wish to lay before you have sprung from the soil of experimental physics, and therein lies their strength. They are radical. Henceforth space by itself, and time by itself, are doomed to fade away into mere shadows, and only a kind of union of the two will preserve an independent reality.' He ended as follows: 'The validity without exception of the world postulate [i.e., the relativity postulates], I like to think, is the true nucleus of an electromagnetic image of the world, which, discovered by Lorentz, and further revealed by Einstein, now lies open in the full light of day' [M6]. It is hardly surprising that these opening and closing statements caused a tremendous stir among his listeners, though probably few of them followed the lucid remarks he made in the body of the speech. Minkowski did not live to see his lecture appear in print. In January 1909 he died of appendicitis. Hilbert called him 'a gift of heaven' when he spoke in his memory [H2].

The rapid growth of Einstein's reputation in scientific circles dates from about 1908. In July 1909 the University of Geneva conferred the title of doctor honoris causa 'à Monsieur Einstein, Expert du Bureau Fédéral de la Propriété intellectuelle.' I do not know what citation accompanied this degree. However, Charles Guye, then professor of experimental physics at Geneva, must have had a hand in this. Since Guye's interests centered largely on the velocity dependence of beta-ray energies, it is probable that Einstein received this first of many honors because of relativity.

---

*Einstein told this to V. Bargmann, whom I thank for in turn relating it to me.

**The text of this colloquium was prepared for publication by Sommerfeld. It appeared in 1915 [M4], long after Minkowski's death. This paper is not included in Minkowski collected works (published in 1911) [M5].

Early in 1912, Wilhelm Wien, Nobel laureate in physics for 1911, wrote to Stockholm to make the following recommendation for the year 1912:* 'I propose to award the prize in equal shares to H. A. Lorentz in Leiden and A. Einstein in Prague. As my motivation for this proposal, I would like to make the following observations. The principle of relativity has eliminated the difficulties which existed in electrodynamics and has made it possible to predict for a moving system all electromagnetic phenomena which are known for a system at rest.' After enumerating some features of the theory he continued, 'From a purely logical point of view, the relativity principle must be considered as one of the most significant accomplishments ever achieved in theoretical physics. Regarding the confirmation of the theory by experiment, in this respect the situation resembles the experimental confirmation of the conservation of energy. [Relativity] was discovered in an inductive way, after all attempts to detect absolute motion had failed. . . . While Lorentz must be considered as the first to have found the mathematical content of the relativity principle, Einstein succeeded in reducing it to a simple principle. One should therefore assess the merits of both investigators as being comparable. . . .'

Then and later the special theory would have its occasional detractors. However, Wien's excellent account shows that it had taken the real pros a reasonably short time to realize that the special theory of relativity constituted a major advance.

7d. Einstein and the Special Theory After 1905

The fifth section of Einstein's review paper on relativity, completed in 1907, deals with gravitation and contains this statement: 'The principle of the constancy of the light velocity can be used also here [i.e., in the presence of gravitation] for the definition of simultaneity, provided one restricts oneself to very small light paths' [E3]. Einstein already knew then that the special theory was only a beginning (see Chapter 9). This largely explains why the special theory per se soon faded from the center of his interests. Also, he was not one to follow up on his main ideas with elaborations of their detailed technical consequences. In addition, from 1908 until some time in 1911 the quantum theory rather than relativity was uppermost in his mind (see Chapter 10).

Apart from review articles and general lectures, Einstein's work on the consequences of the special theory was over by 1909. I shall confine myself to giving a short chronology of his post-1905 papers on this subject. This work is discussed and set in context by Pauli [P1, P2].

1906. Discussion of center-of-gravity motion in special relativity [E10] (see especially [M1] for a detailed discussion of this subject).

*See Chapter 30.

1906. A comment on the possibilities for determining the quantity $(1 - v^2/c^2)$ in beta-ray experiments [E21].

1907. A remark on the detectability of the transverse Doppler effect [E5].

1907. Brief remarks on Ehrenfest's query concerning rigid bodies: 'To date both the dynamics and the kinematics of the rigid body ... must be considered unknown' [E22].

1907. Earlier Einstein had derived the expression $mc^2(\gamma - 1)$ for the kinetic energy. Now he introduces the form γmc^2 for the total energy. Furthermore, the transformation of energy and momentum in the presence of external forces (i.e., for open systems) is derived.* Further ruminations about the rigid body: 'If relativistic electrodynamics is correct, then we are still far from having a dynamics for the translation of rigid bodies' [E23]. In this paper Einstein also expresses an opinion concerning the bearing of his recent light-quantum hypothesis on the validity of the free Maxwell equations. It seemed to him that these equations should be applicable as long as one deals with electromagnetic energy amounts or energy transfers which are not too small, just as—he notes—the laws of thermodynamics may be applied as long as Brownian-motion-type effects (fluctuations) are negligible.

1907. The review paper [E3]. This is the transitional paper from the special to the general theory of relativity. Among the points discussed and not mentioned in the foregoing are (1) the remark that the total electric charge of a closed system is Lorentz invariant, (2) comments on the beta-ray experiments of Kaufmann, a topic to be discussed in the next section and, (3) a discussion of relativistic thermodynamics.**

1908–10. Papers with Laub on the relativistic electrodynamics of ponderable media [E18, E19] (see [P1] or [P2], Sections 33, 35).

A further comment on this subject appeared in 1909 [E25]. In 1910, Einstein published a brief note on the nonrelativistic definition of the ponderomotive force in a magnetic field [E26].

This concludes the brief catalog of Einstein's later contributions to special relativity. (I have already mentioned that in 1935 [E12] and again in 1946 [E13] he gave alternative derivations of $E = mc^2$.) In later years he reviewed the special theory on several occasions, starting with the first lecture he gave at a physics conference [E27], and again in 1910 [E28], 1911 [E29], 1914 [E30], 1915 [E31], and 1925 [E32]. Special relativity is, of course, discussed in his book *The Meaning of Relativity* [E33]. The first newspaper article he ever wrote deals largely with the special theory [E34]; he wrote reviews of books bearing on this subject, in praise of writings by Brill [E35], Lorentz [E35], and Pauli [E36].

---

*See [P1] or [P2], Section 43.

**For a discussion of the early contributions to this subject, see [P1] or [P2], Sections 46–49; see also [E24]. For a subsequent severe criticism of these papers, see [O2]. Since this subject remains controversial to this day (see, e.g., [L7]), it does not lend itself as yet to historic assessment.

We have now discussed special relativity from its nineteenth century antecedents to Einstein's motivation, his paper of 1905 and its sequels, and the early reactions to the new theory. I shall not discuss the further developments in classical special relativity. Its impact on modern physics is assessed in papers by Wolfgang Panofsky [P11] and Edward Purcell [P12].

Remaining unfinished business, mainly related to the roles of Einstein, Lorentz, and Poincaré, will be discussed in Chapter 8. By way of transition, let us consider the problem of electromagnetic mass.

7e. Electromagnetic Mass: The First Century*

Long before it was known that the equivalence of energy and inertial mass is a necessary consequence of the relativity postulates and that this equivalence applies to all forms of energy, long before it was known that the separate conservation laws of energy and of mass merge into one, there was a time when dynamic rather than kinematic arguments led to the notion of electromagnetic mass, a form of energy arising specifically in the case of a charged particle coupled to its own electromagnetic field. The electromagnetic mass concept celebrates its first centennial as these lines are written. The investigations of the self-energy problem of the electron by men like Abraham, Lorentz, and Poincaré have long since ceased to be relevant. All that has remained from those early times is that we still do not understand the problem.

'A close analogy to this question of electromagnetic mass is furnished by a simple hydrodynamic problem,' Lorentz told his listeners at Columbia University early in 1906 [L8]. The problem he had in mind was the motion of a solid, perfectly smooth sphere of mass m_0 moving uniformly with a velocity $\vec{v}$ in an infinite, incompressible, ideal fluid. Motions of this kind had been analyzed as early as 1842 by Stokes [S4]. Stokes had shown that the kinetic energy E and the momentum p of the system are given by $E = \frac{1}{2}mv^2$ and $p = mv$, where $m = m_0 + \mu$. The parameter μ—the induced, or hydrodynamic, mass—depends on the radius of the sphere and the density of the fluid. The analogy to which Lorentz referred was first noted by J. J. Thomson, who in 1881 had studied the problem 'of a charged sphere moving through an unlimited space filled with a medium of specific inductive capacity K. . . . The resistance [to the sphere's motion] . . . must correspond to the resistance theoretically experienced by a solid in moving through a perfect fluid' [T2]. Thomson calculated the kinetic energy of the system for small velocities and found it to be of the form $E = \frac{1}{2}mv^2$, where $m = m_0 + \mu$: 'The effect of the electrification is the same as if the mass of the sphere were

*Some of the material of this section was presented earlier in an article on the history of the theory of the electron [P13].

increased. . . .' Thus he discovered the electromagnetic mass μ, though he did not give it that name. The reader will enjoy repeating the calculation he made for the μ of the earth electrified to the highest potential possible without discharge.

Continuing his Columbia lecture, Lorentz remarked, 'If, in the case of the ball moving in the perfect fluid, we were obliged to confine ourselves to experiments in which we measure the external forces applied to the body and the accelerations produced by them, we should be able to determine the effective mass $[m_0 + \mu]$, but it would be impossible to find the values of m_0 and $[\mu]$ separately. Now, it is very important that in the experimental investigation of the motion of an electron, we can go one step farther. This is due to the fact that the electromagnetic mass is not a constant but increases with velocity' [L8].

Not long after Thomson made his calculations, it became clear that the energy of the charged sphere has a much more complicated form than $\frac{1}{2}mv^2$ if effects depending on v/c are included (see, e.g., [H3, S5, S6]). The charged hard-sphere calculations to which Lorentz referred in his lectures were those performed in Goettingen by Max Abraham, whose results seemed to be confirmed by experiments performed by his friend Walter Kaufmann, also in Goettingen.*

There is a tragic touch to the scientific career of both these men. In 1897, Kaufmann had done very good cathode-ray experiments which led him to conclude: 'If one makes the plausible assumption that the moving particles are ions, then e/m should have a different value for each substance and the deflection [in electric and magnetic fields] should depend on the nature of the electrodes or on the nature of the gas [in the cathode tube]. Neither is the case. Moreover, a simple calculation shows that the explanation of the observed deflections demands that e/m should be about 10^7, while even for hydrogen $[e/m]$ is only about 10^4' [K2]. Had Kaufmann added one conjectural sentence to his paper, completed in April 1897, he would have been remembered as an independent discoverer of the electron. On the 30th of that same month, J. J. Thomson gave a lecture on cathode rays before the Royal Institution in which he discussed his own very similar results obtained by very similar methods but from which he drew a quite firm conclusion: 'These numbers seem to favor the hypothesis that the carriers of the charges are smaller than the atoms of hydrogen' [T3]. It seems to me that Kaufmann's paper deserves to be remembered even though he lacked Thomson's audacity in making the final jump toward the physics of new particles.

As for Abraham, he was a very gifted theoretical physicist (Einstein seriously considered him as his successor when in 1914 he left the ETH for Berlin), but it was his fate to be at scientific odds with Einstein, in regard both to the special theory and the general theory of relativity—and to lose in both instances. We shall encounter him again in Chapter 13.

I return to the electromagnetic mass problem. Kaufmann was the first to study experimentally the energy–velocity relation of electrons. In 1901 he published a paper on this subject, entitled 'The Magnetic and Electric Deflectability of Bec-

*For details about this episode, see [G1].

querel Rays [i.e., β-rays] and the Apparent Mass of the Electron' [K3]. Stimulated by these investigations, Abraham soon thereafter produced the complete
answers for the electromagnetic energy (E_{elm}) and the electromagnetic momentum
(p_{elm}) of an electron considered as a hard sphere with charge e and radius a and
with uniform charge distribution ($\beta = v/c$, $\mu = 2e^2/3ac^2$):

$$E_{\text{elm}} = \frac{e^2}{2a}\left(\frac{1}{\beta}\ln\frac{1+\beta}{1-\beta} - 1\right) \approx \frac{e^2}{2a} + \frac{1}{2}\mu v^2 + \cdots \qquad (7.29)$$

$$p_{\text{elm}} = \frac{e^2}{2ac\beta}\left(\frac{1+\beta^2}{2\beta}\ln\frac{1+\beta}{1-\beta} - 1\right) \approx \mu v + \cdots \qquad (7.30)$$

At the 74th Naturforscherversammlung, held in Karlsbad in September 1902,
Kaufmann presented his latest experimental results [K4]. Immediately after him,
Abraham presented his theory [A1]. Kaufmann concluded that 'the dependence
[of E on v] is exactly represented by Abraham's formula.' Abraham said, 'It now
becomes necessary to base the dynamics of the electrons from the outset on electromagnetic considerations' (in 1903 he published his main detailed article on the
rigid electron [A2]). One sees what Lorentz meant in his Columbia lectures: if it
would have been true, if it could have been true, that the E–v relation were
experimentally exactly as given by Eq. 7.29, then two things would have been
known: the electron is a little rigid sphere and its mass is purely electromagnetic
in origin.

Such was the situation when in 1904 Lorentz proposed a new model: the electron at rest is again a little sphere, but it is subject to the FitzGerald–Lorentz
contraction [L9]. This model yields a velocity dependence different from Eqs. 7.29
and 7.30:

$$E_{\text{elm}} = \gamma\mu_o c^2\left(1 + \frac{\beta^2}{3}\right) \approx \mu_o c^2 + \frac{1}{2}\mu_1 v^2 + \cdots \qquad (7.31)$$

$$p_{\text{elm}} = \gamma\mu v \approx \mu v + \cdots \qquad (7.32)$$

where $\mu_o = 3\mu/4$, $\mu_1 = 5\mu/4$, and μ is as in Eqs. 7.29 and 7.30. Lorentz, aware
of Kaufmann's results and their agreement with Abraham's theory, remarked that
his equations ought to agree 'nearly as well . . . if there is not to be a most serious
objection to the theory I have now proposed' and did some data-fitting which led
him to conclude that there was no cause for concern.

In order to understand Lorentz's equations (Eqs. 7.31 and 7.32) and Poincaré's
subsequent proposal for a modification of these results, it is helpful to depart
briefly from the historic course of events and derive Lorentz's results from the
transformation properties of the electromagnetic energy momentum tensor density
$T_{\mu\nu}$ [P13]. With the help of that quantity we can write (in the Minkowski
metric)*

---

*As usual, we assume the electron to move in the x direction. Equations 7.33 and 7.34 were first
published in 1911 by von Laue [L10].

$$E_{\text{elm}} = \int T_{44} d\vec{x} = \gamma \left[\int T_{44}(0) d\vec{x}_0 - \beta^2 \int T_{11}(0) d\vec{x}_0 \right] \qquad (7.33)$$

$$p_{\text{elm}} = -\frac{i}{c} \int T_{14} d\vec{x} = \frac{\gamma v}{c^2} \left[\int T_{44}(0) d\vec{x}_0 - \int T_{11}(0) d\vec{x}_0 \right] \qquad (7.34)$$

where '0' refers to the rest frame. Since $T_{\mu\nu}$ is traceless and since the rest frame is spatially isotropic, these transformation relations at once yield Eqs. 7.31 and 7.32.

Dynamic rather than kinematic arguments had led to the concept of electromagnetic mass. Dynamic rather than kinematic arguments led Poincaré to modify Lorentz's model. In his brief paper published in June 1905, Poincaré announced, 'One obtains . . . a possible explanation of the contraction of the electron by assuming that the deformable and compressible electron is subject to a sort of constant external pressure the action of which is proportional to the volume variation' [P14]. In his July 1905 memoir he added, 'This pressure is proportional to the fourth power of the experimental mass of the electron' [P15]. In Chapter 6, I discussed the kinematic part of these two papers. More important to Poincaré was the dynamic part, the 'explanation of the contraction of the electron.' It is not for nothing that both papers are entitled 'Sur la Dynamique de l'Électron.'

In modern language, Poincaré's dynamic problem can be put as follows. Can one derive the equations for a Lorentz electron and its self-field from a relativistically invariant action principle and *prove* that this electron, a sphere at rest, becomes an ellipsoid when in uniform motion in the way Lorentz had *assumed* it did? Poincaré first showed that this was impossible. But he had a way out. 'If one wishes to retain [the Lorentz theory] and avoid intolerable contradictions, one must assume a special force which explains both the contraction [in the direction of motion] and the constancy of the two [other] axes' [P15].

Poincaré's lengthy arguments can be reduced to a few lines with the help of $T_{\mu\nu}$. Write Eq. 7.31 in the form

$$E_{\text{elm}} = \gamma \mu c^2 - PV \qquad (7.35)$$

where $V = 4\pi a^3 / 3\gamma$ is the (contracted) volume of the electron and $P = 3\mu c^2 / 16\pi a^3$ is a scalar pressure. Add a term $\rho P \delta_{\mu\nu}$, the 'Poincaré stress,' to $T_{\mu\nu}$, where $\rho = 1$ inside the electron and zero outside. This term cancels the $-PV$ term in E_{elm} for all velocities, it does not contribute to P_{elm}, and it serves to obtain the desired contraction. Assume further—as Poincaré did—that the mass of the electron is purely electromagnetic. Then $\mu \sim e^2/a$ and $P \sim \mu/a^3 \sim \mu^4$, his result mentioned earlier. Again in modern language, the added stress makes the finite electron into a closed system. Poincaré did not realize how highly desirable are the relations

$$E_{\text{elm}} = \gamma \mu c^2 \qquad P_{\text{elm}} = \gamma \mu v \qquad (7.36)$$

which follow from his model! (See [M7] for a detailed discussion of the way Poincaré proceeded.)

Next we must return to Kaufmann. Stimulated by the new theoretical developments, he refined his experiments and in 1906 announced new results: 'The measurements are incompatible with the Lorentz-Einstein postulate. The Abraham equation and the Bucherer equation* represent the observations equally well ...' [K5].

These conclusions caused a stir among the theoretical experts. Planck discussed his own re-analysis of Kaufmann's data at a physics meeting in 1906 [P16]. He could find no flaw, but took a wait-and-see attitude. So did Poincaré in 1908 [P17]. Lorentz vacillated: The experiments 'are decidedly unfavorable to the idea of a contraction, such as I attempted to work out. Yet though it seems very likely that we shall have to relinquish it altogether, it is, I think, worthwhile looking into it more closely ...' [L12]. Einstein was unmoved: 'Herr Kaufmann has determined the relation between [electric and magnetic deflection] of β-rays with admirable care. ... Using an independent method, Herr Planck obtained results which fully agree with [the computations of] Kaufmann. ... It is further to be noted that the theories of Abraham and Bucherer yield curves which fit the observed curve considerably better than the curve obtained from relativity theory. However, in my opinion, these theories should be ascribed a rather small probability because their basic postulates concerning the mass of the moving electron are not made plausible by theoretical systems which encompass wider complexes of phenomena' [E3]. Soon after this was written, experimental confirmation for $E = m\gamma c^2$ was obtained by Bucherer [B7]. Minkowski was delighted. To introduce a rigid electron into the Maxwell theory, he said, is like going to a concert with cotton in one's ears [M8]. The issue remained controversial, however. Wien, in his letter to the Nobel committee, commented early in 1912, 'Concerning the new experiments on cathode and β-rays, I would not consider them to have decisive power of proof. The experiments are very subtle, and one cannot be sure whether all sources of error have been excluded.' The final experimental verdict in favor of relativity came in the years 1914-16.**

Special relativity killed the classical dream of using the energy-momentum-velocity relations of a particle as a means of probing the dynamic origins of its mass. The relations are purely kinematic. The classical picture of a particle as a finite little sphere is also gone for good. Quantum field theory has taught us that particles nevertheless have structure, arising from quantum fluctuations. Recently, unified field theories have taught us that the mass of the electron is certainly not purely electromagnetic in nature.

But we still do not know what causes the electron to weigh.

---

*Alfred Bucherer [B5] and Langevin [L11] had independently invented an extended electron model with FitzGerald-Lorentz contraction but with constant volume. This model was analyzed further by Poincaré [P15] and by Ehrenfest [E37]. In 1908 Bucherer informed Einstein that his, Bucherer's, experiments had led him to abandon his own model in favor of the relativity prediction [B6].

**See [P1] or [P2], Section 29, for detailed references to the experimental literature up to 1918.

References

A1. M. Abraham, *Phys. Zeitschr.* **4,** 57 (1902).

A2. ——, *AdP* **10,** 105 (1903).

B1. M. Born, *Die Relativitätstheorie Einsteins.* Springer, Berlin, 1921. Translated as *Einstein's Theory of Relativity* (H. L. Brose, Tran.). Methuen, London, 1924.

B2. O. M. Bilaniuk, V. K. Deshpande, and E. C. G. Sudarshan, *Am. J. Phys.* **30,** 718, (1962).

B3. F. E. Brasch, *Library of Congress Quarterly* **2** (2), 39 (1945).

B4. W. Braunbeck, *Z. Phys.* **107,** 1 (1937).

B5. A. H. Bucherer, *Mathematische Einführung in die Elektronentheorie,* pp. 57–8. Teubner, Leipzig, 1904.

B6. ——, letters to A. Einstein, September 7, 9, and 10, 1908.

B7. ——, *Phys. Zeitschr.* **9,** 755 (1908).

E1. A. Einstein, *AdP* **17,** 891 (1905).

E2. ——, letter to C. Habicht, spring 1905, undated.

E3. ——, *Jahrb. Rad. Elektr.* **4,** 411 (1907).

E4. ——, *Phys. Zeitschr.* **12,** 509 (1911).

E5. ——, *AdP* **23,** 197 (1907).

E5a. ——, *Astr. Nachr.* **199,** 7, 47, (1914).

E6. ——, *PAW,* 1916, p. 423; *Naturw.* **6,** 697 (1918).

E7. ——, *AdP* **17,** 132 (1905).

E8. —— and V. Bargmann, *Ann. Math.* **45,** 1 (1944).

E9. ——, *AdP* **18,** 639 (1905).

E10. ——, *AdP* **20,** 627; footnote on p. 633 (1906).

E11. ——, [E3], p. 442.

E12. ——, *Bull. Am. Math. Soc.* **41,** 223 (1935).

E13. ——, *Technion J.* **5,** 16 (1946).

E14. ——, letter to C. Habicht, fall 1905, undated.

E15. ——, [E3], p. 443.

E16. ——, *Arch. Sci. Phys. Nat.* **29,** 5, 125 (1910), see esp. p. 144.

E17. P. Ehrenfest, *AdP* **23,** 204 (1907).

E18. A. Einstein and J. J. Laub, *AdP* **26,** 532 (1908); corrections in *AdP* **27,** 232 (1908) and **28,** 445 (1909).

E19. ——, ——, *AdP* **26,** 541 (1908).

E20. ——, *Die Grundlage der Allgemeinen Relativitätstheorie,* introduction. Barth, Leipzig, 1916.

E21. ——, *AdP* **21,** 583 (1906).

E22. ——, *AdP* **23,** 206 (1907).

E23. ——, *AdP* **23,** 371 (1907).

E24. ——, *Science* **80,** 358 (1934).

E25. ——, *AdP* **28,** 885 (1909).

E26. ——, *Arch. Sci. Phys. Nat.* **30,** 323 (1910).

E27. ——, *Phys. Zeitschr.* **10,** 817 (1909).

E28. ——, *Arch. Sci. Phys. Nat.* **29,** 5, 125 (1910).

E29. ——, *Viertelj. Schrift Naturf. Ges. Zürich* **56,** 1 (1911).

E30. ——, *Scientia* **15,** 337 (1914).

E31. —— in *Kultur der Gegenwart* (E. Lecher, Ed.), Vol.1, p. 251. Teubner, Leipzig, 1915.

E32. ——, [E31], 2nd edn., Vol. 1, p. 783.

E33. ——, *The Meaning of Relativity;* 5th edn. Princeton University Press, Princeton, N.J., 1956.

E34. ——, *Die Vossische Zeitung,* April 26, 1914.

E35. ——, *Naturw.* **2,** 1018 (1914).

E36. ——, *Naturw.* **10,** 184 (1922).

E37. P. Ehrenfest, *Phys. Zeitschr.* **7,** 302 (1906).

F1. P. Frank, *Sitz. Ber. Akad. Wiss. Wien.* IIa, **118,** 373 (1909), esp. p. 382.

F2. G. Feinberg, *Phys. Rev.* **159,** 1089 (1967); **D17,** 1651 (1978).

G1. S. Goldberg, *Arch. Hist. Ex. Sci.* **7,** 7 (1970).

H1. F. Hasenöhrl, *AdP* **15,** 344 (1904); **16,** 589 (1905).

H2. D. Hilbert in H. Minkowski, *Ges. Abh.* (see [M5]), Vol. 1. p. xxxi.

H3. O. Heaviside, *Phil. Mag.* **27,** 324 (1889).

K1. H. A. Kramers, *Quantum Mechanics* (D. ter Haar, Tran.), Sec. 57. Interscience, New York, 1957.

K2. W. Kaufmann, *AdP* **61,** 545 (1897).

K3. ——, *Goett. Nachr.,* 1901, p. 143.

K4. ——, *Phys. Zeitschr.* **4,** 54 (1902).

K5. ——, *AdP* **19,** 487 (1906).

L1. M. von Laue, *AdP* **23,** 989 (1907).

L2. H. A. Lorentz, *Versuch einer Theorie der Electrischen and Optischen Erscheinungen in Bewegten Körpern.* Brill, Leiden, 1895. Reprinted in *Collected Papers,* Vol. 5, p. 1. Nyhoff, the Hague, 1937.

L3. P. Langevin, *J. de Phys.* **3,** 553 (1913).

L4. M. Laue, *Das Relativitätsprinzip.* Vieweg, Braunschweig, 1911.

L5. G. N. Lewis and R. Tolman, *Phil. Mag.* **18,** 510 (1909).

L6. J. J. Laub, letter to A. Einstein, February 2, 1908.

L7. P. T. Landsberg, *Phys. Rev. Lett.* **45,** 149 (1980).

L8. H. A. Lorentz, *The Theory of Electrons,* p. 40. Teubner, Leipzig, 1909.

L9. ——, *Proc. R. Ac. Amsterdam* **6,** 809 (1904); *Collected Papers,* Vol. 5, p. 172.

L10. M. von Laue, *AdP* **35,** 124 (1911).

L11. P. Langevin, *Rev. Gén. Sci.* **16,** 257 (1905).

L12. H. A. Lorentz, [L8], p. 213.

M1. C. Møller, *The Theory of Relativity,* Chap. 2. Oxford University Press, Oxford, 1952.

M2. Maja Einstein, *Albert Einstein, Beitrag für sein Lebensbild,* Florence, 1924, unpublished.

M3. K. von Mosengeil, *AdP* **22,** 867 (1907). Reprinted in Planck, *Abhandlungen,* Vol. 2, p. 138.

M4. H. Minkowski, *AdP* **47,** 927 (1915).

M5. ——, *Goett. Nachr.,* 1908, p. 53. Reprinted in *Gesammelte Abhandlungen von Herman Minkowski,* Vol. 2, p. 352. Teubner, Leipzig, 1911.

M6. ——, *Phys. Zeitschr.* **10,** 104 (1909); *Ges. Abh.,* Vol. 2, p. 431.

M7. A. I. Miller, *Arch. Hist. Ex. Sci.* **10,** 207 (1973).

M8. H. Minkowski, *Phys. Zeitschr.* **9,** 762 (1908).

O1. T. Ogawa, *Jap. St. Hist. Sci.* **18,** 73 (1979).

O2. H. Ott, *Z. Phys.* **175,** 70 (1963).

P1. W. Pauli, *Encyklopädie der Mathematischen Wissenschaften,* Vol. 5. Part 2, p. 539. Teubner, Leipzig, 1921.

P2. ——, *Theory of Relativity* (G. Field, Tran.). Pergamon Press, London, 1958.

P3. W. K. H. Panofsky and M. Phillips, *Classical Electricity and Magnetism,* Chap. 15. Addison-Wesley, Reading, Mass., 1955.

P4. W. Pauli, *Wissenschaftlicher Briefwechsel,* Vol. 1, pp. 296–312. Springer, New York, 1979.

P5. See e.g., [P3]., Chap. 11.

P6. M. Planck, *Verh. Deutsch. Phys. Ges.* **4,** 136 (1906); see also *PAW,* 1907, p. 542; *AdP* **26,** 1 (1908).

P7. W. Pauli, [P1] or [P2], Sec. 41.

P7a. M. Planck, *Wissenschaftliche Selbstbiographie.* Barth, Leipzig, 1948. Reprinted in M. Planck, *Physikalische Abhandlungen und Vorträge,* Vol. 3, p. 374. Vieweg, Braunschweig, 1958.

P8. ——, *Phys. Zeitschr.* **7,** 753 (1906); *Abhandlungen,* Vol. 2, p. 121.

P9. ——, [P6], Sec. 12.

P10. ——, letter to A. Einstein, July 6, 1907.

P11. W. K. H. Panofsky in Proc. Einstein Centennial Symposium at Princeton, 1979, p. 94. Addison-Wesley, Reading, Mass., 1980.

P12. E. M. Purcell, [P11], p. 106.

P13. A. Pais in *Aspects of Quantum Theory* (A. Salam and E. P. Wigner, Eds.), p. 79. Cambridge University Press, Cambridge, 1972.

P14. H. Poincaré, *C. R. Ac. Sci. Paris* **140,** 1504 (1905); *Oeuvres de Henri Poincaré,* Vol. 9, p. 489. Gauthier-Villars, Paris, 1954.

P15. ——, *Rend. Circ. Mat. Palermo* **21,** 129 (1906); *Oeuvres,* Vol. 9, p. 494; see esp. Sec. 8.

P16. M. Planck, *Phys. Zeitschr.* **7,** 753 (1906); *Abhandlungen,* Vol. 2, p. 121.

P17. H. Poincaré, *Rev. Gén. Sci.* **19,** 386, 1908; *Oeuvres,* Vol. 9, p. 551.

R1. H. P. Robertson, *Rev. Mod. Phys.* **21,** 378 (1949).

R2. E. Rutherford, J. Chadwick, and C. D. Ellis, *Radiations From Radioactive Substances,* p. 531. Cambridge University Press, Cambridge, 1930.

S1. A. Sommerfeld, Ed., *The Principle of Relativity,* p. 37. Dover, New York.

S2. Se, p. 130.

S3. Se, p. 131.

S4. G. G. Stokes, *Mathematical and Physical Papers,* Vol. 1, p. 17. Johnson, New York, 1966.

S5. G. Searle, *Phil. Trans. Roy. Soc.* **187,** 675 (1896).

S6. A. Schuster, *Phil. Mag.* **43,** 1 (1897).

T1. L. H. Thomas, *Nature* **117,** 514 (1926); *Phil. Mag.* **3,** 1 (1927).

T2. J. J. Thomson, *Phil. Mag.* **11,** 229 (1881).

T3. —— in *The Royal Institute Library of Science, Physical Sciences,* Vol. 5, p. 36. Elsevier, New York, 1970.

U1. G. E. Uhlenbeck and S. Goudsmit, *Naturw.* **13,** 953 (1925).

U2. ——, *Phys. Today* **29** (6), 43 (1976).

8

The Edge of History

1. A New Way of Thinking. On April 6, 1922, the Societé Française de Philosophie (which Henri Poincaré had helped found) convened for a discussion of the special and the general theories of relativity. Among those in attendance were the mathematicians Elie Cartan, Jacques Hadamard, and Paul Painlevé, the physicists Jean Becquerel, Albert Einstein, and Paul Langevin, and the philosophers Henri Bergson, Léon Brunschvicg, Edouard LeRoy, and Emile Meyerson. In the course of the discussions, Bergson expressed his admiration for Einstein's work: 'I see [in this work] not only a new physics, but also, in certain respects, a new way of thinking' [B1].

Special relativity led to new modes of philosophical reflection. It also gave rise to new limericks, such as the one about the young lady from Wight. However, first and foremost this theory brought forth a new way of thinking in physics itself, new because it called for a revision of concepts long entrenched in the physics and chemistry of the classical period. In physics the great novelties were, first, that the recording of measurements of space intervals and time durations demanded more detailed specifications than were held necessary theretofore and, second, that the lessons of classical mechanics are correct only in the limit $v/c \ll 1$. In chemistry the great novelty was that Lavoisier's law of mass conservation and Dalton's rule of simply proportionate weights were only approximate but nevertheless so good that no perceptible changes in conventional chemistry were called for. Thus relativity turned Newtonian mechanics and classical chemistry into approximate sciences, not diminished but better defined in the process.

Today these revisions seem harmless and are easy to teach. To Einstein they came rather abruptly, but only after years of unsuccessful thinking. His postulates were obvious to him once he had conceived them. When I talked with him about those times of transition, he expressed himself in a curiously impersonal way. He would refer to the birth of special relativity as 'den Schritt,' the step.

It was otherwise in the case of Lorentz and Poincaré. Each of them had struggled hard with these same problems, made important steps toward their solution, and garnered deep insights along the way. But neither of them had quite made the final transitional steps. In later years all three men, Einstein, Lorentz, and Poincaré, reacted to the special theory of relativity in ways which arouse curiosity.

Why, on the whole, was Einstein so reticent to acknowledge the influence of the Michelson–Morley experiment on his thinking? Why could Lorentz never quite let go of the aether? Why did Poincaré never understand special relativity? These questions lead us to the edge of history.

It is natural to suppose but wrong to conclude that the use of the term *the edge of history* implies that its user has a clear picture and sharp definition of what history is. History deals with happenings in the past. The history of a period is an account of that period based on a selective sampling of dates and facts from a pool of information which, it is safe to assume, is incomplete. The selective factor is necessary as well as unavoidably subjective. Therefore one cannot speak of *the* history of a period. An historian can definitely be wrong but often cannot be sure of being right. That much is clear. Also, the knowledge of selected facts and dates is necessary but not sufficient if one is not content—and one should not be—with some insight into what happened but wishes to inquire further how 'it' happened. In the case of the history of discovery, questions like, Why did A create what he did, why did B readily accept what A created, why did C resist A's new ideas? are fascinating. In my many years of immersion in theoretical physics I have known A's, B's, and C's. Though their concerns may not have been as profound as relativity, I often found it baffling to answer such questions as those just raised. Creation, acceptance, and resistance, whether in science or in other areas, are acts and attitudes the whys of which can be grasped only if one knows, along with facts, how the minds of A and B and C work. Who knows whether he knows?

However, while the answers to the A-B-C questions are elusive and deliciously conjectural, the same is not necessarily true for the questions themselves. Returning to Einstein, Lorentz, and Poincaré, the questions I raised about them are the result of patient reading of their papers. The questions themselves are therefore distilled from an historical record, and I do not think it is at all bold to call them part of history. Their answers, it seems to me, are beyond history. Somewhere between the question and the answer lies history's edge, a term I have now defined with more precision than history itself. In what follows I shall not entirely refrain from indulging in a bit of extrahistorical speculation regarding the answers.

First, however, a few more facts.

2. Einstein and the Literature.   Einstein's 1907 article [E1] for the *Jahrbuch der Radioaktivität und Elektronik* was written at the invitation of Johannes Stark, the founder and editor of that series. In agreeing to review relativity theory, Einstein wrote to Stark, 'I should note that unfortunately I am not in a position to orient myself about *everything* that has been published on this subject, because the library is closed in my free time. Apart from my own papers, I know of a paper by Lorentz (1904), one by Cohn, one by Mosengeil, and two by Planck.* I would be much obliged if you could point out further relevant publications to me, if such are known to you' [E2]**. This letter, as well as an earlier one to

---

*All these papers are referred to in Chapters 6 and 7.

**This letter was published in an article by Hermann [H1].

Besso [E3], shows that access to the literature was difficult for the man from the patent office. In his reply to Einstein's letter, Stark mentioned work by Planck, von Laue, and himself and added, 'Apart from these papers and those mentioned by you, I do not know of any others either' [S1]. Thus neither Einstein nor Stark was aware of Poincaré's long paper bearing on relativity, completed in July 1905 and published in the 1906 volume of *Rendiconti del Circolo matematico di Palermo* [P1]. Minkowski referred to this article on November 5, 1907, in his lecture† before the Goettinger Mathematische Verein [M1]. It is therefore certain that this publication was in circulation in December 1907, the time at which Einstein completed his review, and *a fortiori* in March 1908, when he added some corrections and comments to the review [E4]. Nevertheless, especially in view of the exchange between Einstein and Stark, I see no grounds for thinking that in 1907 Einstein knew of Poincaré's paper and chose to ignore it.

I believe, however, that Einstein's complaint about his difficulties in getting hold of books and journals, while no doubt genuine, is only a secondary factor in the understanding of his handling of existing literature. The truth of the matter is that he did not much care. Read for example what he wrote in the introduction to a paper published in 1906: 'It seems to me to be in the nature of the subject, that what is to follow might already have been partially clarified by other authors. However, in view of the fact that the questions under consideration are treated here from a new point of view, I believed I could dispense with a literature search which would be very troublesome for me, especially since it is to be hoped that other authors will fill this gap, as was commendably done by Herr Planck and Herr Kaufmann on the occasion of my first paper on the principle of relativity' [E5].* This statement is not arrogant if, and only if, arrogance is a mark of insecurity. To me these lines express ebullience, total self-assurance, and a notable lack of taste.**

The period during which Einstein was unaware of Poincaré's technical writing on relativity now stretches into 1908. I noted in Section 6b that by 1905 Einstein had already read Poincaré's *La Science et l'Hypothèse,* in which it is conjectured that the undetectability of the earth's motion relative to the aether should hold to

---

†See Section 7c.

*"Es scheint mir in der Natur der Sache zu liegen, dasz das Nachfolgende zum Teil bereits von anderen Autoren klargestellt sein dürfte. Mit Rücksicht darauf jedoch, dasz hier die betreffenden Fragen von einem neuen Gesichtspunkt aus behandelt sind, glaubte ich, von einer für mich sehr umständlichen Durchmusterung der Literatur absehen zu dürfen, zumal zu hoffen ist, dasz diese Lücke von anderen Autoren noch ausgefüllt werden wird, wie dies in dankenswerter Weise bei meiner ersten Arbeit über das Relativitätsprinzip durch Hrn. Planck und Hrn. Kaufmann bereits geschehen ist."

**Einstein was evidently able to get to the literature if he set his mind to it. A number of journals are quoted in his 1907 paper [E1], including even the *American Journal of Science* of 1887 in which the Michelson–Morley experiment was reported. I would not be surprised if Einstein had copied that reference from one of Lorentz's papers. Also, in 1906 Einstein mentioned [E6] a paper by Poincaré [P2] which came to his attention because it appeared in a Festschrift for Lorentz.

all orders in v/c and also in which critical comments are made on the naive use
of simultaneity. It cannot be said, however, that the content of Einstein's June
1905 paper depends in any technical sense on these important remarks by Poincaré. Others in Einstein's position might perhaps have chosen to mention Poincaré
at the earliest opportunity. However, it does not seem to me that Einstein had
compelling reasons to do so in 1905. I shall return soon to what Einstein had to
say about Poincaré in later years. Here I note that Poincaré's name appears only
once in a paper by Einstein on relativity, to wit, in 'Geometrie und Erfahrung,'
the text of a lecture he gave in 1921 on general relativity [E7] in which he praises
'der tiefe und scharfsinnige Poincaré,' the deep and sharp-witted P., for his ideas
on non-Euclidean geometry—ideas which, incidentally, are found in Chapter 3
of *La Science et l'Hypothèse*.

3. *Lorentz and the Aether.*   To Lorentz simplicity meant simple dynamics.
As an important example of the Lorentz style, consider his reaction to Kaufmann's
result of 1901–6 about the purely electromagnetic origin of the electron's mass*:
'With a view to simplicity, it will be best to admit Kaufmann's conclusion, or
hypothesis, if we prefer so to call it, that the negative electrons have no material
mass at all. This is certainly one of the most important results of modern physics
...' [L1]. I believe that Lorentz clung to the idea of a purely electromagnetic
electron mass for the rest of his life.

Lorentz's words about Kaufmann are found in his 1906 Columbia lectures, the
publication of which was held up for three years 'on account of my wish to give
some further development to the subject' [L2]. Despite this considerable delay,
'Einstein's principle of relativity [has not] received an adequate treatment' [L2].
This is indeed true. For example, Lorentz still opines that the contraction of rods
has a dynamic origin. There is no doubt that he had read and understood Einstein's papers by then. However, neither then nor later was he prepared to accept
their conclusions as the definitive answer to the problems of the aether. With his
customary clarity, he stated his own credo in the course of lectures given at the
Teyler Foundation in Haarlem in 1913 [L3]:

'According to Einstein, it has no meaning to speak of motion relative to the
aether. He likewise denies the existence of absolute simultaneity.

'It is certainly remarkable that these relativity concepts, also those concerning
time, have found such a rapid acceptance.

'The acceptance of these concepts belongs mainly to epistemology. . . . It is certain, however, that it depends to a large extent on the way one is accustomed to
think whether one is most attracted to one or another interpretation. As far as this
lecturer is concerned, he finds a certain satisfaction in the older interpretations,
according to which the aether possesses at least some substantiality, space and time
can be sharply separated, and simultaneity without further specification can be
spoken of. In regard to this last point, one may perhaps appeal to our ability of

*See Section 7e.

imagining arbitrarily large velocities. In that way, one comes very close to the concept of absolute simultaneity.

'Finally, it should be noted that the daring assertion that one can never observe velocities larger than the velocity of light contains a hypothetical restriction of what is accessible to us, [a restriction] which cannot be accepted without some reservation.'

It is clear beyond doubt that Lorentz's imagination was the classical imagination. Light moves with a velocity c km/s. There is no difficulty in imagining a velocity equal to $c + 1$ km/s. The classical mind asserts, the relativistic mind denies, that a velocity which can be imagined mathematically can necessarily be reached physically.

As I understand Lorentz, he was a leader in theoretical physics who fully grasped all the physical and mathematical aspects of the special theory of relativity but who nevertheless could not quite take leave of a beloved classical past. This attitude has nothing to do with personality conflicts. Those were alien to him. Einstein and Poincaré always spoke in praise of him, Lorentz always reciprocated. Nor did he hesitate to make clear where he had been in error: 'The chief cause of my failure [in discovering special relativity] was my clinging to the idea that only the variable t can be considered as the true time and that my local time t' must be regarded as no more than an auxiliary mathematical quantity,' he wrote in a note added to the second edition of his Columbia lectures [L4]. In a draft* of a letter to Einstein, written in January 1915 [L5], Lorentz wrote the following about the FitzGerald–Lorentz contraction: 'I added the remark that one arrives at this hypothesis if one extends to other forces what one can already say about the influence of a translation on electrostatic forces. If I had stressed this more, then the hypothesis would have given much less of an impression of having been invented ad hoc.' Lorentz never fully made the transition from the old dynamics to the new kinematics.**

4. *Poincaré and the Third Hypothesis.* In April 1909 Poincaré gave a series of six lectures [P3] in Goettingen. In the last of these, entitled 'La Mécanique Nouvelle,' the lecturer dealt with questions bearing on relativity. At first glance the reader of this text may experience surprise at not finding any mention of Einstein, whose theory was four years old by then. On closer scrutiny, he will find that this absence is justified. Poincaré does not describe Einstein's theory.

The new mechanics, Poincaré said, is based on three hypotheses. The first of these is that bodies cannot attain velocities larger than the velocity of light. The second is (I use modern language) that the laws of physics shall be the same in all inertial frames. So far so good. Then Poincaré introduces a third hypothesis: 'One

---

*This draft was discovered in 1979 by A. Kox in one of Lorentz's notebooks. I am grateful to Dr Kox for drawings my attention to this text.

**According to Born, 'Lorentz . . . probably never became a relativist at all, and only paid lip service to Einstein at times, to avoid arguments' [B2].

needs to make still a third hypothesis, much more surprising, much more difficult to accept, one which is of much hindrance to what we are currently used to. A body in translational motion suffers a deformation in the direction in which it is displaced. . . . However strange it may appear to us, one must admit that the third hypothesis is perfectly verified.' It is evident that as late as 1909 Poincaré did not know that the contraction of rods is a consequence of the two Einstein postulates. Poincaré therefore did not understand one of the most basic traits of special relativity.

Should one give Poincaré the benefit of the doubt and assume that his reference to a third hypothesis was made only for pedagogical reasons? This, I think, would be too far-fetched. Moreover, if one rereads his earlier papers in the light of what has just been noted, one finds a distinct similarity in the way he treats the FitzGerald–Lorentz contraction. I repeat what Poincaré said in St Louis in 1904 [P4]. On that occasion he also introduced in essence the first two postulates and then added, 'Unfortunately, [this reasoning] is not sufficient and complementary hypotheses are necessary; one must assume that bodies in motion suffer a uniform contraction in their direction of motion.' One rereads the grand memoir in the *Rendiconti di Palermo* [P1] and finds an admirable discussion of the Lorentz transformation but no mention that these transformations imply the contraction of rods; the emphasis in that paper is on dynamics. It is likewise the case in a semipopular account of relativity which Poincaré wrote in 1908 [P5].

My own assessment of Poincaré's contributions to relativity coincides with what was said about him during the opening remarks of the meeting in Paris of the Societé Française de Philosophie, referred to earlier: 'The solution anticipated by Poincaré was given by Einstein in his memoir of 1905 on special relativity. He accomplished the revolution which Poincaré had foreseen and stated at a moment when the development of physics seemed to lead to an impasse' [L6].

5. *Whittaker and the History of Relativity.*   In 1910, Edmund Whittaker published a book entitled *History of the Theories of Aether and Electricity* [W1]. This work covers the period from Descartes to the close of the nineteenth century. Colleagues more knowledgeable on this period than I, confirm my impression that it is a masterpiece. Forty years later, a revised edition of this book came out. At that time Whittaker also published a second volume dealing with the period from 1900 to 1926 [W2]. His treatment of the special theory of relativity in the latter volume shows how well the author's lack of physical insight matches his ignorance of the literature. I would have refrained from commenting on his treatment of special relativity were it not for the fact that his book has raised questions in many minds about the priorities in the discovery of this theory. Whittaker's opinion on this point is best conveyed by the title of his chapter on this subject: 'The Relativity Theory of Poincaré and Lorentz.'* Born had given Whittaker fair warning [B3]. Einstein's reaction was, 'I do not have to read the thing. . . . If he manages to convince others, that is their own affair' [B4].

---

*Whittaker's obituary of Einstein written for the Royal Society is no work of art either [W3].

6. *Lorentz and Poincaré.*   Every paper by Poincaré dealing with the principle of relativity acknowledges Lorentz's pioneering role. In his Goettingen lectures, Poincaré called him one of the *'grands démolisseurs'* of Newtonian mechanics (I wonder if Lorentz would have agreed with that) and referred once again to his 'very ingenious invention' of the idea of a local time.

Conversely, Lorentz had high esteem for Poincaré. In his major article of 1904 he acknowledged the stimulus of Poincaré's criticism (expressed at the Paris Congress of 1900) to the effect that too many independent hypotheses had been introduced in his earlier work [L7]. Later he wrote to Poincaré acknowledging receipt of 'the important memoir on the dynamics of the electron' [L8]. In Volume 38 of the *Acta Mathematica,* devoted in its entirety to appreciations of the late Poincaré, Lorentz gave a detailed analysis of the Palermo paper [L9] in which, incidentally, an imaginary time coordinate ($x_4 = ict$) is introduced for the first time. Regarding Poincaré's contributions to the principles of relativity, Lorentz's view is balanced, as always. In both editions of the Columbia lectures, Poincaré appears only in connection with the stress terms he invented. In a letter to Einstein, Lorentz reminisced about the origins of the special theory: 'I felt the need for a *more general* theory, which I tried to develop later [i.e., in 1904] and which you (and to a lesser extent Poincaré) formulated' [L5].

7. *Lorentz and Einstein.*   As Einstein told me more than once, Lorentz was to him the most well-rounded and harmonious personality he had met in his entire life. Einstein's thoughts and feelings about Lorentz were a blend of respect, love, and awe. 'I admire this man as no other, I would say I love him,' he wrote to Laub in 1909 [E8]. In a letter to Grossmann, he called Lorentz 'our greatest colleague' [E9]. To Lorentz himself he wrote, 'You will surely feel that I feel an unbounded admiration for you' [E10]. In a memorial service held at the University of Leiden shortly after Lorentz's death, Einstein was one of the speakers: 'The enormous significance of his work consisted therein, that it forms the basis for the theory of atoms and for the general and special theories of relativity. The special theory was a more detailed exposé of those concepts which are found in Lorentz's research of 1895' [E11].

Lorentz's life centered on Arnhem, Leiden, and Haarlem. He was forty-four years old when he attended his first international physics conference, just across the Dutch border. At that same age, Einstein had already lived in four countries and had held four professorships in succession. He, the bird of passage, must at times have been wistful about the Dutch upper-middle-class stability and serenity of Lorentz's existence.

Lorentz's esteem for Einstein was extremely high as well. In Chapter 12, I shall have more to relate about the interactions between these two men at the time that Lorentz almost got Einstein to accept a permanent position in Holland.

8. *Poincaré and Einstein.*   Why did Poincaré not mention Einstein in his Goettingen lectures? Why is there no paper by Poincaré in which Einstein and relativity are linked? It is inconceivable that Poincaré would have studied Einstein's papers of 1905 without understanding them. It is impossible that in 1909

(the year he spoke in Goettingen) he would never have heard of Einstein's activities in this area. Shall I write of petulance or professional envy? I shall not, since my reader's speculations are as good as my own. Could it be that Poincaré had had a mere glance at Einstein's papers and had concluded too hastily that he knew all that already and that there was nothing new there? Possibly. It would be neither far-fetched nor a unique occurrence. In his book *The Anxiety of Influence*, Harold Bloom writes, 'Strong poets make . . . history by misreading one another, so as to clear imaginative space for themselves,' and speaks of 'strong poets, major figures with the persistence to wrestle with their strong precursors even to the death' [B5].* In such respects I see little difference between strong poets and strong creative personalities in any other domain. Poincaré's reaction to Riemann [K1] and Einstein's to Hilbert (to be discussed in Chapter 14) may be cases in point. In any event, the questions are interesting and based on fact, the answers are beyond certain reach. In my opinion, it is more significant that Poincaré until shortly before his death remained silent about Einstein than that Einstein until shortly before his death remained silent about Poincaré. In closing the case of Poincaré and Einstein, I offer their final statements with only minor comments of my own.

Alexander Moszkowski begins his biography of Einstein [M2] by recalling that on October 13, 1910, Poincaré gave a lecture before the Berliner Wissenschaftliche Verein about 'die neue Mechanik' (Poincaré was quite comfortable with the German language). 'In this lecture it happened for the first time that we heard the name Albert Einstein.' Poincaré spoke of 'the beginning of a current which, as he confessed, had disturbed the equilibrium of his earlier opinions.' Alas, we are not told in what way the speaker referred to Einstein.

Einstein and Poincaré met (for the first and last time, I believe) at the first Solvay Conference, held in Brussels in October 1911. About this encounter Einstein reported as follows to a friend: 'Poincaré war (gegen die Relativitätstheorie) einfach allgemein ablehnend, zeigte bei allem Scharfsinn wenig Verständnis für die Situation' [E12].** It is apparent once again that Poincaré either never understood or else never accepted the special theory of relativity.

Shortly thereafter, the authorities at the ETH, in the course of their preparations for offering Einstein a professorship, asked Poincaré for an opinion about him. Poincaré replied, 'Monsieur Einstein is one of the most original minds I have known; in spite of his youth he already occupies a very honorable position among the leading scholars of his time. We must especially admire in him the ease with which he adapts himself to new concepts and his ability to infer all the consequences from them. He does not remain attached to the classical principles and, faced with a physics problem, promptly envisages all possibilities. This is trans-

---

*I would like to thank Sara Pais for directing me to Bloom's book.

**P. was simply generally antipathetic (in regard to relativity theory) and showed little understanding for the situation despite all his sharp wit.

lated immediately in his mind into an anticipation of new phenomena, susceptible some day to experimental verification. I would not say that all his expectations will resist experimental check when such checks will become possible. Since he is probing in all directions, one should anticipate, on the contrary, that most of the roads he is following will lead to dead ends; but, at the same time, one must hope that one of the directions he has indicated will be a good one; and that suffices' [P6].

That, as best I know, is the single and final judgment on Einstein that Poincaré left us. Twice, having met Einstein and written this letter, did he comment on relativity [P7, P8]. Twice did he mention Lorentz but not Einstein, though he referred to Einstein in connection with the photo effect on the second of these occasions. That was in an address given on April 11, 1912. He died unexpectedly three months later.

In 1919, the mathematician Mittag-Leffler wrote to Einstein, asking him to contribute an article to the *Acta Mathematica* volume in honor of Poincaré [M3]. Four months later, Einstein responded. The letter had reached him after a long delay and 'it might be too late' now [E14]. Mittag-Leffler replied that Einstein could still send a paper if he cared to do so [M4]. Two and a half months later, Einstein replied that obligations and travel prevented him from contributing, adding that his decision 'should be considered as nothing but high respect for the task' [E14].

In December 1920, a *New York Times* correspondent interviewed Einstein in his home on the Haberlandstrasse in Berlin. In reply to a question about the origins of relativity theory, Einstein said, 'It was found that [Galilean invariance] would not conform to the rapid motions in electrodynamics. This led the Dutch professor Lorentz and myself to develop the theory of special relativity . . .' [E15]. An additional mention of Poincaré's pioneering ideas might have been gracious. In an interview with *Le Figaro* in 1921, he expressed his great admiration for Poincaré, however [E16].

In the early 1950s, I once asked Einstein how Poincaré's Palermo paper had affected his thinking. Einstein replied that he had never read that paper. I owned a copy—a second-hand exemplar of the Gauthier-Villars reprint—and asked if he would like to borrow that. Yes, he said, he would. I brought it to him. It was never returned to me. Some time after Einstein's death, I asked Helen Dukas if she would please look for it. It had vanished. . . .

Perhaps he did read it. In 1953 Einstein received an invitation to attend the forthcoming Bern celebration of the fiftieth anniversary of special relativity. Einstein wrote back that his health did not permit him to plan such a trip. In this letter Einstein mentions for the first time (as far as I know) Poincaré's role in regard to the special theory: 'Hoffentlich wird dafür gesorgt dasz die Verdienste von H. A. Lorentz und H. Poincaré bei dieser Gelegenheit ebenfalls sachgemass gewürdigt werden'* [E17]. The Bern conference took place shortly after Ein-

*I hope that one will also take care on that occasion to honor suitably the merits of L. and P.

stein's death. The task of speaking about Lorentz and Poincaré fell to Born (who had attended Poincaré's Goettingen lecture). He did not acquit himself well.**

Two months before his death, Einstein gave his fair and final judgment: 'Lorentz had already recognized that the transformations named after him are essential for the analysis of Maxwell's equations, and Poincaré deepened this insight still further . . .' [E18].

9. *Coda: The Michelson–Morley Experiment.* In concluding this account of the history of special relativity, I return to its origins. Toward the end of Section 6a, I promised to comment further on Einstein's reticence in acknowledging the influence of the Michelson–Morley experiment on his thinking. I now do so.

In a letter to an historian, written a year before his death, Einstein expressed himself for the last time on this subject: 'In my own development, Michelson's result has not had a considerable influence. I even do not remember if I knew of it at all when I wrote my first paper on the subject (1905). The explanation is that I was, for general reasons, firmly convinced that there does not exist absolute motion and my problem was only how this could be reconciled with our knowledge of electrodynamics. One can therefore understand why in my personal struggle Michelson's experiment played no role, or at least no decisive role' [E19].

Why this need not to remember or, at best, to underplay this influence?

Just over twenty years before Einstein wrote this late letter, just under twenty years after his creation of the special theory, he gave a lecture at Oxford entitled 'On the Method of Theoretical Physics' [E20], in the course of which he said, 'It is my conviction that pure mathematical construction enables us to discover the concepts and the laws connecting them, which give us the key to the understanding of the phenomena of Nature.' It seems to me that here Einstein grossly overestimates the capabilities of the human mind, even of one as great as his own. It is true that the theoretical physicist who has no sense of mathematical elegance, beauty, and simplicity is lost in some essential way. At the same time it is dangerous and can be fatal to rely exclusively on formal arguments. It is a danger from which Einstein himself did not escape in his later years.

The emphasis on mathematics is so different from the way the young Einstein used to proceed. What wrought this change? Obviously, his realization that Riemannian geometry lay waiting for him as he groped his way to general relativity must have deeply affected his subsequent thinking. Could it be, however, that the conviction expressed in Oxford had even earlier roots?

Stepping beyond the edge of history, I offer the thought that, just barely visible, the origins of Einstein's later attitude toward the discovery of concepts by purely mathematical thinking may go back to 1905. The kinematic part of his June paper has the ideal axiomatic structure of a finished theory, a structure which had

---

**'The reasoning used by Poincaré was just the same as that which Einstein introduced in his first paper of 1905. . . . Does this mean that Poincaré knew all this before Einstein? It is possible . . .' [B6].

abruptly dawned on him after a discussion with Besso. Is it possible that this
experience was so overwhelming that it seared his mind and partially blotted out
reflections and information that had been with him earlier, as the result of deep-
seated desires to come closer to the divine form of pure creation? Of course that
is possible. Of course neither I nor anyone else will ever know whether it is true.
And of course Einstein could never have been of any help in finding out.

References

B1.. H. Bergson, *Bull. Soc. Fran. Phil.* **22,** 102 (1922).
B2. M. Born, *The Born–Einstein Letters* (I. Born, Tran.), p. 198. Walker and Cy,
     New York, 1971.
B3. ——, letter to A. Einstein, September 26, 1953; [B2], p. 197.
B4. ——, [B2], p. 199.
B5. H. Bloom, *The Anxiety of Influence,* p. 5. Oxford University Press, Oxford, 1973.
B6. M. Born, *Helv. Phys. Acta Suppl.* **4,** 244 (1956).
E1. A. Einstein, *Jahrb. Rad. Elektr.* **4,** 411 (1907).
E2. ——, letter to J. Stark, September 25, 1907.
E3. ——, letter to M. Besso, March 17, 1903; *EB,* p. 13.
E4. ——, *Jahrb. Rad. Elektr.* **5,** 18 (1908).
E5. ——, *AdP* **23,** 371 (1907)
E6. ——, *AdP* **20,** 627 (1906).
E7. ——, *PAW,* 1921, p. 123. An extended version was published by Springer, Berlin,
     1921.
E8. ——, letter to J. Laub, May 19, 1909.
E9. ——, letter to M. Grossmann, December 10, 1911.
E10. ——, letter to H. A. Lorentz, November 23, 1911.
E11. ——, *Math.-Naturw. Blätt.* **22,** 24 (1928).
E12. ——, letter to H. Zangger, November 15, 1911.
E13. ——, letter to M. G. Mittag-Leffler, April 12, 1920.
E14. ——, letter to M. G. Mittag-Leffler, July 21, 1920.
E15. ——, *The New York Times,* December 3, 1920.
E16. ——, letter to A. Sommerfeld, January 28, 1922. Reprinted in *Albert Einstein/
     Arnold Sommerfeld Briefwechsel* (A. Hermann, Ed.), p. 99. Schwabe Verlag, Stutt-
     gart, 1968.
E17. ——, letter to A. Mercier, November 9, 1953.
E18. ——, letter to C. Seelig, February 19, 1955; Se, p. 114.
E19. ——, letter to F. C. Davenport, February 9, 1954.
E20. ——, *On the Method of Theoretical Physics.* Oxford University Press, Oxford,
     1933.
H1. A. Herman, *Sudhoffs Archiv.* **50,** 267 (1966).
K1. F. Klein, *Vorlesungen über die Entwicklung der Mathematik im 19 Jahrhundert,*
     Vol. 1, pp. 374–80, Springer, New York, 1979.
L1. H. A. Lorentz, *Theory of Electrons* (1st edn.), p. 43. Teubner, Leipzig, 1909.
L2. ——, [L1], preface.
L3. ——, *Das Relativitätsprinzip,* p. 23. Teubner, Leipzig, 1920.

L4. ——, [L1], 2nd edn., 1915, p. 321.
L5. ——, draft of letter to A. Einstein, January 1915, undated.
L6. X. Léon in [B1], p. 93.
L7. H. A. Lorentz, *Proc. Roy. Soc. Amsterdam* **6,** 809 (1904). Reprinted in *H. A. Lorentz, Collected Papers,* Vol. 5, p. 172. Nyhoff, the Hague, 1937.
L8. ——, letter to H. Poincaré, March 8, 1906. Reprinted in A. I. Miller's contribution to the Proceedings of the Jerusalem Einstein Centennial Symposium, March 1979.
L9. ——, *Acta Math.* **38,** 293 (1921).
M1. H. Minkowski, *AdP* **47,** 927 (1915).
M2. A. Moszkowski, *Einstein,* p. 15. Fontane, Berlin, 1921–2.
M3. M. G. Mittag-Leffler, letter to A. Einstein, December 16, 1919.
M4. ——, letter to A. Einstein, May 3, 1920.
P1. H. Poincaré, *Rend. Circ. Mat. Palermo,* **21,** 129 (1906). Reprinted in *Oeuvres de Henri Poincaré,* Vol. 9, p. 494. Gauthier-Villars, Paris, 1954.
P2. ——, *Arch. Néerl.* **5,** 252 (1900); *Oeuvres,* Vol. 9, p. 464. Also in *Recueil de Travaux Offerts à H. A. Lorentz.* Nyhoff, the Hague, 1900.
P3. ——, *Sechs Vorträge aus der Reinen Mathematik und Mathematischen Physik.* Teubner, Leipzig, 1910.
P4. ——, *Bull. Sci. Math.* **28,** 302 (1904).
P5. ——, *Rev. Gén. Sci.* **19,** 386 (1908); *Oeuvres,* Vol. 9, p. 551.
P6. ——, letter to a colleague at the ETH, undated, probably November 1911.
P7. ——, *Scientia* **12,** 159 (1912). Reprinted in *Dernières Pensèes,* Chap. 2. Flammarion, Paris, 1913.
P8. ——, *J. de Phys.* **5,** 347 (1912). Reprinted *Dernières Pensées,* Chap. 7.
S1. J. Stark, letter to A. Einstein, October 4, 1907, published in [H1].
W1. E. T. Whittaker, *History of the Theories of Aether and Electricity.* Longman, Green, London, 1910.
W2. E. T. Whittaker, *History of the Theories of Aether and Electricity,* Vol. 2. Nelson & Sons, New York, 1953.
W3. E. T. Whittaker, *Biogr. Mem. Fell. Roy. Soc.* **1,** 37 (1955).

IV
RELATIVITY,
THE GENERAL THEORY

9

'The Happiest Thought of my Life'

Musz es sein? Es musz sein.

The February 17, 1921, issue of *Nature* is almost completely devoted to relativity. It appeared at a time when 'in two cases predicted [by general relativity] phenomena for which no satisfactory alternative explanation is forthcoming have been confirmed by observation, and the third is still a subject of inquiry' [L1]. The first two phenomena are the precession of the perihelion of Mercury and the bending of light by the sun. Both effects had been calculated by Einstein in 1915. The first agreed very well indeed with long-known observations. The second had waited until 1919 for confirmation. The third was the red shift of radiation, the experimental magnitude of which was still under advisement in 1921.

This issue of *Nature* appeared at a time when Einstein was already recognized as a world figure, not only by the physics community but by the public at large. Its opening article is by Einstein and begins, 'There is something attractive in presenting the evolution of a sequence of ideas in as brief a form as possible . . .' [E1]. There follow papers by Dyson and Crommelin, the astronomers, by Jeans, Lorentz, Lodge, and Eddington, the physicists, and by Hermann Weyl, the mathematician. Also included are the inevitable philosophical contributions. This issue of the journal had been long in coming. The plan for it was conceived a few weeks after the historic November 6, 1919, joint meeting of the Royal Society and the Royal Astronomical Society in London, at which the results of the May 1919 eclipse expeditions had been reported as being in agreement with Einstein's theory. In that same month, Einstein had been approached for a contribution to *Nature* [L2]. It was he who by his efforts to be 'as brief as possible' caused much delay. In January 1920 his article was almost ready 'but has become so long that I doubt very much whether it can appear in *Nature*' [E2]. It did not. His short paper which eventually did appear [E1] is quite different from his original manuscript, entitled 'Grundgedanken und Methoden der Relativitätstheorie in ihrer Entwicklung dargestellt.' That paper was never published but has survived. The original manuscript is now in the Pierpont Morgan Library in New York City and in what follows is referred to as the Morgan manuscript.

It is a most interesting document. For once Einstein shares with the reader not only his thoughts but also his feelings. At one point he explains how in 1907 the preparation of a review article led him to ask in what way the Newtonian theory of gravitation would have to be modified in order that its laws would fit special relativity. 'When, in 1907, I was working on a comprehensive paper on the special theory of relativity for the *Jahrbuch der Radioaktivität und Elektronik,* I had also to attempt to modify the Newtonian theory of gravitation in such a way that its laws would fit in the [special relativity] theory. Attempts in this direction did show that this could be done, but did not satisfy me because they were based on physically unfounded hypotheses.' (More on these attempts in Chapter 13.) He goes on as follows:

> Then there occurred to me the 'glücklichste Gedanke meines Lebens,' the happiest thought of my life, in the following form. The gravitational field has* only a relative existence in a way similar to the electric field generated by magnetoelectric induction. *Because for an observer falling freely from the roof of a house there exists*—at least in his immediate surroundings—*no gravitational field* [his italics]. Indeed, if the observer drops some bodies then these remain relative to him in a state of rest or of uniform motion, independent of their particular chemical or physical nature (in this consideration the air resistance is, of course, ignored). The observer therefore has the right to interpret his state as 'at rest.'
>
> Because of this idea, the uncommonly peculiar experimental law that in the gravitational field all bodies fall with the same acceleration attained at once a deep physical meaning. Namely, if there were to exist just one single object that falls in the gravitational field in a way different from all others, then with its help the observer could realize that he is in a gravitational field and is falling in it. If such an object does not exist, however—as experience has shown with great accuracy—then the observer lacks any objective means of perceiving himself as falling in a gravitational field. Rather he has the right to consider his state as one of rest and his environment as field-free relative to gravitation.
>
> The experimentally known matter independence of the acceleration of fall is therefore a powerful argument for the fact that the relativity postulate has to be extended to coordinate systems which, relative to each other, are in nonuniform motion.

Let us now turn to Section V of Einstein's 1907 review article [E3], received by the editor on December 4 of that year. It is here that he begins the long road from the special theory to the general theory of relativity. Let us follow him on that road, marked by trials, by errors, and by long pauses, until finally, on November 25, 1915, the structure of the general theory as we now know it lay before him.

---

*At this point, the original text contains a few words which Einstein clearly had forgotten to delete.

I mentioned in Chapter 7 the contributions Einstein made to special relativity after the completion of his September 1905 paper on that subject. Some of these sequels appeared in 1906 and early 1907. In that period he also added to his 1905 work on Brownian motion (Chapter 5). However, his main activities during that time concerned the quantum theory. In 1906 he gave his own interpretation of Planck's 1900 work on the quantum theory and completed the fundamental paper on the quantum theory of the specific heats of solids (Chapters 19 and 20).

His first important paper on relativity theory after 1905 is the 1907 review. This article was written at the request of Stark, the editor of the *Jahrbuch*. On September 25, 1907, Einstein had accepted this invitation [E4]. On November 1, Einstein further wrote to Stark: 'I am now ready with the first part of the work for your *Jahrbuch*; I am working zealously on the second [part] in my unfortunately scarce spare time' [E5]. Since this second part contains the remarks on gravitation, it seems most probable that Einstein's 'happiest thought' came to him sometime in November 1907. We certainly know where he was when he had this idea. In his Kyoto lecture he told the story:

> I was sitting in a chair in the patent office at Bern when all of a sudden a thought occurred to me: 'If a person falls freely he will not feel his own weight.' I was startled. This simple thought made a deep impression on me. It impelled me toward a theory of gravitation. [I1]

Was Einstein first drawn to gravitation because he wanted to *include* it in special relativity or because he saw that he could *extend* special relativity with its help? The way I read the quoted lines from the Morgan manuscript, the answer would seem to be that, by asking for the inclusion, he at once or almost at once came upon the extension. That is also Einstein's own recollection, again found in the Kyoto lecture: 'In 1907, while I was writing a review of the consequences of special relativity ... I realized that all the natural phenomena could be discussed in terms of special relativity except for the law of gravitation. I felt a deep desire to understand the reason behind this. ... It was most unsatisfactory to me that, although the relation between inertia and energy is so beautifully derived [in special relativity], there is no relation between inertia and weight. I suspected that this relationship was inexplicable by means of special relativity' [I1]. The absence of the equation for the static Newtonian gravitational potential Φ:

$$\Delta\Phi = 4\pi G\rho \tag{9.1}$$

(where ρ is the matter density and G the Newtonian gravitational constant) in the 1907 review indicates that the generalization of this equation to special relativity was not his ultimate purpose. Equation 9.1 does not appear in his papers until February 1912 [E6], but by then he already knew that this equation is not generally true even in the static case, as we shall see in Chapter 11.

Three main issues are raised in Section V of the Jahrbuch article.

1. The Equivalence Principle. 'Is it conceivable that the principle of relativity also holds for systems which are accelerated relative to each other?' That is Einstein's starting question, 'which must occur to everyone who has followed the applications of the relativity principle.' Then he gives the standard argument. A reference frame Σ_1 is accelerated in the x direction with a constant acceleration γ. A second frame Σ_2 is at rest in a homogeneous gravitational field which imparts an acceleration $-\gamma$ in the x direction to all objects. 'In the present state of experience, we have no reason to assume that . . . Σ_1 and Σ_2 are distinct in any respect, and in what follows we shall therefore *assume* the *complete* [my italics] physical equivalence of a gravitational field and the corresponding acceleration of the reference frame [Σ_1]. This assumption extends the principle of relativity to the case of uniformly accelerated motion of the reference frame.' Einstein noted that his review was not the place for a thorough discussion of the questions which now arose. Nevertheless, he made a beginning by applying his new postulate to the Maxwell equations, always for uniform acceleration. He did not raise the question of the further extension to nonuniform acceleration until 1912, the year he first referred to his hypothesis as the 'equivalence principle' [E7].

2. *The Gravitational Red Shift.*   Many textbooks on relativity ascribe to Einstein the method of calculating the red shift by means of the Doppler effect of light falling from the top to the bottom of an upwardly accelerating elevator. That is indeed the derivation he gave in 1911 (Chapter 11). However, he was already aware of the red shift in 1907. The derivation he gave at that time is less general, more tortured, and yet, oddly, more sophisticated. It deserves particular mention because it contains the germ of two ideas that were to become cornerstones of his final theory: the existence of local Lorentz frames and the constancy of the velocity of light for infinitesimally small paths. The argument, restricted to small velocities, small uniform accelerations, and small time intervals, runs as follows.

Consider two coordinate systems S (x,y,z,t) and Σ (ξ,η,ζ,τ) which at one time are coincident and which both have velocity $v = 0$ (the symbols in parentheses denote the respective space–time coordinates). At that one time, synchronize a network of clocks in S with each other and with a similar network in Σ. The time of coincidence of S and Σ is set at $t = \tau = 0$. System S remains at rest, while Σ starts moving in the x direction with a constant acceleration γ. Introduce next a third system S' (x',y',z',t') which relative to S moves with uniform velocity v in the x direction in such a way that, for a certain *fixed* time t, $x' = \xi$, $y' = \eta$, $z' = \zeta$. Thus, $v = \gamma t$. Imagine further that at the time of coincidence of S' and Σ all clocks in S' are synchronized with those in Σ.

I. Consider a time interval δ after the coincidence of S' and Σ. This interval is so small that all effects $O(\delta^2)$ are neglected. What is the rate of the clocks in S' relative to those in Σ if γ is so small that all effects $O(\gamma^2)$ can also be neglected? One easily sees that, given all the assumptions, the influence of relative displacement, relative velocity, and acceleration on the relative rates of the clocks in Σ and S' are all of second or higher order. Thus in the infinitesimal interval δ, we can still use the times of the clocks in the local Lorentz frame S' to describe the rate of the Σ clocks. Therefore, 'the principle of the constancy of the light velocity can be . . . used for the definition of simultaneity if one restricts oneself to small light paths.' The trick of using three coordinate systems is ingenious. On the one hand, S and S' are inertial frames and so one can use special relativity. On the other hand, during a small time interval the measurements in S' can be identified with those in Σ up to higher-order effects.

II. How do clocks in two distinct space points of Σ run relative to each other? At $t = \tau = 0$, the two Σ clocks were synchronous with each other and with clocks in S. The two points in Σ move in the same way relative to S. Therefore the two Σ clocks remain synchronous relative to S. But then (by special relativity) they are not synchronous relative to S' and thus, by (I), not synchronous relative to each other. We can now *define* the *time* τ *of* Σ by singling out *one* clock in Σ—say, the one at the origin —and for that clock setting $\tau = t$. Next, with the help of (I) we can define simultaneity in Σ by using S': the simultaneity condition of events 1 and 2 in Σ is

$$t_1 - \frac{vx_1}{c^2} = t_2 - \frac{vx_2}{c^2} \tag{9.2}$$

where, again, $v = \gamma t = \gamma \tau$. Let 1 correspond to the origin of Σ and 2 to a space point $(\xi,0,0)$ where the clock reading is called σ. Introduce one last approximation: the time τ of S' $-$ Σ coincidence is also taken small so that $O(\tau^2)$ effects are negligible. Then $x_2 - x_1 = x_2' - x_1' = \xi$, $t_1 \equiv \tau$, $t_2 \equiv \sigma$, so that Eq. 9.2 becomes

$$\sigma = \tau \left(1 + \frac{\gamma \xi}{c^2} \right) \tag{9.3}$$

a formula that is found—albeit derived differently—in modern textbooks.

The application of the equivalence principle to this equation is also familiar. It says that for a resting frame in a homogeneous gravitational field in the ξ direction:

$$\sigma = \tau \left(1 + \frac{\Phi}{c^2} \right) \tag{9.4}$$

where Φ is the gravitational potential energy difference between $(\xi,0,0)$ and the origin. [Note. Here and in what follows gravitational energy always refers to unit mass so that Φ has the dimension (velocity)^2.]

Einstein at once turned to the physics of Eq. 9.4: 'There are "clocks" which are available at locations with distinct gravitational potential and whose rates can be controlled very accurately; these are the generators of spectral lines. It follows from the preceding that light coming from the solar surface . . . has a longer wavelength than the light generated terrestrially from the same material on earth.' To this well-known conclusion, he appended a footnote: '*Here one assumes that* [*Eq. 9.4*] *also holds for an inhomogeneous gravitational field*' [my italics]. This assumption was of cardinal importance for Einstein's further thinking. He would explore its further consequences in 1911.

3. Maxwell's Equations; Bending of Light; Gravitational Energy = mc². Indomitably Einstein goes on. He tackles the Maxwell equations next. His tools are the same as those just described for the red shift. Again he compares the description in S with the one in Σ, using the local inertial frame S' as an intermediary. The steps are straightforward. I omit the details and state only his results.

Einstein finds, first, that the Maxwell equations in Σ have the same form as in S, but with the velocity of light c in S replaced by:

$$c\left(1 + \frac{\gamma\xi}{c^2} \right) = c\left(1 + \frac{\Phi}{c^2} \right) \tag{9.5}$$

in Σ. 'It follows from this that the light rays which do not run in the ξ direction are bent by the gravitational field.' Second, he examines the energy conservation law in Σ and finds 'a very notable result. An energy E [defined as an energy for the case of no gravitational field] . . . contributes to the total energy an additional position dependent amount

$$\frac{E}{c^2}\gamma\xi = \frac{E}{c^2}\Phi \tag{9.6}$$

In a gravitational field, one must associate with every energy E an additional position-dependent energy which equals the position-dependent energy of a "ponderable" mass of magnitude E/c^2. The law [$E = mc^2$] . . . therefore holds not only for inertial but also for gravitational mass.'

As said, the *Jahrbuch* article was received by the editor on December 4. On December 24, Einstein wrote to Conrad Habicht:

> At this time I am [again] busy with considerations on relativity theory in connection with the law of gravitation. . . . I hope to clear up the so-far unexplained secular changes of the perihelion length of Mercury . . . [but] so far it does not seem to work. [E8]

I own two mementos of Einstein, which I cherish. One is his last pipe. Its head is made of clay, its stem is a reed. Helen Dukas presented it to me some time in 1955. The other is the galley proof of Appendix II, 'Generalized Theory of Gravitation,' which appeared first in the 1950 edition of his *The Meaning of Relativity*. On the opening page of the proofs, the following words are written in a slightly shaky hand: 'Pauli: nach Einsichtnahme bitte Pais geben. A. E.,' P.: after perusal please give to P. I was in my thirties when that 1950 book came out. I read it then and have reread it once every few years, always with the same thought as I turn the pages. Does the man never stop?

Now I react similarly to the *Jahrbuch* article, which I first read at a later age. This review does not have the perfection of the 1905 paper on special relativity. The approximations are clumsy and mask the generality of the conclusions. Einstein was the first to say so, in 1911. The conclusion about the bending of light is qualitatively correct, quantitatively wrong—though, in 1907, not yet logically wrong. Einstein was the first to realize this, in 1915. Despite all that, I admire this article at least as much as the perfect relativity paper of 1905, not so much for its details as for its courage.

Einstein's treatment of simultaneity in 1905 was the result of many years of thinking that had led him to a new physical interpretation of global Lorentz invariance. Only two years later, he realized that the extension of the principle of special relativity demanded a reevaluation of the validity of this most precious tool. In 1907, he already clearly knew that there was something amiss with this invariance if his equivalence principle was to hold up in all generality. He did not know then that Lorentz invariance was to return in a new, local version. Others might have shied away from the equivalence principle in order to retain the global invariance. Not so Einstein. With a total lack of fear he starts on the new road. For the next eight years he has no choice. He has to go on. From then on also his style changes. If the work of 1905 has the quality of Mozart, then the work of 1907–15 is reminiscent of Beethoven. The quotation at the head of this chapter is the motto of the last movement of Beethoven's opus 135: Must it be? It must be.

References

E1. A. Einstein, *Nature* **106**, 782 (1921).
E2. ——, letter to R. W. Lawson, January 22, 1920.
E3. ——, *Jahrb. Rad. Elektr.* **4**, 411 (1907).
E4. ——, letter to J. Stark, September 25, 1907, quoted in [H1].
E5. ——, letter to J. Stark, November 1, 1907, quoted in [H1].
E6. ——, *AdP* **38**, 355 (1912).
E7. ——, [E6], p. 365.
E8. ——, letter to K. Habicht, December 24, 1907.
H1. A. Hermann, *Sudhoff's Archiv.* **50**, 267 (1966).
I1. J. Ishiwara, *Einstein Koēn-Roku.* Tokyo-Tosho, Tokyo, 1977.
L1. R. W. Lawson, *Nature* **106**, 781 (1921).
L2. ——, letter to A. Einstein, November 26, 1919.

10

Herr Professor Einstein

10a. From Bern to Zürich

Soon after December 1907 Einstein began his academic career.

His first step, then a common one, was to apply for a Privatdozentship. This was not a faculty position and no salary was provided by a university or any other official body. To be Privatdozent meant only to have the right to teach at the university where one was appointed. The only remuneration was a small fee paid by each course attendant. It used to be said often in those times that a university career could be contemplated only if one was independently wealthy or married to a well-to-do person. Neither applied to Einstein. That is perhaps why nothing had come of his earlier intent to seek such a post [E1].

In 1907 he decided nevertheless to apply while retaining his position at the patent office. On June 17 he sent a letter to the cantonal authorities in Bern enclosing copies of his PhD thesis, of seventeen published papers (including, of course, the harvest of 1905), and a curriculum vitae. Several faculty members spoke in favor of the application when the matter came up for discussion.* But rules are rules. For whatever reason, Einstein had omitted to follow the requirement to send along with his application a Habilitationsschrift, a not hitherto published scientific article. Accordingly, the request was denied until such time as Herr Einstein saw fit to produce such a document [F1]. Einstein procrastinated. In January 1908 he wrote to Grossmann, asking him the best way to apply for a vacant high school position: 'Can I visit there to give an oral demonstration of my laudable personality as teacher and citizen? Wouldn't I probably make a bad impression (no Swiss-German, Semitic looks, etc.)? Would it make sense if I were to extol my scientific papers on that occasion?' [E1a]. Perhaps he never applied, perhaps he was rejected. At any rate, early in 1908 he finally produced his Habilitationsschrift and on February 28 a letter was drawn up informing young Doctor Einstein that his application had been accepted and that he had been granted the *venia docendi,* the right to teach [F2]. Einstein was for the first time a member of the academic community.

His main job at the patent office forced him to lecture at odd hours. In the summer semester of 1908 he taught the kinetic theory of heat on Saturday and

---

*The professor of experimental physics was opposed to the idea, however [E1a].

Tuesday mornings from seven to eight to an audience of three friends, including Besso. His second and last course was given in the winter semester of 1908–9. Each Wednesday evening from six to seven he lectured to four listeners. His sister Maja would occasionally drop in. After two years at the University of Berlin, she was now attending the University of Bern. It was there that on December 21, 1908, the next main academic event in the Einstein family took place. On that day Maja received her PhD magna cum laude on a thesis in Romance languages [E1b].

The topic of Einstein's second course, the theory of radiation, was also the subject of his Habilitationsschrift: 'Consequences for the Constitution of Radiation of the Energy Distribution Law of Blackbody Radiation' [F3]. This paper was never published nor was its manuscript ever found. Its content may well have been incorporated in the reports 'On the Current Status of the Radiation Problem,' published early in 1909 [E2], and "On the Development of Our Views Concerning the Nature and Constitution of Radiation,' which followed later that same year [E3]. These two papers are not just survey articles. They contain highly important new physics. Forty years later, Pauli said of the second report that it 'can be considered as one of the landmarks in the development of theoretical physics' [P1]. In Chapter 21 I shall come back in detail to these two papers. Suffice it to say here that they are Einstein's most important contributions in the period from 1908 to 1911.

The first of these two papers was completed in Bern, the second one in Zürich. Meanwhile Einstein had obtained his first faculty post, associate professor of theoretical physics at the University of Zürich. It was a newly created position. There had been no professor of theoretical or mathematical physics since Clausius had left the university in 1867 [R1]. The proposal to the faculty written by Alfred Kleiner clearly shows Einstein's rapidly growing renown: 'Today Einstein ranks among the most important theoretical physicists and has been recognized rather generally as such since his work on the relativity principle . . . uncommonly sharp conception and pursuit of ideas . . . clarity and precision of style. . . .' [S1].

Einstein must have been aware of this appreciation. Perhaps, also, he may have sensed some of the following sentiments expressed in a part of the final faculty report*: 'These expressions of our colleague Kleiner, based on several years of personal contact, were all the more valuable for the committee as well as for the faculty as a whole since Herr Dr Einstein is an Israelite and since precisely to the Israelites among scholars are ascribed (in numerous cases not entirely without cause) all kinds of unpleasant peculiarities of character, such as intrusiveness, impudence, and a shopkeeper's mentality** in the perception of their academic position. It should be said, however, that also among the Israelites there exist men who do not exhibit a trace of these disagreeable qualities and that it is not proper,

---

*It is, of course, highly improbable that Einstein ever saw this report.

**'. . . Zudringlichkeit, Unverschämtheit, Krämerhaftigkeit . . .'

therefore, to disqualify a man only because he happens to be a Jew. Indeed, one occasionally finds people also among non-Jewish scholars who in regard to a commercial perception and utilization of their academic profession develop qualities which are usually considered as specifically "Jewish." Therefore neither the committee nor the faculty as a whole considered it compatible with its dignity to adopt anti-Semitism as a matter of policy† and the information which Herr Kollege Kleiner was able to provide about the character of Herr Dr Einstein has completely reassured us' [S1a]. Opinions such as these of course do not describe just Zürich in 1909 but western civilization in the early twentieth century.

The secret faculty vote of March 1909 on the Einstein appointment was ten in favor, one abstention. On July 6, 1909, Einstein submitted his resignation to the patent office. Two days later a new mark of rising eminence: the University of Geneva bestowed on him his first honorary doctorate.* On October 15 he commenced his new university position; on the 22nd he, Mileva, and Hans Albert were registered as residing at Moussonstrasse 12. That same month the new associate professor and doctor *honoris causa* attended, at age thirty, his first physics conference, at Salzburg. At this meeting he gave the report so highly praised by Pauli. On December 11, 1909, he gave, for the first but not the last time in his life, an inaugural address, this one entitled 'On the Role of Atomic Theory in the New Physics.' Einstein's salary in his new position was 4500 SF per annum, the same amount he had received as a technical expert second class in Bern.

New reponsibilities awaited him: six to eight hours of teaching and seminars per week, students to be taken care of, among them Hans Tanner, his first PhD student, who did not get his degree with Einstein, however.** He appeared in class in somewhat shabby attire, wearing pants that were too short and carrying with him a slip of paper the size of a visiting card on which he had sketched his lecture notes [S2]. In his later years, Einstein used to say that he did not enjoy teaching. 'He [E.] obviously enjoyed explaining his ideas to others, and was exceptionally good at it because of his own way of thinking in intuitive and informal terms. What he presumably found irksome was the need to prepare and present material that was not at the moment at the center of his interest. Thus the preparation of lectures would interfere with his own thought' [S3].

In his Zürich period, from October 1909 to March 1911, Einstein published eleven papers on theoretical physics, including the one on critical opalescence. He also was active as an experimentalist. In his Bern days, he had published a paper that contained the idea for an apparatus intended to measure small voltages [E4].

---

†'. . . den "Antisemitismus" als Prinzip auf ihre Fahne zu schreiben. . . .'

*Marie Curie and Ostwald were also among the recipients of honorary degrees.

**After Einstein left for Prague, Tanner went to Basel, where he got his degree in 1912. Another student, Hermann Schuepp, was given a PhD thesis topic by Herzog before Einstein arrived at Zürich. Einstein acted as the referee for this thesis, which was accepted by the faculty on December 21, 1909 [D1].

In Bern he had tried to follow up experimentally on this idea in 'a small laboratory for electrostatic experiments which I have concocted with primitive means' [E5]. Einstein's fellow Olympia member, Konrad Habicht, and the latter's brother Paul became interested. In the university laboratory in Zürich, they constructed a 'Maschinchen,' little machine, as Einstein affectionately called his gadget. In their paper the Habichts state that 'the . . . experiments were performed in collaboration with A. Einstein' [H1]. Einstein followed the further development with lively interest [E6]. (For more on the little machine, see Chapter 29.)

Einstein and his family moved to Prague in March 1911. The family was a foursome by then. On July 28, 1910, a second son had been born to Albert and Mileva. They named him Eduard and called him Tede or Tedel; their nickname for the two boys was 'die Bärchen,' the little bears. 'Eduard inherited from his father the facial traits and the musical talents, from his mother the tendency to melancholy' [S4]. In later years Eduard cared much for the arts. He wrote poetry. He wanted to become a psychiatrist and studied medicine but did not reach his goal. His life came to a sad end.*

10b. Three and a Half Years of Silence

Einstein first stated the equivalence principle in 1907. In 1915 he presented the general theory of relativity as we now know it. This much I learned long ago from Pauli's encyclopedia article, and also that Einstein arrived at his final version 'nach langen Irrwegen,' after having followed wrong tracks for a long time [P2]. I therefore imagined an Einstein engrossed in his new ideas of 1907 and laboring unremittingly from 1907 until 1915 to incorporate into a full-fledged theory the generalization from invariance under uniform motion to invariance under general motion. Not until I read his publications and especially his correspondence of that period did I realize that I was wrong.

Einstein remained silent on gravitation from December 1907 until June 1911, a few months after he had settled in Prague.

One can think of many reasons for this. It was an interval of conspicuous commotion. There was a new baby in the family. There were three career changes, first from technical expert to Privatdozent in Bern to associate professor in Zürich and then, as we shall see, to full professor in Prague. There was a new style of doing physics: in collaboration, first with Laub, then with the Habicht brothers, then with Ludwig Hopf. Lecturing took time and effort: 'I am *very* occupied with the courses, so that my *real* free time is less than in Bern' [E7]. All of these factors could have contributed to digressions from the main course. It was also a period in which Einstein experienced a rapid rise to fame and in which he established

*Helen Dukas tells me that Einstein recognized rather early signs of dementia praecox in his younger son. After many vicissitudes, Eduard was institutionalized in the Burghölzli Hospital in Zürich, where he died in 1965.

his first contacts with larger segments of the physics community. Such circumstances often lead to a slackening of creative tensions. All these events combined might well have sufficed for others to desist from starting a truly major new program in research. Yet, I think, all this has little if anything to do with Einstein's silence on gravitation.

Indeed, if he was silent on that subject, he was not silent on physics as a whole. New research continued during the years in question. There were the papers with Laub on special relativity, the papers with Hopf on classical radiation theory, and the difficult paper on critical opalescence. He invented his little machine. Above all, there were the papers on quantum physics already mentioned, highly creative in content. All this work hardly gives the impression of a man who is sidetracked and cannot find time for serious thinking.

There is, of course, nothing unusual about the fact that Einstein did not publish anything new about gravitation between 1908 and 1911. It could mean simply that he thought about the problem but did not find anything novel to communicate. More curious is the fact that he twice gave surveys of relativity theory without mentioning gravitation or the equivalence principle and its remarkable implications: the red shift and the bending of light. The first of these surveys was his report at the Salzburg conference, which included a survey of relativity theory, 'of the consequences of which I would like to mention only a single one' [E3] (namely, $E = mc^2$), but quantum theory rather than relativity theory was the main issue. The second survey was given in 1910. It is a detailed document, forty-four printed pages long [E8]. There is no mention of relatively accelerated systems. Again this is not too surprising. Even the special theory was still so new that it may have seemed advisable to confine the explications to the case of uniform relative motion.

However, even such pedagogical motives fail to explain one fact which I find truly significant. Throughout his career Einstein was accustomed to writing to one or more colleagues or friends about scientific problems which at any given time were important to him. With a refreshing frankness, he would share with them not only the delights of a new insight but also the troubles of being stuck. It would not in the least have been out of style for Einstein to write to one of his friends: I am preoccupied with the gravitation problem, it mystifies me and I am not getting anywhere. In fact, I am quite sure that he would have written in this vein if, between 1908 and 1911, this problem had really nagged him. Yet, as far as I know, in his scientific correspondence during this period, mention is made only once of gravitation and the related new issues. These same letters also made clear to me the reason for Einstein's silence on the equivalence principle and its consequences: it was not gravitation that was uppermost in his mind. It was the quantum theory.

Some examples may show the intensity of Einstein's concern with quantum physics during that period. Sometime in 1908 he wrote to Laub, 'I am incessantly busy with the question of the constitution of radiation. . . . This quantum problem is so uncommonly important and difficult that it should be the concern of everybody. I did succeed in inventing something which formally corresponds to [a quantum theory], but I have conclusive grounds to consider it nonsense' [E9]. To Stark, July 1909: 'You can hardly imagine how much trouble I have taken to invent a satisfactory mathematical treatment of the quantum theory' [E10]. To Besso, November 1909: 'Reflected little and unsuccessfully about light-quanta' [E11]. Again to Besso, one month later, he writes about attempts to modify Maxwell's equations in such a way that the new equations would have light-quantum solutions: 'Here perhaps lies the solution of the light-quantum problem' [E12]. To Laub, that same day: "I have not yet found a solution of the light-quantum question. All the same I will try to see if I cannot work out this favorite problem of mine' [E13].* Also to Laub, March 1910: 'I have found some interesting things about quanta, but nothing is complete yet' [E14].

In the summer of 1910 Einstein wrote to Laub about his long review article [E8]: '[This paper] contains only a rather broad exposé of the epistemological foundations of the relativity theory' [E15]. This would have been as good an occasion as any to reflect on the new epistemology of the equivalence principle, but Einstein does not do so. Rather he adds, a few lines later, 'I have not come further with the question of the constitution of light.' In November he writes again to Laub: 'Currently I have great expectations of solving the radiation problem . . .' [E16]. A week later, once more to Laub: 'Once again I am getting nowhere with the solution of the light-quantum problem' [E17]. In December, to Laub: 'The enigma of radiation will not yield' [E18]. Finally, by May 1911 he is ready to give up for the time being; he writes to Besso: 'I do not ask anymore whether these quanta really exist. Nor do I attempt any longer to construct them, since I now know that my brain is incapable of fathoming [the problem] this way' [E19].

One month later, in June 1911, he was back to gravitation theory.

It would, of course, be absurd to suppose that Einstein did not think about gravitation at all during those three and a half years. A letter he wrote to Sommerfeld from Bern, just before taking up his post in Zürich, shows that he had indeed done so:

> 'The treatment of the uniformly rotating rigid body seems to me to be very important because of an extension of the relativity principle to uniformly rotating systems by trains of thought which I attempted to pursue for uniformly accelerated translation in the last section of . . . my paper [of 1907]. [E20]**

That isolated remark, important as it is, does not change my opinion that Einstein was concentrating in other directions during this period. In later years, Einstein himself tended to be uncommunicative about his thoughts on gravitation during

---

*Ich will sehen ob ich dieses Lieblingsei doch nicht ausbrüten kann.

**See also [S5]. I shall return in the next chapter to the influence of the problem of rotating bodies on Einstein's thinking.

that time. In the Gibson lecture on the origins of the general theory of relativity, given in Glasgow in June 1933, he says,

> 'If [the equivalence principle] was true for all processes, it indicated that the principle of relativity must be extended to include nonuniform motions of the coordinate systems if one desired to obtain an unforced and natural theory of the gravitational field. From 1908 until 1911 I concerned myself with considerations of this nature, which I need not describe here' [E21].

In his major scientific autobiographical notes of 1949 [E22], he remains silent about those particular years. His final autobiographical sketch, written a few months before his death, contains the following statement: 'From 1909 to 1912, while I had to teach theoretical physics at the universities of Zürich and Prague, I puzzled incessantly about the problem [of gravitation]' [E23]. This is indeed borne out by letters he wrote to his friends after the middle of 1911, but not by the letters prior to that time. Indeed, it seems evident that until he reached Prague, he considered—and, it should be said, for many good reasons—the riddles of the quantum theory far more important and urgent than the problem of gravitation. In sharp contrast, from then until 1916 there are only a few minor papers on the quantum theory while his correspondence shows clearly that now the theory of gravitation is steadily on his mind. I would not go so far as to say that this intense preoccupation is the only reason he did not at once participate in the new quantum dynamics initiated by Bohr in 1913. But it must have been a heavily contributing factor.

Let us next join Einstein in Prague.

References

D1. C. Dür, letter to R. Jost, November 29, 1979.

E1. A. Einstein, letter to M. Besso, January 1903; *EB,* p. 3.

E1a. ——, letter to M. Grossmann, January 3, 1908.

E1b. M. Einstein, 'Beiträge zur Überlieferung des Chevaliers du Cygne und der Enfance Godefroi,' Druck, Erlangen, 1910.

E2. A. Einstein, *Phys. Zeitschr.* **10,** 185 (1909).

E3. ——, *Phys. Zeitschr.* **10,** 817 (1909).

E4. ——, *Phys. Zeitschr.* **9,** 216 (1908).

E5. ——, letter to J. Stark, December 14, 1908. Reprinted in A. Hermann, *Sudhoffs Archiv.* **50,** 267 (1966).

E6. —— in *EB* pp. 42, 47, 464.

E7. ——, letter to M. Besso, November 17, 1909; *EB*, p. 16.

E8. ——, *Arch. Sci. Phys. Nat.* **29,** 5, 125 (1910).

E9. ——, letter to J. Laub, 1908, undated.

E10. ——, letter to J. Stark, July 31, 1909. Reprinted in A. Hermann, [E5].

E11. ——, letter to M. Besso, November 17, 1909; *EB*, p. 16.

E12. ——, letter to M. Besso, December 31, 1909; *EB*, p. 18.

E13. ——, letter to J. Laub, December 31, 1909.

E14. ——, letter to J. Laub, March 16, 1910.

E15. ——, letter to J. Laub, Summer 1910, undated.

E16. ——, letter to J. Laub, November 4, 1910.

E17. ——, letter to J. Laub, November 11, 1910.

E18. ——, letter to J. Laub, December 28, 1910.

E19. ——, letter to M. Besso, May 13, 1911; *EB*, p. 19.

E20. ——, letter to A. Sommerfeld, September 29, 1909.

E21. ——, *'The Origins of the General Theory of Relavitity.'* Jackson, Wylie, Glasgow, 1933.

E22. —— in *Albert Einstein, Philosopher–Scientist* (P. A. Schilpp, Ed.). Tudor, New York, 1949.

E23. —— in *Helle Zeit, dunkle Zeit* (C. Seelig, Ed.). Europa Verlag, Zürich, 1956.

F1. M. Flückiger, *Einstein in Bern,* pp. 114ff. Paul Haupt Verlag, Bern, 1974.

F2. ——, [F1], p. 123.

F3. ——, [F1], p. 118.

H1. C. and P. Habicht, *Phys. Zeitschr.* **11,** 532 (1910).

P1. W. Pauli in *Albert Einstein: Philosopher–Scientist,* p. 149.

P2. —— in *Encyklopädie der Mathematische Wissenschaften,* Vol. V, 2, Sec. 56. Teubner Verlag, Leipzig, 1921.

R1. G. Rasche and H. Staub, *Viertelj. Schrift Naturf. Ges. Zürich* **124,** 205 (1979).

S1. Se, p. 166.

S1a. C. Stoll, letter to H. Ernst, March 4, 1909.

S2. Se, p. 171.

S3. E. G. Straus, lecture delivered at the Einstein Centennial Celebration, Yeshiva University, September 18, 1979.

S4. Se, p. 192.

S5. J. Stachel in *General Relativity and Gravitation,* GRG Society Einstein Centennial Volume, Vol. 1, p. 1. Plenum Press, New York, 1980.

11

The Prague Papers

11a. From Zürich to Prague

'I will most probably receive a call from a large university to be full professor with a salary significantly better than I have now. I am not yet permitted to say *where* it is' [E1]. So Einstein wrote to his mother on April 4, 1910, less than half a year after he had begun his associate professorship in Zürich. The call he expected was supposed to come from the Karl-Ferdinand University, the German university in Prague. He had to be discreet since the search committee convened in January had not even made a proposal to the faculty yet. The experimentalist Anton Lampa, committee chairman and Einstein's strong advocate, had sounded him out beforehand. The committee report dated April 21, 1910, proposed three candidates and stated that all of them were willing to accept a formal offer. Einstein was the first choice. This report quotes a glowing recommendation by Planck: '[Einstein's work on relativity] probably exceeds in audacity everything that has been achieved so far in speculative science and even in epistemology; non-Euclidean geometry is child's play by comparison.' Planck went on to compare Einstein to Copernicus [H1].

The news spread. In July 1910 the Erziehungsrat (board of education) petitioned the government of the Canton Zürich. It was noted that, according to experts, Einstein was one of the few authorities in theoretical physics; that students from the ETH were coming to the University of Zürich to attend his lectures; that he was teaching six to eight hours per week instead of the customary four to six; and that efforts should be made to keep him in Zürich. An annual raise of 1000 SF was proposed. The petition was granted [P1].

It would appear that Einstein was eager to go to Prague, however. In the summer of 1910 he wrote to Laub, 'I did not receive the call from Prague. I was only proposed by the faculty; the ministry has not accepted my proposal because of my Semitic descent' [E2]. (I have seen no documents to this effect.) In October he wrote to Laub that the appointment seemed pretty certain [E3], but in December he wrote that there had been no word from Prague yet [E4]. However, on January 6, 1911, His Imperial and Apostolic Majesty Franz Joseph formally approved the appointment, effective April 1. Einstein was notified by letter, dated January 13 [H1]. Prior to the beginning of his appointment, he had to record his religious affiliation. The answer *none* was unacceptable. He wrote 'Mosaisch'

[F1]. On January 10, he sent his letter of resignation, which was accepted on February 10 [P2]. In February Einstein visited Lorentz in Leiden. In March he and his family arrived in Prague [S1].

It is mildly puzzling to me why Einstein made this move. He liked Zürich. Mileva liked Zürich. He had colleagues to talk to and friends to play music with. He had been given a raise. He must have known that in the normal course of events further promotion was to be expected. Prague was not an active center of theoretical physics. However, a letter by Kleiner to a colleague may indicate that there were other considerations. 'After my statements about his conduct some time ago (after which he wanted to apologize, which I once again prevented), Einstein knows that he cannot expect personal sympathy from the faculty representatives. I would think you may wait until he submits his resignation before you return to this matter . . .' [K1]. I do not know what the cause of friction was.

'I have here a splendid institute in which I work comfortably,' Einstein wrote to Grossmann soon after his arrival in Prague [E5]. Ludwig Hopf, his assistant from Zürich, had accompanied him but left soon afterward for a junior position in Aachen. What little I know about Emil Nohel, Hopf's successor, is found in Chapter 29. In the summer of 1911, Besso came for a visit [E6]. In February 1912 Einstein and Ehrenfest met personally for the first time in Prague [K2]. Otto Stern availed himself of his independent means to join Einstein there, after having received his PhD with Sackur in Breslau [S2], and stayed with Einstein from 1912 to 1914, first in Prague, then in Zürich.

'My position and my institute give me much joy,' Einstein wrote to Besso, but added, 'Nur die Menschen sind mir so fremd,' (Only the people are so alien to me) [E7]. It appears that Einstein was never quite comfortable in Prague. When he arrived at the Institute, a porter would greet him with a bow and a 'your most obedient servant', a servility that did not agree with him. He was bothered by bureaucracy. 'Infinitely much paperwork for the most insignificant Dreck,' he wrote to one friend [E5] and, 'Die Tintenscheisserei ist endlos,' to another [E7a]. His wife was not at ease either [F2]. In Einstein's day, there were four institutions of higher learning in Prague, two universities and two institutes of technology, one Czech and one German each. As Stern later recalled: 'At none [of these institutions] was there anyone with whom Einstein could talk about the matters which really interested him . . . he was completely isolated in Prague . . .' [J1].

Einstein's stay in Prague lasted sixteen months. Ehrenfest was his first choice as his successor. This proposal came to naught because of Ehrenfest's refusal to state a religious affiliation [K3]. Eventually Philipp Frank was named to this post on Einstein's recommendation. Frank stayed in Prague until 1938.* In the next chapter I shall describe Einstein's return to Zürich. First, however, let us have a look at his physics during the Prague period.

*See Frank's biography [F1] for other details about Einstein's Prague period.

11b. 1911. The Bending of Light is Detectable

> Do not Bodies act upon Light at a distance, and by their action
> bend its Rays; and is not this action *(caeteris paribus)* strongest
> at the least distance?
>
> ISAAC NEWTON: *Opticks*, Query 1

Einstein finally broke his silence about gravitation in June 1911 [E8]. He had
become dissatisfied with his presentation of 1907 [E9]. 'More than that, I now
realize that one of the most important consequences of those considerations is amenable to experimental verification.' This is the bending of light. He had already
been aware of this phenomenon in 1907. However, at that time he had thought
only of terrestrial experiments as a means of its observation and had concluded
that these would be too hard to perform (still true to this day). Meanwhile it had
dawned on him that deflection of light by the sun could be detectable. He also had
other new conclusions to report.

The resulting paper, 'On the Influence of Gravitation on the Propagation of
Light,' is included in *Das Relativitätsprinzip,* which first appeared in 1913, a
handy little book (English translation, [L1]). Its later editions contain contributions to relativity theory by Lorentz, Minkowski, Einstein, and Weyl. The book
has two flaws. First, there is no contribution by Poincaré. Poincaré's memoir of
1905 is lengthy and does not readily fit into this small volume. However, a fragment could easily have been included, especially since one of Lorentz's papers does
appear in abridged form. A second shortcoming of the book is the absence of the
brief Section V of Einstein's 1907 article [E9]. Either this piece should have been
included along with his 1911 article or else both should have been omitted, since
the finer points of the 1911 paper cannot be understood without the approximations he had used in 1907.

In the 1911 paper Einstein cautioned his readers, 'Even if the theoretical foundation is correct, the relations derived here are valid only in first approximation,'
but did not add an explicit statement about the nature of this approximation. He
had yet to acquire the skill of reiterating conclusions from his own earlier work.

This is not surprising. Prior to Einstein's involvement with gravitation, each
one of his papers is transparent and self-contained (with the possible exception of
his earliest writing on the foundations of statistical mechanics) though his readers
may occasionally have to go to some effort to realize that. We have seen on various
earlier occasions that Einstein did not go to great trouble to search the literature
for contributions by others, but that was no particular hindrance to an understanding of what he himself had to communicate. Of course, he would return now and
then to a subject he had discussed earlier, but then the new contribution would
again be self-contained. We know that sometimes he had thought long and hard
before gaining a new insight, as in the case of special relativity. Yet little if any
sign of the preceding struggle is found in the resulting papers, which rather give
the impression of a man hugely enjoying himself. From 1907 until 1916, this light

touch and this element of closure is missing. His style of writing changes. Instead of statements made with characteristic finality, we find reports on work in progress.

Turning to the first of the Prague papers, I should evidently begin with the approximations to which Einstein referred. His problem was and remained to find a way to give meaning to simultaneity for the case of uniformly accelerated systems. To this end, he used once again the approximate methods of 1907. Thus in 1911 the three coordinate systems S, Σ, and S' discussed in Chapter 9 reappear.* Recall that Σ is in constant acceleration relative to S and that the inertial frame S' is at one, and only one, time coincident with Σ. As indicated earlier, the strategy was to relate the clocks in S' to those in S by a Lorentz transformation and then, for a tiny time interval, to identify the clock readings in S' with those in Σ. This is not a rigorous procedure, as we saw in Chapter 9. The approximations explained there are the ones that also apply to the paper now under consideration.

In 1911 the four main issues were the same as in 1907: the equivalence principle, the gravity of energy, the red shift, and the bending of light. The main equations in these two papers are also nearly all identical. However, Einstein now had new thoughts about each one of these four questions.

THE EQUIVALENCE PRINCIPLE

Let the frame S be at rest and let it carry a homogeneous gravitational field in the negative z direction. Σ is a field-free frame that moves with a constant acceleration relative to S in the positive z direction. Einstein first reminds the reader of the equivalence of Newton's mechanical laws in both frames. Then he rephrases this principle as follows. 'One can speak as little of the *absolute acceleration* of the reference frame as one can of the *absolute velocity* in the ordinary [special] relativity theory' (his italics). From this he concludes that 'according to this theory, the equal fall of all bodies in a gravitational field is *self-evident*' (my italics).

This seemingly innocent new twist is typical. Einstein had the gift of learning something new from ancient wisdom by turning it around. In the present instance, instead of following the reasoning—experimentally known equal time of fall $\rightarrow$ meaninglessness of constant absolute acceleration—he reverses the direction of the arrow of logic. Thus in 1911 we discern the first glimpses of the new Einstein program: to derive the equivalence principle from a new theory of gravitation. This cannot be achieved within the framework of what he called the ordinary relativity theory, the special theory. Therefore one must look for a new theory not only of gravitation but also of relativity. Another point made in this paper likewise bears on that new program. 'Of course, one cannot replace an *arbitrary* gravita-

*In the 1911 paper, Einstein denotes the frames S, Σ, and S' by K, K', and K_o, respectively. For ease of presentation, I continue to use his earlier notation.

tional field by a state of motion without gravitational field, as little as one can transform to rest by means of a relativity transformation all points of an arbitrarily moving medium.' This statement would continue to be true in the ultimate general theory of relativity.

Einstein concluded his comments on the equivalence principle by stressing again the great heuristic significance of the assumption that it is true for all physical phenomena rather than for point mechanics only.

THE GRAVITY OF ENERGY; THE RED SHIFT

In 1907 Einstein had noted that an electromagnetic field is the source not only of inertial energy but also of an equal amount of gravitational energy (Chapter 9). He had reached this conclusion by studying the structure of the Maxwell equations in the frame Σ. He was now ready to elaborate on this result, but without recourse to anything as specific as the electromagnetic origins of the energy in question. His new and broader view was based on general considerations regarding conservation laws. Consider (he said) the energy increase by an amount E of an arbitrary body. According to the special theory, there is a corresponding increase E/c^2 of its inertial mass. This leads to the 'so satisfactory' conclusion that the law of conservation of mass merges with the law of conservation of energy. Suppose now (he continues) that there were no corresponding increase of the gravitational mass of the body. Then one would have to maintain a separate conservation law of gravitational mass while, at the same time, there would no longer exist a separate conservation law for inertial mass. 'This must be considered as very improbable.' Not only the very existence of the equivalence principle but also the gravitational properties of energy point to the incompleteness of the special theory: 'The usual relativity theory [by itself] yields no argument from which we might conclude that the weight of a body depends on its energy content.' However, this dependence on energy can be derived in a rather general way if, in addition, we invoke the equivalence principle. 'We shall show . . . that the hypothesis of the equivalence of the systems [S and Σ] yields the gravity of energy as a necessary consequence. Then he gives the following argument. (At this point the reader may like to refresh his memory concerning the coordinate systems described in Chapter 9.)

Let there be a light receiver S_1 in the origin of the frame Σ and an emitter at a distance h along the positive z axis, also in Σ. The emitter S_2 emits an amount E_2 of radiation energy at just that moment in which the frame S' is coincident with Σ. The radiation will arrive at S_1 approximately after a time h/c. At that time, S_1 has the velocity $\gamma h/c$ relative to S', γ being the acceleration of Σ. Recall that clocks in Σ are judged by using the inertial frame S'. Einstein could therefore use a result of his 1905 paper on special relativity [E10]: the energy E_1 arriving at S_1 is larger than E_2:

$$E_1 = E_2\left(1 + \frac{v}{c}\right) = E_2\left(1 + \frac{\gamma h}{c^2}\right) \qquad (11.1)$$

Now go to the frame S with its gravitational field. In that frame, we install the same equipment S_1 and S_2 in the same relative positions as in Σ. Then Eq. 11.1 and the equivalence principle yield

$$E_1 = E_2 + \frac{E_2}{c^2}(\phi_2 - \phi_1) \qquad (11.2)$$

where ϕ_1 and ϕ_2 are the gravitational potential at positions 1 and 2, respectively. This is the energy conservation law for the transmission process. It implies that to an energy E there corresponds a gravitational mass E/c^2, the desired result.

Next Einstein treated the red shift in a similar way. First work in Σ. Let the light emitted at S_2 have the frequency ν_2. After having traveled the approximate time h/c, this light is received at S_1 with frequency ν_1. To find the connection between ν_2 and ν_1, work in S'. Then the well-known linear Doppler effect formula gives

$$\nu_1 = \nu_2\left(1 + \frac{\gamma h}{c^2}\right) \qquad (11.3)$$

The equivalence principle tells us what happens in S:

$$\nu_1 = \nu_2\left(1 + \frac{\phi}{c^2}\right) \qquad \phi = \phi_2 - \phi_1 \qquad (11.4)$$

Assume that this equation also holds for inhomogeneous fields. Let 2 be the sun and 1 the earth. Then ϕ is negative. A red shift is seen on earth such that $\Delta\nu/\nu \approx 10^{-6}$.

I next interrupt the discussion of the Prague paper in order to make two comments. First, Einstein derives Eq. 11.2 for the energy shift; then he starts 'all over again' and derives the frequency shift (Eq. 11.4). It is no accident, I am sure, that he did *not* derive only one of these equations and from there go to the other one with the help of

$$E = h\nu \qquad (11.5)$$

He had had something to do with Eq. 11.5. It cannot have slipped his mind; the quantum theory never slipped his mind. However, it was Einstein's style forever to avoid the quantum theory if he could help it—as in the present case of the energy and the frequency shift. In Chapter 26 I shall come back to discuss at some length this attitude of his, a main clue to the understanding of his destiny as a physicist.

Second, in good texts on general relativity the red shift is taught twice. In a first go-around, it is noted that the red shift follows from special relativity and the equivalence principle only. Then, after the tensor equations of general relativity have been derived and the equivalence principle has been understood to hold strictly only in the small, the red shift is returned to and a proof is given that it is sufficient for the derivation of the previous result to consider only the leading deviations of g_{44} from its flat-space–time value. If the text is modern enough, one is treated next to the niceties of second-order effects and to the extreme cases where expansions break down. All this should be remembered in order to grasp better Einstein's plight in 1911. He knows that special relativity is to be incorporated into a more profound theory, but he does not know yet how to do that. With care he manipulates his three coordinate systems in order to obtain Eqs. 11.1–11.4. He knows very well that these equations are approximations, but he does not know to what.

THE BENDING OF LIGHT

What and how can we measure? That prime question of science has a *double entendre*. First of all it means, What is conceptually interesting and technically feasible? Taken in that sense, Einstein's remarks on the red shift and the deflection of light had given direction to the phenomenology of general relativity even before that theory existed. The question has also a second meaning, What is a meaningful measurement as a matter of principle? Also in that sense Einstein had contributed by his re-analysis of simultaneity in 1905. In 1907 the study of the Maxwell equations in accelerated frames had taught him that the velocity of light is no longer a universal constant in the presence of gravitational fields. When he returned to this problem in 1911 he left aside, once again, these earlier dynamic considerations. Instead, he turned to the interpretation of Eq. 11.4.

'Superficially seen, [this equation] seems to state something absurd. If light is steadily transmitted from S_2 to S_1, then how can a different number of periods per second arrive at S_1 than were emitted in S_2? The answer is simple, however.' The apparent trouble lay not with the number of periods but with the second: one must examine with the greatest care what one means by the rate of clocks in an inhomogeneous gravitational field. This demands an understanding of the following three facts of time.

The Clock Factory.   One must first construct 'gleich beschaffene Uhren,' identically functioning clocks, to use Einstein's language. He does not state how this is done. However, his subsequent arguments make sense only if the following procedure is adopted. Construct a clock factory in a (sufficiently small) region of space in which the gravitational field is constant. Synchronize the clocks by some standard procedure. Transport these clocks, one of them (U_1) to a position 1, another one (U_2) to a position 2, etc.

Local Experiments.   Observe the frequency of a spectral line generated at 1 with the clock U_1. Call this frequency $\nu(1,1)$ (produced at 1, measured with U_1).

Next determine $\nu(2,2)$, the frequency of the same* spectral line produced at 2, measured with U_2. One will find (Einstein asserts) that $\nu(1,1) = \nu(2,2)$, 'the frequency is independent of where the light source and the [local] clock are placed.'

[Remark. This statement is not true in all rigor: even though we still cannot calculate the displacement of spectral lines caused by local external gravitational fields (we have no theory of quantum gravity!), we do know that such a displacement must exist; it should be small within our neighborhood.]

Global Experiments. Determine $\nu(2,1)$, the frequency of the same spectral line produced at 2 but now measured at 1 with U_1. As Eq. 11.4 implies, $\nu(2,1) \neq \nu(1,1)$. Yet, Einstein insists, we should continue to accept the physical criterion that the number of wave crests traveling between 2 and 1 shall be independent of the absolute value of time. This is quite possible since 'nothing forces us to the assumption that the ["gleich beschaffene"] clocks at different gravitational potentials [i.e., at 1 and at 2] should run equally fast.' (Recall that the synchronization was achieved in the factory.)

The conclusion is inevitable: the compatibility of Eq. 11.4 with the physical criterion implies that the clock U_2 in 2 runs slower by a factor $(1 + \phi/c^2)$ than U_1 in 1. This is, of course, compatible with $\nu(2,2) = \nu(1,1)$ since the spectral frequency in 2 also decreases by the same factor. After all, the spectral line is nothing but a clock itself. In other words, as a result of the transport to places of different gravitational field strength, clocks become 'verschieden beschaffen,' differently functioning. This leads to a 'consequence of . . . fundamental significance':

$$c_1 = c_2\left(1 + \frac{\phi}{c^2}\right) \tag{11.6}$$

where c_1 and c_2 are the local light velocities at 1 and 2 (the difference between c_1 and c_2 is assumed to be small, so that the symbol c in Eq. 11.6 may stand for either c_1 or c_2). Thus Einstein restored sanity, but at a price. 'In this theory the principle of the constancy of light velocity does not apply in the same way as in . . . the usual relativity theory.'

The final result of the paper is the application of Eq. 11.6 to the deflection of a light ray coming from 'infinity' and moving in the field of a gravitational point source (i.e., a $1/r$ potential). From a simple application of Huyghens' principle, Einstein finds that this ray when going to 'infinity' has suffered a deflection α toward the source given (in radians) by

$$\alpha = \frac{2GM}{\Delta c^2} \tag{11.7}$$

where G is the gravitational constant, M the mass of the source, Δ the distance of closest approach, and c the (vacuum) light velocity. For a ray grazing the sun,

---

*I trust that the term *the same* will not cause confusion.

$\Delta \approx 7 \times 10^{10}$ cm, $M \approx 2 \times 10^{33}$ g, and $\alpha = 0\rlap{.}''87$ (Einstein found $0\rlap{.}''83$). This is the answer to which four years later he would supply a further factor of 2.

The paper ends with a plea to the astronomers: 'It is urgently desirable that astronomers concern themselves with the question brought up here, even if the foregoing considerations might seem insufficiently founded or even adventurous.'

From this time on, Einstein writes to his friends of his hopes and fears about gravitation, just as we saw him do earlier about the quantum theory. Shortly after he completed the paper discussed above, he wrote to Laub:

> The relativistic treatment of gravitation creates serious difficulties. I consider it probable that the principle of the constancy of the velocity of light in its custom-ary version holds only for spaces with constant gravitational potential. [E11]

Evidently he did not quite know yet what to believe of his most recent work. However, he was certain that something new was needed. A few months later, he wrote to his friend Heinrich Zangger, director of the Institute for Forensic Med-icine at the University of Zürich: 'Just now I am teaching the foundations of the poor deceased mechanics, which is so beautiful. What will her successor look like? With that [question] I torment myself incessantly' [E12].

I conclude this section by paying my respects to the German geodete and astron-omer Johann Georg von Soldner, who in 1801 became the first to answer New-ton's query on the bending of light [S3]. 'No one would find it objectionable, I hope, that I treat a light ray as a heavy body. . . . One cannot think of a thing which exists and works on our senses that would not have the property of matter,' Soldner wrote.* He was motivated by the desire to check on possible corrections in the evaluation of astronomical data. His calculations are based on Newton's emission theory, according to which light consists of particles. On this picture the scattering of light by the sun becomes an exercise in Newtonian scattering theory. For small mass of the light-particles, the answer depends as little on that mass as Einstein's wave calculation depends on the light frequency. Soldner made the scat-tering calculation, put in numbers, and found $\alpha = 0\rlap{.}''84$!!

In 1911 Einstein did not know of Soldner's work. The latter's paper was in fact entirely unknown in the physics community until 1921. In that turbulent year, Lenard, in one of his attempts to discredit Einstein, reproduced part of Soldner's paper in the *Annalen der Physik* [L2], together with a lengthy introduction in which he also claimed priority for Hasenöhrl in connection with the mass–energy equivalence.** Von Laue took care of Lenard shortly afterward [L3].

---

*I have seen not his original paper but only an English translation that was recently published together with informative historical data [J2].

**See Section 7b.

11c. 1912. Einstein in No Man's Land

Another eight months passed before Einstein made his next move in the theory of gravitation. A scientific meeting at Karlsruhe, summer lectures at Zürich, and a few minor papers kept him busy in the meantime. But principally he was once again otherwise engaged by the quantum theory. This time, however, it was not so much because that seemed the more compelling subject to him. Rather he had taken on the obligation to prepare a major report on quantum physics for the first Solvay Congress (October 30 to November 3, 1911). 'I am harassed by my drivel for the Brussels Congress,' he wrote to Besso [E13]. He did not look forward to the 'witches' sabbath in Brussels [E14].

He found the congress interesting and especially admired the way in which Lorentz presided over the meetings. 'Lorentz is a marvel of intelligence and fine tact. A living work of art! He was in my opinion still the most intelligent one among the theoreticians present' [E12]. He was less impressed with the outcome of the deliberations: ' . . . but no one knows anything. The whole affair would have been a delight to Jesuit fathers' [E12]. 'The congress gave the impression of a lamentation at the ruins of Jerusalem' [E15]. Obviously, these were references to the infringements of quantum physics on classically conditioned minds. Einstein gave the final address at the congress. His assigned subject was the quantum theory of specific heats. In actual fact, he critically discussed all the problems of quantum theory as they were known to exist at a time when the threats and promises of the hydrogen atom were yet to be revealed. I shall return to this subject in Chapter 20. As to Einstein's contribution, drivel it was not.

Then, in rapid succession, Einstein readied two papers on gravitation, one in February 1912 [E16] and one in March 1912 [E17] (referred to in this section as I and II, respectively). These are solid pieces of theoretical analysis. It takes some time to grasp their logic. Yet these 1912 papers give the impression less of finished products than of well-developed sketches from a notebook. Their style is irresolute. The reasons for this are clear. In 1907 and 1911 Einstein had stretched the kinematic approach to gravitation to its limits. This time he embarked on one of the hardest problems of the century: to find the new gravitational dynamics. His first steps are taken gingerly.

These are also the last papers in which time is warped but space is flat. Already, for the first time in Einstein's published work, the statement appears in paper I that this treatment of space

> is not obviously permissible but contains physical assumptions which might ultimately prove to be incorrect; for example, [the laws of Euclidean geometry] most probably do not hold in a uniformly rotating system in which, because of the Lorentz contraction, the ratio of the circumference to the diameter should be different from π if we apply our definition of lengths.

All the same, Einstein continued to adhere to flat space. It is perhaps significant that, immediately following the lines just quoted, he continued, 'The measuring rods as well as the coordinate axes are to be considered as rigid bodies. This is permitted even though the rigid body cannot possess real existence.' The sequence of these remarks may lead one to surmise that the celebrated problem of the rigid body in the special theory of relativity stimulated Einstein's step to curved space, later in 1912.*

It would be as ill-advised to discuss these papers in detail as to ignore them altogether. It is true that their particular dynamic model for gravitation did not last. Nevertheless, these investigations proved not to be an idle exercise. Indeed, in the course of his ruminations Einstein made a number of quite remarkable comments and discoveries that were to survive. I shall display these in the remainder of this chapter, labeling the exhibits A to F. However, in the course of the following discussion, I shall hold all technicalities to a minimum.

Einstein begins by reminding the reader of his past result that the velocity of light is not generally constant in the presence of gravitational fields:

A. ' ... this result excludes the general applicability of the Lorentz transformation.'

At once a new chord is struck. Earlier he had said (I paraphrase), 'Let us see how far we can come with Lorentz transformations.' Now he says, 'Lorentz transformations are not enough.'

B. 'If one does not restrict oneself to [spatial] domains of constant c, then the manifold of equivalent systems as well as the manifold of the transformations which leave the laws of nature unchanged will become a larger one, but in turn these laws will be more complicated' [!!].

Let us next unveil Einstein's first dynamic Ansatz for a theory of gravitation, to which he was led by Eq. (11.6). He begins by again comparing a homogeneous field in the frame $S(x,y,z,t)$ with the accelerated frame $\Sigma(\xi,\eta,\zeta,\tau)$.** For small τ —terms $O(\tau^3)$ are neglected—he finds

$$x = \xi + \frac{ac}{2}\tau^2 \qquad y = \eta \qquad z = \zeta \qquad t = c\tau \qquad (11.8)$$

and the important relation

$$c = c_o + a\xi \qquad (11.9)$$

in which c_o is fixed by the speed of the clock at the origin of Σ; ac_o is the acceleration of this origin relative to S. Thus $\Delta c = 0$ in Σ. By equivalence $\Delta c = 0$ in S (the Δ's are the respective Laplacians). 'It is plausible to assume that $[\Delta c = 0]$

---

*This point of view has been developed in more detail by Stachel [S4].

**I use again the notations of Chapter 9, which are not identical with those in I. In the frame S, the light velocity is taken equal to unity.

is valid in every mass-free static gravitational field.' The next *assumption* concerns the modification of this equation in the presence of a density of matter ρ:

$$\Delta c = kc\rho \tag{11.10}$$

where k is a constant. The source must be static: 'The equations found by me shall refer only to the static case of masses at rest' [E18].

This last remark, referring to the gravitational field equation, does not preclude the study of the motion of a mass point under the action of the external static field c. This motion (Einstein finds) is given by

$$\frac{d}{dt}\left(\frac{\dot{\vec{x}}}{c} \bigg/ \sqrt{1 - \frac{v^2}{c^2}}\right) = -\vec{\nabla}c \bigg/ \sqrt{1 - \frac{v^2}{c^2}} \tag{11.11}$$

where $v^2 \equiv \dot{\vec{x}}^2$. For what follows, it is important to note in what sense this equation satisfies the equivalence principle: if c is given by Eq. 11.9, then Eq. 11.11 can be transformed to a force-free equation in the accelerated frame Σ.

Einstein derived Eq. 11.11 in I by a method which need not concern us. It is quite important, on the other hand, to note a comment he made about Eq. 11.11 in a note added in proof to paper II. There he showed that this equation can be derived from the variational principle:

$$\delta \int ds = 0 \tag{11.12}$$
$$ds^2 = c^2dt^2 - dx^2 - dy^2 - dz^2 \tag{11.13}$$

Earlier, Planck had applied Eq. 11.12 to special relativistic point mechanics [P3], where, of course, c in Eq. 11.13 is the usual constant light velocity in vacuum. Einstein was stirred by the fact that Eqs. 11.12 and 11.13 still apply if c is a static field!

C. 'Also, here it is seen—as was shown for the usual relativity theory by Planck—that the equations of analytical mechanics have a significance which far exceeds that of the Newtonian mechanics.'

It is hard to doubt that this insight guided Einstein to the ultimate form of the mechanical equations of general relativity, in which Eq. 11.12 survives, while Eq. 11.13 is generalized further.

Paper II is largely devoted to the question of how the electromagnetic field equations are affected by the hypothesis that c is a field satisfying Eq. 11.6. The details are of no great interest except for one remark. The field c, of course, enters into the Maxwell equations. Hence, there is a coupling between the gravitational field and the electromagnetic field. However, the latter is not static in general, whereas the gravitational field is static by assumption. Therefore '[the equations] might be inexact . . . since the electromagnetic field might be able to influence the gravitational field in such a way that the latter is no longer a static field.'

It is conceivable that some of my readers, upon reflecting on this last statement, may ask the same question I did when I first read paper II. What possessed Einstein? Why would he ever write about a static gravitational field coupled to a nonstatic Maxwell field and hope to make any sense? I would certainly have asked him this question, were it not for the fact that I never laid eyes on these papers until many years after the time I knew him. I can offer nothing better than the reply I imagine he might have given me.

The time is about 1950. Einstein speaks: 'Ja, wissen Sie, that time in Prague, that was the most confusing period in my life as far as physics was concerned. Before I wrote down my equation $\Delta c = kc\rho$, I had, of course, thought of using the Dalembertian instead of the Laplacian. That would look more elegant. I decided against that, however, because I already knew that gravitation would have to lead me beyond the Lorentz transformations. Thus I saw no virtue in writing down $\Box c = kc\rho$, since Lorentz invariance was no longer an obvious criterion to me, especially in the case of the dynamics of gravitation. For that reason, I never believed what Abraham and others were doing at that time. Poor Abraham. I did not realize, I must admit, that one can derive an equation for a time-dependent scalar gravitational field that does satisfy the weak equivalence principle. No, that has nothing to do with the wrong value for the perihelion obtained from a scalar theory. That came some years later. I thought again about a scalar theory when I was at first a bit overawed by the complexity of the equations which Grossmann and I wrote down a little later. Yes, there was confusion at that time, too. But it was not like the Prague days. In Zürich I was sure that I had found the right starting point. Also, in Zürich I believed that I had an argument which showed that the scalar theory, you know, the Nordström theory, was in conflict with the equivalence principle. But I soon realized that I was wrong. In 1914 I came to believe in fact that the Nordström theory was a good possibility.

'But to come back to Prague. The only thing I believed firmly then was that one had to incorporate the equivalence principle in the fundamental equations. Did you know that I had not even heard of the Eötvös experiments at that time? Ah, you knew that. Well, there I was. There was no paradox of any kind. It was not like the quantum theory in those days. Those Berlin experiments on blackbody radiation had made it clear that something was badly amiss with classical physics. On the other hand, there was nothing wrong with the equivalence principle and Newton's theory. One was perfectly compatible with the other. Yet I was certain that the Newtonian theory was successful but incomplete. I had not lost my faith in the special theory of relativity either, but I believed that that theory was likewise incomplete. So what I did in Prague was something like this. I knew I had to start all over again, as it were, in constructing a theory of gravitation. Of course, Newtonian theory as well as the special theory had to reappear in some approximate sense. But I did not know how to proceed. I was in no-man's land. So I decided to analyze static situations first and then push along until inevitably I would reach some contradictions. Then I hoped that these contradictions would in turn teach me what the next step might be. Sehen Sie, the way I thought then about Newtonian theory is not so different from the way I think now about quantum mechanics. That, too, seens to me to be a naive theory, and I think people should try to start all over again, first reconsidering the nonrelativistic theory, just as I did for gravitation in Prague. . . .'*

Here my fabrications end. I now return to the 1912 papers in order to add three final exhibits.

The inclusion of electromagnetism forced Einstein to generalize the meaning of ρ in Eq. 11.10, since the electromagnetic energy has a gravitating mass equivalent:

D. The source of the gravitational field had to be 'the density of ponderable matter augmented with the [locally measured] energy density.'

Applied to a system of electrically-charged particles and electromagnetic fields, this would seem to mean that ρ should be replaced by the sum of a 'mechanical' and an electromagnetic term. Einstein denoted this sum by the new symbol σ. However, a paradox arose. On closer inspection, he noted that the theory does not satisfy the conservation laws of energy and momentum, 'a quite serious result which leads one to entertain doubt about the admissibility of the whole theory developed here.' However, he found a way in which this paradox could be resolved.

E. 'If every energy density . . . generates a (negative) divergence of the lines of force of gravitation, then this must also hold for the energy density of gravitation itself.' This led him to the final equation for his field c:

$$\Delta c = k\left[c\sigma + \frac{1}{2\,k}\frac{(\vec{\nabla}c)^2}{c} \right] \qquad (11.14)$$

He went on to show that the second term in the brackets is the gravitational field energy density and that the inclusion of this new term guaranteed validity of the conservation laws. From then on, he was prepared for a nonlinear theory of the gravitational field!

It had been a grave decision to make this last modification of the c-field equation, Einstein wrote, 'since [as a result] I depart from the foundation of the unconditional equivalence principle.' Recall the discussion following Eq. 11.9: it was that equation and the equivalence principle which had led him to $\Delta c = 0$ in the source-free case. This same reasoning does not apply to Eq. 11.14 with $\sigma = 0$! What was the moral?

> **F.** It seems that [the equivalence principle] holds only for infinitely small fields. . . . Our derivations of the equation of motion of the material point and of the electromagnetic [field] are not illusory since [Eqs. 11.8 and 11.9 were] applied only to infinitely small space domains.

This is the dawn of the correct formulation of equivalence as a principle that holds only locally.

---

*The references to other physicists in this piece of fiction have their basis in reality, as will become clear in later chapters.

Let us summarize the Prague papers.* By the spring of 1912, Einstein knew of the red shift and the deflection of light. He had realized that the Lorentz transformations are not generally applicable, that a larger invariance group was needed, and that the laws of physics would have to be correspondingly more complicated. From the study of a primitive scalar model field theory, his attention had been drawn to the generality of the variational principle $\delta \int ds = 0$ for mechanical systems. He understood that the sources of the gravitational field were not just ponderable matter but also field energy. He realized that gravitational field energy is to be included as a source and that the gravitational field equations were therefore bound to be nonlinear. He saw that the equivalence principle apparently held only locally. As yet, he had no theory of gravitation. But he had learned a lot of physics.

References

E1. A. Einstein, letter to Pauline Einstein, April 4, 1910.
E1a. ——, letter to M. Besso, March 6, 1952; *EB,* p. 464.
E2. ——, letter to J. Laub, summer 1910, undated.
E3. ——, letter to J. Laub, October 11, 1910.
E4. ——, letter to J. Laub, December 28, 1910.
E5. ——, letter to M. Grossmann, March 1911.
E6. ——, letter to H. Zangger, August 24, 1911.
E7. ——, letter to M. Besso, May 13, 1911; *EB,* p. 19.
E7a. ——, letter to A. Stern, March 17, 1912.
E8. ——, *AdP* **35,** 898 (1911).
E9. ——, *Jahrb. Rad. Elektr.* **4,** 411 (1907).
E10. ——, *AdP* **17,** 891 (1905), Sec. 8.
E11. ——, letter to J. Laub, August 10, 1911.
E12. ——, letter to H. Zangger, November 16, 1911.
E13. ——, letter to M. Besso, September 11, 1911; *EB,* p. 26.
E14. ——, letter to M. Besso, September 21, 1911; *EB,* p. 32.
E15. ——, letter to M. Besso, December 26, 1911; *EB,* p. 40.
E16. ——, *AdP* **38,** 355 (1912).
E17. ——, *AdP* **38,** 443 (1912).
E18. ——, letter to P. Ehrenfest, June 7, 1912.
E19. ——, *Viertelj. Schrift Ger. Medizin,* **44,** 37 (1912).
F1. P. Frank, *Albert Einstein, Sein Leben und Seine Zeit,* p. 137, Vieweg, Braunschweig, 1979.
F2. ——, [F1], p. 169.
H1. J. Havránek, *Acta Univ. Carolinae* **17,** 105 (1977).
J1. R. Jost, *Viertelj. Schrift. Naturf. Ges. Zürich* **124,** 7 (1979).
J2. S. Jaki, *Found. Phys.* **8,** 927 (1978).

*A short third paper on the c-field theory, also written in Prague [E19], will be discussed later.

K1. A. Kleiner, letter to an unidentified colleague, January 18, 1911. The original is in the Staatsarchiv des Kantons Zürich.

K2. M. J. Klein, *Paul Ehrenfest,* Vol. 1, p. 176. North Holland, Amsterdam, 1970.

K3. ——, [K2], p. 178.

L1. H. A. Lorentz, A. Einstein, H. Minkowski, and H. Weyl, *The Principle of Relativity* (W. Perrett and G. B. Jeffery, Trans.). Dover, New York.

L2. P. Lenard, *AdP* **65,** 593 (1921).

L3. M. von Laue, *AdP* **66,** 283 (1922).

P1. *Protokoll des Regierungsrates,* No. 1226, July 14, 1910.

P2. *Protokoll des Regierungsrates,* No. 247, February 10, 1911.

P3. M. Planck, *Verh. Deutsch. Phys. Ges.* **8,** 136 (1906).

S1. Se, p. 204.

S2. O. Stern, see *Biogr. Mem. Nat. Ac. Sci.* **43,** 215 (1973).

S3. J. G. von Soldner, *Berliner Astr. Jahrb.,* 1804, p. 161.

S4. J. Stachel in *General Relativity and Gravitation,* GRG Society Einstein Centennial Volume, Vol. 1, p. 1. Plenum Press, New York, 1980.

12

The Einstein-Grossmann
Collaboration

In memoriam: Marcel Grossmann

12a. From Prague to Zürich

Grossmann appeared in previous chapters as the helpful fellow student who made his course notes available to Einstein, as the helpful friend who together with his father paved the way for Einstein's appointment at the patent office in Bern, and as the friend to whom Einstein dedicated his doctoral thesis. It is now time to get better acquainted with him.

Grossmann, a descendant of an old Swiss family, was born in 1878 in Budapest, where his father was employed. He spent his first fifteen years there, then went to Switzerland, where he finished high school. Thereupon he studied at the ETH from 1896 to 1900, together with Einstein. During the next seven years, he taught high school, first in Frauenfeld and then in Basel. In that period he finished his thesis, 'On the Metrical Properties of Collinear Structures,' which earned him his doctoral degree at the University of Zürich, and published two geometry books for high school students and three papers on non-Euclidean geometry, his favorite subject. These papers contain very pretty planimetric constructions which, we are told, were praised by one no less than Hilbert [S1]. After a six-year pause, he published another four papers on related subjects in the years 1910–12. He presented one of these at the fifth international congress of mathematicians in Cambridge, England, in August 1912 [G1]. The mentioned papers are his entire scientific output prior to the collaboration with Einstein, which began a few months after the Cambridge conference. Evidently none of his prior research had any bearing on differential geometry or tensor analysis.

Grossmann had meanwhile joined the mathematics faculty at the ETH in Zürich, first as a stand-in and then, in 1907, as a full professor of geometry. Soon thereafter, he began to organize summer courses for high school teachers. In 1910 he became one of the founders of the Swiss Mathematical Society. The next year he was appointed dean of the mathematics–physics section of the ETH.

One of the first acts of the uncommonly young dean was to sound out Einstein as to whether he might be interested in returning to Zürich, this time to the ETH. Grossmann's letter is lost but not Einstein's reply: 'I am certainly prepared in principle to accept a teaching position at your [ETH]. I am extraordinarily happy about the prospect of returning to Zürich. This prospect has led me in recent days not to accept a call which reached me [from] the University of Utrecht' [E1]. A positive outcome of Grossmann's initiative appeared to be assured. Speedy action was called for, however. Einstein was now in great demand. The offer from Utrecht, made by Willem Julius, 'one of the most original exponents of solar physics' [E2], was only the first of several he received in 1911 and 1912. None of these swayed him. Zürich was where he wanted to be. Even before any official action had been taken, he telegraphed Zangger, 'Habe Grossmann zugesagt,' Have said yes to G. [E3]. Zangger himself wrote to the authorities, urging quick action, especially because he had heard that an offer from Vienna might be forthcoming [S2]. Einstein also wrote to Zangger of an offer (which he declined) to lecture at Columbia University in New York in the fall of 1912 [E4].

On January 23, 1912, the ETH authorities sent their recommendation for a ten-year appointment [S3] to the federal Department of the Interior. It included recommendations from Marie Curie ('one is entitled to have the highest hopes for him and to see in him one of the first theoreticians of the future') and from Poincaré (already mentioned in Chapter 8). The authorities quickly accepted the proposal, and on February 2 Einstein could write to Alfred Stern, 'Two days ago I received the call from the [ETH] (halleluia!) and have already announced here my k. k.* departure' [E5]. And so, in the fall of 1912, Einstein began the next phase of his academic career.

It was to last for only three semesters. Berlin was beckoning even before he arrived in Zürich. In the spring of 1912, Emil Warburg, the eminent director of the Physikalisch Technische Reichsanstalt, asked him to join the staff of his institute. The formalities concerning the Zürich appointment had been completed by then. The offer from Vienna also came through after the ETH decision had been made. 'I declined to take anything into consideration until I had settled in Zürich,' Einstein wrote to Zangger, whom he had informed of the Berlin and Vienna overtures [E6].

There was one man who at that time came close to changing Einstein's mind and perhaps his destiny: Lorentz. During the Solvay conference in October 1911, Lorentz asked Einstein what the prospects were of his coming to Utrecht [L1]. Perhaps it was not clear to Einstein whether Lorentz would actually have liked to see a foreigner occupy the chair in Utrecht. At any rate, upon his return to Prague he wrote to Lorentz, 'I write this letter to you with a heavy heart, as one who has done a kind of injustice to his father . . .' and added, 'If I had known that you wanted me to go to Utrecht then I would have gone' [E7]. Lorentz replied

*k. k. = kaiserlich und königlich = imperial and royal, the adjectives referring to the Austro-Hungarian empire.

that Einstein should accept his post in Zürich cheerfully and in good spirits [L1]. Soon thereafter, Lorentz the father figure spoke again. On February 29, 1912, Einstein wrote to Zangger, 'I was called to Leiden by Lorentz to be his successor. It was good that I was already committed to Zürich, for, if not, I would have had to go there' [E8]. The Leiden position went to Ehrenfest, who took over in the fall of 1912. Some time in 1913 Einstein sent Ehrenfest a letter which must often have given its recipient food for thought: 'When Lorentz called me at that time I experienced an undeniable shudder' [E9].

12b. From scalar to tensor

In August 1912, Einstein and his family arrived back in Zürich. On the tenth of that month they were officially registered as residents of an apartment at Hofstrasse 116. Some time between August 10 and August 16, it became clear to Einstein that Riemannian geometry is the correct mathematical tool for what we now call general relativity theory. The impact of this abrupt realization was to change his outlook on physics and physical theory for the rest of his life. The next three years were the most strenuous period in his scientific career.

In order to appreciate what happened in August 1912, it is essential to know that before his arrival in Zürich Einstein had already concluded that the description of gravitation in terms of the single scalar c-field of the Prague days had to go and that a new geometry of physical space–time was needed. I am convinced that he arrived in Zürich with the knowledge that not just one but ten gravitational potentials were needed. This opinion is based on some remarks in Einstein's papers; on a study of all the letters from the period March–August 16, 1912, which are in the Einstein archives in Princeton; and on recollections by myself and by Ernst Gabor Straus, Einstein's assistant from 1944 to 1948, of conversations with Einstein.

To begin with, let us recall that the second of the 1912 papers discussed in the previous chapter [E10] was completed in March. Toward the end of that month, Einstein wrote to Besso, 'Recently, I have been working furiously on the gravitation problem. It has now reached a stage in which I am ready with the statics. I know nothing as yet about the dynamic field, that must follow next. . . . Every step is devilishly difficult' [E11].* Yet his initial response to the finished part, the static case, was strongly positive. From Prague he wrote to Ehrenfest, 'The investigations on the statics of gravitation are ready and satisfy me very much. I really believe I have found a piece of truth. I am now thinking about the dynamic case, one again going from the special to the general' [E12]. This undated letter was certainly written in 1912 and most probably before the middle of May, since by that time, Einstein had become less assured. On May 20 he wrote to Zangger, 'The investigations on gravitation have led to some satisfactory results, although

*This important letter is not contained in the *EB* volume of their correspondence.

until now I have been unable to penetrate beyond the *statics* of gravitation' [E13]. Soon thereafter, there are hints of difficulties: 'The further development of the theory of gravitation meets with great obstacles' (... stösst auf grosse Hindernisse) [E14]. This undated letter to Zangger also contains a reference to von Laue's discovery of X-ray diffraction. Since Einstein wrote congratulations to von Laue in June [E15], it is most probable that the letter to Zangger was written in that same month. Another letter, certainly written in June, contains a similar comment: 'The generalization [of the static case] appears to be very difficult' [E16]. These repeated references to his difficulties are never accompanied by expressions of doubt about his conclusions concerning the red shift and the bending of light. He never wavered in his opinion that these phenomena were to be part of the future physics. For example, he wrote in June, 'What do the colleagues say about giving up the principle of the constancy of the velocity of light? Wien tries to help himself by questioning the gravitational [action of] energy. That, however, is untenable ostrich politics' [E16]. It is my understanding that Einstein was sure he was moving in the right direction but that he gradually came to the conviction that some essential theoretical tools were lacking.

There is a brief and cryptic statement in the last paper Einstein wrote in Prague, in July, which indicates that he was onto something new. This paper (a polemic against Abraham to which I shall return later) contains the following phrase: 'The simple physical interpretation of the space–time coordinates will have to be forfeited, and it cannot yet be grasped *what form the general space– time transformation equations could have* [my italics]. I would ask all colleagues to apply themselves to this important problem!' [E17]. Observe the exclamation mark at the end of this sentence. I do not know how often such a symbol is found in Einstein's writings, but I do know that it occurs only rarely.

On August 10, as said, Einstein registered as a Zürich resident. On August 16, he writes a letter to Hopf. Gone are the remarks about devilish difficulties and great obstacles. Instead, he writes, 'Mit der Gravitation geht es glänzend. Wenn nicht alles trügt habe ich nun die allgemeinsten Gleichungen gefunden' [E18].*

What happened in July and early August 1912?

Two statements by Einstein tell the story. In his Kyoto address (December 1922), he said, 'If all [accelerated] systems are equivalent, then Euclidean geometry cannot hold in all of them. To throw out geometry and keep [physical] laws is equivalent to describing thoughts without words. We must search for words before we can express thoughts. What must we search for at this point? This problem remained insoluble to me until 1912, when I suddenly realized that Gauss's theory of surfaces holds the key for unlocking this mystery. I realized that Gauss's surface coordinates had a profound significance. However, I did not know

---

*'It is going splendidly with gravitation. If it is not all deception, then I have found the most general equations.' One Einstein biographer wrote *general* for *most general* [S4], a nontrivial modification of this crucial phrase.

at that time that Riemann had studied the foundations of geometry in an even more profound way. I suddenly remembered that Gauss's theory was contained in the geometry course given by Geiser when I was a student. . . . I realized that the foundations of geometry have physical significance. My dear friend the mathematician Grossmann was there when I returned from Prague to Zürich. From him I learned for the first time about Ricci and later about Riemann. So *I asked my friend whether my problem could be solved by Riemann's theory* [my italics], namely, whether the invariants of the line element could completely determine the quantities I had been looking for' [I1].

Regarding the role of Carl Friedrich Geiser,* it is known that Einstein attended at least some of Geiser's lectures [K2]. Toward the end of his life, he recalled his fascination with Geiser's course [S5] on 'Infinitesimalgeometrie' [E19]. Grossmann's notebooks (preserved at the ETH) show that Geiser taught the Gaussian theory of surfaces.

I believe that this first encounter with differential geometry played a secondary role in Einstein's thinking in 1912. During long conversations with Einstein in Prague, the mathematician Georg Pick expressed the conjecture that the needed mathematical instruments for the further development of Einstein's ideas might be found in the papers by Ricci and Levi-Civita [F1]. I doubt that this remark made any impression on Einstein at that time. He certainly did not go to the trouble of consulting these important papers during his Prague days.

Einstein's second statement on the July–August period was made in 1923: 'I had the decisive idea of the analogy between the mathematical problem of the theory [of general relativity] and the Gaussian theory of surfaces only in 1912, however, after my return to Zürich, without being aware at that time of the work of Riemann, Ricci, and Levi-Civita. This [work] was first brought to my attention by my friend Grossmann *when I posed to him the problem of looking for generally covariant tensors whose components depend only on derivatives of the coefficients* $[g_{\mu\nu}]$ *of the quadratic fundamental invariant* $[g_{\mu\nu}dx^\mu dx^\nu]$' (my italics) [E20].

We learn from these two statements that even during his last weeks in Prague Einstein already knew that he needed the theory of invariants and covariants associated with the differential line element

$$ds^2 = g_{\mu\nu}dx^\mu dx^\nu \tag{12.1}$$

in which the ten quantities $g_{\mu\nu}$ are to be considered as *dynamic fields* which in some way describe gravitation. Immediately upon his arrival in Zürich, he must have told Grossmann of the problems he was struggling with. It must have been at that time that he said, 'Grossmann, Du musst mir helfen, sonst werd' ich verrückt!' [K2], G., you must help me or else I'll go crazy! With Grossmann's help,

---

*Geiser was a competent and influential mathematician who did much to raise the level of the mathematics faculty at the ETH [K1]. His successor was Hermann Weyl.

the great transition to Riemannian geometry must have taken place during the week prior to August 16, as is indicated by Einstein's letter to Hopf.

These conclusions are in harmony with my own recollections of a discussion with Einstein in which I asked him how the collaboration with Grossmann began. I have a vivid though not verbatim memory of Einstein's reply: he told Grossmann of his problems and asked him to please go to the library and see if there existed an appropriate geometry to handle such questions. The next day Grossmann returned (Einstein told me) and said that there indeed was such a geometry, Riemannian geometry. It is quite plausible that Grossmann needed to consult the literature since, as we have seen, his own field of research was removed from differential geometry.

There is a curiously phrased expression of thanks to Grossmann which, I believe, comes close to confirming this recollection of mine. It is found at the end of the introduction to Einstein's first monograph on general relativity, written in 1916: 'Finally, grateful thoughts go at this place to my friend the mathematician Grossmann, who by his help not only saved me the study of the relevant mathematical literature but also supported me in the search for the field equations of gravitation' [E21].

Finally, there is a recollection which I owe to Straus [S6], who also remembers that Einstein was already thinking about general covariance when he met Grossmann. Einstein told Grossmann that he needed a geometry which allowed for the most general transformations that leave Eq. 12.1 invariant. Grossmann replied that Einstein was looking for Riemannian geometry. (Straus does not recall that Einstein had asked Grossmann to check the literature.) But, Grossmann added, that is a terrible mess which physicists should not be involved with. Einstein then asked if there were any other geometries he could use. Grossmann said no and pointed out to Einstein that the differential equations of Riemannian geometry are nonlinear, which he considered a bad feature. Einstein replied to this last remark that he thought, on the contrary, that was a great advantage. This last comment is easily understood if we remember that Einstein's Prague model had taught him that the gravitational field equations *had* to be nonlinear since the gravitational field necessarily acts as its own source (see Eq. 11.14).

Having discussed *what* happened in July and early August 1912, I turn to the question of *how* it happened. Einstein gave the answer in 1921:

> The decisive step of the transition to generally covariant equations would certainly not have taken place [had it not been for the following consideration]. Because of the Lorentz contraction in a reference frame that rotates relative to an inertial frame, the laws that govern rigid bodies do not correspond to the rules of Euclidean geometry. Thus Euclidean geometry must be abandoned if noninertial frames are admitted on an equal footing. [E22]

Let us pursue Einstein's 'decisive step' a little further.

In June Einstein had written to Ehrenfest from Prague, 'It seems that the equivalence [principle] can hold only *for infinitely small* systems [and] that there-fore Born's accelerated *finite* system cannot be considered as a static gravitational field, that is, it cannot be generated by masses at rest. A rotating ring does not generate a static field in this sense, although it is a field that does not change with time. . . . In the theory of electricity, my case corresponds to the electrostatic field; on the other hand, the general static case would, in addition, include the analog of a static magnetic field. I am not that far yet. The equations found by me must refer only to the static case of masses at rest. Born's field of finite extension does not fall in this category. It has not yet become clear to me why the equivalence principle fails for *finite* fields (Born)' [E23].* Einstein was not the greatest expert in following the scientific literature, but he apparently did know Born's main paper of 1909 on the relativistic treatment of rigid bodies [B1]. At the Salzburg conference in the fall of 1909, Born's presentation of his work on the rigid body [B2] immediately preceded Einstein's own report on the constitution of radiation [E25], and it is known that the two men used that occasion for private discussions on scientific topics of so much common concern [B3]. In June 1912 Einstein was brooding over Born's earlier work, as his letter to Ehrenfest shows. I find this fascinating since Born's formalism of 1909 manifestly has Riemannian traits! It seems sufficiently interesting to explain how this came about.

The two main points of Born's work are (1) to define rigidity as a limiting property of a continuously deformable medium (ignoring all aspects of its atomic constitution) and (2) to define rigidity only as a differential, not as a global, prop-erty. Born considered first the case of nonrelativistic Newtonian mechanics. Let ξ^i ($i = 1,2,3$) denote the cartesian coordinates of some point in the medium at the time $t = 0$. The distance ds between two points ξ^i and $\xi^i + d\xi^i$ at $t = 0$ is given by

$$ds^2 = \sum_{i=1}^{3} (d\xi^i)^2 \tag{12.2}$$

Let $x^i(\xi^i,t)$ be the coordinates at time t of the point that was at ξ^i at $t = 0$. Follow the so-called Lagrangian method, in which the functions x^i are used to describe the history of every particle of the fluid [L2]. At t, the distance ds between two infinitesimally close points is given by $ds^2 = \Sigma(dx^i)^2$. Since

$$dx^i = \sum_{j} \frac{\partial x^i}{\partial \xi^j} d\xi^j \tag{12.3}$$

---

*In a short paper entitled 'Does There Exist a Gravitational Action Analogous to the Electrodyn-amic Induction Effect?' [E24], published in the *Quarterly for Forensic Medicine,* Einstein briefly pursued the electromagnetic analogy mentioned in his letter to Ehrenfest. This uncommon choice of journal was made in order to contribute to a Festschrift for Zangger. It may also indicate that Ein-stein felt less than secure about his results.

we have

$$ds^2 = \sum_{k,l=1}^{3} p_{kl}(\xi,t)d\xi^k d\xi^l \tag{12.4}$$

$$p_{kl}(\xi,t) = \sum_{i,j} \frac{\partial x^i}{\partial \xi^k} \frac{\partial x^j}{\partial \xi^l} \delta_{ij} \tag{12.5}$$

The p_{kl} are in general time-dependent *fields* which satisfy $p_{kl}(\xi,0) = \delta_{kl}$. In the Newtonian case, Born's infinitesimal rigidity condition is given by $dp_{kl}/dt = 0$. This is an invariance condition: ds^2 remains the same at all times and has forever the magnitude given by the Euclidean expression (Eq. 12.2).

Born attempted next to generalize from the Newtonian to the special relativistic case by means of a 'relativistic Lagrangian method.' Instead of the $x^i(\xi^i,t)$, he introduced $x^\mu(\xi^\mu)$, $x^4 = ict$ ($\xi^4 = ic\tau$ is the proper time) and we have

$$dx^\mu = \sum_{\mu=1}^{4} \frac{\partial x^\mu}{\partial \xi^\nu} d\xi^\nu \tag{12.6}$$

The Minkowskian line element

$$ds^2 - \Sigma(dx^\mu)^2 \tag{12.7}$$

becomes, when expressed in Lagrangian coordinates,

$$ds^2 = \Sigma A_{\mu\nu}(\xi^\nu) d\xi^\mu d\xi^\nu \tag{12.8}$$

Consider those world points which are simultaneous as seen by an observer moving with four-velocity u^μ with the volume element $d\xi^\mu$: $u_\mu d\xi^\nu \partial x^\mu/\partial \xi^\nu = 0$. Use this relation to eliminate $d\xi^4$ from Eq. 12.8. Then Eq.12.8 can be written in the form of Eq. 12.4 with the rigidity condition $dp_{kl}/d\tau = 0$. Ehrenfest [E26] and Herglotz [H1] noted that Born's relativistic local rigidity criterion for a volume element of a body in general motion can be phrased as follows. Relative to an observer at rest, that volume element suffers a Lorentz contraction corresponding to the instantaneous velocity of the center of that volume element. For our purposes, it is of no relevance to discuss the paradoxes to which this approach gives rise for the case of a *finite* body—the case to which Einstein referred in his June 7 letter to Ehrenfest. The interested reader can find more on this subject in Pauli's encyclopedia article [P1].

Born's reasoning can be transcribed as follows. In the Newtonian case, introduce a three-dimensional manifold on which Eq. 12.4 defines a Riemannian metric. The transformations (Eq. 12.3) are point transformations linear in the differentials which leave ds^2 invariant. The p_{kl} are determined by the dynamics that governs the motions of the medium. Generalize to four dimensions.

I now return to Einstein. In his papers, he remained silent on the specific problem of the rigid body until 1916 [E27]. Could it be, however, that Born's formalism had given him the inspiration for general covariance?

However this may be, after his first dicussions with Grossmann, Einstein had found the correct starting point for general relativity. The real work could now begin. Hard days lay ahead. In October Einstein wrote to Sommerfeld:

> At present I occupy myself exclusively with the problem of gravitation and now believe that I shall master all difficulties with the help of a friendly mathematician here. But one thing is certain, in all my life I have labored not nearly as hard, and I have become imbued with great respect for mathematics, the subtler part of which I had in my simple-mindedness regarded as pure luxury until now. Compared with this problem, the original relativity is child's play. [E28]

12c. The collaboration

The Einstein–Grossmann paper (referred to here as EG), published in 1913 [E29], contains profound physical insight into the nature of measurement, some correct general relativistic equations, some faulty reasoning, and clumsy notation.

First some remarks about the notation. The concepts of covariant and contravariant tensors are introduced, but all tensor indices are written as subscripts. For example, the covariant metric tensor is denoted by $g_{\mu\nu}$, its contravariant counterpart by $\gamma_{\mu\nu}$. In 1914 Einstein abandoned this miserable notation. 'Following Ricci and Levi-Civita, we denote the contravariant character in such a way that we place the index in the upper position' [E30]. Even then he excluded the coordinate differentials dx^μ from this rule. Nor does EG contain the modern convention that summation over repeated indices is automatically understood. This rule was introduced in 1916—by none other than Einstein himself [E31]. Later he said in jest to a friend, 'I have made a great discovery in mathematics; I have suppressed the summation sign every time that the summation must be made over an index which occurs twice. . . .' [K2]. I do not believe it will serve the reader if I push historical accuracy to the point of adhering to the EG notations. Instead, I shall transcribe the EG equations into their modern form by adopting the notations and conventions of Weinberg's book on gravitation and cosmology [W1]. All technicalities that can be covered by a reference to that text will be omitted.

In EG, Einstein expresses his indebtedness to Mach for inspiring some of his ideas. Comments on the influence of Mach on Einstein, an important subject in its own right, will be deferred till Chapter 15.

As we have seen, the equivalence principle in its primitive form (equality of gravitational and inertial mass for a material object) was Einstein's guide ever since 1907. It is characteristic, because of his limited acquaintance with the literature, that only five years later would he become aware of the precision measurements of Roland the Baron Eötvös of Vásárosnamény that showed the high degree of accuracy of the equality of inertial and gravitational mass. He discussed the

Eötvös experiments for the first time in EG, concluding that 'the physical identity of gravitational and inertial mass ... possesses a high degree of probability.'*

After these prefatory remarks, I turn to Grossmann's contribution to EG. 'Einstein grew up in the Christoffel–Ricci tradition,' Christian Felix Klein wrote in his history of mathematics in the nineteenth century [K3]. This masterwork explains how from a mathematical point of view general relativity may be considered as one of the culmination points in a noble line of descendance starting with the work of Carl Friedrich Gauss, moving on to Georg Friedrich Bernhard Riemann, and from there to Elwin Bruno Christoffel, Gregorio Ricci-Curbastro, Tullio Levi-Civita, and others. I hope my readers will derive the same enjoyment as I did in reading these original papers as well as Klein's history. I would further recommend the essays by Dirk Struik on the history of differential geometry [S7]. I restrict my own task to explaining how Einstein 'grew up.' The two principal references in Grossmann's contribution to EG are the memoir 'On the Transformation of Homogeneous Differential Forms of the Second Degree' by Christoffel [C1], written in Zürich in 1869, and the comprehensive review paper of 1901 on the 'absolute differential calculus' [R2] by Ricci and his brilliant pupil Levi-Civita.

Grossman's contribution consists of a lucid exposition of Riemannian geometry and its tensor calculus. In addition, he gives mathematical details in support of some of Einstein's arguments. He begins with a discussion of the invariance of the line element (Eq. 12.1) under the transformation

$$dx^\mu = a_\nu^\mu \, dx'^\nu \qquad a_\nu^\mu = \frac{\partial x^\mu}{\partial x'^\nu} \tag{12.9}$$

$$g'_{\mu\nu} = a_\mu^\lambda a_\nu^\rho g_{\lambda\rho} \tag{12.10}$$

Then follow the definitions of tensors, the principal manipulations of tensor algebra (as in [W3]), the use of the metric tensor to relate covariant and contravariant tensors, and the description of covariant differentiation ('Erweiterung'). Recall that the covariant derivative $V^\mu_{;\lambda}$ of a contravariant vector V^μ is given by

$$V^\mu_{;\lambda} = \frac{\partial V^\mu}{\partial x^\lambda} + \Gamma^\mu_{\lambda\nu} V^\nu \tag{12.11}$$

where the affine connection ('Christoffel Drei-Indizes Symbol') $\Gamma^\mu_{\lambda\nu}$ is a nontensor given by [W4]

$$\Gamma^\mu_{\lambda\nu} = \frac{1}{2} g^{\mu\sigma} \left(\frac{\partial g_{\sigma\lambda}}{\partial x^\nu} + \frac{\partial g_{\sigma\nu}}{\partial x^\lambda} - \frac{\partial g_{\lambda\nu}}{\partial x^\sigma} \right) \tag{12.12}$$

---

*For an account of the precursors of Eötvös and of the latter's experiments, see [W2]. For a description of improved results of more recent vintage, see the papers by Dicke and collaborators [R1] and by Braginskii and Panov [B4].

Of particular interest for EG is the covariant divergence of a second-rank tensor $T^{\mu\nu}$ [W5],

$$\theta^{\nu} \equiv T^{\mu\nu}_{;\mu} = \frac{1}{\sqrt{g}} \frac{\partial}{\partial x^{\mu}} (\sqrt{g} T^{\mu\nu}) + \Gamma^{\nu}_{\mu\lambda} T^{\mu\lambda} \tag{12.13}$$

where

$$g \equiv - \det g_{\mu\nu} \tag{12.14}$$

For a symmetric $T^{\mu\nu}$ we have:

$$\theta_{\rho} = g_{\rho\nu}\theta^{\nu} = \frac{1}{\sqrt{g}} \frac{\partial}{\partial x^{\mu}} (\sqrt{g}\, g_{\rho\nu} T^{\mu\nu}) - \frac{1}{2} \frac{\partial g_{\mu\nu}}{\partial x^{\rho}} T^{\mu\nu} \tag{12.15}$$

a relation that Einstein used in the discussion of energy–momentum conservation. As a further instance of covariant differentiation, the equation

$$g_{\mu\nu;\rho} = 0 \tag{12.16}$$

should be mentioned [W6]. This is one of the relations that threw Einstein off the track for some time.

Grossmann devotes a special section to antisymmetric tensors. He notes that Eq. 12.13 implies that

$$F^{\mu\nu}_{;\nu} = \frac{1}{\sqrt{g}} \frac{\partial}{\partial x^{\nu}} (\sqrt{g} F^{\mu\nu}) \qquad \text{if } F^{\mu\nu} = -F^{\nu\mu} \tag{12.17}$$

He also points out that $\epsilon^{\alpha\beta\gamma\delta}/\sqrt{g}$ is a contravariant fourth-rank tensor derived from the Levi-Civita symbol $\epsilon^{\alpha\beta\gamma\delta} = +1(-1)$ if $\alpha\beta\gamma\delta$ is an even (odd) permutation of 0123, zero otherwise.* As a result

$$F^{\alpha\beta*} \equiv \epsilon^{\alpha\beta\gamma\delta} F_{\gamma\delta}/\sqrt{g} \tag{12.18}$$

is a tensor, the dual of $F_{\gamma\delta}$.

Grossmann's concluding section starts as follows. 'The problem of the formulation of the differential equations of a gravitation field draws attention to the differential invariants ... and ... covariants of ... $ds^2 = g_{\mu\nu}dx^{\mu}dx^{\nu}$.' He then presents to Einstein the major tensor of the future theory: the 'Christoffel four-index symbol,' now better known as the Riemann–Christoffel tensor [W7]:

$$R^{\lambda}_{\mu\nu\kappa} \equiv \frac{\partial \Gamma^{\lambda}_{\mu\nu}}{\partial x^{\kappa}} - \frac{\partial \Gamma^{\lambda}_{\mu\kappa}}{\partial x^{\nu}} + \Gamma^{\eta}_{\mu\nu} \Gamma^{\lambda}_{\kappa\eta} - \Gamma^{\eta}_{\mu\kappa} \Gamma^{\lambda}_{\nu\eta} \tag{12.19}$$

---

*For definiteness, $\epsilon^{\alpha\beta\gamma\delta}$ is defined in a locally cartesian system where 0 denotes the time direction, 123 the space directions.

From this tensor 'it is ... possible to derive a second-rank tensor of the second order [in the derivatives of $g_{\mu\nu}$],' the Ricci tensor:

$$R_{\mu\nu} \equiv R^{\lambda}_{\mu\lambda\nu} = \frac{\partial \Gamma^{\lambda}_{\mu\lambda}}{\partial x^{\nu}} - \frac{\partial \Gamma^{\lambda}_{\mu\nu}}{\partial x^{\lambda}} + \Gamma^{\alpha}_{\mu\lambda}\Gamma^{\lambda}_{\nu\alpha} - \Gamma^{\alpha}_{\mu\nu}\,\Gamma^{\lambda}_{\lambda\alpha} \qquad (12.20)$$

Having come this close, Grossmann next makes a mistake to which I shall return in the course of describing Einstein's contributions to EG, a topic which should be prefaced by stating Grossmann's agreement with Einstein. 'With pleasure, he [G.] was ready to collaborate on this problem under the condition, however, that he would not have to assume any responsibility for any assertions or interpretations of a physical nature' [E32].

Einstein begins by stating his desideratum: to generalize the theory of relativity in such a way that his earlier result on the variability of the light velocity in an inhomogeneous static gravitational field [E33] shall be contained as a special case. Without preliminaries, he turns at once to the demand of general covariance: the motion of a mass point shall be determined by Eqs. 11.12 and 12.1, which I copy:

$$\delta \int ds = 0 \qquad (12.21)$$
$$ds^2 = g_{\mu\nu}dx^{\mu}dx^{\nu} \qquad (12.22)$$

These equations shall be invariant under the transformations (Eqs. 12.9 and 12.10), and ds^2 shall be an 'absolute invariant.' Then he goes on to state the principle of equivalence as we know it today: there is a special transformation of the type (Eq. 12.9):

$$dx^{\mu} = a^{\mu}_{\nu}d\xi^{\nu} \qquad (12.23)$$

that brings the quadratic form (Eq. 12.22) locally on principal axes:

$$ds^2 = \eta_{\mu\nu}d\xi^{\mu}d\xi^{\nu} \qquad (12.24)$$
$$\eta_{11} = \eta_{22} = \eta_{33} = -\eta_{00} = 1 \qquad \eta_{\mu\nu} = 0, \quad \mu \neq \nu \qquad (12.25)$$

This local coordinate frame in which the gravitational field has been transformed away acts as a free-falling infinitesimal laboratory. Time and space measurements can be performed locally in this frame by the same methods used in the special theory of relativity.* It follows that in terms of the general dx^{μ}, as in Eq. 12.22, 'the corresponding natural distance can be determined only when the $g_{\mu\nu}$ which determine the gravitational field are known. . . . The gravitational field influences the measuring bodies . . . in a definite way.' With these words, he states the broad program of the general theory of relativity.

---

*The specifications of the actual rods and clocks suited for this purpose are delicate [M1]. This author must confess to an occasional doubt as to whether this problem has as yet been fully understood on the atomic and subatomic levels.

Einstein uses Eqs. 12.21 and 12.22 to discuss the properties of the energy and momentum of a matter distribution with mass m (m being 'a characteristic constant independent of the gravitational potential'). In particular he derives the expression

$$\theta_{\mu\nu} = \rho_0 \frac{dx^\mu}{ds} \frac{dx^\nu}{ds} \qquad (12.26)$$

for the energy–momentum tensor of pressureless matter, where $\rho_0 = m/V_0$ and $V_0 = d\vec{\xi}$ is the rest-volume element of the material distribution. His next advance is made with the help of Grossmann's Eq. 12.15. He conjectures that the energy–momentum conservation laws must be of the generally covariant form

$$\frac{1}{\sqrt{g}} \frac{\partial}{\partial x^\mu} (\sqrt{g}\, \theta_\rho^\mu) - \frac{1}{2} \frac{\partial g_{\mu\nu}}{\partial x^\rho} \theta^{\mu\nu} = 0 \qquad (12.27)$$

in which the second term expresses the action of the gravitational field on matter.

The geodesic equation of motion

$$\frac{d^2 x^\mu}{d\tau^2} + \Gamma_{\lambda\nu}^\mu \frac{dx^\lambda}{d\tau} \frac{dx^\nu}{d\tau} = 0 \qquad (12.28)$$

[$d\tau = (-g_{\mu\nu} dx^\mu dx^\nu)^{1/2}$ is the proper time] for a particle with nonvanishing mass is *not* found in EG (Einstein first derived this equation in 1914). It is important to note this absence, since the two authors experienced some difficulty in recognizing the connection between their work and the Newtonian limit. For later purposes, it is helpful to recall how this limit is found for the equation of motion (Eq. 12.28) [W8]: (1) neglect $d\vec{x}/d\tau$ relative to $dt/d\tau$ (slow motion); (2) put $\partial g_{\mu\nu}/\partial t = 0$ (stationarity); (3) write

$$g_{\mu\nu} = \eta_{\mu\nu} + h_{\mu\nu} \qquad (12.29)$$

and retain only first-order terms in $h_{\mu\nu}$ (weak-field approximation). Then one obtains the Newtonian equation

$$\ddot{\vec{x}} = -\vec{\nabla}\phi \qquad (12.30)$$

where $\phi = -h_{00}/2$ is the Newtonian potential, so that

$$g_{00} = -(1 + 2\phi) \qquad (12.31)$$

Nevertheless, though the discussion of the motion of matter was not complete, all was going well so far, and the same continued to be true for electrodynamics. Indeed, EG contains the correct generally covariant form of the Maxwell equations:

$$\frac{1}{\sqrt{g}} \frac{\partial}{\partial x^\nu} (\sqrt{g} F^{\mu\nu}) = J^\mu \qquad (12.32)$$

$$\frac{1}{\sqrt{g}} \frac{\partial}{\partial x^{\nu}} \left(\sqrt{g} F^{\mu\nu*} \right) = 0 \qquad (12.33)$$

(see Eqs. 12.17 and 12.18). There remained the last question: what are the field equations of gravitation itself? Einstein guessed correctly that 'the needed generalization [of the Newtonian equations] should be of the form

$$\kappa\theta_{\mu\nu} = \Gamma_{\mu\nu} \qquad (12.34)$$

where ... $\Gamma_{\mu\nu}$ is a ... tensor of the second rank which is generated by differential operations from the fundamental tensor $g_{\mu\nu}$.'

Then the trouble began.

12d. The Stumbling Block

Clearly, Einstein and Grossmann were in quest of a tensor $\Gamma_{\mu\nu}$ of such a kind that the Newton–Poisson equation

$$\Delta \phi = 4\pi G\rho \qquad (12.35)$$

would emerge as a limiting case. This, Einstein said, was impossible as long as one requires, in the spirit of Eq. 12.35 that $\Gamma_{\mu\nu}$ be no higher than second order in the derivatives of the $g_{\mu\nu}$. Two arguments are given for this erroneous conclusion. The first one, found in Einstein's part, can be phrased as follows. One needs a generalization of div grad ϕ. The generalization of the gradient operator is the covariant differentiation. The generalization of ϕ is $g_{\mu\nu}$. But the covariant derivative of $g_{\mu\nu}$ vanishes (Eq. 12.16)! In Einstein's words, 'These operations [the covariant version of div grad] degenerate when they are applied to ... $g_{\mu\nu}$. From this, it seems to follow that the sought-for equations will be covariant only with respect to a certain group of transformations ... which for the time being is unknown to us.'

The second argument, contained in Grossmann's part, is also incorrect. As was mentioned above, Grossmann saw that the Ricci tensor (Eq. 12.20) might well be a candidate for $\Gamma_{\mu\nu}$ in Eq. 12.34. However, according to Grossmann, 'it turns out ... that this tensor does not reduce to $\Delta\phi$ in the special case of the weak gravitational field.' Reluctantly, the conclusion is drawn in EG that the invariance group for the gravitational equations has to be restricted to linear transformations only ($\partial x^{\alpha}/\partial x'^{\beta}$ is independent of x^{μ}), since then, it is argued, $\partial/\partial x^{\mu}(g^{\mu\nu}\partial g_{\rho\sigma}/\partial x^{\nu})$ does transform like a tensor, which, moreover, reduces to $\Box g_{\rho\sigma}$ in the weak-field limit given by Eq. 12.29. 'If the field is static and if only g_{44} varies [as a function of $\bar{x}$], then we arrive at the case of Newton's gravitation theory.' The troublesome Eq. 12.16 had been evaded!

Einstein also gave a 'physical argument' for the impossibility of generally covariant equations for the gravitational field. This argument, though of course incorrect, is nevertheless quite important. Consider (he says) a four-dimensional space–time domain divided into two parts, L_1 and L_2. The source $\theta_{\mu\nu}$ of the gravitational field (see Eq. 12.34) shall be nonzero only in L_1. Nevertheless, $\theta_{\mu\nu}$ determines the $g_{\mu\nu}$ in all of L by means of Eq. 12.34. Make a generally covariant transformation $x_\mu \rightarrow x'_\mu$ such that $x_\mu = x'_\mu$ in L_1 while, at least in part of L_2, $x_\mu \neq x'_\mu$. Then $g_{\mu\nu} \neq g'_{\mu\nu}$ in that part of L_2. The source $\theta_{\mu\nu}$ remains unchanged: $\theta_{\mu\nu} = \theta'_{\mu\nu}$ in L_1 while, in L_2, $\theta_{\mu\nu}$ once it is equal to zero stays equal to zero. Therefore, general covariance implies that more than one $g_{\mu\nu}$ distribution is possible for a given $\theta_{\mu\nu}$ distribution. *'If—as was done in this paper—the requirement is adhered to that the* $g_{\mu\nu}$ *are completely determined by the* $\theta_{\mu\nu}$, *then one is forced to restrict the choice of reference system'* (my italics). (Note that the above transformation $x_\mu \rightarrow x'_\mu$ is not allowed if the transformation is linear!) This reasoning is quite correct. Then what had gone wrong?

Einstein's 'physical argument' is irrelevant. The $g_{\mu\nu}$ are *not* completely determined by $\theta_{\mu\nu}$. His predicament was, put most succinctly, that *he did not know the Bianchi identities.* Let us consider the final form for Eq. 12.34, which he was to derive in 1915:

$$R_{\mu\nu} - 1/2\, g_{\mu\nu}R = -\kappa T_{\mu\nu} \tag{12.36}$$

where $R_{\mu\nu}$ is given by Eq. 12.20 and $R = R^{\mu\nu}g_{\mu\nu}$. The left-hand side satisfies the four Bianchi identities

$$(R^{\mu\nu} - 1/2\, g^{\mu\nu}R)_{;\nu} = 0 \tag{12.37}$$

Because of these relations, Eq. 12.36 does not determine the $g^{\mu\nu}$ uniquely—just as the Maxwell equations do not determine the electromagnetic potentials uniquely [W9]. The $g_{\mu\nu}$ are determined only up to a transformation $g_{\mu\nu} \rightarrow g'_{\mu\nu}$ corresponding to an arbitrary coordinate transformation $x_\mu \rightarrow x'_\mu$. Einstein still had to understand that this freedom expresses the fact that the choice of coordinates is a matter of convention without physical content. *That* he knew by 1915—although even then he still did not know the Bianchi identities (Chapter 15).

We now also understand Grossmann's difficulty with the Newtonian limit. Use Eq. 12.29 and define $h'_{\mu\nu} = h_{\mu\nu} - \frac{1}{2}\eta_{\mu\nu}\eta_{\alpha\beta}h^{\alpha\beta}$. Then Eq. 12.35 becomes

$$\Box h'_{\mu\nu} - \frac{\partial^2 h'_{\mu\alpha}}{\partial x^\nu \partial x^\alpha} - \frac{\partial^2 h'_{\nu\alpha}}{\partial x^\mu \partial x^\alpha} + \eta_{\mu\nu}\frac{\partial^2 h'_{\alpha\beta}}{\partial x^\alpha \partial x^\beta} = -\kappa T_{\mu\nu} \tag{12.38}$$

an intransparent relation. However, one is *free* to choose a coordinate frame in which

$$\frac{\partial h'_{\mu\alpha}}{\partial x^\alpha} = 0 \tag{12.39}$$

In the static weak-field limit, all components of $R_{\mu\nu}$ except R_{00} are negligible and (see Eq. 12.31)

$$R_{00} \approx \Delta g_{00}/2 = -\Delta\phi \qquad (12.40)$$

the desired result.

Einstein did not at once perceive the apparent restrictions on general covariance as a flaw. He felt that the problem had been solved. Early in 1913 he wrote to Ehrenfest. 'The gravitation affair has been clarified to my *full satisfaction* (namely, the circumstance that the equations of the gravitational field are covariant only for *linear* transformations). One can specifically prove that *generally covariant* equations which *completely* determine the [gravitational] field from the matter tensor cannot exist at all. What can be more beautiful than that this necessary specialization follows from the conservation laws?' (his italics) [E34].

This concludes a sketch of the arguments by which Einstein and Grossmann arrived at a hybrid theory in which some basic elements of the ultimate theory are already in evidence. I shall omit as of less interest the calculations which led them to explicit expressions for $\theta_{\mu\nu}$ and $\Gamma_{\mu\nu}$ in Eq. 12.34 that satisfy the conservation laws. The effort had been immense. Apologizing to Ehrenfest for a long silence, Einstein wrote in May 1913, 'My excuse lies in the literally superhuman efforts I have devoted to the gravitational problem. I now have the inner conviction that I have come upon what is correct and also that a murmur of indignation will go through the rows of colleagues when the paper appears, which will be the case in a few weeks' [E35].

I have now come to the end of the more complex and adventurous part of Einstein's road to the general theory of relativity. It began in 1907 with the equivalence principle, then there were the years of silence, then came the Prague papers about the c field, and finally the collaboration with Grossmann. In 1913 the theory was, of course, far from its logical completion. But the remaining story of Einstein's contributions is much more straightforward. It consists mainly of the recognitions that general covariance *can* be implemented, that the Ricci tensor *is* the clue to the right gravitational equations, and that there are the three classical successes of the theory. All this will be discussed in later chapters.

12e. The Aftermath

In 1905 Einstein had dedicated his doctoral thesis to Grossmann. In 1955 he dedicated his last published autobiographical sketch [E32] to the same old friend, long since deceased. The brief remainder of this chapter is devoted to the tale of Einstein and Grossmann from the times following their epochal collaboration until shortly before Einstein's death.

On September 9, 1913, first Einstein then Grossmann read papers before the annual meeting of the Swiss Physical Society [E36, G2]. These papers are simplified versions of EG and contain nothing substantially new. Einstein had already moved to Berlin when their next and last joint paper came out [E37]. In this work, they returned to the gravitational equations to ask, What are the most general transformations admissible under the assumption that the $g_{\mu\nu}$ are completely determined by the field equations? In EG they had shown that the demand of linearity was sufficient for this purpose. Now they found that *some* nonlinear transformations are admissible as well (including accelerations of various kinds). Actually, they were getting closer to the correct answers: their unjustified criterion of uniquely determined $g_{\mu\nu}$ is expressed by a set of four not generally covariant constraints. As is now well known, four constraints with this property (the so-called coordinate conditions) are indeed required in the correct general theory in order to eliminate the ambiguities in the $g_{\mu\nu}$ by means of the choice of some particular coordinate system [W10].

All publications by Grossmann during the next seven years deal with pedagogical and political subjects. Among social issues to which he devoted himself during the First World War was aid to students of all nations who had been taken prisoners of war. Between 1922 and 1930 he wrote another five papers on his favorite subject: descriptive geometry.

By 1920, the first signs of the disease that would fell him, multiple sclerosis, had already appeared. By 1926 the symptoms were severe. His daughter Elsbeth Grossmann told me that from then on he had difficulties speaking. In 1927 he had to resign his professorship at the ETH.

In 1931 Grossmann wrote his last paper [G3]. It is a polemic, without formulae, against the concepts of parallel displacement (Levi-Civita), absolute parallelism (Cartan), and distant parallelism (Einstein). The paper originated as a reaction to what Grossmann was told by a friend about a lecture by Einstein on unified field theory. Grossmann asserts that there are logical objections to all the concepts just mentioned. One cannot but feel sad upon reading this paper. Its contents were discussed in a correspondence between Einstein and Grossmann that is friendly yet strained. Einstein also wrote to Cartan, urging him not to answer Grossmann publicly [E38]; Cartan agreed [C2].*

After Grossmann's death in 1936, Einstein wrote a moving and deeply respectful letter to his widow [E39] about Grossmann's 'gruesome fate after early years rich in work and aspiration.' He writes of Grossmann 'the exemplary student . . . having good relations with the teachers . . . . I, separate and dissatisfied, not very popular.' He writes of Grossmann's helping him to obtain a job, 'without which I would not have died but might have spiritually wasted away.' He writes of 'the joint feverish work a decade later.' And adds, 'Aber eines ist doch schön. Wir waren und blieben Freunde durchs Leben hindurch.'**

*These two letters are contained in the published Cartan-Einstein correspondence [C3].

**But one thing is really beautiful. We were and remained friends throughout life.

I have a sense of regret that Einstein did not do something for which he had often demonstrated a talent and sensitivity: to write an obituary shortly after Grossmann's death. He did so later. In 1955 he wrote of Grossmann, of their collaboration, and of how the latter had 'checked through the literature and soon discovered that the mathematical problem had already been solved by Riemann, Ricci, and Levi-Civita. . . . Riemann's achievement was the greatest one.' In this article, Einstein wrote, 'The need to express at least once in my life my gratitude to Marcel Grossmann gave me the courage to write this . . . autobiographical sketch' [E32].

References

B1. M. Born, *AdP* **30**, 1 (1909).
B2. ——, *Phys. Zeitschr.* **10**, 814 (1909).
B3. ——, *Phys. Zeitschr.* **11**, 233 (1910).
B4. V. B. Braginskii and V. I. Panov, *Societ. Phys. JETP* **34**, 463 (1972).
C1. E. B. Christoffel, *Z. Math.* **70**, 46 (1869).
C2. E. Cartan, letter to A. Einstein, June 24, 1931.
C3. *Cartan–Einstein Correspondence on Absolute Parallelism* (R. Debever, Ed.). Princeton University Press, Princeton, N.J., 1979.
E1. A. Einstein, letter to M. Grossmann, November 18, 1911.
E2. ——, *Astrophys. J.* **63**, 196 (1926).
E3. ——, telegram to H. Zangger, November 20, 1911.
E4. ——, letter to H. Zangger, January 27, 1912.
E5. ——, letter to A. Stern, February 2, 1912.
E6. ——, letter to H. Zangger, Spring 1912.
E7. ——, letter to H. A. Lorentz, November 23, 1911.
E8. ——, letter to H. Zangger, February 29, 1912.
E9. ——, letter to P. Ehrenfest, 1913, undated.
E10. ——, *AdP* **38**, 443 (1912).
E11. ——, letter to M. Besso, March 26, 1912.
E12. ——, letter to P. Ehrenfest, 1912, undated.
E13. ——, letter to H. Zangger, May 20, 1912.
E14. ——, letter to H. Zangger, 1912, undated.
E15. ——, postcard to M. von Laue, June 10, 1912.
E16. ——, letter to L. Hopf, June 12, 1912.
E17. ——, *AdP* **38**, 1059 (1912).
E18. ——, letter to L. Hopf, August 16, 1912.
E19. —— in *Helle Zeit, dunkle Zeit* (C. Seelig, Ed.), p. 10. Europa Verlag, Zürich, 1956.
E20. *Einstein a Praha* (J. Bicak, Ed.), p. 42. Prometheus, Prague, 1979.
E21. ——, *Die Grundlage der Allgemeinen Relativitätstheorie*, p. 6. J. A. Barth, Leipzig, 1916.
E22. ——, *Geometrie und Erfahrung*. Springer, Berlin, 1921; also *PAW*, 1921, p. 123.
E23. ——, letter to P. Ehrenfest, June 7, 1912.
E24. ——, *Viertelj. Schrift Ger. Medizin* **44**, 37 (1912).
E25. ——, *Phys. Zeitschr.* **10**, 817 (1909).

E26. P. Ehrenfest, *Phys. Zeitschr.* **10**, 918 (1909).

E27. A. Einstein, *AdP* **49**, 769 (1916).

E28. ——, letter to A. Sommerfeld, October 29, 1912. See A. Hermann, *Einstein/Sommerfeld Briefwechsel*, p. 26. Schwabe Verlag, Stuttgart., 1968.

E29. —— and M. Grossmann, *Z. Math. Physik.* **62**, 225 (1913).

E30. —— *PAW*, 1914, p. 1030.

E31. ——, *AdP* **49**, 769 (1916), Sec. 5.

E32. —— in *Helle Zeit, dunkle Zeit* (C. Seelig, Ed.). Europa Verlag, Zürich, 1956.

E33. ——, *AdP* **38**, 443 (1912).

E34. ——, letter to P. Ehrenfest, 1913, undated.

E35. ——, letter to P. Ehrenfest, May 28, 1913.

E36. —— *Viertelj. Schrift Naturf. Ges. Zürich* **58**, 284 (1913). An abbreviated version appears in *Verh. Schw. Naturf. Ges.* **96**, 137 (1914), and a French translation in *Arch. Sci. Phys. Nat.* **37**, 5 (1914).

E37. —— and M. Grossmann, *Z. Math. Physik.* **63**, 215 (1915).

E38. ——, letter to E. Cartan, June 13, 1931.

E39. ——, letter to Mrs M. Grossmann, September 26, 1936.

F1. Ph. Frank, *Albert Einstein; Sein Leben und seine Zeit*, p. 141. Vieweg, Braunschweig, 1979.

G1. M. Grossmann, *Proceedings of the 5th International Congress of Mathematicians*, August 1912, p. 66. Cambridge University Press, Cambridge, 1913.

G2. ——, *Viertelj. Schrift Naturf. Ges. Zürich* **58**, 291 (1913).

G3. ——, *Viertelj. Schrift Naturf. Ges. Zürich* **76**, 42 (1931).

H1. G. Herglotz, *AdP* **31**, 393 (1909).

I1. J. Ishiwara, *Einstein Kōen-Roku.* Tokyo-Tosho, Tokyo, 1977.

K1. L. Kollros, *Verh. Schw. Naturf. Ges.* **115**, 522 (1934).

K2. ——, *Helv. Phys. Acta Suppl.* **4**, 271 (1956).

K3. F. Klein, *Vorlesungen über die Entwicklung der Mathematik im 19. Jahrhundert*, Vol. 2, p. 189. Springer, New York, 1979.

L1. H. A. Lorentz, letter to A. Einstein, December 6, 1911.

L2. H. Lamb, *Hydrodynamics* (6th edn.), p. 12. Dover, New York.

M1. C. W. Misner, K. S. Thorne, and J. A. Wheeler, *Gravitation,* p. 393. Freeman, San Francisco, 1973.

P1. W. Pauli in *Encyklopädie der Mathematischen Naturwissenschaften*, Vol. V, 2, Sec. 45, Teubner, Leipzig, 1921.

R1. P. G. Roll, R. Krotkov, and R. H. Dicke, *Ann. Phys.* **26**, 442 (1964).

R2. G. Ricci and T. Levi-Civita, *Math. Ann.* **54**, 125 (1901).

S1. W. Saxer, *Viertelj. Schr. Naturf. Ges. Zürich* **81**, 322 (1936).

S2. Se, p. 226.

S3. Se, pp. 227–33.

S4. Se, p. 242.

S5. Se, p. 38.

S6. E. G. Straus, discussion with A. Pais, December 11, 1979.

S7. D. J. Struik, *Isis* **19**, 92 (1932); **20**, 161 (1933).

W1. S. Weinberg, *Gravitation and Cosmology.* Wiley, New York, 1972 (quoted as W hereafter).

W2. W, pp. 11–13.

 W3. W, pp. 93–8.
 W4. W, pp. 75, 103–6.
 W5. W, pp. 98, 107.
 W6. W, p. 105.
 W7. W, p. 133.
 W8. W, p. 77.
 W9. W, p. 161.
W10. W, p. 162.

13

Field Theories of Gravitation: the First Fifty Years

13a. Einstein in Vienna

It did not take Einstein long to realize that the collaboration with Grossmann [E1] had led to some conclusions that defeated the very task he had set himself. Let us briefly recapitulate the developments in his thinking about gravitation up to the spring of 1913. Late in 1907 he discovered the singular position of gravitation in the theory of relativity. He realized that the question was not how to incorporate gravitation into the special theory but rather how to use gravitation as a means of breaking away from the privileged position of covariance for uniform relative motion to covariance for general motion. In his Prague days, the analysis of the motion of light in an inhomogeneous gravitational field taught him that the light velocity depends on the gravitational potential and that therefore the framework of the special theory of relativity was too narrow [E2]. Toward the end of his stay in Prague, the technical concept of general covariance took shape in his mind and the fundamental role of the metric tensor as the carrier of gravitation became clear. The first steps toward the tensor theory of gravitation, taken with Grossmann, led him to conclude that the gravitational field equations can be covariant only with respect to linear transformations.

By August 1913, it had become clear to him that this last result spelled disaster. He expressed this in a letter to Lorentz: ...'My faith in the reliability of the theory still fluctuates.... The gravitational equations unfortunately do not have the property of general covariance. Only their covariance for linear transformations is assured. However, the whole faith in the theory rests on the conviction that acceleration of the reference system is equivalent to a gravitational field. Thus, if not all systems of equations of the theory ... admit transformations other than linear ones, then the theory contradicts its own starting point [and] all is up in the air' (sie steht dann in der Luft) [E3].

Thoughts such as these must have been on Einstein's mind when he traveled to Vienna, where on September 23 he had to present a paper before the Natur-forscherversammlung.* He was going to report not only on his own work but also

---

*At that meeting, Einstein met and complimented Friedrich Kottler, who had been the first to write the Maxwell equations in generally covariant form, though not in connection with a theory of gravitation [K1]. Kottler's later involvement with general relativity was less successful [E3a].

on the gravitation theory which the Finnish physicist Gunnar Nordström had been developing since 1912. Furthermore, he was going to comment on yet another recent gravitation theory, this one by Abraham (whom we encountered earlier in the discussion of special relativity). He would also be confronted, he knew, with still a further theory of gravity of recent vintage, one by Gustav Mie.* In one way or another, this outpouring of gravitation theories in the years 1912 and 1913 was a consequence of Einstein's Prague papers. Abraham had proposed to extend Einstein's theory of variable light velocity in a static gravitational field to the nonstatic case. Nordström had raised another question: could not the equivalence principle be incorporated in a relativistic theory with constant light velocity? Mie's theory was yet another variant in which c is constant. These activities during 1911–13 do not by any means mark the beginnings of the search for a field theory of gravitation, however. As a preface to the discussion of the confused situation at the Vienna congress of 1913 let us briefly go back half a century.

The search began with Maxwell's remarks on a vector theory of gravitation. These are found tucked away in his great memoir, *A Dynamical Theory of the Electromagnetic Field,* completed in 1864, the purpose of which is 'to explain the [electromagnetic] action between distant bodies without assuming the existence of forces capable of acting directly at sensible distances. The theory I propose may therefore be called a theory of the Electromagnetic Field . . .' [M1]. After devoting some forty printed pages to this problem, Maxwell abruptly and briefly turns to gravitation: 'After tracing to the action of the surrounding medium both the magnetic and the electric attractions and repulsions, and finding them to depend on the inverse square of the distance, we are naturally led to inquire whether the attraction of gravitation, which follows the same law of the distance, is not also traceable to the action of a surrounding medium.' But how can one explain, Maxwell asks, that the gravitational force is attractive whereas the force between electric charges of the same sign is repulsive? He notes that this requires an ad hoc change of sign when going from the electromagnetic to the gravitational ponderomotive force (recall: this is a vector theory). Therefore the gravitational energy also needs an additional minus sign. This leads to paradoxes: 'the presence of dense bodies influences the medium so as to diminish this energy [of the medium] wherever there is a resultant attraction. As I am unable to understand in what way a medium can possess such properties, I cannot go any further in this direction in searching for the cause of gravitation.'

Maxwell's wise words were not generally heeded, not even by physicists of great stature. Oliver Heaviside discussed the gravitational–electromagnetic analogy without mentioning the negative energy difficulty [H1]. So, remarkably, did Lorentz, in one of his rare speculative papers [L1], written in 1900. He proposed that the repulsive forces between two particles with respective charges $(+e, +e)$ equal those for $(-e, -e)$ but are slightly weaker (in absolute magnitude) than the attractive force for the case $(+e, -e)$. Then if one has, for example, two

---

*References to other work on gravitation from that period are found in a review by Abraham [A1]

neutral particles at rest, each composed of a pair of subunits $(+e, -e)$, there is a residual Newtonian attraction between them. The formalism of his theory consists of a doubled set of Maxwell equations and ponderomotive forces (the latter with coefficients adjusted to give the desired behavior for the various charge combinations). Nowhere in this strange paper is it noted that there exists a doubling of conservation laws, one for charge and one for gravitational rest mass. Lorentz calculated velocity-dependent corrections to Newton's law and went as far as evaluating their influence (too small) on the perihelion of Mercury. A few others also examined the consequences of this theory [G1, W1]. In 1908 Poincaré mentioned Lorentz's gravitation theory as an example of a field theory that is compatible with the requirements of special relativity [P1].*

As late as 1912, it was still necessary to show that all these vector theories made no sense because of Maxwell's negative energy difficulty. At that time Abraham pointed out that the equilibrium of a gravitational oscillator is unstable [A2]: the amplitude of the slightest oscillation increases with emission of gravitational field energy; there is radiation enhancement rather than radiation damping. Thus the vector theories were buried at just about the time attention shifted to scalar theories.

This brief period began with Einstein's paper of June 1911, in which he showed that the velocity of light cannot generally be treated as a universal constant in a static gravitational field [E4]. Half a year later, Abraham made the first attempt to extend this conclusion to nonstatic fields [A3]. He tried the impossible: to incorporate this idea of a nonconstant light velocity into the special theory of relativity. He generalized the Newtonian equation for a point particle, $\vec{K} = -\vec{\nabla}\varphi = \vec{a}$, where $\vec{K}$ is the gravitational force acting on a unit of mass, φ the potential, and $\vec{a}$ the acceleration, to

$$K_\mu = -\frac{\partial \Phi}{\partial x^\mu} = \dot{u}_\mu \tag{13.1}$$

where u_μ is the four-velocity and the dot denotes differentiation with respect to the proper time τ. The function Φ is supposed to satisfy an equation of the type

$$\Box \Phi = \rho \tag{13.2}$$

where Φ and ρ are scalar fields. The four-velocity u_μ satisfies

$$u_\mu u^\mu = -c^2 \tag{13.3}$$

From Eqs. 13.1 and 13.3,

$$u^\mu \frac{\partial \Phi}{\partial x^\mu} = \frac{d\Phi}{d\tau} = c\frac{dc}{d\tau} \tag{13.4}$$

---

*Poincaré had already emphasized the need for a relativistic theory of gravitation in his memoir of 1905 [P2], in which he discussed some general kinematic aspects of the problem without commitment to a specific model. See also Minkowski [M2].

since c is not a constant. Hence

$$c_1^2 - c_2^2 = 2(\Phi_1 - \Phi_2) \qquad (13.5)$$

or, approximately,

$$c_1 = c_2 \left(1 + \frac{\Phi_1 - \Phi_2}{c^2} \right) \qquad (13.6)$$

which is Einstein's equation of 1911 (see Eq. 11.6). No use is made of Eq. 13.2 in this derivation. The latter equation looks invariant with respect to special relativity, but of course it is not, since c is variable. Abraham commented on this in his next communication: 'The variability of c implies that the Lorentz group holds only in the infinitesimally small' [A4], a statement that was almost at once disproved by Einstein [E5].

A debate began in the *Annalen der Physik* which, from Abraham's side, lacked style and substance. In a first comment [A5], Abraham noted that relativity was threatening the healthy development of physics since 'it was clear to the sober observer that this theory could never lead to a complete world picture if it were not possible ... to incorporate gravity.' He added that Einstein had given 'the death blow to relativity' by discarding the unconditional validity of Lorentz invariance.* 'Someone who, like this author [A.], has had to warn repeatedly against the siren song of this theory will greet with satisfaction [the fact] that its originator has now convinced himself of its untenability.' Abraham acknowledged the correctness of Einstein's technical objections to his work. In a later paper [A6], he unveiled his 'second theory': 'I would prefer to develop the new theory of gravitation without entering into [a discussion of] the space–time problem.' Abraham now gives up Lorentz invariance altogether and introduces an absolute reference system (see also [A1], p. 488).

Einstein shot right back, though in measured language: '[Special] relativity has a wide range of applicability [and is] an important advance; I do not believe it has impeded the progress of physics. ... There is not the slightest ground to doubt the general validity of the relativity principle [for uniform motion]' [E6]. He expressed his own views about the difficult and as yet unsolved problem of gravity by making a comparison: 'In my opinion, the situation [regarding gravity] does not indicate the failure of the [special] relativity principle, just as the discovery and correct interpretation of Brownian motion did not lead one to consider thermodynamics and hydrodynamics as heresies.' He added that he himself did not yet understand how the equivalence principle was to be implemented in general.

Abraham did not give up and published a rebuttal [A7]. It adds nothing substantially new and is vicious: '[Einstein] craves credit for the future theory of relativity.' In reply, Einstein published a five-line statement in which he declared

---

*Note that these comments preceded the publication of the Einstein–Grossman paper [E1].

that the public debate was closed as far as he was concerned [E7]. To a friend he described Abraham's theory as 'a stately horse which lacks three legs' [E8].

I would have disregarded the Abraham–Einstein polemic were it not for the fact that Abraham was a very good physicist. Einstein considered him to have the best understanding of gravitation among his colleagues [E9]. Abraham's 1914 review of gravitation theories is excellent [A1]. When in 1913 Einstein decided to leave Zürich for Berlin, he suggested to Zangger that Abraham be considered as his successor [E10].* But, he added, 'I believe that they will proceed without me because I have espoused the cause of the feared Abraham.'

Abraham had a great and unfortunate talent for creating difficulties for himself, especially because of his biting sarcasm. Between himself and his visions stood forever the figure of his demon: Einstein. He understood relativity but could not find peace with it. He cannot be called a major scientist but should be remembered nevertheless as a figure representing the tragic element which accompanies scientific transition. He died in 1923 of a brain tumor. Born and von Laue jointly wrote his obituary: 'He was an honorable opponent who fought with honest weapons and who did not cover up a defeat by lamentation and nonfactual arguments. The abstractions of Einstein were deeply repugnant to him; he loved his absolute aether, his field equations, his rigid electron, as a youth does his first flame, whose memories cannot be erased by later experiences. But he remained clearheaded . . . his objections rested on basic convictions regarding physics . . . and not on lack of knowledge' [B1].

To return to the developments prior to the publication of the Einstein–Grossmann paper, late in 1912 Nordström in Helsingfors (Helsinki) came forth with an ingenious idea [N1]. Since both Einstein and Abraham experienced so much trouble from the Φ-dependence of c, why not try to find a theory of gravitation in which c is independent of Φ and remains a universal constant in the familiar way? As I have noted repeatedly, Einstein correctly saw from the beginning that the incorporation of gravity meant the end of the unconditional validity of special relativity. All the same, Nordström's question was an eminently sensible one for its time. It is peculiar that this line of thought had remained unexplored (or at least had not been discussed in the scientific literature) until October 1912.

As we saw from Abraham's mishandling of Eqs. 13.1–13.4, the problem is not quite trivial. Nordström's idea was to let not c but, instead, mass depend on Φ. For general mass m, he rewrote Eq. 13.1 (which referred to unit mass) as follows:

$$ mK_\mu = -m \frac{\partial \Phi}{\partial x^\mu} = \frac{d}{d\tau}(mu_\mu) = m\dot{u}_\mu + \dot{m}u_\mu \qquad (13.7) $$

The novelty of his theory lies in the $\dot{m}$ term. From Eq. 13.7 and the obviously unchanged Eq. 13.3, one finds

$$ mu^\mu \frac{\partial \Phi}{\partial x^\mu} = m \frac{d\Phi}{d\tau} = c^2 \frac{dm}{d\tau} \qquad (13.8) $$

*On May 17, 1912, Einstein wrote to Wien that Abraham had become a 'convert' to his theory.

whence

$$m = m_0 \exp (\Phi/c^2) \tag{13.9}$$

Note further that Eqs. 13.7 and 13.8 yield

$$-\frac{\partial \Phi}{\partial x^\mu} = \dot{u}_\mu + \frac{u_\mu}{c^2} \dot{\Phi} \tag{13.10}$$

in which m has disappeared. Equations 13.10 and 13.2 form the basis of Nord-ströms first theory, in which he identified ρ with the 'rest mass density' [N2]. I shall leave aside further details of this theory, which left much to be desired, and turn at once to his 'second theory', which he proposed in 1913 [N3]. Though it was not to survive, it deserves to be remembered as the first logically consistent relativistic field theory of gravitation ever formulated.

The main idea (which Nordström owed to von Laue and Einstein) is that the only possible source for his scalar gravitational field is

$$T = \eta_{\mu\nu} T^{\mu\nu} \tag{13.11}$$

the trace of the energy momentum tensor $T^{\mu\nu}$ ($\eta_{\mu\nu}$ is, as usual, the Minkowski metric). All the physical conclusions of the theory are due to Nordström himself. I shall not follow his derivations, however, but instead describe the simple trick, reported by Einstein at the Vienna meeting [E11], which leads rapidly to the desired result.

In Eq. 13.10, put $\Phi = c^2 \ln \psi$. Then

$$\frac{\partial \psi}{\partial x^\mu} + \frac{1}{c^2} \frac{d}{d\tau} (u_\mu \psi) = 0 \tag{13.12}$$

This equation can be derived from the variational principle

$$\delta \int \psi d\tau_0 = 0 \qquad d\tau_0^2 = -\eta_{\mu\nu} dx^\mu dx^\nu \tag{13.13}$$

Once one has a variational principle, one can derive the equation for the energy momentum tensor of a particle with rest mass m and rest volume V ($\rho = m/V$), where the particle is treated as a continuum distributed over the rest volume V:

$$T^{\mu\nu} = \frac{\rho\psi}{c^2} u^\mu u^\nu \tag{13.14}$$

and for its divergence

$$\frac{\partial T^{\mu\nu}}{\partial x^\nu} = -\rho \frac{\partial \psi}{\partial x_\mu} \tag{13.15}$$

Equation 13.14 yields $T^\mu_\mu \equiv T = -\rho\psi$ and hence Eq. 13.15 becomes

$$\frac{\partial T^{\mu\nu}}{\partial x^\nu} = T \frac{1}{\psi} \frac{\partial \psi}{\partial x_\mu} \tag{13.16}$$

in which all reference to a particle with mass m has disappeared. Einstein proposed to consider Eq. 13.16 to hold *whatever* material (and electromagnetic) system generates $T^{\mu\nu}$. Put

$$-\psi \Box \psi = \kappa T \qquad (13.17)$$

This is Nordström's 'second' field equation. It follows from Eqs. 13.16 and 13.17 that

$$\frac{\partial(T^{\mu\nu} + t^{\mu\nu})}{\partial x^\nu} = 0 \qquad (13.18)$$

where

$$t^{\mu\nu} = \frac{1}{\kappa}\left[\frac{\partial\psi}{\partial x_\mu}\frac{\partial\psi}{\partial x_\nu} - \frac{1}{2}\eta^{\mu\nu}\left(\frac{\partial\psi}{\partial x_\lambda}\frac{\partial\psi}{\partial x^\lambda}\right)\right] \qquad (13.19)$$

is the energy momentum tensor of the gravitational field. Thus the theory is Lorentz invariant and also satisfies the conservation laws.

Now to the equivalence principle. Consider a totally static closed system. This obeys (integrated over the system) $\int T^i_i d\vec{x} = 0$ (i = 1, 2, 3). Hence, $\int T d\vec{x} = -E/c^2$, where E is its total energy. The same relation is also true for a system in statistical equilibrium provided E is considered as the time average, over the system.* Go to the static weak-field limit, $\psi/c^2 = 1 + \phi/c^2$, where ϕ is the Newtonian potential. Then Eq. 13.17 becomes

$$\Delta\phi = -\frac{\kappa E}{c^4} \qquad (13.20)$$

and we have the desired result that the gravitational mass is proportional to the total energy of the system.** As Einstein put it later, in this theory the equivalence principle is a statistical law [E12].

About one quarter of Einstein's Vienna report, 'On the Current Status of the Gravitation Problem,' is devoted to Nordström's work.† He commented only briefly on Abraham's contributions, noting that he considered it a requirement of any future theory that special relativity be incorporated and that Abraham had not done so. When in the subsequent discussion Mie remarked that Nordström's theory was an outgrowth of Abraham's work, Einstein replied: psychologically yes, logically no. The incorporation of the equivalence principle was another desi-

---

*See [L2]. The average is to be taken over a time that evens out pressure fluctuations.

**This is the weak equivalence principle in the sense of Dicke, who further showed that the Nordström theory does not satisfy the strong equivalence principle, according to which in a nonrotating free-falling laboratory the laws of physics are those of gravity-free space, assumed to be everywhere the same [D1].

†Einstein also used this occasion to withdraw an objection to the scalar theory which he had raised in his paper with Grossmann [E1]. For other comments on scalar gravitation, see [W2].

deratum stressed by Einstein. 'In the context [of a theory of gravitation], the Eöt-vös experiment plays a role similar to that of the Michelson experiment for uniform motion.' When Mie asked afterward why Einstein had not mentioned his, Mie's, work, Einstein replied that he would discuss only theories which, unlike Mie's, satisfy the equivalence principle.* The bulk of Einstein's report was of course devoted to his recent work with Grossmann. It added little to what has already been described here. At Vienna, Mie was Einstein's principal antagonist. Shortly after this meeting, Mie wrote a further critique on Einstein's theory [M4], to which Einstein replied by giving arguments that were in part incorrect: once again he stressed the inevitability of the invariance of the gravitational equations for linear transformations only [E13].

In summary, prior to 1912 no attempt to construct a field theory of gravitation had led anywhere. Toward the end of 1913 the situation was thoroughly confused. Nordström's was the only consistent theory of gravitation. Most physicists were ready to accept special relativity. A few were willing to concede the fundamental role of the equivalence principle, but others thought that an exaggeration. There is no evidence that anyone shared Einstein's views concerning the limitations imposed by gravitation on special relativity, nor that anyone was ready to follow his program for a tensor theory of gravitation. Only Lorentz had given him some encouragement. 'I am happy that you receive our investigation [E.-Grossmann] with favor,' Einstein wrote in the same letter in which he had expressed his own doubts about the status of his theory [E3].

Despite these reservations, Einstein was in a combative mood. Commenting on the criticisms by Abraham and Mie, he wrote, 'I enjoy it that this affair is at least taken up with the requisite animation. I enjoy the controversies. Figaro mood: "Will der Herr Graf ein Tänzlein wagen? Er soll's nur sagen! Ich spiel ihm auf"' [E14].** He felt sure that the four-dimensional pseudo-Euclidean description needed revision. 'I enjoy it that colleagues occupy themselves at all with the theory, although for the time being with the purpose of killing it. . . . On the face of it, Nordström's theory . . . is much more plausible. But it, too, is built on the a priori Euclidean four-dimensional space, the belief in which amounts, I feel, to something like a superstition' [E15]. In March 1914, he expressed himself as follows about his own efforts. 'Nature shows us only the tail of the lion. But I do not doubt that the lion belongs to it even though he cannot at once reveal himself because of his enormous size' [E16].†

---

*In Mie's theory [M3], the ratio of gravitational and inertial mass depends on physical parameters such as velocity and temperature. Also, there is neither a red shift nor a bending of light. I do not discuss this complicated theory here (it contains two scalar fields) because it does not contain conceptually interesting points of view.

**Would the Count like to dare a little dance? Let him but say so! I'll play him a tune.

†See Chapter 14 for comments by Einstein in 1914 on the Nordström theory and [E17] for his reminiscences on scalar theories.

The portrait of Einstein the scientist in 1913 is altogether remarkable. He has no compelling results to show for his efforts. He sees the limitations of what he has done so far. He is supremely confident of his vision. And he stands all alone. It seems to me that Einstein's intellectual strength, courage, and tenacity to continue under such circumstances and then to be supremely vindicated a few years later do much to explain how during his later years he would fearlessly occupy once again a similar position, in his solitary quest for an interpretation of quantum mechanics which was totally at variance with commonly held views.

13b. The Einstein–Fokker Paper

Adriaan Daniel Fokker received his PhD degree late in 1913 under Lorentz. His thesis dealt with Brownian motions of electrons in a radiation field [F1] and contains an equation which later became known as the Fokker–Planck equation. After this work was completed, Lorentz sent Fokker to Zürich to work with Einstein. The resulting collaboration lasted one semester only. It led to one brief paper which is of considerable interest for the history of general relativity because it contains Einstein's first treatment of a gravitation theory in which general covariance is strictly obeyed [E18].

The authors first rewrite Eq. 13.13:

$$\delta \int d\tau = 0 \qquad d\tau^2 = - g_{\mu\nu} dx^\mu dx^\nu \qquad g_{\mu\nu} = \psi^2 \eta_{\mu\nu} \qquad (13.21)$$

from which they conclude that the Nordström theory is a special case of the Einstein–Grossmann theory, characterized by the additional requirement that the velocity of light be constant. Yet the theory is, of course, more general than special relativity. In particular, it follows from Eq. 13.21 that neither the real rate dt of a transportable clock nor the real length dl of a transportable rod have the special relativistic values dt_0 and dl_0, respectively. Rather (as Nordström already knew) $dt_0 = dt/\psi$, $dl_0 = dl/\psi$, compatible with the ψ-independence of the light velocity.

This paper is particularly notable for its new derivation of the field equation (Eq. 13.17). 'From the investigation by mathematicians of differential tensors,' this field equation must be of the form (they state)

$$R = \text{const. T} \qquad (13.22)$$

where

$$R = g^{\mu\nu} R_{\mu\nu} \qquad (13.23)$$

is the curvature scalar derived from the Ricci tensor $R_{\mu\nu}$ (Eq. 12.20) in which the $g_{\mu\nu}$ are, of course, given (in the present instance) by Eq. 13.21. Einstein and Fokker go on to prove that Eq. 13.22 (with the constant adjusted) is equivalent to Eq. 13.17!

The paper concludes with the following remark: 'It is plausible that the role which the Riemann–Christoffel tensor plays in the present investigation would also open a way for a derivation of the Einstein–Grossmann gravitation equations in a way independent of physical assumptions. The proof of the existence or nonexistence of such a connection would be an important theoretical advance.' A final footnote states that one of the reasons given by Einstein and Grossmann [E1] for the nonexistence of such a connection was incorrect, namely, the allegedly wrong weak-field properties of the Ricci tensor (Chapter 12).

Thus, early in 1914, just fifty years after Maxwell's first attempt at a gravitation field theory, Einstein was not yet quite there but he was closing in, as the final remark of the Einstein–Fokker paper clearly indicates. That it took him almost another two years before he had the final answer was due in part to important changes which were about to take place in his personal life, as we shall see next.

References

A1. M. Abraham, *Jahrb. Rad. Elekt.* **11**, 470 (1914).
A2. ——, *Arch. Math. Phys.* **20**, 193 (1912).
A3. ——, *Phys. Zeitschr.* **13**, 1, 4 (1912).
A4. ——, *Phys. Zeitschr.* **13**, 310 (1912).
A5. ——, *AdP* **38**, 1056 (1912).
A6. ——, *Phys. Zeitschr.* **13**, 793 (1913).
A7. ——, *AdP* **39**, 444 (1912).
B1. M. Born and M. von Laue, *Phys. Zeitschr.* **24**, 49 (1923).
D1. R. H. Dicke, *Ann. Phys.* **31**, 235 (1965).
E1. A. Einstein and M. Grossmann, *Z. Math. Physik.* **62**, 225 (1913).
E2. ——, *AdP* **38**, 355, 443 (1912).
E3. ——, letter to H. A. Lorentz, August 14, 1913.
E3a. ——, *AdP* **51**, 639, (1916).
E4. ——, *AdP* **35**, 898 (1911).
E5. ——, *AdP* **38**, 355 (1912), Sec. 4.
E6. ——, *AdP* **38**, 1059 (1912).
E7. ——, *AdP* **39**, 704 (1912).
E8. ——, letter to L. Hopf, August 16, 1912.
E9. ——, letter to M. Besso, late 1913; *EB*, p. 50.
E10. ——, two letters to H. Zangger; one, undated, from late 1913 or early 1914 and the other dated July 7, 1915.
E11. ——, *Phys. Zeitschr.* **14**, 1249 (1913); **15**, 108 (1914).
E12. ——, *Scientia* **15**, 337 (1914).
E13. ——, *Phys. Zeitschr.* **15**, 176 (1914).
E14. ——, letter to H. Zangger, undated, late 1913 or early 1914.
E15. ——, letter to E. Freundlich, undated, early 1914.
E16. ——, letter to H. Zangger, March 10, 1914.
E17. —— in *Albert Einstein, Philosopher–Scientist* (P. Schilpp, Ed.), pp. 63–5. Tudor, New York, 1949.
E18. —— and A. D. Fokker, *AdP* **44**, 321 (1914).
F1. A. D. Fokker, *Phys. Zeitschr.* **15**, 96 (1914).

G1. R. Gans, *Phys. Zeitschr* **6,** 803 (1905).

H1. O. Heaviside, *Electromagnetic Theory* (3rd edn.), Vol. 1, p. 455. Chelsea, New York, 1971.

K1. F. Kottler, *Wiener Ber.* **121,** 1659 (1912).

L1. H. A. Lorentz, *Collected Works,* Vol. 5, p. 198. Nyhoff, The Hague, 1934.

L2. M. von Laue, *Das Relativitätsprinzip,* (2nd edn.), p. 208. Vieweg, Braunschweig, 1913.

M1. J. C. Maxwell, *Collected Papers,* Vol. 1, p. 570. Dover, New York, 1952.

M2. H. Minkowski, *Goett. Nachr.,* 1908, p. 53, Anhang.

M3. G. Mie, *AdP* **40,** 1 (1913), Sec. 5.

M4. ——, *Phys. Zeitschr.* **15,** 115, 169 (1914).

N1. G. Nordström, *Phys. Zeitschr.* **13,** 1126 (1912).

N2. ——, *AdP* **40,** 856 (1913).

N3. ——, *AdP* **42,** 533 (1913).

P1. H. Poincaré, *Oeuvres,* Vol. 9, p. 551. Gauthier-Villars, Paris, 1954.

P2. ——, [P1], p. 494, Sec. 9.

W1. F. Wacker, *Phys. Zeitschr.* **7,** 300 (1906).

W2. M. Wellner and G. Sandri, *Am. J. Phys.* **28,** 36 (1963).

14

The Field Equations of Gravitation

14a. From Zürich to Berlin

On November 25, 1915, Einstein presented to the physics–mathematics section of the Prussian Academy of Sciences a paper in which 'finally the general theory of relativity is closed as a logical structure' [E1]. The title of that paper is identical with the heading of the present chapter, in which it is described how his field equations reached their final form.

Einstein was still a professor at the ETH when he presented his report to the Vienna meeting discussed in Chapter 13. However, by then he had already decided to leave Zürich.

In the spring of 1913, Planck and Nernst had come to Zürich for the purpose of sounding out Einstein about his possible interest in moving to Berlin. A combination of positions was held out to him: membership in the Prussian Academy with a special salary to be paid, half by the Prussian government and half by the physics–mathematics section of the Academy from a fund maintained with outside help, a professorship at the University of Berlin with the right but not the obligation to teach, and the directorship of a physics institute to be established. The new institute was to be under the auspices of the Kaiser Wilhelm Gesellschaft, an organization founded in 1911 to support basic research with the aid of funds from private sources.*

Much later, Einstein recalled an interesting exchange between himself and Planck during this Zürich visit. 'Planck had asked him what he was working on, and Einstein described general relativity as it was then. Planck said, "As an older friend I must advise you against it for in the first place you will not succeed; and even if you succeed, no one will believe you." ' [S1].

Einstein reacted rapidly and positively to the approach from Berlin. His correspondence from that period makes abundantly clear the principal reason for his interest in this offer. Neither then nor later was he averse to discussing physics issues with younger colleagues and students; but he had had enough of teaching classes. All he wanted to do was think. The catalogue of PhD theses awarded at

---

*This physics institute started its activities in 1917. In 1921, von Laue took over the main day-to-day responsibilities.

the ETH shows that he had acted as Korreferent* for four theses, all in experimental physics, but had not taken on PhD students in theoretical physics.

Encouraged by Einstein's response, Planck, Nernst, Rubens, and Warburg joined in signing a formal laudatio, the statement supporting a proposal for membership, which was presented to the academy on June 12, 1913 [K1]. On July 3, the physics–mathematics section voted on the proposal. The result was twenty-one for, one against [K2]. A number of arrangements remained to be worked out, but already in July 1913 Einstein wrote to a friend that he was going to be in Berlin by the spring of 1914 [E2]. In August he wrote to Lorentz, 'My cordial thanks for your friendly congratulations concerning the new position. I could not resist the temptation to accept a position which frees me of all obligations so that I can devote myself freely to thinking' (Grübelei) [E3]. To similar good wishes by Ehrenfest, he replied that he 'accepted this odd sinecure because it got on my nerves to give courses, whereas there [in Berlin] I do not have to lecture' [E4]. To Zangger he mentioned that contact with the colleagues in Berlin might be stimulating. 'In particular, the astronomers are important to me (at this time)' [E5]. This was in obvious reference to his current interest in the red shift and the bending of light.

In a letter [K3] sent to the academy on December 7, 1913, Einstein formally accepted membership and declared that he wished to begin his new position in April 1914. On February 9, 1914, he gave a farewell talk before the Physical Society of Zürich, in which he noted that 'we have progressed as little in the theory of gravitation as the physicists of the eighteenth century when they knew only Coulomb's law' [E6]. He mentioned the Nordström and the Einstein–Grossmann theories, remarked that the former is simpler and more plausible but does not shed any light on the relativity of nonuniform motion, and expressed the hope that the bending of light (present in the Einstein–Grossmann theory, absent in the Nordström theory) would soon lead to an experimental choice between these two possibilities.

The Einsteins left Zürich in late March 1914. Einstein went for a brief visit to Leiden and from there to Berlin, which was to be his home until December 1932. His wife and children went for a few weeks to Locarno [E7] and then joined him in Berlin, but not for long. Soon after Mileva's arrival, the Einsteins separated. I do not know what precipitated this course of events at that particular moment. But the marriage had been an unhappy one. Einstein never put all the blame for that on Mileva. With inner resistance, he had entered an undertaking which eventually went beyond his strength [E7a]. Now Mileva and the boys were to return to Zürich. Einstein saw them off at the station. 'Weinend ist er vom Bahnhof zurückgegangen'.** His love for his boys endured. For many years he would reg-

---

*The acceptance of an ETH thesis required formal approval by both a principal examiner (Referent) and a coexaminer (Korreferent). Einstein acted in the latter capacity for the theses of Karl Renger, Hans Renker, Elsa Frenkel, and August Piccard.

**'He wept as he returned from the railway station.' (H. Dukas, private communication).

ularly take them on holiday trips. These contacts were not always easy, since Mileva never reconciled herself to the separation and subsequent divorce. In later times, after Einstein's remarriage, the sons would visit and stay with their father in Berlin.

Soon after the separation, Einstein moved into a bachelor apartment at Wittelsbacherstrasse 13. Early in April he wrote to Ehrenfest, 'It is pleasant here in Berlin. A nice room . . . my relations here give me great joy, especially a "Cousine" [female cousin] of my age to whom I am attached by a long friendship' [E8]. A year later he told Zangger, 'Concerning my personal circumstances, I have never been as peaceful and happy as I am now. I live a retiring life, yet not a lonely one thanks to the loving care of a "Cousine" who in fact drew me to Berlin' [E9].* We shall hear more about this cousin in Chapter 16.

By the time Einstein arrived in Berlin, he was already a man of great renown, though not yet the stellar figure he was to become five years later. It was therefore natural that soon after his arrival, he would be approached by the editors of *Die Vossische Zeitung,* a major German daily newspaper, with the request that he explain something of his work to their readers. Einstein accepted. On April 26, 1914, his first newspaper article appeared, entitled 'Vom Relativitätsprinzip,' About the relativity principle [F10]. It is nicely written and deals mainly with topics in the special theory. Its last paragraph begins with the question, 'Is the [special] relativity theory sketched above essentially complete or does it represent only a first step of a farther-reaching development?' Einstein remarked that the second alternative appeared to him to be the correct one but added that 'on this point, the views even of those physicists who understand relativity theory are still divided.'**

This divergence in views on the future of relativity theory, characteristic for the period 1913–15, was much in evidence on the occasion of Einstein's inaugural address before the Prussian Academy, on July 2, 1914 [E12]. After expressing his gratitude for the opportunity given him to devote himself 'fully to scientific study, free of the excitements and cares of a practical profession,' he turned to the major current issues in physics. He spoke in praise of Planck, whose 'quantum hypothesis overthrew classical mechanics for the case of sufficiently small masses moving with sufficiently small velocities and large accelerations. . . . Our position regarding the basic laws of these [molecular] motions is similar to that of the pre-Newtonian astronomers in regard to planetary motions.' Then he went on to relativity theory and observed that the special theory 'is not fully satisfactory from the theoretical point of view because it gives a preferred position to uniform motion.'

Planck replied [P1], welcoming Einstein and remarking, 'I know you well enough to dare say that your real love belongs to that direction of work in which

---

*' . . . die mich ja überhaupt nach Berlin zog.'

**A 1915 review of relativity theory by Einstein [E11] has the same tenor as his newspaper article. It is almost entirely devoted to the special theory and toward the end contains phrases nearly identical to the ones just quoted.

the personality can unfold itself in the freest possible way.' Then he, too, addressed the question of the preferred uniform motions in the special theory. 'In my opinion, one could just as well take the opposite view [of Einstein's] and look upon the preferred position of uniform motion as precisely a very important and valuable characteristic of the theory'. For, Planck notes, natural laws always imply certain restrictions on infinitely many possibilities. 'Should we consider Newton's law of attraction unsatisfactory because the power 2 plays a preferred role?' Could one perhaps not relate the preferred uniform motion to 'the special privilege which indeed singles out the straight line among all other spatial curves'?! These are not impressive comments. However, one must side with Planck when he courteously and justly chided Einstein, noting that in the latter's general theory not all coordinate systems are on an equal footing anyway, 'as you yourself have proved only recently.' Planck ended by expressing the hope that the expedition planned to observe the solar eclipse of August 21, 1914, would provide information about the bending of light predicted (not yet correctly) by Einstein. These hopes were dashed by the outbreak of the First World War.

Einstein's productivity was not affected by the deep troubles of the war years, which, in fact, rank among the most productive and creative in his career. During this period, he completed the general theory of relativity, found the correct values for the bending of light and the displacement of the perihelion of Mercury, did pioneering work on cosmology and on gravitational waves, introduced his A and B coefficients for radiative transitions, found a new derivation of Planck's radiation law—and ran into his first troubles with causality in quantum physics. During the war he produced, in all, one book and about fifty papers, an outpouring all the more astounding since he was seriously ill in 1917 and physically weakened for several years thereafter.

This intense scientific activity did not banish from Einstein's mind a genuine and intense concern for the tragic events unfolding in the world around him. On the contrary, the period of 1914–18 marks the public emergence of Einstein the radical pacifist, the man of strong moral convictions who would never shy away from expressing his opinions publicly, whether they were popular or not. Early in the war, he and a few other scholars signed a 'manifesto to Europeans' criticizing scientists and artists for having 'relinquished any further desire for the continuance of international relations' and calling 'for all those who truly cherish the culture of Europe to join forces. . . . We shall endeavor to organize a League of Europeans' (an effort that came to naught). This appears to be the first political document to which Einstein lent his name. He also joined the pacifist Bund Neues Vaterland, League of the New Fatherland.* It gave him joy to find colleagues who 'stand above the situation and do not let themselves be driven by the murky

* *Einstein on Peace* by Otto Nathan and Heinz Norden describes in detail Einstein's political activities during the First World War [N1]. The quotations from the manifesto are taken from that book, which contains its full text.

currents of [our] time. . . . Hilbert regrets . . . having neglected to foster international relations more. . . . Planck does all he can to keep the chauvinist majority
of the Academy in check. I must say that in this respect the hostile nations are
well matched' [E13].

The strength of Einstein's own convictions was not lessened by the amused
detachment with which throughout his life he regarded human folly. 'I begin to
feel comfortable amid the present insane tumult (wahnsinnige Gegenwartsrum-
mel), in conscious detachment from all things which preoccupy the crazy community (die verrückte Allgemeinheit). Why should one not be able to live con-
tentedly as a member of the service personnel in the lunatic asylum? After all, one
respects the lunatics as the ones for whom the building in which one lives exists.
Up to a point, one can make one's own choice of institution—though the distinction between them is smaller than one thinks in one's younger years' [E14].

Einstein's initial hopes that the voices of reason might prevail yielded to increasing pessimism as the war dragged on. In 1917 he wrote to Lorentz, 'I cannot help
being constantly terribly depressed over the immeasurably sad things which burden our lives. It no longer even helps, as it used to, to escape into one's work in
physics' [E15]. These feelings of dejection may have been enhanced, I think, by
Einstein's own illness at that time.

After this digression on Einstein and the war, I return to the developments in
general relativity. We are in the fall of 1914, at which time Einstein wrote a long
paper for the proceedings of the Prussian Academy [E16]. Its main purpose was
to give a more systematic and detailed discussion of the methods used and the
results obtained in the first paper with Grossmann [E17]. Nearly half the paper
deals with an exposé of tensor analysis and differential geometry. Einstein clearly
felt the need to explain these techniques in his own way; they were as new to him
as to most other physicists. The paper also contains several new touches concerning physics. First of all, Einstein takes a stand against Newton's argument for the
absolute character of rotation (as demonstrated, for example, by Newton's often
reproduced discussion of the rotating bucket filled with water [W1]). Instead, Einstein emphasizes, 'we have no means of distinguishing a "centrifugal field" from
a gravitational field, [and therefore] we may consider the centrifugal field to be a
gravitational field.' The paper contains another advance. For the first time, Einstein derives the geodesic equation of motion of a point particle (cf. Eq. 12.28)
[E18] and shows that it has the correct Newtonian limit (cf. Eq. 12.30) [E19]. He
also shows that his earlier results about the red shift and the bending of light (still
the old value, off by a factor of 2) are contained in the tensor theory [E20]. As a
final positive result, an important comment about the character of space–time
should be mentioned, which (to my knowledge) he makes here for the first time:
'According to our theory, there do not exist independent (selbständige) qualities
of space' [E21].

Regarding the covariance properties of the gravitational field equations, however, there is no progress. If anything, the situation is getting slightly worse.

We saw in Section 12d that early in 1913 Einstein and Grossmann had been unable to find generally covariant gravitational field equations [E17] and that Einstein had given a 'physical argument' for the impossibility of such general covariance. Now, late in 1914, Einstein reproduced this same argument in his long paper. Not only did he still believe it, but he prefaced it with the remark that 'we must restrict this requirement [of general covariance] if we wish to be in full agreement with the law of causality' [E22]. This remark is understandable in the context of Einstein's unjustified criterion that the metric tensor $g_{\mu\nu}$ should be uniquely determined by its source, the energy momentum tensor. In the 1914 paper he returned to the division of space–time into two domains L_1 and L_2, as described in Section 12d. Recall that he had found $g_{\mu\nu} \neq g'_{\mu\nu}$ in the matter-free region L_2. This time, he wrote this inequality in more detail: $g_{\mu\nu}(x) \neq g'_{\mu\nu}(x')$. But, he now adds, $g'_{\mu\nu}(x') = g'_{\mu\nu}(x'(x)) \equiv f_{\mu\nu}(x)$. Anyone familiar with tensor fields will not be shocked by the fact that $g_{\mu\nu}(x) \neq f_{\mu\nu}(x)$. Einstein, on the other hand, concluded from this inequality that generally covariant gravitational field equations are inadmissible. In 1914 not only did he have some wrong physical ideas about causality but in addition he did not yet understand some elementary mathematical notions about tensors [H1]. Once again he insisted that the gravitational field equations can be covariant only under linear transformations.*

Einstein next proceeded to show that this restricted covariance uniquely determines the gravitational Lagrangian, provided that the latter is assumed to be homogeneous and of the second degree in the (ordinary, noncovariant) first derivatives of the $g_{\mu\nu}$ [E24]. In the course of 1915 he realized, however, that this 'argument for the determination of the Lagrange function of the gravitational field was entirely illusory, since it could easily be modified in such a way that [this Lagrangian] . . . could be chosen entirely freely' [E25].

The mathematical details of the October 1914 paper are of no interest for the understanding of the evolution of the general theory and will be omitted. This paper gave rise to a correspondence between Einstein and Levi-Civita, early in 1915. The latter pointed out some technical errors. Einstein was grateful for having these brought to his attention. Above all, however, he was happy to have finally found a professional who took a keen interest in his work. 'It is remarkable how little my colleagues are susceptible to the inner need for a *real* relativity theory. . . . It is therefore doubly gladdening to get to know better a man like you' [E26].

In summary, toward the end of 1914 Einstein could look back on a year which had brought major changes to his personal life and his professional career. He was still essentially alone in his convictions about the future of relativity theory and confused about some of its crucial features. One year later, he had corrected his conceptual errors, completed the theory, and seen others participate actively in its development.

---

*The slight extension of the set of allowed transformations given in the second Einstein–Grossmann paper [E23] (Section 12d) must have been found shortly afterward.

14b. Interlude: Rotation by Magnetization

'I firmly believe that the road taken is in principle the correct one and that later [people] will wonder about the great resistance the idea of general relativity is presently encountering' [E27]. This prophesy was made by Einstein in the first week of 1915. It would be fulfilled before the year was out, but not until Einstein had passed through a crisis followed by an exhausting struggle. Toward the autumn of 1915 he finally realized* that his theory up until then was seriously wrong in several respects.

Meanwhile, early in 1915 he did not publish anything substantially new on relativity.** He did write two review articles, one on relativity theory [E11] and one on the atomic theory of matter [E29], and a short paper on the statistical properties of electromagnetic radiation in thermal equilibrium [E30]. Of more interest are his activities in experimental physics. At that time Einstein made good use of a temporary guest appointment at the Physikalisch Technische Reichsanstalt in Charlottenburg [K4]. 'In my old age, I am acquiring a passion for experiment' [E31]. This passion led to the discovery of the Einstein–de Haas (EdH) effect, the torque induced in a suspended cylinder (made of iron, for example) as a consequence of its being abruptly magnetized. The present interlude is devoted to a brief account of these activities.

Wander Johannes de Haas was a Dutch physicist of Einstein's age. He received his PhD in Leiden, in 1912, with Kamerlingh Onnes. Later that same year, he went to the University of Berlin to work in the laboratory of Henri du Bois.† In August 1913, when Lorentz sent congratulations to Einstein on his forthcoming appointment in Berlin, he must have added (the letter is lost) a query concerning de Haas, as is seen from Einstein's reply: 'At present, I do not know what to do in the matter of your son-in-law, since in Berlin I will have neither an institute nor an assistant.' [E3]. Then came the visiting appointment at the Reichsanstalt. Einstein was now in a position to do something for de Haas—and for Lorentz.¶ I do not know when de Haas joined Einstein at the Reichsanstalt. However, their gyromagnetic experiment was performed 'in a very brief period' [H1a]. De Haas left the Reichsanstalt in April 1915.

Soon after the conclusion of their collaboration, Einstein wrote enthusiastically about the results obtained. 'Scientifically, I have done a wonderful experimental thing this semester, together with Lorentz's son-in-law. We have given firm proof

---

*See Section 14c.

**It is sometimes incorrectly stated that a brief abstract of a talk by Einstein before the Prussian Academy [E28] contains the announcement of the final formulation of his theory as published in November 1915 [D1].

†In October 1912 the Ehrenfests visited de Haas and his wife in Berlin—at the suggestion of Lorentz [K5].

¶On one occasion, Einstein referred in print to de Haas as Herr de Haas–Lorentz [E32].

of the existence of Ampère's molecular currents* (explanation of para- and fer-romagnetism) . . . within the limits of error (about 10 per cent) the experiment yielded in all detail a confirmation of the theory' [E14].** Their experiment, simple in principle, riddled with complexities in practice, gave the first proof of the existence of rotation induced by magnetization. Their result was qualitatively right. However, in the pre-spin days of 1915, any dynamic theory of ferromagnetism had necessarily to be incorrect. Einstein could not know that his theoretical prediction was wrong by a factor of about 2. Since Einstein and de Haas claimed to have found agreement between theory and experiment, their experiment had also to be wrong by a factor of 2. Their estimate of a 10 per cent experimental error had to be too optimistic. As we shall see, the alleged agreement between theory and experiment was largely a theoretical prejudice.

Characteristically, Einstein was unaware of earlier efforts to measure gyromagnetic effects until some time after his own work had been completed [E33]. These attempts go back to Maxwell, who remarked in his treatise of 1873 that 'there is as yet no experimental evidence to show whether the electric current is really a current of a material substance' [M1]. He proposed several methods for testing this idea: acceleration of a conductor should generate a current†; and a magnet should act like a gyroscope, which is the basic idea of the EdH effect [M2]. In 1861 Maxwell himself attempted to detect such gyroscopic effects, but without success.

Two other instances of related work prior to 1915 must be mentioned.†† The theoretical derivation by Einstein in 1915 had already been given in 1907 by Owen Willans Richardson, who had also tried in vain to observe the rotation by magnetization, at Palmer Laboratory in Princeton [R1].¶ In 1909 Samuel Jackson Barnett, then at Tulane University, began the study of the inverse effect, magnetization by rotation, now known as the Barnett effect. I shall next outline the EdH work of 1915 and then state the interesting results obtained by Barnett at about the same time [B2].

Let us first phrase Ampère's hypothesis in modern language.¶¶ The magnetic moment $\vec{M}$ of a magnetized body (assumed at rest) is due to circulating 'hidden

---

*André-Marie Ampère had conjectured around 1820 that magnetism can be considered to be caused by electricity in motion.

**There exists a German [E33], a Dutch [E34], and an English [E35] version of the EdH paper. Each one of these differs slightly from the other two. The statement on the limits of error in each paper agrees in substance with what is said in the letter quoted in the text. All three papers appeared in 1915.

†This effect was first observed in 1916 [T1].

††A detailed early history of gyromagnetic effects is found in papers by Barnett [B1].

¶For some years after 1915, the effect was called the Einstein–Richardson effect.

¶¶In EdH and other early papers, the magnetic moment is defined as cM.

electric currents.' The hidden flow of current is due to a hidden flow of charged matter (electrons) moving in closed orbits. Thus there exists a hidden angular momentum $\vec{J}$, related to $\vec{M}$ by

$$\vec{M} = -\frac{e}{2mc} \cdot g \cdot \vec{J} \tag{14.1}$$

where $-e$ and m are the charge and mass of the electron, respectively. The factor g is now called the Landé factor ($g > 0$ for para- and ferromagnetic substances). In the model of Richardson and Einstein, the value

$$g = 1 \tag{14.2}$$

was obtained by the following reasoning. Consider one electron moving with uniform velocity v in a circular orbit with radius r and circular frequency ν. Then $v = 2\pi r\nu$. The angular momentum has the magnitude $mvr = 2\pi r^2 m\nu$. An amount of electricity $-e\nu$ passes per second through a point of the orbit. The magnetic moment is therefore equal to $(-e\nu)(\pi r^2)/c$. Hence $g = 1$. The same value of g should also hold, it was argued, for a piece of paramagnetic or ferromagnetic matter as long as magnetism is caused by a set of electrons moving independently in circular orbits.

Einstein and de Haas knew well that objections could be raised against this derivation. 'One of these is even more serious than it was in Ampère's days ... circulating electrons must lose their energy by radiation ... the molecules of a magnetic body would therefore lose their magnetic moment. Nothing of the kind having ever been observed, the [Ampère] hypothesis seems irreconcilable with a general validity of the fundamental laws of electromagnetism. It appears ... that ... as much may be said in favour of Ampère's hypothesis as against it and that the question concerns important physical principles' [E35]. Clearly the proof that permanently circulating electrons indeed exist meant far more to Einstein than only the verification of a century-old hypothesis.* So it did to Bohr, whose theory of stationary atomic orbits was only two years old at that time. To Bohr the outcome of the EdH experiment was a confirmation of his own ideas. Later in 1915 he wrote, 'As pointed out by Einstein and de Haas, [their] experiments indicate very strongly that electrons can rotate in atoms without emission of energy radiation' [B3].**

The EdH technique for measuring g consisted in analyzing the motion of an iron cylinder hung vertically (in the z direction; 'up' counted as positive) by means

---

*There was still another reason why Einstein attached great significance to the EdH effect, as is seen especially clearly in a paper he wrote in May 1915 [E32]: he believed (incorrectly) that the persistence of ferromagnetism at zero absolute temperature indicated the existence of a zero point energy of rotation. (In 1913 he had invoked just such a zero point energy in an attempt to explain certain anomalies in the specific heats of diatomic molecules [E36]. By 1915 he knew that his specific heat argument was incorrect, however [F1].)

**The quantum theory is not mentioned in any of the EdH papers, however.

of a wire. A fixed solenoid is placed coaxially around the cylinder. The iron is magnetized by an alternating current run through the solenoid. The change ΔM of the magnetic moment in the z direction induces a change ΔJ in the hidden angular momentum due to the electron motions such that $\Delta M = -eg\Delta J/2mc$. Angular momentum conservation demands that ΔJ be compensated for. Thus the iron cylinder as a whole acquires an angular momentum $-\Delta J$, since this body may be considered rigid. The resulting angular velocity $\Delta \alpha$ would be given by $egQ\Delta\alpha = 2mc\Delta M$ if only the magnetic force were acting on the cylinder (Q being the moment of inertia in the z direction). The true $\Delta \alpha$ results from the interplay between the magnetic driving force and the restoring force due to the attachment of the cylinder to the wire. It is clear that the experiment serves to determine g if the various other magnetic and mechanical parameters are known.

There are many complications. The cylinder has to be hung precisely on its axis; the magnetic field has to be symmetric with respect to the cylinder axis; it also has to be uniform in order to give a simple meaning to ΔM; the effect of the earth's magnetic field needs to be compensated for; there may be effects due to the interaction of the alternating current with some remanent magnetization of the cylinder. No wonder that the cylinder underwent 'the most adventurous motions' [E33]. Einstein and de Haas showed that many of these difficulties could be overcome by an ingenious trick, the resonance method. The cylinder is hung by means of a rather rigid glass wire. The mechanical oscillation frequency of this system is matched with the frequency of the alternating current. The resulting resonance makes it much easier to separate the desired effect from perturbing influences.*

Einstein and de Haas took two sets of measurements. They managed to obtain agreement with their calculated value $g = 1$ by singling out one of these two sets. Six years later—after it was clear that $g = 1$ is not the right value—de Haas described what they had done.** 'The numbers which we found [for g] are 1.45 and 1.02. The second value is nearly equal to the classical value [$g = 1$] so that we thought that experimental errors had made the first value too large. . . . We did not measure the field of the solenoid; we calculated it. . . . We did not measure the magnetism of the cylinder, either; we calculated or estimated it. All this is stated in our original memoir. These preliminary results seemed satisfactory to us, and one can easily understand that we were led to consider the value 1.02 as the better one . . .' [H1a]. I am not aware of a similar confession by Einstein.

This section would not be complete without a few remarks about the transition to the modern era. It is now known that ferromagnetism is almost purely a spin

---

*Additional information was obtained by measuring not only at resonance but also around resonance. The many technical details of the measurement not discussed here can be found in Barnett's article in the *Reviews of Modern Physics* [B1].

**I express the answers in terms of g, thereby slightly changing the wording of de Haas.

effect. The orbital contributions of earlier days have turned out to be nearly entirely quenched. The quantum mechanical theory of ferromagnetism, given by Heisenberg in 1928 [H1b] provided the basis for a refined treatment of the corresponding gyromagnetic effects [H2]. Experimentally, the g value for ferromagnetic materials has been found to lie close to 2 (except for Fe_7S_8) with deviations <10 per cent [S2]. The first experimental indications for $g \approx 2$ were published in 1915 by Barnett (then at Ohio State University). In his earlier-mentioned paper on the Barnett effect [B2], he concluded that 'the magnitude ... is within the experimental error equal to twice the ... value computed,' the latter value being $g = 1$. However, further measurements done by him in 1917 gave $g \approx 1$, 'but the experimental errors ... are such that great importance cannot, in my opinion, be attached to the discrepancies [with his earlier results]' [B4]. In the period 1918–20, three independent measurements of the EdH effect were reported. In chronological order, these came from Princeton [S3], the ETH in Zürich [B5], and Uppsala [A1]. The answers found were $g \approx 1.96$, 1.88, and 1.87, respectively. From that time on, the 'gyromagnetic anomaly' (as it was often called) was firmly established. Inevitably this led to fairly widespread speculations about 'planetary motions of [positively-charged] constituents of nuclei' [B6]. The first one to suspect a connection between the anomalous Zeeman effect and this new gyromagnetic anomaly was Alfred Landé [L1] in 1921, the same year Heisenberg expressed the opinion in a letter to Pauli that $g = 2$ could occur only in ferromagnetic bodies [H3].

Since de Haas was from Leiden, where the spin was discovered, it was only natural that I would ask Uhlenbeck whether the EdH effect had played any role in the discovery of the electron spin by him and Goudsmit (knowing that the effect is not mentioned in their paper). Uhlenbeck replied that he knew of the effect because he was in Leiden but that this subject was not in the center of attention at that time. 'Had Ehrenfest thought it pertinent, he would surely have mentioned it to us.' Thus the EdH effect served to confirm rather than stimulate subsequent theoretical developments.

As to Einstein, his interest in gyromagnetism continued after de Haas's departure. In 1916 he published another paper on the EdH effect. It contains the design of a new experimental arrangement* for determining g [E37]. He also remained interested in the activities at the Reichsanstalt. In 1916 he was appointed member of its Kuratorium (board of governors) and played an active role in the planning and design of its experimental projects [K6].

Let us now return to our main topic, Einstein's final formulation of his theory of general relativity.

---

*The idea was to flip the remanent magnetization of a premagnetized iron cylinder. This method has the advantage that the cylinder is exposed to a magnetic field for such a brief time ($\approx 10^{-3}$ s) that irritating side effects are largely eliminated.

14c. The Final Steps

1. The Crisis.   On the first of January 1916, when it was all over, Einstein wrote
to Lorentz, 'During the past autumn, the gradually dawning realization of the
incorrectness of the old gravitational equations caused me hard times (böse Zei-
ten)' [E25]. It appears that this crisis occurred between late July and early October 1915. For on July 7, 1915, Einstein described to Zangger the subject of lectures he had just given in Goettingen as 'die nun schon sehr geklärte
Gravitationstheorie,' the by now already quite clarified theory of gravitation
[E38]. A week later, he wrote to Sommerfeld about a tentative plan to write a
short treatise on relativity which was to be oriented toward a general theory of
relativity [E39]. But on November 7 he wrote to Hilbert, 'I realized about four
weeks ago that my methods of proof used until then were deceptive' [E40], and
on October 12, to Lorentz, 'In my paper [of October 1914, [E16]], I carelessly
(leichtsinnig) introduced the assumption that [the gravitational Lagrangian] is an
invariant for linear transformations' [E41]. He abandoned this linear invariance
in a series of papers completed in November 1915, which culminate in the final
form of his gravitational equations, presented on November 25. On November 28
he wrote to Sommerfeld: "During the past month I had one of the most exciting
and strenuous times of my life, but also one of the most successful ones' [E42]. All
these statements taken together convince me that Einstein still believed in the 'old'
theory as late as July 1915, that between July and October he found objections
to that theory, and that his final version was conceived and worked out between
late October and November 25. In December he wrote with irony about his earlier
faith in the old version of the theory. 'That fellow Einstein suits his convenience
(Es ist bequem mit dem E.). Every year he retracts what he wrote the year before
. . .' [E43].

What made Einstein change his mind between July and October? Letters to
Sommerfeld [E42] and Lorentz [E25] show that he had found at least three objections against the old theory: (1) its restricted covariance did not include uniform
rotations, (2) the precession of the perihelion of Mercury came out too small by
a factor of about 2, and (3) his proof of October 1914 of the uniqueness of the
gravitational Lagrangian was incorrect. Einstein got rid of all these shortcomings
in a series of four brief articles. 'Unfortunately, I immortalized in [these] academy
papers the last errors made in this struggle' [E42].

2. November the Fourth.   Einstein presents to the plenary session of the Prussian Academy a new version of general relativity 'based on the postulate of covariance with respect to transformations with determinant 1' [E44]. He began this
paper by stating that he had 'completely lost confidence' in the equations proposed
in October 1914 [E16]. At that time he had given a proof of the uniqueness of the
gravitational Lagrangian. He had realized meanwhile that this proof 'rested on
misconception,' and so, he continued, 'I was led back to a more general covariance
of the field equations, a requirement which I had abandoned only with a heavy

heart in the course of my collaboration with my friend Grossmann three years earlier.' (It should be said that in matters of science a heavy heart never lasted very long for Einstein.)

For the last time, I recall that Einstein and Grossmann had concluded [E17] that the gravitational equations could be invariant under linear transformations only and that Einstein's justification for this restriction was based on the belief that the gravitational equations ought to determine the $g_{\mu\nu}$ uniquely, a point he continued to stress in October 1914 [E16]. In his new paper [E44], he finally liberated himself from this three-year-old prejudice. That is the main advance on November 4. His answers were still not entirely right. There was still one flaw, a much smaller one, which he eliminated three weeks later. But the road lay open. He was lyrical. 'No one who has really grasped it can escape the magic of this [new] theory.'

The remaining flaw was, of course, Einstein's unnecessary restriction to unimodular transformations. The reasons which led him to introduce this constraint were not deep, I believe. He simply noted that this restricted class of transformations permits simplifications of the tensor calculus. This is mainly because $\sqrt{g}$ is a scalar under unimodular transformations (cf. Eq. 12.14). Therefore the distinction between tensors and tensor densities no longer exists. As a result, it is possible to *redefine* covariant differentiation for tensors of rank higher than 1. For example, instead of Eq. 12.13, one may use [E45]

$$T^{\mu\nu}_{;\mu} = \frac{\partial T^{\mu\nu}}{\partial x^{\mu}} + \Gamma^{\nu}_{\mu\lambda} T^{\mu\lambda} \qquad (14.3)$$

Equation 12.17 can be similarly simplified. 'The most radical simplification' concerns the Ricci tensor given in Eq. 12.20. Write*

$$R_{\mu\nu} = r_{\mu\nu} + s_{\mu\nu} \qquad (14.4)$$

$$r_{\mu\nu} = -\frac{\partial \Gamma^{\lambda}_{\mu\nu}}{\partial x^{\lambda}} + \Gamma^{\alpha}_{\mu\lambda}\Gamma^{\lambda}_{\nu\alpha} \qquad (14.5)$$

$$s_{\mu\nu} = \frac{\partial v_{\mu}}{\partial x^{\nu}} - \Gamma^{\alpha}_{\mu\nu} v_{\alpha} \qquad (14.6)$$

where [W2]

$$v_{\mu} \equiv \Gamma^{\lambda}_{\lambda\mu} = \frac{\partial \ln \sqrt{g}}{\partial x^{\mu}} \qquad (14.7)$$

v_{μ} is a vector since $\sqrt{g}$ is a scalar; $s_{\mu\nu}$ is the covariant derivative of v_{μ}. Therefore, under unimodular transformations, $R_{\mu\nu}$ decomposes into two parts, $r_{\mu\nu}$ and $s_{\mu\nu}$, each of which separately is a tensor.

---

*The quantities $R_{\mu\nu}$, $r_{\mu\nu}$, $s_{\mu\nu}$ correspond to Einstein's $G_{\mu\nu}$, $R_{\mu\nu}$, $S_{\mu\nu}$ in [E44].

Having described this splitting of the Ricci tensor, Einstein next proposed his penultimate version of the gravitational equations:

$$r_{\mu\nu} = -\kappa T_{\mu\nu} \tag{14.8}$$

covariant under local unimodular transformations. They are a vast improvement over the Einstein–Grossman equations and cure one of the ailments he had diagnosed only recently: unimodular transformations do include rotations with arbitrarily varying angular velocities. In addition, he proved that Eqs. 14.8 can be derived from a variational principle; that the conservation laws are satisfied (here the simplified definitions Eq. 14.3 play a role); and that there exists an identity

$$\frac{\partial}{\partial x^\alpha}\left(g^{\alpha\beta}\frac{\partial \ln \sqrt{g}}{\partial x^\beta}\right) = -\kappa T \tag{14.9}$$

where T is the trace of $T_{\mu\nu}$. He interpreted this equation as a constraint on the $g_{\mu\nu}$. A week later, he would have more to say on this relation.

In the weak-field limit, $g_{\mu\nu} = \eta_{\mu\nu} + h_{\mu\nu}$ (Eq. 12.29), one recovers Newton's law from Eq. 14.8. Einstein's proof of this last statement is by far the most important part of this paper. 'The coordinate system is not yet fixed, since four equations are needed to determine it. *We are therefore free to choose** [my italics]

$$\frac{\partial h^{\mu\nu}}{\partial x^\nu} = 0' \tag{14.10}$$

Then Eqs. 14.8 and 14.10 yield

$$\Box h_{\mu\nu} = 2\kappa T_{\mu\nu} \tag{14.11}$$

which reduces to the Newton–Poisson equation in the static limit.

The phrase italicized in the above quotation shows that Einstein's understanding of general covariance had vastly improved. The gravitational equations do *not* determine the $h_{\mu\nu}$ (hence the $g_{\mu\nu}$) unambiguously. This is *not* in conflict with causality. One may *choose* a coordinate system at one's convenience simply because coordinate systems have no objective meaning. Einstein did not say all this explicitly in his paper. But shortly afterward he explained it to Ehrenfest. 'The apparently compelling nature of [my old causality objection] disappears at once if one realizes that . . . no reality can be ascribed to the reference system' [E43].

3. *November the Eleventh.* A step backward. Einstein proposes [E46] a scheme that is even tighter than the one of a week earlier. Not only shall the theory be invariant with respect to unimodular transformations—which implies that g is a scalar field—but, more strongly, it shall satisfy

$$\sqrt{g} = 1 \tag{14.12}$$

---

*'Wir dürfen deshalb willkürlich festsetzen . . .'. Equation 14.10 is the harmonic coordinate condition in the weak-field limit [W3].

He writes the gravitational equations in the form

$$R_{\mu\nu} = -\kappa T_{\mu\nu} \qquad\qquad (14.13)$$

where $R_{\mu\nu}$ is the full Ricci tensor. However, Eqs. 14.7 and 14.12 imply that $s_{\mu\nu}$ = 0. Thus Eqs. 14.4 and 14.13 give once again Eq. 14.8, the gravitational equations of November 4.

Though not compelling, this new idea may seem simple. It is in fact quite mad. Equation 14.12 together with Eq. 14.9 implies that $T = 0$. The trace of the energy momentum tensor does vanish for electromagnetic fields but not for matter. Thus there seems to be a contradiction, which Einstein proposed to resolve by means of 'the hypothesis that molecular gravitational fields constitute an essential part of matter.' The trace density we 'see' in matter, he suggests, is actually the sum T' of T and the trace of the gravitational field. Then T' can be positive and yet $T = 0$. 'We assume in what follows that the condition $T = 0$ is actually fulfilled.'

During the next two weeks, Einstein believed that his new equation (Eq. 14.12) had brought him closer to general covariance. He expressed this opinion to Hilbert on November 12. 'Meanwhile, the problem has been brought one step forward. Namely, the postulate $\sqrt{g} = 1$ enforces *general* covariance; the Riemann tensor yields directly the gravitational equations. If my current modification . . is justified, then gravitation must play a fundamental role in the structure of matter. Curiosity makes it hard to work!' [E47].

One week later, he remarked that 'no objections of principle' can be raised against Eq. 14.12 [E48]. Two weeks later, he declared that 'my recently stated opinion on this subject was erroneous' [E1].

4. *November the Eighteenth.* Einstein still subscribes to the demands of unimodular invariance and $\sqrt{g} = 1$. On the basis of this 'most radical relativity theory,' he presents two of his greatest discoveries [E48]. Each of these changed his life.

The first result was that his theory 'explains . . . quantitatively . . . the secular rotation of the orbit of Mercury, discovered by Le Verrier, . . . without the need of any special hypothesis.' This discovery was, I believe, by far the strongest emotional experience in Einstein's scientific life, perhaps in all his life. Nature had spoken to him. He had to be right. 'For a few days, I was beside myself with joyous excitement' [E49]. Later, he told Fokker that his discovery had given him palpitations of the heart [F2]. What he told de Haas [F2] is even more profoundly significant: when he saw that his calculations agreed with the unexplained astronomical observations, he had the feeling that something actually snapped in him. . . .

Einstein's discovery resolved a difficulty that was known for more than sixty years. Urbain Jean Joseph Le Verrier had been the first to find evidence for an anomaly in the orbit of Mercury and also the first to attempt to explain this effect. On September 12, 1859, he submitted to the Academy of Sciences in Paris the text of a letter to Hervé Faye in which he recorded his findings [L2]. The perihelion of Mercury advances by thirty-eight seconds per century due to 'some as yet unknown action on which no light has been thrown* . . . a grave difficulty, worthy of attention by astronomers.' The only way to explain the effect in terms of known bodies would be (he noted) to increase the mass of Venus by at least 10 per cent, an inadmissible modification. He strongly doubted that an intramercurial planet, as yet unobserved, might be the cause. A swarm of intramercurial asteroids was not ruled out, he believed. 'Here then, *mon cher confrère,* is a new complication which manifests itself in the neighborhood of the sun.'

Perihelion precessions of Mercury and other bodies** have been the subject of experimental study from 1850 up to the present.† The value 43 seconds per century for Mercury, obtained in 1882 by Simon Newcomb [N1a], has not changed. The present best value is $43''.11 \pm 0.45$ [W4]. The experimental number quoted by Einstein†† on November 18, 1915, was $45'' \pm 5$ [E48].

In the late nineteenth and early twentieth centuries, attempts at a theoretical interpretation of the Mercury anomaly were numerous. Le Verrier's suggestions of an intramercurial planet¶ or planetary ring were reconsidered. Other mechanisms examined were a Mercury moon (again as yet unseen), interplanetary dust, and a possible oblateness of the sun [O2, F3]. Each idea had its proponents at one time or another. None was ever generally accepted. All of them had in common that Newton's $1/r^2$ law of gravitation was assumed to be strictly valid. There were also a number of proposals to explain the anomaly in terms of a deviation from this law. Recall that Newton himself already knew that small deviations from the power -2 would lead to secular perturbations of planetary orbits [N2]. Two kinds of modifications from Newton's law were considered: a slightly different, purely static law [O3] or a $1/r^2$ law corrected with velocity-dependent terms [Z1] (Lorentz's theory of gravitation mentioned in Chapter 13 belongs to this last category). These attempts either failed or are uninteresting because they involve adjustable parameters. Whatever was tried, the anomaly remained puzzling. In his later years, Newcomb tended 'to prefer provisionally the hypothesis that the sun's gravitation is not exactly as the inverse square' [N3].¶¶

Against this background, Einstein's joy in being able to give an explanation 'without any special hypothesis' becomes all the more understandable. The tech-

---

*' . . . dû à quelque action encore inconnue, "cui theoriae lumen nundum accesserit." '

**See, for example, the table in [W4].

†A detailed list of nineteenth century references is found in [O1].

††Einstein took this value from a review by Freundlich [F3]. For his appreciation of Newcomb, see [E49a].

¶In the 1870s, it was briefly thought that such a planet (it was named Vulcan) had actually been seen.

¶¶For a detailed survey of Le Verrier's and Newcomb's work, see [C1].

nicalities of his calculation need not be described in detail since they largely coincide with standard textbook treatments. The following comments will suffice.

a) Einstein started from his field equations

$$r_{\mu\nu} = 0 \qquad (14.14)$$

for empty space (cf. Eq. 14.8) and his general condition $\sqrt{g} = 1$, Eq. 14.12. The modern treatment starts from $R_{\mu\nu} = 0$ and a choice of coordinate system such that $\sqrt{g} = 1$. Either way, the answers for the effect are, of course, the same, a fact Einstein became aware of in the course of preparing his paper [E50].

b) On November 18, he did not yet have the $g_{\mu\nu}R/2$ term in the field equations. This term plays no role in the actual calculations he made, as he himself stressed one week later.

c) The approximation method developed in this paper marks the beginning of post-Newtonian celestial mechanics. Einstein asked for a static isotropic solution of the metric (as it is now called [W5]). His answer: $g_{ik} = -\delta_{ik} - \alpha x_i x_k / r^3$, $g_{i0} = 0$, $g_{00} = -1 + \alpha/r$ $(i,k = 1,2,3)$, where α is an integration constant. He expanded in α/r; $\sqrt{g} = 1$ is satisfied to first order. It suffices to compute Γ^i_{jk} to first order, Γ^i_{00} to second order. The results are inserted in the geodesic equations (Eq. 12.28) and the standard bound-orbit calculation is performed. And so, one week before the general theory of relativity was complete, Einstein obtained for the precession per revolution: $24\pi^3 a^2/T^2 c^2(1 - e^2)$, which yields $43''$/century (a = semimajor axis, T = period of revolution, e = eccentricity; see [W6] for the relation between this result and modern experiment).

d) Two months later, on January 16, 1916, Einstein read a paper [S4] before the Prussian Academy on behalf of Karl Schwarzschild, who was in the German army at the Russian front at that time. The paper contained the exact solution of the static isotropic gravitational field of a mass point, the first instance of a rigorous solution of Einstein's full gravitational field equations. On February 24, 1916, Einstein read another paper by Schwarzschild [S5], this one giving the solution for a mass point in the gravitational field of an incompressible fluid sphere. It is there that the Schwarzschild radius is introduced for the first time. On June 29, 1916, Einstein addressed the Prussian Academy [E51] to commemorate Schwarzschild, who had died on May 11 after a short illness contracted at the Russian front. He spoke of Schwarzschild's great talents and contributions both as an experimentalist and a theorist. He also spoke of Schwarzschild's achievements as director (since 1909) of the astrophysical observatory in Potsdam. He concluded by expressing his conviction that Schwarzschild's contributions would continue to play a stimulating role in science. . . .

I return to the November 18 paper. Einstein devoted only half a page to his second discovery: the bending of light is twice as large as he had found earlier. 'A light ray passing the sun should suffer a deflection of $1''.7$ (instead of $0''.85$).' As is well known [W7], this result can be obtained with the help of the same solutions for $g_{\mu\nu}$ as mentioned above, applied this time to compute unbound orbits.* The discussion of the momentous consequences of this result will be reserved for Chapter 16.

5. *November the Twenty-Fifth* [E1]:

$$R^{\mu\nu} = -\kappa(T^{\mu\nu} - 1/2 \, g^{\mu\nu}T) \tag{14.15}$$

The work is done. The conservation laws are satisfied: $\sqrt{g} = 1$ is no equation of principle but rather an important guide to the choice of convenient coordinate systems. The identity Eq. 14.9, thought earlier to have major physical implications, is replaced by a triviality. The calculations of the week before remain unaffected:

> Any physical theory that obeys special relativity can be incorporated into the general theory of relativity; the general theory does not provide any criterion for the admissibility of that physical theory.... Finally the general theory of relativity is closed as a logical structure.[E1]

Note that Eq. 14.15 is equivalent to $R^{\mu\nu} - g^{\mu\nu}R/2 = -\kappa T^{\mu\nu}$.

In Section 12d, I mentioned that Einstein did not know the Bianchi identities [W8]

$$\left(R^{\mu\nu} - 1/2 \, g^{\mu\nu}R \right)_{;\nu} = 0 \tag{14.16}$$

when he did his work with Grossmann. He *still* did not know them on November 25 and therefore did not realize that the energy–momentum conservation laws

$$T^{\mu\nu}_{;\nu} = 0 \tag{14.17}$$

follow automatically from Eqs. 14.15 and 14.16. *Instead, he used these conservation laws as a constraint on the theory!* I paraphrase his argument. Start from Eq. 14.15 but with the coefficient ½ replaced by a number α to be determined. Differentiate Eq. 14.15 covariantly and use Eq. 14.17. Next take the trace of Eq. 14.15, then differentiate. One finds that $(R^{\mu\nu} + \alpha(1 - 4\alpha)^{-1}g^{\mu\nu}R)_{;\nu} = 0$ (use $g_{\mu\nu;\lambda} = 0$). *Choose coordinates such that* $\sqrt{g} = 1$. See if there is a solution for α. One finds $\alpha = $ ½. Einstein's choice of coordinates is of course admissible, but it is an unnecessary restriction that prevented him from discovering Eq. 14.16 as a generally covariant relation. We shall see in Section 15c how the Bianchi identities finally entered physics.

Einstein's brief belief in Eq. 14.9 may have been a useful mistake, since he had discovered that funny equation by the same compatibility method. In the case of Eq. 14.8, the relations are $r = -\kappa T$ and $r^{\mu\nu}_{;\nu} = 0$. The term on the left-hand side in Eq. 14.9 arose because in the November 4 paper Einstein had redefined his

---

*Einstein inserted those $g_{\mu\nu}$ into $g_{\mu\nu}dx^{\mu}dx^{\nu} = 0$ and then applied Huyghens' principle.

covariant derivatives (cf. Eq. 14.3) in such a way that the conservation laws read $\partial T_\nu^\mu/\partial x^\mu - T^{\alpha\beta}\partial g_{\alpha\beta}/2\partial x^\nu = 0$ instead of Eq. 14.17.

On November 28, Einstein wrote to Sommerfeld that three years earlier he and Grossmann had considered Eq. 14.15 'without the second term on the right-hand side,' but had come to the wrong conclusion that it did not contain Newton's approximation [E42].

On December 10, he wrote to Besso that he was 'zufrieden aber ziemlich kaputt' [E52].*

On June 20, 1933, Einstein, exiled from Germany, gave a lecture at the University of Glasgow on the origins of the general theory of relativity. In concluding this address, he said:

> The years of searching in the dark for a truth that one feels but cannot express, the intense desire and the alternations of confidence and misgiving until one breaks through to clarity and understanding are known only to him who has himself experienced them. [E52a]

14d. Einstein and Hilbert**

To repeat, on November 25 Einstein presented his final version (Eq. 14.15) of the gravitational equations to the Prussian Academy. Five days earlier, David Hilbert had submitted a paper to the Gesellschaft der Wissenschaften in Goettingen [H1] which contained the identical equation but with one qualification. Einstein, having learned the hard way from his mistakes a few weeks earlier, left the structure of $T^{\mu\nu}$ entirely free, except for its transformation and conservation properties. Hilbert, on the other hand, was as specific about gravitational as about all other forces. Correspondingly (and this is the qualification), his $T^{\mu\nu}$ has a definite dynamic form: ' . . . I believe that [my paper] contains simultaneously the solution of the problems of Einstein and of Mie.'

In 1912–13, Mie had proposed a field theory of electromagnetism and matter based on non–gauge-invariant modifications of Maxwell's equations [M4]. It was meant to be a theory of everything but gravitation.† Mie's ideas attracted attention in the second decade of this century but are now of historical interest only and of no relevance to our present subject. Suffice it to say that it was Hilbert's aim to give not just a theory of gravitation but an axiomatic theory of the world. This

---

*Content but rather worn out.

**See also [M3].

†Mie's ideas on gravitation were referred to in Chapter 13. For a comment by Einstein on Mie's electromagnetic theory, see [E52b]. The reader will find clear synopses of Mie's theory in the texts by Pauli [P2] and by Weyl [W9].

lends an exalted quality to his paper, from the title, 'Die Grundlagen der Physik,' The Foundations of Physics, to the concluding paragraph, in which he expressed his conviction that his fundamental equations would eventually solve the riddles of atomic structure. In December 1915, Einstein remarked that Hilbert's commitment to Mie's theory was unnecessary from the point of view of general relativity [E53]. 'Hilbert's Ansatz for matter seems childish to me,' he wrote some time later [E54]. Justified though these criticisms are, Hilbert's paper nevertheless contains a very important and independent contribution to general relativity: the derivation of Eq. 14.15 from a variational principle.

Hilbert was not the first to apply this principle to gravitation. Lorentz had done so before him [L3]. So had Einstein, a few weeks earlier [E44]. Hilbert was the first, however, to state this principle correctly:

$$\delta \int \left(L - \frac{1}{2\kappa} R \right) \sqrt{g}\, d^4x = 0 \qquad (14.18)$$

for infinitesimal variations $g^{\mu\nu}(x) \to g^{\mu\nu}(x) + \delta g^{\mu\nu}(x)$ such that $\delta g^{\mu\nu} = 0$ at the boundary of the integration domain (R is the Riemann curvature scalar, L the matter Lagrangian). It is well known that Eq. 14.18 leads to Eq. 14.15, including the trace term, if L depends on $g^{\mu\nu}$ but not on their derivatives.*

Hilbert's paper also contains the statement (but not the proof!!) of the following theorem. Let J be a scalar function of n fields and let $\delta \int J \sqrt{g}\, d^4x = 0$ for variations $x^{\mu} \to x^{\mu} + \xi^{\mu}(x)$ with infinitesimal ξ^{μ}. Then there exist four relations between the n fields. It is now known* that these are the energy–momentum conservation laws (Eq. 14.17) if $J = L$ and the identities (Eq. 14.16) if $J = R$, but in 1915 that was not yet clear. Hilbert misunderstood the meaning of the theorem as it applied to his theory. Let J correspond to his overall gravitational-electromagnetic Lagrangian. Then J depends on $10 + 4$ fields, the $g_{\mu\nu}$, and the electromagnetic potentials. There are four identities between them. 'As a consequence of . . . the theorem, the four [electromagnetic] equations may be considered as a consequence of the [gravitational] equations. . . . In [this] sense electromagnetic phenomena are gravitational effects. In this observation I see the simple and very surprising solution of the problem of Riemann, who was the first to seek theoretically for the connection between gravitation and light.'** Evidently Hilbert did not know the Bianchi identities either!

These and other errors were expurgated in an article Hilbert wrote in 1924 [H5]. It is again entitled 'Die Grundlagen der Physik' and contains a synopsis of his 1915 paper and a sequel to it [H6], written a year later. Hilbert's collected works, each volume of which contains a preface by Hilbert himself, do not include these two early papers, but only the one of 1924 [H7]. In this last article, Hilbert

---

*See the detailed discussion of variational principles in [W10] and [M5]. The tensor $T^{\mu\nu}$ is defined by $\delta \int L \sqrt{g}\, d^4x = \frac{1}{2} \cdot \int \sqrt{g}\, T^{\mu\nu}(x) \delta g_{\mu\nu}(x) d^4x.$

**Here Hilbert referred to the essay 'Gravitation und Licht' in Riemann's *Nachlass* [R2].

credited Amalie Emmy Noether (who was in Goettingen in 1915) with the proof of the theorem about the four identities; Noether's theorem had meanwhile been published, in 1918 [N4]. By 1924 Lorentz [L4], Felix Klein [K7], Einstein [E55], and Weyl [W11] had also written about the variational methods and the identities to which they give rise (see further Section 15c).

I must return to Einstein and Hilbert, however. The remarkable near simultaneity of their common discovery raises the obvious question of what exchanges took place between them in 1915. This takes me back to the summer of that year. As was mentioned earlier, in late June–early July, Einstein had spent about a week in Goettingen, where he 'got to know and love Hilbert. I gave six two-hour lectures there' [E9].* The subject was general relativity. 'To my great joy, I succeeded in convincing Hilbert and Klein completely' [E56]. 'I am enthusiastic about Hilbert. An important figure . . .,' [E39], he wrote upon his return to Berlin. From the period in which Einstein lectured, it is clear that his subject was the imperfect theory described in his paper of October 1914. I have already mentioned that Einstein made his major advance in October–November 1915. I know much less about the time it took Hilbert to work out the details of the paper he presented on November 20. However, we have Felix Klein's word that, as with Einstein, Hilbert's decisive thoughts came to him also in the fall of 1915—not in Goettingen but on the island of Rügen in the Baltic [K8].

The most revealing source about the crucial month of November is the correspondence during that period between Einstein and Hilbert. Between November 7 and 25, Einstein, otherwise a prolific letter writer, did not correspond with anyone—except Hilbert (if the Einstein archive in Princeton is complete in regard to that period). Let us see what they had to say to each other.

November 7: E. to H. Encloses the proofs of the November 4 paper 'in which I have derived the gravitational equations after I recognized four weeks ago that my earlier methods of proof were deceptive.' Alludes to a letter by Sommerfeld according to which Hilbert had also found objections to his October 1914 paper [E40]. The whole November correspondence may well have been triggered, it seems to me, by Einstein's knowledge that he was not the only one to have found flaws in this earlier work of his.

November 12: E. to H. Communicates the postulate $\sqrt{g} = 1$ (the November 11 paper). Sends along two copies of the October 1914 paper [E47].

November 14: H. to E. Is excited about his own 'axiomatic solution of your grand problem. . . . As a consequence of a general mathematical theorem, the (generalized Maxwellian) electrodynamic equations appear as a mathematical consequence of the gravitational equations so that gravitation and electrodynamics are not distinct at all.' Invites E. to attend a lecture on the subject, which he plans to give on November 16 [H8].

---

*Einstein and Hilbert began corresponding at least as early as October 1912, when Einstein was still in Zürich.

November 15: E. to H. 'The indications on your postcards lead to the greatest expectations.' Apologizes for his inability to attend the lecture, since he is overtired and bothered by stomach pains. Asks for a copy of the proofs of Hilbert's paper [E57].

November 18: E. to H. Apparently Einstein has received a copy of Hilbert's work. 'The system [of equations] given by you agrees—as far as I can see—exactly with what I found in recent weeks and submitted to the Academy' [E58].

November 19: H. to E. Congratulates him for having mastered the perihelion problem. 'If I could calculate as quickly as you, then the electron would have to capitulate in the face of my equations and at the same time the hydrogen atom would have to offer its excuses for the fact that it does not radiate' [H9]. Here, on the day before Hilbert submitted his November 20 paper, the known November correspondence between the two men ends.

Let us come back to Einstein's paper of November 18. It was written at a time in which (by his own admission) he was beside himself about his perihelion discovery (formally announced that same day), very tired, unwell, and still at work on the November 25 paper. It seems most implausible to me that he would have been in a frame of mind to absorb the content of the technically difficult paper Hilbert had sent him on November 18. More than a year later, Felix Klein wrote that he found the equations in that paper so complicated that he had not checked them [K9]. It is true that Hilbert's paper contains the trace term which Einstein had yet to introduce.* But Einstein's method for doing so was, as mentioned earlier, the adaptation of a trick he had already used in his paper of November 4.

Thus it seems that one should not attach much significance either to Einstein's agreeing with Hilbert 'as far as I can see' or to Hilbert's agreeing with Einstein 'as it seems to me' [H4]. I rather subscribe to Klein's opinion that the two men 'talked past each other, which is not rare among simultaneously productive mathematicians' [K10]. (I leave aside the characterization of Einstein as a mathematician, which he never was nor pretended to be.) I again agree with Klein 'that there can be no question of priority, since both authors pursued entirely different trains of thought to such an extent that the compatibility of the results did not at once seem assured' [K11]. I do believe that Einstein was the sole creator of the physical theory of general relativity and that both he and Hilbert should be credited for the discovery of the fundamental equation (Eq. 14.15).

I am not sure that the two protagonists would have agreed.

Something happened between these two men between November 20 and December 20, when Einstein wrote to Hilbert, 'There has been a certain pique between us, the causes of which I do not wish to analyze. I have struggled with complete success against a feeling of bitterness connected with that. I think of you once again with untroubled friendliness and ask you to try to do the same regard-

---

*Hilbert's $T_{\mu\nu}$ has a nonvanishing trace since his L refers to the Mie theory. I find it hard to believe that Einstein went as far as thinking that Hilbert's T had to vanish [E59].

ing me. It is really a shame if two real fellows who have freed themselves to some extent from this shabby world should not enjoy each other' [E60]. The full story may never be known. However, in a reply to a query, E. G. Straus wrote to me, 'Einstein felt that Hilbert had, perhaps unwittingly, plagiarized Einstein's [largely wrong!] ideas given in a colloquium talk at Goettingen.* The way Einstein told it, Hilbert sent a written apology in which he said that '[this talk] had completely slipped his mind ..." [S1]. Whatever happened, Einstein and Hilbert survived. The tone of their subsequent correspondence is friendly. In May 1916 Einstein gave a colloquium on Hilbert's work in Berlin [E61]. On that occasion he must have expressed himself critically about Hilbert's approach.** In May 1917 he told a student from Goettingen, 'It is too great an audacity to draw already now a picture of the world, since there are still so many things which we cannot yet remotely anticipate' [S6], an obvious reference to Hilbert's hopes for a unification of gravitation and electromagnetism. Einstein was thirty-eight when he said that. He was to begin his own program for a picture of the world shortly thereafter. . . .

References

A1. G. Arvidsson, *Phys. Zeitschr.* **21,** 88 (1920).

B1. S. J. Barnett, *Physica* **13,** 241 (1933); *Phys. Zeitschr.* **35,** 203 (1934); *Rev. Mod. Phys.* **7,** 129 (1935).

B2. ——, *Phys. Rev.* **6,** 239 (1915).

B3. N. Bohr, *Phil. Mag.* **30,** 394 (1915).

B4. S. J. Barnett, *Phys. Rev.* **10,** 7 (1917).

B5. E. Beck, *AdP* **60,** 109 (1919).

B6. Cf. W. Braunbeck, *Phys. Zeitschr.* **23,** 307 (1922) and also the discussion at the end of [H1a].

C1. J. Chazy, *La Théorie de la Relativité et la Mécanique Céleste,* Chap. 4. Gauthier-Villars, Paris, 1928.

D1. Cf., e.g., *Dictionary of Scientific Biography,* Vol. 4, pp. 324, 327. Scribner's, New York, 1971.

E1. A. Einstein, *PAW*, 1915, p. 844.

E2. ——, letter to J. Laub, July 22, 1913.

E3. ——, letter to H. A. Lorentz, August 14, 1913.

E4. ——, letter to P. Ehrenfest, undated, probably winter 1913–14.

E5. ——, letter to H. Zangger, March 10, 1914.

E6. ——, *Viertelj. Schr. Naturf. Ges. Zürich* **59,** 4 (1914).

E7. ——, letter to M. Besso, early March 1914; *EB*, p. 52.

*I am forced to assume that this is in reference to the June–July talks, since it is hard to believe that Einstein visited Goettingen in November 1915.

**Einstein to Ehrenfest: 'I don't like Hilbert's presentation ... unnecessarily special ... unnecessarily complicated ... not honest in structure (vision of the Übermensch by means of camouflaging the methods) ...' [E62].

E7a. ——, letter to C. Seelig, May 5, 1952.
 E8. ——, letter to P. Ehrenfest, April 10, 1914.
 E9. ——, letter to H. Zangger, July 7, 1915.
E10. ——, *Die Vossische Zeitung,* April 26, 1914.
E11. —— in *Kultur der Gegenwart* (E. Lecher, Ed.), Vol. 3. Teubner, Leipzig, 1915.
E12. ——, *PAW,* 1914, p. 739.
E13. ——, letter to H. Zangger, July 7, 1915.
E14. ——, letter to H. Zangger, undated, probably spring 1915.
E15. ——, letter to H. A. Lorentz, December 18, 1917.
E16. ——, *PAW,* 1914, p. 1030.
E17. —— and M. Grossmann, *Z. Math. Phys.* **62,** 225 (1913).
E18. ——, [E16], p. 1046, Eq. 23b.
E19. ——, [E16], p. 1083, the second of Eqs. 88.
E20. ——, [E16], p. 1084.
E21. ——, [E16], p. 1085.
E22. ——, [E16], p. 1066.
E23. —— and M. Grossmann, *Z. Math. Phys.* **63,** 215 (1915).
E24. ——, [E16], pp. 1075, 1076, especially Eq. 78.
E25. ——, letter to H. A. Lorentz, January 1, 1916.
E26. ——, letter to T. Levi-Civita, April 14, 1915.
E27. ——, letter to P. Straneo, January 7, 1915.
E28. ——, *PAW,* 1915, p. 315.
E29. —— in *Kultur der Gegenwart* (E. Lecher, Ed.), Vol. 3. Teubner, Leipzig, 1915.
E30. ——, *AdP* **47,** 879 (1915).
E31. ——, letter to M. Besso, February 12, 1915; *EB,* p. 57.
E32. ——, *Naturw.* **3,** 237 (1915).
E33. —— and W. de Haas, *Verh. Deutsch. Phys. Ges.* **17,** 152 (1915); correction, **17,** 203 (1915).
E34. —— and W. de Haas, *Versl. K. Ak. Amsterdam* **23,** 1449 (1915).
E35. —— and W. de Haas, *Proc. K. Ak. Amsterdam* **18,** 696 (1915).
E36. —— and O. Stern, *AdP* **40,** 551 (1913).
E37. ——, *Verh. Deutsch. Phys. Ges.* **18,** 173 (1916).
E38. ——, letter to H. Zangger, July 7, 1915.
E39. ——, letter to A. Sommerfeld, July 15, 1915. Reprinted in *Einstein/Sommerfeld Briefwechsel* (A. Hermann, Ed.), p. 30. Schwabe, Stuttgart, 1968.
E40. ——, letter to D. Hilbert, November 7, 1915.
E41. ——, letter to H. A. Lorentz, October 12, 1915.
E42. ——, letter to A. Sommerfeld, November 28, 1915. Reprinted in *Einstein/Sommerfeld Briefwechsel,* p. 32.
E43. ——, letter to P. Ehrenfest, December 26, 1915.
E44. ——, *PAW,* 1915, p. 778.
E45. ——, [E44], Eq. 5a.
E46. ——, *PAW,* 1915, p. 799.
E47. ——, letter to D. Hilbert, November 12, 1915.
E48. ——, *PAW,* 1915, p. 831.
E49. ——, letter to P. Ehrenfest, January 17, 1916.
E49a. ——, *Science* **69,** 248 (1929).

E50.   ——, [E48], p. 831.
E51.   ——, *PAW*, 1916, p. 768, footnote 1.
E52.   ——, letter to M. Besso, December 10, 1915; *EB*, p. 59.
E52a. ——, *The Origins of the General Theory of Relativity*. Jackson, Wylie, Glasgow, 1933.
E52b. —— and J. Grommer, *PAW*, 1927, p. 3.
E53.   ——, letter to A. Sommerfeld, December 9, 1915. Reprinted in *Einstein/Sommerfeld Briefwechsel*, p. 36.
E54.   ——, letter to H. Weyl, November 23, 1916.
E55.   ——, *PAW*, 1916, p. 1111.
E56.   ——, letter to W. J. de Haas, undated, probably August 1915.
E57.   ——, letter to D. Hilbert, undated, very probably November 15, 1915.
E58.   ——, letter to D. Hilbert, November 18, 1915.
E59.   J. Earman and C. Glymour, *Arch. Hist. Ex. Sci.* **19**, 291 (1978).
E60.   A. Einstein, letter to D. Hilbert, December 20, 1915.
E61.   ——, letter to D. Hilbert, May 25, 1916.
E62.   ——, letter to P. Ehrenfest, May 24, 1916.
F1.   A. D. Fokker, *AdP* **43**, 810 (1914).
F2.   ——, *Ned. Tydschr. Natuurk.* **21**, 125 (1955).
F3.   E. Freundlich, *Astr. Nachr.* **201**, 51 (1915).
H1.   B. Hoffmann, *Proc. Einstein Symposium Jerusalem*, 1979.
H1a.   W. de Haas in *Proceedings of the Third Solvay Conference*, April 1921, p. 206. Gauthier-Villars, Paris, 1923.
H1b.   W. Heisenberg, *Z. Phys.* **49**, 619 (1928).
H2.   S. P. Heims and E. T. Jaynes, *Rev. Mod. Phys.* **34**, 143 (1962).
H3.   W. Heisenberg, letter to W. Pauli, December 17, 1921. See *W. Pauli: Scientific Correspondence*, Vol. 1, p. 48. Springer, New York, 1979.
H4.   D. Hilbert, *Goett. Nachr.*, 1915, p. 395.
H5.   ——, *Math. Ann.* **92**, 1 (1924).
H6.   ——, *Goett. Nachr.*, 1917, p. 53.
H7.   ——, *Gesammelte Abhandlungen*, Vol. 3, p. 258. Springer, New York, 1970.
H8.   ——, two postcards to A. Einstein, November 14, 1915.
H9.   ——, letter to A. Einstein, November 19, 1915.
K1.   C. Kirsten and H. J. Treder, *Albert Einstein in Berlin, 1913–1933*, Vol. I, p. 95. Akademie Verlag, Berlin, 1979. This volume is referred to below as K.
K2.   K, p. 98.
K3.   K, p. 101.
K4.   K, p. 50.
K5.   M. Klein, *Paul Ehrenfest*, Vol. 1, p. 194. North Holland, Amsterdam, 1970.
K6.   K, p. 50.
K7.   F. Klein, *Gesammelte Mathematische Abhandlungen*, Vol. 1, pp. 553, 568, 586. Springer, New York, 1973.
K8.   ——, letter to W. Pauli, May 8, 1921; Pauli correspondence cited in [H3], p. 31.
K9.   ——, [K7], p. 559.
K10.   ——, letter to W. Pauli, March 8, 1921; Pauli correspondence cited in [H3], p. 27.
K11.   ——, [K7], p. 566.

L1. A. Landé, *Z. Phys.* **7,** 398 (1921).

L2. U. J. J. Le Verrier, *C. R. Ac. Sci. Paris* **49,** 379 (1859).

L3. H. A. Lorentz, *Proc. K. Ac. Wetensch. Amsterdam* **23,** 1073 (1915).

L4. ——, *Collected Papers,* Vol. 5, p. 246. Nyhoff, the Hague, 1934.

M1. J. C. Maxwell, *Treatise on Electricity and Magnetism* (1st edn.), Vol. 2, p. 202. Clarendon Press, Oxford, 1873.

M2. ——, *ibid.,* pp. 200–4.

M3. J. Mehra, *Einstein, Hilbert and the Theory of Gravitation.* D. Reidel, Boston, 1974.

M4. G. Mie, *AdP* **37,** 511 (1912); **39,** 1 (1912); **40,** 1 (1913).

M5. C. Misner, K. Thorne, and J. Wheeler, *Gravitation,* Chap. 21. Freeman, San Francisco, 1970.

N1. O. Nathan and H. Norden, *Einstein on Peace,* Chap. 1. Schocken, New York, 1968.

N1a. S. Newcomb. *Astr. Papers of the Am. Ephemeris* **1,** 472 (1882).

N2. I. Newton, *Principia,* liber 1, sectio 9. Best accessible in the University of California Press edition, 1966 (F. Cajori, Ed.).

N3. S. Newcomb, *Encyclopedia Britannica,* Vol. 18, p. 155. Cambridge University Press, Cambridge, 1911.

N4. E. Noether, *Goett. Nachr.,* 1918, pp. 37, 235.

O1. S. Oppenheim, *Encyklopädie der Mathematischen Wissenschaften* Vol. 6, Chap. 22, p. 94. Teubner, Leipzig, 1922.

O2. ——, [O1], Chap. 4.

O3. ——, [O1], Chap. 5.

P1. M. Planck, *PAW,* 1914, p. 742.

P2. W. Pauli, *Relativity Theory,* Sec. 64. Pergamon Press, London, 1958.

R1. O. W. Richardson, *Phys. Rev.* **26,** 248 (1908).

R2. B. Riemann, *Gesammelte Mathematische Werke und Wissenschaftlicher Nachlass* (H. Weber, Ed.), p. 496. Teubner, Leipzig, 1876.

S1. E. G. Straus, letter to A. Pais, October 1979.

S2. G. G. Scott, *Rev. Mod. Phys.* **34,** 102 (1962).

S3. J. Q. Stewart, *Phys. Rev.* **11,** 100 (1918).

S4. K. Schwarzschild, *PAW,* 1916, p. 189.

S5. ———, *PAW,* 1916, p. 424.

S6. Se, p. 261.

T1. R. Tolman and J. Q. Stewart, *Phys. Rev.* **8,** 97 (1916).

W1. See, e.g., S. Weinberg, *Gravitation and Cosmology,* p. 16. Wiley, New York, 1972. This book is quoted as W hereafter.

W2. W, p. 107.

W3. W, p. 163.

W4. W, p. 198.

W5. W, p. 176.

W6. C. M. Will in *General Relativity* (S. Hawking and W. Israel, Eds.), p. 55. Cambridge University Press, New York, 1979.

W7. W, p. 188.

W8. W, p. 147.

W9. H. Weyl, *Space, Time and Matter*, Sec. 28. Dover, New York, 1961.

W10. W, Chap. 12.

W11. H. Weyl, *AdP* **54,** 117 (1917).

Z1. J. Zenneck, *Encyklopädie der Mathematischen Wissenschaften*, Vol. 5, Chap. 2, Part 3. Teubner, Leipzig, 1903.

15

The New Dynamics

15a. From 1915 to 1980

Einstein arrived at the special theory of relativity after thinking for ten years about the properties of light. Electromagnetism was not the only area of physics that attracted his attention during those years. In the intervening time, he also thought hard about statistical mechanics and about the meaning of Planck's radiation law. In addition, he tried his hand at experiments. The final steps leading to his June 1905 paper were made in an intense burst of activity that lasted for less than two months.

Einstein arrived at the general theory of relativity after thinking for eight years about gravitation. This was not the only area of physics which attracted his attention during those years. In the intervening time, he also thought hard about quantum physics and about statistical mechanics. In addition, he tried his hand at experiments. The final steps leading to his November 25, 1915, paper were made in an intense burst of activity that lasted for less than two months.

In every other respect, a comparison of the development of the special and the general theory is a tale of disparities. In June 1905, Einstein at once gave special relativity its ultimate form in the first paper he ever wrote on the subject. By contrast, before November 25, 1915, he had written more than a dozen papers on gravitation, often retracting in later ones some conclusions reached earlier. The November 25 paper is a monumental contribution, of that there can be no doubt. Yet this paper—again in contrast with the paper of June 1905—represents only a first beach-head in new territory, the only sure beacon at its time of publication (but what a beacon) being the one-week-old agreement between theory and experiment in regard to the perihelion precession of Mercury. Both in 1905 and in 1915, Einstein presented new fundamental principles. As I have stressed repeatedly, the theory of 1905 was purely kinematic in character. Its new tenets had already been digested to a large extent by the next generation of physicists. By contrast, general relativity consists of an intricate web of new kinematics and new dynamics. Its one kinematic novelty was perfectly transparent from the start: Lorentz invariance is deprived of its global validity but continues to play a central role as a local invariance. However, the new dynamics contained in the equations of general relativity has not been fully fathomed either during Einstein's life or in the quarter of a century following his death. It is true that since 1915 the under-

266

standing of general relativity has vastly improved, our faith in the theory has grown, and no assured limitations on the validity of Einstein's theory have been encountered. Yet, even on the purely classical level, no one today would claim to have a full grasp of the rich dynamic content of the nonlinear dynamics called general relativity.

Having completed my portrait of Einstein as the creator of general relativity, I turn to a brief account of Einstein as its practitioner. For the present, I exclude his work on unified field theory, a subject that will be dealt with separately in Chapter 17.

As I prepare to write this chapter, my desk is cluttered. Obviously, copies of Einstein's papers are at hand. In addition, I have the following books within reach: Pauli's encyclopedia article on relativity completed in 1920 [P1] as well as its English translation [P2], of particular interest because of the notes Pauli added in the mid-1950s; several editions of Weyl's *Raum, Zeit, Materie* (including the English translation of the fourth edition [W1]), of importance because the variances in the different editions are helpful for an understanding of the evolution of general relativity in the first decade after its creation; the book by North dealing with the history of modern cosmology to 1965 [N1]; the fine source book on cosmology published by the American Association of Physics Teachers [S1]; and, for diversion, the collection of papers on cosmology assembled by Munitz [M1], in which Plato appears as the oldest and my friend Dennis Sciama as the youngest contributor. Taken together, these books are an excellent guide to the decade 1915–25. They enable me to confine myself to a broad outline of this period and to refer the reader to these readily accessible volumes for more details.

There are more books on my desk. The modern texts by Weinberg [W2] and by Misner, Thorne, and Wheeler [M2] (affectionately known as the 'telephone book') serve as sources of information about developments in general relativity during the rest of Einstein's life and the years beyond. Finally, my incomplete little library is brought up to date by a recent report of a workshop on sources and detectors of gravitational radiation [S2], the Einstein centenary survey by Hawking and Israel [H1], the record of the centennial symposium in Princeton [W3], and the two centenary volumes published by the International Society on General Relativity and Gravitation [H2]. I have these five books near me for two reasons, first to remind me that these authoritative and up-to-date reviews of recent developments free me from writing a full history of general relativity up to the present, a task which in any event would far exceed the scope of this book and the competence of its author, and second to remind me that my own understanding would lack perspective if I failed to indicate the enormous changes that have taken place in the ways general relativity is practiced today as compared with the way things were in Einstein's lifetime. I do indeed intend to comment on those changes, but will often urge my reader to consult these recent books for further particulars.

In preparation for the subsequent short sections which deal more directly with Einstein's work, I turn next to a general outline of the entire period from 1915 to the present.

The decade 1915–25 was a period of consolidation and of new ideas. The main advances were the introduction in mathematics of parallel transport by Levi-Civita in 1917 [L1], a concept soon widely used in general relativity; the emergence of a better understanding of the energy–momentum conservation laws as the result of the work by Einstein, Hilbert, Felix Klein, Lorentz, Schroedinger, and Hermann Weyl; Einstein's first papers on gravitational waves; and the pioneering explorations of general relativistic cosmologies by Einstein, Willem de Sitter, and Aleksandr Aleksandrovich Friedmann. The number of participating theoretical physicists is small but growing.

There were also two major experimental developments. The solar eclipse expeditions of 1919 demonstrated that light is bent by an amount close to Einstein's prediction [E1] of November 18, 1915. (I shall return to this event in the next chapter.) The first decade of general relativity ends with the announcement by Edwin Powell Hubble in December 1924 of an experimental result which settled a debate that had been going on for well over a century: the first incontrovertible evidence for the existence of an extragalactic object, Messier 31, the Andromeda nebula [H3].* Theoretical studies of cosmological models received even more important stimulus and direction from Hubble's great discovery of 1929 that the universe is expanding: nebulas are receding with a velocity proportional to their distance. In Hubble's own words, there exists ' . . . a roughly linear relation between velocities and distances. . . . The outstanding feature . . . is . . . the possibility that numerical data may be introduced into discussions of the general curvature of space' [H3a].** Still, the literature on cosmology remained modest in size, though high in quality.† Several attempts to revert to a neo-Euclidean theory of gravitation and cosmology were also made in this period [N4]. These have left no trace.

The number of those actively engaged in research in general relativity continued to remain small in the 1930s, 1940s, and early 1950s. Referring to those years, Peter Bergmann once said to me, 'You only had to know what your six best friends were doing and you would know what was happening in general relativity.' Studies of cosmological models and of special solutions to the Einstein equations con-

---

*A brief history of cosmic distances is found in [W4].

**The history of the antecedents of Hubble's law as well as of the improvements in the determination of Hubble's constant during the next few decades is given in [N2].

†The most detailed bibliography on relativity up to the beginning of 1924 was compiled by Lecat [L2]. See also [N3]. A list of the principal papers on cosmology for the years 1917 to 1932 is found in [R1].

tinued. There was also further research on the problem of motion (which had interested Einstein since 1927), the question of if and how the equations of motion of a distribution of matter can be obtained as a consequence of the gravitational field equations. By and large, throughout this period the advances due to general relativity are perceived to be the 'three successes'—the precession of the perihelion of Mercury, the bending of light, and the red shift—and a rationale for an expanding universe.

However, in the 1930s a new element was injected which briefly attracted attention, then stayed more or less quiescent for a quarter of a century, after which time it became one of general relativity's main themes. Principally as an exercise in nuclear physics, J. Robert Oppenheimer and his research associate Robert Serber decided to study the relative influence of nuclear and gravitational forces in neutron stars [O1].* One of their aims was to improve the estimate made by Lev Davidovich Landau for the limiting mass above which an ordinary star becomes a neutron star. (Landau discussed a model in which this mass is $\approx 0.001 \odot$. He also suggested that every star has an interior neutron core [L2a].) Their work attracted the attention of Richard Chase Tolman. As a result of discussions between Tolman and Oppenheimer and his co-workers, there appeared in 1939, a pair of papers, one by Tolman on static solutions of Einstein's field equations for fluid spheres [T1] and one, directly following it, by Oppenheimer and George Volkoff entitled 'On massive neutron cores' [O2]. In this paper, the foundations are laid for a general relativistic theory of stellar structure. The model discussed is a static spherical star consisting of an ideal Fermi gas of neutrons. The authors found that the star is stable as long as its mass $\lesssim \frac{1}{3} \odot$. (The present best value for a free-neutron gas is $\simeq 0.7 \odot$ and is called the Oppenheimer–Volkoff limit.)** Half a year later, the paper 'On continued gravitational attraction' by Oppenheimer and Hartland Snyder came out [O3]. The first line of its abstract reads, 'When all thermonuclear sources of energy are exhausted, a sufficiently heavy star will collapse; [a contraction follows which] will continue indefinitely.' Thus began the physics of black holes, the name for the ultimate collapsed state proposed by John Archibald Wheeler at a conference held in the fall of 1967 at the Goddard Institute of Space Studies in New York [W5]. At that time, pulsars had just been discovered and neutron stars and black holes were no longer considered 'exotic objects [which] remained a textbook curiosity. . . . Cooperative efforts of radio and optical astronomers [had begun] to reveal a great many strange new things in the sky' [W6].

Which brings us to the change in style of general relativity after Einstein's death.

During Einstein's lifetime, there was not one major international conference

*I am indebted to Robert Serber for a discussion of the papers on neutron stars by Oppenheimer and his collaborators.

**For further details, see [M2], p. 627.

exclusively devoted to relativity theory and gravitation.* The first international conference on relativity convened in Bern, in July 1955, three months after his death. Its purpose was to celebrate the fiftieth anniversary of relativity. Einstein himself had been invited to attend but had to decline for reasons of health. However, he had written to the organizers requesting that tribute be paid to Lorentz and Poincaré. Pauli was in charge of the scientific program. Browsing through the proceedings of the meeting† one will note (how could it be otherwise) that the subjects dealt with are still relativity in the old style. This conference, now known as GR0,‡ had 89 participants from 22 countries. It marked the beginning of a series of international congresses on general relativity and gravitation: GR1 was held in Chapel Hill, N.C. (1957), GR2 in Royaumont (1959), GR3 in Warsaw (1962), GR4 in London (1965), GR5 in Tblisi (1968), GR6 in Copenhagen (1971), GR7 in Tel Aviv (1974), and GR8 in Waterloo, Canada (1977). The most recent one, GR9, took place in Jena in June 1980. The growth of this field is demonstrated by the fact that this meeting was attended by about 800 participants from 53 countries.

What caused this growth and when did it begin? Asked this question, Dennis Sciama replied: 'The Bern Conference was followed two years later by the Chapel Hill Conference organized by Bryce de Witt. . . . This was the real beginning in one sense; that is, it brought together isolated people, showed that they had reached a common set of problems, and inspired them to continue working. The "relativity family" was born then. The other, no doubt more important, reason was the spectacular observational developments in astronomy. This began perhaps in 1954 when Cygnus A—the second strongest radio source in the sky—was identified with a distant galaxy. This meant that (a) galaxies a Hubble radius away could be picked up by radio astronomy (but not optically), (b) the energy needed to power a radio galaxy (on the synchrotron hypothesis) was the rest mass energy $\approx 10^8$ solar masses, that is, 10^{-3} of a galaxy mass. Then came X-ray sources in 1962, quasars in 1963, the 3°K background in 1965, and pulsars in 1967. The black hole in Cygnus X-1 dates from 1972. Another climax was the Kruskal treatment** of the Schwarzschild solution in 1960, which opened the doors to modern black hole theory' [S5]. Thus new experimental developments were a main stim-

---

*The Solvay conferences (which over the years have lost their preeminent status as summit meetings) did not deal with these subjects until 1958 [M3].

†These were published in 1956 as Supplement 4 of *Helvetica Physica Acta*.

‡Some call it GR1, not giving the important Chapel Hill meeting a number. Proceedings were published in the cases of GR0, GR1 (*Rev. Mod. Phys.* **29,** 351–546, 1957), GR2 (*CNRS* Report 1962), GR3 (Conférence Internationale sur les Théories de la Gravitation, Gauthier-Villars, 1964) and GR7 [S3]. Some of the papers presented at the GR conferences after 1970 are found in the journal *General Relativity and Gravitation*.

**Here Sciama refers to the coordinate system introduced independently by Kruskal [K1] and by Szekeres [S4]. For details see [M2], Chapter 31.

ulus for the vastly increased activity and the new directions in general relativity. The few dozen practitioners in Einstein's days are followed by a new generation about a hundred times more numerous.

Now, in 1982, the beginning of a new era described by Sciama has already been followed by further important developments. In June 1980 I attended the GR9 conference in order to find out more about the status of the field. Some of my impressions are found in what follows. Each of the next five sections is devoted to a topic in general relativity in which Einstein himself was active after 1915. In each section I shall indicate what he did and sketch ever so briefly how that subject developed in later years. In the final section, I list those topics which in their entirety belong to the post-Einsteinian era.

15b. The Three Successes

In 1933 Einstein, speaking in Glasgow on the origins of the general theory of relativity [E2], recalled some of his struggles, the 'errors in thinking which caused me two years of hard work before at last, in 1915, I recognized them as such and returned penitently to the Riemann curvature, which enabled me to find the relation to the empirical facts of astronomy.'

The period 1914–15 had been a confusing two years, not only for Einstein but also for those of his colleagues who had tried to follow his gyrations. For example, when in December 1915 Ehrenfest wrote to Lorentz, he referred to what we call the theory of general relativity as 'the theory of November 25, 1915.' He asked if Lorentz agreed with his own understanding that Einstein had now abandoned his arguments of 1914 for the impossibility of writing the gravitational field equations in covariant form [E3]. All through December 1915 and January 1916, the correspondence between Lorentz and Ehrenfest is intense and reveals much about their personalities. Lorentz, aged 62, is calculating away in Haarlem, making mistakes, correcting them, finally understanding what Einstein has in mind. In a letter to Ehrenfest he writes, 'I have congratulated Einstein on his brilliant result' [L3]. Ehrenfest, aged 35, in Leiden, ten miles down the road, is also hard at work on relativity. His reply to Lorentz's letter shows a glimpse of the despair that would ultimately overwhelm him: 'Your remark "I have congratulated Einstein on his brilliant results" has a similar meaning for me as when one Freemason recognizes another by a secret sign' [E4].

Meanwhile Lorentz had received a letter from Einstein in which the latter expressed his happiness with Lorentz's praise. Einstein added, 'The series of my papers about gravitation is a chain of false steps [Irrwegen] which nevertheless by and by led to the goal. Thus the basic equations are finally all right but the derivations are atrocious; this shortcoming remains to be eliminated' [E5]. He went on to suggest that Lorentz might be the right man for this task. 'I could do it myself, since all is clear to me. However, nature has unfortunately denied me the gift of being able to communicate, so that what I write is correct, to be sure, but also thoroughly indigestible.' Shortly afterward, Lorentz once again wrote to Ehrenfest. 'I had written to Einstein that, now that he has reached the acme of his theory, it would be important to give an exposé of its principles in as simple a form as possible, so that every physicist (or anyway many of them) may familiarize himself with its content. I added that I myself would very much like to try doing this but that it would be more beautiful if he did it himself' [L4].

Lorentz's fatherly advice must have been one of the incentives that led Einstein to write his first synopsis of the new theory [E6].* This beautiful, fifty-page account was completed in March 1916. It was well received. This may have encouraged Einstein—who did not communicate all that badly—to do more writing. In December 1916 he completed *Über die spezielle und die allgemeine Relativitätstheorie, gemeinverständlich,*** his most widely known work [E8a]. Demand for it became especially high after the results of the eclipse expedition caused such an immense stir (see Chapter 16). Its tenth printing came out in 1920, the twenty-second in 1972.

Einstein's paper of March 1916 concludes with a brief section on the three new predictions: the red shift, the bending of light, and the precession of the perihelion of Mercury. In the final paragraph of that section is recorded the single major experimental confirmation which at that time could be claimed for the theory: the Mercury anomaly. In 1916 next to nothing was known about the red shift; the bending of light was first observed in 1919.

Commenting on the status of experimental relativity in 1979, David Wilkinson remarked:

> [These] two early successes [—the perihelion precession and the bending of light—were] followed by decades of painfully slow experimental progress. It has taken nearly sixty years finally to achieve empirical tests of general relativity at the one per cent level. Progress . . . required development of technology and experimental techniques well beyond those available in the early 1920s. [W7]

I refer the reader to Wilkinson's paper for further remarks on the technological and sociological aspects of modern relativity experiments. For a summary of the present status of the experimental verification of general relativity (excluding cosmology), the reader should consult the report by Irwin Shapiro wherein it will be found that, within the errors, all is well with the red shift (both astronomically and terrestrially), with the bending of light, with the precession of the perihelia of Mercury and other bodies, and also with the modern refined tests of the equiv-

---

*This article was published both in the *Annalen der Physik* and, also in 1916, as a separate booklet [E7] which went through numerous printings and was also translated into English [E8].

** *On the Special and the General Relativity Theory, a Popular Exposition.* Under this title, the English translation appeared in 1920 (Methuen, London). Einstein used to joke that the book should rather be called 'gemeinunverständlich,' commonly ununderstandable.

I   Einstein at his desk in the Patent office,
Bern, ca. 1905.
(Einstein Archive, Courtesy AIP Niels Bohr Library)

II   The cover of the *Berliner Illustrirte,*
December 14, 1919. The caption reads, in
translation: 'A new great figure in world history: Albert Einstein, whose investigations
signify a complete revision of our concepts of
Nature, and are on a par with the insights of
a Copernicus, a Kepler, and a Newton.'

III   Einstein delivering a lecture
at the Collège de France, 1922.
(Einstein Archive, Courtesy AIP Niels Bohr Library)

IV   Planck and Einstein in Berlin, June 28, 1929, the day on which Planck received
the first, Einstein the second, Planck medal.
(Courtesy AIP Niels Bohr Library)

VI   Albert Einstein, Charlie Chaplin, and Elsa Einstein at the world premiere of 'City
Lights', at the Los Angeles Theater, Los Angeles, January 30, 1931.

VII   Albert and Elsa Einstein near the Grand Canyon,
February 28, 1931.

VIII   Albert Einstein and his sister Maja,
1939. (The woman seen from the back is
the wife of Thomas Mann.)
(Courtesy Mrs. J. W. Brown)

IXa   October 1, 1940: Ceremonies of induction to U.S. citizenship, Trenton, New Jer-
sey. To Einstein's left is his stepdaughter
Margot Einstein.

IXb   Trenton, October 1, 1940: Judge Phillip Forman congratulates Einstein having
sworn him in as U.S. citizen.
(Courtesy Mrs. Phillip Forman)

X   Chico, Helen Dukas, and Einstein in front of 112 Mercer Street (probably taken in the early 1940's). (Courtesy Helen Dukas)

XI   Cake presented to Einstein on his seventieth birthday (1949). The formulae are taken from Appendix II in *The Meaning of Relativity,* Third edition, Princeton University Press, 1950. (Courtesy Helen Dukas)

XII   The last known picture of Einstein,
taken in March 1955, in front
of 112 Mercer Street.
(Einstein Archive, Courtesy United Press International)

alence principle [S6]. In another modern review, the current situation is summarized as follows:

> So far [general relativity] has withstood every confrontation, but new confrontations, in new arenas, are on the horizon. Whether general relativity survives is a matter of speculation for some, pious hope for some, and supreme confidence for others. [W8]

With fervent good wishes and with high hopes for further experiments with rockets, satellites, and planetary probes, I hereby leave the subject of the comparison between theory and experiment in general relativity.

What did Einstein himself have to say in later years about the three successes? I described in the previous chapter his high excitement at the time he found the right value for the precession of the perihelion of Mercury. He still considered this to be a crucial discovery when he sent Lorentz his New Year's wishes for 1916 ('I wish you and yours a happy year and Europe an honest and definitive peace'): 'I now enjoy a hard-won clarity and the agreement of the perihelion motion of Mercury' [E9]. As will be seen in the next chapter, the results of the solar eclipse expeditions in 1919 also greatly stirred him personally. But, as is natural, in later times he tended to emphasize the simplicity of the theory rather than its consequences. In 1930 he wrote, 'I do not consider the main significance of the general theory of relativity to be the prediction of some tiny observable effects, but rather the simplicity of its foundations and its consistency' [E10]. More and more he stressed formal aspects. Again in 1930 he expressed the opinion that the idea of general relativity 'is a purely formal point of view and not a definite hypothesis about nature. . . . Non-[generally] relativistic theory contains not only statements about *things* but [also] statements which refer to things *and* the *coordinate systems* which are needed for their description; also from a logical point of view such a theory is less satisfactory than a relativistic one, the content of which is independent of the choice of coordinates' [E11]. In 1932 he went further: 'In my opinion this theory [general relativity] possesses little inner probability. . . . The field variables $g_{\mu\nu}$ and ϕ_μ [the electromagnetic potentials] do not correspond to a *unified* conception of the structure of the continuum' [E12].

Thus we see Einstein move from the joy of successfully confronting experimental fact to higher abstraction and finally to that discontent with his own achievements which accompanied his search for a unified field theory. He did not live to again use tiny effects for the purpose of advancing physical knowledge. Nor have we to this day recognized any tiny effects which we can be sure pose a threat to the physical principles with which we, perhaps clumsily, operate.

General relativity does predict new tiny effects of a conventional kind, however. One of these caught Einstein's attention in 1936 when R. W. Mandl pointed out to him [M4] that if an observer is perfectly aligned with a 'near' and a 'far' star, then he will observe the image of the far star as an annular ring as a result of the bending of its light by the near star. The idea was, of course, not new. Eddington knew already that one may obtain two pointlike images of the far star if the alignment is imperfect [E12a]. In any event, to Mandl's delight [M5] Einstein went on to publish a calculation of the dependence of the image intensity upon the displacement of the observer from the extended line of centers of the two stars [E12b].* He believed that 'there is no hope of observing this phenomenon.' However, in 1979 it was shown that the apparent double quasar 0957 + 561 A,B is actually the double image of a single quasar [W8a]. An intervening galaxy acts as the gravitational lens [Y1].

15c. Energy and Momentum Conservation; the Bianchi Identities

The collected works of Felix Klein contain a set of papers devoted to the links between geometry on the one hand and group theory and the theory of invariants on the other, his own Erlangen program. The last three articles of this set deal with general relativity. ('For Klein . . . the theory of relativity and its connection with his old ideas of the Erlangen program brought the last flare-up of his mathematical interests and mathematical production' [W9].) One of those three, completed in 1918, is entitled 'On the Differential Laws for the Conservation of Momentum and Energy in the Einstein Theory of Gravitation' [K2]. In its introduction Klein observed, 'As one will see, in the following presentation [of the conservation laws] I really do not any longer need to calculate but only to make use of the most elementary formulae of the calculus of variations.' It was the year of the Noether theorem.

In November 1915, neither Hilbert nor Einstein was aware of this royal road to the conservation laws. Hilbert had come close. I recall here some of his conclusions, discussed in Section 14d. He had derived the gravitational equations from the correct variational principle

$$\delta \int \left(L - \frac{1}{2\kappa} R \right) \sqrt{g}\, d^4x = 0 \tag{15.1}$$

for variations $g_{\mu\nu} \rightarrow g_{\mu\nu} + \delta g_{\mu\nu}$, where the $\delta g_{\mu\nu}$ are infinitesimal and vanish on the boundary of the integration domain. Without proof, he had also stated the theorem that if J is a scalar function of n fields and if

$$\delta \int J \sqrt{g}\, d^4x = 0 \qquad \text{for} \quad x^\mu \rightarrow x^\mu + \xi^\mu \tag{15.2}$$

then there exist four identities between the n fields. He believed that these identities meant that electromagnetism is a consequence of gravitation and failed to see that this theorem at once yields the conservation laws [H4]. In a sequel to his work of 1915, presented in December 1916 [H5], his interpretation of Eq. 15.2 had not changed. (In view of the relations between Hilbert and Einstein, it is of interest to note that in this last paper Hilbert refers to his subject as 'the new

---

*For references to later calculations of this effect, see [S6a].

physics of Einstein's relativity principle' [H6].) As for Einstein, in 1914 [E13] and again on November 4, 1915, [E14] he had derived the field equations of gravitation from a variational principle—but in neither case did he have the correct field equations. In his paper of November 25, 1915, [E15] energy–momentum conservation appears as a constraint on the theory rather than as an almost immediate consequence of general covariance; no variational principle is used.

I repeat one last time that neither Hilbert nor Einstein was aware of the Bianchi identities in that crucial November. Let us see how these matters were straightened out in subsequent years.

The conservation laws are the one issue on which Einstein's synopsis of March 1916 [E6] is weak. A variational principle is introduced but only for the case of pure gravitation; the mathematics is incorrect;* matter is introduced in a plausible but nonsystematic way ([E6], Section 16) and the conservation laws are verified by explicit computation rather than by an invariance argument ([E6], Section 17). In October 1916 Einstein came back to energy–momentum conservation [E16].** This time he gave a general proof (free of coordinate conditions) that for any matter Lagrangian L the energy–momentum tensor $T^{\mu\nu}$ satisfies

$$T^{\mu\nu}_{;\nu} = 0 \qquad\qquad (15.3)$$

as a consequence of the gravitational field equations. I shall return shortly to this paper, but first must note another development.

In August 1917 Hermann Weyl finally decoded the variational principle (Eq. 15.2) [W10]. Let us assume (he said) that the ξ^μ are infinitesimal and that ξ^μ and its derivatives vanish on the boundary of the integration domain. Then for the case that $J = L$, it follows that Eq. 15.3 holds true, whereas if $J = R$ we obtain†

$$(R^{\mu\nu} - \tfrac{1}{2} g^{\mu\nu} R)_{;\nu} = 0 \qquad\qquad (15.4)$$

A correspondence between Felix Klein and Hilbert, published by Klein early in 1918 [K4], shows that also in Goettingen circles it had rapidly become clear that the principle (Eq. 15.2), properly used in the case of general relativity, gives rise to eight rather than four identities, four for $J = L$ and four for $J = R$.

Interestingly enough, in 1917 the experts were not aware that Weyl's derivation of Eq. 15.4 by variational techniques was a brand new method for obtaining a long-known result. Neither Hilbert nor Klein (nor, of course, Einstein) realized that Eq. 15.4, the contracted Bianchi identities, had been derived much earlier, first by the German mathematician Aurel Voss in 1880, then independently by

---

*As Bargmann pointed out to me, Einstein first specializes to the coordinate condition $\sqrt{g} = 1$ and then introduces a variational principle without a Lagrange multiplier for this condition.

**An English translation of this paper is included in the well-known collection of papers by Einstein, Lorentz, Minkowksi, and Weyl [S7].

†For this way of deriving Eqs. 15.3 and 15.4, see [W11]. Other contributions to this subject are discussed in [P3]. For the relation of Weyl's results to those of Klein, see [K3].

Ricci in 1889, and then, again independently, in 1902 by Klein's former pupil Luigi Bianchi.* The name Bianchi appears neither in any of the five editions of Weyl's *Raum, Zeit, Materie* (the fifth edition appeared in 1923) nor in Pauli's review article of 1921 [P1]. In 1920, Eddington wrote in his book *Space, Time and Gravitation*, 'I doubt whether anyone has performed the laborious task of verifying these identities by straightforward algebra' [E17]. The next year he performed this task himself [E18]. In 1922 a simpler derivation was given [J1], soon followed by the remark that Eq. 15.4 follows from

$$R_{\lambda\mu\sigma;\tau} + R_{\lambda\mu\tau;\sigma} + R_{\lambda\mu\sigma\tau;\nu} = 0 \qquad (15.5)$$

now known as *the* Bianchi identities, where $R_{\lambda\mu\nu\sigma}$ is the Riemann curvature tensor [H7].** Harward, the author of this paper, remarked, 'I discovered the general theorem [Eq. 15.5] for myself, but I can hardly believe that it has not been discovered before.' This surmise was, of course, quite correct. Indeed, Eq. 15.5 was the relation discovered by the old masters, as was finally brought to the attention of a new generation by the Dutch mathematicians Jan Schouten and Dirk Struik in 1924: 'It may be of interest to mention that this theorem [Eq. 15.5] is known especially in Germany and Italy as Bianchi's Identity' [S9].

From a modern point of view, the identities 15.3 and 15.4 are special consequences of a celebrated theorem of Emmy Noether, who herself participated in the Goettingen debates on the energy–momentum conservation laws. She had moved to Goettingen in April 1915. Soon thereafter her advice was asked. 'Emmy Noether, whose help I sought in clarifying questions concerning my energy law . . .' Hilbert wrote to Klein [K4]. 'You know that Fräulein Noether continues to advise me in my work,' Klein wrote to Hilbert [K4]. At that time, Noether herself told a friend that a team in Goettingen, to which she also belonged, was performing calculations of the most difficult kind for Einstein but that 'none of us understands what they are good for' [D1]. Her own work on the relation between invariance under groups of continuous transformations and conservation theorems was published in 1918 [N5]. Noether's theorem has become an essential tool in modern theoretical physics. In her own oeuvre, this theorem represents only a sideline. After her death, Einstein wrote of her, 'In the judgment of the most competent living mathematicians, Fräulein Noether was the most significant creative mathematical genius since the higher education of women began' [E19].

Let us return to Einstein's article of October 1916. The principal point of that paper is not so much the differential as the integral conservation laws. As is now

---

*For more historical details, see the second edition of Schouten's book on Ricci calculus [S8].

**Equation 15.4 follows from Eq. 15.5 by contraction and by the use of symmetry properties of the Riemann tensor [W12].

well known, this is not a trivial problem. Equation 15.3 can equivalently be written in the form

$$\frac{\partial \sqrt{g}\, T^{\nu}_{\mu}}{\partial x^{\nu}} - \tfrac{1}{2}\sqrt{g}\, T^{\alpha\beta} \frac{\partial g_{\alpha\beta}}{\partial x^{\mu}} = 0 \qquad (15.6)$$

The second term—which accounts for the possibility of exchanging energy-momentum between the gravitational field and matter—complicates the transition from differential to integral laws by simple integration over spatial domains. Einstein found a way out of this technical problem. He was the first to cast Eq. 15.6 in the form of a vanishing divergence [E16]. He noted that since the curvature scalar R is linear in the second derivatives of the $g_{\mu\nu}$, one can uniquely define a quantity R^* which depends only on the $g_{\mu\nu}$ and their first derivatives by means of the relation

$$\int R\, \sqrt{g}\, d^4x = \int R^* d^4x + \text{surface term} \qquad (15.7)$$

Next define an object t^{ν}_{μ} by

$$t^{\nu}_{\mu} = 1/2 \left(R^* \delta^{\nu}_{\mu} - \frac{\partial R^*}{\partial(\partial g^{\alpha\beta}/\partial x^{\mu})} \frac{\partial g^{\alpha\beta}}{\partial x_{\nu}} \right) \qquad (15.8)$$

With the help of the gravitational field equations, it can be shown that Eq. 15.6 can be cast in the alternative form

$$\frac{\partial}{\partial x^{\mu}} (\sqrt{g}\, T^{\mu}_{\nu} + t^{\mu}_{\nu}) = 0 \qquad (15.9)$$

Therefore, one can define

$$P_{\mu} \equiv \int (\sqrt{g}\, T^{4}_{\mu} + t^{4}_{\mu})\, d^3x \qquad (15.10)$$

as the total energy-momentum of a closed system. Einstein emphasized that, despite appearances, Eq. 15.9 is fully covariant. However, the quantity t^{ν}_{μ} is not a generally covariant tensor density. Rather, it is a tensor only relative to affine transformations.

These results are of particular interest in that they show how Einstein was both undaunted by and quite at home with Riemannian geometry, which he handled with ingenuity. In those years, he would tackle difficult mathematical questions only if compelled by physical motivations. I can almost hear him say, 'General relativity is right. One must be able to give meaning to the total energy and momentum of a closed system. I am going to find out how.' I regard it as no accident that in his October 1916 paper Einstein took the route from Eq. 15.9 to Eq. 15.6 rather than the other way around! For details of the derivation of Eq. 15.9 and the proof that t^{ν}_{μ} is an affine tensor, I refer the reader to Pauli's review article [P4] and the discussion of the energy-momentum pseudotensor by Landau and Lifshitz [L5].

The discovery of Eq. 15.9 marks the beginning of a new chapter in general relativity. New problems arise. Since t^{ν}_{μ} is not a general tensor density, to what extent are the definitions of energy and momentum independent of the choice of coordinate system? During the next two years, this question was discussed by Felix Klein, Levi-Civita, Lorentz, Pauli, Schroedinger, and others,* as well as by Einstein himself, who in 1918 came back to this issue one more time. 'The significance of [Eq. 15.9] is rather generally doubted,' he wrote. He noted that the quantity t^{ν}_{μ} can be given arbitrary values at any given point but that nevertheless the energy and momentum integrated over all space have a definite meaning [E19b]. Later investigations have shown that P_{μ} is well defined provided that the metric suitably approaches the Minkowski metric at spatial infinity.

Many related questions continue to be studied intensely in the era of renewed activity following Einstein's death. Examples: Can one calculate the energy in a finite domain? Can one separate the energy into a gravitational and a nongravitational part? Does purely gravitational energy exist? Is the total energy of a gravitating system always positive? A status report on these questions (many of them not yet fully answered) is found in an article by Trautman [T2]. The last-mentioned question was the subject of a plenary lecture at GR9. This difficult problem (known for years as the positive energy program) arises because t^{ν}_{μ} by itself is not positive definite. It was found in 1979 that positive definiteness of the total energy can nevertheless be demonstrated [S10]. After my return from GR9, I learned that the original proof can be simplified considerably [W13].

15d. Gravitational Waves

At no time during GR9 did I sense more strongly how much general relativity belongs to the future than when I listened to the plenary lectures by Kip Thorne from Pasadena and Vladimir Braginsky from Moscow on the present state of experiments designed to detect gravitational waves. So far such waves have not been found, but perhaps, Thorne said, they will be observed in this century. Fifteen experimental groups, some of them multinational, are preparing for this event.

None of these groups is planning to emulate Hertz's discovery of electromagnetic waves by terrestrial means. The probability of an atomic transition accompanied by gravitational radiation is some fifty powers of 10 less than for photon emission. We have to look to the heavens for the best sources of gravitational radiation, most particularly to exotic, violent, and rare stellar phenomena such as the collapse of star cores into neutron stars or supernovas; or the formation of black holes. Sources like these may produce intensities some fifty powers of 10 higher than what can be attained on earth. Gravitational antennas need to be built which are sensitive enough to overcome stupendous background problems. Work

---

*This early work is described in Pauli [P5]. See also [E19a].

is in progress on acoustical detectors, on improved Weber bars (named after Joseph Weber, whose pioneering work in the 1960s did much to stimulate the present worldwide efforts [W14]) and monocrystals, and on electromagnetic detectors, such as laser interferometers. These devices are designed to explore the frequency range from about 100 Hz to 10 kHz. The use of space probes in the search for gravitational waves (in the range 10^{-2}–10^{-4} Hz) by Doppler tracking is also being contemplated. Detector studies have led to a burgeoning new technology, quantum electronics [C1]. The hope is not just to observe gravitational waves but to use them for a new kind of experimental astronomy. When these waves pass through matter, they will absorb and scatter vastly less even than neutrinos do. Therefore, they will be the best means we may ever have for exploring what happens in the interior of superdense matter. It is anticipated that gravitational wave astronomy may inform us about the dynamics of the evolution of supernova cores, neutron stars, and black holes. In addition, it may well be that gravitational waves will provide us with experimental criteria for distinguishing between the orthodox Einsteinian general relativity and some of its modern variants.

Detailed accounts and literature referring to all these extraordinarily interesting and challenging aspects of gravitational wave physics are found in some of the books mentioned earlier in this chapter. I mention in particular the proceedings of a 1978 workshop [S2], the chapter by Weber in the GRG book [H2], the chapters by Douglass and Braginsky and by Will in the Hawking–Israel book [H1], and the review of reviews completed in 1980 by Thorne [T3]. All these papers reveal a developing interaction between astrophysics, particle physics, and general relativity. They also show that numerical relativity has taken great strides with the help of ever-improving computers.

Einstein contributed the quadrupole formula.

Even before relativity, Lorentz had conjectured in 1900 that gravitation 'can be attributed to actions which do not propagate with a velocity larger than that of light' [L6]. The term *gravitational wave* (onde gravifique) appeared for the first time in 1905, when Poincaré discussed the extension of Lorentz invariance to gravitation [P6]. In June 1916, Einstein became the first to cast these qualitative ideas into explicit form [E20]. He used the weak-field approximation:

$$g_{\mu\nu} = \eta_{\mu\nu} + h_{\mu\nu} \tag{15.11}$$

where $\eta_{\mu\nu}$ is the Minkowski metric, $|h_{\mu\nu}| \ll 1$, and terms of higher order than the first in $h_{\mu\nu}$ are neglected throughout. For the source-free case, he showed that the quantities

$$h'_{\mu\nu} = h_{\mu\nu} - \tfrac{1}{2}\eta_{\mu\nu}\, h^{\alpha}_{\alpha} \tag{15.12}$$

satisfy ($\Box$ is the Dalembertian)

$$\Box h'_{\mu\nu} = 0 \tag{15.13}$$

in a coordinate system for which the 'gauge condition'

$$\frac{\partial h'_{\mu\nu}}{\partial x^\nu} = 0 \qquad (15.14)$$

holds true (Eq. 15.14 is sometimes called the Hilbert condition since Hilbert was the first to prove in general that the coordinate condition Eq. 15.14 can always be satisfied to the first order in $h_{\mu\nu}$ [H5]).

Einstein noted not only that in the weak-field approximation there exist gravitational waves which propagate with light velocity but also that only two of the ten $h'_{\mu\nu}$ have independent physical significance, or, as we now say, that there are only two helicity states. He also pointed out that the existence of radiationless stable interatomic orbits is equally mysterious from the electromagnetic as from the gravitational point of view! 'It seems that the quantum theory will have to modify not only Maxwell's electrodynamics but also the new gravitational theory.' Perhaps this renewed concern with quantum physics spurred him, a few months later, to make one of his great contributions to quantum electrodynamics: in the fall of 1916 he introduced the concepts of spontaneous and induced transitions and gave a new derivation of Planck's radiation law [E21].

In the same June 1916 paper, Einstein also attempted to calculate the amount of gravitational radiation emitted by an excited isolated mechanical system with linear dimensions R. He introduced two further approximations: (1) only wavelengths λ for which $\lambda/R >> 1$ are considered and (2) all internal velocities of the mechanical system are $<< c$. At that time he mistakenly believed that a permanently spherically symmetric mechanical system can emit gravitational radiation. There the matter lay until he corrected this error in 1918 and presented the quadrupole formula [E22]: the energy loss of the mechanical system is given by*

$$-\frac{dE}{dt} = \frac{G}{5c^5} \sum_{i,j} \dddot{Q}_{ij} \dddot{Q}_{ij} \qquad (15.15)$$

where

$$Q_{ij} = \int \rho \left(x_i x_j - \tfrac{1}{3}\delta_{ij} r^2 \right) d^3x \qquad (15.16)$$

is the mass quadrupole moment and ρ the mass density of the source.

After 1918 Einstein returned one more time to gravitational waves. In 1937 he and Rosen studied cylindrical wave solutions of the exact gravitational equations [E23], which were analyzed further in [W15].

---

*Einstein's result was off by a factor of 2. This factor is corrected in Eq. 15.15, which has also been written in modernized form. Dots denote time derivatives. Equation 15.15 represents, of course, the leading term in a gravitational multipole expansion. For a review of this expansion, see [T4].

Do gravitational waves exist? Is the derivation of the quadrupole formula correct? If so, does the formula apply to those extreme circumstances mentioned above, which may offer the most potent sources of gravitational radiation?

There exists an extensive and important literature on these questions, beginning in 1922 with a remark by Eddington, who believed that the waves were spurious and 'propagate ... with the speed of thought' [E24]. In 1937, Einstein briefly thought that gravitational waves do not exist (see Chapter 29). 'Among the present day theoretical physicists there is a strong consensus that gravitational radiation does exist,' one reads in [H8]. At GR9, the validity of the quadrupole formula was the subject of a plenary lecture and a discussion session. In the closing months of 1980, there appeared in the literature 'a contribution to the debate concerning the validity of Einstein's quadrupole formula' [W16].

The difficulties in answering the above questions stem, of course, from the nonlinear nature of gravitation, an aspect not incorporated in Einstein's linearized approximation. No one doubts that Eq. 15.15 holds true (in the long-wavelength, slow-motion approximation) for nongravitational sources of gravitational waves, such as elastically vibrating bars. The hard question is what happens if both material sources and the gravitational field itself are included as sources of gravitational waves. The difficult questions which arise are related in part to the definition of energy localization referred to in the previous section. For a recent assessment of these difficulties see especially [E25] and [R2]. For a less severe judgment, see [T5]. I myself have not struggled enough with these problems to dare take sides.*

Finally, as a gift from the heavens, there comes to us the binary pulsar PSR1913 + 16, 'the first known system in which relativistic gravity can be used as a practical tool for the determination of astrophysical parameters' [W17]. This system offers the possibility of testing whether the quantitative general relativistic prediction of a change in period due to energy loss arising from gravitational quadrupole radiation holds true. At GR9, this loss was reported to be 1.04 ± 0.13 times the quadrupole prediction. This result does, of course, not prove the validity of the quadrupole formula, nor does it diminish the urge to observe gravitational waves directly. It seems more than fair to note, however, that this binary pulsar result strengthens the belief that the quadrupole formula cannot be far off the mark and that the experimental relativists' search for gravitational waves will not be in vain.

15e. Cosmology

> Die Unbegrenztheit des Raumes besitzt ... eine gröszere empirische Gewiszheit als irgend eine aüszere Erfahrung. Hieraus folgt aber die Unendlichkeit keineswegs. . . .
>
> Bernhard Riemann, Habilitationsvortrag, 1854.

*I am grateful to J. Ehlers and P. Havas for enlightening discussions on this group of problems.

1. Einstein and Mach.   Einstein was in the middle of preparing his first synopsis
on general relativity when in February 1916 word reached him that the sufferings
of Mach had come to an end. He interrupted his work and prepared a short article
on Mach [E26] which reached the editors of *Naturwissenschaften* a week before
his synopsis was received by the *Annalen der Physik*. The paper on Mach is not
just a standard obituary. It is the first occasion on which Einstein shows his exceptional talent for drawing with sensitivity a portrait of a man and his work, placing
him in his time and speaking of his achievements and of his frailties with equal
grace.

Mach was successively a professor of mathematics, experimental physics, and
philosophy. In the obituary, Einstein lauded a number of diverse contributions
but reserved his highest praise for Mach's historical and critical analysis of
mechanics [M6], a work that had profoundly influenced him since his student
days [E27], when he was introduced to it by Besso [E28]. He had studied it again
in Bern, together with his colleagues of the Akademie Olympia [S11]. In 1909 he
had written to Mach that of all his writings, he admired this book the most
[E29].* Initially, Mach seems to have looked with favor on relativity, for Einstein
wrote to him, again in 1909, 'I am very pleased that you enjoy the relativity theory'
[E30]. In the obituary, Einstein cited extensively Mach's famous critique of Newton's concepts of absolute space and absolute motion and concluded, 'The cited
places show that Mach clearly recognized the weak sides of classical mechanics
and that he was not far from demanding a general theory of relativity, and that
nearly half a century ago!' [E26]. In his nineteenth century classic, Mach had
indeed criticized the Newtonian view that one can distinguish between absolute
and relative rotation. 'I cannot share this view. For me, only relative motions exist,
and I can see, in this regard, no distinction between rotation and translation,' he
had written [M7].** Einstein had Mach's discussion of rotational motion in mind
when he wrote his own 1916 synopsis: its second section, entitled 'On the Grounds
Which Make Plausible an Extension of the [Special] Relativity Postulate,' begins
with the phrase:

> Classical mechanics, and the special theory of relativity not less, suffer from an
> epistemological shortcoming [the preferred position of uniform translation over
> all other types of relative motion] which was probably emphasized for the first
> time by Mach. [E6]

In 1910, Mach had expressed himself positively about the work of Lorentz,
Einstein, and Minkowski [M8]. Around January 1913, Einstein had written to
him how pleased he was with Mach's 'friendly interest which you manifest for

---

*Four letters from Einstein to Mach have been preserved, none from Mach to Einstein. These letters
are discussed in essays by Herneck [H9] and by Holton [H10], along with more details on the
relations between the two men.

**In this connection, readers may wish to refresh their memory about Newton's rotating bucket
experiment and Mach's analysis thereof; see, e.g., [W18]. In February 1916, Einstein gave a lecture
on the Foucault pendulum [E31].

the new [i.e., the Einstein–Grossmann] theory' [E32]. In his later years, however, Mach turned his back on relativity. In July 1913 he wrote, 'I must ... as assuredly disclaim to be a forerunner of the relativists as I withhold from the atomistic belief of the present day,' and added that to him relativity seemed 'to be growing more and more dogmatical' [M9]. These phrases appear in a book that was not published until 1921. Even so, Einstein's esteem for Mach never faltered. 'There can hardly be any doubt that this [reaction by M.] was a consequence of an absorption capacity diminished by age, since the whole direction of thinking of this theory is in concordance with that of Mach, so that it is justified to consider Mach as the precursor of the general theory of relativity,' he wrote in 1930 [E33]. In the last interview given by Einstein, two weeks before his death, he reminisced with evident pleasure about the one visit he had paid to Mach and he spoke of four people he admired: Newton, Lorentz, Planck, and Mach [C2]. They, and Maxwell, and no others, are the only ones Einstein ever accepted as his true precursors.

In a discussion of Mach's influence on Einstein, it is necessary to make a clear distinction between three themes.

First, Mach's emphasis on the relativity of all motion. As we have just seen, in this regard Einstein's respect was and remained unqualified.

Second, Mach's philosophy or, perhaps better, his scientific methodology. 'Mach fought and broke the dogmatism of nineteenth century physics' is one of the rare approving statements Einstein ever made about Mach's philosophical positions [E34]. In 1922 he expressed himself as follows before a gathering of philosophers. 'Mach's system [consists of] the study of relations which exist between experimental data; according to Mach, science is the totality of these relations. That is a bad point of view; in effect, what Mach made was a catalog and not a system. Mach was as good at mechanics as he was wretched at philosophy.* This short-sighted view of science led him to reject the existence of atoms. It is possible that Mach's opinion would be different if he were alive today' [E35]. His negative opinion of Mach's philosophy changed as little during his later years as did his admiration for Mach's mechanics. Just before his death,

> Einstein said he had always believed that the invention of scientific concepts and the building of theories upon them was one of the creative properties of the human mind. His own view was thus opposed to Mach, because Mach assumed that the laws of science were only an economical way of describing a large collection of facts. [C2]**

---

*'Autant Mach fut un bon méchanicien, autant il fut un déplorable philosophe.'

**In his autobiographical sketch, Einstein mentioned that the critical reasoning required for his discovery of special relativity was decisively furthered by his reading of Mach's philosophical writings [E27]. I would venture to guess that at this point Einstein had once again Mach's mechanics in mind.

The third theme, Mach's conjecture on the dynamic origins of inertia, leads us to Einstein's work on cosmology.

2. Einstein and Mach's Principle.   The central innovation in Mach's mechanics is the abolition of absolute space in the formulation of the law of inertia. Write this law as: A system on which no forces act is either at rest or in uniform motion relative to xxx. Then

xxx =	absolute space	Newton
xxx =	the fixed stars	
	idealized as a	
	rigid system	Mach

'When . . . we say that a body preserves unchanged its direction and velocity *in space,* our assertion is nothing more or less than an abbreviated reference to *the entire universe*' [M10]. Those are Mach's words and italics. He argued further that the reference to the entire universe could be restricted to the heavy bodies at large distances which make up the fixed stars idealized as a rigid system, since the relative motion of the body with regard to nearby bodies averages out to zero.

Mach goes on to raise a new question.* Newton's law of inertia refers to motions that are uniform relative to an absolute space; this law is a *kinematic first principle.* By contrast, his own version of the law of inertia refers to motions of bodies relative to the fixed stars. Should one not seek a *dynamic explanation* of such motions, just as one explains dynamically the planetary orbits by means of gravitational dynamics or the relative motion of electrically-charged particles by means of electrodynamics? These are not Mach's own words. However, this dynamic view is implicit in his query: 'What would become of the law of inertia if the whole of the heavens began to move and the stars swarmed in confusion? How would we apply it then? How would it be expressed then? . . . Only in the case of a shattering of the universe [do] we learn that *all bodies* [his italics] each with its share are of importance in the law of inertia' [M11]. We do not find in Mach's book *how* this importance of all bodies manifests itself; he never proposed an explicit dynamic scheme for his new interpretation of the law of inertia. Mach invented Mach's law of inertia, not Mach's principle. Reading his discourse on inertia is not unlike reading the Holy Scriptures. The text is lucid but one senses, perhaps correctly, perhaps wrongly, a deeper meaning behind the words. Let us see how Einstein read Mach.

Soon after Einstein arrived in Prague and broke his long silence on gravitation, he published a short note entitled 'Does There Exist a Gravitational Action Analogous to the Electrodynamical Induction Effect?' [E36]. In this paper (based on the rudimentary gravitation theory of the Prague days), he showed that if a hollow, massive sphere is accelerated around an axis passing through its center, then the inertial mass of a mass point located at the sphere's center is increased, an effect which foreshadows the Lense–Thirring effect [T6].

*See also [H11].

Enter Mach.

In this note Einstein declared, 'This [conclusion] lends plausibility to the conjecture that the *total* inertia of a mass point is an effect due to the presence of all other masses, due to a sort of interaction with the latter. . . . This is just the point of view asserted by Mach in his penetrating investigations on this subject.' From that time on, similar references to Mach are recurrent. In the Einstein–Grossmann paper we read of 'Mach's bold idea that inertia originates in the interaction of [a given] mass point with all other [masses]' [E37]. In June 1913, Einstein wrote to Mach about the induction effect as well as about the bending of light, adding that, if these effects were found, it would be 'a brilliant confirmation of your ingenious investigations on the foundations of mechanics' [E38]. In his Vienna lecture given in the fall of 1913, Einstein referred again to Mach's view of inertia and named it 'the hypothesis of the relativity of inertia' [E39]. He mentioned neither this hypothesis nor the problem of inertia in any of his subsequent articles until February 1917, when he submitted a paper [E40] which once again marks the beginning of a new chapter in physics: general relativistic cosmology.

A few days before presenting this paper to the Prussian Academy, Einstein had written to Ehrenfest, 'I have . . . again perpetrated something about gravitation theory which somewhat exposes me to the danger of being confined in a madhouse' [E41]. In the paper itself, he mentions the 'indirect and bumpy road' he had followed to arrive at the first cosmological model of the new era, an isotropic, homogeneous, unbounded, but spatially finite static universe. It must have taken him a relatively long time to formulate this theory, since already in September 1916 de Sitter mentions a conversation with Einstein about the possibility 'of an entirely material origin of inertia' and the implementation of this idea in terms of 'a world which of necessity must be finite' [S12].

Einstein's paper is no doubt motivated by Machian ideas. However, he begins with a re-analysis of another problem, the difficulties with a static Newtonian universe.* He remarked that the Newton–Poisson equation

$$\Delta\phi = 4\pi G\rho \qquad (15.17)$$

permits only (average) mass densities ρ which tend to zero faster than $1/r^2$ for $r \rightarrow \infty$, since otherwise the gravitational potential would be infinite and the force on a particle due to all the masses in the universe undetermined. (He realized soon afterward that this reasoning is incorrect [E41a].) He also argued that even if ϕ remains finite for large r, there still are difficulties. For it is still impossible to have a Boltzmann equilibrium distribution of stars as long as the total stellar energy is larger than the energy needed to expel stars one by one to infinity as the result of collisions with other stars during the infinite time the universe has lived. On the other hand (he notes), if Eq. 15.17 is replaced by

$$\Delta\phi - \lambda\phi = 4\pi G\rho \qquad (15.18)$$

*For details and references to cosmology in the nineteenth century, see especially [P7] and [N6]. For broader historial reviews, see [M1] and [M12].

(a proposal which again has nineteenth century origins), where ρ is a uniform density, then the solution

$$\phi = -\frac{4\pi G}{\lambda}\rho \tag{15.19}$$

is dynamically acceptable.

Is it also physically acceptable? Constant ρ means an isotropic, homogeneous universe. In 1917 the universe was supposed to consist of our galaxy and presumably a void beyond. The Andromeda nebula had not yet been certified to lie beyond the Milky Way. Today an individual galaxy is considered as a local disturbance of a distribution which is indeed isotropic and homogeneous, to a degree which itself demands explanation [S13]. Einstein had no such physical grounds for assuming these two properties—except for the fact that, he believed, they led to the first realization of the relativity of inertia in the model he was about to unveil. That this model is of the static variety is natural for its time. In 1917 no large-scale galactic motions were yet known to exist.

Let us return to the transition from Eq. 15.17 to Eq. 15.18. There are three main points in Einstein's paper. First, he performs the very same transition in general relativity, that is, he replaces

$$R_{\mu\nu} - \tfrac{1}{2}g_{\mu\nu}R = -\kappa T_{\mu\nu} \tag{15.20}$$

by

$$R_{\mu\nu} - \tfrac{1}{2}g_{\mu\nu}R - \lambda g_{\mu\nu} = -\kappa T_{\mu\nu} \tag{15.21}$$

Second, he constructs a solution of Eq. 15.21 that resolves the conundrum of the Newtonian infinite. Third, he proposes a dynamic realization of the relativity of inertia. His solution, the Einsteinian universe, had to be abolished in later years. It will nevertheless be remembered as the first serious proposal for a novel topology of the world at large. Let us see how he came to it.

Einstein had applied Eq. 15.20 with great success to the motion of planets, assuming that far away from their orbits the metric is flat. Now he argued that there are two reasons why this boundary condition is unsatisfactory for the universe at large. First, the old problem of the Newtonian infinite remains. Second— and here Mach enters—the flatness condition implies that 'the inertia [of a body] is *influenced* by matter (at finite distances) but *not determined* by it [his italics]. If only a single mass point existed it would have inertia . . . [but] in a consistent relativity theory there cannot be inertia relative to "space" but only inertia of masses relative to each other.' Thus Einstein began to give concrete form to Mach's ideas: since the $g_{\mu\nu}$ determine the inertial action, they should, in turn, be *completely* determined by the mass distribution in the universe. He saw no way of using Eq. 15.20 and meeting this desideratum. Equation 15.21, on the other hand, did provide the answer, it seemed to him,* in terms of the following solution ($i,k = 1, 2, 3$):

*He also noted that this equation preserves the conservation laws, since $g_{\mu\nu;\rho} = 0$.

$$g_{ik} = \delta_{ik} + \frac{x_i x_k}{r^2 - \sum_i x_i^2} \qquad g_{i4} = 0, \quad g_{44} = -1 \qquad (15.22)$$

provided that

$$\lambda = \frac{1}{r^2} = 1/2\,\kappa\rho c^2 = \frac{4\pi G\rho}{c^2} \qquad (15.23)$$

where ρ is a constant mass density. In this Einsteinian universe, the Newtonian infinite no longer causes problems because it has been abolished; three-dimensional space is spherically bounded and has a time-independent curvature. Moreover, if there is no matter, then there is no inertia, that is, *for nonzero* λ, Eq. 15.21 cannot be satisfied if $\rho = 0$. Of course, this solution did not specifically associate inertia with the distant stars, but it seemed a good beginning.

So strongly did Einstein believe at that time in the relativity of inertia that in 1918 he stated as being on equal footing three principles on which a satisfactory theory of gravitation should rest [E42]:

1. The principle of relativity as expressed by general covariance
2. The principle of equivalence
3. Mach's principle (the first time this term entered the literature): 'Das G-Feld ist *restlos* durch die Massen der Körper bestimmt,' that is, the $g_{\mu\nu}$ are completely determined by the mass of bodies, more generally by $T_{\mu\nu}$. In 1922, Einstein noted that others were satisfied to proceed without this criterion and added, 'This contentedness will appear incomprehensible to a later generation, however' [E42a].

In later years, Einstein's enthusiasm for Mach's principle waned and finally vanished. I conclude with a brief chronology of his subsequent involvement with cosmology.

1917. Einstein never said so explicitly, but it seems reasonable to assume that he had in mind that the correct equations should have no solutions at all in the absence of matter. However, right after his paper appeared, de Sitter did find a solution of Eq. 15.21 with $\rho = 0$ [S14, W19]. Thus the cosmological term $\lambda g_{\mu\nu}$ does not prevent the occurrence of 'inertia relative to space.' Einstein must have been disappointed. In 1918 he looked for ways to rule out the de Sitter solution [E42b], but soon realized that there is nothing wrong with it.

1919. Einstein suggests [E43] that perhaps electrically-charged particles are held together by gravitational forces. He starts from Eq. 15.21, assumes that $T_{\mu\nu}$ is due purely to electromagnetism so that $T_\mu^\mu = 0$, and notes that this yields the trace condition $\lambda = R/4$. Thus electromagnetism constrains gravitation. This idea may be considered Einstein's first attempt at a unified field theory. In 1927 he wrote a further short note on the mathematical properties of this model [E44]. Otherwise, as is not unusual for him in his later years, a thought comes, is mentioned in print, and then vanishes without a trace.

1922. Friedmann shows that Eq. 15.20 admits nonstatic solutions with isotropic, homogeneous matter distributions, corresponding to an expanding universe
[F1]. Einstein first believes the reasoning is incorrect [E45], then finds an error
in his own objection [E46] and calls the new results 'clarifying.'

1923. Weyl and Eddington find that test particles recede from each other in
the de Sitter world. This leads Einstein to write to Weyl, 'If there is no quasi-
static world, then away with the cosmological term' [E47].

1931. Referring to the theoretical work by Friedmann, 'which was not influenced by experimental facts' and the experimental discoveries of Hubble, 'which
the general theory of relativity can account for in an unforced way, namely, without a λ term' Einstein formally abandons the cosmological term, which is 'theoretically unsatisfactory anyway' [E48]. In 1932, he and de Sitter jointly make a
similar statement [E49]. He never uses the λ term again [E50].

1954. Einstein writes to a colleague, 'Von dem Mach'schen Prinzip sollte
man eigentlich überhaupt nicht mehr sprechen,' As a matter of fact, one should
no longer speak of Mach's principle at all [E51].

It was to be otherwise. After Einstein, the Mach principle faded but never died.
In the post-Einsteinian era of revitalized interest in general relativity, it has
become an important topic of research. At GR9, a discussion group debated the
issue, in particular what one has to understand by this principle. This question
can arouse passion. I am told that the *Zeitschrift für Physik* no longer accepts
papers on general relativity on the grounds that articles on Mach's principle pro-
voke too many polemical replies. At stake is, for example, whether a theory is then
acceptable only if it incorporates this principle as a fundamental requirement (as
Einstein had in mind in 1918) or whether this principle should be a criterion for
the selection of solutions within a theory that also has non-Machian solutions.* It
must be said that, as far as I can see, to this day Mach's principle has not brought
physics decisively farther. It must also be said that the origin of inertia is and
remains *the* most obscure subject in the theory of particles and fields. Mach's principle may therefore have a future—but not without quantum theory.

15f. Singularities; the Problem of Motion

In 1917 Einstein wrote to Weyl, 'The question whether the electron is to be
treated as a singular point, whether true singularities are at all admissible in the
physical description, is of great interest. In the Maxwell theory one decided on a
finite radius in order to explain the finite inertia of the electron' [E52]. Probably
already then, certainly later, there was no doubt in his mind (except for one brief

---

*For a detailed review of the various versions of the principle and a survey of the literature, see
[G1].

interlude) what the answer to this question was: singularities are anathema. His belief in the inadmissibility of singularities was so deeply rooted that it drove him to publish a paper purporting to show that 'the "Schwarzschild singularity" [at $r = 2GM/c^2$] does not appear [in nature] for the reason that matter cannot be concentrated arbitrarily ... because otherwise the constituting particles would reach the velocity of light' [E53].* This paper was submitted in 1939, two months before Oppenheimer and Snyder submitted theirs on stellar collapse [O3]. Unfortunately, I do not know how Einstein reacted to that paper. As to the big bang, Einstein's last words on that subject were, 'One may ... not assume the validity of the equations for very high density of field and matter, and one may not conclude that the "beginning of expansion" must mean a singularity in the mathematical sense' [E54]. He may very well be right in this.

The scientific task which Einstein set himself in his later years is based on three desiderata, all of them vitally important to him: to unify gravitation and electromagnetism, to derive quantum physics from an underlying causal theory, and to describe particles as singularity-free solutions of continuous fields. I add a comment on this last point (unified field theory and quantum theory will be discussed in later chapters). As Einstein saw it, Maxwell's introduction of the field concept was a revolutionary advance which, however, did not go far enough. It was his belief that, also, in the description of the sources of the electromagnetic field, and other fields, all reference to the Newtonian mechanical world picture should be eradicated. In 1931 he expressed this view in these words:

> In [electrodynamics], the continuous field [appears] side by side with the material particle [the source] as the representative of physical reality. This dualism, though disturbing to any systematic mind, has today not yet disappeared. Since Maxwell's time, physical reality has been thought of as [being] represented by continuous fields, governed by partial differential equations, and not capable of any mechanical interpretation. . . . It must be confessed that the complete realization of the program contained in this idea has so far by no means been attained. The successful physical systems that have been set up since then represent rather a compromise between these two programs [Newton's and Maxwell's], and it is precisely this character of compromise that stamps them as temporary and logically incomplete, even though in their separate domains they have led to great advances. [E55]

That is the clearest expression I know of Einstein's profound belief in a description of the world exclusively in terms of everywhere-continuous fields.

There was a brief period, however, during which Einstein thought that singularities might be inevitable. That was around 1927, when he wrote, 'All attempts

---

*Actually, the singularity at the Schwarzschild radius is not an intrinsic singularity. It was shown later that the Schwarzschild solution is a two-sheeted manifold that is analytically complete except at $r = 0$. Two-sheetedness was first introduced in 1935 by Einstein and Rosen [E53a], who believed, however, that the singularity at $r = 2GM/c^2$ is intrinsic.

290 RELATIVITY, THE GENERAL THEORY

of recent years to explain the elementary particles of nature by means of continuous fields have failed. The suspicion that this is not the correct way of conceiving material particles has become very strong in us after very many failed attempts, about which we do not wish to speak here. Thus, one is forced into the direction of conceiving of elementary particles as singular points or world lines. . . . We are led to a way of thinking in which it is supposed that there are no field variables other than the gravitational and the electromagnetic field (with the possible exception of the 'cosmological term' [!]); instead one assumes that singular world lines exist' [E56]. These phrases are found in a paper, prepared with Jacob Grommer, in which Einstein made his first contribution to the problem of motion. Let us recall what that problem is.

Our knowledge of the left-hand side of the gravitational equations (Eq. 15.20) is complete: $R_{\mu\nu}$ and R are known functions of the $g_{\mu\nu}$ and their derivatives and of nothing else. To this day, our knowledge of the right-hand side, the source $T_{\mu\nu}$, is flimsy. However, the left-hand side satisfies the identities Eq. 15.4. This piece of *purely gravitational information* implies that $T^{\mu\nu}_{;\nu} = 0$. Thus general relativity brings a new perspective to energy–momentum conservation: gravitation *alone* constrains its own sources to satisfy these laws. Consider now, as the simplest instance of such a source, a structureless point particle, a gravitational monopole. Its motion is necessarily constrained by $T^{\mu\nu}_{;\nu} = 0$. Question: In view of these constraints, which are of gravitational origin, does the equation of motion of the source follow from the gravitational field equations alone? In other words, was the separate postulate of geodesic motion, already introduced by Einstein in 1914, unnecessary? Einstein and Grommer showed that this is indeed true for the case of a weak external gravitational field.

A few weeks later, Weyl wrote to Einstein, thanking him for the opportunity to see the galley proofs of his new paper and 'for the support [this paper] gives to my old idea about matter' [W20], adding a reference to an article he had written in 1922 [W21] in which similar conclusions had been reached. Indeed, as was discussed in particular by Havas [H12],* Einstein was one of the independent originators of the problem of motion, but neither the only nor the first one.

Einstein's reply to Weyl is especially interesting because it adds to our understanding of his interest in this problem at that time. 'I attach so much value to the whole business because it would be very important to know whether or not the field equations as such are disproved by the established facts about the quanta [Quantenthatsachen]' [E58]. Recall that we are in 1927, shortly after the discoveries by Heisenberg and Schroedinger.

Einstein's last important contribution to general relativity deals again with the problem of motion. It is the work done with Leopold Infeld and Banesh Hoffmann

---

*Havas's paper, which also contains a simple derivation of the Einstein–Grommer result, is one of several important articles on the problem of motion in modern guise found in a volume edited by J. Ehlers [E57].

on the N-body problem of motion [E59, E60]. In these papers, the gravitational field is no longer treated as external. Instead, it and the motion of its (singular) sources are treated simultaneously. A new approximation scheme is introduced in which the fields are no longer necessarily weak but in which the source velocities are small compared with the light velocity. Their results are not new; the same or nearly the same results were obtained much earlier by Lorentz and Droste, de Sitter, Fock, and Levi-Civita (P. Havas, private communication). The equations obtained have found use in situations where Newtonian interaction must be included. '[These equations] are widely used in analyses of planetary orbits in the solar system. For example, the Cal Tech Jet Propulsion Laboratory uses them, in modified form, to calculate ephemerides for high-precision tracking of planets and spacecraft' [M13].

In his report to GR9 on the problem of motion, Ehlers stressed the difficulties of defining isolated systems in general relativity and the need not to treat the problem of motion as an isolated question. Rather, the problem should be linked with other issues, such as the description of extended bodies and gravitational radiation (see also [E61]).* A particle physicist might like to add that the problem of motion should perhaps not be dissociated from the fact that a body has a Compton wavelength, a parameter of little interest for big things—and vice versa.

15g. What Else Was New at GR9?

The program of GR9 showed that all the topics discussed in the preceding sections continue to be of intense interest. I conclude by listing other subjects discussed at that meeting. Exact solutions are now examined by new analytic methods as well as by computer studies. Other classical interests include the important Cauchy problem.** Current experimental results (notably the huge precession of the periastron of PSR 1913 + 16) and future terrestrial and planetary experiments were discussed, with refined tests of general relativity in mind. There was a debate on relativistic thermodynamics, a controversial subject to this day. There were reports on the fundamental advances of our understanding regarding the general structure of relativity theory, with special reference to singularity theorems, black holes, and cosmic censorship. We were told that the best of all possible universes is still the Friedmann universe, not only in our epoch but since time began. These beginnings (especially the earliest fraction of a second) were reviewed with reference to bary-

---

*For example, it so happens that in the approximation defined by Eqs. 15.11–15.14, sources move with constant velocity (!) [E57].

**Mme Y. Choquet-Bruhat told me that Einstein did not show much interest in this problem when she once discussed it with him.

on asymmetries in the universe. There were discussions on the neutrino contents of the universe and on the $3°K$ background radiation.

And there was discussion of quantum mechanics in general relativistic context, not only of Hawking radiation, the important theoretical discovery of the 1970s that particles are steadily created in the background geometry of a black hole, but also of quantum gravity and supergravity. To the listener at this conference, these last two topics, more than anything else, brought home most strikingly how much still remains to be done in general relativity.

References

C1. C. Caves, K. Thorne, R. Draver, V. Sandberg, and M. Zimmerman, *Rev. Mod. Phys.* **52,** 341 (1980).

C2. I. B. Cohen, *Sci. Amer.,* July 1955, p. 69.

D1. A. Dick, *Elem. Math. Beiheft* 13 (1970).

E1. A. Einstein, *PAW,* 1915, p. 831.

E2. ——, *The Origins of the General Theory of Relativity.* Jackson, Wylie, Glasgow, 1933.

E3. P. Ehrenfest, letter to H. A. Lorentz, December 23, 1915.

E4. ——, letters to H. A. Lorentz, January 12 and 13, 1916.

E5. A. Einstein, letter to H. A. Lorentz, January 17, 1916.

E6. ——, *AdP* **49,** 769 (1916).

E7. ——, *Die Grundlage der Allgemeinen Relativitätstheorie.* Barth, Leipzig, 1916.

E8. —— and H. Minkowski, *The Principle of Relativity* (M. N. Saha and S. N. Bose, Trans.). University of Calcutta, Calcutta, 1920.

E8a. ——, *Uber die Spezielle und die Allgemeine Relativitätstheorie Gemeinverständlich.* Vieweg, Braunschweig, 1917.

E9. ——, letter to H. A. Lorentz, January 1, 1916.

E10. ——, *Forum Phil.* **1,** 173 (1930).

E11. ——, *The Yale University Library Gazette* **6,** 3 (1930).

E12. ——, *Die Quelle* **82,** 440 (1932).

E12a. A. S. Eddington, *Space, Time and Gravitation,* p. 134. Cambridge University Press, Cambridge, 1920.

E12b. A. Einstein, *Science* **84,** 506 (1936).

E13. ——, *PAW,* 1914, p. 1030, Sec. 13.

E14. ——, *PAW,* 1915, p. 778.

E15. ——, *PAW,* 1915, p. 844.

E16. ——, *PAW,* 1916, p. 1111.

E17. A. Eddington, [E12a], p. 209.

E18. A. Eddington, *Espace, Temps et Gravitation,* Partie Théorique, p. 89. Hermann,

E18. A. Eddington, *Espace, Temps et Gravitation,* p. 89. Hermann, Paris, 1921.

E19. A. Einstein, letter to *The New York Times,* May 4, 1935.

E19a. ——, *Phys. Zeitschr.* **19,** 115, 165 (1918).

E19b. ——, *PAW,* 1918, p. 448.

E20. *PAW,* 1916, p. 688.

E21. ——, *Verh. Deutsch. Phys. Ges.* **18,** 318 (1916); *Mitt. Phys. Ges. Zürich* **16,** 47 (1916).

E22. ——, *PAW,* 1918, p. 154.

E23. —— and N. Rosen, *J. Franklin Inst.* **223,** 43 (1937).

E24. A. S. Eddington, *The Mathematical Theory of Relativity* (2nd edn.), p. 130. Cambridge University Press, Cambridge, 1960.

E25. J. Ehlers, A Rosenblum, J. Goldberg, and P. Havas, *Astrophys. J.* **208,** L77 (1976).

E26. A. Einstein, *Naturw.* **17,** 101 (1916).

E27. —— in *Albert Einstein: Philosopher–Scientist* (P. Schilpp, Ed.), p. 21. Tudor, New York, 1949.

E28. ——, letter to M. Besso, March 6, 1952; *EB,* p. 464.

E29. ——, letter to E. Mach, August 9, 1909.

E30. ——, letter to E. Mach, August 17, 1909.

E31. ——, *PAW,* 1916, p. 98.

E32. ——, letter to E. Mach, undated, around January 1913.

E33. ——, letter to A. Weiner, September 18, 1930.

E34. ——, letter to C. B. Weinberg, December 1, 1937.

E35. ——, *Bull. Soc. Fran. Phil.* **22,** 91 (1922); see also *Nature* **112,** 253 (1923).

E36. ——, *Viertelj. Schrift Ger. Medizin* **44,** 37 (1912).

E37. —— and M. Grossmann, *Z. Math. Physik.* **62,** 225, (1914) see p. 228; also, A. Einstein, *Viertelj. Schrift. Naturf. Ges. Zürich* **59,** 4 (1914).

E38. ——, letter to E. Mach, June 25, 1913.

E39. ——, *Phys. Zeitschr.* **14,** 1249 (1913), Sec. 9.

E40. ——, *PAW,* 1917, p. 142.

E41. ——, letter to P. Ehrenfest, February 4, 1917.

E41a. ——, letters to M. Besso, December 1916, August 20, 1918; *EB,* pp. 96, 134.

E42. ——, *AdP* **55,** 241 (1918); also, *Naturw.* **8,** 1010 (1920).

E42a. ——, *AdP* **69,** 436 (1922).

E42b. ——, *PAW,* 1918, p. 270.

E43. ——, *PAW,* 1919, pp. 349, 463.

E44. ——, *Math. Ann.* **97,** 99 (1927).

E45. ——, *Z. Phys.* **11,** 326 (1922).

E46. ——, *Z. Phys.* **16,** 228 (1923).

E47. ——, letter to H. Weyl, May 23, 1923.

E48. ——, *PAW,* 1931, p. 235.

E49. —— and W. De Sitter, *Proc. Nat. Ac. Sci.* **18,** 213 (1932).

E50. ——, *The Meaning of Relativity* (5th edn.), p. 127. Princeton University Press, Princeton, N.J., 1955.

E51. ——, letter to F. Pirani, February 2, 1954; also, D. Sciama in [W3], p. 396.

E52. ——, letter to H. Weyl, January 3, 1917.

E53. ——, *Ann. Math.* **40,** 922 (1939).

E53a. —— and N. Rosen, *Phys. Rev.* **48,** 73 (1935).

E54. [E50] p. 129.

E55. —— in *James Clerk Maxwell,* p. 66. Macmillan, New York, 1931.

E56. —— and J. Grommer, *PAW,* 1927, p. 2.

E57. J. Ehlers (Ed.), *Isolated Gravitating Systems,* Varenna Lectures, Vol 67. Societa Italiana di Fisica, Bologna, 1979.

E58. A. Einstein, letter to H. Weyl, April 26, 1927.

E59. ——, L. Infeld and B. Hoffmann, *Ann Math.* **39,** 65 (1938).

E60. —— and ——, *Ann Math.* **41,** 455 (1940).

E61. J. Ehlers, *Ann N.Y. Ac. Sci.* **336,** 279 (1980).

F1. A. Friedmann, *Z. Phys.* **10,** 377 (1922).

G1. H. F. Goenner, in *Grundlagenproblemen der modernen Physik*, BI Verlag, Mannheim, 1981.

H1. S. W. Hawking and W. Israel (Eds.), *General Relativity, an Einstein Century Survey*. Cambridge University Press, Cambridge, 1979.

H2. A. Held (Ed.), *General Relativity and Gravitation*. Plenum Press, New York, 1980.

H3. E. P. Hubble, *Astrophys. J.* **62,** 409 (1925); **63,** 236 (1926); **64,** 321 (1926).

H3a. ——, *Proc. Nat. Ac. Sci.* **15,** 169 (1929).

H4. D. Hilbert, *Goett. Nachr.*, 1915, p. 395.

H5. ——, *Goett. Nachr.*, 1917, p. 53.

H6. ——, [H5], p. 63.

H7. A. E. Harward, *Phil. Mag.* **44,** 380 (1922).

H8. S. W. Hawking and W. Israel, [H1], p. 90.

H9. F. Herneck, *Einstein und Sein Weltbild,* p. 109. Verlag der Morgen, Berlin, 1976.

H10. G. Holton, *Thematic Origins of Scientific Thought,* p. 219. Harvard University Press, Cambridge, Mass., 1973.

H11. H. Hönl, Einstein Symposium 1965, Ak. Verl. Berlin, 1966, p. 238.

H12. P. Havas in *Isolated Systems in General Relativity* (J. Ehlers, Ed.), p. 74. North Holland, Amsterdam, 1979.

J1. G. B. Jeffery, *Phil. Mag.* **43,** 600 (1922).

K1. M. D. Kruskal, *Phys. Rev.* **119,** 1743 (1960).

K2. F. Klein, *Goett. Nachr.,* 1918, p. 71. Reprinted in *Felix Klein, Gesammelte Mathematische Abhandlungen* (R. Fricke and A. Ostrowski, Eds.), Vol. 1, p. 568. Springer, Berlin, 1921.

K3. ——, [K2], Sec. 8, especially footnote 14.

K4. ——, *Goett. Nachr.,* 1917, p. 469. Reprinted in Fricke and Ostrowski, [K2], Vol. 1, p. 553.

L1. T. Levi-Civita, *Rend. Circ. Mat. Palermo* **42,** 173 (1917).

L2. M. Lecat, *Bibliographie de la Relativité*. Lamertin, Brussels, 1924.

L2a. L. D. Landau, *Nature* **141,** 333 (1938).

L3. H. A. Lorentz, letters to P. Ehrenfest, January 10 and 11, 1916.

L4. ——, letter to P. Ehrenfest, January 22, 1916.

L5. L. D. Landau and E. M. Lifshitz, *The Classical Theory of Fields,* (3rd edn.), p. 304. Addison-Wesley, Reading, Mass., 1971.

L6. H. A. Lorentz, *Proc. K. Ak. Amsterdam* **8,** 603 (1900); *Collected Works,* Vol. 5, p. 198. Nyhoff, the Hague, 1937.

M1. M. K. Munitz, *Theories of the Universe,* The Free Press, Glencoe, Ill., 1957.

M2. C. W. Misner, K. S. Thorne, and J. A. Wheeler, *Gravitation.* Freeman, San Francisco, 1973.

M3. J. Mehra, *The Solvay Conferences on Physics,* Chap. 15. Reidel, Boston, 1975.

M4. R. W. Mandl, letter to A. Einstein, May 3, 1936.

M5. ——, letter to A. Einstein, December 18, 1936.

M6. E. Mach, *Die Mechanik in Ihrer Entwicklung, Historisch-Kritisch Dargestellt.*

Brockhaus, Leipzig, 1883. Translated as *The Science of Mechanics* (4th edn.). Open Court, Chicago, 1919.

M7.   ——, [M6], English translation, pp. 542, 543.

M8.   ——, *Phys. Zeitschr.* **11**, 599 (1910).

M9.   ——, *The Principles of Physical Optics,* preface. Methuen, London, 1926.

M10.   ——, [M6], Chap. 2, Sec. 6, Subsec. 7.

M11.   ——, *History and Root of the Principle of the Conservation of Energy* (2nd edn.; P. Jourdain, Tran.), pp. 78, 79. Open Court, Chicago, 1911.

M12.   C. W. Misner et al., [M2], pp. 752–62.

M13.   ——, [M2], p. 1095.

N1.   J. D. North, *The Measure of the Universe.* Oxford University Press, Oxford, 1965.

N2.   ——, [N1], Chap. 7.

N3.   *Nature* **106**, issue of February 17, 1921.

N4.   J. D. North, [N1], Chaps. 8 and 9.

N5.   E. Noether, *Goett. Nachr.,* 1918, pp. 37, 235.

N6.   J. D. North, [N1], Chap. 2.

O1.   J. R. Oppenheimer and R. Serber, *Phys. Rev.* **54**, 540 (1938).

O2.   —— and G. M. Volkoff, *Phys. Rev.* **55**, 374 (1939).

O3.   —— and H. Snyder, *Phys. Rev.* **56**, 455 (1939).

P1.   W. Pauli, 'Relativitätstheorie,' *Encyklopädie der Mathematischen Wissenschaften.* Teubner, Leipzig, 1921.

P2.   ——, *Theory of Relativity* (G. Field, Tran.). Pergamon Press, London, 1958.

P3.   ——, [P1] or [P2], Sec. 54.

P4.   ——, [P1] or [P2], Secs. 23 and 57.

P5.   ——, [P1] or [P2], Sec. 61.

P6.   H. Poincaré, *C. R. Ac. Sci. Paris* **140**, 1504 (1905); *Oeuvres de H. Poincaré,* Vol. 9, p. 489. Gauthier-Villars, Paris, 1954.

P7.   W. Pauli, [P1] or [P2], Sec. 62.

R1.   H. P. Robertson, *Rev. Mod. Phys.* **5**, 62 (1933).

R2.   A. Rosenblum, *Phys. Rev. Lett.* **41**, 1003 (1978).

S1.   L. S. Shepley and A. A. Strassenberg, *Cosmology.* AAPT, Stony Brook, N.Y., 1979.

S2.   L. L. Smarr (Ed.), *Sources of Gravitational Radiation.* Cambridge University Press, Cambridge, 1979.

S3.   G. Shaviv and J. Rosen (Eds.), *Relativity and Gravitation.* Wiley, New York, 1975.

S4.   G. Szekeres, *Pub. Mat. Debrecen.* **7**, 285 (1960).

S5.   D. W. Sciama letter to A. Pais, October 16, 1979.

S6.   I. I. Shapiro, [W3], p. 115.

S6a.   N. Sanitt, *Nature* **234**, 199 (1971).

S7.   A. Sommerfeld (Ed.), *The Principle of Relativity.* Dover, New York.

S8.   J. Schouten, *Ricci-Calculus* (2nd edn.), p. 146. Springer, Berlin, 1954.

S9.   —— and D. J. Struik, *Phil. Mag.* **47**, 584 (1924).

S10.   R. Schoen and S. T. Yau, *Phys. Rev. Lett.* **43**, 1457 (1979).

S11.   Se, p. 98.

S12.   W. de Sitter, *Proc. K. Ak. Amsterdam* **19**, 527 (1917), footnote on pp. 531, 532.

S13. D. Sciama, [W3], p. 387.

S14. W. de Sitter, *Proc. K. Ak. Amsterdam* **19,** 1217 (1917); **20,** 229 (1917).

T1. R. C. Tolman, *Phys. Rev.* **55,** 364 (1939).

T2. A. Trautman in *Gravitation* (L. Witten, Ed.), p. 169. Wiley, New York, 1962.

T3. K. Thorne, *Rev. Mod. Phys.* **52,** 285 (1980).

T4. ——, *Rev. Mod. Phys.* **52,** 299 (1980).

T5. ——, *Rev. Mod. Phys.* **52,** 290 (1980).

T6. H. Thirring and J. Lense *Phys. Z.* **19,** 156 (1918).

W1. H. Weyl, *Space, Time and Matter* (H. L. Brose, Tran.). Dover, New York, 1951.

W2. S. Weinberg, *Gravitation and Cosmology.* Wiley, New York, 1972.

W3. H. Woolf (Ed.), *Some Strangeness in the Proportion.* Addison-Wesley, Reading, Mass., 1980.

W4. S. Weinberg, [W2], Chap. 14, Sec. 5.

W5. J. A. Wheeler, *Am. Scholar* **37,** 248 (1968); *Am. Scientist* **56,** 1 (1968).

W6. S. Weinberg, [W2], p. 297.

W7. D. T. Wilkinson, [W3], p. 137.

W8. C. M. Will, [H1], Chap. 2.

W8a. D. Walsh, R. F. Carswell, and R. J. Weymann, *Nature* **279,** 381 (1979).

W9. H. Weyl, *Scripta Math.* **3,** 201 (1935).

W10. ——, *AdP* **54,** 117 (1917).

W11. S. Weinberg, [W2], Chap. 12, Secs. 3 and 4.

W12. ——, [W2], Chap. 9, Sec. 8.

W13. E. Witten, *Comm. Math. Phys.* **80,** 381 (1981); see further R. Schoen and S. T. Yau, *Phys. Rev. Lett.* **48,** 369, 1981; G. T. Horowitz and M. J. Perry, *Phys. Rev. Lett.* **48,** 371, 1981.

W14. J. Weber, *Phys. Rev.* **47,** 306 (1960); *Phys. Rev. Lett.* **22,** 1302 (1969).

W15. —— and J. A. Wheeler, *Rev. Mod. Phys.* **29,** 509 (1957).

W16. M. Walker and C. M. Will, *Phys. Rev. Lett.* **22,** 1741 (1980).

W17. C. M. Will, [H1], Chap. 2.

W18. S. Weinberg, [W2], pp. 16, 17.

W19. See, e.g., [W2], pp. 613ff.

W20. H. Weyl, letter to A. Einstein, February 3, 1927.

W21. ——, addendum to a paper by R. Bach, *Math. Zeitschr.* **13,** 134 (1922).

Y1. P. Young, J. E. Gunn, J. Kristian, J. B. Oke, and J. A. Westphal, *Astrophys. J.* **241,** 507 (1980).

V

THE LATER JOURNEY

16

'The Suddenly Famous
Doctor Einstein'

16a. Illness; Remarriage; Death of Mother

Part IV of this book began with an account of Einstein's arrival in Berlin, his separation from Mileva, his reactions to the First World War, and his earliest activities in the political sphere. This was followed by a description of the final phases in the creation of general relativity. In the previous chapter, Einstein's role in the further development of this theory and its impact on later generations of physicists were discussed. In this chapter, I turn to the impact of general relativity on the world at large, an impact that led to the abrupt emergence of Einstein as a charismatic figure and a focus of awe, reverence, and hatred. I also continue the story, begun in Section 14a, of Einstein's years in Berlin. To begin with, I return to the days just after November 1915, when Einstein completed his work on the foundations of general relativity.

As was mentioned before, in December 1915 Einstein wrote to his friend Besso that he was 'zufrieden aber ziemlich kaputt,' satisfied but rather worn out [E1]. He did not take a rest, however. In 1916 he wrote ten scientific papers, including his first major survey of general relativity, his theory of spontaneous and induced emission, his first paper on gravitational waves, articles on the energy–momentum conservation laws and on the Schwarzschild solution, and a new proposal for measuring the Einstein–de Haas effect. He also completed his first semipopular book on relativity. Too much exertion combined with a lack of proper care must have been the chief cause of a period of illness that began sometime in 1917 and lasted several years.

I do not know precisely when this period began, but in February 1917 Einstein wrote to Ehrenfest that he would not be able to visit Holland because of a liver ailment that had forced him to observe a severe diet and to lead a very quiet life [E2]. That quiet life did not prevent him from writing the founding paper on general relativistic cosmology in that same month. Lorentz expressed regret that Einstein could not come; however, he wrote, 'After the strenuous work of recent years, you deserve a rest' [L1]. Einstein's reply shows that his indisposition was not a trivial matter. He mentioned that he could get proper nourishment because of the connections that his family in Berlin maintained with relatives in southern

Germany and added, 'Without this help it would hardly be possible for me to stay here; nor do I know if things can continue the way they are' [E3]. As a Swiss citizen, he was entitled to and did receive food parcels from Switzerland [E4], but that was evidently not enough to compensate for the food shortages in Berlin caused by the war. He did not follow the advice of his doctor, who had urged him to recuperate in Switzerland [E5].

At that stage Elsa Einstein Löwenthal took matters in hand. Elsa, born in 1876 in Hechingen in Hohenzollern, was both a first and a second cousin of Albert's. Rudolf, her father, was a first cousin of Hermann, Albert's father. Fanny, her mother, was a sister of Pauline, Albert's mother. Elsa and Albert had known each other since childhood, when Elsa would visit the relatives in Munich and Albert would come to Hechingen. They had grown fond of each other. In her early twenties, Elsa married a merchant named Löwenthal, by whom she had two daughters, Ilse (b. 1897) and Margot (b. 1899). This brief marriage ended in divorce. When Einstein arrived in Berlin, Elsa and her daughters were living in an upper-floor apartment on Haberlandstrasse No. 5. Her parents lived on lower floors in the same building. Elsa's presence in Berlin had been one of the factors drawing Einstein to that city.

It was principally Elsa who took care of her cousin during his illness. In the summer of 1917, Einstein moved from the Wittelsbacherstrasse to an apartment next to Elsa's. In September he invited Besso to visit him in his spacious and comfortable new quarters [E6]. In December, he wrote to Zangger that he felt much better. 'I have gained four pounds since last summer, thanks to Elsa's good care. She herself cooks everything for me, since this has turned out to be necessary' [E7]. However, he still had to maintain a strict diet and was never sure that severe pains might not return [E8].

Toward the end of the year, his health worsened. It turned out that he was suffering from a stomach ulcer [E9, E10]. For the next several months, he had to stay in bed [E10]. His feelings were at a low ebb: 'The spirit turns lame, the strength diminishes' [E11]. While bedridden, he derived the quadrupole formula for gravitational radiation. In April 1918 he was permitted to go out, but still had to be careful. 'Recently I had a nasty attack, which was obviously caused only because I played the violin for an hour' [E10]. In May he was in bed again, this time with jaundice [E12], but completed a fundamental paper on the pseudotensor of energy–momentum. His dream (in August [E13]) that he had cut his throat with a shaving knife may or may not have been a reaction to his state of health. In November he published an article on the twin paradox. In December he wrote to Ehrenfest that he would never quite regain his full health [E14].

By that time, Albert and Elsa had decided to get married, and therefore Einstein had to institute procedures to obtain a divorce from Mileva [E15]. The divorce decree was issued on February 14, 1919. It stipulated that Mileva would receive, in due course, Einstein's Nobel prize money.*

---

*See further Chapter 30.

Mileva remained in Zürich for the rest of her life. Initially she took on her own family name, Marity, but by decree of the cantonal government of Zürich dated December 24, 1924, she was given permission to revert to the name Einstein. On occasional visits to his children, Einstein would stay in her home. She was a difficult woman, distrustful of other people and given to spells of melancholy. (Her sister Zorka suffered from severe mental illness.) She died in 1948. Some years thereafter Einstein wrote of her, 'She never reconciled herself to the separation and the divorce, and a disposition developed reminiscent of the classical example of Medea. This darkened the relations to my two boys, to whom I was attached with tenderness. This tragic aspect of my life continued undiminished until my advanced age' [E16].

Albert and Elsa were married on June 2, 1919. He was forty, she forty-three. They made their home in Elsa's apartment, to which were added two rooms on the floor above, which served as Einstein's quarters for study and repose. On occasion, his stomach pain would still flare up [E17], but in 1920 he wrote to Besso that he was in good health and good spirits [E18]. Perhaps the most remarkable characteristic of this period of illness is the absence of any lull in Einstein's scientific activity.

Elsa, gentle, warm, motherly, and prototypically bourgeoise, loved to take care of her Albertle. She gloried in his fame. Charlie Chaplin, who first met her in 1931, described her as follows: 'She was a square-framed woman with abundant vitality; she frankly enjoyed being the wife of the great man and made no attempt to hide the fact; her enthusiasm was endearing' [C1]. The affectionate relationship between her husband and her daughters added to her happiness. Albert, the gypsy, had found a home, and in some ways that did him much good. He very much liked being taken care of and also thoroughly enjoyed receiving people at his apartment—scientists, artists, diplomats, other personal friends. In other ways, however, this life was too much for him. A friend and visitor gave this picture: 'He, who had always had something of the bohemian in him, began to lead a middle-class life . . . in a household such as was typical of a well-to-do Berlin family . . . in the midst of beautiful furniture, carpets, and pictures. . . . When one entered . . . one found Einstein still remained a "foreigner" in such a surrounding— a bohemian guest in a middle-class home' [F1]. Elsa gave a glimpse of their life to another visitor: 'As a little girl, I fell in love with Albert because he played Mozart so beautifully on the violin. . . . He also plays the piano. Music helps him when he is thinking about his theories. He goes to his study, comes back, strikes a few chords on the piano, jots something down, returns to his study. On such days, Margot and I make ourselves scarce. Unseen, we put out something for him to eat and lay out his coat. [Sometimes] he goes out without coat and hat, even when the weather is bad. Then he comes back and stands there on the stairs' [S1]. One does not have a sense of much intimacy between the two. The bedroom next to Elsa's was occupied by her daughters; Albert's was down the hall [H1]. Nor do they appear to have been a couple much given to joint planning and deliberation. 'Albert's will is unfathomable,' Elsa once wrote to Ehrenfest [E19]. In marked contrast to her husband, she was conscious of social standing and others' opinions.*

On various occasions, Einstein would utter asides which expressed his reservations on the bliss attendant on the holy state of matrimony. For example, he was once asked by someone who observed him incessantly cleaning his pipe whether he smoked for the pleasure of smoking or in order to engage in unclogging and refilling his pipe. He replied, 'My aim lies in smoking, but as a result things tend to get clogged up, I'm afraid. Life, too, is like smoking, especially marriage' [I1].

Shortly after Elsa died, in 1936, Einstein wrote to Born, 'I have acclimated extremely well here, live like a bear in its cave, and feel more at home than I ever did in my eventful life. This bearlike quality has increased because of the death of my comrade [Kameradin], who was more attached to people [than I]' [E20]. It was not the only time that Einstein wrote about his family with more frankness than grace [E21].

In March 1955, shortly after the death of his lifelong friend Michele Besso, Einstein wrote to the Besso family, 'What I most admired in him as a human being is the fact that he managed to live for many years not only in peace but also in lasting harmony with a woman—an undertaking in which I twice failed rather disgracefully' [E22].

Half a year after Albert and Elsa were married, his mother came to Berlin to die in her son's home.

Pauline's life had not been easy. After her husband's death in 1902 left her with limited means and no income, she first went to stay with her sister Fanny, in Hechingen. Thereafter she lived for a long period in Heilbron in the home of a widowed banker by the name of Oppenheimer, supervising the running of the household and the education of several young children who adored her. Later she managed for a time the household of her widowed brother Jakob Koch, then moved to Lucerne to stay with her daughter, Maja, and the latter's husband, Paul Winteler, at their home at Brambergstrasse 16a. It was to that address that Einstein sent a newspaper clipping 'for the further nourishment of Mama's anyhow already considerable mother's pride' [E23].

While staying with her daughter, Pauline became gravely ill with abdominal cancer and had to be hospitalized at the Sanatorium Rosenau. Shortly thereafter, she expressed the desire to be with her son. In December 1919, Elsa wrote to Ehrenfest that the mother, now deathly ill, would be transported to Berlin [E24]. Around the beginning of 1920, Pauline arrived, accompanied by Maja, a doctor, and a nurse [E25]. She was bedded down in Einstein's study. Morphine treatments affected her mind, but 'she clings to life and still looks good' [E25]. She

*Frank remarks that she was not popular in Berlin circles [F1].

died in February and was buried in the Schöneberg Cemetery in Berlin. Soon thereafter, Einstein wrote to Zangger, 'My mother has died. . . . We are all completely exhausted. . . . One feels in one's bones the significance of blood ties' [E26].

16b. Einstein Canonized

In the early fall of 1919, when Pauline Einstein was in the sanatorium, she received a postcard from her son which began, 'Dear Mother, joyous news today. H. A. Lorentz telegraphed that the English expeditions have actually demonstrated the deflection of light from the sun' [E27]. The telegram that had announced the news to Einstein a few days earlier read, 'Eddington found star displacement at the sun's edge preliminary between nine-tenth second and double that. Many greetings. Lorentz' [L2]. It was an informal communication. Nothing was definitive. Yet Einstein sent almost at once a very brief note to *Naturwissenschaften* for the sole purpose of reporting the telegram he had received [E28]. He was excited.

Let us briefly recapitulate Einstein's progress in understanding the bending of light. 1907. The clerk at the patent office in Bern discovers the equivalence principle, realizes that this principle by itself implies some bending of light, but believes that the effect is too small to ever be observed. 1911. The professor at Prague finds that the effect *can* be detected for starlight grazing the sun during a total eclipse and finds that the amount of bending in that case is 0″.87. He does not yet know that space is curved and that, therefore, his answer is incorrect. He is still too close to Newton, who believed that space is flat and who could have himself computed the 0″.87 (now called the Newton value) from his law of gravitation and his corpuscular theory of light. 1912. The professor at Zürich discovers that space is curved. Several years pass before he understands that the curvature of space modifies the bending of light. 1915. The member of the Prussian Academy discovers that general relativity implies a bending of light by the sun equal to 1″.74, the Einstein value, twice the Newton value. This factor of 2 sets the stage for a confrontation between Newton and Einstein.

In 1914, before Einstein had the right answer, he had written to Besso with typical confidence. 'I do not doubt any more the correctness of the whole system, whether the observation of the solar eclipse succeeds or not' [E29]. Several quirks of history saved him from the embarrassment of banking on the wrong result. An Argentinian eclipse expedition which had gone to Brazil in 1912 and which had the deflection of light on its experimental program was rained out. In the summer of 1914, a German expedition led by Erwin Freundlich and financed by Gustav Krupp, in a less familiar role of benefactor of humanity, headed for the Crimea to observe the eclipse of August 21. (Russian soldiers and peasants were told by their government not to fear evil omens: the forthcoming eclipse was a natural phenomenon [N1].) When the war broke out, the party was warned in time to return and some did so. Those who hesitated were arrested, eventually returned home safely but of course without results [N2]. Frustration continued also after November 18, 1915, the day on which Einstein announced the right bending of 1″74 [E30]. Ten days later, commenting on a new idea by Freundlich for measuring light bending, Einstein wrote to Sommerfeld, 'Only the intrigues of miserable people prevent the execution of this last, new, important test of the theory,' and, most uncharacteristically, signed his letter 'Your infuriated Einstein,' [E31]. An opportunity to observe an eclipse in Venezuela in 1916 had to be passed up because of the war. Early attempts to seek deflection in photographs taken during past eclipses led nowhere. An American effort to measure the effect during the eclipse of June 1918 never gave conclusive results.* It was not until May 1919 that two British expeditions obtained the first useful photographs and not until November 1919 that their results were formally announced.

English interest in the bending of light developed soon after copies of Einstein's general relativity papers were sent from Holland by de Sitter to Arthur Stanley Eddington at Cambridge (presumably these were the first papers on the theory to reach England). In addition, de Sitter's beautiful essay on the subject, published in June 1916 in the *Observatory* [S2], as well as his three important papers in the *Monthly Notices* [S3] further helped to spread the word. So did a subsequent report by Eddington [E33], who in a communication to the Royal Astronomical Society in February 1917 stressed the importance of the deflection of light [E34]. In March 1917 the Astronomer Royal, Sir Frank Watson Dyson, drew attention to the excellence of the star configuration on May 29, 1919, (another eclipse date) for measuring the alleged deflection, adding that 'Mr Hinks has kindly undertaken to obtain for the Society information of the stations which may be occupied' [D1]. Two expeditions were mounted, one to Sobral in Brazil, led by Andrew Crommelin from the Greenwich Observatory, and one to Principe Island off the coast of Spanish Guinea, led by Eddington. Before departing, Eddington wrote, 'The present eclipse expeditions may for the first time demonstrate the weight of light [i.e., the Newton value]; or they may confirm Einstein's weird theory of non-Euclidean space; or they may lead to a result of yet more far-reaching consequences—no deflection' [E35]. Under the heading 'Stop Press News,' the June issue of the *Observatory* contains the text of two telegrams, one from Sobral: 'Eclipse splendid. Crommelin,' and one from Principe: 'Through cloud. Hopeful. Eddington' [01]. The expeditions returned. Data analysis began.** According to a preliminary report by Eddington to the meeting of the British Association held in Bournemouth on September 9–13, the bending of light lay between 0″87 and double that value. Word reached Lorentz.† Lorentz cabled Einstein, whose excite-

*For many details about all these early efforts, see especially [E32].

**I shall not discuss any details of the actual observations or of the initial analysis of the data and their re-analysis in later years. For these subjects, I refer to several excellent articles [B1, E32, M1].

†The news was brought to Leiden by van der Pol, who had attended the Bournemouth meeting [L3].

ment on receiving this news after seven years of waiting will now be clearer. Then came November 6, 1919, the day on which Einstein was canonized.†

Ever since 1905 Einstein had been *beatus,* having performed two first-class miracles. Now, on November 6, the setting, a joint meeting of the Royal Society and the Royal Astronomical Society, resembled a Congregation of Rites.‡ Dyson acted as postulator, ably assisted by Crommelin and Eddington as advocate-procurators. Dyson, speaking first, concluded his remarks with the statement, 'After a careful study of the plates I am prepared to say that they confirm Einstein's prediction. A very definite result has been obtained, that light is deflected in accordance with Einstein's law of gravitation.' Crommelin added further details. Eddington spoke next, stating that the Principe results supported the figures obtained at Sobral, then reciting the two requisite authentic miracles subsequent to Einstein's elevation to *beatus:* the perihelion of Mercury and the bending of light, $1''.98 \pm 0''.30$ and $1''.61 \pm 0''.30$ as observed in Sobral and Principe, respectively. Ludwick Silberstein,* the *advocatus diaboli,* presented the *animadversiones:* 'It is unscientific to assert for the moment that the deflection, the reality of which I admit, is due to gravitation.' His main objection was the absence of evidence for the red shift: 'If the shift remains unproved as at present, the whole theory collapses.' Pointing to the portrait of Newton which hung in the meeting hall, Silberstein admonished the congregation: 'We owe it to that great man to proceed very carefully in modifying or retouching his Law of Gravitation.'

Joseph John Thomson, O.M., P.R.S., in the chair, having been petitioned *instanter, instantius, instantissime,* pronounced the canonization: 'This is the most important result obtained in connection with the theory of gravitation since Newton's day, and it is fitting that it should be announced at a meeting of the Society so closely connected with him. . . . The result [is] one of the highest achievements of human thought.' A few weeks later he added, 'The deflection of light by matter, suggested by Newton in the first of his Queries, would itself be a result of first-rate scientific importance; it is of still greater importance when its magnitude supports the law of gravity put forward by Einstein' [T1].

Even before November 6, Einstein and others already knew that things looked good.

---

†I find the parallels with the rituals of beatification and canonization compelling, even though they are here applied to a living person. Note that a *beatus* may be honored with public cult by a specified diocese or institution (here, the physicists). A canonized person is honored by unrestricted public cult. For these and other terms used, see [N3].

‡The details of the proceedings quoted here are found in an article in the *Observatory* [O2].

*Silberstein, a native of Poland who moved to England and later settled in the United States, was the author of three books on relativity. On several occasions, he was in dogged but intelligent opposition to relativity theory.

On October 22, Carl Stumpf, a psychologist and fellow member of the Prussian Academy, wrote to Einstein, 'I feel compelled to send you most cordial congratulations on the occasion of the grandiose new success of your gravitation theory. With all our hearts, we share the elation which must fill you and are proud of the fact that, after the military-political collapse, German science has been able to score such a victory . . .' [S4].* On November 3 Einstein replied, 'On my return from Holland I find your congratulations. . . . I recently learned in Leiden that the confirmation found by Eddington is also a complete one quantitatively' [E36]. A few days after the joint meeting of November 6, Lorentz sent another telegram to Einstein, confirming the news [L4]. On November 7, 1919, the Einstein legend began.

16c. The Birth of the Legend

'Armistice and treaty terms/Germans summoned to Paris/Devastated France/ Reconstruction progress/War crimes against Serbia.' These are among the headlines on page 11 of the London *Times* of November 7, 1919. Turning to page 12, one finds that column 1 is headed by 'The glorious dead/King's call to his people/ Armistice day observance/Two minutes pause from work' and column 6 by 'Revolution in science/New theory of the universe/Newtonian ideas overthrown.' Halfway down the column, there is the laconic subheading 'Space warped.' In this London *Times* issue, we find the first report to a world worn by war of the happenings at the meetings of the joint societies the day before. The next day, the same paper published a further article on the same subject headlined 'The revolution in science/Einstein v. Newton/Views of eminent physicists,' in which we read, 'The subject was a lively topic of conversation in the House of Commons yesterday, and Sir Joseph Larmor, F.R.S., M.P. for Cambridge University, . . . said he had been besieged by inquiries as to whether Newton had been cast down and Cambridge "done in."' (Hundreds of people were unable to get near the room when Eddington lectured in Cambridge on the new results [E37].) The news was picked up immediately by the Dutch press [N3a, A1]. Daily papers invited eminent physicists to comment. In his lucid way, Lorentz explained general relativity to the readers of the *Nieuwe Rotterdamsche Courant* of November 19, remarking that 'I cannot refrain from expressing my surprise that according to the report in the [London] *Times* there should be so much complaint about the difficulty of understanding the new theory. It is evident that Einstein's little book *"About the Special and General Theory of Relativity in Plain Terms"* did not find its way into England during wartime.'** On November 23 an article by Max Born enti-

---

*I thank A. Hermann for informing me that in October the Berlin papers were already carrying early reports. An article by Alexander Moszkowski entitled 'Die Sonne bracht' es an den Tag' in the *Berliner Tageblatt* of October 8, 1919, must presumably have been based on information from Einstein himself.

**This article appeared later in translation in *The New York Times* [N4].

REVOLUTION IN SCIENCE.

NEW THEORY OF THE UNIVERSE.

NEWTONIAN IDEAS OVERTHROWN.

Yesterday afternoon in the rooms of the Royal Society, at a joint session of the Royal and Astronomical Societies, the results obtained by British observers of the total solar eclipse of May 29 were discussed.

The greatest possible interest had been aroused in scientific circles by the hope that rival theories of a fundamental physical problem would be put to the test, and there was a very large attendance of astronomers and physicists. It was generally accepted that the observations were decisive in the verifying of the prediction of the famous physicist, Einstein, stated by the President of the Royal Society as being the most remarkable scientific event since the discovery of the predicted existence of the planet Neptune. But there was difference of opinion as to whether science had to face merely a new and unexplained fact, or to reckon with a theory that would completely revolutionize the accepted fundamentals of physics

SIR FRANK DYSON, the Astronomer Royal, described the work of the expeditions sent respectively to Sobral in North Brazil and the island of Principe, off the West Coast of Africa. At each of these places, if the weather were propitious on the day of the eclipse, it would be possible to take during totality a set of photographs of the obscured sun and of a number of bright stars which happened to be in its immediate vicinity. The desired object was to ascertain whether the light from these stars, as it passed the sun, came as directly towards us as if the sun were not there, or if there was a deflection due to its presence, and if the latter proved to be the case, what the amount of the deflection was. If deflection did occur, the stars would appear on the photographic plates at a measurable distance from their theoretical positions. He explained in detail the apparatus that had been employed, the corrections that had to be made for various disturbing factors, and the methods by which comparison between the theoretical and the observed positions had been made. He convinced the meeting that the results were definite and conclusive. Deflection did take place, and the measurements showed that the extent of the deflection was in close accord with the theoretical degree predicted by Einstein, as opposed to half that degree, the amount that would follow from the principles of Newton. It is interesting to recall that Sir Oliver Lodge, speaking at the Royal Institution last February, had also ventured on a prediction. He doubted if deflection would be observed, but was confident that if it did take place, it would follow the law of Newton and not that of Einstein.

DR. CROMMELIN and PROFESSOR EDDINGTON, two of the actual observers, followed the Astronomer-Royal, and gave interesting accounts of their work, in every way confirming the general conclusions that had been enunciated.

" MOMENTOUS PRONOUNCEMENT."

So far the matter was clear, but when the discussion began, it was plain that the scientific interest centred more in the theoretical bearings of the results than in the results themselves. Even the President of the Royal Society, in stating that they had just listened to "one of the most momentous, if not the most momentous, pronouncements of human thought," had to confess that no one had yet succeeded in stating in clear language what the theory of Einstein really was. It was accepted, however, that Einstein, on the basis of his theory, had made three predictions. The first, as to the motion of the planet Mercury, had been verified. The second, as to the existence and the degree of deflection of light as it passed the sphere of influence of the sun, had now been verified. As to the third, which depended on spectroscopic observations there was still uncertainty. But he was confident that the Einstein theory must now be reckoned with, and that our conceptions of the fabric of the universe must be fundamentally altered

At this stage Sir Oliver Lodge, whose contribution to the discussion had been eagerly expected, left the meeting.

Subsequent speakers joined in congratulating the observers, and agreed in accepting their results. More than one, however, including Professor Newall, of Cambridge, hesitated as to the full extent of the inferences that had been drawn and suggested that the phenomena might be due to an unknown solar atmosphere further in its extent than had been supposed and with unknown properties. No speaker succeeded in giving a clear non-mathematical statement of the theoretical question.

SPACE "WARPED."

Put in the most general way it may be described as follows : the Newtonian principles assume that space is invariable, that, for instance, the three angles of a triangle always equal, and must equal, two right angles. But these principles really rest on the observation that the angles of a triangle do equal two right angles, and that a circle is really circular. But there are certain physical facts that seem to throw doubt on the universality of these observations, and suggest that space may acquire a twist or warp in certain circumstances, as, for instance, under the influence of gravitation, a dislocation in itself slight and applying to the instruments of measurement as well as to the things measured. The Einstein doctrine is that the qualities of space, hitherto believed absolute, are relative to their circumstances. He drew the inference from his theory that in certain cases actual measurement of light would show the effects of the warping in a degree that could be predicted and calculated. His predictions in two of three cases have now been verified, but the question remains open as to whether the verifications prove the theory from which the predictions were deduced.

tled 'Raum, Zeit und Schwerkraft' appeared in the *Frankfurter Allgemeine Zeitung*. A column by Freundlich in *Die Vossische Zeitung* (Berlin) of November 30 begins as follows: 'In Germany a scientific event of extraordinary significance has not yet found the reaction which its importance deserves.' However, the weekly *Berliner Illustrierte Zeitung* of December 14 carried a picture of Einstein on its cover with the caption 'A new great in world history: Albert Einstein, whose researches, signifying a complete revolution in our concepts of nature, are on a par with the insights of a Copernicus, a Kepler, and a Newton.' As far as I know, the first news in the Swiss papers is found in the *Neue Züricher Zeitung* of December 10, where it is reported that the astronomer Henri Deslandres gave an account of the May 29 observations before the December 8 session of the French Academy of Sciences in which he summarized Einstein's theory by saying that energy attracts energy.

Einstein himself accepted 'with joy and gratefulness' the invitation to write a guest article in the London *Times* of November 28, for this gave him an opportunity for communication 'after the lamentable breach in the former international relations existing among men of science. . . . It was in accordance with the high and proud tradition of English science that English scientific men should have given their time and labour . . . to test a theory that had been completed and published in the country of their enemies in the midst of war.' Referring to an earlier description of him in the London *Times,* he concluded his article as follows: 'By an application of the theory of relativity to the tastes of readers, today in Germany I am called a German man of science and in England I am represented as a Swiss Jew. If I come to be regarded as a *bête noire,* the descriptions will be reversed and I shall become a Swiss Jew for the Germans and a German man of science for the English!' The same *Times* issue carried an editorial reply, 'Dr Einstein pays a well-intended if somewhat superfluous compliment to the impartiality of English science,' to Einstein's first remark, followed by the comments, 'We concede him his little jest. But we note that, in accordance with the general tenor of his theory, Dr Einstein does not supply any absolute description of himself" in reply to his second remark. The best description I know of Einstein in 1919 is the photograph on the cover of the *Berliner Illustrirte,* a picture of an intelligent, sensitive, and sensuous man who is deeply weary—from the strains of intense thinking during the past years, from illnesses from which he has barely recovered, from the pain of watching his dying mother, and, I would think, from the commotion of which he was the center (See Plate II).

November 1919 was not the first time Einstein and relativity appeared in the news. Frank recalls having seen in 1912 a Viennese newspaper with the headlines 'The minute in danger, a sensation of mathematical science' [F2], obviously a reference to the time dilation of special relativity. In 1914 Einstein himself had written a newspaper article on relativity for *Die Vossische Zeitung* [E38]. Thus he was already somewhat of a public celebrity, but only locally in German-speaking countries. It was only in November 1919 that he became a world figure. For example, *The New York Times Index* contains no mention of him until November 9, 1919. From that day until his death, not one single year passed without his name appearing in that paper, often in relation to science, more often in relation to other issues. Thus the birth of the Einstein legend can be pinpointed at November 7, 1919, when the London *Times* broke the news.

The article in *The New York Times* (hereafter called the *Times*) of November 9 was a sensible report which contained only one embellishment. J. J. Thomson was alleged to have said, 'This is one of the greatest—*perhaps the greatest*—of achievements in the history of human thought' The words I italicized were not spoken by Thomson, but they sell better (and may even be true). The *Times* of November 9 contains a lead article on 'World outbreak plotted by Reds for November 7/Lenin's emissaries sought to start rising all over Europe' and a column on Einstein under the sixfold headline 'Lights all askew in the heavens/Men of science more or less agog over results of eclipse observation/Einstein theory triumphs/Stars not where they seem or were calculated to be, but nobody need worry/A book for 12 wise men/No more in all the world could comprehend it, said Einstein when his daring publishers accepted it.' The article reported that 'one of the speakers at the Royal Society's meeting suggested that Euclid was knocked out' (not so, but, again, it sells) and concluded as follows: 'When he [Einstein] offered his last important work to the publishers, he warned them that there were not more than twelve persons in the whole world who would understand it, but the publishers took the risk.' Perhaps this story was invented by a reporter. I think it more probable, however, that this often-quoted statement indeed originated with Einstein himself and was made sometime in 1916, when he published a pamphlet (with Barth in Leipzig) and a 'popular' book on relativity (with Vieweg in Braunschweig). At any rate, when in December 1919 a *Times* correspondent interviewed him at his home and asked for an account of his work that would be accessible to more than twelve people, 'the doctor laughed good-naturedly but still insisted on the difficulty of making himself understood by laymen' [N5].

Editorials in the *Times* now begin to stress that quality of distance between the common man and the hero which is indispensable for the creation and perpetuation of his mythical role. November 11: 'This is news distinctly shocking and apprehensions for the safety of confidence even in the multiplication table will arise. . . . It would take the presidents of two Royal Societies to give plausibility or even thinkability to the declaration that as light has weight space has limits. It just doesn't, by definition, and that's the end of that—for commonfolk, however it may be for higher mathematicians.' November 16: 'These gentlemen may be great astronomers but they are sad logicians. Critical laymen have already objected that scientists who proclaim that space comes to an end somewhere are under obligation to tell us what lies beyond it.' November 18: the *Times* urges its readers not to be offended by the fact that only twelve people can understand the theory of 'the suddenly famous Dr Einstein.' November 25: a news column with the headlines: 'A new physics based on Einstein/Sir Oliver Lodge says it will prevail, and mathematicians will have a terrible time.' November 26: An editorial entitled 'Bad times for the learned.' November 29: A news item headlined 'Can't understand Einstein' reports that 'the London *Times* . . . confesses that it cannot follow the details. . . .' December 7: An editorial, 'Assaulting the absolute,' states that 'the raising of blasphemous voices against time and space threw some [astronomers] into a state of terror where they seemed to feel, for some days at least, that the foundations of all human thought had been undermined.' One cannot fail to notice that some of these statements were made with tongue in cheek. Yet they convey a sense of mystery accompanying the replacement of old wisdom by new order. Transitions such as these can induce fear. When interviewed by the *Times* on relativity theory, Charles Poor, professor of celestial mechanics at Columbia University, said, 'For some years past, the entire world has been in a state of unrest, mental as well as physical. It may well be that the physical aspects of the unrest, the war, the strikes, the Bolshevist uprisings, are in reality the visible objects of some underlying deep mental disturbance, worldwide in character. . . . This same spirit of unrest has invaded science . . . ' [N6].

It would be a misunderstanding of the Einstein phenomenon to attribute these various reactions to a brief and intense shock of the new. The insistence on mystery never waned. One reads in the *Times* ten years later, 'It is a rare exposition of Relativity that does not find it necessary to warn the reader that here and here and here he had better not try to understand' [N7].

The worldwide character of the legend is well illustrated by reports to the Foreign Office from German diplomats stationed in countries visited by Einstein [K1]. Oslo, June 1920: '[Einstein's] lectures were uncommonly well received by the public and the press.' Copenhagen, June 1920: 'In recent days, papers of all opinions have emphasized in long articles and interviews the significance of Professor Einstein, "the most famous physicist of the present." ' Paris, April 1922: ' . . . a sensation which the intellectual snobism of the capital did not want to pass up.' Tokyo, January 1923: 'When Einstein arrived at the station there were such large crowds that the police was unable to cope with the perilous crush . . . at the chrysanthemum festival it was neither the empress nor the prince regent nor the imperial princes who held reception; everything turned around Einstein.' Madrid, March 1923: 'Great enthusiasm everywhere . . . every day the papers devoted columns to his comings and goings. . . .' Rio de Janeiro, May 1925: ' . . . numerous detailed articles in the Brazilian press. . . . ' Montevideo, June 1925: 'He was the talk of the town and a news topic a whole week long. . . .' On April 25, 1921, Einstein was received by President Harding on the occasion of his first visit to the United States. An eyewitness described the mood of the public when Einstein gave a lecture in a large concert hall in Vienna that same year. People were 'in a curious state of excitement in which it no longer matters what one understands but only that one is in the immediate neighborhood of a place where miracles happen' [F3].

So it was, and so it remained everywhere and at all times during Einstein's life. The quality of his science had long since sufficed to command the admiration of his peers. Now his name also became a byword to the general public because of the pictures, verbal and visual, created by that new power of the twentieth century, the media. Some of these images were cheap, some brilliant (as in the blending of kings and apostles into twelve wise men). Einstein's science and the salesmanship of the press were necessary but not sufficient conditions for the creation of the legend, however. Compare, for example, the case of Einstein with the one and only earlier instance in which a major discovery in physics had created a world-wide sensation under the influence of newspapers. That was the case of Roentgen and the X-rays he discovered in 1895. It was the discovery, not the man, that was at the center of attention. Its value was lasting and it has never been forgotten by the general public, but its newsworthiness went from a peak into a gentle steady decline.

The essence of Einstein's unique position goes deeper and has everything to do, it seems to me, with the stars and with language. A new man appears abruptly, the 'suddenly famous Doctor Einstein.' He carries the message of a new order in the universe. He is a new Moses come down from the mountain to bring the law and a new Joshua controlling the motion of heavenly bodies. He speaks in strange tongues but wise men aver that the stars testify to his veracity. Through the ages, child and adult alike had looked with wonder at stars and light. Speak of such new things as X-rays or atoms and man may be awed. But stars had forever been in his dreams and his myths. Their recurrence manifested an order beyond human control. Irregularities in the skies—comets, eclipses—were omens, mainly of evil. Behold, a new man appears. His mathematical language is sacred yet amenable to transcription into the profane: the fourth dimension, stars are not where they seemed to be but nobody need worry, light has weight, space is warped. He fulfills two profound needs in man, the need to know and the need not to know but to believe. The drama of his emergence is enhanced (though this to me seems secondary) by the coincidence—itself caused largely by the vagaries of war—between the meeting of the joint societies and the first annual remembrance of horrid events of the recent past which had caused millions to die, empires to fall, the future to be uncertain. The new man who appears at that time represents order and power. He becomes the θεῖος ἀνήρ, the divine man, of the twentieth century.

In the late years, when I knew him, fame and publicity were a source of amusement and sometimes of irritation to Einstein, whose tribe revered no saints. Photographs and film clips indicate that in his younger years he had the ability to enjoy his encounters with the press and the admiration of the people. As I try to find the best way to characterize Einstein's deeper response to adulation, I am reminded of words spoken by Lord Haldane when he introduced Einstein to an audience at King's College in London on June 13, 1921. On that first visit to

England Einstein stayed in the home of Haldane, whose daughter fainted from excitement the first time the distinguished visitor entered the house. In his introduction, Haldane mentioned that he had been 'touched to observe that Einstein had left his house [that morning] to gaze on the tomb of Newton at Westminster Abbey.' Then he went on to describe Einstein in these words:

> A man distinguished by his desire, if possible, to efface himself and yet impelled by the unmistakable power of genius which would not allow the individual of whom it had taken possession to rest for one moment. [L5]

16d. Einstein and Germany

In April 1914, Einstein set out from Zürich to settle in the capital of the German Empire, a country still at peace. In December 1932, he left Germany for good. In the interim, he lived through a world war. The Empire disintegrated. His own worldwide renown began in 1919, the time of the uncertain rise of the Weimar republic. At the time he left Germany, the republic, too, was doomed.

Fame attracts envy and hatred. Einstein's was no exception. In this instance, these hostile responses were particularly intensified because of his exposed position in a turbulent environment. During the 1920s, he was a highly visible personality, not for one but for a multitude of reasons. He was the divine man. He was a scientific administrator and an important spokesman for the German establishment. He traveled extensively—through Europe, to Japan, to Palestine, through the Americas. And he was a figure who spoke out on nonestablishment issues, such as pacifism and the fate of the Jews.

In the first instance, Einstein's role within the establishment was dictated by his obligations, many of them administrative, to science. He fulfilled all these duties conscientiously, some of them with pleasure. As a member of the renowned Preussische Akademie der Wissenschaften, he published frequently in its *Proceedings,* faithfully attended the meetings of its physics section as well as the plenary sessions, often served on its committees, and refereed dubious communications submitted to its *Proceedings* [K2]. On May 5, 1916, he succeeded Planck as president of the Deutsche Physikalische Gesellschaft. Between then and May 31, 1918, when Sommerfeld took over, he chaired eighteen meetings of this society and addressed it on numerous occasions. On December 30, 1916, he was appointed by imperial decree to the Kuratorium of the Physikalisch Technische Reichsanstalt, a federal institution, and participated in the board's deliberations on the choice of experimental programs [K3]. He held this position until he left Germany. In 1917 he began his duties as director of the Kaiser Wilhelm Institut für Physik, largely an administrative position, the initial task of the institute being to administer grants for physics research at various universities.* (It became a

---

*In the early years, only the astronomer Freundlich held an appointment as scientific staff member of the institute. Freundlich caused Einstein and others a certain amount of trouble [K4].

research institute only after Einstein left Germany.) In 1922 the Akademie appointed him to the board of directors of the astrophysical laboratory in Potsdam [K4]. In that year he was also nominated president of the Einstein Stiftung, a foundation for the promotion of work on experimental tests of general relativity. This Stiftung was eventually housed in a somewhat bizarre-looking new building, the Einstein Turm, situated on the grounds of the astrophysical laboratory in Potsdam. Its main piece of equipment, the Einstein Teleskop, was designed especially for solar physics experiments. Einstein had no formal duties at the University of Berlin. Nevertheless, he would occasionally teach and conduct seminars. He also felt a moral obligation to Zürich, an obligation he fulfilled by giving a series of lectures at its university from January to June 1919.

Einstein held one additional professorial position, this one in Holland. By royal decree of June 24, 1920, a special chair in Leiden was created for him, enabling him to come to that university for short periods of his choosing. On October 27, 1920, Einstein began his new position with an inaugural address on aether and relativity theory.* He came back to Leiden in November 1921, May 1922, October 1924, February 1925, and April 1930, and lectured on several of these occasions. He was comfortable there, walking around in his socks and sweater [U1]. The initial term of appointment was for three years, but kept being extended until it was formally terminated on September 23, 1952 [B2].

Einstein's physics of the 1920s was not only an exercise in administration and the holding of professorships, however. It was also play. With Mühsam he measured the diameter of capillaries; with Goldschmidt he invented a hearing aid; and with Szilard several refrigerating devices.** (for more on these topics, see Chapter 29). But above everything else his prime interest remained with the questions of principle in physics. I shall return to this subject in the next section. First some remarks on Einstein's other activities during the Berlin period.

In the early days of the First World War, Einstein had for the first time publicly advocated the cause of pacifism. He continued to do so from then on. Reaction to this stand was hostile. During the war, the chief of staff of the military district Berlin wrote to the president of police of the city of Berlin, pointing out the dangers of permitting pacifists to go abroad. The list of known pacifists appended to the letter included Einstein's name [K5]. After the war, Einstein the outspoken supranationalist became a figure detested by the growing number of German chauvinists.

Einstein regarded his pacifism as an instinctive feeling rather than the result of

---

*The printed version of this lecture [E39] gives an incorrect date for its delivery. By *aether* Einstein meant the gravitational field (one may wonder if this new name was felicitously chosen). 'The aether of the general theory of relativity is a medium without mechanical and kinematic properties, but which codetermines mechanical and electromagnetic events.'

**Jointly with a Dutch firm, the N.V. Nederlandsche Technische Handelsmaatschappy 'Giro,' Einstein also held a patent for a gyrocompass (Deutsches Reichs Patent 394677) [M2]. He did the work on this device in the mid-1920s.

an intellectual theory [N8]. In the early years, one of his main ideals was the establishment of a United States of Europe. For that reason, he had become an active member of the Bund Neues Vaterland (later renamed the German League for Human Rights), an organization that had advocated European union since its founding in 1914; in 1928 he joined its board of directors. In 1923 he helped found the Freunde des Neuen Russland [K6]. Though mainly interested in cultural exchanges, this group did not fail to interest the police [K7]. In the late 1920s, his pacifism became more drastic as he began expressing himself in favor of the principle of unconditionally refusing to bear arms. Among the numerous manifestos he signed were several that demanded universal and total disarmament. In a message to a meeting of War Resisters' International in 1931, he expressed the opinion that the people should take the issue of disarmament out of the hands of politicians and diplomats [N9].

Writing to Hadamard, Einstein remarked that he would not dare to preach his creed of war resistance to a native African tribe, 'for the patient would have died long before the cure could have been of any help to him' [E40]. It took him rather a long time to diagnose the seriousness of Europe's ailments. (In this regard, he was no rare exception.) It is true that in 1932 he signed an appeal to the Socialist and Communist parties in Germany, urging them to join forces in order to stave off Germany's 'terrible danger of becoming Fascist' [K8], but as late as May 1933, three months after Hitler came to power, Einstein still held to an unqualified antimilitarist position. Thereafter he changed his mind, as will be described in Section 25b.

Einstein's active interest in the fate of the Jews also began in the Berlin period. To him this concern was never at variance with his supranational ideals. In October 1919 he wrote to the physicist Paul Epstein, 'One can be internationally minded without lacking concern for the members of the tribe' [E41]. In December he wrote to Ehrenfest, 'Anti-Semitism is strong here and political reaction is violent' [E42]. He was particularly incensed about the German reaction to Jews who had recently escaped worse fates in Poland and Russia.* 'Incitement against these unfortunate fugitives . . . has become an effective political weapon, employed with success by every demagogue' [E42a]. Einstein knew of their plight especially well, since a number of these refugees literally came knocking at his door for help. To him supranationalism could wait so far as the hunted Jew was concerned. It was another case where the patient would have been dead (and often was) before the cure.

There was another irritant. 'I have always been annoyed by the undignified assimilationist cravings and strivings which I have observed in so many of my [Jewish] friends. . . . These and similar happenings have awakened in me the Jewish national sentiment' [E43]. I am sure that Einstein's strongest source of

---

*Their influx was particularly noticeable in Berlin. In 1900, 11 000 out of the 92 000 Berlin Jews were 'Ostjuden.' In 1925 these numbers were 43 000 out of 172 000 [G1].

identity, after science, was to be a Jew, increasingly so as the years went by. That allegiance carried no religious connotation. In 1924 he did become a dues-paying member of a Jewish congregation in Berlin, but only as an act of solidarity. Zionism to him was above all else a form of striving for the dignity of the individual. He never joined the Zionist organization.

There was one person who more than anyone else contributed to Einstein's awakening: Kurt Blumenfeld, from 1910 to 1914 secretary general of the Executive of World Zionist Organizations, which then had its seat in Berlin, and from 1924 to 1933 president of the Union of German Zionists. Ben Gurion called him the greatest moral revolutionary in the Zionist movement. He belonged to the seventh generation of emancipated German Jewry. In a beautiful essay, Blumenfeld has written of his discussions with Einstein in 1919, of his efforts 'to try to get out of a man what is hidden in him, and never to try to instill in a man what is not in his nature' [B3]. It was Blumenfeld whom Einstein often entrusted in later years with the preparation of statements in his name on Zionist issues. It was also Blumenfeld who was able to convince Einstein that he ought to join Weizmann on a visit to the United States (April 2–May 30, 1921) in order to raise funds for the planned Hebrew University. Blumenfeld understood the man he was dealing with. After having convinced Einstein, he wrote to Weizmann, 'As you know, Einstein is no Zionist, and I beg you not to make any attempt to prevail on him to join our organization. . . . I heard . . . that you expect Einstein to give speeches. Please be quite careful with that. Einstein . . . often says things out of naiveté which are unwelcome to us' [B4].* As to his relations with Weizmann, Einstein once said to me, 'Meine Beziehungen zu dem Weizmann waren, wie der Freud sagt, ambivalent.'**

The extraordinary complexity of Einstein's life in the 1920s begins to unfold, the changes in midlife are becoming clear. Man of research, scientific administrator, guest professor, active pacifist, spokesman for a moral Zionism, fund-raiser in America. Claimed by the German establishment as one of their most prominent members, though nominally he is Swiss.† Suspected by the establishment because of his pacifism. Target for anti-Semitism from the right. Irritant to the German assimilationist Jews because he would not keep quiet about Jewish self-expression. It is not very surprising that under these circumstances Einstein occasionally experienced difficulty in maintaining perspective, as two examples may illustrate. One of these concerns the 1920 disturbances, the other the League of Nations.

On February 12, 1920, disturbances broke out in the course of a lecture given by Einstein at the University of Berlin. The official reason given afterward was that there were too few seats to accommodate everyone. In a statement to the press, Einstein noted that there was a certain hostility directed against him which was

---

*Part of this letter (dated incorrectly) is reproduced in [B3]. The full text is in [B5].

**As F. would say, my relations to W. were ambivalent.

†See especially the events surrounding the awarding of the Nobel prize to Einstein, Chapter 30.

not explicitly anti-Semitic, although it could be interpreted as such [K9]. On August 24, 1920, a newly founded organization, the Arbeitsgemeinschaft deutscher Naturforscher, organized a meeting in Berlin's largest concert hall for the purpose of criticizing the content of relativity theory and the alleged tasteless propaganda made for it by its author.* Einstein attended. Three days later he replied in the *Berliner Tageblatt* [E44], noting that reactions might have been otherwise had he been 'a German national with or without swastika instead of a Jew with liberal international convictions,' quoting authorities such as Lorentz, Planck, and Eddington in support of his work, and grossly insulting Lenard on the front page. One may sympathize. By then, Lenard was already on his way to becoming the most despicable of all German scientists of any stature. Nevertheless, Einstein's article is a distinctly weak piece of writing, out of style with anything else he ever allowed to be printed under his name. On September 6 the German minister of culture wrote to him, expressing his profound regrets about the events of August 24 [K10]. On September 9 Einstein wrote to Born, 'Don't be too hard on me. Everyone has to sacrifice at the altar of stupidity from time to time . . . and this I have done with my article' [E45].

From September 19 to 25, the Gesellschaft der deutschen Naturforscher und Ärzte met in Bad Nauheim. Einstein and Lenard were present. The official record of the meeting shows only that they engaged in useless but civilized debate on relativity [E46]. However, Born recalls that Lenard attacked Einstein in malicious and patently anti-Semitic ways [B6], while Einstein promised Born soon afterward not again to become as worked up as he had been in Nauheim [E46a]. The building in which the meeting was held was guarded by armed police [F4], but there were no incidents.

It would, of course, have been easy for Einstein to leave Germany and find an excellent position elsewhere. He chose not to do so because 'Berlin is the place to which I am most closely tied by human and scientific connections' [E46b].

Invited by the Collège de France, Einstein went to Paris in March 1922 to discuss his work with physicists, mathematicians, and philosophers. Relations between France and Germany were still severely strained, and the trip was sharply criticized by nationalists in both countries. In order to avoid demonstrations, Einstein left the train to Paris at a suburban station [L6]. Shortly after this visit, he accepted an invitation to become a member of the Committee on Intellectual Cooperation of the League of Nations. Germany did not enter the League until 1926, and so Einstein was once again in an exposed position. On June 24 Walter Rathenau, who had been foreign minister of Germany for only a few months, a Jew and an acquaintance of Einstein's, was assassinated. On July 4 Einstein wrote to Marie Curie that he must resign from the committee, since the murder of Rathenau had made it clear to him that strong anti-Semitism did not make him an appropriate member [E47]. A week later he wrote to her of his intention to give up his Akademie position and to settle somewhere as a private

*This organization later published a book entitled *100 Autoren Gegen Einstein* [I2].

individual [E48]. Later that same month he cited 'my activity in Jewish causes and, more generally, my Jewish nationality' as reasons for his resignation [E49]. He was persuaded to stay on, however. In March 1923, shortly after French and Belgian troops occupied the Ruhrgebiet, he resigned again, declaring that the League had neither the strength nor the good will for the fulfillment of its great task [E50]. In 1924 he rejoined, since he now felt that 'he had been guided by a passing mood of discouragement rather than by clear thinking' [E51].*

Evidently Einstein's life and moods were strongly affected by the strife and violence in Germany in the early 1920s. On October 8, 1922, he left with his wife for a five-month trip abroad. 'After the Rathenau murder, I very much welcomed the opportunity of a long absence from Germany, which took me away from temporarily increased danger' [K11]. After short visits to Colombo, Singapore, Hong Kong, and Shanghai, they arrived in Japan for a five-week stay. En route, Einstein received word that he had been awarded the Nobel prize.** On the way back, they spent twelve days in Palestine, then visited Spain, and finally returned to Berlin in February 1923. Another trip in May/June 1925 took them to Argentina, Brazil, and Uruguay. Wherever they came, from Singapore to Montevideo, they were especially feted by local Jewish communities.

It was, one may say, a full life. There came a time when Einstein had to pay Early in 1928, while in Zuoz in Switzerland, he suffered a temporary physical collapse brought on by overexertion. An enlargement of the heart was diagnosed. As soon as practicable, he was brought back to Berlin, where he had to stay in bed for four months. He fully recuperated but remained weak for almost a year. 'Sometimes . . . he seemed to enjoy the atmosphere of the sickroom, since it permitted him to work undisturbed' [R1].

During that period of illness—on Friday, April 13, 1928, to be precise—Helen Dukas began working for Einstein. She was to be his able and trusted secretary for the rest of his life and became a member of the family.

In the summer of 1929, Einstein bought a plot of land in the small village of Caputh, near Berlin, a few minutes' walk from the broad stream of the Havel. On this site a small house was built for the family. It was shortly after his fiftieth birthday,† and several friends joined to celebrate this event by giving him a sailboat. Sailing on the Havel became one of his fondest pleasures.

Not long after his recovery, Einstein was on the road again. He was at Cal Tech from December 1930 till March 1931, and again from December 1931 till March 1932.‡ Those were the years when things began to look bad in Germany.

---

*In 1927, Einstein, Curie, and Lorentz prepared a report for the committee, dealing with an international bureau of meteorology [E52]. Einstein's final resignation from the committee came in April 1932 [D2].

**See Chapter 30.

†The city of Berlin intended to present him with a summer house, but after many altercations, not all of them funny, this plan fell through [R1].

‡This was principally the doing of Millikan, who since 1924 had been urging Einstein to spend part of his time in Pasadena [M3].

In December 1932 the Einsteins left once again for California. As they closed their house in Caputh, Einstein turned to Elsa and said, 'Dreh dich um. Du siehst's nie wieder,' Turn around. You will never see it again. And so it was. What happened thereafter will be described in Section 25b.

I conclude the story of the Berlin days with an anecdote told by Harry, Count Kessler, the chronicler of life in Berlin in the Weimar years. Some time in 1930 the sculptor Maillol came to Berlin. Einstein was one of the guests invited for a lunch in his honor. When Einstein came in Maillol observed, 'Une belle tête; c'est un poète?' And, said Kessler, 'I had to explain to him who Einstein was; he had evidently never heard of him' [K12].

16e. The Later Writings

1. The Man of Culture.   All the papers Einstein published before finishing his work on the formulation of general relativity deal either directly with research or with reviews of research, with minor exceptions: a note in honor of Planck written in 1913 [E53] and reviews of booklets on relativity by Brill and by Lorentz [E53a]. Thereafter, the writings change, very slowly at first. From 1916 to 1920 we find the early eulogies—to Mach, Schwarzschild, Smoluchowski, Leo Arons—and a few more reviews of others' work—of Lorentz's Paris lectures [E54], of Helmholtz's lectures on Goethe [E55], of Weyl's book on relativity [E56]. After 1920 there is a far more noticeable change as he starts writing on public affairs, political issues, education. The more important of these contributions have been reprinted in various collections of Einstein essays. I shall not discuss them here.

After 1920 Einstein wrote fairly often on scientific personalities. He was, of course, an obvious candidate for contributions commemorating Kepler [E57], Newton [E57a], and Maxwell [E58]. In these essays he emphasized points of general principle. On other occasions he clearly enjoyed writing about technical issues, whether of a theoretical or an experimental nature, as, for example, his pieces on Kelvin [E59] and Warburg [E60]. He spoke at Lorentz's grave and commemorated him on other occasions as well [E61]. He wrote tributes [E62] to Ehrenfest, Marie Curie, Nernst, Langevin, and Planck; also to Julius [E63], Edison [E64], Michelson [E65], and Noether [E66]. He wrote in praise of Arago [E67] and Newcomb [E68] and of his friend Berliner [E69]. As I have mentioned before, these portraits show Einstein's keen perception of people and thereby contribute to a composite portrait of Einstein himself. In addition, they make clear that his interest in physics ranged far beyond his own immediate research.

Einstein had a lifelong interest in philosophy. As a schoolboy, he had read Kant. With his friends in Bern he had studied Spinoza's ethics, Hume's treatise of human nature, Mill's system of logic, Avenarius's critique of pure experience, and other philosophical works. As I already remarked in Chapter 1, calling Einstein a philosopher sheds as much light on him as calling him a musician. 'Is not all of philosophy as if written in honey? It looks wonderful when one contemplates it, but when one looks again it is all gone. Only mush remains,' he once said [R2].

Even though Einstein's interest in and impact on philosophy were strong, he himself never wrote articles that may be called philosophical in a technical sense. After 1920 he wrote occasional reviews of or introductions for philosophical works, however. His reviews of books on epistemology by Weinberg [E70] and Winternitz [E71] show his familiarity with Kant. So does the record of his discussions with French philosophers in 1922. When one of these referred to a possible connection between Einstein's ideas and those of Kant, Einstein replied:

> In regard to Kant's philosophy, I believe that every philosopher has his own Kant. . . . Arbitrary concepts are necessary in order to construct science; as to whether these concepts are given *a priori* or are arbitrary conventions, I can say nothing. [E72]

From Einstein's introduction to a new translation of Galileo's *Dialogue* [E73], we see that he had read Plato. He wrote an introduction to a new German translation of Lucretius's *De Rerum Natura* [E74]. He was familiar with Bertrand Russell's theory of knowledge [E75]. His philosophical interests are also manifest in his review of Emile Meyerson's *La Déduction Relativiste* [E76] and his introductions to books by Planck [E77] and Frank [E78]. Among the oriental philosophers, he appreciated Confucius. Once, in Princeton, he fell asleep during a lecture on Zen Buddhism. Perhaps he was tired that evening.

Einstein continued to consider philosophy ennobling in his later years. In 1944 he wrote to Benedetto Croce, 'I would not think that philosophy and reason itself will be man's guide in the foreseeable future; however, they will remain the most beautiful sanctuary they have always been for the select' [E79]

Among the many contributions that show Einstein as a man of culture, I select two for brief additional comments.

The first is his appreciation of Maxwell [E58], one of his precursors. In Einstein's opinion, Maxwell was a revolutionary figure. The purely mechanical world picture was upset by 'the great revolution forever linked with the names Faraday, Maxwell, and Hertz. The lion's share in this revolution was Maxwell's. . . . Since Maxwell's time, physical reality has been thought of as represented by continuous fields. . . . This change in the conception of reality is the most profound and the most fruitful that physics has experienced since the time of Newton.' Elsewhere Einstein wrote of Maxwell, 'Imagine his feelings when the differential equations he had formulated proved to him that electromagnetic fields spread in the form of polarized waves and with the speed of light!' [E80].

The second comment deals with the views on religion [E81]. 'A religious person is devout in the sense that he has no doubt of the significance of those superpersonal objects and goals which neither require nor are capable of rational foundation.' Thus, according to Einstein, 'a legitimate conflict between science and religion cannot exist. . . . Science without religion is lame, religion without science is blind.' By his own definition, Einstein himself was, of course, a deeply religious man.

2. The Man of Science. With the formulation of the field equations of gravitation in November 1915, classical physics (that is, nonquantum physics) reached its perfection and Einstein's scientific career its high point. His oeuvre does not show anything like an abrupt decline thereafter. Despite much illness, his years from 1916 to 1920 were productive and fruitful, both in relativity and in quantum theory. A gentle decline begins after 1920. There is a resurgence toward the end of 1924 (the quantum theory of the monatomic gas). After that, the creative period ceases abruptly, though scientific efforts continue unremittingly for another thirty years.

Who can gauge the extent to which the restlessness of Einstein's life in the 1920s was the cause or the effect of a lessening of creative powers? Many influences were obviously beyond his volition: age, illness, many of his administrative obligations, wordly fame, the violence of the early Weimar period. At the same time, I perceive in his writings after 1916 a natural diminution of creative tension. His activities in public affairs were no doubt the result of a combination of strong inner urges and of those demands on him which are part of the burdens of fame. It is less clear to me to what extent he would have responded to these pressures if physics had been as all-consuming to him as it was in earlier days. It is my impression that, after 1916, Einstein finally had some energy to spare for the world in which he lived. Kessler's chronicles [K12] and Kayser's biography [R1] indicate that participation in Berlin's social life gave him pleasure. So did conversations with statesmen like Rathenau, Stresemann, and Briand, and later Churchill and Roosevelt. Letters (not in the Princeton Archives) written by Einstein in the early 1920s, showing that for several years he had a strong attachment to a younger woman, express emotions for which, perhaps, he had no energy to spare in his marriages. This interlude ended late in 1924, when he wrote to her that he had to seek in the stars what was denied him on earth. That line was written only months before the discovery of quantum mechanics, the time at which a younger generation of physicists took over the lead while Einstein went his own way.

I return to Einstein's physics. Two major items remain to be discussed, unified field theory and quantum theory. I deal with Einstein's work on unified field theory first, since it is a direct outgrowth of general relativity, the last scientific topic treated before the present long digression on the suddenly famous Doctor Einstein. Then I turn to Einstein and the quantum theory, begining once again with events in the year 1905 and continuing from there until his final days.

A line from a letter in 1928 from Einstein to Ehrenfest may serve as an epigraph to the later writings:

> I believe less than ever in the essentially statistical nature of events and have decided to use the little energy still given to me in ways that are independent of the current bustle. [E82]

References

A1. *Algemeen Handelsblad,* November 10, 1919.
B1. B. Bertotti, D. Brill, and R. Krotkov in *Gravitation* (L. Witten, Ed.), p. 1. Wiley, New York, 1962.

B2. A. M. Bienfait-Visser, letter to A. Pais, February 12, 1980.

B3. K. Blumenfeld in *Helle Zeit, dunkle Zeit*, p. 74. Europa Verlag, Zürich, 1956.

B4. ———, letter to C. Weizmann, March 15, 1921; *ETH Bibl. Zürich Hs.* **304,** 201–4.

B5. ———, *Im Kampf um den Zionismus*, p. 66. Deutsches Verlag Anst, Stuttgart, 1968.

B6. M. Born in *Einstein–Born Briefwechsel*, p. 60. Nympenburger, Munich, 1969.

C1. C. Chaplin, *My Autobiography*, p. 346, The Bodley Head, London, 1964.

D1. F. W. Dyson, *M. N. Roy. Astr. Soc.* **77,** 445 (1917).

D2. A. Dufour, letter to A. Einstein, April 23, 1932.

E1. A. Einstein, letter to M. Besso, December 10, 1915; *EB,* p. 59.

E2. ———, letter to P. Ehrenfest, February 14, 1917.

E3. ———, letter to H. A. Lorentz, April 23, 1917.

E4. ———, letter to H. Zangger, March 10, 1917.

E5. ———, letter to M. Besso, May 13, 1917; *EB,* p. 114.

E6. ———, letter to M. Besso, September 3, 1917; *EB,* p. 121.

E7. ———, letter to H. Zangger, December 6, 1917.

E8. ———, letter to P. Ehrenfest, November 12, 1917.

E9. ———, letter to M. Besso, January 5, 1918; *EB,* p. 124.

E10. ———, letter to D. Hilbert, undated, April 1918.

E11. ———, letter to H. Zangger, undated, early 1918.

E12. ———, letter to P. Ehrenfest, May 8, 1918.

E13. ———, letter to M. Besso, August 20, 1918; *EB,* p. 132.

E14. ———, letter to P. Ehrenfest, December 6, 1918.

E15. ———, letter to M. Besso, December 4, 1918; *EB,* p. 145.

E16. ———, letter to C. Seelig, May 5, 1952.

E17. ———, letter to P. Ehrenfest, September 12, 1919.

E18. ———, letter to M. Besso, July 26, 1920; *EB,* p. 151.

E19. E. Einstein, letter to P. Ehrenfest, April 5, 1932.

E20. A. Einstein, letter to M. Born undated, probably 1937; *Einstein–Born Briefwech-sel,* p. 177. Nymphenburger, Munich, 1969.

E21. ———, *Lettres à Maurice Solovine*, p. 134. Gauthier-Villars, Paris, 1956.

E22. ———, letter to V. Besso, March 21, 1955; *EB,* p. 537.

E23. ———, letter to P. Winteler and family, undated, May 1919.

E24. E. Einstein, letter to P. Ehrenfest, December 10, 1919.

E25. A. Einstein, letter to H. Zangger, undated, January 1920.

E26. ———, letter to H. Zangger, undated, March 1920.

E27. ———, postcard to P. Einstein, September 27, 1919.

E28. ———, *Naturw.* **7,** 776 (1919).

E29. ———, letter to M. Besso, undated, March 1914; *EB.* p. 52.

E30. ———, *PAW,* 1915, p. 831.

E31. ———, letter to A. Sommerfeld, November 28, 1915.

E32. J. Earman and C. Glymour, *Hist. St. Phys. Sci.* 11, 49 (1980).

E33. A. S. Eddington, *Report on the Relativity Theory of Gravitation.* Fleetway Press, London, 1918.

E34. ———, *M. N. Roy. Astr. Soc.* **77,** 377 (1917).

E35. ———, *Observatory* **42,** 119 (1919).

E36. A. Einstein, letter to C. Stumpf, November 3, 1919.

E37.   A. S. Eddington, letter to A. Einstein, December 1, 1919.

E38.   A. Einstein, *Die Vossische Zeitung,* April 26, 1914.

E39.   ——, *Aether und Relativitätstheorie.* Springer, Berlin, 1920.

E40.   ——, letter to J. Hadamard, Sept. 24, 1929.

E41.   ——, letter to P. Epstein, October 5, 1919.

E42.   ——, letter to P. Ehrenfest, December 4, 1919.

E42a. ——, *About Zionism* (L. Simon, Tran.), p. 40. Macmillan, New York, 1931.

E43.   ——, [E42a], pp. 41, 43.

E44.   ——, *Berliner Tageblatt,* August 27, 1920.

E45.   ——, letter to M. Born, September 9, 1920.

E46.   —— and P. Lenard, *Phys. Zeitschr.* **21**, 666 (1921).

E46a. ——, letter to M. Born, undated, autumn 1920.

E46b. ——, letter to K. Haenisch, September 8, 1920; [K1], Vol. 1, p. 204.

E47.   ——, letter to M. Curie, July 4, 1921.

E48.   ——, letter to M. Curie, July 11, 1921.

E49.   ——, letter to G. Murray, July 25, 1922.

E50.   ——, letter to the Committee on Intellectual Cooperation, March 21, 1923; *New York Times,* June 28, 1923.

E51.   ——, letter to G. Murray, May 30, 1924.

E52.   ——, M. Curie, and H. A. Lorentz, *Science* **65**, 415 (1927).

E53.   ——, *Naturw.* **1**, 1077 (1913).

E53a. ——, *Naturw.* **2**, 1018 (1914).

E54.   ——, *Naturw.* **4**, 480 (1916).

E55.   ——, *Naturw.* **5**, 675 (1917).

E56.   ——, *Naturw.* **6**, 373 (1918).

E57.   ——, *Frankfurter Zeitung,* November 9, 1930.

E57a. ——, see Refs. [E8]–[E11] in Chap. 1.

E58.   ——, in *James Clerk Maxwell,* p. 66. Cambridge University Press, Cambridge, 1931.

E59.   ——, *Naturw.* **12**, 601 (1924).

E60.   ——, *Naturw.* **10**, 823 (1922).

E61.   ——, *Mein Weltbild,* pp. 32, 35, 39. Europa, Zürich, 1953.

E62.   ——, *Out of My Later Years,* Philosophical Library, New York, 1950.

E63.   ——, *Astrophys. J.* **63**, 196 (1926).

E64.   ——, *Science,* **74**, 404 (1931).

E65.   ——, *Z. Angew. Chemie* 44, 658 (1931).

E66.   ——, *New York Times,* May 4, 1935.

E67.   ——, *Naturw.* **17**, 363 (1929).

E68.   ——, *Science* **69**, 249 (1929).

E69.   ——, *Naturw.* **20**, 913 (1932).

E70.   ——, *Naturw.* **18**, 536 (1930).

E71.   ——, *Deutsche Literaturzeitung,* Heft 1, p. 20, 1924.

E72.   ——, *Bull. Soc. Fran. Philosophie* 22, 91 (1922).

E73.   ——, foreword to Galileo's *Dialogue* (S. Drake, Tran.). University of California Press, Berkeley, 1967.

E74.   ——, introduction to *Lukrez, Von der Natur* (H. Diels, Tran.). Weidmann, Berlin, 1924.

E75. ——, in *The Philosophy of Bertrand Russell* (P. A. Schilpp, Ed.), p. 277. Tudor, New York, 1944.

E76. ——, *Rev. Phil. France* **105**, 161 (1928).

E77. ——, prologue to M. Planck, *Where Is Science Going?* Norton, New York, 1932.

E78. ——, foreword to P. Frank, *Relativity, a Richer Truth.* Beacon Press, Boston, 1950.

E79. ——, letter to B. Croce, June 7, 1944.

E80. ——, *Science* **91**, 487 (1940).

E81. ——, *Nature* **146**, 605 (1941).

E82. ——, letter to P. Ehrenfest, August 23, 1928.

F1. P. Frank, *Einstein, His Life and Times,* p. 124. Knopf, New York, 1953.

F2. ——, *Einstein, Sein Leben und Seine Zeit,* p. 106. Vieweg, Braunschweig, 1979.

F3. ——, [F2], p. 290.

F4. ——, [F2], p. 275.

G1. P. Gay, *Freud, Jews and Other Germans,* p. 172. Oxford University Press, New York, 1978.

H1. F. Herneck, *Einstein Privat,* p. 29. Der Morgen, Berlin, 1978.

I1. J. Ishiwara, *Einstein ko en roku,* p. 193. Tokyo-Tosho, Tokyo, 1978.

I2. H. Israel, E. Ruckhaber, and R. Weinmann (Eds.), *100 Autoren Gegen Einstein.* Voigtlander, Leipzig, 1931.

K1. C. Kirsten and H. J. Treder, *Einstein in Berlin,* Vol. 1, documents 148-60. Akadamie Verlag, Berlin, 1979.

K2. ——, [K1], Vol. 1, documents 59-68.

K3. ——, [K1], Vol. 1, documents 81-7.

K4. ——, [K1], Vol. 1, pp. 22, 54, 58.

K5. ——, [K1], Vol. 1, p. 198.

K6. ——, [K1], Vol. 1, p. 215.

K7. ——, [K1], Vol. 1, p. 219.

K8. ——, [K1], Vol. 1, p. 223.

K9. ——, [K1], Vol. 1, p. 202.

K10. ——, [K1], Vol. 1, p. 210.

K11. ——, [K1], Vol. 1, p. 231.

K12. H. Kessler, *In the Twenties,* p. 396. Holt, Rinehart and Winston, New York, 1976.

L1. H. A. Lorentz, letter to A. Einstein, March 22, 1917.

L2. ——, telegram to A. Einstein, September 27, 1919.

L3. ——, letter to P. Ehrenfest, September 22, 1919.

L4. ——, telegram to A. Einstein, November 10, 1919.

L5. *London Times,* June 14, 1921.

L6. J. Langevin, *Cahiers Fundamenta Scientiae,* No. 93, 1979.

M1. D. F. Moyer in *On the Path of Albert Einstein,* p. 55. Plenum Press, New York, 1979.

M2. K. von Mayrhauser, letter to A. Einstein, October 11, 1926.

M3. R. Millikan, letter to A. Einstein, October 2, 1924.

N1. *New York Times,* August 16, 1914.

N2. *Nature* **94**, 66 (1914).

N3. *New Catholic Encyclopedia,* McGraw-Hill, New York, 1967.

N3a. *Nieuwe Rotterdamsche Courant,* November 9 and 11, 1919.

N4. *New York Times,* December 21, 1919.

N5. *New York Times,* December 3, 1919.

N6. *New York Times,* November 16, 1919.

N7. *New York Times,* January 28, 1928.

N8. O. Nathan and M. Norden, *Einstein on Peace,* p. 98. Schocken, New York, 1968.

N9. ——, [N8], p. 141.

O1. *Observatory,* **42**, 256 (1919).

O2. *Observatory,* **42**, 389 (1919); see also, *Proc. Roy. Soc* **96A**, i (1919).

R1. A. Reiser, *Albert Einstein.* Boni, New York, 1930.

R2. I. Rosenthal-Schneider, *Reality and Scientific Truth,* p. 62. Wayne State University Press, Detroit, 1980.

S1. N. Saz, Forschungen d. Päd. Hochsch. 'Karl Liebknecht,' Naturw. Reihe B, No. 14, p. 59.

S2. W. de Sitter, *Observatory* **39**, 412 (1916).

S3. ——, *M. N. Roy. Astr. Soc.* **76**, 699 (1916); **77**, 155, 481 (1917); **78**, 3, 341 (1917).

S4. C. Stumpf, letter to A. Einstein, October 22, 1919.

T1. J. J. Thomson, *Proc. Roy Soc.* **96 A**, 311 (1919).

T2. M. Talmey, *The Relativity Theory Simplified,* p. 164. Falcon Press, New York, 1932.

U1. G. E. Uhlenbeck in *Some Strangeness in the Proportion* (H. Woolf, Ed.), p. 524. Addison-Wesley, Reading, Mass., 1980.

17

Unified Field Theory

17a. Particles and Fields around 1920

Einstein died early on a Monday morning. The day before, he had asked for his most recent pages of calculations on unified field theory. The awareness of unfinished work was with him, and not just in those final hours when he knew that death was near. It had been so throughout his life. Nearly forty years earlier, he had written to Felix Klein:

> However we select from nature a complex [of phenomena] using the criterion of simplicity, in no case will its theoretical treatment turn out to be forever appropriate (sufficient). Newton's theory, for example, represents the gravitational field in a seemingly complete way by means of the potential ϕ. This description proves to be wanting; the functions $g_{\mu\nu}$ take its place. But I do not doubt that the day will come when that description, too, will have to yield to another one, for reasons which at present we do not yet surmise. I believe that this process of deepening the theory has no limits. [E1]

That was written in 1917, shortly before he began his search for the unification of gravitation and electromagnetism. Those were still the days in which he knew with unerring instinct how to select complexes from nature to guide his scientific steps. Even then he already had a keen taste for mathematical elegance as well, but did not yet believe that formal arguments alone could be relied upon as markers for the next progress in physics. Thus, later in 1917, when Felix Klein wrote to him about the conformal invariance of the Maxwell equations [K1], he replied:

> It does seem to me that you highly overrate the value of formal points of view. These may be valuable when an *already found* [his italics] truth needs to be formulated in a final form, but fail almost always as heuristic aids. [E2]

Nothing is more striking about the later Einstein than his change of position in regard to this advice, given when he was in his late thirties. I do not believe that his excessive reliance in later years on formal simplicity did him much good, although I do not accept the view of some that this change was tragic. Nothing in Einstein's scientific career was tragic, even though some of his work will be remembered forever and some of it will be forgotten. In any event, when Einstein embarked on his program for a unified field theory, his motivation was thoroughly physical. In order to appreciate this, we must first have a brief look at the physics of particles and fields around 1920.

During the second decade of the twentieth century, there were advances in theoretical physics of the highest calibre. Rutherford discovered the atomic nucleus, Bohr the quantum theory of the atom, Einstein general relativity. It was also the time that provided one of the most striking examples of how physicists can temporarily be led astray by the selection of complexes from nature on grounds of simplicity. The case in point is the model of the nucleus built of protons and electrons.

Rutherford had discovered the proton (so baptized in 1919), the nucleus of the lightest atom. Bohr had been the first to realize that beta decay is a process in which electrons are ejected from the nucleus. What then was more obvious than to assume that the nuclear weight was almost entirely due to a number of constituent protons equal to the mass number, with the difference between mass number and charge number equal to the number of constituent electrons? The nucleus must be considered 'as a very complex structure ... consisting of positively-charged particles and electrons, but it is premature (and would serve no useful purpose) to discuss at the present time the possible structure of the nucleus itself' [R1]. Thus Rutherford expressed himself on the structure of the atom during a Royal Society meeting held on March 19, 1914. Even the cautious Rutherford had but one choice for the nature of the internuclear forces. Again in 1914 he wrote, 'The nucleus, though of minute dimensions, is in itself a very complex system consisting of positively and negatively charged bodies bound closely together by intense *electrical* forces' [R2] (my italics). Nuclear binding energy, he conjectured, is an electromagnetic effect. 'As Lorentz has pointed out, the electrical mass of a system of charged particles, if close together, will depend not only on the number of these particles, but on the way their fields interact. For the dimensions of the positive and negative electrons considered [a positive electron being a proton], the packing must be very close in order to produce an appreciable alteration in the mass due to this cause. This may, for example, be the explanation of the fact that the helium atom has not quite four times the mass of the hydrogen atom' [R3].

Thus all forces within the atom, whether peripheral or in its core, were initially perceived to be electrical. This was a natural thought, especially since the nucleus had been discovered to begin with by the observation that the scattering of alpha particles on atoms was dominated by a coulomb interaction between the alpha particle and a near-pointlike atomic core. Not until 1919 did these scatterings give a first intimation that all was not electrical [R4]. Not until 1921 did experiments show beyond doubt that the $1/r^2$ force law breaks down at small distances. 'It is our task to find some field of force which will represent these effects.... The present experiments ... show that the *forces are of very great intensity*' [C1].

These last words (italicized by me) represent the first instance, as best I know, where it is stated in the literature that there are strong interactions. It was the second great discovery by James Chadwick. His first one had been made in 1914: the primary beta spectrum is continuous [C2]. Until well into the 1920s, this continuity was believed to have secondary causes. The neutrino was not postulated until 1929.

Thus nuclear physics began with a nucleus without neutrons, beta decay without neutrinos. Matter was made of protons and electrons. There were neither weak nor strong interactions. In the beginning there was only electromagnetism. And, of course, there was gravitation.

Which brings us back to unified field theory.

When Einstein, Weyl, and others began their work on unified field theory, it was natural to assume that this task consisted exlusively of the union of gravitation with electromagnetism. To be sure, the separateness of these two fields posed no conflicts or paradoxes. There were no puzzles such as the Michelson–Morley experiment nor curious coincidences like the equality of the inertial and the gravitational mass. Nevertheless, it seemed physically well-motivated and appealing to ask, Do nature's only two fields of force, both long-range in character, have a common origin?

Then it came to pass that physics veered toward a different course, neither led nor followed by Einstein. First quantum mechanics and then quantum field theory took center stage. New forces had to be introduced. New particles were proposed and discovered. Amid all these developments, Einstein stayed with the unification of gravitation and electromagnetism, the final task he set himself. This insistence brought the ultimate degree of apartness to his life.

After his death, the urge for unification returned and became widespread, but both the goals and the methods of pursuit are different now. At the end of this chapter I shall comment further on this new look of the unification program. I turn next to an account of Einstein's own efforts at unification. It remains to be seen whether his methods will be of any relevance for the theoretical physics of the future. Certainly this work of his did not produce any results of physical interest. I therefore believe it will suffice to indicate (omitting details as much as possible) the two general directions in which he looked for the realization of his aims. One of these, based on the extension of space-time to a five-dimensional manifold, is discussed in the Section 17c. The other, based on generalizations of the geometry of Riemann, is treated in Section 17e. The discussion of this second category is preceded by a brief excursion into post-Riemannian geometry and a comment on the influence of Einstein's general relativity on mathematics.

In the early 1920s, the structure of the nucleus was an interesting but secondary problem and the unification of forces a minor issue. Quantum phenomena posed the central challenge. Einstein was well aware of this when, at age forty, he began his search for unification. In fact, by then he already believed that the need to unify forces and the need to resolve the quantum paradoxes were *connected* desiderata. In later years, he was one among few to search for unification and one among few to be critical of quantum mechanics. He was unique in holding the view that there was a link between these problem areas. In this chapter, nothing further will be said on Einstein and quantum physics. However, in Chapter 26 I shall return to his hopes for a new dynamics, based on a generalization of general relativity, in which quantum mechanics would be explained rather than postulated.

17b. Another Decade of Gestation

Einstein completed his first paper on unified field theory in January 1922.

Much had happened to him since the strenuous days of November 1915, when he completed his general relativity theory. He had done his share of applying this theory to the energy–momentum conservation problem, to gravitational waves, and to cosmology. He had introduced the A and B coefficients in quantum theory. He had been ill. He had remarried. After November 1919 he had become a world figure. He had been in the midst of turmoil in Germany. And he had made his first trip to the United States. The problem of unification had been on his mind in the intervening years, even though he had not published on this subject. In 1918 he wrote to Weyl, 'Ultimately it must turn out that action densities must not be glued together additively. I too, concocted various things, but time and again I sank my head in resignation' [E3]. His statement to Ehrenfest in 1920, 'I have made no progress in general relativity theory. The electromagnetic field still stands there in unconnected fashion' [E4], expressed both his disbelief in Weyl's theory (to be described in Section 17d) and his conviction that unification is a worthy cause. When he wrote to Weyl in 1922 about unified theories, 'I believe that in order to make real progress one must again ferret out some general principle from nature' [E5], he was still taking his cues from physics.

Nor were his interests in physics in those years confined to general relativity, whether of the orthodox or of the unified variety. His letters of that period to Ehrenfest, always filled with physics ideas that intrigued him, deal largely with the quantum theory. In 1921 he was excited about his new proposal for an experiment to test quantum aspects in Doppler phenomena [E6]. In 1922 he was intrigued by the Stern–Gerlach experiment [E7]. His January 1922 paper on unified field theory, written with Grommer [E8], is never mentioned in these letters, but a few weeks after its completion he wrote of his work with Grommer on quantum problems [E9]. In 1923 he and Ehrenfest worked on the quantum theory of radiative equilibrium [E10], and, together with another friend,* he published his last paper on experimental physics, a determination of the width of

---

*See the entry about Mühsam in Chapter 29.

capillaries in membranes [E11]. Late in 1924 and early in 1925, his three papers on the Bose–Einstein gas were completed (see Chapter 23).

Meanwhile he was not altogether idle in regard to unified field theory. There is the Einstein–Grommer paper of 1922 in response to the Kaluza theory (see Section 17c). There are several papers in 1923 (to be discussed in Section 17e) elaborating an attempt at unification due to Eddington. But it is not until 1925 that we witness his first truly deep immersion in this subject, as he came forth with an invention all his own of a new version of unification.

From that time on, the character of Einstein's scientific output changes. In 1926 he wrote three papers of that playful but not at all flippant variety which he had so often produced in earlier years, one on the meandering of rivers [E12], two on the light emission by canal rays [E13, E14]. They were his last in this genre. The later period begins. He is nearly fifty years old. Occasionally there are papers on conventional general relativity, such as those on the problem of motion. But unified field theory now becomes the main thrust of his efforts, along with the search for an alternative that deprives quantum mechanics of its status as a fundamental theory. I have already alluded to the fact that these two themes were—in his view—intimately related, a subject to which I shall return at more length in Section 26e.

Heisenberg's first paper on matrix mechanics [H1] and Einstein's first privately created unified field theory [E15] were both completed in July 1925; Schroedinger's first paper on wave mechanics in January 1926 [S1]. Einstein's gestation period before he made the real plunge into unified field theory had lasted about a decade, just as it had been for the special and the general theories of relativity. This time, however, it was not he but others who in the end ushered in the new physics. So it was to remain in the next decade, and the next and the next, until he laid down his pen and died. His work on unification was probably all in vain, but he had to pursue what seemed centrally important to him, and he was never afraid to do so. That was his destiny.

Let us see next what he did, first with five-dimensional theories.

17c. The Fifth Dimension

1. Kaluza and Oskar Klein. The two pioneers of unified field theory were both mathematicians. The first unification, based on a generalization of Riemannian geometry in the usual four space–time dimensions, was proposed by Hermann Weyl in 1918 (see Section 17d). With the same aim in mind, and inspired by Weyl's paper, the mathematician and consummate linguist Theodor Kaluza became the first to suggest that unification might be achieved by extending space–time to a five-dimensional manifold.* His one paper on this subject was published

---

*In 1914 Nordström had already proposed to use a five-dimensional space for the unification of electromagnetism with a *scalar* gravitational field [N1].

in 1921 [K2], but he already had this idea in 1919, for in April of that year Einstein wrote to him, 'The idea of achieving [a unified theory] by means of a five-dimensional cylinder world never dawned on me. . . . At first glance I like your idea enormously' [E16]. Still very much in the Machian mood, Einstein added that one ought to examine whether this new theory would allow for a sensible solution of the cosmological problem.* A few weeks later, he wrote to him again, 'The formal unity of your theory is startling'[E18]. In 1921 he communicated Kaluza's work to the Prussian Academy. (I do not know why this publication was delayed so long.)

Kaluza's well-written paper contains nearly all the main points of the five-dimensional approach:

1. The introduction of an invariant line element

$$ds^2 = \gamma_{\mu\nu}dx^\mu dx^\nu \qquad \mu,\nu = 1,\ldots,5 \qquad (17.1)$$

in which the metric tensor $\gamma_{\mu\nu}$ satisfies two constraints. First, the $\gamma_{\mu\nu}$ shall depend only on the space–time coordinates x^i, $i = 1,\ldots,4$:

$$\frac{\partial \gamma_{\mu\nu}}{\partial x^5} = 0 \qquad (17.2)$$

Secondly, γ_{55} is assumed to be a positive numerical invariant that may be normalized such that

$$\gamma_{55} = 1 \qquad (17.3)$$

Thus we deal with a cylinder world, the fifth axis is preferred, the fifth direction is space-like. Equation 17.3 has become known as the cylinder condition.

2. γ_{i5}, a 4-vector field relative to the Riemannian space–time submanifold R_4, is assumed to be proportional to the electromagnetic potential.

3. The field equations are

$$R_{\mu\nu} - \tfrac{1}{2}g_{\mu\nu}R = -\kappa T_{\mu\nu} \qquad (17.4)$$

where $R_{\mu\nu}$ and R are the familiar functions of the $\Gamma^\lambda_{\mu\nu}$ and their first derivatives and $T_{\mu\nu}$ is the energy–momentum tensor *exclusive* of the purely electromagnetic contribution. Kaluza considered only the case where the source is a single point particle with mass m and charge e, $T^{\mu\nu} = mu^\mu u^\nu$, $u^\mu = dx^\mu/ds$, and showed that for $\mu, \nu = i, j$, one obtains the gravitational field equations; $\mu, \nu = i, 5$, yield the Maxwell equations; $\mu, \nu = 5, 5$, reduces to a trivial identity. The identification of the Maxwell equations requires that u^5 be proportional to e/m. Thus mu^μ is the 5-vector of 'momentum–energy–charge.'

4. A geodesic in the cylinder world can be identified with the trajectory of a charged test particle moving in a combined gravitational-electromagnetic field.

*As was mentioned in Section 15e, Einstein had used the cosmological term in 1919 for the purpose of linking electromagnetism to gravitation [E17].

Kaluza proved his results only for the case where the fields are weak (i.e., $g_{\mu\nu} = \eta_{\mu\nu} + h_{\mu\nu}$, $|h_{\mu\nu}| \ll 1$, $\eta_{55} = 1$) and the velocity is small ($v/c \ll 1$). An important advance was made by Oskar Klein, who showed in 1926* that these two constraints are irrelevant [K3]. Unification (at least this version) has nothing to do with weak fields and low velocities. The resulting formulation has since become known as the Kaluza–Klein theory. Its gist can be stated as follows.

1. Start with the quadratic form Eq. 17.1 and demand that it be invariant under a group G_5 of transformations that is the product of the familiar group of point transformation G_4 in R_4 and the group S_1, defined by

$$x_5' = x_5 + f(x^i) \qquad (17.5)$$

The relations 17.2 and 17.3 are invariant under G_5.

2. Define g_{ik} by

$$g_{ik} = \gamma_{ik} - \gamma_{i5}\gamma_{k5} \qquad (17.6)$$

The g_{ik} are symmetric; they are a tensor under G_4 and are invariant under S_1. Thus we can define $g_{ik}\, dx^i dx^k$ as the standard line element in R_4.

3. Define the electromagnetic potentials ϕ_i by

$$\phi_i = \sqrt{2\kappa}\, \gamma_{i5} \qquad (17.6a)$$

They are a four-vector under G_4 and (since Eq. 17.1 is invariant under G_5) they transform under S_1 as

$$\phi_i' = \phi_i - \sqrt{2\kappa}\, \frac{\partial f}{\partial x^i} \qquad (17.7)$$

which shows that S_1 is a geometrized version of the local electromagnetic gauge group.

4. Let $R^{(5)}$ be the curvature scalar in five-space. A straightforward calculation shows that

$$R^{(5)} = R^{(4)} + \frac{\gamma_{55}}{4}\, F^{ik} F_{ik} \qquad (17.8)$$

$$F_{ik} = \frac{\partial \phi_i}{\partial x^k} - \frac{\partial \phi_k}{\partial x^i} \qquad (17.9)$$

where $R^{(4)}$ is the curvature scalar in R_4. Thus $R^{(5)}$ is the unified Lagrangian for gravitation and electromagnetism! Equation 17.8 makes clear why the factor $\sqrt{2\kappa}$ was introduced in Eq. 17.6a and why it is important that γ_{55} be taken *positive* (and normalized to $+1$).

5. In 1926 Klein already believed that the fifth dimension might have something to do with quantization [K4], an idea that stayed with him for many years

---

*In the same year, the five-dimensional unification was discovered independently by Mandel [M1]; see also [M2] and [F1].

[K5]. In particular he noted that the Lagrangian L for a particle with mass m

$$L = \tfrac{1}{2}m \left(\frac{ds}{d\tau} \right)^2 \qquad (17.10)$$

(where ds is given by Eq. 17.1 and where $d\tau$ is the differential proper time) leads to five conjugate momenta p_μ:

$$p_\mu = \frac{\partial L}{\partial(dx^\mu/d\tau)} \qquad (17.11)$$

such that p_5 is constant along a geodesic. For $i = 1, \ldots, 4$, the corresponding equations of motion yield Kaluza's result for the geodesic motion in a gravitational-electromagnetic field (see, e.g., Pauli's review article [P1]) provided one chooses

$$p_5 = \frac{Ne}{c\sqrt{2\kappa}} \qquad (17.12)$$

where Ne is the charge of the particle considered and e is the charge of the electron. Now, Klein argued [K4], since nature tells us that N is an integer, '[Eq. 17.12] suggests that the atomicity of electricity may be interpreted as a quantum theoretical law. In fact, if the five-dimensional space is assumed to be closed in the direction of x^5 with a period l, and if we apply the formalism of quantum mechanics to our geodesics, we shall expect p_5 to be governed by the following rule:

$$p_5 = N\frac{h'}{l} \qquad (17.13)$$

Thus a length l enters the theory, given by

$$l = \frac{hc\sqrt{2\kappa}}{e} = 0.8 \times 10^{-30}\text{cm} \qquad (17.14)$$

Klein conjectured that '[the] smallness [of l] may explain the nonappearance of the fifth dimension in ordinary experiments as the result of averaging over the fifth dimension.'* This same suspicion that there might be some reality to the fifth dimension was also on Einstein's mind when, in the late 1930s, he

---

*In those years immediately following the discovery of quantum mechanics, there were also quite different speculations to the effect that the fifth dimension had something to do with the new mechanics. For example, it was suggested that γ_{55} should be taken as a scalar field (rather than as a constant) which might play the role of the Schroedinger wavefield [G1].

George Uhlenbeck told me, 'I remember that in the summer of 1926, when Oskar Klein told us of his ideas which would not only unify the Maxwell with the Einstein equations but also bring in the quantum theory, I felt a kind of ecstasy! Now one understands the world!'

worked for some years on the Kaluza–Klein theory. However, Einstein had already become actively interested in Kaluza's ideas before the appearance of Klein's papers in 1926.

2. *Einstein and the Kaluza–Klein Theory.* In 1922 Einstein and Grommer addressed the question, Does Eq. 17.4 have any particle-like solutions in the absence of 'sources,' that is, if $T_{\mu\nu} = 0$? It was a question Einstein had pondered earlier in the context of conventional general relativity. For that case we do not know, he reasoned, how to nail down T_{ik} ($i,k = 1, \ldots, 4$) as firmly as the left-hand side of the gravitational equations. Could we do without a T_{ik} altogether? Perhaps, he said, since the equations for pure gravitation are nonlinear. The possibility that there are nonsingular particle-like solutions for vanishing T_{ik} ought to be considered. In what follows, we shall see that time and time again Einstein kept insisting on the existence of singularity-free solutions of source-free equations as a condition that must be met by a theory acceptable to him.

Transcribed to the Kaluza theory, the question of zero T_{ik} becomes the question of zero $T_{\mu\nu}$. Einstein and Grommer [E8] showed that 'the Kaluza theory possesses no centrally symmetric solution which depends on the $g_{\mu\nu}$ only and which might be interpreted as a (singularity-free) electron,' a conclusion which of course has nothing to do with unified field theory per se, since it could equally well have been asked in the context of ordinary general relativity theory.

Einstein's next papers on the five-dimensional theory are two short communications in February 1927 [E19, E20]. I should explain why these papers are a mystery to me. Recall that in 1926 (in April, to be precise) Klein had presented an improved version of the Kaluza theory. In August 1926 Einstein wrote to Ehrenfest that Grommer had drawn his attention to Klein's paper: 'Subject: Kaluza, Schroedinger, general relativity' [E21]. Ten days later, he wrote to him again: 'Klein's paper is beautiful and impressive, but I find Kaluza's principle too unnatural' [E22]. Then come Einstein's own two papers just mentioned, followed by a letter to Lorentz: 'It appears that the union of gravitation and Maxwell's theory is achieved in a completely satisfactory way by the five-dimensional theory (Kaluza–Klein–Fock)' [E23, F1].

There is nothing unusual in Einstein's change of opinion about a theory being unnatural at one time and completely satisfactory some months later. What does puzzle me is a note added to the second paper [E20]: 'Herr Mandel points out to me that the results communicated by me are not new. The entire content is found in the paper by O. Klein.' An explicit reference is added to Klein's 1926 paper [K3]. I fail to understand why he published his two notes in the first place.

Einstein then remained silent on the subject of five dimensions until 1931, when he and Walther Mayer (see Chapter 29) presented a new formalism 'which is psychologically connected with the known theory of Kaluza but in which an extension of the physical continuum to five dimensions is avoided' [E24]. He wrote enthusiastically to Ehrenfest that this theory 'in my opinion definitively solves the problem in the macroscopic domain' [E25] (for the last four words read: excluding quantum phenomena). This was his motivation: 'It is anomalous to replace the four-dimensional continuum by a five-dimensional one and then subsequently to tie up artificially one of these five dimensions in order to account for the fact that it does not manifest itself. We have succeeded in formulating a theory which formally approximates Kaluza's theory without being exposed to the objection just stated. This is accomplished by the introduction of an entirely new mathematical concept' [E26].

The new mathematics presented by Einstein and Mayer in two papers [E24, E27] does *not* involve the embedding of the Riemann manifold R_4 in a five-space. Instead, a five-dimensional vector space M_5 is associated with each point of R_4 and the local Minkowski space (call it M_4) is embedded in the local M_5, which has $(4 + 1)$-metric. Prescriptions are introduced for decomposing tensors in M_5 with respect to M_4. The transport of 5-tensors from one M_5 to another M_5 attached to a neighboring point in R_4 is defined. This involves a five-dimensional connection of which (so it is arranged) some components are identified with the Riemannian connection in R_4 while, in addition, only an antisymmetrical tensor F_{kl} appears, which is identified with the electromagnetic field.* However (as Einstein noted in a letter to Pauli [E28]), one has to *assume* that F_{kl} is the curl of a 4-vector; also, the Einstein–Mayer equations are not derivable from a variational principle. After 1932 we find no trace of this theory in Einstein's work.

In a different environment, he made one last try at a five-dimensional theory. He was in America now. His old friend Ehrenfest was gone. The year was 1938. This time he had in mind not to make x^5 less real than Kaluza–Klein, but more real. At first he worked with Peter Bergmann; later Valentin Bargmann joined them. Altogether, their project was under active consideration for some three years. Bergmann's textbook tells us what the motivation was:

> It appeared impossible for an iron-clad four-dimensional theory ever to account for the results of quantum theory, in particular for Heisenberg's indeterminacy relation. Since the description of a five-dimensional world in terms of a four-dimensional formalism would be incomplete, it was hoped that the indeterminacy of 'four dimensional' laws would account for the indeterminacy relation and that quantum phenomena would, after all, be explained by a [classical] field theory. [B1]

Their approach was along the lines of Klein's idea [K4] that the 5-space is closed in the fifth direction with a fixed period. The group is again G_5 (see Eq. 17.5). The line element (Eq. 17.1), the condition (Eq. 17.3) on γ_{55}, and the definition (Eq. 17.6) of g_{ik} are also maintained, but Eq. 17.2 is generalized. It is still assumed that the γ_{i5} (the electromagnetic potentials) depend only on x^i, but (and this is new) the g_{ik} are allowed to depend periodically on x^5. The resulting formalism is

---

*These rules are summarized in papers by Pauli and Solomon [P2] that have been reproduced in Pauli's collected works [P3].

discussed in much detail in Bergmann's book (see also [B2] and [P1]). Two versions of the theory were considered. In the first one [E29], the field equations are derived from a variational principle. Because of the new x^5 dependence, they are integro-differential equations (an integration over x^5 remains). They also contain several arbitrary constants because the action can contain new invariants (depending on derivatives of the g_{ik} with respect to x^5). In a second version [E30], the variational principle is abandoned and Bianchi identities which constrain these constants are postulated.

In theories of this kind, the g_{ik} can be represented by (the period is normalized to 2π):

$$g_{ik}(x^5, x^i) = \sum_{n=-\infty}^{\infty} g_{ik}^{(n)}(x^i) e^{inx^5}$$

$$g_{ik}^{(-n)} = g_{ik}^{(n)*}$$

(17.15)

Bargmann and Bergmann told me that Einstein thought that the higher Fourier components might somehow be related to quantum fields. He gave up the five-dimensional approach for good when these hopes did not materialize.

3. *Addenda*. Other attempts to use five- or more-dimensional manifolds for a description of the physical world continue to be made.

a) Soon after the Einstein–Mayer theory, another development in five-dimensional theory began, known as projective relativity, to which many authors contributed.* In this theory the space–time coordinates x^i are assumed to be homogeneous functions of degree zero in five coordinates X^μ. A Riemann metric with invariant line element $ds^2 = g_{\mu\nu} dX^\mu dX^\nu$ is introduced in the projective 5-space (which has signature $4 + 1$). The condition

$$g_{\mu\nu} X^\mu X^\nu = 1$$

(17.16)

takes the place of the cylinder condition. The quantities $\gamma_\nu^k = \partial x^k / \partial X^\nu$ project from the 5-space to the 4-space.** One proves that

$$X_\mu = \frac{\sqrt{2\kappa}}{c} \gamma_\mu^k \varphi_k + \frac{1}{F} \frac{\partial F}{\partial X^\mu}$$

(17.17)

where φ_k are the electromagnetic potentials and F is an arbitrary homogeneous function of degree one in the X^μ. Thus the projective coordinates themselves are directly related to the potentials up to a 5-gauge transformation.

The Dirac equation in projective space was discussed by Pauli [P4]. Variational methods were applied to this theory by Pais [P5] with the following results. Let

*For detailed references, see especially [S2]. The best introduction to this subject is a pair of papers by Pauli [P4].

**The mathematical connection between this theory and the Kaluza–Klein theory is discussed in [B1].

$$\delta \int (R - \kappa \mathcal{L}) \sqrt{g} \, d^5X = 0 \tag{17.18}$$

be the variational principle, where R is the 5-curvature scalar. All that is given about $\mathcal{L}$ is that it is a scalar function of field variables and their covariant derivatives. In addition, one *must* admit an explicit dependence of $\mathcal{L}$ on the coordinates X^μ. By extending the Noether methods to this more general situation, one can derive an explicit expression for the source tensor $T^{\mu\nu}$ in terms of $\mathcal{L}$ and derivatives of $\mathcal{L}$ with respect to the fields and to X^μ. This tensor satisfies

$$T^{\mu\nu}_{;\nu} = 0 \tag{17.19}$$

five conservation laws which are shown to be the differential laws for conservation of energy, momentum, and charge.

b) A number of authors, in particular Jordan [J1], have studied an extension of this formalism to the case where the right-hand side of Eq. 17.16 is replaced by a scalar field. Bergmann informed me that he and Einstein also had worked on this generalization [B3].

c) In the 1980s, particle physicists have taken up the study of field equations in $(4 + N)$-dimensional manifolds, where '4' refers to space–time and where the extra N variables span a compact space-like N-dimensional domain which is supposed to be so small as not to influence the usual physics in inadmissible ways. Various values of N are being considered for the purpose of including non-Abelian gauge fields. Some authors advocate dropping constraints of the type 17.2 and 17.3, hoping that the compactness in the additional dimensions will result from 'spontaneous compactification,' a type of spontaneous symmetry breaking. The future will tell what will come of these efforts. It seems fitting to close this section by noting that, in 1981, a paper appeared with the title 'Search for a Realistic Kaluza–Klein Theory' [W1].*

4. Two Options. Einstein spent much less energy on five-dimensional theories than on a second category of unification attempts in which the four-dimensional manifold is retained but endowed with a geometry more general than Riemann's.

At this point the reader is offered two options.

Option 1. Take my word for it that these attempts have led nowhere thus far, skip the next section, skim the two sections thereafter, and turn to the quantum theory.

Option 2. If he is interested in what not only Einstein but also men like Eddington and Schroedinger tried to do with these geometries, turn to the next section.

17d. Relativity and Post-Riemannian Differential Geometry

In his address on general relativity and differential geometry to the Einstein Centennial Symposium in Princeton [C3], the eminent mathematician Shiing-Shen

---

*In that paper, one will find references to other recent work in this direction.

Chern made two statements which apply equally well to the present section: 'It is a strange feeling to speak on a topic of which I do not know half the title', and 'I soon saw the extreme difficulty of his [Einstein's] problem and the difference between mathematics and physics.' Otherwise the overlap between this section and Chern's paper is minor. Chern deals mainly with modern global problems of differential geometry, such as the theory of fiber bundles, subjects which Einstein himself never wrote about or mentioned to me. My own aim is to give an account of unified field theory in Einstein's day, when the concerns were uniquely with local differential geometry and when the now somewhat old-fashioned (and globally inadequate) general Ricci calculus was the main tool. Hence the main purpose of this section: to give the main ideas of this calculus in one easy lesson.* A simple way of doing this is first to consider a number of standard equations and results of Riemannian geometry, found in any good textbook on general relativity, and then to generalize from there.

In Riemannian geometry, we have a line element

$$ds^2 = g_{\mu\nu}dx^\mu dx^\nu \tag{17.20}$$

invariant under all continuous point transformations $x^i \rightarrow x^{i'} = x^{i'}(x^j)$ and a connection $\Gamma^\lambda_{\mu\nu}$ related to the $g_{\mu\nu}$ by

$$\Gamma^\lambda_{\mu\nu} = \tfrac{1}{2}g^{\lambda\sigma}\left(\frac{\partial g_{\sigma\mu}}{\partial x^\nu} + \frac{\partial g_{\sigma\nu}}{\partial x^\mu} - \frac{\partial g_{\mu\nu}}{\partial x^\sigma}\right) \tag{17.21}$$

For later purposes I distinguish two groups of properties.

The First Group

1. A covariant vector field A_μ and a contravariant vector field B^μ transform as

$$A'^\mu = \frac{\partial x'^\mu}{\partial x^\nu} A^\nu \qquad B'_\mu = \frac{\partial x^\nu}{\partial x'^\mu} B_\nu \tag{17.22}$$

from which one deduces the transformation of higher-rank tensors by the standard rules.

2. Contraction of a tensor of rank n (≥ 2) yields a tensor of rank $n - 2$.

3. The covariant derivative of A_μ, defined by

$$A_{\mu;\nu} = \frac{\partial A_\mu}{\partial x^\nu} - \Gamma^\lambda_{\mu\nu}A_\lambda \tag{17.23}$$

is a tensor of the second rank. Covariant derivatives of higher covariant tensors are deduced in the standard way. In particular, $Q_{\mu\nu\lambda}$, defined by

---

*The interested reader is urged to read Schroedinger's wonderful little book on this subject [S3].

$$Q_{\mu\nu\lambda} = g_{\mu\nu;\lambda} \tag{17.24}$$

is a tensor of the third rank.

4. The connection transforms as

$$\Gamma^{\nu'}_{\mu'} = \frac{\partial x'^{\lambda}}{\partial x^{\alpha}} \frac{\partial x^{\beta}}{\partial x'^{\mu}} \frac{\partial x^{\gamma}}{\partial x'^{\nu}} \Gamma^{\alpha}_{\beta\gamma} + \frac{\partial x'^{\lambda}}{\partial x^{\alpha}} \frac{\partial^2 x^{\alpha}}{\partial x'^{\mu} \partial x'^{\nu}} \tag{17.25}$$

5. There is a curvature tensor defined by

$$R^{\lambda}_{\mu\nu\rho} = \frac{\partial \Gamma^{\lambda}_{\mu\nu}}{\partial x^{\rho}} - \frac{\partial \Gamma^{\lambda}_{\mu\rho}}{\partial x^{\nu}} + \Gamma^{\alpha}_{\mu\nu}\Gamma^{\lambda}_{\alpha\rho} - \Gamma^{\alpha}_{\mu\rho}\Gamma^{\lambda}_{\alpha\nu} \tag{17.26}$$

This tensor plays a central role in all unified field theories discussed hereafter.

6. The Ricci tensor $R_{\mu\nu}$ is defined by

$$R_{\mu\nu} = R^{\lambda}_{\mu\lambda\nu} = \frac{\partial \Gamma^{\lambda}_{\mu\lambda}}{\partial x^{\nu}} - \frac{\partial \Gamma^{\lambda}_{\mu\nu}}{\partial x^{\lambda}} + \Gamma^{\alpha}_{\mu\lambda}\Gamma^{\lambda}_{\alpha\nu} - \Gamma^{\alpha}_{\mu\nu}\Gamma^{\lambda}_{\alpha\lambda} \tag{17.27}$$

The Second Group

1.
$$\Gamma^{\lambda}_{\mu\nu} = \Gamma^{\lambda}_{\nu\mu} \tag{17.28}$$

2.
$$\Gamma^{\alpha}_{\alpha\lambda} = \frac{1}{\sqrt{g}} \frac{\partial \sqrt{g}}{\partial x^{\lambda}} \qquad g \equiv - \det g_{\mu\nu} \tag{17.29}$$

3.
$$R_{\mu\nu} = R_{\nu\mu} \tag{17.30}$$

4.
$$Q_{\mu\nu\rho} = 0 \tag{17.31}$$

5. If A^{μ} is a contravariant vector field with a covariant derivative defined by

$$A^{\mu}_{;\nu} = \frac{\partial A^{\mu}}{\partial x^{\nu}} + \tilde{\Gamma}^{\mu}_{\alpha\nu} A^{\alpha} \tag{17.32}$$

then

$$\tilde{\Gamma}^{\mu}_{\alpha\nu} = \Gamma^{\mu}_{\alpha\nu} \tag{17.33}$$

6. The quantity R defined by

$$R = g_{\mu\nu}R^{\mu\nu} \tag{17.34}$$

is a scalar.

7.
$$(R^{\mu\nu} - \tfrac{1}{2}g^{\mu\nu}R)_{;\nu} = 0 \tag{17.35}$$

8. The equations

$$R^{\lambda}_{\mu\nu\rho} = 0 \tag{17.36}$$

are necessary and sufficient conditions for a Riemann space to be everywhere flat (pseudo-Euclidean).

Now comes the generalization. Forget Eqs. 17.20 and 17.21 and the second group of statements. Retain the first group. This leads not to one new geometry but to a new class of geometries, or, as one also says, a new class of connections. Let us note a few general features.

a) There is no longer a metric. There are only connections. Equation 17.25, now *imposed* rather than derived from the transformation properties of $g_{\mu\nu}$, is sufficient to establish that $A_{\mu;\nu}$ and $R_{\mu\nu}$ are tensors. Thus we still have a tensor calculus.

b) A general connection is defined by the 128 quantities $\Gamma^\lambda_{\mu\nu}$ and $\tilde{\Gamma}^\lambda_{\mu\nu}$. If these are given in one frame, then they are given in all frames provided we add the rule that even if $1^\lambda_{\mu\nu} \neq \tilde{\Gamma}^\lambda_{\mu\nu}$ then $\tilde{\Gamma}^\lambda_{\mu\nu}$ still transforms according to Eq. 17.25.

c) In the first group, we retained one reference to $g_{\mu\nu}$, in Eq. 17.24. The reason for doing so is that in these generalizations one often introduces a *fundamental tensor* $g_{\mu\nu}$, but not via the invariant line element. Hence this fundamental tensor no longer deserves the name *metrical tensor*. A fundamental tensor $g_{\mu\nu}$ is nevertheless of importance for associating with *any* contravariant vector A^μ a covariant vector A_μ by the rule $A_\mu = g_{\mu\nu}A^\nu$ and likewise for higher-rank tensors. The $g_{\mu\nu}$ does not in general obey Eq. 17.31, nor need it be symmetric (if it is not, then, of course, $g_{\mu\nu}A^\nu \neq g_{\nu\mu}A^\nu$).

d) Since Eq. 17.28 does not necessarily hold, the order of the μ,ν indices in Eq. 17.23 is important and should be maintained. For unsymmetric $\Gamma^\lambda_{\mu\nu}$, the replacement of $\Gamma^\lambda_{\mu\nu}$ in Eq. 17.23 by $\Gamma^\lambda_{\nu\mu}$ also defines a connection, but a different one.

e) Even if $\Gamma^\lambda_{\mu\nu}$ is symmetric in μ and ν, it does *not* follow that $R_{\mu\nu}$ is symmetric: we may use Eq. 17.27 but not Eq. 17.30. This remark is of importance for the Weyl and Eddington theories discussed in what follows.

f) For *any* symmetric connection, the Bianchi identities

$$R^\lambda_{\mu\nu\rho;\sigma} + R^\lambda_{\mu\sigma\nu;\rho} + R^\lambda_{\mu\rho\sigma;\nu} = 0 \qquad (17.37)$$

are valid.

g) $R^\lambda_{\mu\nu\sigma}$ is still a tensor, but $R^\lambda_{\mu\nu\sigma} = 0$ does not *in general* imply flatness; see the theory of distant parallelism discussed in the next section.

h) We can always contract the curvature tensor to the Ricci tensor, but, in the absence of a fundamental tensor, we cannot obtain the curvature scalar from the Ricci tensor.

i) the *contracted* Bianchi identities Eq. 17.35 are in general not valid, nor even defined. These last two observations already make clear to the physicist that the use of general connections means asking for trouble.

The theory of connections took off in 1916, starting with a paper by the mathematician Gerhard Hessenberg [H2]. These new developments were entirely a consequence of the advent of general relativity, as is seen from persistent reference to that theory in all papers on connections which appeared in the following years, by authors like Weyl, Levi-Civita, Schouten, Struik, and especially Élie Cartan, who introduced torsion in 1922 [C4], and whose memoir 'Sur les Variétés à Connexion Affine et la théorie de la Relativité Généralisée' [C5] is one of the papers which led to the modern theory of fiber bundles [C3]. Thus Einstein's labors had a major impact on mathematics.

The first book on connections, Schouten's *Der Ricci-Kalkül* [S4], published in 1924, lists a large number of connections distinguished (see [S4], p. 75) by the relative properties of $\Gamma^\lambda_{\mu\nu}$ and $\tilde{\Gamma}^\lambda_{\mu\nu}$, the symmetry properties of $\Gamma^\lambda_{\mu\nu}$, and the properties of $Q_{\mu\nu\rho}$. It will come as a relief to the reader that for all unified field theories to be mentioned below, Eq. 17.33 *does hold*. This leads to considerable simplifications since then, and only then, product rules of the kind

$$(A^\lambda B_\lambda)_{;\mu} = A^\lambda_{;\mu} B_\lambda + A^\lambda B_{\lambda;\mu} \tag{17.38}$$

hold true. *Important note*: the orders of indices in Eqs. 17.23 and 17.32 are matched in such a way that Eq. 17.38 is also true for nonsymmetric connections.

Let us consider the Weyl theory of 1918 [W2] as an example of this formalism. This theory is based on Eq. 17.33, on a symmetric (also called affine) connection, and on a symmetric fundamental tensor $g_{\mu\nu}$. However, $Q_{\mu\nu\rho}$ does not vanish. Instead:

$$\left(\frac{\partial}{\partial x^\rho} + \phi_\rho \right) g_{\mu\nu} - g_{\mu\sigma}\Gamma^\sigma_{\nu\rho} - g_{\nu\sigma}\Gamma^\sigma_{\mu\rho} = 0 \tag{17.39}$$

(which reduces to $Q_{\mu\nu\rho} = 0$ for $\phi_\rho = 0$). ϕ_ρ is a 4-vector. This equation is invariant under

$$g'_{\mu\nu} = \lambda g_{\mu\nu} \tag{17.40}$$

$$\phi'_\mu = \phi_\mu - \frac{1}{\lambda}\frac{\partial\lambda}{\partial x^\mu} \tag{17.41}$$

$$\Gamma'^\sigma_{\mu\nu} = \Gamma^\sigma_{\mu\nu} \tag{17.42}$$

where λ is an arbitrary function of x^μ. Equations 17.40–17.42 are compatible since Eq. 17.39 implies that

$$\Gamma^\lambda_{\mu\nu} = \Gamma^{*\lambda}_{\mu\nu} + \frac{1}{2}g^{\lambda\sigma}(g_{\sigma\mu}\phi_\nu + g_{\sigma\nu}\phi_\mu - g_{\mu\nu}\phi_\sigma) \tag{17.43}$$

where $\Gamma^{*\lambda}_{\mu\nu}$ is the Riemannian expression given by the right-hand side of Eq. 17.21. Weyl's group is the product of the point transformation group and the group of λ transformations specified by Eqs. 17.40 and 17.41. The x^λ are unchanged by λ transformations, so that the thing $ds^2 = g_{\mu\nu}dx^\mu dx^\nu \rightarrow \lambda ds^2$. If we dare to think of the thing ds as a length, then length is regauged (in the same sense the word is used for railroad tracks), whence the expression *gauge transformations*, which made its entry into physics in this unphysical way. The quantities $R^\lambda_{\mu\nu\sigma}$ and $F_{\mu\nu}$ defined by

$$F_{\mu\nu} = \frac{\partial \phi_\mu}{\partial x^\nu} - \frac{\partial \phi_\nu}{\partial x^\mu} \qquad (17.44)$$

are both gauge-invariant tensors. So, therefore, is $R_{\mu\nu}$ (which is not symmetric now); R is a scalar but is not gauge invariant: $R' = \lambda^{-1} R$, since $g^{\mu\nu\prime} = \lambda^{-1} g^{\mu\nu}$.

It is obvious what Weyl was after: $F_{\mu\nu}$ is to be the electromagnetic field. In addition, he could show that his group leads automatically to the five conservation laws for energy, momentum, and charge. His is not a unified theory if one demands that there be a unique underlying Lagrangian L that forces the validity of the gravitational and electromagnetic field equations, since to any L one can add an arbitrary multiple of the gauge-invariant scalar $\int F_{\mu\nu} F^{\mu\nu} \sqrt{g} \; d^4x$. For a detailed discussion and critique of this theory, see books by Pauli [P1] and by Bergmann [B1].

When Weyl finished this work, he sent a copy to Einstein and asked him to submit it to the Prussian Academy [W3]. Einstein replied, 'Your ideas show a wonderful cohesion. Apart from the agreement with reality, it is at any rate a grandiose achievement of the mind' [E31]. Einstein was of course critical of the fact that the line element was no longer invariant. The lengths of rods and the readings of clocks would come to depend on their prehistory [E32], in conflict with the fact that all hydrogen atoms have the same spectrum irrespective of their provenance. He nevertheless saw to the publication of Weyl's paper, but added a note in which he expressed his reservations [E33].* Weyl's response was not convincing. Some months later, he wrote to Einstein, '[Your criticism] very much disturbs me, of course, since experience has shown that one can rely on your intuition' [W4].

This theory did not live long. But local gauge transformations survived, though not in the original meaning of regauging lengths and times. In the late 1920s, Weyl introduced the modern version of these transformations: local phase transformations of matter wave functions. This new concept, suitably amplified, has become one of the most powerful tools in theoretical physics.

17e. The Later Journey: a Scientific Chronology

The last period of Einstein's scientific activities was dominated throughout by unified field theory. Nor was quantum theory ever absent from his mind. In all those thirty years, he was as clear about his aims as he was in the dark about the methods by which to achieve them. On his later scientific journey he was like a traveler who is often compelled to make many changes in his mode of transportation in order to reach his port of destination. He never arrived.

The most striking characteristics of his way of working in those years are not all that different from what they had been before: devotion to the voyage, enthu-

---

*In 1921, Einstein wrote a not very interesting note in which he explored, in the spirit of Weyl, a relativity theory in which only $g_{\mu\nu} dx^\mu dx^\nu = 0$ is invariant [E34].

siasm, and an ability to drop without pain, regrets, or afterthought, one strategy and to start almost without pause on another one. For twenty years, he tried the five-dimensional way about once every five years. In between as well as thereafter he sought to reach his goal by means of four-dimensional connections, now of one kind, then of another. He would also spend time on problems in general relativity (as was already discussed in Chapter 15) or ponder the foundations of quantum theory (as will be discussed in Chapter 25).

Returning to unified field theory, I have chosen the device of a scientific chronology to convey how constant was his purpose, how manifold his methods, and how futile his efforts. The reader will find other entries (that aim to round off a survey of the period) interspaced with the items on unification. The entries dealing with the five-dimensional approach, already discussed in Section 17b, are marked with a †. Before I start with the chronology, I should stress that Einstein had three distinct motives for studying generalizations of general relativity. First, he wanted to join gravity with electromagnetism. Second, he had been unsuccessful in obtaining singularity-free solutions of the source-free general relativistic field equations which could represent particles; he hoped to have better luck with more general theories. Third, he hoped that such theories might be of help in understanding the quantum theory (see Chapter 26).

1922.† A study with Grommer on singularity-free solutions of the Kaluza equations.

1923. Four short papers [E35, E36, E37, E38] on Eddington's program for a unified field theory. In 1921 Eddington had proposed a theory inspired by Weyl's work [E39]. As we just saw, Weyl had introduced a connection and a fundamental tensor, both symmetric, as primary objects. In Eddington's proposal only a symmetric $\Gamma^\lambda_{\mu\nu}$ is primary; a symmetric fundamental tensor enters through a back door. A theory of this kind contains a Ricci tensor $R_{\mu\nu}$ that is not symmetric (even though the connection is symmetric). Put

$$R_{\mu\nu} = R^{(+)}_{\mu\nu} + R^{(-)}_{\mu\nu} \tag{17.45}$$

where the first (second) term is the symmetric (antisymmetric) part. Not only is $R^{(-)}_{\mu\nu}$ antisymmetric, it is a curl: according to Eq. 17.27

$$R^{(-)}_{\mu\nu} = \frac{1}{2}\left(\frac{\partial \phi_\mu}{\partial x^\nu} - \frac{\partial \phi_\nu}{\partial x^\mu} \right) \qquad \phi_\mu = \Gamma^\lambda_{\mu\lambda} \tag{17.46}$$

(recall that $R^{(-)}_{\mu\nu} = 0$ in the Riemannian case because of Eq. 17.29). Eddington therefore suggested that $R^{(-)}_{\mu\nu}$ play the role of electromagnetic field.

Note further that

$$ds^2 \equiv \frac{1}{\lambda} R_{\mu\nu} dx^\mu dx^\nu = \frac{1}{\lambda} R^{(+)}_{\mu\nu} dx^\mu dx^\nu \tag{17.47}$$

is a scalar, where λ is some constant. *Define* $g_{\mu\nu}$ by

$$R^{(+)}_{\mu\nu} = \lambda g_{\mu\nu} \tag{17.48}$$

an equation akin to an Einstein equation with a cosmological constant. Then from Eqs. 17.47 and 17.48 we *derive* rather than postulate a metric.

It is all rather bizarre, a Ricci tensor which is the sum of a metric and an electromagnetic field tensor. In 1923 Weyl declared the theory not fit for discussion ('undiskutierbar') [W5], and Pauli wrote to Eddington, 'In contrast to you and Einstein, I consider the invention of the mathematicians that one can found a geometry on an affine connection without a [primary] line element as for the present of no significance for physics' [P6].

Einstein's own initial reaction was that Eddington had created a beautiful framework without content [E40]. Nevertheless, he began to examine what could be made of these ideas and finally decided that 'I must absolutely publish since Eddington's idea must be thought through to the end' [E41]. That was what he wrote to Weyl. Three days later, he wrote to him again about unified field theories: 'Above stands the marble smile of implacable Nature which has endowed us more with longing than with intellectual capacity' [E42].* Thus, romantically, began Einstein's adventures with general connections, adventures that were to continue until his final hours.

Einstein set himself the task of answering a question not fully treated by Eddington: what are the field equations for the forty fundamental $\Gamma^\lambda_{\mu\nu}$ that take the place of the ten field equations for the $g_{\mu\nu}$ in general relativity? The best equations he could find were of the form

$$\Gamma^\lambda_{\mu\nu} = \Gamma^{*\lambda}_{\mu\nu} - \tfrac{1}{2}g_{\mu\nu}i^\lambda + \tfrac{1}{6}(\delta^\lambda_\mu i_\nu + \delta^\lambda_\nu i_\mu) \qquad (17.49)$$

where $\Gamma^{*\lambda}_{\mu\nu}$ is the rhs of Eq. 17.21 and where the i^λ had to be interpreted as the sources of the electromagnetic field. Then he ran into an odd obstacle: it was impossible to derive source-free Maxwell equations! In addition, there was the old lament: 'The theory . . . brings us no enlightenment on the structure of electrons' [E38], there were no singularity-free solutions.

In 1925 Einstein referred to these two objections at the conclusion to an appendix for the German edition of Eddington's book on relativity. 'Unfortunately, for me the result of this consideration consists in the impression that the Weyl–Eddington [theories] are unable to bring progress in physical knowledge' [E43].

1924–5. Three papers on the Bose–Einstein gas, Einstein's last major innovative contribution to physics (see Chapter 23).

1925. Einstein's first homemade unified field theory, also the first example of a publicly expressed unwarranted optimism for a particular version of a unified theory followed by a rapid rejection of the idea. 'After incessant search during the last two years, I now believe I have found the true solution,' he wrote in the opening paragraph of this short paper [E44].

Both the connection and a primary fundamental tensor $g^{\mu\nu}$ are nonsymmetric

---

* ' . . . Darüber steht das marmorne Lächeln der unerbittlichen Natur, die uns mehr Sehnsucht als Geist verliehen hat.'

in this new version. Thus there are eighty fundamental fields, all of which are to be varied independently in his variational principle

$$\delta \int g^{\mu\nu} R_{\mu\nu} \sqrt{g} \, d^4x = 0 \qquad (17.50)$$

where $R_{\mu\nu}$ is once again the Ricci tensor (still a tensor, as was noted earlier). Equation 17.50 looks, of course, very much like the variational principle in general relativity. Indeed, Eq. 17.21 is recovered in the symmetric limit (not surprising since in that case the procedure reduces to the Palatini method [P1]). In the general case, relations between $\Gamma^\lambda_{\mu\nu}$ and $g_{\mu\nu}$ can be obtained only up to the introduction of an arbitrary 4-vector.

Einstein attempted to identify the symmetric part of $g_{\mu\nu}$ with gravitation, the antisymmetric part $\phi_{\mu\nu}$ with the electromagnetic field. However, $\phi_{\mu\nu}$ is in general not a curl. The closest he could come to the first set of Maxwell equations was to show that in the weak-field limit

$$\frac{\partial}{\partial x_\alpha} \left(\frac{\partial \phi_{\mu\nu}}{\partial x^\alpha} + \frac{\partial \phi_{\nu\alpha}}{\partial x_\mu} + \frac{\partial \phi_{\alpha\mu}}{\partial x^\nu} \right) = 0 \qquad (17.51)$$

There the paper ends. Einstein himself realized soon after the publication of this work that the results were not impressive. He expressed this in three letters to Ehrenfest. In the first one, he wrote, 'I have once again a theory of gravitation–electricity; very beautiful but dubious' [E45]. In the second one, 'This summer I wrote a very beguiling paper about gravitation–electricity . . . but now I doubt again very much whether it is true' [E46]. Two days later, 'My work of last summer is no good' [E47]. In a paper written in 1927 he remarked, *'As a result of numerous failures, I have now arrived at the conviction that this road* [Weyl → Eddington → Einstein] *does not bring us closer to the truth'* [E48].

[Remark. Einstein's work was done independently of Cartan, who was the first to introduce nonsymmetric connections (the antisymmetric parts of the $\Gamma^\lambda_{\mu\nu}$ are now commonly known as Cartan torsion coefficients). There is considerable interest by general relativists in theories of this kind, called Einstein–Cartan theories [H3]. Their main purpose is to link torsion to spin. This development has, of course, nothing to do with unification, nor was Einstein ever active in this direction].

1927.† Einstein returns to the Kaluza theory. His improved treatment turns out to be identical with the work of Klein. In January 1928 he writes to Ehrenfest that this is the right way to make progress. 'Long live the fifth dimension' [E49]. Half a year later, he was back at the connections.

1928. All attempts at unification mentioned thus far have in common that one could imagine or hope for standard general relativity to reappear somehow, embedded in a wider framework. Einstein's next try is particularly unusual, since the most essential feature of the 'old' theory is lost from the very outset: the existence of a nonvanishing curvature tensor expressed in terms of the connection by Eq. 17.26.

It began with a purely mathematical paper [E50], a rarity in Einstein's oeuvre, in which he invented distant parallelism (also called absolute parallelism or tele-parallelism). Transcribed in the formalism of the previous section, this geometry looks as follows. Consider a contravariant Vierbein field, a set of four orthonormal vectors h_a^v, $a = 1, 2, 3, 4$; a numbers the vectors, v their components. Imagine that it is possible for this Vierbein *as a whole* to stay parallel to itself upon arbitrary displacement, that is, $h_{a;\mu}^v = 0$ for each a, or, in longhand,

$$\frac{\partial h_a^v}{\partial x^\mu} + \Gamma_{\lambda\mu}^v h_a^\lambda = 0 \tag{17.52}$$

for each a. If this is possible, then one can evidently define the notion of a straight line (not to be confused with a geodesic) and of parallel lines. Let h_{va} be the normalized minor of the determinant of the h_a^v. Then (summation over a is understood)

$$h_{\rho a} h_a^v = \delta_\rho^v \tag{17.53}$$

The notation is proper since h_{va} is a covariant vector field. From Eqs. 17.52 and 17.53 we can solve for the connection:

$$\Gamma_{\lambda\mu}^v = -h_{\lambda a}\frac{\partial h_a^v}{\partial x^\mu} \tag{17.54}$$

from which one easily deduces that

$$R_{v\lambda\sigma}^\mu = 0 \tag{17.55}$$

Thus distant parallelism is possible only for a special kind of nonsymmetric connection in which the sixty-four $\Gamma_{\lambda\mu}^v$ are expressible in terms of sixteen fields and in which the curvature tensor vanishes. When Einstein discovered this, he did not know that Cartan was already aware of this geometry.*

All these properties are independent of any metric. However, one can define an invariant line element $ds^2 = g_{\mu\nu}dx^\mu dx^\nu$ with

$$g_{\mu\nu} = h_{\mu a} h_{va} \tag{17.56}$$

The resulting geometry, a Riemannian geometry with torsion, was the one Einstein independently invented. A week later he proposed to use this formalism for unification [E51a]. Of course, he had to do something out of the ordinary since he had no Ricci tensor. However, he had found a new tensor $A_{\mu\nu}^\lambda$ to play with, defined by

$$A_{v\mu}^\lambda = \Gamma_{v\mu}^\lambda - \Gamma_{v\mu}^{*\lambda} \tag{17.57}$$

where $\Gamma_{\mu\nu}^{*\lambda}$ is defined by the rhs of Eq. 17.21 (it follows from Eq. 17.25 that $A_{\nu\mu}^\lambda$ is a true tensor). He hoped to be able to identify $A_{v\lambda}^\lambda$ with the electromagnetic potential, but even for weak fields he was unable to find equations in which grav-

---

*See a letter from Cartan to Einstein [C6] (in which Cartan also notes that he had alluded to this geometry in a discussion with Einstein in 1922) reproduced in the published Cartan–Einstein correspondence [D1]. In 1929, Einstein wrote a review of this theory [E51] to which, at his suggestion, Cartan added a historical note [C7].

itational and electromagnetic fields are separated, an old difficulty. There the matter rested for several months, when odd things began to happen.

On November 4, 1928, *The New York Times* carried a story under the heading 'Einstein on verge of great discovery; resents intrusion,' followed on November 14 by an item 'Einstein reticent on new work; will not "count unlaid eggs." ' Einstein himself cannot have been the direct source of these rumors, also referred to in *Nature* [N2], since these stories erroneously mentioned that he was preparing a book on a new theory. In actual fact, he was at work on a short paper dealing with a new version of unification by means of distant parallelism. On January 11, 1929, he issued a brief statement to the press stating that 'the purpose of this work is to write the laws of the fields of gravitation and electromagnetism under a unified view point' and referred to a six-page paper he had submitted the day before [E52]. A newspaper reporter added the following deathless prose to Einstein's statement. 'The length of this work—written at the rate of half a page a year—is considered prodigious when it is considered that the original presentation of his theory of relativity [on November 25, 1915] filled only three pages' [N3]. 'Einstein is amazed at stir over theory. Holds 100 journalists at bay for a week,' the papers reported a week later, adding that he did not care for this publicity at all. But Einstein's name was magic, and shortly thereafter he heard from Eddington. 'You may be amused to hear that one of our great department stores in London (Selfridges) has posted on its window your paper (the six pages pasted up side by side) so that passers-by can read it all through. Large crowds gather around to read it!' [E53]. The 'Special Features' section of the Sunday edition of *The New York Times* of February 3, 1929, carried a full-page article by Einstein on the early developments in relativity, ending with remarks on distant parallelism in which his no doubt bewildered readers were told that in this geometry parallelograms do not close.* So great was the public clamor that he went into hiding for a while [N4].

It was much ado about very little. Einstein had found that

$$B_{\mu\nu}^{\lambda} = \Gamma_{\mu\nu}^{\lambda} - \Gamma_{\nu\mu}^{\lambda} \tag{17.58}$$

is a third-rank tensor (as follows at once from Eq. 17.25) and now identified $B_{\lambda\nu}^{\lambda}$ with the electromagnetic potentials. He did propose a set of field equations, but added that 'further investigations will have to show whether [these] will give an interpretation of the physical qualities of space' [E52]. His attempt to derive his equations from a variational principle [E54] had to be withdrawn [E55]. Nevertheless, in 1929 he had 'hardly any doubt' that he was on the right track [E56]. He lectured on his theory in England [E57] and in France [E58] and wrote about distant parallelism in semipopular articles [E59, E60, E61, E62]. One of his coworkers wrote of 'the theory which Einstein advocates with great seriousness and emphasis since a few years' [L1].

---

*Consider four straight lines $L_1,..., L_4$. Let L_1 and L_2 be parallel. Let L_3 intersect L_1 and L_2. Through a point of L_1 not on L_3 draw L_4 parallel to L_3. Then L_4 and L_2 need not intersect.

Einstein's colleagues were not impressed. Eddington [E63] and Weyl [W6] were critical (for other views, see [L2] and [W7]). Pauli demanded to know what had become of the perihelion of Mercury, the bending of light, and the conservation laws of energy–momentum [P7]. Einstein had no good answer to these questions [E64], but that did not seem to overly concern him, since one week later he wrote to Walther Mayer, 'Nearly all the colleagues react sourly to the theory because it puts again in doubt the earlier general relativity' [E65]. Pauli on the other hand, was scathing in a review of this subject written in 1932: '[Einstein's] never-failing inventiveness as well as his tenacious energy in the pursuit of [unification] guarantees us in recent years, on the average, one theory per annum. . . . It is psychologically interesting that for some time the current theory is usually considered by its author to be the "definitive solution" ' [P8].

Einstein held out awhile longer. In 1930 he worked on special solutions of his equations [E66] and began a search for identities which should play a role (without the benefit of a variational principle) similar to the role of the Bianchi identities in the usual theory [E67]. One more paper on identities followed in 1931 [E68]. Then he gave up. In a note to *Science*, he remarked that this was the wrong direction [E26] (for his later views on distant parallelism, see [S5]). Shortly thereafter, he wrote to Pauli, 'Sie haben also recht gehabt, Sie Spitzbube,' You were right after all, you rascal [E69]. Half a year after his last paper on distant parallelism he was back at the five dimensions.

1931–2†. Work on the Einstein–Mayer theory of local 5-vector spaces.

1933. The Spencer lecture, referred to in Chapter 16, in which Einstein expressed his conviction that pure mathematical construction enables us to discover the physical concepts and the laws connecting them [E70]. I cannot believe that this was the same Einstein who had warned Felix Klein in 1917 against overrating the value of formal points of view 'which fail almost always as heuristic aids' [E2].

1935. Work with Rosen and Podolsky on the foundations of the quantum theory.

1935–8. Work on conventional general relativity—alone on gravitational lenses, with Rosen on gravitational waves and on two-sheeted spaces, and with Infeld and Hoffmann on the problem of motion.

1938–41†. Last explorations of the Kaluza–Klein theory, with Bergmann and Bargmann.

The early 1940s. In this period, Einstein became interested in the question of whether the most fundamental equations of physics might have a structure other than the familiar partial differential equations. His work with Bargmann on bivector fields [E71, E72]* must be considered an exploration of this kind. It was not meant to necessarily have anything to do with physics. Other such investigations in collaboration with Ernst Straus [S6] remained unpublished.**

---

*See Chapter 29.

**I am grateful to Professors Bargmann and Straus for discussions about this period.

From 1945 until the end. The final Einstein equations. Einstein, now in his mid-sixties, spent the remaining years of his life working on an old love of his, dating back to 1925: a theory with a fundamental tensor and a connection which are both nonsymmetric. Initially, he proposed [E73] that these quantities be complex but hermitian (see also [E74]). However, without essential changes one can revert to the real nonsymmetric formulation (as he did in later papers) since the group remains the G_4 of real point transformations which do not mix real and imaginary parts of the g's and the Γ's. The two mentioned papers were authored by him alone, as were two other contributions, one on Bianchi identities [E75] and one on the place of discrete masses and charges in this theory [E76]. The major part of this work was done in collaboration, however, first with Straus [E77] (see also [S7]), then with Bruria Kaufman [E78, E79], his last assistant. Shortly after Einstein's death, Kaufman gave a summary of this work at the Bern conference [K6]. In this very clear and useful report is also found a comparison with the near-simultaneous work on nonsymmetric connections by Schroedinger [S3] and by Behram Kursunoglu [K7].*

As the large number of papers intimates, Einstein's efforts to master the nonsymmetric case were far more elaborate during the last decade of his life than they had been in 1925. At the technical level, the plan of attack was modified several times. My brief review of this work starts once again from the general formalism developed in the previous section, where it was noted that the properties of the third-rank tensor $Q_{\mu\nu\rho}$ defined by Eq. 17.24 are important for a detailed specification of a connection. That was Einstein's new point of departure. In 1945 he *postulated* the relation

$$g_{\mu\nu;\rho} \equiv \frac{\partial g_{\mu\nu}}{\partial x^\rho} - g_{\lambda\nu}\Gamma^\lambda_{\mu\rho} - g_{\mu\lambda}\Gamma^\lambda_{\rho\nu} = 0 \qquad (17.59)$$

From the transformation properties of the $g_{\mu\nu}$ (which, whether symmetric or not, transform in the good old way; see Eq. 17.22 and the comment following it) and of the $\Gamma^\lambda_{\mu\nu}$ (Eq. 17.25), it follows that Eq. 17.59 is a covariant postulate. Furthermore, now that we are cured of distant parallelism, we once again have nontrivial curvature and Ricci tensors given by Eqs. 17.26 and 17.27, respectively. In addition Γ_μ, defined by

$$\Gamma_\mu \doteq \tfrac{1}{2}(\Gamma^\lambda_{\mu\lambda} - \Gamma^\lambda_{\lambda\mu}) \qquad (17.60)$$

plays a role; Γ_μ is a 4-vector (use Eq. 17.25) which vanishes identically in the Riemann case. The plan was to construct from these ingredients a theory such that (as in 1925) the symmetric and antisymmetric parts of $g_{\mu\nu}$ would correspond to the metric and the electromagnetic field, respectively, and to see if the theory

---

*Schroedinger treats only the connection as primary and introduces the fundamental tensor via the cosmological-term device of Eddington. Kursunoglu's theory is more like Einstein's but contains one additional parameter. For further references to nonsymmetric connections, see [L3, S8, and T1].

could have particle-like solutions. This plan had failed in 1925. It failed again this time. I summarize the findings.

a) The order of the indices of the Γ's in Eq. 17.59 is important and was chosen such that Eq. 17.59 shall remain valid if $g_{\lambda\mu} \rightarrow g_{\mu\lambda}$ and $\Gamma^\lambda_{\mu\nu} \rightarrow \Gamma^\lambda_{\nu\mu}$. Einstein and Kaufman extended this rule to the nontrivial constraint that all final equations of the theory shall be invariant under this transposition operation. ($R_{\lambda\mu}$ is not invariant under transposition; the final equations are. Note that the indices in Eq. 17.26 have been written in such an order that they conform to the choice made by Einstein and his co-workers.)

b) In the symmetric case, Eq. 17.21 is a consequence of Eq. 17.59. This is not true here.

c) $g_{\mu\nu}$ is a *reducible* representation of the group; the symmetric and antisymmetric parts do not mix under G_4. Therefore, the unification of gravitation and electromagnetism is formally arbitrary. 'For this reason, Pauli sticks out his tongue when I tell him about [the theory]' [E80]. An attempt to overcome this objection by extending G_4 was not successful.*

d) As in 1925, the variational principle is given by Eq. 17.50. After lengthy calculations, Einstein and his collaborators found the field equations to be

$$g_{\mu\nu;\rho} = 0$$
$$\Gamma_\mu = 0 \qquad\qquad (17.61)$$
$$R_{\underline{\mu\nu}} = 0$$
$$R_{\underset{\vee}{\mu\nu};\lambda} + R_{\underset{\vee}{\lambda\mu};\nu} + R_{\underset{\vee}{\nu\lambda};\mu} = 0$$

the first of which is identical with Eq. 17.59, which therefore ceases to be a postulate and becomes a consequence of the variational principle. The $R_{\underline{\mu\nu}}$ and $R_{\underset{\vee}{\mu\nu}}$ are the respective symmetric and antisymmetric parts of $R_{\mu\nu}$.

These are Einstein's final field equations.

In his own words (written in December 1954), 'In my opinion, the theory presented here is the logically simplest relativistic field theory which is at all possible. But this does not mean that nature might not obey a more complex field theory' [E81]. It must be said, however, that, once again, logical simplicity failed not only to produce something new in physics but also to reproduce something old. Just as in 1925 (see Eq. 17.51), he could not even derive the electromagnetic field equations in the weak-field approximation (see [K6], p. 234). It is a puzzle to me why he did not heed this result of his, obtained thirty years earlier. Indeed, none of Einstein's attempts to generalize the Riemannian connection ever produced the free-field Maxwell equations.

In 1949 Einstein wrote a new appendix for the third edition of his *The Meaning of Relativity* in which he described his most recent work on unification. It was

---

*The idea was to demand invariance under $\Gamma^\alpha_{\mu\nu} \rightarrow \Gamma^\alpha_{\mu\nu} + \delta^\alpha_\mu \,\partial\lambda/\partial x^\nu$, where λ is an arbitrary scalar function. This forces $\Gamma^\alpha_{\mu\nu}$ to be nonsymmetric and at the same time leaves $R_{\mu\nu}$ invariant. However, the final equation $\Gamma_\mu = 0$ is not invariant under this new transformation.

none of his doing* that a page of his manuscript appeared on the front page of *The New York Times* under the heading 'New Einstein theory gives a master key to the universe' [N5]. He refused to see reporters and asked Helen Dukas to relay this message to them: 'Come back and see me in twenty years' [N6]. Three years later, Einstein's science made the front page one last time. He had rewritten his appendix for the fourth edition, and his equations (Eq. 17.61) appeared in the *Times* under the heading 'Einstein offers new theory to unify law of the cosmos' [N7].

'It is a wonderful feeling to recognize the unifying features of a complex of phenomena which present themselves as quite unconnected to the direct experience of the senses' [E82]. So Einstein had written to Grossmann, in 1901, after completing his very first paper on statistical physics. This wonderful feeling sustained him through a life devoted to science. It kept him engaged, forever lucid. Nor did he ever lose his sense of scientific balance. The final words on unified field theory should be his own:

> The skeptic will say, 'It may well be true that this system of equations is reasonable from a logical standpoint, but this does not prove that it corresponds to nature.' You are right, dear skeptic. Experience alone can decide on truth. [E83]

17f. A Postscript to Unification, a Prelude to Quantum Theory

The unification of forces is now widely recognized to be one of the most important tasks in physics, perhaps the most important one. It would have made little difference to Einstein if he had taken note of the fact—as he could have—that there are other forces in nature than gravitation and electromagnetism. The time for unification had not yet come.

Pauli, familiar with and at one time active in unified field theory, used to play Mephisto to Einstein's Faust. He was fond of saying that men shall not join what God has torn asunder, a remark which, as it turned out, was more witty than wise. In the 1970s, unification achieved its first indubitable successes. Electromagnetism has been joined not to gravitation but to the weak interactions. Attempts to join these two forces to the strong interactions have led to promising but not as yet conclusive schemes known as grand unified theories.

The unification of gravitation with the other known fundamental forces remains now as much of a dream as it was in Einstein's day. It is just barely possible that supergravity** may have something to do with this supreme union and may end our ignorance, so often justly lamented by Einstein, about $T_{\mu\nu}$.

---

*The Princeton University Press displayed the manuscript at an AAAS meeting in New York City.

**For an authoritative account of the status of supergravity, see [Z1].

In his attempts to generalize general relativity, Einstein had from the very beginning two aims in mind. One of these, to join gravitation to electromagnetism in such a way that the new field theory would yield particle-like singularity-free solutions, was described in the preceding pages.

His second aim was to lay the foundations of quantum physics, to unify, one might say, relativity and quantum theory.

Einstein's vision of the grand synthesis of physical laws will be described toward the end of the next part of this book, devoted to the quantum theory. As that part begins, we are back with the young Einstein in that radiant year 1905.

References

B1. P. Bergmann, *Introduction to the Theory of Relativity*, p. 272, Prentice-Hall, New York, 1942.

B2. ——, *Phys. Today*, March 1979, p. 44.

B3. ——, *Ann. Math.* **49**, 255, (1948).

C1. J. Chadwick and E. S. Bieler, *Phil. Mag.* **42**, 923 (1921).

C2. ——, *Verh. Deutsch. Phys. Ges.* **16**, 383, (1914).

C3. S. Chern, in *Some Strangeness in the Proportion* (H. Woolf, Ed.) p. 271, Addison-Wesley, Reading, Mass., 1980.

C4. E. Cartan, *C. R. Ac. Sci. Paris* **174**, 437, 593 (1922).

C5. ——, *Ann. Ec. Norm.* **40**, 325 (1923); **41**, 1 (1924). reprinted in *Oeuvres Complètes*, Vol. 3, p. 569. Gauthier-Villars, Paris, 1955.

C6. ——, letter to A. Einstein, May 8, 1929.

C7. ——, *Math. Ann.* **102**, 698 (1929).

D1. R. Debever (Ed.), *Elie Cartan–Albert Einstein Letters on Absolute Parallelism*. Princeton University Press, Princeton, N.J., 1979.

E1. A. Einstein, letter to F. Klein, March 4, 1917

E2. ——, letter to F. Klein, December 12, 1917.

E3. ——, letter to H. Weyl, September 27, 1918.

E4. ——, letter to P. Ehrenfest, April 7, 1920.

E5. ——, letter to H. Weyl, June 6, 1922.

E6. ——, *PAW*, 1921, p. 882.

E7. —— and P. Ehrenfest, *Z. Phys.* **11**, 31 (1922).

E8. —— and J. Grommer, *Scripta Jerusalem Univ.* **1**, No. 7 (1923).

E9. ——, letter to P. Ehrenfest, February 20, 1922.

E10. —— and P. Ehrenfest, *Z. Phys.* **19**, 301 (1923).

E11. —— and H. Mühsam, *Deutsch. Medizin. Wochenschr.* **49**, 1012 (1923).

E12. ——, *Naturw.* **14**, 223 (1926).

E13. ——, *Naturw.* **14**, 300 (1926).

E14. ——, *PAW*, 1926, P. 334.

E15. ——, *PAW*, 1925, p. 414.

E16. ——, letter to T. Kaluza, April 21, 1919.

E17. ——, *PAW*, 1919, pp. 349, 463.

E18. ——, letter to T. Kaluza, May 5, 1919.

E19. ——, *PAW*, 1927, p. 23.

E20. ——, *PAW*, 1927, p. 26.

E21. ——, letter to P. Ehrenfest, August 23, 1926.

E22. ——, letter to P. Ehrenfest, September 3, 1926.

E23. ——, letter to H. A. Lorentz, February 16, 1927.

E24. —— and W. Mayer, *PAW*, 1931, p. 541.

E25. ——, letter to P. Ehrenfest, September 17, 1931.

E26. ——, *Science* **74,** 438 (1931).

E27. —— and W. Mayer, *PAW*, 1932, p. 130.

E28. ——, letter to W. Pauli, January 22, 1932.

E29. —— and P. Bergmann, *Ann. Math.* **39,** 683 (1938).

E30. ——, V. Bargmann, and P. Bergmann, *T. von Kármán Anniversary Volume*, p. 212. California Institute of Technology, Pasadena, 1941.

E31. ——, letter to H. Weyl, April 8, 1918.

E32. ——, letter to H. Weyl, April 15, 1918.

E33. ——, *PAW*, 1918, p. 478.

E34. ——, *PAW*, 1921, p. 261.

E35. ——, *PAW*, 1923, p. 32.

E36. ——, *PAW*, 1923, p. 76.

E37. ——, *PAW*, 1923, p. 137.

E38. ——, *Nature* **112,** 448 (1923).

E39. A. S. Eddington, *Proc. Roy. Soc.* **99,** 104 (1921).

E40. A. Einstein, letter to H. Weyl, June 6, 1922.

E41. ——, letter to H. Weyl, May 23, 1923.

E42. ——, letter to H. Weyl, May 26, 1923.

E43. ——, appendix to A. S. Eddington, *Relativitätstheorie*. Springer, Berlin, 1925.

E44. ——, *PAW*, 1925, p. 414.

E45. ——, letter to P. Ehrenfest, August 18, 1925.

E46. ——, letter to P. Ehrenfest, September 18, 1925.

E47. ——, letter to P. Ehrenfest, September 20, 1925.

E48. ——, *Math Ann.* **97,** 99 (1927).

E49. ——, letter to P. Ehrenfest, January 21, 1928.

E50. ——, *PAW*, 1928, p. 217.

E51. ——, *Math Ann.* **102,** 685 (1929).

E51a. ——, *PAW*, 1928, p. 224.

E52. ——, *PAW*, 1929, p. 2.

E53. A. S. Eddington, letter to A. Einstein, February 11, 1929.

E54. A. Einstein, *PAW*, 1929, p. 156.

E55. ——, *PAW*, 1930, p. 18.

E56. —— *Festschrift Prof. Dr. A. Stodola* p. 126. Füssli, Zurich, 1929.

E57. ——, *Science* **71,** 608 (1930).

E58. ——, *Ann. Inst. H. Poincaré* **1,** 1 (1930).

E59. ——, *Die Koralle,* 1930, pp. 486–7.

E60. ——, *Forum Philosophicum* **1,** 173 (1930).

E61. ——, *The Yale University Library Gazette* **6,** 3 (1930).

E62. ——, *Die Quelle* **82,** 440 (1932).

E63. A. S. Eddington, *Nature* **123,** 280 (1929).

E64. A. Einstein, letter to W. Pauli, December 24, 1929.

E65. ——, letter to W. Mayer, January 1, 1930.

E66. —— and W. Mayer, *PAW*, 1930, p. 110.

E67. ——, *PAW*, 1930, p. 401.

E68. —— and W. Mayer, *PAW*, 1931, p. 257.

E69. ——, letter to W. Pauli, January 22, 1932.

E70. ——, *On the Method of Theoretical Physics*. Oxford University Press, Oxford, 1933.

E71. —— and V. Bargmann, *Ann. Math.* **45,** 1 (1944).

E72. ——, *Ann. Math.* **45,** 15 (1944).

E73. ——, *Ann. Math.* **46,** 578 (1945).

E74. ——, *Rev. Mod. Phys.* **20,** 35 (1948).

E75. ——, *Can. J. Math.* **2,** 120 (1950).

E76. ——, *Phys. Rev.* **89,** 321 (1953).

E77. —— and E. Straus, *Ann. Math.* **47,** 731 (1946).

E78. —— and B. Kaufman, *Ann. Math.* **59,** 230 (1954).

E79. —— and ——, *Ann. Math.* **62,** 128 (1955).

E80. ——, letter to E. Schroedinger, January 22, 1946.

E81. ——, *The Meaning of Relativity* (5th edn.), p. 163. Princeton University Press, Princeton, N.J. 1955.

E82. ——, letter to M. Grossmann, April 14, 1901.

E83. ——, *Sci. Am.*, April 1950, p. 17.

F1. V. Fock, *Z. Phys.* **39,** 226 (1926).

G1. F. Gonseth and G. Juret, *C. R. Ac. Sci. Paris* **185,** 448, 535 (1927).

H1. W. Heisenberg, *Z. Phys.* **33,** 879 (1926).

H2. G. Hessenberg, *Math. Ann.* **78,** 187 (1916).

H3. F. Hehl, P. von der Heyde, G. D. Kerlick, and J. Nester, *Rev. Mod. Phys.* **48,** 393 (1976).

J1. P. Jordan, *Schwerkraft und Weltall* (2nd edn.). Vieweg, Braunschweig, 1955.

K1. F. Klein, *Gesammelte Mathematische Abhandungen*, Vol. 1, p. 533. Springer, Berlin, 1921.

K2. T. Kaluza, *PAW*, 1921, p. 966.

K3. O. Klein, *Z. Phys.* **37,** 895 (1926).

K4. ——, *Nature* **118,** 516 (1926).

K5. ——, *Helv. Phys. Acta,* Suppl. IV, 58 (1956).

K6. B. Kaufman, *Helv. Phys. Acta,* Suppl. IV, 227 (1956).

K7. B. Kursunoglu, *Phys. Rev.* **88,** 1369 (1952).

L1. C. Lanczos, *Erg. Ex. Naturw.* **10,** 97 (1931).

L2. T. Levi-Civita, *Nature* **123,** 678 (1929).

L3. A. Lichnerowicz, *Théories Relativistes de la Gravitation et de l'Électromagnétisme,* Chap. 4. Masson, Paris, 1955.

M1. H. Mandel, *Z. Phys.* **39,** 136 (1926).

M2. H. Mandel. *Z. Phys.* **45,** 285 (1927).

N1. G. Nordström, *Phys. Zeitschr.* **15,** 504 (1914).

N2. Nature, **123,** 174 (1929).

N3. *New York Times*, January 12, 1929.

N4. *New York Times*, February 4, 1929.

N5. *New York Times*, December 27, 1949.

N6. *New York Times*, December 28, 1949.

N7. *New York Times*, March 30, 1953.

P1. W. Pauli, *Theory of Relativity* (G. Field, Tran.), Supplementary Note 23. Pergamon Press, London, 1958.

P2. —— and J. Solomon, *J. Phys. Radium* **3**, 452, 582 (1932).

P3. ——, *Collected Scientific papers* (R. Kronig and V. Weisskopf, Eds.), Vol. 2, p. 461. Interscience, New York, 1964.

P4. ——, *AdP* **18,** 305, 337 (1933); *Collected Papers*, Vol. 2, p. 630. Interscience, New York, 1964.

P5. A. Pais, *Physica* **8,** 1137 (1941).

P6. W. Pauli, letter to A. S. Eddington, September 20, 1923. Reprinted in *Scientific Correspondence*, p. 115. Springer, New York, 1979.

P7. ——, letter to A. Einstein, December 19, 1929. reprinted in *Scientific Correspondence*, Vol. 1, p. 526.

P8. ——, *Naturw.* **20,** 186 (1932); *Collected Papers*, Vol. 2. p. 1399.

R1. E. Rutherford, *Proc. Roy. Soc.* **A90,** addendum (1914).

R2. ——, *Scientia* **16,** 337 (1914).

R3. ——, *Phil. Mag.* **27,** 488 (1914).

R4. ——, *Phil. Mag.* **37,** 537 (1919).

S1. E. Schroedinger, *AdP* **79,** 361 (1926).

S2. E. Schmutzer, *Relativistische Physik*, Chap. 10. Teubner, Leibzig, 1968.

S3. E. Schroedinger, *Space-Time Structure*. Cambridge University Press, Cambridge, 1950.

S4. J. Schouten, *Der Ricci-Kalkül*. Springer, Berlin, 1924.

S5. H. Salzer, *Arch. Hist. Ex. Sci.* **12,** 88 (1973).

S6. E. Straus in *Some Strangeness in the Proportion* (H. Woolf, Ed.), p. 483. Addison-Wesley, Reading, Mass., 1980.

S7. E. Straus, *Rev. Mod. Phys.* **21,** 414 (1949).

S8. J. Schouten, *Ricci-Calculus* (2nd edn.), Chap. 3, Sec. 11. Springer, Berlin, 1954.

T1. M. A. Tonnelat, *Einstein's Unified Field Theory*. Gordon and Breach, New York, 1966.

W1. E. Witten, *Nucl. Phys.* **B186,** 412 (1981).

W2. H. Weyl, *PAW*, 1918, p. 465.

W3. ——, letter to A. Einstein, April 5, 1918.

W4. ——, letter to A. Einstein, December 10, 1918.

W5. ——, *Raum, Zeit, Materie* (5th edn.), Appendix 4. Springer, Berlin, 1923.

W6. ——, *Z. Phys.* **56,** 330 (1929).

W7. N. Wiener and M. Vallarta, *Nature* **123,** 317 (1929).

Z1. B. Zumino, *Einstein Symposium Berlin,* p. 114. Springer, New York, 1979.

VI
THE QUANTUM THEORY

Apart, adv., 4. Away from others in action or function; separately, independently, individually. . . .

Oxford English Dictionary

18

Preliminaries

18a. An Outline of Einstein's Contributions

In 1948, I undertook to put together the Festschrift in honor of Einstein's seventieth birthday [R1]. In a letter to prospective contributors, I wrote, 'It is planned that the first article of the volume shall be of a more personal nature and, written by a representative colleague, shall pay homage to Einstein on behalf of all contributors' [P1]. I then asked Robert Andrews Millikan to do the honors, as the senior contributor.* He accepted and his article is written in his customary forthright manner. On that occasion, he expressed himself as follows on the equation $E = h\nu - P$ for the photoelectric effect. 'I spent ten years of my life testing that 1905 equation of Einstein's and contrary to all my expectations, I was compelled in 1915 to assert its unambiguous verification in spite of its unreasonableness, since it seemed to violate everything we knew about the interference of light' [M1].

Physics had progressed, and Millikan had mellowed since the days of his 1915 paper on the photoeffect, as is evidenced by what he wrote at that earlier time: 'Einstein's photoelectric equation . . . appears in every case to predict exactly the observed results. . . . Yet the semicorpuscular theory by which Einstein arrived at his equation seems at present wholly untenable' [M2]; and in his next paper, Millikan mentioned 'the bold, not to say the reckless, hypothesis of an electromagnetic light corpuscle' [M3]. Nor was Millikan at that time the only first-rate physicist to hold such views, as will presently be recalled. Rather, the physics community at large had received the light-quantum hypothesis with disbelief and with skepticism bordering on derision. As one of the architects of the pre-1925 quantum theory, the "old" quantum theory, Einstein had quickly found both enthusiastic and powerful support for one of his two major contributions to this field: the quantum theory of specific heat. (There is no reason to believe that such support satisfied any particular need in him.) By sharp contrast, from 1905 to 1923, he was a man apart in being the only one, or almost the only one, to take the light-quantum seriously.

---

*It was decided later that L. de Broglie, M. von Laue, and P. Frank should also write articles of a personal nature.

The critical reaction to Einstein's light-quantum hypothesis of 1905 is of great importance for an understanding of the early developments in quantum physics. It was also a reaction without parallel in Einstein's scientific career. Deservedly, his papers before 1905 had not attracted much attention. But his work on Brownian motion drew immediate and favorable response. The same is true for relativity. Planck became an advocate of the special theory only months after its publication; the younger generation took note as well. Lorentz, Hilbert, F. Klein, and others had followed the evolution of his ideas on general relativity; after 1915 they and others immediately started to work out its consequences. Attitudes to his work on unified field theory were largely critical. Many regarded these efforts as untimely, but few rejected the underlying idea out of hand. In regard to the quantum theory, however, Einstein almost constantly stood apart, from 1905 until his death. Those years cover two disparate periods, the first of which (1905–1923) I have just mentioned. During the second period, from 1926 until the end of his life, he was the only one, or again nearly the only one, to maintain a profoundly skeptical attitude toward quantum mechanics. I shall discuss Einstein's position on quantum mechanics in Chapter 25, but cannot refrain from stating at once that Einstein's skepticism should not be equated with a purely negative attitude. It is true that he was forever critical of quantum mechanics, but at the same time he had his own alternative program for a synthetic theory in which particles, fields, and quantum phenomena all would find their place. Einstein pursued this program from about 1920 (before the discovery of quantum mechanics!) until the end of his life. Numerous discussions with him in his later years have helped me gain a better understanding of his views.

But let me first return to the days of the old quantum theory. Einstein's contributions to it can be grouped under the following headings.

(a) *The Light-Quantum.* In 1900 Planck discovered the blackbody radiation law without using light-quanta. In 1905 Einstein discovered light-quanta without using Planck's law. Chapter 19 is devoted to the light-quantum hypothesis. The interplay between the ideas of Planck and Einstein is discussed. A brief history of the photoelectric effect from 1887 to 1915 is given. This Chapter ends with a detailed account of the reasons why the light-quantum paper drew such a negative response.

(b) *Specific Heats.* Toward the end of the nineteenth century, there existed grave conflicts between the data on specific heats and their interpretation in terms of the equipartition theorem of classical statistical mechanics. In 1906 Einstein completed the first paper on quantum effects in the solid state. This paper showed the way out of these paradoxes and also played an important role in the final formulation of the third law of thermodynamics. These topics are discussed in Chapter 20.

(c) *The Photon.* The light-quantum as originally defined was a parcel of energy. The concept of the photon as a particle with definite energy and momentum emerged only gradually. Einstein himself did not discuss photon momentum until 1917. Relativistic energy momentum conservation relations involving photons were not written down till 1923. Einstein's role in these developments is discussed in Chapter 21, which begins with Einstein's formulation in 1909 of the particle–wave duality for the case of electromagnetic radiation and also contains an account of his discovery of the A and B coefficients and of his earliest concern with the breakdown of classical causality. The Chapter concludes with remarks on the role of the Compton effect.

The reader may wonder why the man who discovered the relation $E = h\nu$ for light in 1905 and who propounded the special theory of relativity in that same year would not have stated sooner the relation $p = h\nu/c$. I shall comment on this question in Section 25d.

(d)   Einstein's work on quantum statistics is treated in Chapter 23, which also includes a discussion of Bose's contribution.

(e)   Einstein's role as a key transitional figure in the discovery of wave mechanics will be discussed in Chapter 24.

I shall continue the outline of Einstein's contributions to the quantum theory in Section 18c. First, however, I should like to take leave of our main character for a brief while in order to comment on the singular role of the photon in the history of the physics of particles and fields. In so doing, I shall interrupt the historical sequence of events in order to make some comments from today's vantage point.

18b. Particle Physics: The First Fifty Years

Let us leave aside the photon for a while and ask how physicists reacted to the experimental discovery or the theoretical prediction (whichever came first) of other new particles. No detailed references to the literature will be given, in keeping with the brevity of my comments on this subject.

The discovery in 1897 of the first particle, the electron, was an unexpected experimental development which brought to an end the ongoing debate about whether cathode rays are molecular torrents or aetherial disturbances. The answer came as a complete surprise: they are neither, but rather are a new form of matter. There were some initial reactions of disbelief. J. J. Thomson once recalled the comment of a colleague who was present at the first lecture Thomson gave on the new discovery: 'I [T.] was told long afterwards by a distinguished physicist who had been present at my lecture that he thought I had been "pulling their leg"' [T1]. Nevertheless, the existence of the electron was widely accepted within the span of very few years. By 1900 it had become clear that beta rays are electrons as well. The discoveries of the free electron and of the Zeeman effect (in 1896) combined made it evident that a universal atomic constituent had been discovered and that the excitations of electrons in atoms were somehow the sources of atomic spectra.

The discovery of the electron was a discovery at the *outer* experimental frontier.

In the first instance, this finding led to the abandonment of the earlier qualitative concept of the indivisibility of the atom, but it did not require, or at least not at once, a modification of the established corpus of theoretical physics.

During the next fifty years, three other particles entered the scene in ways not so dissimilar from the case of the electron, namely, via unexpected discoveries of an experimental nature at the outer frontier. These are the proton (or, rather, the nucleus), the neutron,* and—just half a century after the electron—the muon, the first of the electron's heavier brothers. As to the acceptance of these particles, it took little time to realize that their coming was, in each instance, liberating. Within two years after Rutherford's nuclear model, Bohr was able to make the first real theoretical predictions in atomic physics. Almost at once after the discovery of the neutron, the first viable models of the nucleus were proposed, and nuclear physics could start in earnest. The muon is still one of the strangest animals in the particle zoo, yet its discovery was liberating, too, since it made possible an understanding of certain anomalies in the absorption of cosmic rays. (Prior to the discovery of the muon, theorists had already speculated about the need for an extra particle to explain these anomalies.)

To complete the particle list of the first half century, there are four more particles (it is too early to include the graviton) which have entered physics—but in a different way: initially, they were theoretical proposals. The first neutrino was proposed in order to save the law of energy conservation in beta radioactivity. The first meson (now called the pion) was proposed as the conveyer of nuclear forces. Both suggestions were ingenious, daring, innovative, and successful—but did not demand a radical change of theory. Within months after the public unveiling of the neutrino hypothesis, the first theory of the weak interactions, which is still immensely useful, was proposed. The meson hypothesis immediately led to considerable theoretical activity as well.

The neutrino hypothesis was generally assimilated long before this particle was actually observed. The interval between the proposal and the first observation of the neutrino is even longer than the corresponding interval for the photon. The meson postulate found rapid experimental support from cosmic-ray data—or so it seemed. More than a decade passed before it became clear that the bulk of these observations actually involved muons instead of pions.

Then there was the positron, 'a new kind of particle, unknown to experimental physics, having the same mass and opposite charge to an electron' [D1]. This particle was proposed in 1931, after a period of about three years of considerable

---

*It is often said, and not without grounds, that the neutron was actually anticipated. In fact, twelve years before its discovery, in one of his Bakerian lectures (1920) Rutherford spoke [R2] of 'the idea of the possible existence of an atom of mass one which has zero nuclear charge.' Nor is there any doubt that the neutron being in the air at the Cavendish was of profound importance to its discoverer, James Chadwick [C1]. Even so, not even a Rutherford could have guessed that his 1920 neutron (then conjectured to be a tightly bound proton–electron system) was so essentially different from the particle that would eventually go by that name.

controversy over the meaning of the negative energy solutions of the Dirac equation. During that period, one participant expressed fear for 'a new crisis in quantum physics'[W1]. The crisis was short-lived, however. The experimental discovery of the positron in 1932 was a triumph for theoretical physics. The positron theory belongs to the most important advances of the 1930s.

And then there was the photon, the first particle to be predicted theoretically.

Never, either in the first half-century or in the years thereafter, has the idea of a new particle met for so long with such resistance as the photon. The light-quantum hypothesis was considered somewhat of an aberration even by leading physicists who otherwise held Einstein in the highest esteem. Its assimilation came after a struggle more intense and prolonged than for any other particle ever postulated. Because never, to this day, has the proposal of any particle but the photon led to the creation of a new *inner* frontier. The hypothesis seemed paradoxical: light was known to consist of waves, hence it could not consist of particles. Yet this paradox alone does not fully account for the resistance to Einstein's hypothesis. We shall look more closely at the situation in Section 19f.

18c. The Quantum Theory: Lines of Influence

The skeleton diagram below is an attempt to reduce the history of the quantum theory to its barest outlines. At the same time, this figure will serve as a guide to the rest of this paper; in it X → Y means 'the work of X was instrumental to an advance by Y.' Arrows marked M and R indicate that the influence went via the theory of matter and radiation, respectively.

If Planck, Einstein, and Bohr are the fathers of the quantum theory, then Gustav Robert Kirchhoff is its grandfather. Since he was the founder of optical spectra analysis (in 1860, together with Robert Bunsen [K1]), an arrow leads from him and Bunsen to Johann Jakob Balmer, the inventor of the Balmer formula [B1]. From Balmer we move to Bohr, the founder of atomic quantum dynamics. Returning to Kirchhoff as the discoverer of the universal character of blackbody radiation [K2], we note that his influence goes via Wien to Planck (see further, Section 19a).

The arrow from Wien to Planck refers to the latter's formulation of his blackbody radiation law and the triangle Wien–Planck–Einstein to the mutual influences which led to the light-quantum hypothesis (Sections 19b–d).

The arrow from Bose to Einstein refers to Bose's work on electromagnetic radiation and its impact on Einstein's contributions to the quantum statistics of a material gas (Chapter 23, wherein Einstein's influence on Dirac is also briefly mentioned).

The triangle Einstein–de Broglie–Schroedinger has to do with the role of Einstein as the transitional figure in the birth of wave mechanics, discussed in Chapter 24.

The *h* marking the arrow from Planck to Bohr serves as a reminder that not

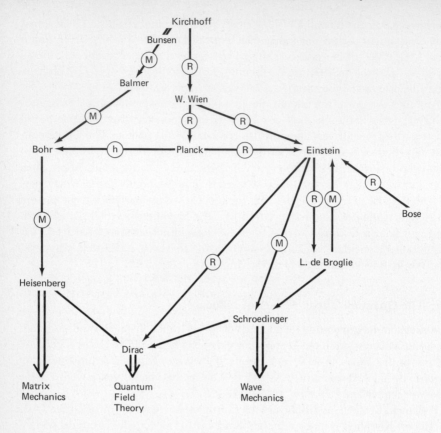

The quantum theory: Lines of influence.

so much the details of Planck's work on radiation as the very introduction by Planck of his new universal constant h was decisive for Bohr's ideas about atomic stability. An account of Bohr's influence on Heisenberg and of Heisenberg's and Schroedinger's impact on Dirac is beyond the scope of the present book.

In the case of Einstein and Bohr, it cannot be said that the work of one induced major advances in the work of the other. Therefore, the simplified diagram does not and should not contain links between them. Nevertheless, for forty years there were influences at work between Einstein and Bohr and these were in fact intense, but on a different plane. In a spirit of friendly and heroic antagonism, these two men argued about questions of principle. Chapter 22 deals with Bohr's resistance to Einstein's idea of the photon. This was but a brief interlude. It ended with the detailed experimental vindication of the photon concept, to which Bohr fully subscribed from then on. Their far more important debate on the foundations of quantum mechanics began in 1927. On these issues, the intellectual resistance and opposition of one against the most basic views held by the other continued unabated until the end of Einstein's life. At issue were the criteria by which one should judge the completeness of the description of the physical world. Their discussions have not affected the evolution of physical theory. Yet theirs will be remembered as one of the great debates on scientific principle between two dominant contemporary figures.

The dialogue between Bohr and Einstein had one positive outcome: it forced Bohr to express the tenets of complementarity in increasingly precise language. This debate will be one of the themes of Chapter 25, which deals with Einstein's objections to quantum mechanics.

A point made earlier bears repeating here: Einstein's own visions on physics issues were often in opposition to the mainstream, but they were never negative. So it was in the case of quantum mechanics. After 1930 he considered this theory to be consistent and successful but incomplete. At the same time, he had his own aspirations for a future theory of particles and fields. I shall try to make clear in Chapter 26 what these were.

I do not believe that Einstein presented valid arguments for the incompleteness of quantum theory, but neither do I think that the times are ripe to answer the question of whether the quantum-mechanical description is indeed complete, since to this day the physics of particles and fields is a subject beset with many unresolved fundamental problems. Among these, there is one that was most dear to Einstein and with which he (and all of us to date) struggled in vain: the synthesis of quantum physics with general relativity. In the survey given in Chapter 2, I noted that we still have far to go in regard to this synthesis. The assessment of Einstein's view of this problem, to be given in Chapter 26, must therefore necessarily be tentative.

References

B1. J. J. Balmer, *AdP* **25,** 80 (1885).
C1. J. Chadwick, *Proceedings Tenth International Conference on the History of Science,* Ithaca, Vol., 1, p. 159. Hermann, Paris, 1962.
D1. P.A.M. Dirac, *Proc. Roy. Soc.* **A133,** 60 (1931).
K1. G. Kirchhoff and R. Bunsen, *Ann. Phys. Chem.* **110,** 160 (1860).
K2. ——, *Ann. Phys. Chem.* **109,** 275 (1860).
M1. R. A. Millikan, *Rev. Mod. Phys.* **21,** 343 (1949).
M2. ——, *Phys. Rev.* **7,** 18 (1916).
M3. ——, *Phys. Rev.* **7,** 355 (1916).
P1. A. Pais, letter dated December 9, 1948.
R1. *Rev. Mod. Phys.* **21**(3) (1949).
R2. E. Rutherford, *Proc. Roy. Soc.* **A97,** 374 (1920).
T1. J. J. Thomson, *Recollections and Reflections,* p. 341. Bell, London, 1936.
W1. H. Weyl, *The theory of groups and quantum mechanics* (2nd edn.), pp. 263–264 and preface. Dover, New York, 1930 (original edition published in 1928 as *Gruppentheorie und Quantenmechanik*).

19

The Light-Quantum

19a. From Kirchhoff to Planck

In the last four months of 1859, there occurred a number of events that were to change the course of science.

On the twelfth of September, Le Verrier submitted to the French Academy of Sciences the text of his letter to Faye concerning an unexplained advance of the perihelion of Mercury (see Section 14c), the effect explained by Einstein in November 1915. On the twenty-fourth of November, a book was published in London entitled *On the Origin of Species by Means of Natural Selection, or the Preservation of Favoured Races in the Struggle for Life,* by Charles Robert Darwin. Meanwhile on the twentieth of October, Gustav Kirchhoff from Heidelberg submitted his observation that the dark D lines in the solar spectrum are darkened still further by the interposition of a sodium flame [K1]. As a result, a few weeks later he proved a theorem and posed a challenge. The response to Kirchhoff's challenge led to the discovery of the quantum theory.

Consider a body in thermal equilibrium with radiation. Let the radiation energy which the body absorbs be converted to thermal energy only, not to any other energy form. Let $E_\nu d\nu$ denote the amount of energy emitted by the body per unit time per cm^2 in the frequency interval $d\nu$. Let A_ν be its absorption coefficient for frequency ν. Kirchhoff's theorem [K2] states that E_ν/A_ν depends only on ν and the temperature T and is independent of any other characteristic of the body:

$$E_\nu/A_\nu = J(\nu, T) \tag{19.1}$$

Kirchhoff called a body perfectly black if $A_\nu = 1$. Thus $J(\nu, T)$ is the emissive power of a blackbody. He also gave an operational definition for a system, the 'Hohlraumstrahlung,' which acts as a perfect blackbody: 'Given a space enclosed by bodies of equal temperature, through which no radiation can penetrate, then every bundle of radiation within this space is constituted, with respect to quality and intensity, as if it came from a completely black body of the same temperature.'

Kirchhoff challenged theorists and experimentalists alike: 'It is a highly important task to find this function [J]. Great difficulties stand in the way of its experimental determination. Nevertheless, there appear grounds for the hope that it has

364

a simple form, as do all functions which do not depend on the properties of individual bodies and which one has become acquainted with before now' [K2].

Kirchhoff's emphasis on the experimental complexities turned out to be well justified. Even the simple property of J that it has one pronounced maximum which moves to lower ν with decreasing T was not firmly established experimentally until about twenty years later [K3]. Experimentalists had to cope with three main problems: (1) to construct manageable bodies with perfectly black properties, (2) to devise radiation detectors with adequate sensitivity, and (3) to find ways of extending the measurements over large frequency domains. Forty years of experimentation had to go by before the data were sufficient to answer Kirchhoff's question.

Kirchhoff derived Eq. 19.1 by showing that its violation would imply the possibility of a *perpetuum mobile* of the second kind. The novelty of his theorem was not so much its content as the precision and generality of its proof, based exclusively on the still-young science of thermodynamics. A quarter of a century passed before the next theoretical advance in blackbody radiation came about.

In 1879 Josef Stefan conjectured on experimental grounds that the total energy radiated by a hot body varies with the fourth power of the absolute temperature [S1]. This statement is not true in its generality. The precise formulation was given in 1884, when Boltzmann (then a professsor of experimental physics in Graz) proved theoretically that the strict T^4 law holds only for bodies which are black. His proof again involved thermodynamics, but combined this time with a still younger branch of theoretical physics: the electromagnetic theory of Maxwell.

For the case of Hohlraumstrahlung, the radiation is homogeneous, isotropic, and unpolarized, so that

$$J(\nu, T) = (c/8\pi)\rho(\nu, T) \qquad (19.2)$$

where $\rho(\nu, T)$, the spectral density, is the energy density per unit volume for frequency ν. In this case, the Stefan–Boltzmann law reads (V is the volume of the cavity)

$$E(T) = V \int \rho(\nu, T)d\nu = aVT^4 \qquad (19.3)$$

This law was the very first thermodynamic consequence derived from Maxwell's theorem, according to which the numerical value of the radiation pressure equals one third of the energy per unit volume. When in 1893 Wilhelm Wien proved his displacement law [W1]

$$\rho(\nu, T) = \nu^3 f(\nu/T) \qquad (19.4)$$

one had come as far as possible on the basis of thermodynamics and general electromagnetic theory. (Proofs of Eqs. 19.3 and 19.4 are found in standard texts.)

Meanwhile, proposals for the correct form of ρ had begun to appear as early as the 1860s. All these guesses may be forgotten except for one, Wien's exponential law, proposed in 1896 [W2]:

$$\rho = \alpha\nu^3 e^{-\beta\nu/T} \qquad\qquad (19.5)$$

Experimental techniques had sufficiently advanced by then to put this formula to the test. This was done by Friedrich Paschen from Hannover, whose measurements (very good ones) were made in the near infrared, $\lambda = 1-8\ \mu m$ (and $T = 400-1600$ K). He published his data in January 1897. His conclusion: 'It would seem very difficult to find another function [of ν and T, Eq. 19.5] that represents the data with as few constants' [P1]. For a brief period, it appeared that Wien's law was the final answer. But then, in the year 1900, this conclusion turned out to be premature and the correct response to Kirchhoff's challenge was found. Two factors were decisive. One was a breakthrough in experimental techniques in the far infrared. The other was the persistence and vision of Planck.

It happened in Berlin. At the Physikalisch Technische Reichsanstalt, at that time probably the world's best-equipped physics laboratory, two teams were independently at work on blackbody radiation experiments. The first of these, Otto Lummer and Ernst Pringsheim, had tackled the problem in an as yet unexplored wavelength region, $\lambda = 12-18\ \mu m$ (and $T = 300-1650$ K). In February 1900 they stated their conclusion: Wien's law fails in that region [L1].* The second team, consisting of Heinrich Rubens and Ferdinand Kurlbaum, moved even farther into the infrared: $\lambda = 30-60\ \mu m$ (and $T = 200-1500°$C). They arrived at the same conclusion [R1].

I need to say more about the latter results, but I should like to comment first on the role of experiment in the discovery of the quantum theory. The Rubens–Kurlbaum paper is a classic. The work of these authors, as well as that of Paschen and of Lummer and Pringsheim, was of a pioneering nature. By the middle of the nineteenth century, wavelengths had been measured up to $\lambda \approx 1.5\mu m$. Progress was slow in the next forty years, as demonstrated by a question raised by Samuel Pierpont Langley in a lecture given in 1885 before the AAAS meeting in Ann Arbor: 'Does [the] ultimate wavelength of 2.7 μm which our atmosphere transmits correspond to the lowest [frequency] which can be obtained from any terrestrial source?' [L2]. The great advance came in the 1890s. The first sentence of the first paper in the first issue of the *Physical Review* reads as follows: 'Within a few years the study of obscure radiation has been greatly advanced by systematic inquiry into the laws of dispersion of the infrared rays.' This was written in 1893, by Ernest Fox Nichols. At about that time, new techniques were developed which culminated in the 'Reststrahlen,' residual rays, method of Rubens and Nichols [R2]: one eliminates short wavelengths from a beam of radiation by subjecting it to numerous reflections on quartz or other surfaces. This procedure leads to the isolation of the long wavelengths in the beam. These experimental developments are of fundamental importance for our main subject, the quantum theory, since they were crucial to the discovery of the blackbody radiation law.

---

*There had been earlier indications of deviations from Wien's law, but these were not well documented.

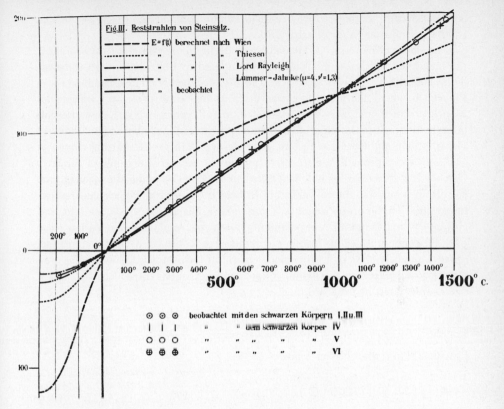

Fig.III. Reststrahlen von Steinsalz.

Sample of the Rubens–Kurlbaum data which led Planck to guess his radiation formula [R1]. ρ is plotted versus T for $\lambda = 51.2\mu$m. ("berechnet nach" means "computed after", "beobachtet" means "observed".) The curves marked "Wien" and "Lord Rayleigh" refer to best fits to the Eqs. (19.5), (19.17), respectively. The curves marked "Thiesen" and "Lummer-Jahnke" refer to theoretical proposals which are not discussed in this book. Planck's formula is not yet plotted.

The paper by Rubens and Kurlbaum was presented to the Prussian Academy on October 25, 1900. The figure above shows some of the measured points they recorded* and some theoretical curves with which they compared their findings. One of these was the Wien curve, which did not work. Neither did a second curve, proposed by Rayleigh (I shall return to Rayleigh's work in section 19c). I shall leave aside the two other comparison curves they drew and turn to the all-important 'fifth formula, given by Herr M. Planck after our experiments had already

---

*These refer to observations at $\lambda = 51.2\mu$m. This wavelength was isolated by multiple reflections off rock salt. The blackbody radiation intensity is plotted as a function of T. (Recall that after multiple reflection, those specific frequencies predominantly survive which correspond to the ionic vibrations in the crystal lattice chosen as reflector.)

been concluded ... [and which] reproduces our observations [from −188° to 1500°C] within the limits of error' [R1].

Kirchhoff had moved from Heidelberg to Berlin to take the chair in theoretical physics. After his death, this position was offered to Boltzmann, who declined. Then Heinrich Hertz was approached; he also declined. The next candidate was Planck, to whom the offer of extraordinarius (associate professor) was made. Planck accepted and was soon promoted to full professor. His new position brought him close to the experimental developments outlined above. This nearness was to be one of the decisive factors in the destiny of this most unusual man.

Planck most probably* discovered his law in the early evening of Sunday, October 7. Rubens and his wife had called on the Plancks on the afternoon of that day. In the course of the conversation, Rubens mentioned to Planck that he had found $\rho(\nu, T)$ to be proportional to T for small ν. Planck went to work after the visitors left and found an interpolation between this result and Wien's law, Eq. 19.5. He communicated his formula by postcard to Rubens that same evening and stated it publicly [P3] in a discussion remark on October 19, following the presentation of a paper by Kurlbaum. Expressed in notations introduced by Planck two months later, he proposed that

$$\rho(\nu, T) = \frac{8\pi h\nu^3}{c^3} \frac{1}{e^{h\nu/kT} - 1} \tag{19.6}$$

Equation 19.6 contains Wien's law of 1896:

$$\rho(\nu, T) = \frac{8\pi h\nu^3}{c^3} e^{-h\nu/kT} \qquad \text{for } \frac{h\nu}{kT} \gg 1 \tag{19.7}$$

which is indeed correct in the quantum regime $h\nu/kT \gg 1$, a condition that is well satisfied in Paschen's experiment mentioned earlier ($h\nu/kT \approx 15$ for $T = 1000$ K and $\lambda = 1$ μm). Strange as it may sound, the quantum theory was discovered only after classical deviations from the quantum regime had been observed in the far infrared.

It would do grave injustice to Planck if I left the reader with the impression that Planck's discovery was exclusively the result of interpolating experimental data. For years, it had been his ambition to derive the correct radiation law from first principles. Thus the rapidity of his response to Ruben's remark is less surprising than the correctness of his answer. I must refrain from discussing Planck's earlier research (cf. [K4]), nor shall I describe how he made his guess. However, it is very important for an understanding of Einstein's starting point in 1905 and of the subsequent reactions to the light-quantum hypothesis to give a brief account of Planck's activities from October to December 1900, the heroic period of his life.

*Here I rely on the obituary of Rubens by Gerhard Hettner [H1], himself an experimental expert on blackbody radiation. Hettner's account differs slightly from the recollections that Planck himself wrote in his late eighties [P2].

Even if Planck had stopped after October 19, he would forever be remembered as the discoverer of the radiation law. It is a true measure of his greatness that he went further. He wanted to interpret Eq. 19.6. That made him the discoverer of the quantum theory. I shall briefly outline the three steps he took [P4].

The Electromagnetic Step. This concerns a result Planck had obtained some time earlier [P5]. Consider a linear oscillator with mass m and charge e in inter-action with a monochromatic, periodic electric field (with frequency ω) in the direction of its motion. The equation of motion is

$$m\ddot{x} + fx - \frac{2e^2}{3c^3}\dddot{x} = eF \cos 2\pi\omega t \tag{19.8}$$

Let ν denote the frequency of the free oscillator, $f/m = (2\pi\nu)^2$. Consider in par-ticular the case in which the radiation damping due to the $\dddot{x}$ term is very small, that is, $\gamma \ll \nu$, where $\gamma = 8\pi^2 e^2 \nu^2 / 3mc^3$. Then one may approximate $\dddot{x}$ by $-(2\pi\nu)^2\dot{x}$. The solution of Eq. 19.8 can be written (see [P6]) $x = C \cos (2\pi\omega t - \alpha)$. One can readily solve for C and α. The energy E of the oscillator equals $m(2\pi\nu)^2 C^2 / 2$, and one finds that

$$E = \frac{e^2 F^2}{2m} \frac{1}{4\pi(\nu - \omega)^2 + \gamma^2} \tag{19.9}$$

Next, let the electric field consist of an incoherent isotropic superposition of fre-quencies in thermal equilibrium at temperature T. In that case, the equilibrium energy U of the oscillator is obtained by replacing the electric field energy density $F^2/2$ in Eq. 19.9 by $4\pi\rho(\omega, T)d\omega/3$ and by integrating over ω:

$$U = \frac{4\pi e^2}{3m} \int \frac{\rho(\omega, T)d\omega}{4\pi(\nu - \omega)^2 + \gamma^2} \tag{19.10}$$

Since γ is very small, the response of the oscillator is maximal if $\omega = \nu$. Thus we may replace $\rho(\omega, T)$ by $\rho(\nu, T)$ and extend the integration from $-\infty$ to $+\infty$. This yields

$$\rho(\nu, T) = \frac{8\pi\nu^2}{c^3} U(\nu, T) \tag{19.11}$$

This equation for the joint equilibrium of matter and radiation, one of Planck's important contributions to classical physics, was the starting point for his discovery of the quantum theory. As we soon shall see, this same equation was also the point of departure for Einstein's critique in 1905 of Planck's reasoning and for his quan-tum theory of specific heats.

The Thermodynamic Step. Planck concluded from Eq. 19.11 that it suffices to determine U in order to find ρ. (There is a lot more to be said about this seemingly innocent statement; see Section 19b.) Working backward from Eqs. 19.6 and 19.11, he found U. Next he determined the entropy S of the linear oscillator by integrating $TdS = dU$, where T is to be taken as a function of U (for fixed ν). This yields

$$S = k\left[\left(1 + \frac{U}{h\nu}\right)\ln\left(1 + \frac{U}{h\nu}\right) - \frac{U}{h\nu}\ln\frac{U}{h\nu}\right] \qquad (19.12)$$

Equation 19.6 follows if one can derive Eq. 19.12.

The Statistical Step. I should rather say, what Planck held to be a statistical step. Consider a large number N of linear oscillators, all with frequency ν. Let $U_N = NU$ and $S_N = NS$ be the total energy and entropy of the system, respectively. Put $S_N = k\ln W_N$, where W_N is the thermodynamic probability. Now comes the quantum postulate.

The total energy U_N is supposed to be made up of *finite* energy elements ϵ: $U_N = P\epsilon$, where P is a large number. Define W_N to be the number of ways in which the P *indistinguishable* energy elements can be distributed over N *distinguishable* oscillators. Example: for $N = 2$, $P = 3$, the partitions are $(3\epsilon,0)$, $(2\epsilon,\epsilon)$, $(\epsilon,2\epsilon)$, $(0,3\epsilon)$. In general,

$$W_N = \frac{(N - 1 + P)!}{P!(N - 1)!} \qquad (19.13)$$

Insert this in $S_N = k\ln W_N$, use $P/N = U/\epsilon$, $S_N = NS$ and apply the Stirling approximation. This gives

$$S = k\left[\left(1 + \frac{U}{\epsilon}\right)\ln\left(1 + \frac{U}{\epsilon}\right) - \frac{U}{\epsilon}\ln\frac{U}{\epsilon}\right] \qquad (19.14)$$

It follows from Eqs. 19.4 and 19.11, and from $TdS = dU$, that S is a function of U/ν only. Therefore

$$\epsilon = h\nu \qquad (19.15)$$

Thus one recovers Eq. 19.12. And that is how the quantum theory was born. This derivation was first presented on December 14, 1900 [P4].

From the point of view of physics in 1900 the logic of Planck's electromagnetic and thermodynamic steps was impeccable, but his statistical step was wild. The latter was clearly designed to argue backwards from Eqs. 19.13–19.15 to 19.12. In 1931 Planck referred to it as 'an act of desperation. . . . I had to obtain a positive result, under any circumstances and at whatever cost' [H2]. Actually there were two desperate acts rather than one. First, there was his unheard-of step of attaching physical significance to finite 'energy elements' [Eq. 19.15]. Second, there was his equally unheard-of counting procedure given by Eq. 19.13. In Planck's opinion, 'the electromagnetic theory of radiation does not provide us with any starting point whatever to speak of such a probability [W_N] in a definite sense' [P7]. This statement is, of course, incorrect. As will be discussed in Section 19b, the classical equipartition theorem could have given him a quite definite method for determining all thermodynamic quantities he was interested in—but would not have given him the answer he desired to derive.

However, let us leave aside for the moment what Planck did not do or what he might have done and return to his unorthodox handling of Boltzmann's principle. In his papers, Planck alluded to the inspiration he had received from Boltzmann's statistical methods.* But in Boltzmann's case the question was to determine the most probable way in which a fixed number of *distinguishable* gas molecules with fixed total energy are distributed over cells in phase space. The corresponding counting problem, discussed previously in Section 4b, has nothing to do with Planck's counting of partitions of *indistinguishable* objects, the energy elements. In fact, this new way of counting, which prefigures the Bose Einstein counting of a quarter century later, cannot be justified by any stretch of the classical imagination. Planck himself knew that and said so. Referring to Eq. 19.13, he wrote:

> Experience will prove whether *this hypothesis* [my italics] is realized in nature. [P7]**

Thus the only justification for Planck's two desperate acts was that they gave him what he wanted. His reasoning was mad, but his madness has that divine quality that only the greatest transitional figures can bring to science. It cast Planck, conservative by inclination, into the role of a reluctant revolutionary. Deeply rooted in nineteenth century thinking and prejudice, he made the first conceptual break that has made twentieth century physics look so discontinuously different from that of the preceding era. Although there have been other major innovations in physics since December 1900, the world has not seen since a figure like Planck.

From 1859 to 1926, blackbody radiation remained a problem at the frontier of theoretical physics, first in thermodynamics, then in electromagnetism, then in the old quantum theory, and finally in quantum statistics. From the experimental point of view, the right answer had been found by 1900. As Pringsheim put it in a lecture given in 1903, 'Planck's equation is in such good agreement with experiment that it can be considered, at least to high approximation, as the mathematical expression of Kirchhoff's function' [P8]. That statement still holds true. Subsequent years saw only refinements of the early results.

The quality of the work by the experimental pioneers can best be illustrated by the following numbers. In 1901 Planck obtained from the available data the value $h = 6.55 \times 10^{-27}$ erg·s for his constant [P9]. The modern value is 6.63×10^{-27}. For the Boltzmann constant, he found $k = 1.34 \times 10^{-16}$ erg·K^{-1}; the present best value is 1.38×10^{-16}. Using his value for k, he could determine Avogadro's number N from the relation $R = Nk$, where R is the gas constant. Then from Faraday's law for univalent electrolytes, $F = Ne$, he obtained the value $e = 4.69 \times 10^{-10}$ esu [P7]. The present best value is 4.80×10^{-10}. At the time of Planck's

---

*In January 1905 and again in January 1906, Planck proposed Boltzmann for the Nobel prize.
**The interesting suggestion has been made that Planck may have been led to Eq. 19.13 by a mathematical formula in one of Boltzmann's papers [K4].

determination of e, J. J. Thomson [T1] had measured the charge of the electron with the result $e = 6.5 \times 10^{-10}$! Not until 1908, when the charge of the alpha particle was found to be 9.3×10^{-10} [R3] was it realized how good Planck's value for e was.

From the very start, Planck's results were a source of inspiration and bewilderment to Einstein. Addressing Planck in 1929, he said 'It is twenty-nine years ago that I was inspired by his ingenious derivation of the radiation formula which ... applied Boltzmann's statistical method in such a novel way' [E1]. In 1913, Einstein wrote that Planck's work 'invigorates and at the same time makes so difficult the physicist's existence. . . . It would be edifying if we could weigh the brain substance which has been sacrified by the physicists on the altar of the [Kirchhoff function]; and the end of these cruel sacrifices is not yet in sight!' [E2]. Of his own earliest efforts, shortly after 1900, to understand the quantum theory, he recalled much later that 'all my attempts . . . to adapt the theoretical foundations of physics to this [new type of] knowledge failed completely. It was as if the ground had been pulled from under one, with no firm foundation to be seen anywhere' [E3].

From my discussions with Einstein, I know that he venerated Planck as the discoverer of the quantum theory, that he deeply respected him as a human being who stood firm under the inordinate sufferings of his personal life and of his country, and that he was grateful to him: 'You were the first to advocate the theory of relativity' [E1]. In 1918 he proposed Planck for the Nobel prize.* In 1948, after Planck's death, Einstein wrote, 'This discovery [i.e., the quantum theory] set science a fresh task: that of finding a new conceptual basis for all of physics. Despite remarkable partial gains, the problem is still far from a satisfactory solution' [E4].

Let us now return to the beginnings of the quantum theory. Nothing further happened in quantum physics after 1901 until Einstein proposed the light-quantum hypothesis.

19b. Einstein on Planck: 1905.
The Rayleigh–Einstein–Jeans Law

The first sentence on the quantum theory published by Einstein was written in the month of March, in the year 1905. It is the title of his first paper on light-quanta, 'On a heuristic point of view concerning the generation and conversion of light' [E5, A1]. (In this chapter, I shall call this paper the March paper.) Webster's Dictionary contains the following definition of the term heuristic: 'providing aid and direction in the solution of a problem but otherwise unjustified or incapable of justification.' Later on, I shall mention the last sentence published by Einstein on scientific matters, also written in March, exactly one half-century

*See Chapter 30.

later. It also deals with the quantum theory. It has one thing in common with the opening sentence mentioned above. They both express Einstein's view that the quantum theory is provisional in nature. The persistence of this opinion of Einstein's is one of the main themes of this book. Whatever one may think of the status of the quantum theory in 1955, in 1905 this opinion was, of course, entirely justified.

In the March paper, Einstein referred to Eq. 19.6 as 'the Planck formula, which agrees with all experiments to date.' But what was the meaning of Planck's derivation of that equation? 'The imperfections of [that derivation] remained at first hidden, which was most fortunate for the development of physics' [E3]. The March paper opens with a section entitled 'on a difficulty concerning the theory of blackbody radiation,' in which he put these imperfections in sharp focus.

His very simple argument was based on two solid consequences of classical theory. The first of these was the Planck equation (Eq. 19.11). The second was the equipartition law of classical mechanics. Applied to U in Eq. (19.11), that is, to the equilibrium energy of a one-dimensional material harmonic oscillator, this law yields

$$U(v, T) = (R/N) T \qquad (19.16)$$

where R is the gas constant, N Avogadro's number, and R/N ($= k$) the Boltzmann constant (for a number of years, Einstein did not use the symbol k in his papers). From Eqs. 19.10 and 19.16, Einstein obtained

$$\rho(v, T) = \frac{8\pi v^2}{c^3} \frac{R}{N} T \qquad (19.17)$$

and went on to note that this classical relation is in disagreement with experiment and has the disastrous consequence that $a = \infty$, where a is the Stefan–Boltzmann constant given in Eq. 19.3.

'If Planck had drawn this conclusion, he would probably not have made his great discovery,' Einstein said later [E3]. Planck had obtained Eq. 19.11 in 1897. At that time, the equipartition law had been known for almost thirty years. During the 1890s, Planck had made several errors in reasoning before he arrived at his radiation law, but none as astounding and of as great an historical significance as his fortunate failure to be the first to derive Eq. 19.17. This omission is no doubt related to Planck's decidedly negative attitude (before 1900) towards Boltzmann's ideas on statistical mechanics.

Equation 19.17, commonly known as the Rayleigh–Jeans law, has an interesting and rather hilarious history, as may be seen from the following chronology of events.

June 1900.   There appears a brief paper by Rayleigh [R4]. It contains for the first time the suggestion to apply to radiation 'the Maxwell–Boltzmann doctrine of the partition of energy' (i.e., the equipartition theorem). From this doctrine, Rayleigh goes on to derive the relation $\rho = c_1 v^2 T$ but does not evaluate the constant c_1. It should be stressed that Rayleigh's derivation of this result had the distinct advantage over Planck's reasoning of dispensing altogether with the latter's material oscillators.* Rayleigh also realizes that this relation should be interpreted as a limiting law: 'The suggestion is then that $[\rho = c_1\nu^2 T]$, rather than [Wien's law, Eq. 19.5] may be the proper form *when* $[T/\nu]$ is *great*' (my italics).** In order to suppress the catastrophic high frequency behavior, he introduces next an ad hoc exponential cutoff factor and proposes the overall radiation law

$$\rho(\nu, T) = c_1\nu^2 T \exp(-c_2\nu/T) \qquad (19.18)$$

This expression became known as the Rayleigh law. Already in 1900 Rubens and Kurlbaum (and also Lummer and Pringsheim) found this law wanting, as was seen on page 367.

Thus the experimentalists close to Planck were well aware of Rayleigh's work. One wonders whether or not Planck himself knew of this important paper, which appeared half a year before he proposed his own law. Whichever may be the case, in 1900 Planck did not refer to Rayleigh's contribution.†

March 17 and June 9, 1905.   Einstein gives the derivation of Eq. 19.17 discussed previously. His paper is submitted March 17 and appears on June 9.

May 6 and 18, 1905.   In a letter to *Nature* (published May 18), Rayleigh returns to his $\nu^2 T$ law and now computes c_1. His answer for c_1 is off by a factor of 8 [R5].

June 5, 1905.   James Hopwood Jeans adds a postscript to a completed paper, in which he corrects Rayleigh's oversight. The paper appears a month later [J1]. In July 1905 Rayleigh acknowledges Jeans' contribution [R6].

It follows from this chronology (not that it matters much) that the Rayleigh–Jeans law ought properly to be called the Rayleigh–Einstein–Jeans law.

The purpose of this digression about Eq. 19.17 is not merely to note who said what first. Of far greater interest is the role this equation played in the early reactions to the quantum theory. From 1900 to 1905, Planck's radiation formula was generally considered to be neither more nor less than a successful representation of the data (see [B1]). Only in 1905 did it begin to dawn, and then only on

---

*Planck derived his radiation law in a circuitous way via the equilibrium properties of his material oscillators. He did so because of his simultaneous concern with two questions, How is radiative equilibrium established? What is the equilibrium distribution? The introduction of the material oscillators would, Planck hoped, show the way to answer both questions. Rayleigh wisely concentrated on the second question only. He considered a cavity filled with 'aetherial oscillators' assumed to be in equilibrium. This enabled him to apply equipartition directly to these radiation oscillators.

**This same observation was also made independently by Einstein in 1905 [E5].

†Neither did Lorentz, who in 1903 gave still another derivation of the $\nu^2 T$ law [L3]. The details need not concern us. It should be noted that Lorentz gave the correct answer for the constant c_1. However, he did not derive the expression for c_1 directly. Rather he found c_1 by appealing to the long-wavelength limit of Planck's law.

a few, that a crisis in physics was at hand [E6]. The failure of the Rayleigh–Einstein–Jeans law was the cause of this turn of events.

Rayleigh's position on the failure of Eq. 19.17 as a universal law was that 'we must admit the failure of the law of equipartition in these extreme cases' (i.e., at high frequencies) [R5]. Jeans took a different view: the equipartition law is correct but 'the supposition that the energy of the ether is in equilibrium with that of matter is utterly erroneous in the case of ether vibrations of short wavelength under experimental conditions' [J2]. Thus Jeans considered Planck's constant h as a phenomenological parameter well-suited as an aid in fitting data but devoid of fundamental significance. The nonequilibrium-versus-failure-of-equipartition debate continued for a number of years [H2]. The issue was still raised at the first Solvay Congress in 1911, but by then the nonequilibrium view no longer aroused much interest.

The March paper, the first of Einstein's six papers written in 1905, was completed almost exactly one year after he had finished the single article he published in 1904 [E7], in which Planck is mentioned for the first time (see Section 4c). The middle section of that paper is entitled 'On the meaning of the constant κ in the kinetic atomic energy,' κ being half the Boltzmann constant. In the final section, 'Application to radiation,' he had discussed energy fluctuations of radiation near thermal equilibrium. He was on his way from studying the second law of thermodynamics to finding methods for the determination of k or—which is almost the same thing—Avogadro's number N. He was also on his way from statistical physics to quantum physics. After the 1904 paper came a one-year pause. His first son was born. His first permanent appointment at the patent office came through. He thought long and hard in that year, I believe. Then, in Section 2 of the March paper, he stated the first new method of the many he was to give in 1905 for the determination of N: compare Eq. 19.17 with the long-wavelength experimental data. This gave him

$$N = 6.17 \times 10^{23} \qquad (19.19)$$

This value is just as good as the one Planck had found from his radiation law, but, Einstein argued, if I use Eq. 19.17 instead of Planck's law (Eq. 19.6), then I understand from accepted first principles what I am doing.

Einstein derived the above value for N in the light-quantum paper, completed in March 1905. One month later, in his doctoral thesis, he found $N = 2.1 \times 10^{23}$. He did not point out either that the March value was good or that the April value left something to be desired, for the simple reason that N was not known well at that time. I have already discussed the important role that Einstein's May 1905 method, Brownian motion, played in the consolidation of the value for N.

We now leave the classical part of the March paper and turn to its quantum part.

19c. The Light-Quantum Hypothesis and the Heuristic Principle

I mentioned in Chapter 3 that the March paper was Einstein's only contribution that he himself called revolutionary. Let us next examine in detail what this revolution consisted of.

In 1905, it was Einstein's position that Eq. 19.6 agreed with experiment but not with existing theory, whereas Eq. 19.17 agreed with existing theory but not with experiment. He therefore set out to study blackbody radiation in a new way 'which is not based on a picture of the generation and propagation of radiation'— that is, which does not make use of Planck's equation (Eq. 19.11). But then something had to be found to replace that equation. For that purpose, Einstein chose to reason 'im Anschluss an die Erfahrung,' phenomenologically. His new starting point was the experimentally known validity of Wien's guess (Eq. 19.5) in the region of large $\beta\nu/T$, the Wien regime. He extracted the light-quantum postulate from an analogy between radiation in the Wien regime and a *classical* ideal gas of material particles.

Einstein began by rederiving in his own way the familiar formula for the finite reversible change of entropy S at constant T for the case where n gas molecules in the volume v_0 are confined to a subvolume v:

$$S(v, T) - S(v_0, T) = \frac{R}{N} \ln \left(\frac{v}{v_0} \right)^n \qquad (19.20)$$

Two and a half pages of the March paper are devoted to the derivation and discussion of this relation. What Einstein had to say on this subject was described following Eq. 4.15.

Now to the radiation problem. Let $\phi(\nu, T) d\nu$ be the entropy density per unit volume in the frequency interval between ν and $\nu + d\nu$. Then (ρ is again the spectral density)

$$\frac{\partial \phi}{\partial \rho} = \frac{1}{T} \qquad (19.21)$$

Assume that Wien's guess (Eq. 19.5) is applicable. Then

$$\phi = -\frac{\rho}{\beta\nu} \left(\ln \frac{\rho}{\alpha\nu^3} - 1 \right) \qquad (19.22)$$

Let the radiation be contained in a volume v. Then $S(\nu,v,T) = \phi v d\nu$ and $E(\nu, v, T) = \rho v d\nu$ are the total entropy and energy in that volume in the interval ν to $\nu + d\nu$, respectively. In the Wien regime, S follows trivially from Eq. 19.22 and one finds that

$$S(\nu,v,T) - S(\nu,v_0,T) = \frac{E}{\beta\nu} \ln \left(\frac{v}{v_0} \right) = \frac{R}{N} \ln \left(\frac{v}{v_0} \right)^{NE/R\beta\nu} \qquad (19.23)$$

Compare Eqs. 19.23 and 19.20 and we have Einstein's

> *Light-quantum hypothesis:* Monochromatic radiation of low density [i.e., within the domain of validity of the Wien radiation formula] behaves in thermodynamic respect as if it consists of mutually independent energy quanta of magnitude $R\beta v/N$ ($\beta = h/k$, $R/N = k$, $R\beta v/N = h v$).

This result, which reads like a theorem, was nevertheless a hypothesis since it was based on Wien's guess, which itself still needed proof from first principles. To repeat, the derivation is based on a blend of purely classical theoretical physics with a piece of experimental information that defies description in classical terms. The genius of the light-quantum hypothesis lies in the intuition for choosing the right piece of experimental input and the right, utterly simple, theoretical ingredients. One may wonder what on earth moved Einstein to think of the volume dependence of the entropy as a tool for his derivation. That choice is less surprising if one recalls* that a year earlier the question of volume dependence had seemed quite important to him for the analysis of the energy fluctuations of radiation.

Einstein's introduction of light-quanta in the Wien regime is the first step toward the concept of radiation as a Bose gas of photons. Just as was the case for Planck's derivation of his radiation law, Einstein's derivation of the light-quantum hypothesis grew out of statistical mechanics. The work of both men has a touch of madness, though of a far more subtle kind in Einstein's case. To see this, please note the words *mutually independent* in the formulation of the hypothesis. Since 1925, we have known (thanks to Bose and especially to Einstein) that the photon gas obeys Bose statistics for *all* frequencies, that the statistical independence of energy quanta is *not* true in general, and that the gas analogy which makes use of the Boltzmann statistics relation (Eq. 19.20) is not true in general either. We also know that it is important *not* to assume—as Einstein had tacitly done in his derivation—that the number of energy quanta is in general conserved. However, call it genius, call it luck, in the Wien regime the counting according to Boltzmann and the counting according to Bose happen to give the same answer while nonconservation of photons effectively plays no role. This demands some explanation, which I shall give in Chapter 23.

So far there is still no revolution. The physicist of 1905 could take or leave the light-quantum hypothesis as nothing more than a curious property of pure radiation in thermal equilibrium, without any physical consequence. Einstein's extraordinary boldness lies in the step he took next, a step which, incidentally, gained him the Nobel prize in 1922.

> *The heuristic principle:* If, in regard to the volume dependence of the entropy, monochromatic radiation (of sufficiently low density) behaves as a discrete medium consisting of energy quanta of magnitude $R\beta v/N$, then this suggests an inquiry as to whether the laws of the generation and conversion of light are also constituted as if light were to consist of energy quanta of this kind.

*See the discussion following Eq. 4.14.

In other words, the light-quantum hypothesis is an assertion about a quantum property of free electromagnetic radiation; the heuristic principle is an extension of these properties of light to the interaction between light and matter. That, indeed, was a revolutionary step.

I shall leave Einstein's applications of the heuristic principle to Section 19e and shall describe next how, in 1906, Einstein ceased assiduously avoiding Planck's equation (Eq. 19.11) and embraced it as a new hypothesis.

19d. Einstein on Planck: 1906

In 1906 Einstein returned once more to Planck's theory of 1900. Now he had much more positive things to say about Planck's radiation law. This change in attitude was due to his realization that 'Planck's theory makes implicit use of the . . . light-quantum hypothesis' [E8]. Einstein's reconsideration of Planck's reasoning and of its relation to his own work can be summarized in the following way:

1. Planck had used the $\rho - U$ relation, Eq. 19.11, which follows from classical mechanics and electrodynamics.
2. Planck had introduced a quantization related to U, namely, the prescription $U = Ph\nu/N$ (see Eqs. 19.12–19.15).
3. If one accepts step 2, which is alien to classical theory, then one has no reason to trust Eq. 19.11, which is an orthodox consequence of classical theory.
4. Einstein had introduced a quantization related to ρ: the light-quantum hypothesis. In doing so, he had not used the $\rho - U$ relation (Eq. 19.11).
5. The question arises of whether a connection can be established between Planck's quantization related to U and Einstein's quantization related to ρ.

Einstein's answer was that this is indeed possible, namely, by introducing a *new assumption:* Eq. 19.11 is also valid in the quantum theory! Thus he proposed to trust Eq. 19.11 even though its theoretical foundation had become a mystery when quantum effects are important. He then re-examined the derivation of Planck's law with the help of this new assumption. I omit the details and only state his conclusion. 'We must consider the following theorem to be the basis of Planck's radiation theory: the energy of a [Planck oscillator] can take on only those values that are integral multiples of $h\nu$; in emission and absorption the energy of a [Planck oscillator] changes by jumps which are multiples of $h\nu$.' Thus already in 1906 Einstein correctly guessed the main properties of a quantum mechanical material oscillator and its behavior in radiative transitions. We shall see in Section 19f that Planck was not at all prepared to accept at once Einstein's reasoning, despite the fact that it lent support to his own endeavors. As to Einstein himself, his acceptance of Planck's Eq. 19.11, albeit as a hypothesis, led to a major advance in his own work: the quantum theory of specific heats, to be discussed in the next chapter.

19e. The Photoelectric Effect: The Second Coming of h

The most widely remembered part of Einstein's March paper deals with his interpretation of the photoelectric effect. The present discussion of this subject is organized as follows. After a few general remarks, I sketch its history from 1887 to
1905. Then I turn to Einstein's contribution. Finally I outline the developments
up to 1916, by which time Einstein's predictions were confirmed.

These days, photoelectron spectroscopy is a giant field of research with its own
journals. Gases, liquids, and solids are being investigated. Applications range from
solid state physics to biology. The field has split into subdisciplines, such as the
spectroscopy in the ultraviolet and in the X-ray region. In 1905, however, the
subject was still in its infancy. We have a detailed picture of the status of photoelectricity a few months before Einstein finished his paper on light-quanta: the
first review article on the photoelectric effect, completed in December 1904 [S2],
shows that at that time photoelectricity was as much a frontier subject as were
radioactivity, cathode ray physics, and (to a slightly lesser extent) the study of
Hertzian waves.

In 1905 the status of experimental techniques was still rudimentary in all these
areas; yet in each of them initial discoveries of great importance had already been
made. Not surprisingly, an experimentalist mainly active in one of these areas
would also work in some of the others. Thus Hertz, the first to observe a photoelectric phenomenon (if we consider only the so-called external photoelectric
effect), made this discovery at about the same time he demonstrated the electromagnetic nature of light. The high school teachers Julius Elster and Hans Geitel
pioneered the study of photoelectric effects in vacuum tubes and constructed the
first phototubes [E9]; they also performed fundamental experiments in radioactivity. Pierre Curie and one of his co-workers were the first to discover that photoelectric effects can be induced by X-rays [C1]. J. J. Thomson is best remembered for his discovery of the electron in his study of cathode rays [T2]; yet
perhaps his finest experimental contribution deals with the photoeffect.

Let us now turn to the work of the pioneers.

1887: Hertz. Five experimental observations made within the span of one
decade largely shaped the physics of the twentieth century. In order of appearance,
they are the discoveries of the photoelectric effect, X-rays, radioactivity, the Zeeman effect, and the electron. The first three of these were made accidentally. Hertz
found the photoeffect when he became intrigued by a side effect he had observed
in the course of his investigations on the electromagnetic wave nature of light
[H3]. At one point, he was studying spark discharges generated by potential differences between two metal surfaces. A primary spark coming from one surface
generates a secondary spark on the other. Since the latter was harder to see, Hertz
built an enclosure around it to eliminate stray light. He was struck by the fact
that this caused a shortening of the secondary spark. He found next that this effect
was due to that part of the enclosure that was interposed between the two sparks.

It was not an electrostatic effect, since it made no qualitative difference whether the interposed surface was a conductor or an insulator. Hertz began to suspect that it might be due to the light given off by the primary spark. In a delightful series of experiments, he confirmed his guess: light can produce sparks. For example, he increased the distance between the metal surfaces until sparks ceased to be produced. Then he illuminated the surfaces with a nearby electric arc lamp: the sparks reappeared. He also came to the (not quite correct) conclusion that 'If the observed phenomenon is indeed an action of light, then it is only one of ultraviolet light.'

1888: Hallwachs. Stimulated by Hertz's work, Wilhelm Hallwachs showed next that irradiation with ultraviolet light causes uncharged metallic bodies to acquire a positive charge [H4].

The earliest speculations on the nature of the effect predate the discovery of the electron in 1897. It was suggested in 1889 that ultraviolet light might cause specks of metallic dust to leave the metal surface [L4].

1899: J. J. Thomson. Thomson was the first to state that the photoeffect induced by ultraviolet light consists of the emission of electrons [T3]. He began his photoelectric studies by measuring the e/m of the particles produced by light, using the same method he had applied to cathode rays two years earlier (the particle beams move through crossed electric and magnetic fields). His conclusion: 'The value of m/e in the case of ultraviolet light. . . . is the same as for cathode rays.' In 1897 he had been unable to determine m or e separately for cathode rays. Now he saw his way clear to do this for photoelectrons. His second conclusion: 'e is the same in magnitude as the charge carried by the hydrogen atom in the electrolysis of solutions.'

Thomson's method for finding e is of major interest, since it is one of the earliest applications of cloud chamber techniques. His student Charles Thomson Rees Wilson had discovered that charged particles can form nuclei for condensation of supersaturated water vapor. Thomson applied this method to the determination of the number of charged particles by droplet counting. Their total charge was determined electrometrically. In view of these technical innovations, his value for e (6.8×10^{-10} esu) must be considered very respectable.

1902: Lenard. In 1902 Philip Lenard studied the photoeffect using a carbon arc light as a source. He could vary the intensity of his light source by a factor of 1000. He made the crucial discovery that the electron energy showed 'not the slightest dependence on the light intensity' [L5]. What about the variation of the photoelectron energy with the light frequency? One increases with the other; nothing more was known in 1905 [S2].

1905: Einstein. On the basis of his heuristic principle, Einstein proposed the following 'simplest picture' for the photoeffect. A light-quantum gives all its energy to a single electron, and the energy transfer by one light-quantum is independent of the presence of other light-quanta. He also noted that an electron ejected from the interior of the body will in general suffer an energy loss before it reaches the surface. Let E_{max} be the electron energy for the case where this energy loss is zero. Then, Einstein proposed, we have the relation (in modern notation)

$$E_{max} = h\nu - P \tag{19.24}$$

where ν is the frequency of the incident (monochromatic) radiation and P is the work function, the energy needed to escape the surface. He pointed out that Eq. 19.24 explains Lenard's observation of the light intensity independence of the electron energy.

Equation 19.24 represents the second coming of h. This equation made very new and very strong predictions. First, E should vary linearly with ν. Second, the slope of the (E,ν) plot is a universal constant, independent of the nature of the irradiated material. Third, the value of the slope was predicted to be Planck's constant determined from the radiation law. None of this was known then.

Einstein gave several other applications of his heuristic principle: (1) the frequency of light in photoluminescence cannot exceed the frequency of the incident light (Stokes's rule) [E5]; (2) in photoionization, the energy of the emitted electron cannot exceed $h\nu$, where ν is the incident light frequency [E5];* (3) in 1906, he discussed the application to the inverse photoeffect (the Volta effect) [E8]; (4) in 1909, he treated the generation of secondary cathode rays by X-rays [E11]; (5) in 1911, he used the principle to predict the high-frequency limit in Bremsstrahlung [E12].

1915: Millikan; the Duane–Hunt Limit. In 1909, a second review paper on the photoeffect appeared [L6]. We learn from it that experiments were in progress to find the frequency dependence of E_{max} but that no definite conclusions could be drawn as yet. Among the results obtained during the next few years, those of Arthur Llewellyn Hughes, J. J. Thomson's last student, are of particular interest. Hughes found a linear E–ν relation and a value for the slope parameter that varied from 4.9 to 5.7 $\times$ 10^{-27}, depending on the nature of the irradiated material [H5]. These and other results were critically reviewed in 1913 and technical reservations about Hughes's results were expressed [P10]. However, soon thereafter Jeans stated in his important survey of the theory of radiation [J3] that 'there is almost general agreement' that Eq. 19.24 holds true. Opinions were divided, but evidently experimentalists were beginning to close in on the Einstein relation.

In the meantime, in his laboratory at the University of Chicago, Millikan had already been at work on this problem for several years. He used visible light (a set of lines in the mercury spectrum); various alkali metals served as targets (these are photosensitive up to about $0.6\mu m$). On April 24, 1914, and again on April 24, 1915, he reported on the progress of his results at meetings of the American Physical Society [M1, M2]. A long paper published in 1916 gives the details of the

*In 1912, Einstein [E10] noted that the heuristic principle could be applied not only to photonionization but also in a quite similar way to photochemical processes.

experiments and a summary of his beautiful results: Eq. 19.24 holds very well and 'Planck's h has been photoelectrically determined with a precision of about 0.5% and is found to have the value $h = 6.57 \times 10^{-27}$.'

The Volta effect also confirmed the heuristic principle. This evidence came from X-ray experiments performed in 1915 at Harvard by William Duane and his assistant Franklin Hunt [D1]. (Duane was one of the first biophysicists in America. His interest in X-rays was due largely to the role they play in cancer therapy.) Working with an X-ray tube operated at a constant potential V, they found that the X-ray frequencies produced have a sharp upper limit ν given by $eV = h\nu$, as had been predicted by Einstein in 1906. This limiting frequency is now called the Duane–Hunt limit. They also obtained the respectable value $h = 6.39 \times 10^{-27}$.

In Section 18a, I mentioned some of Millikan's reactions to these developments. Duane and Hunt did not quote Einstein at all in their paper. I turn next to a more systematic review of the responses to the light-quantum idea.

19f. Reactions to the Light-Quantum Hypothesis

Comments by Planck, Nernst, Rubens, and Warburg written in 1913 when they proposed Einstein for membership in the Prussian Academy will set the right tone for what follows next. Their recommendation, which expressed the highest praise for his achievements, concludes as follows. 'In sum, one can say that there is hardly one among the great problems in which modern physics is so rich to which Einstein has not made a remarkable contribution. That he may sometimes have missed the target in his speculations, as, for example, in his hypothesis of light-quanta, cannot really be held too much against him, for it is not possible to introduce really new ideas even in the most exact sciences without sometimes taking a risk' [K5].

1. Einstein's Caution. Einstein's letters provide a rich source of his insights into physics and people. His struggles with the quantum theory in general and with the light-quantum hypothesis in particular are a recurring theme. In 1951 he wrote to Besso, 'Die ganzen 50 Jahre bewusster Grübelei haben mich der Antwort der Frage "Was sind Lichtquanten" nicht näher gebracht' [E13].*

Throughout his scientific career, quantum physics remained a crisis phenomenon to Einstein. His views on the nature of the crisis would change, but the crisis would not go away. This led him to approach quantum problems with great caution in his writings—a caution already evident in the way the title of his March paper was phrased. In the earliest years following his light-quantum proposal, Einstein had good reasons to regard it as provisional. He could formulate it clearly only in the domain $h\nu/kT \gg 1$, where Wien's blackbody radiation law holds. Also,

---

*All these fifty years of pondering have not brought me any closer to answering the question, What are light quanta?

he had used this law as an experimental fact without explaining it. Above all, it was obvious to him from the start that grave tensions existed between his principle and the wave picture of electromagnetic radiation—tensions which, in his own mind, were resolved neither then nor later. A man as perfectly honest as Einstein had no choice but to emphasize the provisional nature of his hypothesis. He did this very clearly in 1911, at the first Solvay congress, where he said, 'I insist on the provisional character of this concept [light-quanta] which does not seem reconcilable with the experimentally verified consequences of the wave theory' [E12].

It is curious how often physicists believed that Einstein was ready to retract. The first of these was his admirer von Laue, who wrote Einstein in 1906, 'To me at least, any paper in which probability considerations are applied to the vacuum seems very dubious'[L7], and who wrote him again at the end of 1907, 'I would like to tell you how pleased I am that you have given up your light-quantum theory' [L8]. In 1912 Sommerfeld wrote, 'Einstein drew the most far-reaching consequences from Planck's discovery [of the quantum of action] and transferred the quantum properties of emission and absorption phenomena to the structure of light energy in space without, as I believe, maintaining today his original point of view [of 1905] in all its audacity' [S3]. Referring to the light-quanta, Millikan stated in 1913 that Einstein 'gave ... up, I believe, some two years ago' [M3], and in 1916 he wrote, 'Despite ... the apparently complete success of the Einstein equation [for the photoeffect], the physical theory of which it was designed to be the symbolic expression is found so untenable that Einstein himself, I believe, no longer holds to it' [M4].

It is my impression that the resistance to the light-quantum idea was so strong that Einstein's caution was almost hopefully mistaken for vacillation. However, judging from his papers and letters, I find no evidence that he at any time withdrew any of his statements made in 1905.

2. *Electromagnetism: Free Fields and Interactions.*   Einstein's March paper is the second of the revolutionary papers on the old quantum theory. The first one was, of course, Planck's of December 1900 [P4]. Both papers contained proposals that flouted classical concepts. Yet the resistance to Planck's ideas—while certainly not absent—was much less pronounced and vehement than in the case of Einstein. Why?

First, a general remark on the old quantum theory. Its main discoveries concerned quantum rules for stationary states of matter and of pure radiation. By and large, no comparable breakthroughs occurred in regard to the most difficult of all questions concerning electromagnetic phenomena: the interaction between matter and radiation. There, advances became possible only after the advent of quantum field theory, when the concepts of particle creation and annihilation were formulated. Since then, progress on the interaction problems has been enormous. Yet even today this is not by any means a problem area on which the books are closed.

As we saw in Section 19a, when Planck introduced the quantum in order to describe the spectral properties of pure radiation he did so by a procedure of quantization applied to matter, to his material oscillators. He was unaware of the fact that his proposal implied the need for a revision of the classical radiation field itself. His reasoning alleged to involve only a modification of the interaction between matter and radiation. This did not seem too outlandish, since the interaction problem was full of obscurities in any event. By contrast, when Einstein proposed the light-quantum he had dared to tamper with the Maxwell equations for free fields, which were believed (with good reason) to be much better understood. Therefore, it seemed less repugnant to accept Planck's extravaganzas than Einstein's.

This difference in assessment of the two theoretical issues, one raised by Planck, one by Einstein, is quite evident in the writings of the leading theorists of the day. Planck himself had grave reservations about light-quanta. In 1907 he wrote to Einstein:

> I am not seeking the meaning of the quantum of action [light-quanta] in the vacuum but rather in places where absorption and emission occur, and [I] assume that what happens in the vacuum is rigorously described by Maxwell's equations. [P11]

A remark by Planck at a physics meeting in 1909 vividly illustrates his and others' predilections for 'leaving alone' the radiation field and for seeking the resolution of the quantum paradoxes in the interactions:

> I believe one should first try to move the whole difficulty of the quantum theory to the domain of the interaction between matter and radiation. [P12]

In that same year, Lorentz expressed his belief in 'Planck's hypothesis of the energy elements' but also his strong reservations regarding 'light-quanta which retain their individuality in propagation' [L9].

Thus by the end of the first decade of the twentieth century, many leading theorists were prepared to accept the fact that the quantum theory was here to stay. However, the Maxwell theory of the free radiation field, pure and simple, provided neither room for modification (it seemed) nor a place to hide one's ignorance, in contrast with the less transparent situation concerning the interaction between matter and radiation. This position did not change much until the 1920s and remained one of the deepest roots of resistance to Einstein's ideas.

3. *The Impact of Experiment.* The first three revolutionary papers on the old quantum theory were those by Planck [P4], Einstein [E5], and Bohr [B2]. All three contained proposals that flouted classical concepts. Yet the resistance to the ideas of Planck and Bohr—while certainly not absent—was much less pronounced and vehement than in the case of Einstein. Why? The answer: because of the impact of experiment.

Physicists—good physicists—enjoy scientific speculation in private but tend to frown upon it when done in public. They are conservative revolutionaries, resisting innovation as long as possible and at all intellectual cost, but embracing it when the evidence is incontrovertible. If they do not, physics tends to pass them by.

I often argued with Einstein about reliance on experimental evidence for confirmation of fundamental new ideas. In Chapter 25, I shall have more to say on that issue. Meanwhile, I shall discuss next the influence of experimental developments on the acceptance of the ideas of Planck, Bohr, and Einstein.

First, Planck. His proximity to the first-rate experiments on blackbody radiation being performed at the Physikalisch Technische Reichsanstalt in Berlin was beyond doubt a crucial factor in his discovery of 1900 (though it would be very wrong to say that this was the only decisive factor). In the first instance, experiment also set the pace for the acceptance of the Planck formula. One could (and did and should) doubt his derivation, as, among others, Einstein did in 1905. At the same time, however, neither Einstein nor any one else denied the fact that Planck's highly nontrivial universal curve admirably fitted the data. Somehow he had to be doing something right.

Bohr's paper [B2] of April 1913 about the hydrogen atom was revolutionary and certainly not at once generally accepted. But there was no denying that his expression $2\pi^2 e^4 m/h^3 c$ for the Rydberg constant of hydrogen was remarkably accurate (to within 6 per cent, in 1913). When, in October 1913, Bohr was able to give for the ratio of the Rydberg constants for singly ionized helium and hydrogen an elementary derivation that was in agreement with experiment to five significant figures [B3], it became even more clear that Bohr's ideas had a great deal to do with the real world. When told of the helium/hydrogen ratio, Einstein is reported to have said of Bohr's work, 'Then it is one of the greatest discoveries' [H6].

Einstein himself had little to show by comparison.

To be sure, he had mentioned a number of experimental consequences of his hypothesis in his 1905 paper. But he had no curves to fit, no precise numbers to show. He had noted that in the photoelectric effect the electron energy E is constant for fixed light frequency ν. This explained Lenard's results. But Lenard's measurements were not so precise as to prevent men like J. J. Thomson and Sommerfeld from giving alternative theories of the photoeffect of a kind in which Lenard's law does not rigorously apply [S4]. Einstein's photoelectric equation, $E = h\nu - P$, predicts a linear relation between E and ν. At the time Einstein proposed his heuristic principle, no one knew how E depended on ν beyond the fact that one increases with the other. Unlike Bohr and Planck, Einstein had to wait a decade before he saw one of his predictions, the linear E–ν relation, vindicated, as was discussed in the previous section. One immediate and salutary effect of these experimental discoveries was that alternative theories of the photoeffect vanished from the scene.

Yet Einstein's apartness did not end even then.

I have already mentioned that Millikan relished his result on the photoeffect but declared that, even so, the light quantum theory 'seems untenable' [M5]. In

1918, Rutherford commented on the Duane–Hunt results, 'There is at present no physical explanation possible of this remarkable connection between energy and frequency' [R7]. One can go on. The fact of the matter is that, even after Einstein's photoelectric law was accepted, almost no one but Einstein himself would have anything to do with light-quanta.

This went on until the early 1920s, as is best illustrated by quoting the citation for Einstein's Nobel prize in 1922: 'To Albert Einstein for his services to theoretical physics and especially for his discovery of the law of the photoelectric effect' [A2]. This is not only an historic understatement but also an accurate reflection on the consensus in the physics community.

To summarize: the enormous resistance to light-quanta found its roots in the particle–wave paradoxes. The resistance was enhanced because the light-quantum idea seemed to overthrow that part of electromagnetic theory believed to be best understood: the theory of the free field. Moreover, experimental support was long in coming and, even after the photoelectric effect predictions were verified, light-quanta were still largely considered unacceptable. Einstein's own emphasis on the provisional nature of the light-quantum hypothesis tended to strengthen the reservations held by other physicists.

Right after March 1905, Einstein sat down and wrote his doctoral thesis. Then came Brownian motion, then special relativity, and then the equivalence principle. He did not return to the light-quantum until 1909. However, in 1906 he made another important contribution to quantum physics, his theory of specific heats. This will be the subject of the next chapter. We shall return to the light-quantum in Chapter 21.

References

A1. A. B. Arons and M. B. Peppard, *Am. J. Phys.* **33,** 367 (1965).
A2. S. Arrhenius in *Nobel Lectures in Physics,* Vol. 1, p. 478. Elsevier, New York, 1965.
B1. U. Benz, *Arnold Sommerfeld,* p. 74. *Wissenschaftliche Verlagsgesellschaft,* Stuttgart, 1975.
B2. N. Bohr, *Phil. Mag.* **26,** 1 (1913).
B3. ——, *Nature* **92,** 231 (1913).
C1. P. Curie and G. Sagnac, *C. R. Acad. Sci. Paris* **130,** 1013 (1900).
D1. W. Duane and F. L. Hunt, *Phys. Rev.* **6,** 166 (1915).
E1. A. Einstein, *Forschungen und Fortschritte* **5,** 248 (1929).
E2. ——, *Naturw.* **1,** 1077 (1913).
E3. ——, in *Albert Einstein: Philosopher–Scientist* (P. A. Schilpp, Ed.), p. 2. Tudor, New York, 1949.
E4. ——, in *Out of My Later Years,* p. 229. Philosophical Library, New York, 1950.
E5. ——, *AdP* **17,** 132 (1905).
E6. ——, *Naturw.* **1,** 1077 (1913).
E7. ——, *AdP* **14,** 354 (1904).

E8. ——, *AdP* **20,** 199 (1906).

E9. J. Elster and H. Geitel, *AdP* **41,** 166 (1890).

E10. A. Einstein, *AdP* **37,** 832 (1912); **38,** 881, 888 (1912).

E11. ——, *Phys. Zeitschr.* **10,** 817 (1909).

E12. ——, in *Proceedings of the First Solvay Congress* (P. Langevin and M. de Broglie, Eds.), p. 443. Gauthier-Villars, Paris, 1912.

E13. ——, letter to M. Besso, December 12, 1951, EB p. 453.

H1. G. Hettner, *Naturw.* **10,** 1033 (1922).

H2. A. Hermann, *Frühgeschichte der Quantentheorie 1899–1913,* p. 32. Mosbach, Baden, 1969.

H3. H. Hertz, *AdP* **33,** 983 (1887).

H4. W. Hallwachs, *AdP* **33,** 310 (1888).

H5. A. L. Hughes, *Trans. Roy. Soc.* **212,** 205 (1912).

H6. G. de Hevesy, letter to E. Rutherford, October 14, 1913. Quoted in A. S. Eve, *Rutherford,* p. 226. Cambridge University Press, Cambridge, 1939.

J1. J. H. Jeans, *Phil. Mag.* **10,** 91 (1905).

J2. ——, *Nature* **72,** 293 (1905).

J3. ——, *The Electrician,* London, 1914, p. 59.

K1. G. Kirchhoff, *Monatsber. Berlin,* 1859, p. 662.

K2. ——, *Ann. Phys. Chem.* **109,** 275 (1860)

K3. H. Kangro, *History of Planck's Radiation Law.* Taylor and Francis, London, 1976.

K4. M. Klein in *History of Twentieth Century Physics.* Academic Press, New York, 1977.

K5. G. Kirsten and H. Körber, *Physiker über Physiker,* p. 201. Akademie Verlag, Berlin, 1975.

L1. O. Lummer and E. Pringsheim, *Verh. Deutsch. Phys. Ges.* **2,** 163 (1900).

L2. S. P. Langley, *Phil. Mag.* **21,** 394 (1886).

L3. H. A. Lorentz in *Collected Works,* Vol. 3, p. 155. Nyhoff, the Hague, 1936.

L4. P. Lenard and M. Wolf, *AdP* **37,** 443 (1889).

L5. ——, *AdP* **8,** 149 (1902).

L6. R. Ladenburg, *Jahrb. Rad. Elektr.* **17,** 93, 273 (1909).

L7. M. von Laue, letter to A. Einstein, June 2, 1906.

L8. ——, letter to A. Einstein, December 27, 1907.

L9. H. A. Lorentz, letter to W. Wien, April 12, 1909. Quoted in [H2], p. 68.

M1. R. A. Millikan, *Phys. Rev.* **4,** 73 (1914).

M2. ——, *Phys. Rev.* **6,** 55 (1915).

M3. ——, *Science* **37,** 119 (1913).

M4. ——, *Phys. Rev.* **7,** 355 (1916).

M5. ——, *Phys. Rev.* **7,** 18 (1916).

P1. W. Paschen, *AdP* **60,** 662 (1897).

P2. M. Planck in *M. Planck, Physikalische Abhandlungen und Vorträge* (M. von Laue, Ed.), Vol. 3, p. 374. Vieweg, Braunschweig, 1958.

P3. ——, *Verh. Deutsch. Phys. Ges.* **2,** 202 (1900): *Abhandlungen,* Vol. 1, p. 687.

P4. ——, *Verh. Deutsch. Phys. Ges.* **2,** 237 (1900); *Abhandlungen,* Vol. 1, p. 698.

P5. ——, *AdP* **1,** 69 (1900); *Abhandlungen,* Vol. 1, p. 614.

P6. W. Pauli, *Collected Scientific Papers,* Vol. 1, pp. 602–7. Interscience, New York, 1964.

P7. M. Planck, *AdP* **4,** 553 (1901); *Abhandlungen,* Vol. 1, p. 717.

P8. E. Pringsheim, *Arch. Math. Phys.* **7,** 236 (1903).

P9. M. Planck, *AdP* **4,** 564 (1901); *Abhandlungen,* Vol. 1, p. 728.

P10. R. Pohl and L. Pringsheim, *Phil. Mag.* **26,** 1017 (1913).

P11. M. Planck, letter to A. Einstein, July 6, 1907.

P12. ——, *Phys. Zeitschr.* **10,** 825 (1909).

R1. H. Rubens and F. Kurlbaum, *PAW,* 1900, p. 929.

R2. —— and E. F. Nichols, *AdP* **60,** 418 (1897).

R3. E. Rutherford and H. Geiger, *Proc. Roy. Soc.* **A81,** 162 (1908).

R4. J. W. S. Rayleigh, *Phil. Mag.* **49,** 539 (1900).

R5. ——, *Nature* **72,** 54 (1905).

R6. ——, *Nature,* **72,** 243 (1905).

R7. E. Rutherford, *J. Röntgen Soc.* **14,** 81 (1918).

S1. J. Stefan, *Sitzungsber. Ak. Wiss. Wien, Math. Naturw. Kl, 2 Abt.* **79,** 391 (1879).

S2. E. von Schweidler, *Jahrb. Rad. Elektr.* **1,** 358 (1904).

S3. A. Sommerfeld, *Verh. Ges. Deutsch. Naturf. Ärzte* **83,** 31 (1912).

S4. R. H. Stuewer, *The Compton Effect,* Chap. 2. Science History, New York, 1975.

T1. J. J. Thomson, *Phil. Mag.* **48,** 547 (1899).

T2. ——, *Phil. Mag.* **44,** 269 (1897).

T3. ——, *Phil. Mag.* **48,** 547 (1899).

W1. W. Wien, *PAW,* 1893, p. 55.

W2. ———, *AdP* **58,** 662 (1896).

20

Einstein and Specific Heats

The more success the quantum theory has, the sillier it looks.
A. Einstein in 1912

20a. Specific Heats in the Nineteenth Century

By the end of the first decade of the twentieth century, three major quantum theoretical discoveries had been made. They concern the blackbody radiation law, the light-quantum postulate, and the quantum theory of the specific heat of solids. All three arose from statistical considerations. There are, however, striking differences in the time intervals between these theoretical advances and their respective experimental justification. Planck formulated his radiation law in an uncommonly short time after learning about experiments in the far infrared that complemented earlier results at higher frequencies. It was quite a different story with the light-quantum. Einstein's hypothesis was many years ahead of its decisive experimental tests. As we shall see next, the story is quite different again in the case of specific heats. Einstein's first paper on the subject [E1], submitted in November 1906, contains the qualitatively correct explanation of an anomaly that had been observed as early as 1840: the low value of the specific heat of diamond at room temperature. Einstein showed that this can be understood as a quantum effect. His paper contains one graph, the specific heat of diamond as a function of temperature, reproduced here below, which represents the first published graph in the history of the quantum theory of the solid state. It also represents one of only three instances I know of in which Einstein published a graph to compare theory with experiment (another example will be mentioned in Section 20b).

In order to recognize an anomaly, one needs a theory or a rule or at least a prejudice. As I just mentioned, peculiarities in specific heats were diagnosed more than half a century before Einstein explained them. It was also known well before 1906 that specific heats of gases exhibited even more curious properties. In what way was diamond considered so exceptional? And what about other substances? For a perspective on Einstein's contributions, it is necessary to sketch the answer to these questions. I therefore begin with a short account of specific heats in the nineteenth century.

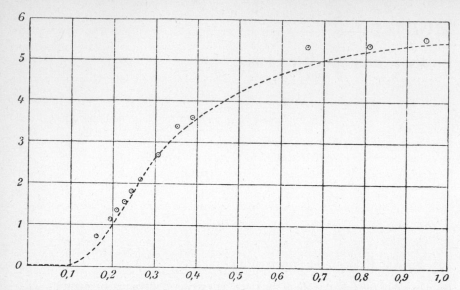

The first published graph dealing with the quantum theory of the solid state: Einstein's expression for the specific heat of solids [given in Eq. 20.4] plotted versus $h\nu/kT$. The little circles are Weber's experimental data for diamond. Einstein's best fit to Weber's measurements corresponds to $h\nu/k \cong 1300K$.

The story begins in 1819, when two young Frenchmen, Pierre Louis Dulong and Alexis Thérèse Petit, made an unexpected discovery during the researches in thermometry on which they had been jointly engaged for a number of years. For a dozen metals and for sulfur (all at room temperature), they found that c, the specific heat per gram-atom* (referred to as the specific heat hereafter), had practically the same value, approximately 6 cal/mole·deg [P1]. They did, of course, not regard this as a mere coincidence: 'One is allowed to infer [from these data] the following law: the atoms of all simple bodies [elements] have exactly the same heat capacity.' They did not restrict this statement to elements in solid form, but initially believed that improved experiments might show their law to hold for gases also. By 1830 it was clear, however, that the rule could at best apply only to solids.

Much remained to be learned about atomic weights in those early days of modern chemistry. In fact, in several instances Dulong and Petit correctly halved values of atomic weights obtained earlier by other means in order to bring their data into line with their law [F1]. For many years, their rule continued to be an important tool for atomic weight determinations.

*To be precise, these and other measurements on solids to be mentioned hereafter refer to c_p at atmospheric pressure. Later on, a comparison will be made with theoretical values for c_v. This requires a tiny correction to go from c_p to c_v. This correction will be ignored [L1].

It became clear rather soon, however, that even for solid elements the Dulong–Petit rule is not as general as its propounders had thought. Amedeo Avogadro was one of the first to remark on deviations in the case of carbon, but his measurements were not very precise [A1].* Matters got more serious in 1840, when two Swiss physicists, Auguste de la Rive and François Marcet, reported on studies of carbon. In particular, they had obtained 'not without difficulty and expense' an amount of diamond powder sufficient to experiment with, for which they found $c \approx 1.4$ [R1]. At almost the same time, diamond was also being studied by Henri Victor Regnault, who more than any other physicist contributed to the experimental investigations of specific heats in the nineteenth century. His value: $c \simeq 1.8$ [R2]. Regnault's conclusion about carbon was unequivocal: it is 'a complete exception among the simple bodies: it does not satisfy the general law which [relates] specific heats and atomic weights.' During the next twenty years, he continued his studies of specific heats and found many more deviations from the general law, though none as large as for diamond.

We now move to the 1870s, when Heinrich Friedrich Weber,** then in Berlin, made the next advance. He began by re-analyzing the data of de la Rive and Marcet and those of Regnault and came to the correct conclusion that the different values for the specific heat of diamond found by these authors were not due to systematic errors. However, the de la Rive–Marcet value referred to a temperature average from 3° to 14°C whereas Regnault's value was an average from 8° to 98°C. Weber noted that both experiments could be correct if the specific heat of carbon were to vary with temperature [W1]! Tiny variations in specific heats with temperature had long been known for some substances (for example, water) [N1]. In contrast, Weber raised the issue of a very strong temperature dependence—a new and bold idea. His measurements for twelve different temperatures between 0° and 200°C confirmed his conjecture: for diamond c varied by a factor of 3 over this range. He wanted to continue his observations, but it was March and, alas, there was no more snow for his ice calorimeter. He announced that he would go on with his measurements 'as soon as meteorological circumstances permit.' The next time we hear from Weber is in 1875, when he presented his beautiful specific heat measurements for boron, silicon, graphite, and diamond, from −100° to 1000°C [W2]. For the case of diamond, c varied by a factor of 15 between these limits.

By 1872, Weber had already made a conjecture which he confirmed in 1875: at high T one gets close to the Dulong–Petit value. In Weber's words, 'The three

---

*In 1833 Avogadro obtained $c \simeq 3$ for carbon at room temperature. This value is too high. Since it was accidentally just half the Dulong–Petit value, Avogadro incorrectly conjectured 'that one must reduce the atom [i.e., the atomic weight] of sulfur and metals in general by [a factor of] one half' [A1].

**Weber was Einstein's teacher, whom we encountered in Chapter 3. Einstein's notebooks of Weber's lectures are preserved. They do not indicate that as a student Einstein knew of Weber's results.

curious exceptions [C, B, Si] to the Dulong–Petit law which were until now a cause for despair have been eliminated: the Dulong–Petit law for the specific heats of solid elements has become an unexceptional rigorous law' [W2]. This is, of course, not quite true, but it was distinct progress. The experimental points on page 390 are Weber's points of 1875.*

In 1872, not only Weber, but also a second physicist, made the conjecture that the Dulong–Petit value $c \approx 6$ would be reached by carbon at high temperatures: James Dewar. His road to the carbon problem was altogether different: for reasons having to do with solar temperatures, Dewar became interested in the boiling point of carbon. This led him to high-temperature experiments, from which he concluded [D1] that the mean specific heat of carbon between 0° and 2000°C equals about 5 and that 'the true specific heat [per gram] at 2000°C must be at least 0.5, so that at this temperature carbon would agree with the law of Dulong and Petit.'**

Dewar's most important contribution to our subject deals with very low temperatures. He had liquefied hydrogen in 1898. In 1905 he reported on the first specific heat measurements in the newly opened temperature region. It will come as no surprise that diamond was among the first substances he chose to study. For this case, he found the very low average value $c \approx 0.05$ in the interval from 20 to 85 K. 'An almost endless field of research in the determination of specific heats is now opened,' Dewar remarked in this paper [D2]. His work is included in a detailed compilation by Alfred Wigand [W3] of the literature on the specific heats of solid elements that appeared in the same issue of the *Annalen der Physik* as Einstein's first paper on the quantum theory of specific heats. We are therefore up to date in regard to the experimental developments preceding Einstein's work.

The theoretical interpretation of the Dulong–Petit rule is due to Boltzmann. In 1866 he grappled unsuccessfully with this problem [B2]. It took another ten years before he recognized that this rule can be understood with the help of the equipartition theorem of classical statistical mechanics. The simplest version of that theorem had been known since 1860: the average kinetic energy equals $kT/2$ for each degree of freedom.† In 1871 Boltzmann showed that the average kinetic energy equals the average potential energy for a system of particles each one of which oscillates under the influence of external harmonic forces [B4]. In 1876 he applied these results to a three-dimensional lattice [B5]. This gave him an average energy $3RT \simeq 6$ cal/mol. Hence c_v, the specific heat at constant volume, equals

---

*By the end of the nineteenth century, it was clear that the decrease in c with temperature occurs far more generally than just for C, B, and Si [B1].

**There followed a controversy about priorities between Weber and Dewar, but only a very mild one by nineteenth century standards. In any event, there is no question that the issues were settled only by Weber's detailed measurements in 1875.

†This result (phrased somewhat differently) is due to John James Waterston and Maxwell [M1]. For the curious story of Waterston's contribution, see [B3].

6 cal/mol·deg. Thus, after half a century, the Dulong–Petit value had found a theoretical justification! As Boltzmann himself put it, his result was in good agreement with experiment 'for all simple solids with the exception of carbon, boron* and silicon.' Boltzmann went on to speculate that these anomalies might be a consequence of a loss of degrees of freedom due to a 'sticking together' at low temperatures of atoms at neighboring lattice points. This suggestion was elaborated by others [R3] and is mentioned by Wigand in his 1906 review as the best explanation of this effect. I mention this incorrect speculation only in order to stress one important point: before Einstein's paper of 1906, it was not realized that the diamond anomaly was to be understood in terms of the failure (or, rather, the inapplicability) of the classical equipartition theorem. Einstein was the first one to state this fact clearly.

By sharp contrast, it was well appreciated that the equipartition theorem was in trouble when applied to the specific heat of gases. This was a matter of grave concern to the nineteenth century masters. Even though this is a topic that does not directly bear on Einstein's work in 1906, I believe it will be useful to complete the nineteenth century picture with a brief explanation of why gases caused so much more aggravation.

The reasons were clearly stated by Maxwell in a lecture given in 1875:

> The spectroscope tells us that some molecules can execute a great many different kinds of vibrations. They must therefore be systems of a very considerable degree of complexity, having far more than six variables [the number characteristic for a rigid body] . . . Every additional variable increases the specific heat. . . . Every additional degree of complexity which we attribute to the molecule can only increase the difficulty of reconciling the observed with the calculated value of the specific heat. I have now put before you what I consider the greatest difficulty yet encountered by the molecular theory. [M2]

Maxwell's conundrum was the mystery of the missing vibrations. The following oversimplified picture suffices to make clear what troubled him. Consider a molecule made up of n structureless atoms. There are $3n$ degrees of freedom, three for translations, at most three for rotations, and the rest for vibrations. The kinetic energy associated with each degree of freedom contributes $kT/2$ to c_v. In addition, there is a positive contribution from the potential energy. Maxwell was saying that this would almost always lead to specific heats which are too large. As a consequence of Maxwell's lecture, attention focused on monatomic gases, and, in 1876, the equipartition theorem scored an important success: it found that $c_p/c_v \approx 5/3$ for mercury vapor, in accordance with $c_v = 3R/2$ and the ideal gas rule $c_p - c_v = R$ [K1]. It had been known since the days of Regnault** that several

---

*The good professor wrote *bromine* but meant *boron.*

**A detailed review of the specific heats of gases from the days of Lavoisier until 1896 is found in Wüllner's textbook [W4].

diatomic molecules (including hydrogen) have a c_v close to $5R/2$. It was not yet recognized by Maxwell that this is the value prescribed by the equipartition theorem for a rigid dumbbell molecule; that observation was first made by Boltzmann [B5]. The equipartition theorem was therefore very helpful, yet, on the whole, the specific heat of gases remained a murky subject.

Things were getting worse. Already before 1900, instances were being found in which c_v depended (weakly) on temperature [W4], in flagrant contradiction with classical concepts. No wonder these results troubled Boltzmann. His idea about the anomalies for the specific heats of solids could not work for gases. Molecules in dilute gases hardly stick together! In 1895 he suggested a way out: the equipartition theorem is correct for gases but does not apply to the combined gas–aether system because there is no thermal equilibrium: 'The entire ether has not had time to come into thermal equilibrium with the gas molecules and has in no way attained the state which it would have if it were enclosed for an infinitely long time in the same vessel with the molecules of the gas' [B6].

Kelvin took a different position; he felt that the classical equipartition theorem was wrong. He stuck to this belief despite the fact that his attempts to find flaws in the theoretical derivation of the theorem had of course remained unsuccessful. 'It is . . . not quite possible to rest contented with the mathematical verdict not proved and the experimental verdict not true in respect to the Boltzmann–Maxwell doctrine,' he said in a lecture given in 1900 before the Royal Institution [K2]. He summarized his position by saying that 'the simplest way to get rid of the difficulties is to abandon the doctrine' [K3].

Lastly, there was the position of Rayleigh: the proof of the equipartition theorem is correct and there *is* thermal equilibrium between the gas molecules and the aether. Therefore there is a crisis. 'What would appear to be wanted is some escape from the destructive simplicity of the general conclusion [derived from equipartition]' [R4].

Such was the state of affairs when Einstein took on the specific heat problem.

20b. Einstein

Until 1906, Planck's quantum had played a role only in the rather isolated problem of blackbody radiation. Einstein's work on specific heats [E1] is above all important because it made clear for the first time that quantum concepts have a far more general applicability. His 1906 paper is also unusual because here we meet an Einstein who is quite prepared to use a model he knows to be approximate in order to bring home a point of principle. Otherwise this paper is much like his other innovative articles: succinctly directed to the heart of the matter.

Earlier in 1906 Einstein had come to accept Planck's relation (Eq. 19.11) between ρ and the equilibrium energy U as a new physical assumption (see Section 19d). We saw in Section 19a that Planck had obtained the expression

$$U(v,T) = \frac{\xi kT}{\exp\xi - 1} \qquad \xi = \frac{hv}{kT} \tag{20.1}$$

by introducing a prescription that modified Boltzmann's way of counting states. Einstein's specific heat paper begins with a new prescription for arriving at the same result. He wrote U in the form*

$$U(v,T) = \frac{\int Ee^{-E/kT}\omega(E,v)\,dE}{\int e^{-E/kT}\omega(E,v)\,dE} \tag{20.2}$$

The exponential factor denotes the statistical probability for the energy E. The weight factor ω contains the dynamic information about the density of states between E and $E + dE$. For the case in hand (linear oscillators), ω is trivial in the classical theory: $\omega(E,v) = 1$. This yields the equipartition result $U = kT$. Einstein proposed a new form for ω. Let $\epsilon = hv$. Then ω shall be different from zero only when $n\epsilon < E < n\epsilon + \alpha$, $n = 0, 1, 2, \ldots$ 'where α is infinitely small compared with ϵ,' and such that

$$\int_{n\epsilon}^{n\epsilon+\alpha} \omega\,dE = A \tag{20.3}$$

for all n, where the value of the constant A is irrelevant. Mathematically, this is the forerunner of the δ-function! Today we write $\omega(E,v) = \sum_n \delta(E - nhv)$.

From Eqs. 20.2 and 20.3 we recover Eq. 20.1. This new formulation is important because for the first time the statistical and the dynamic aspects of the problem are clearly separated. 'Degrees of freedom must be weighed and not counted,' as Sommerfeld put it later [S1].

In commenting on his new derivation of Eq. 20.1, Einstein remarked, 'I believe we should not content ourselves with this result' [E1] If we must modify the theory of periodically vibrating structures in order to account for the properties of radiation, are we then not obliged to do the same for other problems in the molecular theory of heat, he asked. 'In my opinion, the answer cannot be in doubt. If Planck's theory of radiation goes to the heart of the matter, then we must also expect to find contradictions between the present [i.e., classical] kinetic theory and experiment in other areas of the theory of heat—contradictions that can be resolved by following this new path. In my opinion, this expectation is actually realized.'

Then Einstein turned to the specific heat of solids, introducing the following model of a three-dimensional crystal lattice. The atoms on the lattice points oscillate independently, isotropically, harmonically, and with a single frequency v

---

*I do not always use the notations of the original paper.

around their equilibrium positions (volume changes due to heating and contributions to the specific heat due to the motions of electrons within the atoms are neglected, Einstein notes). He emphasized that one should of course not expect rigorous answers because of all these approximations.

The First Generalization. Einstein applied Eq. 20.2 to his three-dimensional oscillators. In thermal equilibrium, the total energy of a gram-atom of oscillators equals $3NU(\nu, T)$, where U is given by Eq. 20.1 and N is Avogadro's number. Hence,

$$c_v = 3R \frac{\xi^2 e^\xi}{(e^\xi - 1)^2} \tag{20.4}$$

which is Einstein's specific heat formula.

The Second Generalization. For reasons of no particular interest to us now, Einstein initially believed that his oscillating lattice points were electrically charged ions. A few months later, he published a correction to his paper, in which he observed that this was an unnecessary assumption [E2] (In Planck's case, the linear oscillators had of course to be charged!). Einstein's correction freed the quantum rules (in passing, one might say) from any specific dependence on electromagnetism.

Einstein's specific heat formula yields, first of all, the Dulong–Petit rule in the high-temperature limit. It is also the first recorded example of a specific heat formula with the property

$$c_v(T) \rightarrow 0 \quad \text{as} \quad T \rightarrow 0 \tag{20.5}$$

As we shall see in the next section, Eq. 20.5 played an important role in the ultimate formulation of Nernst's heat theorem.

Einstein's specific heat formula has only one parameter. The only freedom is the choice of the frequency* ν, or, equivalently, the 'Einstein temperature' T_E, the value of T for which $\xi = 1$. As was mentioned before, Einstein compared his formula with Weber's points for diamond. Einstein's fit can be expressed in temperature units by $T_E \approx 1300$ K, for which 'the points lie indeed almost on the curve.' This high value of T_E makes clear why a light and hard substance like diamond exhibits quantum effects at room temperature (by contrast, $T_E \approx 70$ K for lead).

By his own account, Einstein took Weber's data from the Landolt–Bornstein tables. He must have used the 1905 edition [L2], which would have been readily available in the patent office. These tables do not yet contain the earlier-mentioned results by Dewar in 1905. Apparently Einstein was not aware of these data in 1906 (although they were noted in that year by German physicists [W3]). Perhaps that was fortunate. In any case, Dewar's value of $c_v \approx 0.05$ for diamond refers

---

*In a later paper, Einstein attempted to relate this frequency to the compressibility of the material [E3].

to an average over the range $\xi \approx 0.02-0.07$. This value is much too large to be accommodated (simultaneously with Weber's points) by Einstein's Eq. 20.4: the exponential drop of c_v as $T \rightarrow 0$, predicted by that equation, is far too steep.

Einstein did become aware of this discrepancy in 1911, when the much improved measurements by Nernst showed that Eq. 20.4 fails at low T [N2]. Nernst correctly ascribed the disagreement to the incorrectness of the assumption that the lattice vibrations are monochromatic. Einstein himself explored some modifications of this assumption [E4]. The correct temperature dependence at low temperatures was first obtained by Peter Debye; for nonmetallic substances, c_v $\rightarrow 0$ as T^3 [D3]. Einstein had ended his active research on the specific heats of solids by the time the work of Debye and the more exact treatment of lattice vibrations by Max Born and Theodore von Kármán appeared [B7]. These further developments need therefore not be discussed here.

However, in 1913 Einstein returned once again to specific heats, this time to consider the case of gases. This came about as the result of important experimental advances on this subject which had begun in 1912 with a key discovery by Arnold Eucken. It had long been known by then that $c_v \approx 5$ for molecular hydrogen at room temperature. Eucken showed that this value decreased with decreasing T and that $c_v \approx 3$ at $T \approx 60$ K [E5]. As is well known today, this effect is due to the freezing of the two rotational degrees of freedom of this molecule at these low temperatures. In 1913 Einstein correctly surmised that the effect was related to the behavior of these rotations and attempted to give a quantitative theory. In a paper on this subject, we find another instance of curve fitting by Einstein [E6]. However, this time he was wrong. His answer depended in an essential way on the incorrect assumption that rotational degrees of freedom have a zero point energy.*

In 1925 Einstein was to turn his attention one last time to gases at very low temperatures, as we shall see in Section 23b.

20c. Nernst: Solvay I**

'As the temperature tends to absolute zero, the entropy of a system tends to a universal constant that is independent of chemical or physical composition or of other parameters on which the entropy may depend. The constant can be taken to be zero.' This modern general formulation of the third law of thermodynamics implies (barring a few exceptional situations) that specific heats tend to zero as T $\rightarrow 0$ (see [H2]). The earliest and most primitive version of the 'heat theorem' was presented in 1905, before Einstein wrote his first paper on specific heats. The final

---

*In 1920 Einstein announced a forthcoming paper on the moment of inertia of molecular hydrogen [E7]. That paper was never published, however,
**The preparation of this section was much facilitated by my access to an article by Klein [K4] and a book by Hermann [H1].

form of the third law was arrived at and accepted only after decades of controversy and confusion.* For the present account, it is important to note the influence of Einstein's work on this evolution.

On December 23, 1905, Hermann Walther Nernst read a paper at the Goettingen Academy entitled 'On the Computation of Chemical Equilibria from Thermal Measurements.' In this work he proposed a new hypothesis for the thermal behavior of liquids and solids at absolute zero [N3]. For our purposes, the 1905 hypothesis is of particular interest as it applies to a chemically homogeneous substance. For this case, the hypothesis states in essence that the entropy difference between two modifications of such a substance (for example, graphite and diamond in the case of carbon) tends to zero as $T \rightarrow 0$. Therefore it does not exclude a nonzero specific heat at zero temperatures. In fact, in 1906 Nernst assumed that all specific heats tend to 1.5 cal/deg at $T = 0$ [N3, N4]. However, he noted that he had no proof of this statement because of the absence of sufficient low-temperature data. He stressed that it was a 'most urgent task' to acquire these [N3]. Nernst's formidable energies matched his strong determination. He and his collaborators embarked on a major program for measuring specific heats at low temperatures. This program covered the same temperature domain already studied by Dewar, but the precision was much greater and more substances were examined. One of these was diamond, obviously.

By 1910 Nernst was ready to announce his first results [N5]. From his curves, 'one gains the clear impression that the specific heats become zero or at least take on very small values at very low temperatures. This is in qualitative agreement with the theory developed by Herr Einstein. . .'

Thus, the order of events was as follows. Late in 1905 Nernst stated a primitive version of the third law. In 1906 Einstein gave the first example of a theory that implies that $c_v \rightarrow 0$ as $T \rightarrow 0$ for solids. In 1910 Nernst noted the compatibility of Einstein's result with 'the heat theorem developed by me.' However, it was actually Planck who, later in 1910, took a step that 'not only in form but also in content goes a bit beyond [the formulation given by] Nernst himself.' In Planck's formulation, the specific heat of solids and liquids does go to zero as $T \rightarrow 0$ [P2]. It should be stressed that neither Nernst nor Planck gave a proof of the third law. The status of this law was apparently somewhat confused, as is clear from Einstein's remark in 1914 that 'all attempts to derive Nernst's theorem theoretically in a thermodynamic way with the help of the experimental fact that the specific heat vanishes at $T = 0$ must be considered to have failed.' Einstein went on to remark—rightly so—that the quantum theory is indispensable for an understanding of this theorem [E8]. In an earlier letter to Ehrenfest, he had been sharply critical of the speculations by Nernst and Planck [E9].

Nernst's reference to Einstein in his paper of 1910 was the first occasion on

---

*Simon has given an excellent historical survey of this development [S2].

which he acknowledged the quantum theory in his publications. His newly aroused interest in the quantum theory was, however, thoroughly pragmatic. In an address (on the occasion of the birthday of the emperor), he said:

> At this time, the quantum theory is essentially a computational rule, one may well say a rule with most curious, indeed grotesque, properties. However, . . . it has borne such rich fruits in the hands of Planck and Einstein that there is now a scientific obligation to take a stand in its regard and to subject it to experimental test.

He went on to compare Planck with Dalton and Newton [N6]. Also in 1911, Nernst tried his hand at a needed modification of Einstein's Eq. 20.4 [N7].

Nernst was a man of parts, a gifted scientist, a man with a sense for practical applications, a stimulating influence on his students, and an able organizer. Many people disliked him. But he commanded respect 'so long as his egocentric weakness did not enter the picture' [E10]. He now saw the need for a conference on the highest level to deal with the quantum problems. His combined talents as well as his business relations enabled him to realize this plan. He found the industrialist Ernest Solvay willing to underwrite the conference. He planned the scientific program in consultation with Planck and Lorentz. On October 29, 1911, the first Solvay Conference convened. Einstein was given the honor of being the final speaker. The title of his talk: 'The Current Status of the Specific Heat Problem.' He gave a beautiful review of this subject—and used the occasion to express his opinion on the quantum theory of electromagnetic radiation as well. His contributions to the latter topic are no doubt more profound than his work on specific heats. Yet his work on the quantum theory of solids had a far greater immediate impact and considerably enlarged the audience of those willing to take quantum physics seriously.

Throughout the period discussed in the foregoing, the third law was applied only to solids and liquids. Only in 1914 did Nernst dare to extend his theorem to hold for gases as well. Eucken's results on the specific heat of molecular hydrogen were a main motivation for taking this bold step [N8]. Unlike the case for solids, Nernst could not point to a convincing theoretical model of a gas with the property $c_v \to 0$ as $T \to 0$. So it was to remain until 1925, when the first model of this kind was found. Its discoverer: Einstein (Section 23b).

Einstein realized, of course, that his work on the specific heats of solids was a step in the right direction. Perhaps that pleased him. It certainly puzzled him. In 1912 he wrote the following to a friend about his work on the specific heat of gases at low temperatures:

> In recent days, I formulated a theory on this subject. *Theory* is too presumptuous a word—it is only a groping without correct foundation. The more success the quantum theory has, the sillier it looks. How nonphysicists would scoff if they were able to follow the odd course of developments! [E11]

References

A1. A. Avogadro, *Ann. Chim. Phys.* **55,** 80 (1833), especially pp. 96–8.

B1. U. Behn, *AdP* **48,** 708 (1893).

B2. L. Boltzmann, *Wiener Ber.* **53,** 195 (1866). Reprinted in *Wissenschaftliche Abhandlugen von L. Boltzmann* (F. Hasenöhrl, Ed.), Vol. 1, p. 20, Reprinted by Chelsea, New York, 1968. These collected works are referred to below as *WA.*

B3. S. G. Brush, *The Kind of Motion We Call Heat,* Vol. 1, Chap 3; Vol. 2, Chap. 10. North Holland, Amsterdam, 1976.

B4. L. Boltzmann, *Wiener Ber.* **63,** 679, (1871); *WA,* Vol. 1, p. 259.

B5. ——, *Wiener Ber.* **74,** 553, (1876); *WA,* Vol 2, p. 103.

B6. ——, *Nature* **51,** 413, (1895); *WA,* Vol. 3, p. 535.

B7. M. Born and T. von Kármán, *Phys. Zeitschr.* **13,** 297, (1912); **14,** 15 (1913).

D1. J. Dewar, *Phil. Mag.* **44,** 461 (1872).

D2. ——, *Proc. Roy. Soc. London* **76,** 325 (1905).

D3. P. Debye, *AdP* **39,** 789 (1912).

E1. A. Einstein, *AdP* **22,** 180 (1907).

E2. ——, *AdP* **22,** 800 (1907).

E3. ——, *AdP* **34,** 170 (1911).

E4. ——, *Ad* **35,** 679, (1911).

E5. A. Eucken, *PAW,* 1912, p. 141.

E6. A. Einstein and O. Stern, *AdP* **40,** 551 (1913).

E7. ——, *PAW,* 1920, p. 65.

E8. ——, *Verh. Deutsch. Phys. Ges.* **16,** 820 (1914).

E9. ——, letter to *P.* Ehrenfest, April 25, 1912.

E10. ——, *Sci. Monthly* **54,** 195 (1942).

E11. ——, letter to H. Zangger, May 20, 1912.

F1. R. Fox, *Brit. J. Hist. Sci.* **4,** 1 (1968).

H1. A. Hermann, *Frühgeschichte der Quantentheorie, 1899–1913.* Mosbach, Baden, 1969.

H2. K. Huang, *Statistical Mechanics,* p. 26. Wiley, New York, 1963.

K1. A. Kundt and E. Warburg, *AdP* **157,** 353 (1876).

K2. Kelvin, *Baltimore Lectures,* Sec. 27. Johns Hopkins University Press, Baltimore, 1904.

K3. ——, [K2], p. xvii.

K4. M. Klein, *Science* **148,** 173 (1965).

L1. G. N. Lewis, *J. Am. Chem. Soc.* **29,** 1165, 1516 (1907).

L2. H. Landolt and R. Bornstein, *Physikalisch Chemische Tabellen* (3rd ed.), p. 384. Springer, Berlin, 1905.

M1. J. C. Maxwell, *The Scientific Papers of J. C. Maxwell* (W. P. Niven , Ed.), Vol. 1, p. 377. Dover, New York.

M2. —— [M1], Vol. 2, p. 418.

N1. F. E. Neumann, *AdP* **23,** 32 (1831).

N2. W. Nernst, *PAW,* 1911, p. 306.

N3. ——, *Gött. Nachr.,* 1906, p. 1.

N4. ——, *PAW,* 1906, p. 933.

N5. ——, *PAW,* 1910, p. 262.

N6. ——, *PAW*, 1911, p. 65.

N7. —— and F. Lindemann, *PAW*, 1911, p. 494.

N8. ——, *Z. Elektrochem.* **20,** 397 (1914).

P1. A. T. Petit and P. L. Dulong, *Ann. Chim. Phys.* **10,** 395 (1819).

P2. M. Planck, *Vorlesungen über Thermodynamik* (3rd Edn.), introduction and Sec. 292. Von Veit, Leipzig, 1911.

R1. A. de la Rive and F. Marcet, *Ann. Chim. Phys.* **75,** 113 (1840).

R2. H. V. Regnault, *Ann. Chim. Phys.* **1,** 129 (1841), especially pp. 202–5.

R3. F. Richarz, *AdP* **48,** 708 (1893).

R4. J. W. S. Rayleigh, *Phil. Mag.* **49,** 98 (1900).

S1. A. Sommerfeld, *Gesammelte Schriften,* Vol. 3, p. 10. Vieweg, Braunschweig, 1968.

S2. F. Simon, *Yearbook Phys. Soc. London,* 1956, p. 1.

W1. H. F. Weber, *AdP* **147,** 311 (1872).

W2. ——, *AdP* **154,** 367, 533 (1875).

W3. A. Wigand, *AdP* **22,** 99 (1907).

W4. A. Wüllner, *Lehrbuch der Experimentalphysik,* Vol. 2, p. 507. Teubner, Leipzig, 1896.

21

The Photon

21a. The Fusion of Particles and Waves and Einstein's Destiny

I now continue the tale of the light-quantum, a subject on which Einstein published first in 1905, then again in 1906. Not long thereafter, there began the period I earlier called 'three and a half years of silence,' during which he was again intensely preoccupied with radiation and during which he wrote to Laub, 'I am incessantly busy with the question of radiation. . . . This quantum question is so uncommonly important and difficult that it should concern everyone' [E1]. Our next subject will be two profound papers on radiation published in 1909. The first one [E2] was completed while Einstein was still a technical expert second class at the patent office. The second one [E3] was presented to a conference at Salzburg in September, shortly after he had been appointed associate professor in Zürich. These papers are not as widely known as they should be because they address questions of principle without offering any new experimental conclusion or prediction, as had been the case for the first light-quantum paper (photoeffect) and the paper on specific heats.

In 1909 Kirchhoff's theorem was half a century old. The blackbody radiation law had meanwhile been found by Planck. A small number of physicists realized that its implications were momentous. A proof of the law did not yet exist. Nevertheless, 'one cannot think of refusing [to accept] Planck's theory,' Einstein said in his talk at Salzburg. That was his firmest declaration of faith up to that date. In the next sentence, he gave the new reason for his conviction: Geiger and Rutherford's value for the electric charge had meanwhile been published and Planck's value for e had been 'brilliantly confirmed' (Section 19a).

In Section 4c, I explained Einstein's way of deriving the energy fluctuation formula

$$\langle \epsilon^2 \rangle = kT^2 \frac{\partial \langle E \rangle}{\partial T} \tag{21.1}$$

where $\langle \epsilon^2 \rangle$ is the mean square energy fluctuation and $\langle E \rangle$ the average energy for a system in contact with a thermal bath at temperature T. As is so typical for Einstein, he derived this statistical physics equation in a paper devoted to the quantum theory, the January 1909 paper. His purpose for doing so was to apply this result to energy fluctuations of blackbody radiation in a frequency interval between ν and $\nu + d\nu$. In order to understand how this refinement is made, consider a small subvolume v of a cavity filled with thermal radiation. Enclose v with a wall that prevents all frequencies but those in $d\nu$ from leaving v while those in $d\nu$ can freely leave and enter v. We may then apply Eq. 21.1 with $\langle E \rangle$ replaced by $\rho v d\nu$, so that $\langle \epsilon^2 \rangle$ is now a function of ν and T and we have

$$\langle \epsilon^2(\nu, T) \rangle = kT^2 v d\nu (\partial\rho/\partial T) \tag{21.2}$$

This equation expresses the energy fluctuations in terms of the spectral function ρ in a way that is independent of the detailed form of ρ. Consider now the following three cases.

1. ρ is given by the Rayleigh–Einstein–Jeans law (eq. 19.17). Then

$$\langle \epsilon^2(\nu, T) \rangle = \frac{c^3}{8\pi\nu^2} \rho^2 v d\nu \tag{21.3}$$

2. ρ is given by the Wien law (Eq. 19.7). Then

$$\langle \epsilon^2(\nu, T) \rangle = h\nu\rho v d\nu \tag{21.4}$$

3. ρ is given by the Planck law (Eq. 19.6). Then

$$\langle \epsilon^2(\nu, T) \rangle = \left(h\nu\rho + \frac{c^3}{8\pi\nu^2} \rho^2 \right) v d\nu \tag{21.5}$$

(I need not apologize for having used the same symbol ρ in the last three equations even though ρ is a different function of ν and T in each of them.)*

In his discussion of Eq. 21.5, Einstein stressed that 'the current theory of radiation is incompatible with this result.' By current theory, he meant, of course, the classical wave theory of light. Indeed, the classical theory would give only the second term in Eq. 21.5, the 'wave term' (compare Eqs. 21.5 and 21.3). About the first term of Eq. 21.5, Einstein had this to say: 'If it alone were present, it would result in fluctuations [to be expected] if radiation were to consist of independently moving pointlike quanta with energy $h\nu$.' In other words, compare Eqs. 21.4 and 21.5. The former corresponds to Wien's law, which in turn holds in the regime in which Einstein had introduced the light-quantum postulate.

Observe the appearance of a new element in this last statement by Einstein. The word *pointlike* occurs. Although he did not use the term in either of his 1909 papers, he now was clearly thinking of quanta as particles. His own way of referring to the particle aspect of light was to call it 'the point of view of the Newtonian emission theory.' His vision of light-quanta as particles is especially evident in a letter to Sommerfeld, also dating from 1909, in which he writes of 'the ordering of the energy of light around discrete points which move with light velocity' [E4].

*Equations 21.3 and 21.4 do not explicitly occur in Einstein's own paper.

Equation 21.5 suggests (loosely speaking) that the particle and wave aspects of radiation occur side by side. This is one of the arguments which led Einstein in 1909 to summarize his view on the status of the radiation theory in the following way!*

> I already attempted earlier to show that our current foundations of the radiation theory have to be abandoned. . . . It is my opinion that the next phase in the development of theoretical physics will bring us a theory of light that can be interpreted as a kind of fusion of the wave and the emission theory. . . . [The] wave structure and [the] quantum structure . . . are not to be considered as mutually incompatible. . . . It seems to follow from the Jeans law [Eq. 19.17] that we will have to modify our current theories, not to abandon them completely.

This fusion now goes by the name of complementarity. The reference to the Jeans law we would now call an application of the correspondence principle.

The extraordinary significance for twentieth century physics of Einstein's summing up hardly needs to be stressed. I also see it as highly meaningful in relation to the destiny of Einstein the scientist if not of Einstein the man. In 1909, at age thirty, he was prepared for a fusion theory. He was alone in this. Planck certainly did not support this vision. Bohr had yet to arrive on the scene. Yet when the fusion theory arrived in 1925, in the form of quantum mechanics, Einstein could not accept the duality of particles and waves inherent in that theory as being fundamental and irrevocable. It may have distressed him that one statement he made in 1909 needed revision: moving light-quanta with energy $h\nu$ are not pointlike. Later on, I shall have to make a number of comments on the scientific reasons that changed Einstein's apartness from that of a figure far ahead of his time to that of a figure on the sidelines. As I already indicated earlier, I doubt whether this change can be fully explained on the grounds of his scientific philosophy alone.

(As a postscript to the present section, I add a brief remark on Einstein's energy fluctuation formula. Equations 21.3–21.5 were obtained by a statistical reasoning. One should also be able to derive them in a directly dynamic way. Einstein himself had given qualitative arguments for the case of Eq. 21.3. He noted that the fluctuations come about by interference between waves with frequencies within and without the $d\nu$ interval. A few years later, Lorentz gave the detailed calculation, obtaining Eq. 21.3 from classical electromagnetic theory [L1]. However, difficulties arose with attempts to derive the Planck case (Eq. 21.5) dynamically. These were noted in 1919 by Leonard Ornstein and Frits Zernike, two Dutch experts on statistical physics [O1]. The problem was further elaborated by Ehrenfest [E5].

*In the following quotation, I combine statements made in the January and in the October paper.

It was known at that time that one can obtain Planck's expression for ρ by introducing the quantum prescription* that the electromagnetic field oscillators could have only energies $nh\nu$. However, both Ornstein and Zernike, and Ehrenfest found that the same prescription applied to the fluctuation formula gave the wrong answer. The source of the trouble seemed to lie in Einstein's entropy additivity assumption (see Eq. 4.21). According to Uhlenbeck (private communication), these discrepancies were for some years considered to be a serious problem. In their joint 1925 paper, Born, Heisenberg, and Jordan refer to it as a fundamental difficulty [B1]. In that same paper, it was shown, however, that the new quantum mechanics applied to a set of noninteracting oscillators does give the Einstein answer. The noncommutativity of coordinates and momenta plays a role in this derivation. Again, according to Uhlenbeck (private communication), the elimination of this difficulty was considered one of the early successes of quantum mechanics. (It is not necessary for our purposes to discuss subsequent improvements on the Heisenberg–Born–Jordan treatment.))**

21b. Spontaneous and Induced Radiative Transitions

After 1909 Einstein continued brooding about the light-quantum for almost another two years. As mentioned in Chapter 10, in May 1911 he wrote to Besso, 'I do not ask anymore whether these quanta really exist. Nor do I attempt any longer to construct them, since I now know that my brain is incapable of fathoming the problem this way' [E6]. For the time being, he was ready to give up. In October 1911 Einstein (now a professor in Prague) gave a report on the quantum theory to the first Solvay Congress [E7], but by this time general relativity had already become his main concern and would remain so until November 1915. In 1916, he returned once again to blackbody radiation and made his next advance. In November 1916 he wrote to Besso, 'A splended light has dawned on me about the absorption and emission of radiation' [E8]. He had obtained a deep insight into the meaning of his heuristic principle, and this led him to a new derivation of Planck's radiation law. His reasoning is contained in three papers, two of which appeared in 1916 [E9, E10], the third one early in 1917 [E11]. His method is based on general hypotheses about the interaction between radiation and matter. No special assumptions are made about intrinsic properties of the objects which interact with the radiation. These objects 'will be called molecules in what follows' [E9]. (It is completely inessential to his arguments that these molecules could be Planck's oscillators!)

Einstein considered a system consisting of a gas of his molecules interacting with electromagnetic radiation. The entire system is in thermal equilibrium.

*The elementary derivation due to Debye is found in Section 24c.

**The reader interested in these further developments is referred to a paper by Gonzalez and Wergeland, which also contains additional references to this subject [G1].

Denote by E_m the energy levels of a molecule and by N_m the equilibrium number of molecules in the level E_m. Then

$$N_m = p_m \exp(-E_m/kT) \tag{21.6}$$

where p_m is a weight factor. Consider a pair of levels E_m, E_n, $E_m > E_n$. Einstein's new hypothesis is that the total number dW of transitions in the gas per time interval dt is given by

$$dW_{mn} = N_m(\rho B_{mn} + A_{mn})dt \qquad \text{for m} \to \text{n} \tag{21.7}$$
$$dW_{nm} = N_n\rho B_{nm}dt \qquad \text{for n} \to \text{m} \tag{21.8}$$

The A coefficient corresponds to spontaneous transitions m $\to$ n, which occur with a probability that is independent of the spectral density ρ of the radiation present. The B terms refer to induced emission and absorption. In Eqs. 21.7 and 21.8, ρ is a function of ν and T, where 'we shall assume that a molecule can go from the state E_n to the state E_m by absorption of radiation with a definite frequency ν, and [similarly] for emission' [E9]. Microscopic reversibility implies that $dW_{mn} = dW_{nm}$. Using Eq. 21.6, we therefore have

$$A_{mn}p_m = \rho\{B_{nm}p_n \exp[(E_m - E_n)/kT] - B_{mn}p_m\} \tag{21.9}$$

(Note that the second term on the right-hand side corresponds to induced emission. Thus, if there were no induced emission we would obtain Wien's law.) Einstein remarked that 'the constants A and B could be computed directly if we were to possess an electrodynamics and mechanics modified in the sense of the quantum hypothesis' [E9]. That, of course, was not yet the case. He therefore continued his argument in the following way. For fixed $E_m - E_n$ and $T \to \infty$, we should get the Rayleigh-Einstein-Jeans law (Eq. 19.17). This implies that

$$B_{nm}p_n = B_{mn}p_m \tag{21.10}$$

whence

$$\rho = \alpha_{mn} \{\exp[(E_m - E_n)/kT] - 1\}^{-1} \tag{21.11}$$

where $\alpha_{mn} = A_{mn}/B_{mn}$. Then he concluded his derivation by appealing to the universality of ρ and to Wien's displacement law, Eq. 19.4: 'α_{mn} and $E_m - E_n$ cannot depend on particular properties of the molecule but only on the active frequency ν, as follows from the fact that ρ must be a universal function of ν and T. Further, it follows from Wien's displacement law that α_{mn} and $E_m - E_n$ are proportional to the third and first powers of ν, respectively. Thus one has

$$E_m - E_n = h\nu \tag{21.12}$$

where h denotes a constant' [E9].

The content of Eq. 21.12 is far more profound than a definition of the symbol

ν (and h). It is a compatibility condition. Its physical content is this: in order that Eqs. 21.7 and 21.8 may lead to Planck's law, it is necessary that the transitions m $\leftrightarrows$ n are accompanied by a single monochromatic radiation quantum. By this remarkable reasoning, Einstein therefore established a bridge between blackbody radiation and Bohr's theory of spectra.

About the assumptions he made in the above derivation, Einstein wrote, 'The simplicity of the hypotheses makes it seem probable to me that these will become the basis of the future theoretical description.' That turned out to be true.

Two of the three papers under discussion [E10, E11] contained another result, one which Einstein himself considered far more important than his derivation of the radiation law: light-quanta carry a momentum $h\nu/c$. This will be our next topic.

21c. The Completion of the Particle Picture

1. Light-Quantum and Photon. A photon is a state of the electromagnetic field with the following properties.
1. It has a definite frequency ν and a definite wave vector $\vec{k}$.
2. Its energy E,

$$E = h\nu \tag{21.13}$$

and its momentum $\vec{p}$,

$$\vec{p} = h\vec{k} \tag{21.14}$$

satisfy the dispersion law

$$E = c|\vec{p}| \tag{21.15}$$

characteristic of a particle of zero rest mass.*
3. It has spin one and (like all massless particles with nonzero spin) two states of polarization. The single particle states are uniquely specified by these three properties [W1].

The number of photons is in general not conserved in particle reactions and decays. I shall return to the nonconservation of photon number in Chapter 23, but would like to note here an ironic twist of history. The term *photon* first appeared in the title of a paper written in 1926: 'The Conservation of Photons.' The author: the distinguished physical chemist Gilbert Lewis from Berkeley. The subject: a speculation that light consists of 'a new kind of atom . . . uncreatable and inde-structible [for which] I . . . propose the name photon' [L2]. This idea was soon forgotten, but the new name almost immediately became part of the language. In

---

*There have been occasional speculations that the photon might have a tiny nonzero mass. Direct experimental information on the photon mass is therefore a matter of interest. The best determinations of this mass come from astronomical observations. The present upper bound is 8×10^{-49} g [D1]. In what follows, the photon mass is taken to be strictly zero.

October 1927 the fifth Solvay conference was held. Its subject was 'électrons et photons.'

When Einstein introduced light-quanta in 1905, these were *energy* quanta satisfying Eq. 21.13. There was no mention in that paper of Eqs. 21.15 and 21.14. In other words, the full-fledged particle concept embodied in the term *photon* was not there all at once. For this reason, in this section I make the distinction between light-quantum ('$E = h\nu$ only') and photon. The dissymmetry between energy and momentum in the 1905 paper is, of course, intimately connected with the origins of the light-quantum postulate in equilibrium statistical mechanics. In the statistical mechanics of equilibrium systems, important relations between the overall energy and other macroscopic variables are derived. The overall momentum plays a trivial and subsidiary role. These distinctions between energy and momentum are much less pronounced when fluctuations around the equilibrium state are considered. It was via the analysis of statistical fluctuations of blackbody radiation that Einstein eventually came to associate a definite momentum with a light-quantum. That happened in 1916. Before I describe what he did, I should again draw the attention of the reader to the remarkable fact that it took the father of special relativity theory twelve years to write down the relation $p = h\nu/c$ side by side with $E = h\nu$. I shall have more to say about this in Section 25d.

2. *Momentum Fluctuations: 1909.* Einstein's first results bearing on the question of photon momentum are found in the two 1909 papers. There he gave a momentum fluctuation formula that is closely akin to the energy fluctuation formula Eq. 21.5. He considered the case of a plane mirror with mass m and area f placed inside the cavity. The mirror moves perpendicular to its own plane and has a velocity v at time t. During a small time interval from t to $t + \tau$, its momentum changes from mv to $mv - Pv\tau + \Delta$. The second term describes the drag force due to the radiation pressure (P is the corresponding friction constant). This force would eventually bring the mirror to rest were it not for the momentum fluctuation term Δ, induced by the fluctuations of the radiation pressure. In thermal equilibrium, the mean square momentum $m^2\langle v^2 \rangle$ should remain unchanged over the interval τ. Hence* $\langle \Delta^2 \rangle = 2mP\tau\langle v^2 \rangle$. The equipartition law applied to the kinetic energy of the mirror implies that $m\langle v^2 \rangle = kT$. Thus

$$\langle \Delta^2 \rangle = 2P\tau kT \tag{21.16}$$

Einstein computed P in terms of ρ for the case in which the mirror is fully transparent for all frequencies except those between ν and $\nu + d\nu$, which it reflects perfectly. Using Planck's expression for ρ, he found that

$$\langle \Delta^2 \rangle = \frac{1}{c}\left[\rho h\nu + \frac{c^3\rho^2}{8\pi\nu^2} \right] f\tau \, d\nu \tag{21.17}$$

*Terms $O(\tau^2)$ are dropped, and $\langle v\,\Delta \rangle = 0$ since v and Δ are uncorrelated.

The parallels between Eqs. 21.5 and 21.17 are striking. The respective first terms dominate if $h\nu/kT \gg 1$, the regime in which ρ is approximated by Wien's exponential law. Recall that Einstein had said of the first term in Eq. 21.5 that it corresponds to 'independently moving pointlike quanta with energy $h\nu$.' One might therefore expect that the first term in Eq. 21.17 would lead Einstein to state, in 1909, the 'momentum quantum postulate': monochromatic radiation of low density behaves in regard to pressure fluctuations as if it consists of mutually independent momentum quanta of magnitude $h\nu/c$. It is unthinkable to me that Einstein did not think so. But he did not quite say so.

What he did say was, 'If the radiation were to consist of very few extended complexes with energy $h\nu$ which move independently through space and which are independently reflected—a picture that represents the roughest visualization of the light-quantum hypothesis—then as a consequence of fluctuations in the radiation pressure there would act on our plate only such momenta as are represented by the first term of our formula [Eq. 21.17].' He did not refer explicitly to momentum quanta or to the relativistic connection between $E = h\nu$ and $p = h\nu/c$. Yet a particle concept (the photon) was clearly on his mind, since he went on to conjecture that 'the electromagnetic fields of light are linked to singular points similar to the occurrence of electrostatic fields in the theory of electrons' [E3]. It seems fair to paraphrase this statement as follows: light-quanta may well be particles in the same sense that electrons are particles. The association between the particle concept and a high degree of spatial localization is typical for that period. It is of course not correct in general.

The photon momentum made its explicit appearance in that same year, 1909. Johannes Stark had attended the Salzburg meeting at which Einstein discussed the radiative fluctuations. A few months later, Stark stated that according to the light-quantum hypothesis, 'the total electromagnetic momentum emitted by an accelerated electron is different from zero and . . . in absolute magnitude is given by $h\nu/c$' [S1]. As an example, he mentioned Bremsstrahlung, for which he wrote down the equation

$$m_1\vec{v}_1 + m_2\vec{v}_2 = m_1\vec{v}_1' + m_2\vec{v}_2' + \frac{h\nu}{c^2}\vec{c} \qquad (21.18)$$

the first occasion on record in which the photon enters explicitly into the law of momentum conservation for an elementary process.

3. Momentum Fluctuations: 1916. Einstein himself did not explicitly introduce photon momentum until 1916, in the course of his studies on thermal equilibrium between electromagnetic radiation and a molecular gas [E10, E11]. In addition to his new discussion of Planck's law, Einstein raised the following problem. In equilibrium, the molecules have a Maxwell distribution for the translational velocities. How is this distribution maintained in time considering the fact that the molecules are subject to the influence of radiation pressure? In other words, what is the Brownian motion of molecules in the presence of radiation?

Technically, the following issue arises. If a molecule emits or absorbs an amount ϵ of radiative energy all of which moves in the same direction, then it experiences a recoil of magnitude ϵ/c. There is no recoil if the radiation is not directed at all, as for a spherical wave. Question: What can one say about the degree of directedness of the emitted or absorbed radiation for the system under consideration? Einstein began the discussion of this question in the same way he had treated the mirror problem in 1909. Instead of the mirror, he now considered molecules that all move in the same direction. Then there is again a drag force, $Pv\tau$, and a fluctuation term, Δ. Equipartition gives again $m\langle v^2 \rangle = kT$, and one arrives once more at Eq. 21.16.

Next comes the issue of compatibility. With the help of Eqs. 21.7 and 21.8, Einstein could compute separately expressions for $\langle \Delta^2 \rangle$ as well as for P in terms of the A and B terms and ρ, where ρ is now given by Planck's law.* I shall not reproduce the details of these calculations, but do note the crux of the matter. In order to obtain the same answer for the quantities on both sides of Eq. 21.16, he had to invoke a condition of directedness: 'if a bundle of radiation causes a molecule to emit or absorb an energy amount $h\nu$, then a momentum $h\nu/c$ is transferred to the molecule, directed along the bundle for absorption and opposite the bundle for [induced] emission' [E11]. (The question of spontaneous emission is discussed below.) Thus Einstein found that consistency with the Planck distribution (and Eqs. 21.7 and 21.8) requires that the radiation be fully directed (this is often called Nadelstrahlung). And so with the help of his trusted and beloved fluctuation methods, Einstein once again produced a major insight, the association of momentum quanta with energy quanta. Indeed, if we leave aside the question of spin, we may say that *Einstein abstracted not only the light-quantum but also the more general photon concept entirely from statistical mechanical considerations.*

21d. Earliest Unbehagen about Chance

Einstein prefaced his statement about photon momentum just quoted with the remark that this conclusion can be considered 'als ziemlich sicher erwiesen,' as fairly certainly proven. If he had some lingering reservations, they were mainly due to his having derived some of his equations on the basis of 'the quantum theory, [which is] incompatible with the Maxwell theory of the electromagnetic field' [E11]. Moreover, his momentum condition was a sufficient, not a necessary, condition, as was emphasized by Pauli in a review article completed in 1924: 'From Einstein's considerations, it could . . . not be seen with complete certainty that his assumptions were the only ones that guarantee thermodynamic–statistical equilibrium' [P1]. Nevertheless, his 1917 results led Einstein to drop his caution and reticence about light-quanta. They had become real to him. In a letter to

---

*In 1910, Einstein had made a related calculation, together with Hopf [E12]. At that time, he used the classical electromagnetic theory to compute $\langle \Delta^2 \rangle$ and P. This cast Eq. 21.16 into a differential equation for ρ. Its solution is Eq. 19.17.

Besso about the needle rays, he wrote, 'Damit sind die Lichtquanten so gut wie gesichert' [E13].* And, in a phrase contained in another letter about two years later, 'I do not doubt anymore the *reality* of radiation quanta, although I still stand quite alone in this conviction,' he underlined the word 'Realität' [E14].

On the other hand, at about the same time that Einstein lost any remaining doubts about the existence of light-quanta, we also encounter the first expressions of his Unbehagen, his discomfort with the theoretical implications of the new quantum concepts in regard to 'Zufall,' chance. This earliest unease stemmed from the conclusion concerning spontaneous emission that Einstein had been forced to draw from his consistency condition (Eq. 21.16): the needle ray picture applies not only to induced processes (as was mentioned above) but also to spontaneous emission. That is, in a spontaneous radiative transition, the molecule suffers a recoil $h\nu/c$. However, the recoil direction cannot be predicted! He stressed (quite correctly, of course) that it is 'a weakness of the theory . . . that it leaves time and direction of elementary processes to chance' [E11]. What decides when the photon is spontaneously emitted? What decides in which direction it will go?

These questions were not new. They also apply to another class of emission processes, the spontaneity of which had puzzled physicists since the turn of the century: radioactive transformations. A spontaneous emission coefficient was in fact first introduced by Rutherford in 1900 when he derived** the equation $dN = -\lambda N dt$ for the decrease of the number N of radioactive thorium emanation atoms in the time interval dt [R2]. Einstein himself drew attention to this similarity: 'It speaks in favor of the theory that the statistical law assumed for [spontaneous] emission is nothing but the Rutherford law of radioactive decay' [E9]. I have written elsewhere about the ways physicists responded to this baffling lifetime problem [P2]. I should now add that Einstein was the first to realize that the probability for spontaneous emission is a nonclassical quantity. No one before Einstein in 1917 saw as clearly the depth of the conceptual crisis generated by the occurrence of spontaneous processes with a well-defined lifetime. He expressed this in prophetic terms:

> The properties of elementary processes required by [Eq. 21.16] make it seem almost inevitable to formulate a truly quantized theory of radiation. [E11]

Immediately following his comment on chance, Einstein continued, 'Nevertheless, I have full confidence in the route which has been taken' [E11]. If he was confident at that time about the route, he also felt strongly that it would be a long one. The chance character of spontaneous processes meant that something was amiss with classical causality. That would forever deeply trouble him. As early as March 1917, he had written on this subject to Besso, 'I feel that the real joke that the eternal inventor of enigmas has presented us with has absolutely not been

*With that, [the existence of] light-quanta is practically certain.

**Here a development began which, two years later, culminated in the transformation theory for radioactive substances [R1].

understood as yet' [E15]. It is believed by nearly all of us that the joke was understood soon after 1925, when it became possible to calculate Einstein's A_{mn} and B_{mn} from first principles. As I shall discuss later, Einstein eventually accepted these principles but never considered them to be *first* principles. Throughout the rest of his life, his attitude was that the joke has not been understood as yet. One further example may show how from 1917 on he could not make his peace with the quantum theory. In 1920 he wrote as follows to Born:

> That business about causality causes me a lot of trouble, too. Can the quantum absorption and emission of light ever be understood in the sense of the complete causality requirement, or would a statistical residue remain? I must admit that there I lack the courage of a conviction. However, I would be very unhappy to renounce complete causality. [E16]

21e. An Aside: Quantum Conditions for Nonseparable Classical Motion

In May 1917, shortly after Einstein finished his triple of papers on the quantum theory of radiation, he wrote an article on the restrictions imposed by the 'old' quantum theory on classically allowed orbits in phase space [E17], to which he added a brief mathematical sequel a few months later [E18]. He never returned to this subject nor, for a long time, did others show much interest in it. However, recently the importance and the pioneering character of this work has been recognized by mathematicians, quantum physicists, and quantum chemists. The only logic for mentioning this work at this particular place is that it fits with the time sequence of Einstein's contributions to quantum physics.

What Einstein did was to generalize the Bohr–Sommerfeld conditions for a system with l degrees of freedom. These conditions are $\int p_i \, dq_i = n_i h$, $i = 1, \ldots, l$, where the q_i are the coordinates, the p_i their conjugate momenta, and the n_i the integer quantum numbers. These conditions had been derived for the case where one can find a coordinate system in which the classical motion is separable in the coordinates. Thus, the conditions, if at all realizable, depend on the choice of a suitable coordinate system. Einstein found a coordinate-invariant generalization of these conditions which, moreover, did not require the motion to be separable, but only to be multiply periodic. The generalization of this result has become a problem of interest to mathematicians. Its relevance to modern physics and chemistry stems from the connection between the orbits of the old quantum theory and the semiclassical (WKB) limit of quantum mechanics. For example, a semiclassical treatment of the nuclear motion in a molecule can be combined with a Born–Oppenheimer treatment of the electronic motion. For references to recent literature, see, e.g., [B2] and [M1].

21f. The Compton Effect

I return to the photon story and come to its dénouement.

Since, after 1917, Einstein firmly believed that light-quanta were here to stay, it is not surprising that he would look for new ways in which the existence of photons might lead to observable deviations from the classical picture. In this he did not succeed. At one point, in 1921, he thought he had found a new quantum criterion [E19], but it soon turned out to be a false lead [E20, K1]. In fact, after 1917 nothing particularly memorable happened in regard to light-quanta until capital progress was achieved* when Arthur Compton [C1] and Debye [D2] independently derived the relativistic kinematics for the scattering of a photon off an electron at rest:

$$h\vec{k} = \vec{p} + h\vec{k}' \tag{21.19}$$
$$hc|\vec{k}| + mc^2 = hc|\vec{k}'| + (c^2p^2 + m^2c^4)^{1/2} \tag{21.20}$$

Why were these elementary equations not published five or even ten years earlier, as well they could have been? Even those opposed to quantized radiation might have found these relations to their liking since (independent of any quantum dynamics) they yield at once significant differences from the classical theories of the scattering of light by matter** and therefore provide simple tests of the photon idea.

I have no entirely satisfactory answer to this question. In particular, it is not clear to me why Einstein himself did not consider these relations. However, there are two obvious contributing factors. First, because photons were rejected out of hand by the vast majority of physicists, few may have felt compelled to ask for tests of an idea they did not believe to begin with. Second, it was only in about 1922 that strong evidence became available for deviations from the classical picture. This last circumstance impelled both Compton and Debye to pursue the quantum alternative.† Debye, incidentally, mentioned his indebtedness to Einstein's work on needle radiation [D2]. Compton in his paper does not mention Einstein at all.

The same paper in which Compton discussed Eqs. 21.19 and 21.20 also contains the result of a crucial experiment. These equations imply that the wavelength difference $\Delta\lambda$ between the final and the initial photon is given by

$$\Delta\lambda = (h/mc)(1 - \cos\theta) \tag{21.21}$$

where θ is the photon scattering angle. Compton found this relation to be satisfied

---

*Einstein attached great importance to an advance in another direction that took place in the intervening years: the effect discovered by Otto Stern and Walther Gerlach [E21]. Together with Ehrenfest, he made a premature attempt at its interpretation [E22].

**For details on these classical theories, see Stuewer's fine monograph on the Compton effect [S2].

†Nor is it an accident that these two men came forth with the photon kinematics at about the same time. In his paper, Debye acknowledges a 1922 report by Compton in which the evidence against the classical theory was reviewed. A complete chronology of these developments in 1922 and 1923 is found in [S2], p. 235. For a detailed account of the evolution of Compton's thinking, see [S2], Chapter 6.

within the error.* The quality of the experiment is well demonstrated by the value he obtained for the Compton wavelength: $h/mc \approx 0.0242$ Å, which is within less than one per cent of the modern value (for the current state of the subject, see [W2]). Compton concluded, 'The experimental support of the theory indicates very convincingly that a radiation quantum carries with it directed momentum as well as energy.'**

This discovery 'created a sensation among the physicists of that time' [A1]. There were the inevitable controversies surrounding a discovery of such major proportions. Nevertheless, the photon idea was rapidly accepted. Sommerfeld incorporated the Compton effect in his new edition of *Atombau und Spektrallinien* with the comment, 'It is probably the most important discovery which could have been made in the current state of physics' [S3].

What about Einstein's response? A year after Compton's experiments, Einstein wrote a popular article for *Berliner Tageblatt,* which ends as follows: 'The positive result of the Compton experiment proves that radiation behaves as if it consisted of discrete energy projectiles, not only in regard to energy transfer but also in regard to Stosswirkung (momentum transfer)' [E24]. Here then, in projectile (that is, particle) language, is the 'momentum postulate,' phrased in close analogy to the energy quantum postulate in 1905. In both cases, we encounter the phraseology, 'Radiation . . . behaves . . . as if it consists of. . . .'

Still, Einstein was not (and would never be) satisfied. There was as yet no real theory. In the same article he also wrote, 'There are therefore now two theories of light, both indispensable, and—as one must admit today despite twenty years of tremendous effort on the part of theoretical physicists—without any logical connection.'

The years 1923–24 mark the end of the first phase of Einstein's apartness in relation to the quantum theory. Yet there remained one important bastion of resistance to the photon, centering around Niels Bohr.

References

A1. S. K. Allison, *Biogr. Mem. Nat. Acad. Sci.* **38,** 81 (1965).
B1. M. Born, W. Heisenberg, and P. Jordan, *Z. Phys.* **35,** 557 (1925).
B2. M. V. Berry, *Ann. N.Y. Ac. Sci.* **357,** 183 (1980).
C1. A. H. Compton, *Phys. Rev.* **21,** 483 (1923).
D1. L. Davis, A. S. Goldhaber, and M. M. Nieto, *Phys. Rev. Lett.* **35,** 1402 (1975).
D2. P. Debye, *Phys. Zeitschr.* **24,** 161 (1923).

*K-line X-rays from a molybdenum anticathode were scattered off graphite. Compton stressed that one should use only light elements as scatterers so that the electrons will indeed be quasi-free. Scattered X-rays at 45°, 90°, and 135° were analyzed.

**The work of Compton and Debye led Pauli to extend Einstein's work of 1917 to the case of radiation in equilibrium with free electrons [P3]. Einstein and Ehrenfest subsequently discussed the connection between Pauli's and Einstein's Stosszahlansatz [E23].

E1. A. Einstein, letter to J. Laub, undated, 1908. Quoted in Se, p. 103.

E2. ——, *Phys. Zeitschr.* **10,** 185 (1909).

E3. ——, *Phys. Zeitschr.* **10,** 817 (1909).

E4. ——, letter to A. Sommerfeld, September 29, 1909.

E5. P. Ehrenfest, *Z. Phys.* **34,** 362 (1925).

E6. A. Einstein, letter to M. Besso, May 13, 1911; *EB,* p. 19.

E7. ——, in *La Théorie du Rayonnement et les Quanta* (P. Langevin and M. de Broglie, Eds.), p. 407. Gauthier-Villars, Paris, 1912.

E8. ——, letter to M. Besso, November 18, 1916; *EB,* p. 78.

E9. ——, *Verh. Deutsch. Phys. Ges.* **18,** 318 (1916).

E10. ——, *Mitt. Phys. Ges. Zürich* **16,** 47 (1916).

E11. ——, *Phys. Zeitschr.* **18,** 121 (1917).

E12. ——, and L. Hopf, *AdP* **33,** 1105 (1910).

E13. ——, letter to M. Besso, September 6, 1916; *EB,* p. 82.

E14. ——, letter to M. Besso, July 29, 1918; *EB,* p. 130.

E15. ——, letter to M. Besso, March 9, 1917.

E16. ——, letter to M. Born, January 27, 1920; in M. Born (Ed.), *The Born–Einstein Letters,* p. 23. Walker, New York, 1971.

E17. ——, *Verh. Deutsch. Phys. Ges.* **19,** 82 (1917).

E18. ——, *PAW,* 1917, p. 606.

E19. ——, *PAW,* 1921, p. 882.

E20. ——, *PAW,* 1922, p. 18.

E21. ——, letter to M. Besso, May 24, 1924; *EB,* p. 201.

E22. ——, and P. Ehrenfest, *Z. Phys.* **11,** 31 (1922).

E23. —— and ——, *Z. Phys.* **19,** 301 (1923).

E24. ——, *Berliner Tageblatt,* April 20, 1924.

G1. J. J. Gonzales and H. Wergeland, *K. Nor. Vidensk. Selsk. Skr.,* No. 4, 1973.

K1. M. Klein, *Hist. St. Phys. Sci.* **2,** 1 (1970).

L1. H. A. Lorentz, *Les Théories Statistiques en Thermodynamique,* p. 59. Teubner, Leipzig, 1916.

L2. G. N. Lewis, *Nature* **118,** 874 (1926).

M1. R. A. Marcus, *Ann. N.Y. Ac. Sci.* **357,** 169 (1980).

O1. L. S. Ornstein and F. Zernike, *Proc. K. Ak. Amsterdam* **28,** 280 (1919).

P1. W. Pauli, *Collected Scientific Papers,* Vol. 1, p. 630. Interscience, New York, 1964.

P2. A. Pais, *Rev. Mod. Phys.* **49,** 925 (1977).

P3. W. Pauli, *Z. Phys.* **18,** 272 (1923).

R1. E. Rutherford and F. Soddy, *Phil. Mag.* **4,** 370, 569 (1902).

R2. —— and ——, *Phil. Mag.* **49,** 1 (1900).

S1. J. Stark, *Phys. Zeitschr.* **10,** 902 (1909).

S2. R. H. Stuewer, *The Compton Effect.* Science History, New York, 1975.

S3. A. Sommerfeld, *Atombau und Spektrallinien* (4th ed.), p. VIII. Vieweg, Braunschweig, 1924.

W1. E. P. Wigner, *Ann. Math.* **40,** 149 (1939).

W2. B. Williams (Ed.), *Compton Scattering.* McGraw-Hill, New York, 1977.

22

Interlude: The BKS Proposal

Sie haben sich heiss und innig geliebt.
Helen Dukas

In January 1924, Niels Bohr, Hendrik Anton Kramers, and John Clarke Slater submitted to the *Philosophical Magazine* an article [B1] that contained drastic theoretical proposals concerning the interaction of light and matter. It was written after Compton's discovery, yet it rejected the photon. It was also written after Einstein and Bohr had met. This chapter on the BKS proposal serves a twofold purpose. It is a postscript to the story of the photon and a prelude to the Bohr–Einstein dialogue which will occupy us more fully later on.

I have already mentioned that Einstein was immediately and strongly impressed by Bohr's work of 1913. The two men did not yet know each other at that time. A number of years were to pass before their first encounter; meanwhile, they followed each other's published work. Also, Ehrenfest kept Einstein informed of the progress of Bohr's thinking. 'Ehrenfest tells me many details from Niels Bohr's Gedankenküche [thought kitchen]; his must be a first-rate mind, extremely critical and far-seeing, which never loses track of the grand design' [E1]. Einstein remained forever deeply respectful of Bohr's pioneering work. When he was nearly seventy, he wrote 'That this insecure and contradictory foundation [of physics in the years from 1910 to 1920] was sufficient to enable a man of Bohr's unique instinct and tact to discover the major laws of the spectral lines and of the electron shells of the atoms together with their significance for chemistry appeared to me like a miracle—and appears to me as a miracle even today. This is the highest form of musicality in the sphere of thought' [E2].

Einstein and Bohr finally met in the spring of 1920, in Berlin. At that time, they both had already been widely recognized as men of destiny who would leave their indelible marks on the physics of the twentieth century. The impact of their encounter was intense and went well beyond a meeting of minds only. Shortly after his visit, Einstein wrote to Bohr, 'Not often in life has a human being caused me such joy by his mere presence as you did' [E3]. Two days later, he wrote to Ehrenfest, 'Bohr was here, and I am as much in love with him as you are. He is like an extremely sensitive child who moves around in this world in a sort of trance' [E4]. The next month, Bohr wrote to Einstein, 'To meet you and to talk with you was one of the greatest experiences I ever had' [B2]. Some years later, Einstein began a letter to Bohr, 'Lieber oder viehmehr geliebter Bohr,' Dear or rather beloved Bohr [E5]. Once when I talked with Helen Dukas about the strong tie between these two men, she made the comment that is at the head of this chapter: 'They loved each other warmly and dearly.'

Those also were the years of scientific harmony between the two men. In 1922 Einstein wrote to Ehrenfest, 'At present, I am reading a major lecture by Bohr* which makes his world of thought wonderfully clear. He is truly a man of genius. It is fortunate to have someone like that. I have full confidence in his way of thinking' [E6]. Einstein was particularly impressed at that time with Bohr's enunciation and handling of the correspondence principle [E6], a concept on which he and Bohr were able to see eye to eye, then and later.

All who have known Bohr will be struck by the perceptive characterization Einstein gave of him much later. 'He utters his opinions like one perpetually groping and never like one who believes to be in the possession of definite truth' [E7]. Bohr's style of writing makes clear for all to see how he groped and struggled. 'Never express yourself more clearly than you think,' he used to admonish himself and others. Bohr's articles are sometimes dense. Having myself assisted him on a number of occasions when he was attempting to put his thoughts on paper, I know to what enormous lengths he went to find the most appropriate turn of phrase. I have no such first-hand information about the way Einstein wrote. But, again for all to see, there are the papers, translucent. The early Einstein papers are brief, their content is simple, their language sparse. They exude finality even when they deal with a subject in flux. For example, no statement made in the 1905 paper on light-quanta needs to be revised in the light of later developments.

The first meeting of Einstein and Bohr took place in 1920, some years before they found themselves at scientific odds on profound questions of principle in physics. They did not meet very often in later times. They did correspond but not voluminously. I was together a few times with both of them some thirty years after their first encounter, when their respective views on the foundations of quantum mechanics had long since become irreconcilable. Neither the years nor later events had ever diminished the mutual esteem and affection in which they held one another.

Let us now turn to the BKS proposal.

As already stressed in Section 19f, it was the position of most theoretical physicists during the first decades of the quantum era that the conventional continuous description of the free radiation field should be protected at all cost and that the quantum puzzles concerning radiation should eventually be resolved by a revision

---

*This was presumably the text of Bohr's contribution to the third Solvay conference (April 1921). Because of ill health, Bohr did not deliver that lecture in person [B3].

of the properties of interaction between radiation and matter. The BKS proposal represents the extreme example of this position. Its authors suggested that radiative processes have highly unconventional properties 'the cause of [which] we shall not seek in any departure from the electrodynamic theory of light as regards the laws of propagation in free space, but in the peculiarities of the interaction between the virtual field of radiation and the illuminated atoms' [B1]. Before describing these properties, I should point out that the BKS paper represents a program rather than a detailed research report. It contains no formalism whatsoever.* This program was not to be the right way out of the difficulties of the old quantum theory, yet the paper had a lasting impact in that (as we shall see) it stimulated important experimental developments. Let us discuss next the two main paradoxes addressed in BKS.

The first paradox. Consider an atom that emits radiation in a transition from a higher to a lower state. BKS assume that in this process 'energy [is] of two kinds, the continuously changing energy of the field and the discontinuously changing atomic energy' [S2]. But how can there be conservation of an energy that consists of two parts, one changing discontinuously, the other continuously? The BKS answer [B1]: 'As regards the occurrence of transitions, which is the essential feature of the quantum theory, we abandon . . . a direct application of the principles of conservation of energy and momentum.' Energy and momentum conservation, they suggested, does not hold true for individual elementary processes but should hold only statistically, as an average over many such processes.

The idea of energy nonconservation had already been on Bohr's mind a few years prior to the time of the BKS proposal [B5].** However, it was not Bohr but Einstein who had first raised—and rejected—this possibility. In 1910 Einstein wrote to a friend, 'At present, I have high hopes for solving the radiation problem, and that without light quanta. I am enormously curious as to how it will work out. One must renounce the energy principle in its present form' [E9]. A few days later he was disenchanted. 'Once again the solution of the radiation problem is getting nowhere. The devil has played a rotten trick on me' [E10]. He raised the issue one more time at the 1911 Solvay meeting, noting that his formula for the energy fluctuations of blackbody radiation could be interpreted in two ways. 'One can choose between the [quantum] structure of radiation and the negation of an absolute validity of the energy conservation law.' He rejected the second alternative. 'Who would have the courage to make a decision of this kind? . . . We shall agree that the energy principle should be retained' [E11]. Others, however, were apparently not as convinced. In 1916 the suggestion of statistical energy conser-

*The same is true for a sequel to this paper that Bohr wrote in 1925 [B4]. Schroedinger [S1] and especially Slater [S2] did make attempts to put the BKS ideas on a more formal footing. See also Slater's own recollections of that period [S3].

**A letter from Ehrenfest to Einstein shows that Bohr's thoughts had gone in that direction at least as early as 1922 [E8].

vation was taken up by Nernst [N1].* Not later than January 1922, Sommerfeld remarked that the 'mildest cure' for reconciling the wave theory of light with quantum phenomena would be to relinquish energy conservation [S4]. Similar speculations were made by other physicists as well [K1]. Thus the BKS proposal must be regarded as an attempt to face the consequences of an idea that had been debated for quite some time.

In order to understand Bohr's position in 1924, it is above all important to realize that to him the correspondence principle was the principal reliable bridge between classical and quantum physics. However, the correspondence principle is, of course, no help in understanding light-quanta: the issue of photons versus waves lies beyond that principle. The photon–wave duality was the earliest known instance of what was later to be called a complementary situation. The BKS theory, with its rejection of photons and its insistence on the continuous picture of light at the price of nonconservation, historically represents the last stand of the old quantum theory. For very good reasons, this proposal was characterized some years later by one of the principal architects of quantum mechanics as representing the height of the crisis in the old quantum theory [H1]. Nor was nonconservation of energy and momentum in individual processes the only radical proposal made by BKS.

The Second Paradox.   Another question that had troubled Einstein since 1917 (as we have seen) was, How does an electron know when to emit radiation in making a spontaneous transition?

In its general form, the BKS answer to this question was that there is no truly spontaneous emission. They associated with an atom in a given state a 'virtual radiation field' that contains all the possible transition frequencies to other stationary states and assumed that 'the transitions which in [the Einstein theory of 1917] are designated as spontaneous are, in our view, *induced* [my italics] by the virtual field.' According to BKS, the spontaneous transition to a specific final state is connected with the virtual field mechanism 'by probability laws analogous to those which in Einstein's theory hold for induced transitions.' In this way, 'the atom is under no necessity of knowing what transitions it is going to make ahead of time' [S2]. Thus, spontaneous emission is ascribed to the action of the virtual field, but this action is noncausal. I shall not discuss details of the BKS picture of induced emission and absorption and other radiative processes. Suffice it to say that all of these are supposed to be due to virtual fields and that in all of these causality is abandoned. In a paper completed later in 1924, Slater [S2] noted that the theory 'has unattractive features . . . [but] it is difficult at the present stage to see how [these are] to be avoided.'

But what about the Compton effect? The successfully verified Eq. 21.21 rests on the conservation laws Eqs. 21.19 and 21.20. However (BKS argued), these

---

*The title of Nernst's paper is (in translation) 'On an attempt to revert from quantum-mechanical considerations to the assumption of continuous energy changes.'

equations do hold in the average and the experiment on $\Delta\lambda$ refers only to the average change of the wavelength. In fact, at the time of the BKS proposal, *there did not exist any direct experimental proof of energy–momentum conservation or of causality in any individual process.* This is one of the reasons why the objections to BKS (held by many, 'perhaps the majority' of physicists [P1]* were initially expressed in a somewhat muted fashion. Thus, Pauli wrote to Bohr that he did not believe in the latter's theory but that 'one cannot prove anything logically and also the available data are not sufficient to decide for or against your view' [P1]. All this was to change soon.

There was a second reason, I believe, for the subdued character of comments by others. The physics community was witness to a rare occurrence. Einstein, of course, did not care at all for BKS. Earlier he had given thought to energy non-conservation and rejected it. To give up strict causality went deeply against his grain. Thus Einstein and Bohr, the two leading authorities of the day, were locked in conflict (the word *conflict* was used by Einstein himself**). To take sides meant choosing between the two most revered physicists. Ideally, personal considerations of this kind ought to play no role in matters scientific, but this ideal is not always fully realized. Pauli reflected on this in a letter concerning the BKS issue: 'Even if it were psychologically possible for me to form a scientific opinion on the grounds of some sort of belief in authority (which is not the case, however, as you know), this would be logically impossible (at least in this case) since here the opinions of two authorities are so very contradictory' [P1].

Even the interaction between the two protagonists was circumspect during that period. They did not correspond on the BKS issue [E12]. Nor (as best I know) were there personal meetings between them in those days, even though Bohr had told Pauli repeatedly how much he would like to know Einstein's opinion [P1]. Heisenberg wrote to Pauli that he had met Einstein in Goettingen and that the latter had 'a hundred objections' [H2]. Sometime later, Pauli also met Einstein, whereupon he sent Bohr a detailed list of Einstein's criticisms [P1].

Einstein had given a colloquium on this paper, at which he had raised objections. The idea (he wrote Ehrenfest) 'is an old acquaintance of mine, which I do not hold to be an honest fellow, however' (. . . den ich aber für keinen reellen Kerl halte) [E13]. At about that time, he drew up a list of nine objections, which I shall not reproduce here in detail. Samples: 'What should condition the virtual field which corresponds to the return of a previously free electron to a Bohr orbit? (very questionable). . . . Abandonment of causality as a matter of principle should be permitted only in the most extreme emergency' [E14]. The causality issue

---

*Born, Schroedinger, and R. Ladenburg were among the physicists who initially believed that BKS might be a step in the right direction.

**On October 25, 1924, the Danish newspaper *Politiken* carried an item on the Bohr–Einstein controversy. This led the editor of a German newspaper to send a query to Einstein [J1]. Einstein sent a brief reply [E12], acknowledging that a conflict existed and adding that no written exchanges between himself and Bohr had resulted.

(which had already plagued him for seven years by then) was the one to which he took exception most strongly. He confided to Born that the thought was unbearable to him that an electron could choose freely the moment and direction in which to move [E15]. This causality question would continue to nag him long after experiment revealed that the BKS answers to both paradoxes were incorrect.

The Experimental Verdict on Causality.   The BKS ideas stimulated Walther Bothe and Hans Geiger to develop counter coincidence techniques for the purpose of measuring whether, as causality demands, the secondary photon and the knock-on electron are produced simultaneously in the Compton effect [B6]. Their result: these two particles are both created in a time interval $\lesssim 10^{-3}$ s [B7, B8]. Within the limits of accuracy, causality had been established and the randomness of the relative creation times demanded by BKS disproved. Since then, this time interval has been narrowed down experimentally to $\lesssim 10^{-11}$ s [B9].

The Experimental Verdict on Energy–Momentum Conservation.   The validity of these conservation laws in individual elementary processes was established for the Compton effect by Compton and A. W. Simon. From cloud chamber observations on photoelectrons and knock-on electrons, they could verify the validity of the relation

$$\tan\phi = -\left[\left(1 + \frac{h\nu}{mc^2}\right)\tan\frac{1}{2}\theta\right]^{-1} \qquad (22.1)$$

in individual events, where ϕ, θ are the scattering angles of the electron and photon, respectively, and ν is the incident frequency [C1].

And so the last resistance to the photon came to an end. Einstein's views had been fully vindicated. The experimental news was generally received with great relief (see, e.g., [P2]*). Bohr took the outcome in good grace and proposed 'to give our revolutionary efforts as honorable a funeral as possible' [B10]. He was now prepared for an even more drastic resolution of the quantum paradoxes. In July 1925 he wrote, 'One must be prepared for the fact that the required generalization of the classical electrodynamic theory demands a profound revolution in the concepts on which the description of nature has until now been founded' [B4].

These remarks by Bohr end with references to de Broglie's thesis and also to Einstein's work on the quantum gas (the subject of the next chapter): the profound revolution had begun.

References

B1. N. Bohr, H. A. Kramers, and J. C. Slater, *Phil. Mag.* **47,** 785 (1924).
B2. ——, letter to A. Einstein, June 24, 1920.
B3. *Niels Bohr, Collected Works* (L. Rosenfeld, Ed.), Vol. 3, pp. 28, 357. North Holland, New York, 1976.

*Pauli's own description of BKS, written early in 1925, can be found in his collected works [P3].

B4. N. Bohr, *Z. Phys.* **34**, 142 (1925).

B5. ——, *Z. Phys.* **13**, 117 (1923), especially Sec. 4.

B6. W. Bothe and H. Geiger, *Z. Phys.* **26**, 44 (1924).

B7. —— and ——, *Naturw.* **13**, 440 (1925).

B8. —— and ——, *Z. Phys.* **32**, 639 (1925).

B9. A. Bay, V. P. Henri, and F. McLennon, *Phys. Rev.* **97**, 1710 (1955).

B10. N. Bohr, letter to R. H. Fowler, April 21, 1925.

C1. A. H. Compton and A. W. Simon, *Phys. Rev.* **26**, 889 (1925).

E1. A. Einstein, postcard to M. Planck, October 23, 1919.

E2. —— in *Albert Einstein: Philosopher–Scientist* (P. A. Schilpp, Ed.). Tudor, New York, 1949.

E3. ——, letter to N. Bohr, May 2, 1920.

E4. ——, letter to P. Ehrenfest, May 4, 1920.

E5. ——, letter to N. Bohr, January 11, 1923.

E6. ——, letter to P. Ehrenfest, March 23, 1922.

E7. ——, letter to B. Becker, March 20, 1954.

E8. P. Ehrenfest, letter to A. Einstein, January 17, 1922.

E9. A. Einstein, letter to J. J. Laub, November 4, 1910.

E10. ——, letter to J. J. Laub, November 7, 1910.

E11. —— in *Proceedings First Solvay Conference* (P. Langevin and M. de Broglie, Ed.) pp. 429, 436. Gauthier-Villars, Paris, 1912.

E12. ——, letter to K. Joel, November 3, 1924.

E13. ——, letter to P. Ehrenfest, May 31, 1924.

E14. ——, undated document in the Einstein archives, obviously written in 1924.

E15. ——, letter to M. Born, April 29, 1924. Reprinted in *The Born–Einstein Letters* (M. Born, Ed.), p. 82. Walker, New York, 1971.

H1. W. Heisenberg, *Naturw.* **17**, 490 (1929).

H2. ——, letter to W. Pauli, June 8, 1924; see [P1], p. 154.

J1. K. Joel, letter to A. Einstein, October 28, 1924.

K1. M. Klein, *Hist. St. Phys. Sci.* **2**, 1 (1970).

N1. W. Nernst, *Verh. Deutsch. Phys. Ges.* **18**, 83 (1916).

P1. W. Pauli, letter to N. Bohr, October 2, 1924. Reprinted in *W. Pauli, Scientific Correspondence* (A. Hermann, K. v. Meyenn, and V. Weisskoff, Eds.), Vol. 1, p. 163. Springer, New York, 1979.

P2. ——, letter to H. A. Kramers, July 27, 1925; see [P1], p. 232.

P3. ——, *Collected Scientific Papers,* Vol. 1, pp. 83–6. Interscience, New York, 1964.

S1. E. Schroedinger, *Naturw.* **36**, 720 (1924).

S2. J. C. Slater, *Phys. Rev.* **25**, 395 (1925).

S3. ——, *Int. J. Quantum Chem.* **1s**, 1 (1967).

S4. A. Sommerfeld, *Atombau und Spektrallinien* (3rd edn.), p. 311. Vieweg, Braunschweig, 1922.

23

A Loss of Identity:
the Birth of Quantum Statistics

23a. From Boltzmann to Dirac

This episode begins with a letter dated June 1924 [B1], written by a young Bengali. His name was Satyendra Nath Bose. The five papers he had published by then were of no particular distinction. The subject of his letter was his sixth paper. He had sent it to the *Philosophical Magazine*. A referee had rejected it [B2]. Bose's letter was addressed to Einstein, then forty-five years old and already recognized as a world figure by his colleagues and by the public at large. In this chapter I describe what happened in the scientific lives of these two men during the six months following Einstein's receipt of Bose's letter. For Bose the consequences were momentous. Virtually unknown before, he became a physicist whose name will always be remembered. For Einstein this period was only an interlude.* He was already deeply engrossed in his search for a unified theory. Such is the scope of his oeuvre that his discoveries in those six months do not even rank among his five main contributions, yet they alone would have sufficed for Einstein to be remembered forever.

Bose's sixth paper deals with a new derivation of Planck's law. Along with his letter, he had sent Einstein a copy of his manuscript, written in English, and asked him to arrange for publication in the *Zeitschrift für Physik,* if he thought the work of sufficient merit. Einstein acceded to Bose's request. He personally translated the paper into German and submitted it, adding as a translator's note: 'In my opinion, Bose's derivation of the Planck formula constitutes an important advance. The method used here also yields the quantum theory of the ideal gas, as I shall discuss elsewhere in more detail.'

The purpose of this chapter is not to discuss the history of quantum statistics but rather to describe Einstein's contribution to the subject. Nevertheless, I include a brief outline of Bose's work for numerous reasons. (1) It will give us some insight into what made Einstein deviate temporarily from his main pursuits. (2) It will facilitate the account of Einstein's own research on the molecular gas. That work

*In 1925 Einstein said of his work on quantum statistics, 'That's only by the way' [S1].

is discussed in Section 23b with the exception of one major point, which is reserved for the next chapter: Einstein's last encounter with fluctuation questions. (3) It will be of help in explaining Einstein's ambivalence to Bose's work. In a letter to Ehrenfest, written in July, Einstein did not withdraw, but did qualify his praise of Bose's paper: Bose's 'derivation is elegant but the essence remains obscure' [E1]. (4) It will help to make clear how novel the photon concept still was at that time and will throw an interesting sidelight on the question of photon spin.

Bose recalled many years later that he had not been aware of the extent to which his paper defied classical logic. (Such a lack of awareness is not uncommon in times of transition, but it is not the general rule. Einstein's light-quantum paper of 1905 is a brilliant exception.) 'I had no idea that what I had done was really novel. . . . I was not a statistician to the extent of really knowing that I was doing something which was really different from what Boltzmann would have done, from Boltzmann statistics. Instead of thinking of the light-quantum just as a particle, I talked about these states. Somehow this was the same question which Einstein asked when I met him [in October or November 1925]: how had I arrived at this method of deriving Planck's formula?' [M1].

In order to answer Einstein's question and to understand what gave Bose the idea that he was doing what Boltzmann would have done, I need to make a brief digression.

As was discussed in Section 4b, both logically and historically classical statistics developed via the sequence

fine-grained counting → course-grained counting

This is, of course, the logic of quantum statistics as well, but its historical development went the reverse way, from coarse-grained to fine-grained. For the oldest quantum statistics, the Bose–Einstein (BE) statistics, the historical order of events was as follows.

1924–5. Introduction of a new coarse-grained counting, first by Bose, then by Einstein. These new procedures are the main subject of this chapter.

1925–6. Discovery of nonrelativistic quantum mechanics. It is not at once obvious how the new theory should be supplemented with a fine-grained counting principle that would lead to BE statistics [H1].

1926. This principle is discovered by Paul Adrien Maurice Dirac. Recall first Boltzmann's fine-grained counting formula for his discrete model of a classical ideal gas consisting of N particles with total energy E. Let there be n_i particles with energy ϵ_i (see section 4b, especially Eq. 4.4 and Eq. 4.5):

$$N = \sum_i n_i \qquad E = \sum_i \epsilon_i n_i \qquad (23.1)$$

Then the corresponding number w of microstates is given by

$$w = N! \left(\prod_i n_i! \right)^{-1} \qquad \text{(Boltzmann statistics)} \qquad (23.2)$$

We owe to Dirac the observation that in the BE case, Eq. 23.2 must be replaced by

$$w = 1 \qquad \text{(BE statistics)} \qquad (23.3)$$

only the single microstate that is symmetric in the N particles is allowed. Dirac went on to show that Eq. 23.3 leads to the blackbody radiation law, Eq. 19.6 [D1]. Thus he brought to an end the search—which had lasted just over a quarter of a century—for the foundations of Planck's law.

Equation 23.3 was of course not known at the time Bose and Einstein completed the first papers ever written on quantum statistics. Theirs was guesswork, but of an inspired kind. Let us turn first to Bose's contribution.

23b. Bose

The paper by Bose [B3] is the fourth and last of the revolutionary papers of the old quantum theory (the other three being by, respectively, Planck [P1], Einstein [E2], and Bohr [B4]). Bose's arguments divest Planck's law of all supererogatory elements of electromagnetic theory and base its derivation on the bare essentials. It is the thermal equilibrium law for particles with the following properties: they are massless, they have two states of polarization, the number of particles is not conserved, and the particles obey a new statistics. In Bose's paper, two new ideas enter physics almost stealthily. One, the concept of a particle with two states of polarization, mildly puzzled Bose. The other is the nonconservation of photons. I do not know whether Bose even noticed this fact. It is not explicitly mentioned in his paper.

Bose's letter to Einstein begins as follows: 'Respected Sir, I have ventured to send you the accompanying article for your perusal. I am anxious to know what you think of it. You will see that I have ventured to deduce the coefficient $8\pi\nu^2/c^3$ in Planck's law independent of the classical electrodynamics . . .' [B1]. Einstein's letter to Ehrenfest contains the phrase, 'the Indian Bose has given a beautiful derivation of Planck's law, including the constant [i.e., $8\pi\nu^2/c^3$]' [E1]. Neither letter mentions the other parts of Planck's formula. Why this emphasis on $8\pi\nu^2/c^3$?

In deriving Planck's law, one needs to know the number of states Z^s in the frequency interval between ν^s and $\nu^s + d\nu^s$. It was customary to compute Z^s by counting the number of standing waves in a cavity with volume V. This yields

$$Z^s = 8\pi(\nu^s)^2 V d\nu^s / c^3 \qquad (23.4)$$

Bose was so pleased because he had found a new derivation of this expression for Z^s which enabled him to give a new meaning to this quantity in terms of particle language. His derivation rests on the replacing of the counting of wave frequencies by the counting of cells in one-particle phase space. He proceeded as follows. Integrate the one-particle phase space element $d\vec{x}d\vec{p}$ over V and over all momenta between p^s and $p^s + dp^s$. Supply a further factor 2 to count polarizations. This produces the quantity $8\pi V(p^s)^2 dp^s$, which equals $h^3 Z^s$ by virtue of the relation $p^s = h\nu^s/c$. Hence Z^s is the number of cells of size h^3 contained in the particle phase space region being considered. How innocent it looks, yet how new it was. Recall that the kinematics of the Compton effect had been written down only about a year and a half earlier. Here was a new application of $p = h\nu/c$!

Before I turn to the rest of Bose's derivation, I shall comment briefly on the subject of photon spin. When Bose introduced his polarization factor of 2, he noted that 'it seems required' to do so. This slight hesitation is understandable. Who in 1924 had ever heard of a particle with two states of polarization? For some time, this remained a rather obscure issue. After the discovery of the electron spin, Ehrenfest asked Einstein 'to tell [him] how the analogous hypothesis is to be stated for light-corpuscles, in a relativistically correct way' [E3]. As is well known, this is a delicate problem since there exists, of course, no rest frame definition of spin in this instance. Moreover, gauge invariance renders ambiguous the separation into orbital and intrinsic angular momentum (see, e.g., [J1]). It is not surprising, therefore, that in 1926 the question of photon spin seemed quite confusing to Einstein. In fact, he went so far as to say that he was 'inclined to doubt whether the angular momentum law can be maintained in the quantum theory. At any rate, its significance is much less deep than that of the momentum law' [E4]. I believe that this is an interesting comment on the state of the art some fifty years ago and that otherwise not too much should be made of it.

Let us return to Bose. His new interpretation of Z^s was in terms of 'number of cells,' not 'number of particles.' This must have led him to follow Boltzmann's counting but to replace everywhere 'particles' by 'cells,' a procedure he neither did nor could justify—but which gave the right answer. It may help to understand Bose's remark that he did not know that he was 'doing something which was really different from what Boltzmann would have done, from Boltzmann statistics,' if I recall at this point Boltzmann's coarse-grained counting, which is discussed at more length in Section 4b.

Boltzmann. Partition N particles with total energy E over the one-particle phase space cells $\omega_1, \omega_2, \ldots$ There are N_A particles in ω_A. Their mean energy is E_A. We have

$$N = \sum_A N_A \qquad E = \sum_A E_A N_A \qquad (23.5)$$

The relative probability W of this coarse-grained state is

$$W = N! \prod_A \frac{\omega_A^{N_A}}{N_A!} \qquad (23.6)$$

The equilibrium entropy S is given by

$$S = k \ln W_{\max} + C \qquad (23.7)$$

where C is a constant and W_{max} follows from the extremal conditions

$$\sum \delta N_A (\ln \omega_A - \ln N_A + \lambda - \beta^{-1} E_A) = 0 \qquad (23.8)$$

which incorporate the constraints (a) hold N fixed and (b) hold E fixed.

Bose. Partition Z^s into numbers p_r^s, where p_r^s is defined as the number of cells which contain r quanta with frequency ν^s. Let there be N^s photons in all with this frequency and let E be the total energy. Then

$$Z^s = \sum_r p_r^s \qquad (23.9)$$

$$N^s = \sum_r r p_r^s \qquad (23.10)$$

$$E = \sum_s N^s h \nu^s \qquad (23.11)$$

and

$$N = \sum_s N^s \qquad (23.12)$$

is the total number of photons. Next Bose introduced his new coarse-grained counting:

$$W = \prod_s \frac{Z^s!}{p_0^s! p_1^s! \cdots} \qquad (23.13)$$

He then maximized W as a function of the p_r^s holding Z^s and E fixed so that

$$\sum_{s,r} \delta p_r^s \left(1 + \ln p_r^s + \lambda^s + \frac{1}{\beta} r h \nu^s \right) = 0 \qquad (23.14)$$

and then derived Planck's law for $E(\nu, T)$ by standard manipulations—and therewith concluded his paper without further comments.

Bose considered his *Ansatz* (Eq. 23.13) to be 'evident' [B3]. Nothing is further from the truth. I venture to guess that to him the cell counting (Eq. 23.13) was the perfect analog of Boltzmann's particle counting (Eq. 23.6) and that his cell constraint, hold Z^s fixed, was similarly the analog of Boltzmann's particle constraint, hold N fixed. Likewise, the two Lagrange parameters in Eq. 23.14 are his analogs of the parameters in Eq. 23.8. Bose's replacement of fixed N by fixed Z^s already implies that N is not conserved. The final irony is that the constraint of fixed Z^s is irrelevant: if one drops this constraint, then one must drop λ^s in Eq. 23.14. Even so, it is easily checked that one still finds Planck's law! This is in accordance with the now-familiar fact that Planck's law follows from Bose statistics with E held fixed as the *only* constraint. In summary, Bose's derivation introduced three new features:

1. Photon number nonconservation.
2. Bose's cell partition numbers p_r^s are defined by asking how many particles are in a cell. Boltzmann's axiom of distinguishability is gone.
3. The *Ansatz* (Eq. 23.13) implies statistical independence of cells. Statistical independence of particles is gone.

The astounding fact is that Bose was correct on all three counts. (In his paper, he commented on none of them.) I believe there had been no such successful shot in the dark since Planck introduced the quantum in 1900. Planck, too, had counted in strange ways, as was subtly recalled by Einstein in his review, written in 1924, of a new edition of Planck's *Wärmestrahlung:* 'Planck's law [was] derived ... by postulating statistical laws in the treatment of the interaction between ponderable matter and radiation which appear to be justified on the one hand because of their simplicity, on the other hand because of their analogy to the corresponding relations of the classical theory' [E5].

Einstein continued to be intrigued by Bose's paper. In an address given in Lucerne on October 4, 1924, before the Schweizerische Naturforschende Gesellschaft, he stressed 'the particular significance for our theoretical concepts' of Bose's new derivation of Eq. 23.4 [E6]. By this time, he had already published his own first paper on quantum statistics.

23c. Einstein

As long as Einstein lived, he never ceased to struggle with quantum physics. As far as his constructive contributions to this subject are concerned, they came to an end with a triple of papers, the first published in September 1924, the last two in early 1925. In the true Einsteinian style, their conclusions are once again reached by statistical methods, as was the case for all his important earlier contributions to the quantum theory. The best-known result is his derivation of the Bose–Einstein condensation phenomenon. I shall discuss this topic next and shall leave for the subsequent section another result contained in these papers, a result that is perhaps not as widely remembered even though it is more profound.

First, a postscript to Einstein's light-quantum paper of 1905.

Its logic can be schematically represented in the following way.

$$\text{Einstein 1905:} \quad \left. \begin{array}{l} \text{Wien's law} \\[2mm] \text{Gas analogy} \end{array} \right\} \rightarrow \text{Light-quanta}$$

An issue raised in Section 19c should be dealt with now. We know that BE is the correct statistics when radiation is treated as a photon gas. Then how could Einstein have correctly conjectured the existence of light-quanta using Boltzmann statistics? Answer: according to BE statistics, the most probable value $\langle n_i \rangle$ of n_i for photons is given by $\langle n_i \rangle = [\exp(h\nu_i/kT) - 1]^{-1}$. This implies that $\langle n_i \rangle \ll 1$ in the Wien regime $h\nu_i \gg kT$. Therefore, up to an irrelevant* factor $N!$, Equations 23.2 and 23.3 coincide in the Wien limit. This asymptotic relation in the Wien region fully justifies, *ex post facto,* Einstein's extraordinary step forward in 1905!

Bose's reasoning in 1924 went as follows:

$$\text{Bose 1924:} \quad \left.\begin{array}{l} \text{Photons} \\ \\ \text{Quantum statistics} \end{array}\right\} \rightarrow \text{Planck's law}$$

and in 1924–5 Einstein came full circle:

$$\text{Einstein 1924–5:} \quad \left.\begin{array}{l} \text{Bose statistics} \\ \\ \text{Photon analogy} \end{array}\right\} \rightarrow \text{The quantum gas}$$

It was inevitable, one might say, that he would do so. 'If it is justified to conceive of radiation as a quantum gas, then the analogy between the quantum gas and a molecular gas must be a complete one' [E7].

In his 1924 paper [E8], Einstein adopted Bose's counting formula (Eq. 23.13), but with two modifications. He needed, of course, the Z^s appropriate for nonrelativistic particles with mass m:

$$h^3 Z^s = 2\pi V (2m)^{3/2} (E^s)^{1/2} \, dE^s \qquad (23.15)$$
$$2mE^s = (p^s)^2$$

Second (and unlike Bose!), he needed the constraint that N be held fixed. This is done by adding a term

$$- r\ln A \qquad (23.16)$$

inside the parentheses of Eq. 23.14.** One of the consequences of the thus modified Eq. 23.14 is that the Lagrange multiplier ($-\ln A$) is determined by

$$N = \sum_s N^s = \sum_s \left[\frac{1}{A} \exp\left(\frac{E^s}{kT}\right) - 1 \right]^{-1} \qquad (23.17)$$

Hence, Einstein noted, the 'degeneracy parameter' A must satisfy

$$A \leqslant 1 \qquad (23.18)$$

In his first paper [E8], Einstein discussed the régime in which A does not reach

---

*The $N!$ is irrelevant since it affects only C in Eq. 23.7. The constant C is interesting nevertheless. For example, its value bears on the possibility of defining S in such a way that it becomes an extensive thermodynamic variable. The interesting history of these normalization questions has been discussed in detail by M. Klein [K1].

**The term A^{-1} is defined as $\exp(-\mu/kT)$, where μ is the chemical potential. Einstein, of course, never introduced the superfluous λ^s into the parenthetical term. In Eqs. 23.16–23.22, I deviate from Einstein's notation.

the critical value unity. He proceeded to the continuous limit, in which the sum in Eq. 23.17 is replaced by an integral over phase space, and found

$$\text{if } A < 1: \qquad \frac{1}{v} = \frac{\phi_{3/2}(A)}{3}$$

$$\frac{p}{kT} = \frac{\phi_{5/2}(A)}{3} \qquad (23.19)$$

$$\phi_n(A) = \sum_{m=1}^{\infty} m^{-n} A^m$$

with $v = V/N$. He then discussed the region $A \ll 1$, where the equation of state (obtained by eliminating A between Eqs. 23.19) shows perturbative deviations from the classical ideal gas. All this is good physics, though unusually straightforward for a man like Einstein.

In his second paper [E7], the most important one of the three, Einstein began with the $v - T$ relation at $A = 1$:

$$kT_0 = \frac{h^2}{2m \, [v_0 \phi_{3/2}(1)]^{3/2}} \qquad (23.20)$$

and asked what happens if T drops below T_0 (for given v_0). His answer:

> I maintain that, in this case, a number of molecules steadily growing with increasing density goes over in the first quantum state (which has zero kinetic energy) while the remaining molecules distribute themselves according to the parameter value $A = 1$.... A separation is effected; one part condenses, the rest remains a 'saturated ideal gas.' [E7]

He had come upon the first purely statistically derived example of a phase transition, which is now called Bose–Einstein condensation. I defer a few comments on this phenomenon to the next section and turn to other important facets of the three Einstein papers.

1. Einstein on Statistical Dependence.   After the papers by Bose [B3] and the first one by Einstein [E8] came out, Ehrenfest and others objected (so we read in Einstein's second paper [E7]) that 'the quanta and molecules, respectively, are not treated as statistically independent, a fact that is not particularly emphasized in our papers' (i.e., [B3] and [E8]). Einstein replied, 'This [objection] is entirely correct' [E7]. He went on to stress that the differences between the Boltzmann and the BE counting 'express indirectly a certain hypothesis on a mutual influence of the molecules which for the time being is of a quite mysterious nature.' With this remark, Einstein came to the very threshold of the quantum mechanics of identical particle systems. The mysterious influence is, of course, the correlation induced by the requirement of totally symmetric wave functions.

2. Einstein on Indistinguishability.   In order to illustrate further the differences between the new and the old counting of macrostates, Einstein cast W in a form alternative to Eq. 23.13. He counted the number of ways in which N^s indistinguishable particles in the dE^s interval can be partitioned over the Z^s cells. This yields

$$W = \prod_s \frac{(N^s + Z^s - 1)!}{N^s! \, (Z^s - 1)!}$$ (23.21)

Einstein's Eq. 23.21 rather than Bose's Eq. 23.13 is the one now used in all textbooks.

3. *Einstein on the Third Law of Thermodynamics.* As was noted at the end of Section 20c, in 1914 Nernst introduced the hypothesis that the third law of thermodynamics applies to gases. It was also mentioned that no sensible model of a gas with that property was available at that time. In 1925 Einstein made his last contribution to thermodynamics by pointing out that the BE gas does satisfy the third law. (A Boltzmann gas does not do so, Einstein remarked.) Indeed, since all particles go into the zero energy state as $T \rightarrow 0$, we have in this limit $N^0 = N$, all other $N^s = 0$. Hence $W \rightarrow 1$ and $S \rightarrow 0$ as $T \rightarrow 0$. It was as important to him that a molecular BE gas yield Nernst's law as that a BE photon gas yield Planck's law.

4. *Einstein and Nonconservation of Photons.* After 1917 Einstein ceased to write scientific articles on questions related to radiation.* The only mention of radiation in the 1924–5 papers is that 'the statistical method of Herr Bose and myself is by no means beyond doubt, but seems only *a posteriori* justified by its success for the case of radiation' [E11].

There can be no doubt that he must have noted the nonconservation of photons. In his language, this is implemented by putting $A = 1$ in Eq. 23.16. Yet I have not found any reference to nonconservation, either in his scientific writings or in the correspondence I have seen. I cannot state with certainty why he chose to be silent on this and all further issues regarding photons. However, I do believe that it is a fair guess that Einstein felt he would have nothing fundamental to say about photons until such time as he could find his own way of dealing with the lack of causality he had noted in 1917. Such a time never came.

Other physicists had followed Einstein's work on quantum statistics with interest. Lorentz invited him to speak on this subject at the 1927 Solvay congress. Einstein's reply, written in June 1927, may serve as a most appropriate preliminary to my subsequent discussion of quantum mechanics.

> I recall having committed myself to you to give a report on quantum statistics at the Solvay congress. After much reflection back and forth, I come to the conviction that I am not competent [to give] such a report in a way that really

---

*Except for a brief refutation of an objection to his work on needle radiation [E9]. I found a notice by Einstein in 1930 announcing a new paper on radiation fluctuations [E10]. This paper was never published, however.

corresponds to the state of things. The reason is that I have not been able to participate as intensively in the modern development of the quantum theory as would be necessary for this purpose. This is in part because I have on the whole too little receptive talent for fully following the stormy developments, in part also because I do not approve of the purely statistical way of thinking on which the new theories are founded. . . . Up until now, I kept hoping to be able to contribute something of value in Brussels; I have now given up that hope. I beg you not to be angry with me because of that; I did not take this lightly but tried with all my strength. . . . Perhaps Herr Fermi in Bologna . . . or Langevin . . . could do a good job. [E12]

23d. Postscript on Bose–Einstein Condensation

(1) In December 1924, Einstein wrote to Ehrenfest, 'From a certain temperature on, the molecules "condense" without attractive forces, that is, they accumulate at zero velocity. The theory is pretty, but is there also some truth to it?' [E13].

(2) In 1925, Einstein mentioned hydrogen, helium, and the electron gas as the best possible candidates in which to observe his condensation phenomenon [E7]. In 1925, these were, of course, sensible proposals. Recall that the Fermi–Dirac statistics was not discovered* until 1926 [F1, D1], following Pauli's enunciation of the exclusion principle in 1925 [P2]. Even then, it took some time until it was sorted out when BE and FD statistics apply respectively: referring to Dirac's paper [D1], Pauli wrote in December 1926, 'We shall take the point of view also advocated by Dirac, that the Fermi, and not the Einstein–Bose, statistics applies to the material gas' [P3]. These matters were cleared up by 1927.

(3) In his 1925 paper, Einstein did not call the condensation phenomenon a phase transition. According to Uhlenbeck (private communication), nobody realized in 1925 that the existence of a phase transition was a 'deep' problem. In 1926, Uhlenbeck himself raised an objection to Einstein's treatment of the condensation problem [U1]. This critique was to lead to a more precise theoretical formulation of the conditions under which phase transitions can occur. Uhlenbeck noted that the quantity N^0 in Eq. 23.17 $\to \infty$ as $A \to 1$ (for fixed T); hence also $N \to \infty$. Thus, if $A \to 1$, it is impossible to implement the constraint that N is a fixed finite number. Therefore $A = 1$ can be reached only asymptotically and there is no two-phase regime.

Uhlenbeck recently described the communications between Ehrenfest and Einstein on this question [U2]. Uhlenbeck and Einstein were both right, however. The point is that a sharp phase transition can occur only in the so-called thermodynamic limit $N \to \infty$, $V \to \infty$, v fixed. This view emerged in a morning-long debate that took place during the van der Waals Centenary Conference in November 1937. The issue was, Does the partition function contain the information necessary to describe a sharp phase transition? The transition implies the

---

*Dirac has given a charming account of the time sequence of these discoveries [D2].

existence of analytically distinct parts of isotherms. It was not clear how this could come about. The debate was inconclusive, and Kramers, the chairman, put the question to a vote. Uhlenbeck recalls that the ayes and nays were about evenly divided. However, Kramers' suggestion to go to the thermodynamic limit was eventually realized to be the correct answer. Shortly afterward, Uhlenbeck withdrew his objections to Einstein's result, in a joint paper with his gifted student, the late Boris Kahn (a Nazi victim) [K2].

(4) Until 1928, the BE condensation had 'the reputation of having only a purely imaginary character' [L1]. Recall that the HeI–HeII phase transition was not discovered until 1928, by Willem Hendrik Keesom [K3]. In 1938, Fritz London proposed interpreting this helium transition as a BE condensation. Experimentally, the transition point lies at 2.19 K. It is most encouraging that Eq. 23.20 gives $T = 3.1$ K [L2]. It is generally believed but not proved that the difference between these two values is due to the neglecting of intermolecular forces in the theoretical derivations.

References

B1. S. N. Bose, letter to A. Einstein, June 4, 1924.

B2. W. Blanpied, *Am. J. Phys.* **40**, 1212 (1972).

B3. S. N. Bose, *Z. Phys.* **26**, 178 (1924).

B4. N. Bohr, *Phil. Mag.* **26**, 1 (1913).

D1. P. A. M. Dirac, *Proc. Roy. Soc.* **112**, 661 (1926).

D2. ——, *History of Twentieth Century Physics,* Varenna Summer School, pp. 133–4. Academic Press, New York, 1977.

E1. A. Einstein, letter to P. Ehrenfest, July 12, 1924.

E2. ——, *AdP* **17**, 132 (1905).

E3. P. Ehrenfest, letter to A. Einstein, April 7, 1926.

E4. A. Einstein, letter to P. Ehrenfest, April 12, 1926.

E5. ——, *Deutsche Literaturzeitung,* 1924, p. 1154.

E6. ——, *Verh. Schw. Naturf. Ges.* **105**, 85 (1924).

E7. ——, *PAW,* 1925, p. 3.

E8. ——, *PAW,* 1924, p. 261.

E9. ——, *Z. Phys.* **31**, 784 (1925).

E10. ——, *PAW,* 1930, p. 543.

E11. ——, *PAW,* 1925, p. 18.

E12. ——, letter to H. A. Lorentz, June 17, 1927.

E13. ——, letter to P. Ehrenfest, November 29, 1924.

F1. E. Fermi, *Z. Phys.* **36**, 902 (1926).

H1. W. Heisenberg, *Z. Phys.* **38**, 411 (1926).

J1. J. M. Jauch and F. Rohrlich, *The Theory of Photons and Electrons,* p. 40. Addison-Wesley, Reading, Mass., 1955.

K1. M. Klein, Proc. Kon. Ned. Akad. Wetensch. Amsterdam, **62**, 41, 51 (1958).

K2. B. Kahn and G. E. Uhlenbeck, *Physica* **4**, 399 (1938).

K3. W. H. Keesom, *Helium.* Elsevier, New York, 1942.

L1. F. London, *Nature* **141,** 643 (1938).

L2. ——, *Phys. Rev.* **54,** 1947 (1938).

M1. J. Mehra, *Biogr. Mem. Fell. Roy. Soc.* **21,** 117 (1975).

P1. M. Planck, *Verh. Deutsch. Phys. Ges.* **2,** 237 (1900).

P2. W. Pauli, *Z. Phys.* **31,** 625 (1925).

P3. ——, *Z. Phys.* **41,** 81 (1927).

S1. E. Salaman, *Encounter,* April 1979, p. 19.

U1. G. E. Uhlenbeck, 'Over Statistische Methoden in de Theorie der Quanta,' PhD thesis, Nyhoff, the Hague, 1927.

U2. ——, *Proceedings Einstein Centennial Symposium 1979* (H. Woolf, Ed.). Addison-Wesley, Reading, Mass., 1980.

24

Einstein as a Transitional Figure: The Birth of Wave Mechanics

We now leave the period of the old quantum theory and turn to the time of transition, during which matter waves were being discussed by a tiny group of physicists at a time when matter wave mechanics had not yet been discovered. This period begins in September 1923 with two brief communications by Louis de Broglie to the French Academy of Sciences [B1, B2]. It ends in January 1926 with Schroedinger's first paper on wave mechanics [S1]. The main purpose of this chapter is to stress Einstein's key role in these developments, his influence on de Broglie, de Broglie's subsequent influence on him, and, finally, the influence of both on Schroedinger.

Neither directly nor indirectly did Einstein contribute to an equally fundamental development that preceded Schroedinger's discovery of wave mechanics: the discovery of matrix mechanics by Heisenberg [H1]. Therefore, I shall have no occasion in this book to comment in any detail on Heisenberg's major achievements.

24a. From Einstein to de Broglie

During the period that began with Einstein's work on needle rays (1917) and ended with Debye's and Compton's papers on the Compton effect (1923), there were a few other theoreticians also doing research on photon questions. Of those, the only one* whose contribution lasted was de Broglie.

De Broglie had finished his studies before the First World War. In 1919, after a long tour of duty with the French forces, he joined the physics laboratory headed by his brother Maurice, where X-ray photoeffects and X-ray spectroscopy were the main topics of study. Thus he was much exposed to questions concerning the nature of electromagnetic radiation, a subject on which he published several papers. In one of these [B6], de Broglie evaluated independently of Bose (and

---

*The other ones I know of are Brillouin [B3], Wolfke [W1], Bothe [B4], Bateman [B5], and Ornstein and Zernike [O1].

published before him) the density of radiation states in terms of particle (photon) language. That was in October 1923—one month after his enunciation of the epochal new principle that particle–wave duality should apply not only to radiation but also to matter. 'After long reflection in solitude and meditation, I suddenly had the idea, during the year 1923, that the discovery made by Einstein in 1905 should be generalized by extending it to all material particles and notably to electrons' [B7].

He made the leap in his September 10, 1923, paper [B1]: $E = h\nu$ shall hold not only for photons but also for electrons, to which he assigns a 'fictitious associated wave.' In his September 24 paper [B2], he indicated the direction in which one 'should seek experimental confirmations of our ideas': a stream of electrons traversing an aperture whose dimensions are small compared with the wavelength of the electron waves 'should show diffraction phenomena.'

Other important aspects of de Broglie's work are beyond the scope of this book (for more details, see, e.g.. [K1]). The mentioned articles were extended to form his doctoral thesis [B7], which he defended on November 25, 1924. Einstein received a copy of this thesis from Langevin, who was one of de Broglie's examiners. A letter to Lorentz (in December) shows that Einstein was impressed and also that he had found a new application of de Broglie's ideas:

> A younger brother of . . . de Broglie has undertaken a very interesting attempt to interpret the Bohr–Sommerfeld quantum rules (Paris dissertation 1924). I believe it is a first feeble ray of light on this worst of our physics enigmas. I, too, have found something which speaks for his construction. [E1]

24b. From de Broglie to Einstein

In 1909 and again in 1917, Einstein had drawn major conclusions about radiation from the study of fluctuations around thermal equilibrium. It goes without saying that he would again examine fluctations when, in 1924, he turned his attention to the molecular quantum gas.

In order to appreciate what he did this time, it is helpful to again present the formula (Eq. 21.5) given earlier for the mean square energy fluctuation of electromagnetic radiation:

$$\langle\epsilon^2\rangle = \left(\rho h\nu + \frac{c^3\rho^2}{8\pi\nu^2}\right) V d\nu \tag{24.1}$$

Put $V\rho d\nu = n(\nu)h\nu$ and $\langle\epsilon^2\rangle = \Delta(\nu)^2(h\nu)^2$. The term $n(\nu)$ can be interpreted as the average number of quanta in the energy interval $d\nu$, and $\Delta(\nu)^2$ as the mean square fluctuation of this number. One can now write Eq. 24.1 in the form

$$\Delta(\nu)^2 = n(\nu) + \frac{n(\nu)^2}{Z(\nu)} \tag{24.2}$$

where $Z(\nu)$ is the number of states per interval $d\nu$ given in Eq. 23.4. In his paper submitted on January 8, 1925, Einstein showed that Eq. 24.2 holds equally well for his quantum gas, as long as one defines ν in the latter case by $E = h\nu = p^2/2m$ and uses Eq. 23.15 instead of Eq. 23.4 for the number of states [E2].

When discussing radiation in 1909, Einstein recognized the second term of Eq. 24.1 as the familiar wave term and the first one as the unfamiliar particle term. When in 1924 he revisited the fluctuation problem for the case of the quantum gas, he noted a reversal of roles. The first term, at one time unfamiliar for radiation, was now the old fluctuation term for a Poisson distribution of (distinguishable) particles. What to do with the second term (which incorporates indistinguishability effects of particles) for the gas case? Since this term was associated with waves in the case of radiation, Einstein was led to 'interpret it in a corresponding way for the gas, by associating with the gas a radiative phenomenon' [E2]. He added, 'I pursue this interpretation further, since I believe that here we have to do with more than a mere analogy.'

But what were the waves?

At this point, Einstein turned to de Broglie's thesis [B7], 'a very notable publication.' He suggested that a de Broglie-type wavefield should be associated with the gas and pointed out that this assumption enabled him to interpret the second term in Eq. 24.2. Just as de Broglie had done, he also noted that a molecular beam should show diffraction phenomena but added that the effect should be extremely small for manageable apertures. He also remarked that the de Broglie wavefield had to be a scalar (the polarization factor is 2 for Eq. 23.4, as noted above, but it is 1 for Eq. 23.15!).

It is another of Einstein's feats that he would be led to state the necessity of the existence of matter waves from the analysis of fluctuations. One may wonder what the history of twentieth century physics would have looked like had Einstein pushed the analogy still further. However, with the achievement of an independent argument for the particle–wave duality of matter, the twenty-year period of highest scientific creativity in Einstein's life, at a level probably never equalled, came to an end.

Postscript, Summer 1978.   In the course of preparing this chapter, I noticed a recollection by Pauli of a statement made by Einstein during a physics meeting held in Innsbruck in 1924. According to Pauli, Einstein proposed in the course of that meeting 'to search for interference and diffraction phenomena with molecular beams' [P1]. On checking the dates of that meeting, I found them to be September 21–27. This intrigued me. Einstein arrived at the particle–wave duality of matter via a route that was independent of the one taken by de Broglie. The latter defended his thesis in November. If Pauli's memory is correct, then Einstein made his remark about two months prior to that time. Could he have come upon the wave properties of matter independently of de Broglie? After all, Einstein had been thinking about the molecular gas since July. The questions arise, When did

Einstein become aware of de Broglie's work? In particular, when did he receive de Broglie's thesis from Langevin? Clearly, it would be most interesting to know what Professor de Broglie might have to say about these questions. Accordingly I wrote to him. He was kind enough to reply. With his permission, I quote from his answers.

De Broglie does not believe that Einstein was aware of his three short publications [B1, B2, B3] written in 1923. 'Nevertheless, since Einstein would receive the *Comptes Rendus* and since he knew French very well, he might have noticed my articles' [B8]. De Broglie noted further that he had given Langevin the first typed copy of his thesis early in 1924. 'I am certain that Einstein knew of my Thèse since the spring of 1924' [B9]. This is what happened. 'When in 1923 I had written the text of the Thèse de Doctorat which I wanted to present in order to obtain the Doctorat ès Sciences, I had three typed copies made. I handed one of these to M. Langevin so that he might decide whether this text could be accepted as a Thèse. M. Langevin, probablement un peu étonné par la nouveauté de mes idées,* asked me to furnish him with a second typed copy of my Thèse for transmittal to Einstein. It was then that Einstein declared, after having read my work, that my ideas seemed quite interesting to him. This made Langevin decide to accept my work' [B8].

Thus, Einstein was not only one of the three fathers of the quantum theory, but also the sole godfather of wave mechanics.

24c. From de Broglie and Einstein to Schroedinger

Late in 1925, Schroedinger completed an article entitled 'On Einstein's Gas Theory' [S2]. It was his last paper prior to his discovery of wave mechanics. Its contents are crucial to an understanding of the genesis of that discovery [K2].

In order to follow Schroedinger's reasoning, it is necessary to recall first a derivation of Planck's formula given by Debye in 1910 [D1]. Consider a cavity filled with radiation oscillators in thermal equilibrium. The spectral density is $8\pi\nu^2\epsilon(\nu, T)/c^3$, where ϵ is the equilibrium energy of a radiation field oscillator with frequency ν. Debye introduced the quantum prescription that the only admissible energies of the oscillator shall be $nh\nu$, $n = 0, 1, 2, \ldots$. In equilibrium, the nth energy level is weighted with its Boltzmann factor. Hence $\epsilon = \Sigma nh\nu y^n/\Sigma y^n$, $y = \exp(-h\nu/kT)$. This yields Planck's law.**

Now back to Schroedinger. By his own admission, he was not much taken with the new BE statistics [S2]. Instead, he suggested, why not evade the new statistics

---

*Probably a bit astonished by the novelty of my ideas.

**This derivation differs from Planck's in that the latter quantized material rather than radiation oscillators. It differs from Bose's photon gas derivation in that here the energy $nh\nu$ is interpreted as the nth state of a single oscillator, not (as was done in Chapter 23) as a state of n particles with energy $h\nu$.

by treating Einstein's molecular gas according to the Debye method? That is, why not start from a wave picture of the gas and superimpose on that a quantization condition à la Debye? Now comes the key sentence in the article: 'That means nothing else but taking seriously the de Broglie–Einstein wave theory of moving particles' [S2]. And that is just what Schroedinger did. It is not necessary to discuss further details of this article, which was received by the publisher on December 25, 1925.

Schroedinger's next paper was received on January 27, 1926 [S1]. It contains his equation for the hydrogen atom. Wave mechanics was born. In this new paper, Schroedinger acknowledged his debt to de Broglie and Einstein:

> I have recently shown [S2] that the Einstein gas theory can be founded on the consideration of standing waves which obey the dispersion law of de Broglie. . . . The above considerations about the atom could have been presented as a generalization of these considerations.

In April 1926, Schroedinger again acknowledged the influence of de Broglie and 'brief but infinitely far-seeing remarks by Einstein' [S3].

References

B1. L. de Broglie, *C. R. Acad. Sci. Paris* **177,** 507 (1923).

B2. ——, *C. R. Acad. Sci. Paris* **177,** 548 (1923).

B3. L. Brillouin, *J. de Phys.* **2,** 142 (1921).

B4. W. Bothe, *Z. Phys.* **20,** 145 (1923).

B5. H. Bateman, *Phil. Mag.* **46,** 977 (1923).

B6. L. de Broglie, *C. R. Acad. Sci. Paris* **177,** 630 (1923).

B7. ——, preface to his reedited 1924 PhD thesis, *Recherches sur la Théorie des Quanta*, p. 4. Masson, Paris, 1963.

B8. ——, letter to A. Pais, August 9, 1978.

B9. ——, letter to A. Pais, September 26, 1978.

D1. P. Debye, *AdP* **33,** 1427 (1910).

E1. A. Einstein, letter to H. A. Lorentz, December 16, 1924.

E2. ——, *PAW*, 1925. p. 3.

H1. W. Heisenberg, *Z. Phys.* **33,** 879 (1926).

K1. F. Kubli, *Arch. Hist. Ex. Sci.* **7,** 26 (1970).

K2. M. Klein, *Nat. Phil.* **3,** 1 (1964).

O1. L. S. Ornstein and F. Zernike, *Proc. K. Akad. Amsterdam* **28,** 280 (1919).

P1. W. Pauli in *Albert Einstein: Philosopher–Scientist* (P. A. Schilpp, Ed.), p. 156. Tudor, New York, 1949.

S1. E. Schroedinger, *AdP* **79,** 361 (1926).

S2. ——, *Phys. Zeitschr.* **27,** 95 (1926).

S3. ——, *AdP* **79,** 734, (1926); footnote on p. 735.

W1. M. Wolfke, *Phys. Zeitschr.* **22,** 315 (1921).

25

Einstein's Response to the New Dynamics

Everyone familiar with modern physics knows that Einstein's attitude regarding quantum mechanics was one of skepticism. No biography of him fails to mention his saying that God does not throw dice. He was indeed given to such utterances (as I know from experience), and stronger ones, such as 'It seems hard to look in God's cards. But I cannot for a moment believe that He plays dice and makes use of "telepathic" means (as the current quantum theory alleges He does)' [E1]. However, remarks such as these should not create the impression that Einstein had abandoned active interest in quantum problems in favor of his quest for a unified field theory. Far from it. In fact, even in the search for a unified theory, the quantum riddles were very much on his mind, as I shall discuss in Chapter 26. In the present chapter, I shall describe how Einstein's position concerning quantum mechanics evolved in the course of time. To some extent this is reflected in his later scientific papers. It becomes evident more fully in several of his more autobiographical writings and in his correspondence. My own understanding of his views has been helped much by discussions with him.

To begin with, I turn to the period 1925–31, during which he was much concerned with the question, Is quantum mechanics consistent?

25a. 1925–31: The Debate Begins

Schroedinger was not the only one who had profited from the study of Einstein's three papers on the new gas theory. Half a year before Schroedinger's first paper on wave mechanics, Walter Elsasser, likewise acknowledging the stimulus of Einstein's articles, suggested that slow electrons would be ideally suited for testing '[Einstein's] assumption that to every translational motion of a particle one must associate a wavefield which determines the kinematics of the particle' [E2]. He also pointed out that the existing experimental results of Ramsauer, Davisson and Kunsman, and others already seemed to give evidence of diffraction and interference of matter waves. Heisenberg wrote to Pauli that, after having studied Einstein's papers, he was enthusiastic about Elsasser's ideas [H1].

Also Einstein himself continued thinking about the meaning of wavefields, old and new. Eugene Wigner, who was in Berlin in 1925, told me that Einstein had at that time the idea of wavefields serving as 'Führungsfelder,' guiding fields, for light-quanta or other particles, one field for each particle. 'Einstein, though in a way he was fond of [this idea], never published it' [W1] since his idea of one field per particle was incompatible with strict energy–momentum conservation—a difficulty which was overcome when Schroedinger introduced one guiding field, the Schroedinger wave function, for joint particle configurations.

As was mentioned earlier, Einstein considered his work on the quantum gas only a temporary digression. During the very early days of quantum mechanics,* we find him 'working strenuously on the further development of a theory on the connection between gravitation and electricity' [E3]. Yet the great importance of the new developments in quantum theory was not lost on him. Bose, who visited Berlin in November 1925, recalled that 'Einstein was very excited about the new quantum mechanics. He wanted me to try to see what the statistics of light-quanta and the transition probabilities of radiation would look like in the new theory' [M1]. It was not Bose but Dirac who answered that question by giving the dynamic derivation of expressions for Einstein's A and B coefficients in a paper in which he laid the foundations of quantum electrodynamics [D1]. Initially, Einstein's reaction to Dirac's contributions was decidedly negative. In 1926 he wrote to Ehrenfest, 'I have trouble with Dirac. This balancing on the dizzying path between genius and madness is awful' [E4], and again, a few days later, 'I don't understand Dirac at all (Compton effect)' [E5]. Some years later, however, he wrote admiringly of 'Dirac, to whom, in my opinion, we owe the most logically perfect presentation of [quantum mechanics]' [E6].

Let us return to the fall of 1925. Einstein's deep interest in quantum mechanics must have led him to write to Heisenberg soon after the publication of the latter's paper [H2].** All the letters from Einstein to Heisenberg have been lost. However, a number of letters from Heisenberg to Einstein are extant. One of these (dated November 30, 1925) is clearly in response to an earlier letter from Einstein to Heisenberg in which Einstein appears to have commented on the new quantum mechanics. One remark by Heisenberg is of particular interest. 'You are probably right that our formulation of quantum mechanics is more adapted to the Bohr–Kramers–Slater attitude, but this [BKS theory] constitutes, in fact, one aspect of the radiation phenomena. The other is your light-quantum theory, and we have the hope that the validity of the energy and momentum laws in our quantum mechanics will one day make possible the connection with your theory' [H4]. I find it remarkable that Einstein apparently sensed that there was some connection between the BKS theory and quantum mechanics. No such connection exists, of

---

*Recall that Heisenberg's first paper on this subject was completed in July 1925, Schroedinger's in January 1926.

**The two men met for the first time in the spring of 1926. See [H3] for an attempt at reconstruction of their early discussions.

course. Nevertheless, the BKS proposal contains statistical features,* as we have seen. Could Einstein have surmised as early as 1925 that some statistical element is inherent in the quantum mechanical description?

During the following months, Einstein vacillated in his reaction to the Heisenberg theory. In December 1925 he expressed misgivings [E7], but in March 1926 he wrote to the Borns, 'The Heisenberg–Born concepts leave us all breathless and have made a deep impression on all theoretically oriented people. Instead of a dull resignation, there is now a singular tension in us sluggish people' [E8]. The next month he expressed again his conviction that the Heisenberg–Born approach was off the track. That was in a letter in which he congratulated Schroedinger on his new advance [E9]. In view of the scientific links between Einstein's and Schroedinger's work, it is not surprising that Einstein would express real enthusiasm about wave mechanics: 'Schroedinger has come out with a pair of wonderful papers on the quantum rules', he wrote in May 1926 [E10]. It was the last time he would write approvingly about quantum mechanics.

There came a parting of ways.

Nearly a year passed after Heisenberg's paper before there was a first clarification of the conceptual basis of quantum mechanics. It began with Born's observation in June 1926 that the absolute square of a Schroedinger wave function is to be interpreted as a probability density. Born's brief and fundamental paper goes to the heart of the problem of determinism. Regarding atomic collisions he wrote:

> One does not get an answer to the question, What is the state after collision? but only to the question, How probable is a given effect of the collision? . . . From the standpoint of our quantum mechanics, there is no quantity [Grösze] which causally fixes the effect of a collision in an individual event. Should we hope to discover such properties later . . . and determine [them] in individual events? . . . I myself am inclined to renounce determinism in the atomic world, but that is a philosophical question for which physical arguments alone do not set standards. [B1]

One month later, Born wrote a more elaborate sequel to this paper, in which he pointed out that the starting point of his considerations was 'a remark by Einstein on the relation between [a] wavefield and light-quanta; he [E.] said approximately that waves are there only to point out the path to the corpuscular light-quanta,

---

*Heisenberg remarked much later that 'the attempt at interpretation by Bohr, Kramers, and Slater nevertheless contained some very important features of the later correct interpretation [of quantum mechanics],' [H5]. I do not share this view, but shall not argue the issue beyond what has been said in Chapter 22.

and spoke in this sense of a "Gespensterfeld"', ghost field [B2], clearly a reference to Einstein's idea of a 'Führungsfeld.' Shortly thereafter, Born wrote to Einstein:

> My idea to consider Schroedinger's wavefield as a 'Gespensterfeld' in your sense of the word proves to be more useful all the time. . . . The probability field propagates, of course, not in ordinary space but in phase space (or configuration space). [B3]*

Once more, but now for the last time, we encounter Einstein as a transitional figure in the period of the birth of quantum mechanics.

Born's papers had a mixed initial reception. Several leading physicists found it hard if not impossible to swallow the abandonment of causality in the classical sense, among them Schroedinger. More than once, Bohr mentioned to me that Schroedinger told him he might not have published his papers had he been able to foresee what consequences they would unleash.** Einstein's position in the years to follow can be summarized succinctly by saying that he took exception to every single statement in Born's papers and in the letter Born subsequently wrote to him. His earliest expressions of lasting dissent I know of date from December 1926 and are, in fact, contained in his reply to one of Born's letters: 'Quantum mechanics is very impressive. But an inner voice tells me that it is not yet the real thing. The theory produces a good deal but hardly brings us closer to the secret of the Old One. I am at all events convinced that *He* does not play dice. Waves in $3n$-dimensional space whose velocity is regulated by potential energy (e.g., rubber bands) . . . ' [E11].

'Einstein's verdict . . . came as a hard blow' to Born [B4]. There are other instances as well in which Einstein's reactions were experienced with a sense of loss, of being abandoned in battle by a venerated leader. Thus Goudsmit told me of a conversation that took place in mid-1927 (to the best of his recollection [G1]) between Ehrenfest and himself. In tears, Ehrenfest said that he had to make a choice between Bohr's and Einstein's position and that he could not but agree with Bohr. Needless to say, Einstein's reactions affected the older generation more intensely than the younger.

Of the many important events in 1927, four are particularly significant for the present account.

February 1927. In a lecture given in Berlin, Einstein is reported to have said that 'what nature demands from us is not a quantum theory or a wave theory; rather, nature demands from us a synthesis of these two views which thus far has exceeded the mental powers of physicists' [E12]. At this point in the developments, as others are about to take over, it should be recalled one more time that as early

---

*This important letter is not included in the published Born–Einstein correspondence. I thank John Stachel for drawing my attention to its existence.

**Schroedinger retained reservations on the interpretation of quantum mechanics for the rest of his life [S1].

as 1909 Einstein had been the first to stress the need for incorporating a particle–wave duality in the foundations of physical theory (see Section 21a).

March 1927.   Heisenberg states the uncertainty principle [H6]. (In this paper, Heisenberg, too, referred to 'Einstein's discussions of the relation between waves and light-quanta.') In June 1927 Heisenberg writes a letter to Einstein which begins, 'Many cordial thanks for your kind letter; although I really do not know anything new, I would nevertheless like to write once more why I believe that indeterminism, that is, the nonvalidity of rigorous causality, is *necessary* [his italics] and not just consistently possible' [H7]. This letter is apparently in response to another lost letter by Einstein, triggered, most probably, by Heisenberg's work in March. I shall return to Heisenberg's important letter in Chapter 26. I mention its existence at this point only in order to emphasize once again that Einstein did not react to these new developments as a passive bystander. In fact, at just about that time, he was doing his own research on quantum mechanics (his first, I believe). 'Does Schroedinger's wave mechanics determine the motion of a system completely or only in the statistical sense?'* he asked. Heisenberg had heard indirectly that Einstein 'had written a paper in which you ... advocate the view that it should be possible after all to know the orbits of particles more precisely than I would wish.' He asked for more information 'especially because I myself have thought so much about these questions and only came to believe in the uncertainty relations after many pangs of conscience, though now I am entirely convinced' [H8]. Einstein eventually withdrew his paper.

September 16, 1927.   At the Volta meeting in Como (Einstein had been invited but did not attend), Bohr enunciates for the first time the principle of complementarity: 'The very nature of the quantum theory ... forces us to regard the space–time coordination and the claim of causality, the union of which characterizes the classical theories, as complementary but exclusive features of the description, symbolizing the idealization of observation and definition, respectively' [B5].

October 1927.   The fifth Solvay Conference convenes. All the founders of the quantum theory were there, from Planck, Einstein, and Bohr to de Broglie, Heisenberg, Schroedinger, and Dirac. During the sessions, 'Einstein said hardly anything beyond presenting a very simple objection to the probability interpretation. ... Then he fell back into silence' [B5a]. As was mentioned in Chapter 23, Einstein had declined an invitation to give a paper on quantum statistics at that conference.

However, the formal meetings were not the only place for discussion. All participants were housed in the same hotel, and there, in the dining room, Einstein was much livelier. Otto Stern has given this first-hand account**:

---

*This is the title of a paper Einstein submitted for the May 5, 1927, meeting of the Prussian Academy in Berlin. The records show that the paper was in print when Einstein requested by telephone that it be withdrawn. The unpublished manuscript is in the Einstein archive. See also [K1].

**In a discussion with Res Jost, taped on December 2, 1961. I am very grateful to Jost for making available to me a transcript of part of this discussion.

Einstein came down to breakfast and expressed his misgivings about the new quantum theory, every time [he] had invented some beautiful experiment from which one saw that [the theory] did not work. . . . Pauli and Heisenberg, who were there, did not pay much attention, 'ach was, das stimmt schon, das stimmt schon' [ah, well, it will be all right, it will be all right]. Bohr, on the other hand, reflected on it with care and in the evening, at dinner, we were all together and he cleared up the matter in detail.

Thus began the great debate between Bohr and Einstein. Both men refined and sharpened their positions in the course of time. No agreement between them was ever reached. Between 1925 and 1931, the only objection by Einstein that appeared in print in the scientific literature is the one at the 1927 Solvay conference [E13]. However, there exists a masterful account of the Bohr–Einstein dialogue during these years, published by Bohr in 1949 [B6]. I have written elsewhere about the profound role that the discussions with Einstein played in Bohr's life [P1].

The record of the Solvay meeting contains only minor reactions to Einstein's comments. Bohr's later article analyzed them in detail. Let us consider next the substance of Einstein's remarks.

Einstein's opening phrase tells more about him than does many a book: 'Je dois m'excuser de n'avoir pas approfondi la mécanique des quanta,' I must apologize for not having penetrated quantum mechanics deeply enough [E13]*.

He then went on to discuss an experiment in which a beam of electrons hits a fixed screen with an aperture in it. The transmitted electrons form a diffraction pattern, which is observed on a second screen. Question: does quantum mechanics give a complete description of the individual electron events in this experiment? His answer: this cannot be. For let A and B be two distinct spots on the second screen. If I know that an individual electron arrives at A, then I know instantaneously that it did not arrive at B. But this implies a peculiar instantaneous action at a distance between A and B contrary to the relativity postulate. Yet (Einstein notes) in the Geiger–Bothe experiment on the Compton effect [B7], there is no limitation of principle to the accuracy with which one can observe coincidences in individual processes, and that without appeal to action at a distance. This circumstance adds to the sense of incompleteness of the description for diffraction.

Quantum mechanics provides the following answer to Einstein's query. It does apply to individual processes, but the uncertainty principle defines and delimits the optimal amount of information obtainable in a given experimental arrange-

*The original German text reads, 'Ich [bin] mir des Umstandes bewusst dass ich in das Wesen der Quantenmechanik nicht tief genug eingedrungen bin' [E14].

ment. This delimitation differs incomparably from the restrictions on information inherent in the coarse-grained description of events in classical statistical mechanics. There the restrictions are wisely self-imposed in order to obtain a useful approximation to a description in terms of an ideally knowable complete specification of momenta and positions of individual particles. In quantum mechanics, the delimitations mentioned earlier are not self-imposed but are renunciations of first principle (on the fine-grained level, one might say). It is true that one would need action at a distance if one were to insist on a fully causal description involving the localization of the electron at every stage of the experiment on hand. Quantum mechanics denies that such a description is called for and asserts that, in this experiment, the final position of an individual electron cannot be predicted with certainty. Quantum mechanics nevertheless makes a prediction in this case concerning the probability of an electron arriving at a given spot on the second screen. The verification of this prediction demands, of course, that the 'one-electron experiment' be repeated as often as necessary to obtain this probability distribution with the desired accuracy.

Nor is there a conflict with Geiger–Bothe, since now one refers to another experimental arrangement in which localization in space–time is achieved, but this time at the price of renouncing information on sharp energy–momentum properties of the particles observed in coincidence. From the point of view of quantum mechanics, these renunciations are expressions of laws of nature. They are also applications of the saying, 'Il faut reculer pour mieux sauter,' It is necessary to take a step back in order to jump better. As we shall see, what was and is an accepted renunciation to others was an intolerable abdication in Einstein's eyes. On this score, he was never prepared to give up anything.

I have dwelt at some length on this simple problem since it contains the germ of Einstein's position, which he stated more explicitly in later years. Meanwhile, the debate in the corridors between Bohr and Einstein continued during the sixth Solvay Conference (on magnetism) in 1930. This time Einstein thought he had found a counterexample to the uncertainty principle. The argument was ingenious. Consider a box having in one of its walls a hole that can be opened or closed by a shutter controlled by a clock inside the box. The box is filled with radiation. Weigh the box. Set the shutter to open for a brief interval during which a single photon escapes. Weigh the box again, some time later. Then (in principle) one has found to arbitrary accuracy both the photon energy and its time of passage, in conflict with the energy–time uncertainty principle.

'It was quite a shock for Bohr . . . he did not see the solution at once. During the whole evening he was extremely unhappy, going from one to the other and trying to persuade them that it couldn't be true, that it would be the end of physics if Einstein were right; but he couldn't produce any refutation. I shall never forget the vision of the two antagonists leaving the club [of the Fondation Universitaire]: Einstein a tall majestic figure, walking quietly, with a somewhat ironical smile,

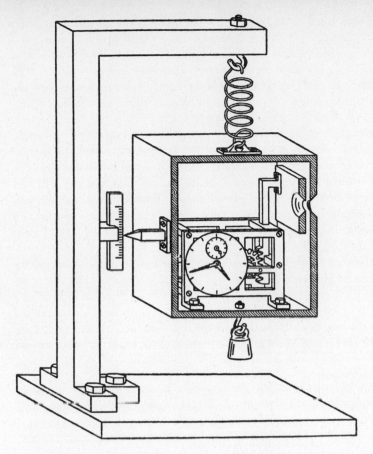

Bohr's drawing of Einstein's clock-in-the-box experiment [B6]. (Reproduced with the kind permission of Professor A. Schilpp.)

and Bohr trotting near him, very excited.... The next morning came Bohr's triumph' [R1].

Bohr later illustrated his arguments [B6] with the help of the experimental arrangement reproduced above. The initial weighing is performed by recording the position of the pointer attached to the box relative to the scale attached to the fixed frame. The loss of weight resulting from the escape of the photon is compensated by a load (hung underneath the box) that returns the pointer to its initial position with a latitude Δq. Correspondingly, the weight measurement has an uncertainty Δm. The added load imparts to the box a momentum which we can measure with an accuracy Δp delimited by $\Delta p \Delta q \approx h$. Obviously $\Delta p < tg\Delta m$, where t is the time taken to readjust the pointer and g is the gravitational acceleration. Thus, $tg\Delta m\Delta q > h$. Next, Bohr used the red shift formula*: the uncertainty Δq of the position of the clock in the gravitational field implies an uncertainty $\Delta t = c^{-2}gt\Delta q$ in the determination of t. Hence, $c^2\Delta m\Delta t = \Delta E\Delta t > h$. Thus the accuracy with which the energy of the photon is measured restricts the precision with which its moment of escape can be determined, in accordance with the uncertainty relations for energy and time.

Note that every one of the many details in the figure serves an experimental purpose: the heavy bolts fix the position of the scale along which the pointer moves, the spring guarantees the mobility of the box in the gravitational field, the weight attached to the box serves to readjust its position, and so on. There was nothing fanciful in Bohr's insistence on such details. Rather he had them drawn in order to illustrate that, since the results of all physical measurements are expressed in classical language, it is necessary to specify in detail the tools of measurement in that language as well.

After this refutation by Bohr, Einstein ceased his search for inconsistencies. By 1931 his position on quantum mechanics had undergone a marked change.

First of all, his next paper on quantum mechanics [E15], submitted in February 1931, shows that he had accepted Bohr's criticism.** It deals with a new variant of the clock-in-the-box experiment. Experimental information about one particle is used to make predictions about a second particle. This paper, a forerunner of the Einstein–Podolsky–Rosen article to be discussed below, need not be remembered for its conclusions.†

A far more important expression of Einstein's opinions is found in a letter he wrote the following September. In this letter, addressed to the Nobel committee in Stockholm, Einstein nominated Heisenberg and Schroedinger for the Nobel prize. In his movitation, he said about quantum mechanics, 'Diese Lehre enthält nach meiner Überzeugung ohne Zweifel ein Stück endgültiger Wahrheit.'‡ Einstein himself was never greatly stirred by honors and distinctions. Even so, his nominations reveal a freedom of spirit and a generosity of mind. In addition, they show most clearly his thoughts: he came to accept that quantum mechanics was not an aberration but rather a truly professional contribution to physics.

---

*Recall that the only ingredients for the derivation of this formula are the special relativistic time dilation and the equivalence principle.

**The Gedankenexperiment in this paper involved a time measurement. The authors take care to arrange things so that 'the rate of the clock . . . is not disturbed by the gravitational effects involved in weighing the box.'

†The authors are 'forced to conclude that there can be no method for measuring the momentum of a particle without changing its value,' a statement which, of course, is unacceptable.

‡'I am convinced that this theory undoubtedly contains a part of the ultimate truth.' Einstein had already proposed Heisenberg and Schroedinger in 1928, and proposed Schroedinger again in 1932 (see Chapter 31).

Not that from then on he desisted from criticizing quantum mechanics. He had recognized it to be part of the truth, but was and forever remained deeply convinced that it was not the whole truth. From 1931 on, the issue for him was no longer the consistency of quantum mechanics but rather its completeness.

During the last twenty-five years of life, Einstein maintained that quantum mechanics was incomplete. He no longer believed that quantum mechanics was wrong but did believe that the common view of the physics community was wrong in ascribing to the postulates of quantum mechanics a degree of finality that he held to be naive and unjustified. The content and shape of his dissent will gradually unfold in what follows.

In November 1931 Einstein gave a colloquium in Berlin 'on the uncertainty relation' [E16]. The report of this talk does not state that Einstein objected to Heisenberg's relations. Rather it conveys a sense of his discomfort about the freedom of choice to measure precisely either the color of a light ray or its time of arrival. My friend Casimir has written to me about a colloquium Einstein gave in Leiden, with Ehrenfest in the chair [C1] (this must have been in November 1930). In his talk, Einstein discussed several aspects of the clock-in-the-box experiments. In the subsequent discussion, it was mentioned that no conflict with quantum mechanics existed. Einstein reacted to this statement as follows: 'Ich weiss es, widerspruchsfrei ist die Sache schon, aber sie enthält meines Erachtens doch eine gewisse Härte' (I know, this business is free of contradictions, yet in my view it contains a certain unreasonableness).

By 1933 Einstein had stated explicitly his conviction that quantum mechanics does not contain logical contradictions. In his Spencer lecture, he said of the Schroedinger wave functions: 'These functions are supposed to determine in a mathematical way only the probabilities of encountering those objects in a particular place or in a particular state of motion, if we make a measurement. This conception is logically unexceptionable and has led to important successes' [E17].

It was in 1935 that Einstein stated his own desiderata for the first time in a precise form. This is the criterion of objective reality, to which he subscribed for the rest of his life. By 1935 Einstein was settled in Princeton. At this point, I interrupt the account of the quantum theory in order to describe what happened to Einstein and his family from 1932 to 1945.

25b. Einstein at Princeton

Einstein settled permanently in the United States in October 1933. His thoughts of leaving Germany had begun to take shape two years earlier, however. In December 1931, he wrote in his travel diary: 'Today, I made my decision essentially to give up my Berlin position' [E18]. He was on board ship at that time, en route to his first stay in Pasadena. It was an atmosphere conducive to reflecting on the recent happenings in Germany. A year earlier, the National Socialists had made a stunning advance, increasing their number of seats in the Reichstag from twelve to one hundred and seven.

Einstein's decision to move to Princeton was the result of three meetings with Abraham Flexner [F1]. The first of these was unplanned. Early in 1932, Flexner had come to Pasadena to discuss with faculty members at CalTech his project for a new center of research, The Institute for Advanced Study. On that occasion, he was introduced to Einstein. The two men discussed the Institute plan in general terms. When they met again in Oxford, in the spring of 1932, Flexner asked if Einstein himself might be interested in joining the Institute. At their third meeting, in Caputh in June 1932, Einstein said he was enthusiastic about coming, provided he could bring his assistant, Walther Mayer; for himself he requested an annual salary of $3000. 'He asked . . . "could I live on less"?' [F2]. Formal negotiations began at once [E19]. The appointment was approved in October 1932 [I1]. His salary was set at $15000 per year. The remarkable story of the negotiations concerning Walther Mayer is found in Chapter 29.

Einstein originally intended to spend five months of the year in Princeton and the rest of the time in Berlin [K2]. It never worked out that way. New elections in July 1932 gave the Nazis 230 Reichstag seats. It was the following December that Einstein told his wife that she would never see Caputh again (section 16d). On December 10, 1932, the Einsteins, accompanied by thirty pieces of luggage, left Bremerhaven on board the steamer Oakland, once again bound for California. As it turned out, it was their permanent departure from Germany.

On January 30, 1933, Hitler came to power. Three days later, Einstein still wrote to the secretariat of the Prussian Academy concerning his salary arrangements [K3]. The situation deteriorated rapidly, however, and in a letter dated March 28, 1933, Einstein sent his resignation to the Akademie in Berlin [K4].* A week earlier, *The New York Times* had reported that 'one of the most perfect raids of recent German history was carried out' [N1]. The SA had raided the Einsteins' Caputh home to search for hidden weapons. According to the *Times*, all they found was a breadknife.

March 28 was also the day on which the Einsteins arrived in Antwerp, returning from California. They had to return to Europe because Einstein had obligations and because arrangements had to be made for the move to Princeton, which now, of course, was to be their only home. Family and friends helped them find a temporary European abode, the villa Savoyard in Le Coq sur Mer on the Belgian coast. There they were joined by Ilse and Margot, who had meanwhile gone to Paris. Helen Dukas came from Zürich, Walther Mayer from Vienna. Their establishment was completed by two guards (assigned by the Belgian government) who were to watch over their safety. Rumors were rife of planned attempts on Einstein's life.

Practical arrangements were made. Einstein's son-in-law Rudolf Kayser saw

---

*On April 21 he also resigned from the Bavarian Academy.

to it that Einstein's papers in Berlin were saved and sent to the Quai d'Orsay by French diplomatic pouch. Furniture from the home on the Haberlandstrasse was prepared for shipment (and arrived safely in Princeton some time later). Einstein traveled. He lectured several times in Brussels; he went to Zürich, where he saw his son Eduard for the last time; he went to Oxford, where on June 10 he gave the Spencer lecture, which I have often quoted [E17].

Two days later, he lectured again in Oxford and on June 20 was in Glasgow to give the first Gibson lecture, dealing with the origins of general relativity [E20].* During a brief second visit to England, in July, he met with Churchill and other prominent personalities. Meanwhile, offers for academic positions reached him from several sides. Weizmann asked him to come to Jerusalem. Einstein refused outright because he was highly critical of the Hebrew University's administration. He was approached by Leiden and Oxford. Offers for chairs came from Madrid and Paris.

In the midst of these happenings, Einstein and Mayer managed to do a little physics and complete two papers on semivectors, which they sent from Le Coq to Holland for publication in the Royal Dutch Academy proceedings [E21, E22]. These were sequels to a joint paper they had finished a few days before Einstein had set off for Pasadena [E23]. This work was stimulated by Ehrenfest's insistence on a better understanding of the relation between single-valued and double-valued representations of the Lorentz group [E23]. In response, this is what they did. Associate a 2×2 matrix X to a special relativistic 4-vector x_μ:

$$X = \begin{pmatrix} x_0 + x_3 & x_1 - ix_2 \\ x_1 + ix_2 & x_0 - x_3 \end{pmatrix} \tag{25.1}$$

so that $\det X$ equals the vector's (invariant length)^2. Transform X by

$$X' = AXB \tag{25.2}$$

where A and B are complex 2×2 matrices. This transformation is length-preserving if $\det A \, \det B = 1$. Scale in such a way that $\det A = 1$; then $\det A = \det B = 1$. With these constraints, Eq. 25.2 represents the general complex Lorentz group excluding reflections; reality preservation demands that $B = A^\dagger$. Under the transformation

$$X' = AX \tag{25.3}$$

each of the two columns of X transforms into itself. These columns, called semivectors by Einstein and Mayer, are double-valued representations of the proper Lorentz group; up to linear combinations they are spinors.** Not all of this was new [K5], but it was nice work, done independently. They went on to relate semi-

---

*A report in *The New York Times* [N2] that Einstein was present at a Zionist Congress in Prague in August is incorrect.

**The detailed connection between semivectors and spinors was discussed by Bargmann [B8].

vectors to the Dirac equation and to generalize the formalism to general relativity. Their studies of semivector pairs led them to believe that for 'the first time . . . an explanation has been given for the existence of two electric elementary particles of different mass, with charges that are [equal and] opposite' [E21], a conclusion that did not survive.*

On September 9 Einstein left the Continent for good. Le Coq was too close to the German border for his safety. Again he went to England, where he spent a few quiet weeks in the country. On October 3 he addressed a mass meeting in London, chaired by Rutherford, which was designed to draw attention to the need for aid to scholars in exile [N3]. Then it was time to go. Ilse and Margot returned to Paris. Elsa, Helen Dukas, and Walther Mayer** boarded the *Westmoreland* in Antwerp. On October 7 Einstein joined them in Southampton. Carrying visitors' visas, the four of them set out for a new life.

On October 17 they arrived in New York and were met at quarantine by Edgar Bamberger and Herbert Maass, trustees of the Institute, who handed Einstein a letter from Flexner, the Institute's first director. The letter read in part: 'There is no doubt whatsoever that there are organized bands of irresponsible Nazis in this country. I have conferred with the local authorities . . . and the national government in Washington, and they have all given me the advice . . . that your safety in America depends upon silence and refraining from attendance at public functions. . . . You and your wife will be thoroughly welcome at Princeton, but in the long run your safety will depend on your discretion' [F3]. The party was taken by special tug from quarantine to the Battery. From there, they were driven directly to Princeton, where rooms at the Peacock Inn were waiting for them. A few days later, the Einsteins and Helen Dukas moved to a rented house at 2 Library Place. There they stayed until 1935, when Einstein bought the house at 112 Mercer Street from Mary Marden, paying for it in cash. In the autumn of that year, they moved in. It was to be Einstein's last home. In 1939 Mussolini's racial laws forced Einstein's sister, Maja Winteler, to leave the small estate outside Florence which Einstein had bought for her and her husband, Paul. Maja came to live with her brother in Princeton. Paul moved in with the Michaele Bessos in Geneva.

Death struck in the early years. Ilse died in Paris after a painful illness. Thereafter Margot joined her family in Princeton. In May 1935 Einstein and his wife as well as Margot and her husband† sailed for Bermuda, in order to obtain immigrant visas upon reentry. This was Einstein's last trip outside the United States. Not long thereafter, Elsa became gravely ill. She died on December 20, 1936, of heart disease.

---

*These papers are rather bizarre since the authors were aware of the recent discovery of the positron [E21].

**One biographer's story [C2] that Mayer had joined Einstein in England is incorrect.

†Margot was briefly married to Dimitri Marianoff.

In 1938 Einstein's son Hans Albert came to the United States. In 1926 he had obtained the diploma as civil engineer at the ETH. In 1928 he married Frida Knecht in Dortmund, where he worked for some years as a steel designer. In 1930 their son Bernhard Caesar was born, Einstein's first grandchild. In 1936, Hans Albert obtained his PhD degree at the ETH. From 1947 to 1971 he was professor of hydraulic engineering at the University of California in Berkeley. About his father's influence on him, he once remarked, 'Probably the only project he ever gave up on was me. He tried to give me advice, but he soon discovered that I was too stubborn and that he was just wasting his time' [N3a].

Shortly after arriving in the United States, Einstein gave the Queen of Belgium his early impressions of Princeton: 'A quaint ceremonious village of puny demi-gods on stilts' [E24]. A year and a half later he wrote to her again: 'I have locked myself into quite hopeless scientific problems—the more so since, as an elderly man, I have remained estranged from the society here' [E25]. After he came to the United States, his charisma did not wane. In January 1934 he and Elsa had stayed with the Roosevelts at the White House and had spent a night in the Franklin Room. There were the same odd demands on his energies and time, as, for example, when he was asked to write a letter for a time capsule to be placed at the site of the New York World's Fair and to be opened in the year 6369 (he did [N4]). But Princeton, small, genteel, was not like the Berlin of the Weimar days, large, vibrant, and perverse. Even a man with a strong inner life like Einstein had to adjust himself to a new environment. He did, and very well. The more peaceful new life began to grow on him. There was music in the home. He found old friends and made new ones. He could be seen on Carnegie Lake in the small sailboat he had bought, which had been christened *Tinnef* by Helen Dukas (Yiddish for 'cheaply made'). The name stuck. He never owned a car nor did he ever learn to drive. There were occasional trips to New York and to other cities. There were vacations, on the shores of Long Island or in the Adirondacks. In 1936 Einstein took out his citizenship papers. On October 1, 1940, in Trenton, he, Margot, and Helen Dukas were sworn in as United States citizens by that wonderful judge Phillip Forman. (I cherish his memory; he inducted me, too.) On the following November 5, the three of them waited their turn to vote in the Roosevelt–Willkie election.

Einstein went on with his physics. What he did in those years was described in other chapters and will be returned to in the next section. The Institute did not yet have its own buildings when he arrived. He and other faculty members were given space in Princeton University's 'old' Fine Hall (now the Gest Institute of Oriental Studies). After 1939 they moved to the Institute's newly built Fuld Hall. His only official duty was to attend faculty meetings. This he did until his retirement at age 65, in 1944, and continued to do until early 1950. A number of people came to work with him. These we shall meet in Chapter 29. He was readily accessible to all who wanted to discuss science with him.

THE QUANTUM THEORY

During the years 1933–45 Einstein spoke out less on political issues than he had done before or would do again after the war.* The reasons for this relative quietude are obvious. In the early years he was not yet a U.S. citizen. When the war came there was only one issue: to win it. From 1933 until after the war he desisted from advocating world disarmament and conscientious objection. 'Organized power can be opposed only by organized power. Much as I regret this, there is no other way' [N6]. During the war years he acted as occasional consultant to the Navy Bureau of Ordnance.

Much has been written about Einstein's letters to President Roosevelt on the importance of the development of atomic weapons [E26]. Opinions on the influence of these letters are divided.** It is my own impression that this influence was marginal. It is true that Roosevelt appointed a three-man Advisory Committee on Uranium on the same day he replied to Einstein's first letter. However, he only decided to go ahead with full scale atomic weapons development in October 1941. At that time he was mainly influenced, I believe, by the British efforts. It was not until then that Secretary of War Stimson heard about the project for the first time [S2]. In his later years, Einstein himself said more than once that he regretted having signed these letters. 'Had I known that the Germans would not succeed in producing an atomic bomb, I would not have lifted a finger' [V1].

The story of Einstein in Princeton will be continued and concluded in Chapter 27. Before returning to objective reality, I mention one anecdote of Einstein's early years in the United States, a story I owe to Helen Dukas.

During a speech by a high official at a major reception for Einstein, the honored guest took out his pen and started scribbling equations on the back of his program, oblivious to everything. The speech ended with a great flourish. Everybody stood up, clapping hands and turning to Einstein. Helen whispered to him that he had to get up, which he did. Unaware of the fact that the ovation was for him, he clapped his hands, too, until Helen hurriedly told him that he was the one for whom the audience was cheering.

25c. Einstein on Objective Reality

In his Como address, Bohr had remarked that quantum mechanics, like relativity theory, demands refinements of our everyday perceptions of inanimate natural phenomena. 'We find ourselves here on the very path taken by Einstein of adapting our modes of perception borrowed from the sensations to the gradually deepening knowledge of the laws of Nature' [B5]. Already then, in 1927, he emphasized that we have to treat with extreme care our use of language in recording the results of observations that involve quantum effects. 'The hindrances met with on this path originate above all in the fact that, so to say, every word in the language

*See [N5] for some of Einstein's opinions during the period 1933–45.

**For comments by General Groves, I. I. Rabi, and E. P. Wigner see [L1].

refers to our ordinary perception.' Bohr's deep concern with the role of language in the appropriate interpretation of quantum mechanics never ceased. In 1948 he put it as follows:

> Phrases often found in the physical literature, as 'disturbance of phenomena by observation' or 'creation of physical attributes of objects by measurements,' represent a use of words like 'phenomena' and 'observation' as well as 'attribute' and 'measurement' which is hardly compatible with common usage and practical definition and, therefore, is apt to cause confusion. As a more appropriate way of expression, one may strongly advocate limitation of the use of the word *phenomenon* to refer exclusively to observations obtained under specified circumstances, including an account of the whole experiment. [B9]

This usage of *phenomenon,* if not generally accepted, is the one to which nearly all physicists now subscribe.

In contrast to the view that the concept of phenomenon *irrevocably* includes the specifics of the experimental conditions of observation, Einstein held that one should seek for a deeper-lying theoretical framework which permits the description of phenomena independently of these conditions. That is what he meant by the term *objective reality.* After 1933 it was his almost solitary position that quantum mechanics is logically consistent but that it is an incomplete manifestation of an underlying theory in which an objectively real description is possible.

In an article written in 1935 with Boris Podolsky and Nathan Rosen [E27], Einstein gave reasons for his position by discussing an example, simple as always. This paper 'created a stir among physicists and has played a large role in philosophical discussion' [B10].* It contains the following definition. 'If without in any way disturbing a system we can predict with certainty (i.e., with a probability equal to unity) the value of a physical quantity, then there exists an element of physical reality corresponding to this physical quantity.' The authors then consider the following problem. Two particles with respective momentum and position variables (p_1, q_1) and (p_2, q_2) are in a state with definite total momentum $P = p_1 + p_2$ and definite relative distance $q = q_1 - q_2$. This, of course, is possible since P and q commute. The particles are allowed to interact. Observations are made on particle 1 long after the interaction has taken place. Measure p_1 and one knows p_2 without having disturbed particle 2. Therefore (in their language), p_2 is an element of reality. Next, measure q_1 and one knows q_2 again without having disturbed particle 2. Therefore q_2 is also an element of reality, so that both p_2 and q_2 are elements of reality. But quantum mechanics tells us that p_2 and q_2 cannot simultaneously be elements of reality because of the noncommutativity of the

---

*This stir reached the press. On May 4, 1935, *The New York Times* carried an article under the heading 'Einstein attacks quantum theory,' which also includes an interview with another physicist. Its May 7 issue contains a statement by Einstein in which he deprecated this release, which did not have his authorization.

momentum and position operators of a given particle. Therefore quantum mechanics is incomplete.

The authors stress that they 'would not arrive at our conclusion if one insisted that two . . . physical quantities can be regarded as simultaneous elements of reality *only when they can be simultaneously measured or predicted*' (their italics). Then follows a remark that is the key to Einstein's philosophy and which I have italicized in part:

> This [simultaneous predictability] makes the reality of p_2 and q_2 depend upon the process of measurement carried out on the first system which does not disturb the second system in any way. *No reasonable definition of reality could be expected to permit this.*

The only part of this article that will ultimately survive, I believe, is this last phrase, which so poignantly summarizes Einstein's views on quantum mechanics in his later years. The content of this paper has been referred to on occasion as the Einstein–Podolsky–Rosen paradox. It should be stressed that this paper contains neither a paradox nor any flaw of logic. It simply concludes that objective reality is incompatible with the assumption that quantum mechanics is complete. This conclusion has not affected subsequent developments in physics, and it is doubtful that it ever will.

'It is only the mutual exclusion of any two experimental procedures, permitting the unambiguous definition of complementary physical quantities which provides room for new physical laws,' Bohr wrote in his rebuttal [B11]. He did not believe that the Einstein–Podolsky–Rosen paper called for any change in the interpretation of quantum mechanics. Most physicists (myself included) agree with this opinion.

This concludes an account of Einstein's position. He returned to his criterion for objective reality in a number of later papers [E28, E29, E30, E31], in which he repeated the EPR argument on several occasions. These papers add nothing substantially new. In one of them [E30], he discussed the question of whether the quantum-mechanical notion of phenomenon should also apply to bodies of everyday size. The answer is, of course, in the affirmative.

Bohr was, of course, not the only one to express opposition to objective reality; nor was Einstein the only one critical of the complementarity interpretation.* I have chosen to confine myself to the exchanges between Einstein and Bohr because I believe that Einstein's views come out most clearly in juxtaposing them with Bohr's. Moreover, I am well acquainted with their thoughts on these issues because of discussions with each of them. Bohr was in Princeton when he put the

---

*In 1950 Einstein mentioned Schroedinger and von Laue as the only ones who shared his views [E32]. There were many others who at that time (and later) had doubts about the complementarity interpretation, but their views and Einstein's did not necessarily coincide or overlap (see [E33]). Note also that the term *hidden variable* does not occur in any of Einstein's papers or letters, as far as I know.

finishing touches to his 1949 article [B6], and we discussed these matters often at that time. (It was during one of these discussions that Einstein sneaked in to steal some tobacco [P1].) However, it needs to be stressed that other theoretical physicists and mathematicians have made important contributions to this area of problems. Experimentalists have actively participated, as well. A number of experimental tests of quantum mechanics in general and also of the predictions of specific alternative schemes have been made.* This has not led to any surprises.

It has been stressed many times that, in order to follow Einstein's thinking, it is necessary to see him both as a critic and as a visionary. In this chapter the critic has been portrayed. In the next we meet the visionary.

References

B1. M. Born, *Z. Phys.* **37,** 863 (1926).
B2. ——, *Z. Phys.* **38,** 803 (1926).
B3. ——, letter to A. Einstein, November 30, 1926.
B4. *The Born–Einstein Letters,* p. 130. Walker, New York, 1971.
B5. N. Bohr, *Nature* **121,** 580 (1928).
B5a. L. de Broglie, *New Perspectives in Physics,* p. 150. Basic, New York, 1962.
B6. N. Bohr in *Albert Einstein: Philosopher–Scientist* (P. Schilpp, Ed.), p. 199. Tudor, New York, 1949.
B7. W. Bothe and H. Geiger, *Naturw.* **13,** 440 (1925) *Z. Phys.* **32,** 639 (1925).
B8. V. Bargmann, *Helv. Phys. Acta* **7,** 57, (1933).
B9. N. Bohr, *Dialectica* **2,** 312 (1948).
B10. ——, [B6], p. 232.
B11. ——, *Phys. Rev.* **48,** 696 (1935).
C1. H. B. G. Casimir, letter to A. Pais, December 31, 1977.
C2. R. W. Clark, *Einstein: The Life and Times,* p. 603. Avon Books, New York, 1971.
D1. P.A.M. Dirac, *Proc. Roy. Soc.* **A114,** 243 (1927).
E1. A. Einstein, letter to C. Lanczos, March 21, 1942.
E2. W. Elsasser, *Naturw.* **13,** 711 (1925).
E3. A. Einstein, letter to R. A. Millikan, September 1, 1925.
E4. ——, letter to P. Ehrenfest, August 23, 1926.
E5. ——, letter to P. Ehrenfest, August 28, 1926.
E6. ——, in *James Clark Maxwell,* p. 66. Macmillan, New York, 1931.
E7. ——, letter to M. Besso, December 25, 1925; *EB,* p. 215.
E8. ——, letter to H. Born, March 7, 1926. Reprinted in *The Born–Einstein Letters* (M. Born, Ed.), p. 91. Walker, New York, 1971.
E9. ——, letter to E. Schroedinger, April 26, 1926. Reprinted in *Letters on Wave Mechanics* (M. Klein, Ed.). Philosophical Library, New York, 1967.
E10. ——, letter to M. Besso, May 1, 1926; *EB,* p. 224.

*Typically, these tests deal with variants of the EPR arrangement, such as long-range correlations between spins or polarizations. I must admit to being insufficiently familiar with the extensive theoretical and experimental literature of these topics. My main guides have been a book by Jammer [J1] and a review article by Pipkin [P2]. Both contain extensive references to other literature.

E11. ——, letter to M. Born, December 4, 1926; *The Born–Einstein Letters*, p. 90.

E12. ——, *Z. Angew. Chemie* **40,** 546 (1927).

E13. ——,in *Proceedings of the Fifth Solvay Conference*, p. 253. Gauthier-Villars, Paris, 1928.

E14. ——, letter to H. A. Lorentz, November 21, 1927.

E15. ——, R. Tolman, and B. Podolsky, *Phys. Rev.* **37,** 780 (1931).

E16. ——, *Z. Angew. Chemie* **45,** 23 (1932).

E17. ——,*On the Method of Theoretical Physics.* Oxford University Press, New York, 1933. Reprinted in *Phil. Sci.* **1,** 162 (1934).

E18. ——, personal travel diary, December 6, 1931.

E19. ——, letter to A. Flexner, June 8, 1932.

E20. ——,*Origins of the General Theory of Relativity.* Glasgow University, Publ. No. 30, 1933.

E21. ——, and W. Mayer, *Proc. K. Ak. Amsterdam* **36,** 497 (1933).

E22. ——, and——, *Proc. K. Ak. Amsterdam* **36,** 615 (1933).

E23. ——, and——, *PAW*, 1932, p. 522.

E24. ——, letter to Queen Elizabeth of Belgium, November 20, 1933.

E25. ——, letter to Queen Elizabeth of Belgium, February 16, 1935.

E26. ——,letters to F. D. Roosevelt, August 2, 1939; March 7, 1940. Reprinted in [N3], pp. 294, 299.

E27. ——, B. Podolsky, and N. Rosen, *Phys. Rev.* **47,** 777 (1935).

E28. ——, *Dialectica* **2,** 320 (1948).

E29. ——, in *Albert Einstein: philosopher–scientist* (P. Schilpp, Ed.). Tudor, New York, 1949.

E30. ——, in *Scientific Papers Presented to Max Born,* Hafner, New York, 1951. p. 33.

E31. —— in *Louis de Broglie, Physicien et Penseur,* p. 5. Michel, Paris, 1953.

E32. ——, letter to E. Schroedinger, December 22, 1950.

E33. ——, letter to M. Born, May 12, 1952.

F1. A. Flexner, *I Remember.* Simon and Schuster, New York, 1940.

F2. ——, *The New York Times,* April 19, 1955.

F3. ——, letter to A. Einstein, October 13, 1933.

G1. S. Goudsmit, letter to A. Pais, January 16, 1978.

H1. W. Heisenberg, postcard to W. Pauli, June 29, 1925. Reprinted in *W. Pauli Scientific Correspondence,* Vol. 1, p. 229. Springer, New York, 1979.

H2. ——, *Z. Phys.* **33,** 879 (1926).

H3. ——, *Der Teil und das Ganze,* pp. 90–100. Piper, Munich, 1969.

H4. ——, letter to A. Einstein, November 30, 1925.

H5. ——,in *Niels Bohr and the Development of Physics* (W. Pauli, Ed.), p. 12. McGraw-Hill, New York, 1955.

H6. ——, *Z. Phys.* **43,** 172 (1927).

H7. ——, letter to A. Einstein, June 10, 1927.

H8. ——, letter to A. Einstein, May 19, 1927.

I1. The Institute for Advanced Study, excerpt from minutes, October 10, 1932.

J1. M. Jammer, *The Philosophy of Quantum Mechanics.* Wiley, New York, 1974.

K1. C. Kirsten and H. J. Treder, *Einstein in Berlin,* Vol. 2. p. 268. Akademie, Berlin, 1979.

K2. —— and ——, [K1], Vol. 1, p. 241.

K3. —— and ——, [K1], Vol. 1, p. 242.

K4. —— and ——, [K1], Vol. 1, p. 246.

K5. F. Klein, *Vorlesungen über die Entwicklung der Mathematik im 19 Jahrhundert*, Vol. 2, Chap. 2, Sec. 2. Springer, New York, 1979.

L1. A. B. Lerner, *Einstein and Newton*, pp. 212–15. Lerner, Minneapolis, 1973.

M1. J. Mehra, *Biogr. Mem. Fell. Roy. Soc.* **21**, 117 (1975).

N1. *New York Times,* March 20, 1933.

N2. *New York Times,* August 22, 1933.

N3. O. Nathan and M. Norden, *Einstein on Peace,* p. 236. Schocken, New York, 1968.

N3a. *New York Times*, July 27, 1973.

N4. *New York Times,* September 16, 1938.

N5. O. Nathan and M. Norden, [N3], Chaps. 8–10.

N6. ——and——, [N3], p. 319.

P1. A. Pais in *Niels Bohr,* p. 215. North-Holland, Amsterdam, 1967.

P2. F. M. Pipkin, *Adv. At. Mol. Phys.* **14**, 281 (1978).

R1. L. Rosenfeld in *Proceedings of the Fourteenth Solvay Conference,* p. 232. Interscience, New York, 1968.

S1. W. T. Scott, *Erwin Schroedinger,* University of Massachusetts Press, Amherst, 1967.

S2. H. L. Stimson, *On active Service in Peace and War,* Chap. 23. Harper New York 1947.

V1. A. Vallentin, *The Drama of Albert Einstein,* p. 278. Doubleday, New York, 1954.

W1. E. P. Wigner, *Proceedings,* Einstein Centennial Conference at Princeton, p. 461. Addison-Wesley, Reading, Mass., 1980.

26
Einstein's Vision

26a. Einstein, Newton, and Success

Einstein's lasting conviction that quantum mechanics was not a theory of principle did not impede him from recognizing that this theory was highly successful. As early as 1927, he publicly expressed his judgment that wave mechanics is 'in amazing agreement with the facts of experience' [E1]. In 1936 he wrote, 'It seems clear . . . that the Born statistical interpretation of the quantum theory is the only possible one' [E2], and in 1949 declared, 'The statistical quantum theory [is] the most successful theory of our period' [E3]. Then why was he never convinced by it?

I believe Einstein indirectly answered this question in his 1933 Spencer lecture—perhaps the clearest and most revealing expression of his way of thinking in later life. The key is to be found in his remarks on Newton and classical mechanics. In this lecture [E4], Einstein noted that 'Newton felt by no means comfortable about the concept of absolute space, . . . of absolute rest . . . [and] about the introduction of action at a distance.' Then he went on to refer to the success of Newton's theory in these words: 'The enormous practical success of his theory may well have prevented him and the physicists of the eighteenth and nineteenth centuries from recognizing the fictitious character of the principles of his system.' It is important to note that by fictitious Einstein meant free inventions of the human mind. Whereupon he compared Newton's mechanics with his own work on general relativity: 'The fictitious character of the principles is made quite obvious by the fact that it is possible to exhibit two essentially different bases [Newtonian mechanics and general relativistic mechanics] each of which in its consequences leads to a large measure of agreement with experience.' (Remember that these words were spoken long before it was realized how markedly the predictions of Newtonian mechanics differ from those of general relativity when strong gravitational fields come into play.)

In the Spencer lecture, Einstein mentioned the success not only of classical mechanics but also of the statistical interpretation of quantum theory. 'This conception is logically unexceptionable and has led to important successes.' But, he added, 'I still believe in the possibility of giving a model of reality which shall represent events themselves and not merely the probability of their occurence.'

From this lecture as well as from discussions with him on the foundations of quantum physics, I have gained the following impression. Einstein tended to compare the successes of classical mechanics with those of quantum mechanics. In his view both were on a par, being successful but incomplete. For more than a decade, Einstein had pondered the single question of how to extend the invariance under uniform translations to general motions. His resulting theory, general relativity, had led to only small deviations from Newton's theory. (Instances where these deviations are large were discussed only much later.) He was likewise prepared for the survival of the practical successes of quantum mechanics, with perhaps only small modifications. He was also prepared to undertake his own search for objective reality, fearless of how long it would take. It is quite plausible that the very success of his highest achievement, general relativity, was an added spur to Einstein's apartness. Yet it should not be forgotten that this trait characterized his entire oeuvre and style.

The crux of Einstein's thinking on the quantum theory was not his negative position in regard to what others had done, but rather his deep faith in his own distinct approach to the quantum problems. His beliefs may be summarized as follows:

(1) Quantum mechanics represents a major advance, and yet it is only a limiting case of a theory which remains to be discovered:

> There is no doubt that quantum mechanics has seized hold of a beautiful element of truth and that it will be a touchstone for a future theoretical basis in that it must be deducible as a limiting case from that basis, just as electrostatics is deducible from the Maxwell equations of the electromagnetic field or as thermodynamics is deducible from statistical mechanics. [E2]

(2) One should not try to find the new theory by beginning with quantum mechanics and trying to refine or reinterpret it:

> I do not believe that quantum mechanics will be the starting point in the search for this basis, just as one cannot arrive at the foundations of mechanics from thermodynamics or statistical mechanics. [E2]

(3) Instead—and this was Einstein's main point—*one should start all over again,* as it were, and endeavor to obtain the quantum theory as a by-product of a general relativistic theory or a generalization thereof. Starting all over again had never daunted him. That is the single most important link between the early and the late Einstein. His reverence for Lorentz had not held him back from rejecting the latter's dynamic views on the contraction of rods and on the interpretation of Fizeau's experiment. His reverence for Newton had not prevented him from rejecting absolute space. The relativity theories, his own greatest successes, his theories of principle, had been arrived at by making fresh starts. He was going to do that again for the quantum theory, and never mind the time it might take. In 1950 he wrote to Born, 'I am convinced of [objective reality] although, up to now, *success* is against it' [E5].

It was a solitary position. Einstein knew that. Nor was he oblivious to other's reactions. 'I have become an obstinate heretic in the eyes of my colleagues,' he wrote to one friend [E6], and to another, 'I am generally regarded as a sort of petrified object, rendered blind and deaf by the years. I find this role not too distasteful, as it corresponds very well with my temperament' [E7]. He knew, and on occasion would even say, that his road was a lonely one [E8], yet he held fast. 'Momentary success carries more power of conviction for most people than reflections on principle' [E9].

Einstein was neither saintly nor humorless in defending his position on the quantum theory. On occasion he could be acerbic. At one time, he said that Bohr thought very clearly, wrote obscurely, and thought of himself as a prophet [S1]. Another time he referred to Bohr as a mystic [E10]. On the other hand, in a letter to Bohr, Einstein referred to his own position by quoting an old rhyme: 'Über die Reden des Kandidaten Jobses/Allgemeines Schütteln des Kopses' [E11].*There were moments of loneliness. 'I feel sure that you do not understand how I came by my lonely ways' [E12]. He may not have expressed all his feelings on these matters. But that was his way. 'The essential of the being of a man of my type lies precisely in *what* he thinks and *how* he thinks, not in what he does or suffers' [E3].

Einstein's apartness in regard to the foundations of quantum physics predates the discovery of quantum mechanics. That is the second most important link between the early and the later Einstein. I shall enlarge on this in Section 26c, but first some final comments on the subject of Chapter 2: Einstein's general attitude toward the quantum and relativity theories.

26b. Relativity Theory and Quantum Theory

It is a very striking characteristic of Einstein's early scientific writing that he left relativity theory separate from quantum theory, even on occasions where it would have been natural and straightforward to connect them. This separation is already evident in his very first paper on special relativity, in which he noted, 'It is remarkable that the energy and frequency of a light complex vary with the state of motion of the observer according to the same law' [E13]. Here was an obvious opportunity to refer to the relation $E = h\nu$ of his paper on light-quanta, finished only a few months earlier. But Einstein did not do that. Also, in the September 1905 paper on relativity [E14], he referred to radiation but not to light-quanta. In his 1909 address at Salzburg, Einstein discussed his ideas both on relativity theory and on quantum theory but kept these two areas well separated [E15]. As we saw in Section 21c, in his 1917 paper Einstein ascribed to light-quanta an energy $E = h\nu$ and a momentum $p = h\nu/c$. This paper concludes with the remark, 'Energy and momentum are most intimately related; therefore, a theory can be

*Roughly: There was a general shaking of heads concerning the words of candidate Jobs.

considered justified only if it has been shown that according to [the theory] the momentum transferred by radiation to matter leads to motions as required by thermodynamics' [E16]. Why is only thermodynamics mentioned; why not relativity also? Because, I believe, to him relativity was to such an extent the revealed truth that in his view the phenomenological and provisional quantum theory was not yet ripe enough, perhaps not yet worthy enough, to be brought into contact with relativity arguments.

So it was in the days of the old quantum theory. So it remained after quantum mechanics came along. In the previous section, I noted that Einstein considered quantum mechanics to be highly successful. I should now be more precise and add that this opinion of his applied exclusively to nonrelativistic quantum mechanics. I know from experience how difficult it was to discuss quantum field theory with him. He did not believe that nonrelativistic quantum mechanics provided a secure enough basis for relativistic generalizations [E17, E18]. Relativistic quantum field theory was repugnant to him [B1]. Walter Thirring has written to me of conversations with Einstein in which 'his objections became even stronger when it concerned quantum field theory, and he did not believe in any of its consequences' [T1]. Valentin Bargmann has told me that at one time Einstein asked him for a private survey of quantum field theory, beginning with second quantization. Bargmann did so for about a month. Thereafter Einstein's interest waned.

The preceding remarks on quantum field theory refer principally to its special relativistic version. In the time capsule of Section 2b, I inserted the comment that to this day the synthesis of quantum theory and general relativity is beset with conceptual difficulties. Was *that* what bothered Einstein? It was not, as is best seen from the closing phrases of his tribute to Maxwell:

> 'I incline to the belief that physicists will not be permanently satisfied with . . . an indirect description of Reality, *even if the* [quantum] *theory can be fitted successfully to the General Relativity* postulates [my italics]. They would then be brought back to the attempt to realize that programme which may suitably be called Maxwell's: the description of Physical Reality by fields which satisfy without singularity a set of partial differential equations. [E19]

'That programme' is uniquely Einstein's. His main point was that one should not start out by accepting the quantum postulates as primary rules and then proceed to fit these rules to general relativity. Instead, he believed one should start with a classical field theory, a unified field theory, and demand of that theory that the quantum rules should emerge as constraints imposed by that theory itself.

In the next and final section on the quantum theory, I shall outline *how* Einstein hoped to achieve this. The question of *why* he harbored such expectations brings us to another edge of history. A definitive answer cannot be given. As a personal opinion, it seems to me that making great discoveries can be accompanied by trauma, and that the purity of Einstein's relativity theories had a blinding effect on him. He almost said so himself: 'To the discoverer . . . the constructions of his imagination appear so necessary and so natural that he is apt to treat them not as the creations of his thoughts but as given realities' [E4]. His insistence on objective reality is a perfect example of such a mental process.

Finally, I should like to reiterate my own view that Einstein's technical objections to quantum mechanics are unfounded, but that I do not know whether either quantum mechanics or general relativity is complete, or whether their desired synthesis can be consummated simply by welding together their respective sets of postulates.

26c. Überkausalität

In 1923 Einstein published an article entitled 'Does field theory offer possibilities for the solution of the quantum problem?' [E20]. It begins with a reminder of the successes achieved in electrodynamics and general relativity theory in regard to a causal description: events are causally determined by differential equations combined with initial conditions on a spacelike surface. However, Einstein continued, this method cannot be applied to quantum problems without further ado. As he put it, the discreteness of the Bohr orbits indicates that initial conditions cannot be chosen freely. Then he asked, Can one nevertheless implement these quantum constraints in a (causal) theory based on partial differential equations? His answer: 'Quite certainly: we must only "overdetermine" the field variables by [appropriate] equations.' Next he stated his program, based on three requirements: (1) general covariance, (2) the desired equations should at least be in accordance with the gravitational and the Maxwell theory, and (3) the desired system of equations which overdetermines the fields should have static, spherically symmetric solutions which describe the electron and proton. If this overdetermination can be achieved, then 'we may hope that these equations co-determine the mechanical behavior of the singular points (electrons) in such a way that the initial conditions of the field and the singular points are also subject to restrictive conditions.' He went on to discuss a tentative example and concluded, 'To me, the main point of this communication is the idea of overdetermination.'

By 1923 Einstein had already been brooding about these ideas for a number of years. In 1920 he had written to Born, 'I do not seem able to give tangible form to my pet idea [meine Lieblingsidee], which is to understand the structure of the quanta by redundancy in determination, using differential equations,' [E21].This is the earliest reference to his strategy that I am aware of. It would seem likely that ideas of this kind began to stir in him soon after 1917, when he had not only completed the general theory of relativity but had also discovered the lack of causality in spontaneous emission [E16]. The early response of others to these attempts by Einstein was recorded by Born: 'In those days [early 1925], we all thought that his objective ... was attainable and also very important' [B2]. Einstein himself felt that he had no choice. 'The road may be quite wrong, but it must be tried' [E22].

feeling sure that in nature is actualized the ideal of mathematical simplicity' [E4]. As early as 1927, Heisenberg stressed, in a letter to Einstein, that the latter's concept of simplicity and the simplicity inherent in quantum mechanics cannot be realized at the same time. 'If I have understood correctly your point of view, then you would gladly sacrifice the simplicity [of quantum mechanics] to the principle of [classical] causality. Perhaps we could comfort ourselves [with the idea that] the dear Lord could go beyond [quantum mechanics] and maintain causality. I do not really find it beautiful, however, to demand more than a physical description of the connection between experiments' [H1].

As Einstein's life drew to a close, doubts about his vision arose in his mind.

'The theory of relativity and the quantum theory ... seem little adapted to fusion into one unified theory,' he remarked in 1940 [E34]. He wrote to Born, probably in 1949, 'Our respective hobby-horses have irretrievably run off in different directions. ... Even I cannot adhere to [mine] with absolute confidence' [E35]. In the early 1950s, he once said to me that he was not sure whether differential geometry was to be the framework for further progress, but if it was then he believed he was on the right track.* To his dear friend Besso he wrote in 1954, 'I consider it quite possible that physics cannot be based on the field concept, i.e., on continuous structures. In that case, *nothing* remains of my entire castle in the air, gravitation theory included, [and of] the rest of modern physics' [E37]. I doubt whether any physicist can be found who would not agree that this judgment is unreasonably harsh. In one of the last of the many introductions Einstein wrote for books by others, he said:

> My efforts to complete the general theory of relativity ... are in part due to the conjecture that a sensible general relativistic [classical] field theory might perhaps provide the key to a more complete quantum theory. This is a modest hope, but certainly not a conviction. [E38]

But, as Helen Dukas told me, Einstein once said at the dinner table (she did not recall the year) that he thought physicists would understand him a hundred years later. Nor can I escape the impression that he was thinking about himself when he wrote the following lines about Spinoza:

> Although he lived three hundred years before our time, the spiritual situation with which Spinoza had to cope peculiarly resembles our own. The reason for this is that he was utterly convinced of the causal dependence of all phenomena, at a time when the success accompanying the efforts to achieve a knowledge of the causal relationship of natural phenomena was still quite modest. [E39].

---

*V. Bargmann informs me that Einstein made similar remarks to him in the late 1930s. A related comment is found in a letter to Infeld: 'I tend more and more to the opinion that one cannot come further with a continuum theory' [E36].

Einstein kept thinking about quantum theory until the very end. He wrote his last autobiographical sketch in Princeton, in March 1955, about a month before his death. Its final sentences deal with the quantum theory.

> It appears dubious whether a [classical] field theory can account for the atomistic structure of matter and radiation as well as of quantum phenomena. Most physicists will reply with a convinced 'No,' since they believe that the quantum problem has been solved in principle by other means. However that may be, Lessing's comforting word stays with us: the aspiration to truth is more precious than its assured possession. [E40]

References

B1. M. Born, letter to A. Einstein, October 10, 1944.

B2. ——(Ed.), *The Born–Einstein Letters,* p. 88. Walker, New York, 1971.

E1. A. Einstein, Smithsonian Institution Report for 1927, p. 201; *Naturw.* **15,** 273 (1927).

E2. ——, *J. Franklin Inst.* **221,** 313 (1936).

E3. ——in *Albert Einstein: Philosopher–Scientist* (P. A. Schilpp, Ed.). Tudor, New York, 1949.

E4. ——, *On the Method of Theoretical Physics.* Oxford University Press, New York, 1933. Reprinted in *Phil. Sci.* **1,** 162 (1934).

E5. ——, letter to M. Born, September 15, 1950.

E6. ——, letter to M. Besso, August 8, 1949; *EB,* p. 407.

E7. ——, letter to M. Born, April 12, 1949.

E8. ——, letter to M. Born, March 18, 1948.

E9. ——, letter to M. Besso, July 24, 1949; *EB,* p. 402.

E10. ——, letter to E. Schroedinger, August 9, 1939.

E11. ——, letter to N. Bohr, April 4, 1949.

E12. ——, letter to M. Born, March 18, 1948.

E13. ——, *AdP* **17,** 891 (1905).

E14. ——, *AdP* **18,** 639 (1905).

E15. ——, *Phys. Zeitschr.* **10,** 817 (1909).

E16. ——, *Phys. Zeitschr.* **18,** 121 (1917).

E17. ——, letter to M. Born, March 22, 1934.

E18. ——, letter to A. Sommerfeld, December 14, 1946.

E19. ——in *James Clark Maxwell,* p. 66. Macmillan, New York, 1931.

E20. ——, *PAW,* 1923, p. 359.

E21. ——, letter to M. Born, March 3, 1920.

E22. ——, letter to M. Besso, January 5, 1924; *EB,* p. 197.

E23. ——, *Forschungen und Fortschritte* **5,** 248 (1929).

E24. ——, letter to M. Besso, July 28, 1925; *EB,* p. 209.

E25. ——, letter to M. Besso, August 1942; *EB,* p. 366.

E26. ——, letter to M. Besso, August 16, 1949; *EB,* p. 409.

E27. ——, letter to L. de Broglie, February 8, 1954.

E28. ——and J. Grommer *PAW,* 1927, p. 2.

E29.   ——, *PAW,* 1927, p. 235.

E30.   ——, *Science* **71,** 608 (1930).

E31.   ——, *Science* **74,** 438 (1931).

E32.   ——and N. Rosen, *Phys. Rev.* **48,** 73 (1935).

E33.   ——, *Physica* **5,** 330 (1925).

E34.   ——, *Science* **91,** 487 (1940).

E35.   ——, letter to M. Born, undated, probably written in 1949.

E36.   ——, letter to L. Infeld, March 6, 1941.

E37.   ——, letter to M. Besso, August 10, 1954; *EB,* p. 525.

E38.   ——in *Louis de Broglie, Physicien et Penseur.* Albin Michel, Paris, 1953.

E39.   ——, introduction to R. Kayser, *Spinoza, Portrait of a Spiritual Hero,* p. xi, Philo-sophical Library, New York, 1946.

E40.   ——in *Helle Zeit, dunkle Zeit* (C. Seelig, Ed.). Europa Verlag Zürich, 1956.

H1.   W. Heisenberg, letter to A. Einstein, June 10, 1927.

P1.   W. Pauli, *Phys. Zeitschr.* **20,** 457 (1919).

S1.   R. S. Shankland, *Am. J. Phys.* **31,** 47 (1963).

T1.   W. Thirring, letter to A. Pais, November 29, 1977.

U1.   G. E. Uhlenbeck, *Physics Today* **29** (6), 43 (1976).

VII
JOURNEY'S END

27

The Final Decade

Einstein's mind continued to be intensely active and fully alert until the very end of his life. During the last ten years, however, his age, the state of his health, his never-ending urge to do physics, and the multitude of his extra-scientific involvements called for economy in the use of his energies and time. He kept to simple routines as much as possible. He would come down for breakfast at about nine o'clock, then read the morning papers. At about ten-thirty he would walk to The Institute for Advanced Study, stay there until one o'clock, then walk home. I know of one occasion when a car hit a tree after its driver suddenly recognized the face of the beautiful old man walking along the street, his black woollen knit cap firmly planted on his long white hair. After lunch he would go to bed for a few hours. Then he would have a cup of tea, work some more or attend to his mail or receive people for discussions of nonpersonal matters. He took his evening meal between six-thirty and seven. Thereafter he would work again or listen to the radio (there was no television in his home) or occasionally receive a friend. He normally retired between eleven and twelve. Every Sunday at noon he listened to a news analysis broadcast by Howard K. Smith. Guests were never invited at that hour. On Sunday afternoons there would be walks or drives in some friend's car. Only seldom would he go out to a play or a concert, very rarely to a movie. He would occasionally attend a physics seminar at Palmer Laboratory, causing the awed hush I mentioned before. In those last years, he no longer played the violin but improvised daily on the piano. He also had stopped smoking his beloved pipes [D1].

At the beginning of his last decade Einstein, sixty-six years old, shared his home on Mercer Street with his sister Maja, his stepdaughter Margot, and Helen Dukas, who took care of everything from mail to meals. Soon after the end of the war, Maja began making preparations for rejoining her husband, Paul, who then was living with the Bessos in Geneva [E1]. It was not to be. In 1946 she suffered a stroke and remained bedridden thereafter. Her situation deteriorated; in the end she could no longer speak, though her mind remained clear. Every night after dinner, Einstein would go to the room of his sister, who was so dear to him, and read to her. She died in the Mercer Street home in June 1951.

Physics remained at the center of Einstein's being in the final decade, during which, as I described earlier, he concentrated exclusively on unified field theory and on questions of principle regarding the quantum theory. His published work during that period includes eight papers on unified field theory; a contribution to *Dialectica,* written at the instigation of Pauli, in which he explained his views on quantum mechanics [E2]; and his necrology, as he called it, the important essay entitled 'Autobiographisches' [E3]. On rare occasions, he would give a seminar about his work at the Institute. In order to avoid curiosity-seekers, especially the press, announcements of such talks were made only by word of mouth. The seminars themselves were lucid, inconclusive, and other-worldly. Those were the days of striking advances in quantum electrodynamics and unexpected discoveries of new particles, days in which the gap between Einstein's physics and the physics of younger generations was ever widening.

At no time did Einstein immerse himself more in problems of policy and politics than during the years following the end of the Second World War. 'The war is won but peace is not,' he told an audience in December 1945 [E4]. He regarded the post-war world as dangerously unstable and believed that new modes of governance were called for. 'The first atomic bomb destroyed more than the city of Hiroshima. It also exploded our inherited, outdated political ideas' [E5]. As early as September 1945, he suggested that 'the only salvation for civilization and the human race lies in the creation of a world government, with security of nations founded upon law' [E6]. In his opinion, such a world government should be given powers of decision which would be binding on the member states. He was skeptical of the United Nations because it lacked such powers. World government remained a theme with variations to which he returned time and again in his remaining years. He repeated it in 1950 in a message 'on the moral obligation of a scientist': 'Mankind can be saved only if a supranational system, based on law, is created to eliminate the methods of brute force' [E7]. That, he believed, is what man should strive for, even if the environment were hostile to such ideals. 'While it is true that an inherently free and scrupulous person may be destroyed, such an individual can never be enslaved or made to serve as a blind tool' [E7]. In several instances,* celebrated in their day, he advocated civil disobedience. 'It is my belief that the problem of bringing peace to the world on a supranational basis will be solved only by employing Gandhi's method on a large scale' [E8]. 'What ought the minority of intellectuals to do against [the] evil [of suppressing freedom of teaching]? Frankly, I can see only the revolutionary way of non-cooperation in the sense of Gandhi's' [E9]. These statements, dating from the ugly McCarthy period, were rather uncommon for that time.

Einstein further believed in the necessity 'to advance the use of atomic energy

---

*In a letter concerning a conscientious objector [N1] and in another one to William Frauenglass, a high-school teacher who had been called to appear before the House Committee on Un-American Activities [N2].

THE FINAL DECADE 475

in ways beneficial to mankind [and] to diffuse knowledge and information about atomic energy . . . in order that an informed citizenry may intelligently determine and shape its action to serve its own and mankind's best interest,' as it is put in the charter of the Emergency Committee of Atomic Scientists, a group of which he was the chairman during its brief existence.* In 1954 Einstein sided with the overwhelming majority of atomic scientists who publicly condemned the United States government's actions in the security case against Oppenheimer.

Einstein's political views in the post-war years centered, I believe, on the themes just described. The reader interested in a more complete picture of his actions and beliefs is referred once again to the book *Einstein on Peace* [N1], in which the documentation of this period, covering hundreds of pages, illustrates how much effort Einstein devoted in his last years to issues dealing with the world's future. Some of his suggestions were perhaps unrealistic, other perhaps premature. Certain it is, though, that they originated from a clear mind and strong moral convictions.

Two further issues, bearing on Einstein's political views but going much deeper, must be mentioned. He never forgave the Germans. 'After the Germans massacred my Jewish brothers in Europe, I will have nothing further to do with Germans. . . . It is otherwise with those few who remained firm within the range of the possible' [E10]. To him those few included Otto Hahn, Max von Laue, Max Planck, and Arnold Sommerfeld.

Einstein was devoted to the cause of Israel, even though on occasion he was publicly critical of its government. He spoke of Israel as 'us' and of the Jews as 'my people.' It appears to me that Einstein's Jewish identity emerged ever more strongly as he grew older. He may never have found a place that truly was home to him. But he did find the tribe to which he belonged.

During the last years of his life, Einstein was not well.

For a number of years, he had had attacks of pain in the upper abdomen. These lasted usually two days, were accompanied by vomiting, and recurred every few months. In the fall of 1948, the surgeon Rudolf Nissen,** who had been called in for consultation, diagnosed an abdominal growth the size of a grapefruit. He suggested an experimental laparotomy, to which Einstein consented. On December 12 he entered the Jewish Hospital in Brooklyn. Dr Nissen performed the operation and discovered that the growth was an aneurysm in the abdominal aorta. The aneurysm was intact, its lining was firm. Corrective measures were counterindicated. Einstein stayed in the hospital until the incision had sufficiently healed.

---

*The committee was incorporated in August 1946. Its other members were R. Bacher, H. Bethe, E. Condon, T. Hogness, L. Szilard, H. Urey, and V. Weisskopf. This group became inactive in January 1949.

**Here I use an informal account by Dr Nissen [N3].

The nurse's notes indicate that he invariably responded to inquiries about his health by saying that he felt well. He left the hospital on January 13, 1949.

About a year and a half later, it was found that the aneurysm was growing. From then on, 'we around him knew . . . of the sword of Damocles hanging over us. He knew it, too, and waited for it, calmly and smilingly' [D2].

On March 18, 1950, Einstein put his signature to his last will and testament. He appointed his friend, the economist Otto Nathan as executor. Nathan and Helen Dukas were named trustees of all his letters, manuscripts, and copyrights with the understanding that all his papers would eventually be turned over to the Hebrew University. Other dispositions included the bequests of his books to Helen Dukas and of his violin to his grandson Bernhard Caesar.

Among the other legatees were his sons, Hans Albert, then a professor of engineering at Berkeley, and Eduard, then confined to the psychiatric hospital Burghölzli in Zürich. Their mother, Mileva, had died in Zürich on August 4, 1948. My picture of Mileva has remained rather vague. Among the many difficulties which beset her life, the poor mental health of Eduard must have been a particularly heavy burden. She saw 'Tede' regularly until the end of her life. Eduard died in Burghölzli in 1965, Hans Albert in Berkeley in 1973.

Among the many events in later years, I single out one.

Chaim Weizmann, the first president of Israel, died on November 9, 1952. Thereupon the Israeli government decided to offer the presidency to Einstein, who first heard this news one afternoon from *The New York Times*. What happened next has been described by a friend who was with Einstein that evening. 'About nine o'clock a telegram was delivered . . . from the Israeli ambassador in Washington, Mr Abba Eban. The highly elaborate terms of the telegram . . . made it quite plain that the earlier report must be true, and the little quiet household was much ruffled. "This is very awkward, very awkward," the old gentleman was explaining while walking up and down in a state of agitation which was very unusual with him. He was not thinking of himself but of how to spare the Ambassador and the Israeli government embarrassment from his inevitable refusal. . . . He decided not to reply by telegram but to call Washington at once. [He got] through to the Ambassador, to whom he spoke briefly and almost humbly made plain his position' [M1].

The end came in 1955.

In March of that year, Einstein had occasion to remember three old friends. He wrote to Kurt Blumenfeld, 'I thank you belatedly for having made me conscious of my Jewish soul' [E11]. He wrote his last autobiographical sketch [E12], a contribution to a special issue of the *Schweizerische Hochschulzeitung* published on the occasion of the centenary of the ETH. In this note, he mentioned 'the need to express at least once in my life my gratitude to Marcel Grossmann,' the friend whose notebooks he had used as a student, who had helped him to get a job at the patent office, to whom he had dedicated his doctoral thesis, and with whom he had written his first paper on the tensor theory of general relativity. In the same month Michele Besso died, another trusted friend from his student days, later his colleague at the patent office, and his sounding board in the days of special relativity. In a letter to the Besso family, Einstein wrote, 'Now he has gone a little ahead of me in departing from this curious world' [E13].

On April 11 he lent for the last time his name to a pacifist manifesto—this one drawn up by Bertrand Russell—in which all nations are urged to renounce nuclear weapons [N4].

On the morning of Wednesday, April 13, the Israeli consul called on Einstein at his home in order to discuss the draft of a statement Einstein intended to make on television and radio on the occasion of the forthcoming anniversary of Israel's independence. The incomplete draft [N5] ends as follows. 'No statesman in a position of responsibility has dared to take the only promising course [toward a stable peace] of supranational security, since this would surely mean his political death. For the political passions, aroused everywhere, demand their victims.' These may well be the last phrases Einstein committed to paper.

That afternoon Einstein collapsed at home. The aneurysm had ruptured. Guy K. Dean, his personal physician, was called immediately. That evening, two medical friends of Einstein's were called to Princeton from New York: Rudolf Ehrmann, who had been his physician in Berlin, and Gustav Bucky, a radiologist. On Thursday Frank Glenn, a cardiac and aortic surgeon from New York Hospital, was also called in for consultation. After the doctors had deliberated, Einstein asked Dr Dean if it would be a horrible death. Perhaps, one does not know, he was told. Perhaps it will be minutes, perhaps hours, perhaps days [D3]. 'He was very stoical under pain,' Dr Dean said a few days later [D4]. During this period, Einstein often resisted being given morphine injections and firmly refused all suggestions for an operation. 'I want to go when *I* want. It is tasteless to prolong life artificially; I have done my share, it is time to go. I will do it elegantly' [D2]. On Friday he was moved to Princeton Hospital. That evening a call was made to his son Hans Albert in Berkeley, who immediately left for Princeton and arrived on Saturday afternoon. 'On Saturday and Sunday, I was together quite a lot with my father, who much enjoyed my company' [E14]. On Saturday Einstein called the house to ask for his glasses. On Sunday he called for writing material [D3]. That evening he appeared to be resting comfortably.

Alberta Rozsel, a night nurse at the hospital, was the last person to see Einstein alive. At 1:10 a.m. on April 18, 'Mrs Rozsel noted that he was breathing differently. She summoned another nurse, who helped her roll up the head of the bed. Right after the other nurse left, Dr. Einstein mumbled in German. Then, as Mrs Rozsel put it, "he gave two deep breaths and expired"' [D4]. It was 1:15 in the morning.

The news was made public at 8 a.m. The autopsy performed that morning*

---

*By Dr Thomas F. Harvey, who removed the brain, part of which now rests in a bottle somewhere in Weston, Missouri [W1].

showed that death had been caused by 'a big blister on the aorta, which broke finally like a worn-out inner tube' [D4]. Later that morning, Hermann Weyl came to the hospital, where he and Dr Dean spoke to reporters.

At 2 p.m. the body was removed to the Mather Funeral Home in Princeton and from there, ninety minutes later, to the Ewing Crematorium in Trenton, where twelve people close to Einstein gathered.* One of them spoke briefly, reciting lines from Goethe's *Epilog zu Schiller's Glocke*. The body was cremated immediately thereafter. The ashes were scattered at an undisclosed place.

References

D1. H. Dukas, letter to C. Seelig, Bibl. ETH, Zürich, HS 304:133.

D2. ——, letter to A. Pais, April 30, 1955.

D3. ——, letter to C. Seelig, May 8, 1955; Bibl. ETH, Zürich, HS 304:90.

D4. G. K. Dean, *The New York Times,* April 19, 1955.

E1. A. Einstein, letter to M. Besso, April 21, 1946; *EB,* p. 376.

E2. ——, *Dialectica* **2,** 320 (1948).

E3. ——in *Albert Einstein: Philosopher–Scientist* (P. A. Schilpp, Ed.), p. 2. Tudor, New York, 1949.

E4. ——, *The New York Times,* December 11, 1945.

E5. ——, co-signing a statement published in *The New York Times,* October 10, 1945.

E6. ——, *The New York Times,* September 15, 1945.

E7. ——, *Impact* **1,** 104 (1950).

E8. ——, letter to G. Nellhaus, March 20, 1951.

E9. ——, letter to W. Frauenglass, published in *The New York Times,* June 12, 1953.

E10. ——, letter to A. Sommerfeld, December 14, 1946.

E11. ——, letter to K. Blumenfeld, March 25, 1955.

E12. ——, *Schweizerische Hochschulzeitung* **28,** 1955, special issue. Reproduced with a small deletion in *Helle Zeit, dunkle Zeit* (C. Seelig, Ed.). Europa, Zürich, 1956.

E13. ——, letter to V. Besso, March 21, 1955; *EB,* p. 537.

E14. H. A. Einstein, letter to C. Seelig, April 18, 1955; Bibl. ETH, Zürich, HS 304:566.

M1. D. Mitrany, *Jewish Observer and Middle East Review,* April 22, 1955.

N1. O. Nathan and M. Norden, *Einstein on Peace,* p. 542. Schocken, New York, 1968.

N2. —and—, [N1], p. 546.

N3. R. Nissen, letter to C. Seelig, June 29, 1955; Bibl. ETH, Zürich, HS 304:906/911.

N4. O. Nathan and M. Norden, [N1], p. 631.

N5. —and—, [N1], pp. 643–4.

S1. C. Seelig in *Helle Zeit, dunkle Zeit,* p. 86. Europa Verlag, Zürich, 1956.

W1. N. Wade, *Science* **213,** 521 (1981).

*Their names are found in [S1].

28
Epilogue

I saw Einstein for the last time in December 1954.

As he had not been well, he had for some weeks been absent from the Institute, where he normally spent a few hours each morning. Since I was about to take a term's leave from Princeton, I called Helen Dukas and asked her to be kind enough to give my best wishes to Professor Einstein. She suggested I come to the house for a brief visit and a cup of tea. I was, of course, glad to accept. After I arrived, I went upstairs and knocked at the door of Einstein's study. There was his gentle 'Come.' As I entered, he was seated in his arm chair, a blanket over his knees, a pad on the blanket. He was working. He put his pad aside at once and greeted me. We spent a pleasant half hour or so; I do not recall what was discussed. Then I told him I should not stay any longer. We shook hands, and I said goodbye. I walked to the door of the study, not more than four or five steps away. I turned around as I opened the door. I saw him in his chair, his pad back on his lap, a pencil in his hand, oblivious to his surroundings.

He was back at work.

VIII

APPENDICES

29

Of Tensors and a Hearing Aid
and Many Other Things:
Einstein's Collaborators

All of Einstein's major papers are his alone. However, over the years he had a remarkably large number, more than thirty, of co-workers. Einstein did not like crowds, never cared for teaching classes, and did not create a school. But he loved to talk physics, as was illustrated in such delightful ways during the session of the Einstein symposium in Princeton devoted to 'working with Einstein' [W1]. The four men who reminisced on that occasion had all worked with him during the 1930s and 1940s. Their respective collaborative efforts all dealt with general relativity and unified field theory, Einstein's exclusive interests during that period. All of them were men much younger than Einstein who had come to him in the formative stages of their development.

It was not quite like that in earlier times. Along with the younger physicists who came even in those days, Einstein also had collaborators who belonged to his own generation, men like Laub, the Habicht brothers, Grossmann, Ehrenfest, Bucky, Mühsam, and Tolman. Pauli, though twenty years younger than Einstein, was already a mature physicist when he and Einstein wrote a joint paper. Furthermore, in the early days, even though relativity was already a main topic of concern, there was a greater variety of research subjects that interested Einstein. For example, he is the co-author of experimental papers dealing with refrigerators, a hearing aid, gyromagnetism, and the permeability of membranes for colloids. It would appear that in the early years Einstein had more fun.

To understand Einstein the physicist, it would be of some interest to organize a reunion, albeit on paper only, of all his collaborators.* It is the purpose of this appendix to do so. The format will be a series of thumb-nail sketches in which the nature of the various collaborations are stated and in which it is indicated what became of the people who worked with Einstein.**

*I believe but cannot certify that the list of collaborators given in what follows is complete. I do not include men such as Besso, with whom Einstein had important scientific discussions not accompanied or followed by a joint enterprise.

**See also [P1] for an account of Einstein's earliest scientific collaborations.

1. Jakob Johann Laub. b. 1872, Jägerndorf, Austria. PhD with W. Wien in Würzburg, November, 1906. Laub published on special relativity as early as 1907 [L1]. At the beginning of 1908, he wrote to Einstein in Bern, asking if he could work with him [L2]. The resulting collaboration led to two papers on the electrodynamics of ponderable media [E1, E2].* In 1910, Laub wrote the first major review article on the experimental basis of special relativity [L3]. He became professor of physics in La Plata, Argentina. Later, he joined the Foreign Service of Argentina and was the Argentinian ambassador to Poland at the time of the German invasion in 1939. d. 1962, Fribourg, Switzerland.

2. Walter Ritz. b. 1878, Sion, Switzerland. PhD in Goettingen with Voigt, 1902. Privatdozent in Goettingen from 1908, the year in which he discovered the combination principle for line spectra. Ritz did not accept special relativity, but rather believed in the need to give up the notion of a field described by partial differential equations (see [P2], Sec. 3). Ritz and Einstein published one very brief joint paper, written in April 1909. I stretch the notion of collaboration by including it, since it is a tersely phrased joint communiqué in which both men state what they have agreed to differ on. The issue was whether advanced and retarded solutions of the electromagnetic field equations are both admissible types of solutions. 'Ritz considers the restriction to the . . . retarded potentials as one of the roots of the second law [of thermodynamics], whereas Einstein believes that the irreversibility rests exclusively on probability grounds' [R1]. The life of Ritz, a gifted man, was short and beset with much illness. d. 1909, Goettingen.

3. and 4. The Habicht Brothers. Johann Conrad, b. 1876, and Franz Paul, b. 1884, both in Schaffhausen, Switzerland.** Conrad was one of the members of the Akademie Olympia in Bern. He obtained a doctorate in mathematics in 1903, then became a high school teacher, first in Schiers (Graubünden), then in Schaffhausen, where he died in 1958. Paul, an engineer, founded a small factory for the production of electrical and acoustical equipment. He, too, died in Schaffhausen, in 1948.

As the result of a note on voltage fluctuations in a condensor, 'a phenomenon similar to Brownian motion' [E3], that Einstein wrote in 1907, he became interested in the possibility of amplifying small voltage differences. He conceived the idea of using for this purpose a condensor with variable capacity which is charged at low voltage and maximum capacity, then discharged at a higher voltage and at minimum capacity into another condensor. This process was to be repeated with the help of a set of condensors coupled in series. It was his hope that this electrostatic device might be of use for research in radioactivity. In December 1907 Einstein wrote to Conrad that Paul planned to build this 'Maschinchen,' (little machine), as Einstein always affectionately called it, in his own laboratory. Ein-

*These papers are discussed in [P2], Secs. 33,35.

**Biographical details about Conrad and Paul Habicht and found in [H1] and [R2], respectively. I am indebted to H. Lieb, Staatsarchivar from Schaffhausen, for directing me to these articles.

stein was quite excited about his invention and at one time must have even considered patenting it. 'I am very curious how much can be achieved—I have rather high hopes. I have dropped the patent, mainly because of the lack of interest of the manufacturer [?]' [E4]. A few months later, he published his proposal [E5] and in 1908 tried to construct his own Maschinchen [E6]. In 1910 the Habicht brothers published the results of experiments 'performed together with A. Einstein at the laboratory of the University of Zürich,' in which Einstein's idea was realized with the help of a set of six rotating condensors [H2]. Einstein still continued to take a lively interest in the project after his own work had gone in other directions. In 1911 [E7] and again in 1912 [E8], he wrote from Prague to Besso about the great success Paul had had in demonstrating the apparatus in Berlin.

Rapid advances in amplification technology overtook Einstein's design, however. After Paul's death in 1948, Einstein wrote to Conrad, 'The memory awakens of old days in which I worked with your brother on the . . . little machine. . . . It was wonderful [Schön war es], even though nothing useful came of it' [E9].

5. *Ludwig Hopf.* b. 1884, Nürnberg. PhD with Sommerfeld in 1909. Hopf met Einstein in September 1909 at the Salzburg physics meeting and soon joined him at the University of Zürich as his assistant. Together they wrote two papers on classical statistical aspects of radiation, including the problem of the motion of a resonator in a radiation field [E10, E11]. Hopf arranged a meeting between Einstein and Carl Jung, the psychoanalyst [S1]. In 1911 Hopf accompanied Einstein to Prague. Later that year he accepted an assistantship at the Technische Hochschule in Aachen, where he eventually became a professor in hydrodynamics and aerodynamics. He did important work in these fields, contributed to the *Handbuch der Physik* [H3], and was co-author of a highly esteemed textbook on aerodynamics [F1]. He lost his position at Aachen in 1934 because he was a non-Aryan. Soon thereafter he moved to Dublin as professor of mathematics at Trinity College. d. 1939, Dublin.

6. *Emil Nohel.* Assistant to Einstein in Prague. Nothing is recorded about him in the literature except for a few brief comments in the biography by Philipp Frank: 'Nohel . . . was the son of a small Jewish farmer, and as a boy he walked behind the plow. He had the quiet poise of a peasant rather than the nervous personality so often found among the Jews . . .' [F2]. I am grateful to Y. Nohel from Haifa for providing me with more details about his father. With his permission, I quote from his letter to me [N1].

Emil Nohel was born in the small Czech village of Mcelly, the son of a farmer.* He received a German education in Prague, where he entered the German University in 1904. Anton Lampa, the professor of experimental physics in Prague, advised the young student not to take physics as a main subject 'since all the original work had already been done, the laws had been established, and important new developments were not be be expected.' Nohel therefore took mathematics as

*In the 1860s, it became legal for Jews to acquire land in that region.

his major subject and physics as a secondary subject. After Einstein arrived in Prague, he took Nohel as his assistant upon Lampa's recommendation. There is no record of Nohel's subsequent research. 'The many hours Einstein and my father spent together in Einstein's study, his world view and character left a lasting impression on my father. . . . He was fond of Einstein's first wife and regretted their separation.' Nohel got his PhD in 1912 or 1913. After Einstein's return to Zürich, Nohel became a mathematics teacher at the Handelsakademie in Vienna, a post he retained until the Anschluss of 1938. From 1938 to 1940 he was first a teacher, then the principal of the Chayes Gymnasium, the only remaining secondary school which Jewish children could attend in Vienna. In 1942 he was interned in Theresienstadt (Teresin). He is mentioned in studies of life in the camp as being active in educational work. After the rest of his family died in Teresin, he voluntarily joined his sister upon deportation to the extermination camps. Letters by Nohel to his son were deposited in the Yad va-Shem Memorial Archives in Jerusalem. Einstein attempted to help Nohel but without success [E12].

7. *Otto Stern.*   b. 1888, Sohrau, upper Silesia, (now Zory in Poland). PhD in 1912 in physical chemistry with Otto Sackur in Breslau. Stern came to Prague with his own independent means to join Einstein and accompanied him to Zürich when Einstein took up his position at the ETH. Einstein and Stern wrote a joint paper dealing with an attempt (unsuccessful) to interpret anomalies in the specific heats of gases at low temperatures [E13]. Helped by Einstein's advocacy, Stern became Privatdozent in Zürich in 1913. The next year he moved to Frankfurt, where the Stern-Gerlach experiments were performed in 1920-2. His discovery of the anomalous magnetic moment of the proton was made in Hamburg in 1933. Stern left Germany after the Nazis came to power, to become research professor of physics at the Carnegie Institute of Technology (now Carnegie-Mellon University) in Pittsburgh. In 1944 he received the 1943 Nobel prize in physics 'for his contributions to the molecular ray method and the discovery of the magnetic moment of the proton.' After his retirement in 1946, he divided his time between Berkeley and Zürich. When Jost and I visited him in Berkeley in the early 1960s, he told us with tears in his eyes of the beautiful days with Einstein in Prague.* d. 1969, Berkeley.

8. *Marcel Grossmann.*   b. 1878, Budapest. Fellow student of Einstein at the ETH, 1896-1900. PhD in 1902 with Fiedler in Zürich. Grossmann and his father were instrumental in getting Einstein appointed to the patent office in Bern. In 1905 Einstein dedicated his PhD thesis to the younger Grossmann. The Einstein-Grossmann collaboration is discussed at length in Chapter 12. d. 1936, Zürich. Einstein remembered Grossmann with gratitude in his last autobiographical sketch [E14].**

*See also [S2].

**For other biographical details about Grossmann, see [K1] and [S3].

9. *Adriaan Daniel Fokker.* b. 1887, Buitenzorg, Dutch East Indies, (now Bogor, Indonesia). PhD in 1913 with Lorentz in Leiden on the Brownian motion of an electron in a radiation field [F3]. This work led to the Fokker–Planck equation for Gaussian Markov processes. Fokker worked with Einstein in Zürich during the winter semester in 1913–14. Their joint paper on the Nordström theory of gravitation [E15] was discussed in Section 13b. In later years, Fokker wrote several papers on relativity as well as a Dutch textbook on that subject. He became the curator of the Teyler Foundation in Haarlem and concurrently held a professorship at Leiden. He was a passionate advocate of 31-tone music and of the purity of the Dutch language. d. 1972, Beekbergen, Holland.

10. *Wander Johannes de Haas.* b. 1878, Lisse, Holland. PhD in 1912 with Kamerlingh Onnes in Leiden. Soon after obtaining this degree, de Haas and his wife (née Geertruida Luberta Lorentz, the oldest of the three children of H. A. Lorentz) went to Berlin, where he worked first in the laboratory of Henri du Bois and then with Einstein at the Physikalisch Technische Reichsanstalt. This led to the discovery of the Einstein–de Haas effect, as described in Section 14b. In 1925 de Haas succeeded Kamerlingh Onnes at Leiden. He was a leading and productive figure in experimental low-temperature physics. He retired from his Leiden position in 1948. d. 1960, Bilthoven, Holland.

11. *Jakob Grommer.* b. Brest-Litovsk, a Russian town in the year (not known to me) of Grommer's birth, a Polish town from 1921 to 1939 (Grommer held a Polish passport at one time), now Brest in the U.S.S.R. As a young man, Grommer devoted himself exclusively to the study of the Talmud.* A burning interest in mathematics brought him to Goettingen. According to Helen Dukas, Grommer spoke only Yiddish when he arrived in Germany. In Goettingen 'he aroused the curiosity of the mathematicians soon after his arrival. In an incredibly short time, he not only acquired a deep knowledge of mathematics but also managed to write a doctoral thesis which is considered outstanding by insiders. . . . If one considers that he was disfigured as the result of a malignant disease** and that he was, moreover, physically weak, then one can appreciate how uncommon the talents were which this man brought along into this world' [E16].

Grommer worked with Einstein for ten years, the longest period any person collaborated with him. The first mention of him is in Einstein's 1917 paper on cosmology [E17]. Six years later, they published a joint paper in which it was shown that the Kaluza theory does not admit centrally symmetric singularity-free solutions [E18]. Shortly thereafter, Einstein mentioned Grommer's work again in one of his own papers [E19]. In 1925 Einstein wrote that Grommer had 'faithfully assisted me in recent years with all calculations in the area of general relativity

---

*This was stated by Einstein in a note written in 1953 [E16] at the request of an Israeli committee that was preparing a book on the history of the Jews of Brest-Litovsk [C1].

**Grommer suffered from elephantiasis or a related ailment. Einstein mentioned that this affliction often made Grommer irritable.

theory' [E20]. In 1927 they wrote a joint paper on the problem of motion in general relativity (see Chapter 15) [E21]. Another acknowledgment [E22] indicates that Grommer was in Berlin at least as late as 1928. Funds for his support came in part from the Kaiser Wilhelm Institut [K2]. While in Germany, Grommer worked on the preparation of a mathematics and physics textbook in Hebrew for use in high schools in Palestine. Weizmann had authorized financial support for this project [R3]. In the late 1920s, Grommer accepted a university position in Minsk. In 1929 he wrote to Einstein from Minsk that some of his lectures were given in Russian, others in Yiddish [G1]. He was later elected to the Bielorussian Academy of Sciences in Minsk. d. 1933, Minsk.

12. Paul Ehrenfest.   b. 1880, Vienna. PhD in Vienna in 1904 with Boltzmann. Ehrenfest first met Einstein in Prague in 1912. Their deep friendship lasted until Ehrenfest's death. In 1922 they wrote a joint paper on the Stern–Gerlach effect, in which the pre-quantum mechanical difficulties of understanding this phenomenon are clearly demonstrated [E23]. Another joint paper, written the next year, deals with an extension of Einstein's earlier work on spontaneous and induced emission and absorption of radiation to two-photon states, with an application to the Compton effect [E24]. From 1913 to 1933 Ehrenfest was professor of theoretical physics in Leiden. d. 1933, Amsterdam, by his own hand. 'Paul Ehrenfest, in memoriam,' one of Einstein's finest and most moving pieces of prose, was written to honor a friend and 'the best teacher in our profession I have ever known.'* In this note Einstein shows his great sensitivity to the fate of physics and physicists.

*13. Hans Mühsam** *   b. 1876, Berlin. In 1900 Mühsam passed his final medical examinations, started a private practice, and became a staff member at the Jewish Hospital in Berlin. He first met Einstein in 1915. 'At that time, his name was little known in lay circles' [M1]. The meeting came about because of a chance encounter between the Mühsams and Elsa Einstein. On that occasion Mühsam told Elsa that he had heard of Albert Einstein and that she, Elsa, had a famous name. When Einstein heard of this, he became curious and got in touch with the Mühsams. A friendship developed. The men would go on Sunday hikes during which they discussed physics and also medical and biological problems [S4].

In 1923 Einstein and Mühsam wrote a joint paper on the experimental determination of the permeability of filters [E26]. The purpose of the experiment was to find the maximum diameter of colloidal particles capable of permeating a given rigid membrane. The membrane consists of the walls of a tube that is open at one

---

*Einstein's article on Ehrenfest was originally published in the *Almanak van het Leidsche Studentencorps* in 1934. Its English version is found in one of his collections of essays [E25].

**I obtained most of the biographical information about Mühsam from letters by him and his wife, Minna, to Carl Seelig. These letters are now in the Historisch-Wissenschaftliche Sammlung in the main library of the ETH in Zürich.

end. The open end is connected to an air pump. The empty tube is hung in a bath of aether (chosen for its low capillary constant σ). The aether fills the membrane pores. The air pump serves to increase the pressure inside the tube until, at a pressure p, air bubbles begin to appear in the aether. Then $p = 4\sigma/d$. Here d is the diameter of the widest membrane pores and is therefore the optimal colloidal diameter to be determined. The authors record the results of experiments in which diameters of about 1 μm were obtained.

The friendship between the two men grew and became very important in Einstein's life. 'For a long period, Einstein visited us daily in Berlin' [M2]. Mrs Mühsam wrote to Seelig after her husband's death, 'Do you know that Einstein once said to me, "First comes your husband, then for a long while comes nothing, and only then come all other people"?' [M3]. I have reasons to believe that Mühsam became Einstein's closest confidant in the Berlin days. It was to Mühsam that Einstein told the story of having, at age twelve, composed songs in honor of God which he would sing to himself on his way to school [S5] (see Chapter 3). When Mühsam once asked what would have become of Einstein if he had been born the son of poor Russian Jews, Einstein replied that he would probably have become a rabbi [S6]. Mühsam could have informed us better than anyone else about personal events which may well have contributed to Einstein's becoming a figure who went his lonely separate way in physics after 1926.

Einstein and Mühsam kept in touch after the Einsteins had settled in the United States and the Mühsams had fled from Germany to Israel. A letter from Einstein in 1942 still shows personal touches: 'I have become a lonely old chap who is mainly known because he does not wear socks and who is exhibited as a curiosum on special occasions' [E27]. In that same letter, he also writes about his work: 'In regard to work, I am more fanatic than ever and really hope to have solved my old problem of the unity of the physical field. However, it is like an airship with which one can sail around in the clouds without seeing clearly how to land in reality, that is, on earth.' Mühsam died in Haifa in 1957.

14. Leo Szilard. b. 1898, Budapest. He went to Berlin for his university education. 'As soon as it became clear to Szilard that physics was his real interest, he introduced himself, with characteristic directness, to Albert Einstein. I believe it was largely Szilard's doing that Einstein gave a seminar on statistical mechanics. . . . The seminar was a unique experience for most participants; it also inspired, I believe, Szilard's doctoral dissertation' [W2]. PhD in Berlin in 1922 with von Laue. Until 1933 Szilard worked at one of the Kaiser Wilhelm Institutes in Berlin. From 1928 to 1933 he was also Privatdozent at the University.

Einstein and Szilard made a considerable number of joint patent applications, eight German (November 1927–December 1930), six British (December 1927–December 1929), one U.S. (December 16, 1927), one to Einstein's old patent office in Bern (December 21, 1928), and one Dutch (December 27, 1928). All applications were granted except for two of the British ones. All the German patents were awarded after Einstein had left that country. In 1927 Einstein authorized Szilard to apply in his own name for patents abroad of some of their joint ventures [E28].

A detailed discussion of these patents is found in Szilard's collected papers [F4].* Briefly, the task Einstein and Szilard had set for themselves was to devise a noiseless household refrigerator. Their principal novelty was the so-called Einstein-Szilard pump, later described by Einstein in general terms. 'By means of an alternating electric current, a magnetic guide field is generated which moves a liquid mixture of sodium and potassium. This mixture moves in alternating directions inside a casing and acts as the piston of a pump; the refrigerant [inside the casing] is thus mechanically liquified and cold is generated by its re-evaporation' [E29]. It appears that the inventors received a modest amount of money for their work [S7], but it did not make them rich. 'As it turned out, such refrigerators were never commercially utilized because of the rapid advances made in mechanical refrigerators which eliminated their objectionable noise, the dangers from leakage of the poisonous refrigerant, and erratic operation' [F4]. However, there were other applications. 'For many years there did not appear to be any other practical use for such pumping systems, but with the advent of atomic energy their need became evident (first to Szilard), and much effort has since been expended in their further development' [F4].

In 1933 Szilard went to England. In 1938 he settled in the United States. His first position was at Columbia University. He then moved to Chicago, where he participated in the first nuclear reactor project. In 1946 he was appointed professor of biophysics at the Enrico Fermi Institute in Chicago. 'In his work in biology, Szilard finally reached his full potential' [W2]. He had a strongly developed political conscience. On August 2, 1939, he and Eugene Wigner called on Einstein to urge him to bring the need for action on the development of atomic weapons to the attention of President Roosevelt. This visit led to the letter drafted by Szilard and signed by Einstein which was handed to Roosevelt on October 11, 1939. Later, Szilard suggested that Einstein write a second letter to the president, urging him to speed up these activities. A letter to this effect was sent on March 7, 1940. d. 1964, La Jolla, California.

15. *Rudolf Goldschmidt.*** b. 1876, Neubukow (Mecklenburg-Schwerin), Germany. Engineering diploma in 1898. From 1899 to 1909, Goldschmidt worked in England with such electrotechnical firms as Westinghouse. Upon his return to Germany, he became first Privatdozent, later professor, in Darmstadt. One of his main achievements was the invention of the high-frequency apparatus

*See also [K3], [M4], and [M5]. The Swiss patent is mentioned in [F5] and [M5], not in [F4].

**I am grateful to Professor Goldschmidt's daugther-in-law Rose Goldie from New Malden, Surrey, England, and to Horst Melcher from Potsdam for information which was of great help to me in the preparation of this note on the Einstein–Goldschmidt patent. I first became aware of this patent through Professor Melcher's papers [M4, M5].

used in the first radiotelegraphic link between Germany and the United States, opened on June 19, 1914, with an exchange of telegrams between Wilhelm II and Woodrow Wilson.

In the 1920s, Goldschmidt was director of an industrial research laboratory in Berlin-Moabit. He held many patents. One of these, German patent 590783, held jointly with Einstein, has the following history. An acquaintance of Einstein, a distinguished singer, had become hard of hearing. In 1928 Einstein asked Goldschmidt's assistance in developing a new type of hearing aid for her. At that time, he sent his friend one of his poetic creations:

> Ein biszchen Technik dann und wann
> Auch Grübler amusieren kann.
> Drum kühnlich denk ich schon so weit:
> Wir legen noch ein Ei zu zweit.*

The final patent is entitled 'Device, especially for sound-reproduction equipment, in which changes of an electric current generate movements of a magnetized body by means of magnetostriction.' It was issued on January 10, 1934. Einstein's address is given as 'Earlier in Berlin, present residence unknown.'

Goldschmidt emigrated to England in 1934 and in later years kept up a correspondence with Einstein. d. 1950, Bournemouth, England.

16. Cornelius Lanczos. (born Kornel Loewy, the name later Hungarianized). b. 1892, Szekesfehervar, Hungary. PhD in 1921 with Rudolf Ortvay in Szeged. Lanczos corresponded with Einstein from 1919 on and had already written over a dozen papers on general relativity when he came to work with Einstein. In 1928, Einstein wrote to Erwin Madelung in Frankfurt am Main, asking if it would be possible for Lanczos to have a year's leave of absence from his position as an assistant and Privatdozent at the University of Frankfurt in order to work with Einstein on problems in unified field theory [E30]. A week later, Lanczos wrote to Einstein, 'Young Bethe is being considered as my deputy' [L4]. Lanczos arrived in Berlin in November 1928 for a one-year period. There are no joint papers. Einstein refers to Lanczos' work in one of his articles on distant parallelism [E31], a subject on which Lanczos wrote a review two years later [L5].

Lanczos returned to Frankfurt at the end of 1929. His distinguished career included a professorship at Purdue (1931–46), a period of work in industry, and, after 1954, a professorship at the Institute for Advanced Studies in Dublin. He wrote a number of books, three of which deal with Einstein, his oeuvre, and his influence [L6, L7, L8]. d. 1974, Budapest.

17. Hermann Müntz. I have only a few biographical notes on Müntz. He was born in Poland and later became a German citizen [M6]. He corresponded

---

*In prose translation: A bit of technique now and then/Can also amuse thinkers./Therefore, audaciously I'm thinking far ahead: One day we'll produce something good together.

with Einstein at least as early as 1927. In 1928 Einstein wrote to him on distant parallelism: 'This mathematically so natural theory is worthy of serious consideration, especially in view of the current desperate state of theoretical physics' [E32]. Müntz came to work with Einstein during the period Lanczos was there. Both men were supported by stipends from the Notgemeinschaft Deutscher Wissenschaftler [K4].* Einstein acknowledged Müntz's work in two papers on distant parallelism [E31, E33]. In 1929 Müntz became professor of mathematics at the University of Leningrad, where he received an honorary doctorate in 1935. After declining to become a Soviet citizen, Müntz had to leave the Soviet Union in 1937 [M7]. In 1938 he arrived in Sweden. Einstein contacted several Jewish agencies in attempts to obtain financial support for him. I do not know what became of him after 1938.

18. Walther Mayer.   b. 1887, Graz, Austria. Studied at the ETH in Zürich and at the universities of Vienna, Paris, and Goettingen. PhD in 1912 in Vienna, where he became Privatdozent in 1926. In 1929 he completed a book on Riemannian geometry, part of a textbook on differential geometry [D1].

After the departure of Lanczos and Müntz, Einstein contacted Richard von Mises in Vienna to ask if he knew of someone interested in working with him. In December 1929, von Mises recommended Mayer [M8]. The Einstein-Mayer collaboration started soon after and was at once a success. In January 1930 Einstein requested a stipend for Mayer from the Preussische Akademie [K5]. In February 1930 they published their first joint paper, on static solutions of the distant parallelism theory [E34]. Einstein must rapidly have concluded that he wanted to keep Mayer close to him, for in June he wrote to the mathematician Ludwig Bieberbach in Berlin, asking if a job for Mayer could be found [E35]. In October Einstein presented to the Prussian Academy a paper by him and Mayer in which a new unified field theory was proposed, one based on a four-dimensional space-time continuum with a five-dimensional tangent space attached at each point [E36].** Mayer (as well as Helen Dukas) accompanied the Einsteins on their first trip to California (December 1930–March 1931), since Einstein did not wish to interrupt the collaboration. Right after their return, a sequel to the October 1930 paper was submitted [E37]. In December 1932 they completed their last joint paper to be published in Germany. It deals with semi-vectors and spinors [E38] and was the last paper published by Einstein in the Sitzungsberichte of the Preussische Akademie.

Meanwhile, in October 1932, Einstein had been appointed professor at The Institute for Advanced Study with the understanding that his first period in Princeton would start in October 1933. Throughout the negotiations with Abra-

---

*This fund existed from 1920 to 1934 under the presidency of Friedrich Schmidt-Ott. Its purpose was to give financial support to promising young PhD's and Privatdozente who could not manage to start their academic career without outside aid.

**See Chapter 17.

ham Flexner, the first director of the Institute, Einstein insisted on an appointment for Mayer as an essential condition for his own acceptance of the new position. After other conditions of his professorship had been settled to mutual satisfaction, Einstein wrote to Flexner, 'Now my only wish is that Herr Dr W. Mayer, my excellent co-worker, will receive an appointment that is formally independent of my own. Until now, he has suffered very much from the fact that his abilities and achievements have not found their deserved recognition. He must be made to feel that he is being appointed because of his own achievements and not for my sake' [E39].

The next two Einstein–Mayer papers again dealt with semi-vectors [E40, E41]. They were produced during their stay at Le Coq sur Mer in Belgium (see Section 25b). At that time, the spring of 1933, Mayer's Princeton appointment had still not been settled, and Einstein wrote to Flexner urging him to exercise care in the choice of people he might approach for opinions on Mayer [E42]. A subsequent letter to Flexner shows that Einstein could put the pressure on if he wanted to: 'You will by now have learned through the press that I have accepted a chair at Madrid University. . . . In view of my relations to the Spanish government, I feel it is my duty to write to you about my assistant, Professor W. Mayer. The Spanish government has conceded me the right to recommend to them a mathematician to be appointed as full professor under my direction. Now, as I have very great regard for Professor Mayer's abilities, not only as my collaborator but also as an independent researcher in pure mathematics whose achievements are notable and valuable, he would be the right man to take up such a professorship. He would not have thought of asking me to recommend him for this post had he not felt it as a set-back that he was appointed to your Institute not as a full professor but only as an associate professor with a salary that hardly corresponds to his merits and his needs. I therefore find myself in a difficult position: either to recommend him for Spain or to ask you whether you could possibly extend his appointment to a full professorship. This would be the only way of retaining him for your Institute and for a collaboration with me. I would deplore it very much indeed if I were deprived of his valuable collaboration; and his absence from the Institute might even create some difficulties for my own work. Besides, his resignation would be a great loss to your Institute' [E43].

The very high importance which Einstein still attached to the collaboration with Mayer is also evident from his reply to a proposal by Flexner that Mayer arrive in Princeton some weeks before Einstein would be there: '[This] would severely impair our joint work . . . [since] we would be torn away from each other [voneinander gerissen] for a whole month . . .' [E44].

Einstein prevailed, and Mayer was given a tenured position with the title of associate, the only appointment of its kind ever made by the Institute. The entire collaboration of Einstein and Mayer in the United States consists of one joint paper, the last one on semi-vectors [E45]. After 1934 Mayer returned to his own pursuits in pure mathematics. It is my understanding that he no longer wished to be associated with work on unified field theory and that he believed his career would best be furthered by independent work. I knew him during the last years of his life, a gentle and somewhat diffident figure with an office on the third floor in Fuld Hall. d. 1948, Princeton.

19. Richard Chase Tolman. b. 1881, West Newton, Massachusetts. PhD in physical chemistry in 1910 with Arthur Noyes. Professor at California Institute of Technology 1922. Author of two books on relativity theory [T1, T2]. During Einstein's first visit to California, Tolman collaborated with Ehrenfest and Podolsky on a study of the gravitational field produced by light [E46] and with Einstein and Podolsky on a less-than-successful study of the measurement problem in quantum mechanics [E47]. d. 1948, Pasadena, California.

20. Willem de Sitter. b. 1872, Sneek, Holland. PhD in Groningen with Jacobus Kapteyn. Proposed the 'de Sitter universe' in 1917. Director of the Leiden astronomical observatory 1919–34. During Einstein's second visit to California, he published a joint note with de Sitter [E48] in which a cosmologically flat universe is proposed (without cosmological term and with zero pressure). d. 1934, Leiden.

21. Boris Podolsky. b. 1896, Taganrog, Russia. Emigrated to the United States in 1913. PhD with Paul Epstein at CalTech 1928. Podolsky met Einstein in Pasadena in 1931 and collaborated with him and Tolman. He was in Charkov in the early 1930s where he worked with Fock and Dirac on quantum electrodynamics. He was a member of The Institute for Advanced Study in 1934–35, when the Einstein–Podolsky–Rosen collaboration took place [E49] (Section 25c). In this paper, the term *wave function* is used. I was sure that Einstein had not done the actual writing, since he would invariably use the expression *psi-function* instead. Nathan Rosen told me that the paper was written by Podolsky. Later Podolsky became research professor at the Xavier University in Cincinnati [D2]. d. 1966, Cincinnati.

22. Nathan Rosen. b. 1909, Brooklyn, New York. ScD at MIT in 1932. Rosen wrote his master's thesis on distant parallelism and then went to Princeton to work on theoretical molecular physics.* While in Princeton, he solicited Einstein's opinion on his master's thesis. This contact led to a period of collaboration. Rosen was a member of The Institute for Advanced Study in 1934–5. The first joint paper was the Einstein–Podolsky–Rosen article, the main idea of which came from Rosen. This was followed two months later by a paper on singularity-free solutions of the combined gravitational and electromagnetic field [E50]. In 1936 they published a note on the general relativistic two-body problem [E51] and in 1937 a paper on cylindrical gravitational waves [E52].

In the course of working on this last problem, Einstein believed for some time that he had shown that the rigorous relativistic field equations do not allow for the existence of gravitational waves [I1, S2]. After he found the mistake in the argu-

*I am indebted to Nathan Rosen for telling me of his experiences.

ment, the final manuscript was prepared and sent to the *Physical Review*. It was returned to him accompanied by a lengthy referee report in which clarifications were requested. Einstein was enraged and wrote to the editor that he objected to his paper being shown to colleagues prior to publication [E53]. The editor courteously replied that refereeing was a procedure generally applied to all papers submitted to his journal, adding that he regretted that Einstein may not have been aware of this custom [T3]. Einstein sent the paper to the *Journal of the Franklin Institute* and, apart from one brief note of rebuttal [E54], never published in the *Physical Review* again.

The final version of the gravitational wave paper was completed in 1937. At that time Rosen was in the Soviet Union, where Einstein had helped him to obtain a temporary position. He had written to Vyacheslev Molotov, at that time the chairman of the Council of People's Commissars, asking him to facilitate Rosen's projects [E55]. The little man with the pince-nez must have replied to the good professor, for shortly afterward Einstein wrote again to Molotov to thank him for his help [E56]. Since 1952 Rosen has been professor at the Technion in Haifa.

23. Gustav Bucky. b. 1880, Leipzig. Bucky, a physician specializing in radiology, met the Einsteins in Berlin in the course of treating Ilse Kayser-Einstein. The Buckys and the Einsteins became friends after the two families moved to the United States. On October 27, 1936, the two men obtained joint patent No. 2,058,562 from the U.S. patent office for a photoelectric device. An open photoelectric eye in the front of a camera takes in the object to be photographed as the camera is pointed and automatically moves a screen of varying transparency in front of the camera lens. d. 1963, New York.

24. Leopold Infeld. b. 1898, Cracow. PhD in 1921 with Ladislas Natanson in Cracow. In his student days, Infeld once called on Einstein in Berlin [I1] and corresponded with him from 1927 on. In 1934 Einstein wrote an introduction to a popular scientific book by Infeld [E57]. Infeld was a member of The Institute for Advanced Study in 1936–7, and he and Einstein wrote three joint articles [E58, E59, E60] on the problem of motion in general relativity, the first one being the well-known Einstein–Infeld–Hoffmann paper mentioned in Chapter 15. In 1938 Einstein and Infeld wrote *The Evolution of Physics,* a popular scientific book written to help Infeld financially [E61]. In his autobiography, *Quest,* Infeld wrote about his days with Einstein. Einstein was not enthusiastic about this book. 'One should not undertake anything which endangers the tenuous bridge of confidence between people' [E62]. Infeld was professor at the University of Toronto from 1938 to 1950 and at the University of Warsaw from 1950 until his death. d. 1968, Warsaw.

25. Banesh Hoffmann. b. 1906, Richmond, England. In 1929 Hoffmann started work on projective relativity with Veblen. PhD in 1932 with Veblen at Princeton. A member of The Institute for Advanced Study in 1935–7. Hoffmann co-authored the aforementioned paper with Einstein and Infeld [E58]. He has been professor at Queens College in New York City since 1952 and is author of an excellent popular biography of Einstein [H4] and, together with Helen Dukas, of a book on memorable pronouncements by Einstein [D3].*

26. *Peter Gabriel Bergmann.*   b. 1915, Berlin. PhD in 1936 in Prague with Philipp Frank, who recommended him to Einstein. Bergmann worked with Einstein from 1936 to 1941. They published two joint papers on the five-dimensional unification of electromagnetism and gravitation (Kaluza–Klein theory), the second one in collaboration with Bargmann [E63, E64]. Einstein wrote an introduction to Bergmann's textbook on relativity [E65]. Since 1950, Bergmann has held a professorate at Syracuse University.

27. *Valentin Bargmann.*   b. 1908, Berlin, of Russian parents. PhD in 1936 with Gregor Wentzel in Zürich. German citizen from 1925 until deprived of German citizenship in 1934. Member of The Institute for Advanced Study 1937–46. Bargmann and Einstein published two papers together, the one with Bergmann just mentioned [E64] and a paper on bivectors [E66].** [Bivectors are quantities $T_{\mu\nu}(x_1, x_2)$, depending on a pair of space–time points, transforming under general coordinate transformations like the product $A_\mu(x_1)B_\nu(x_2)$, where $A_\mu(x_1)$ and $B_\nu(x_2)$ are ordinary 4-vector fields.] Bargmann became professor at the University of Pittsburg and, afterwards, professor of mathematical physics at Princeton University.

28. *Wolfgang Pauli.*   b. 1900, Vienna. PhD in 1921 with Sommerfeld in Munich. Einstein wrote a laudatory review [E68] of Pauli's review article [P2] on relativity theory. Pauli spent the years 1940–6 at The Institute for Advanced Study in order to escape the menaces of war. In 1943 he wrote a joint paper with Einstein [E69] in which it was proved that any everywhere regular and static solution of the source-free gravitational equations which behaves at large distances like a Schwarzschild solution must have a vanishing Schwarzschild mass. (A similar theorem was shown to hold in the Kaluza–Klein theory.)†

It will be obvious that this brief comment is not in any way meant to do justice to Pauli's contributions and influence in regard to relativity theory and relativistic quantum theory. For a survey of Pauli's oeuvre, see [E71]. d. 1958, Zürich.

29. *Ernst Gabor Straus.*   b. 1922, Munich. Assistant to Einstein 1944–8. At the time Straus came to work with Einstein, the latter was much interested in the problem of finding generalizations of general relativity that are not based on differential geometry. He also discussed these matters with Pauli at that time. Two examples of such generalizations (about which Einstein never published) are found in Straus's reminiscences [W1]. A joint paper on the influence of the expansion of space on the gravitational fields surrounding individual stars was written

*The reader is urged to read the reminiscences of Hoffmann, Bargmann, Bergmann, and Straus in [W1].

**Einstein also wrote a sequel to this paper [E67].

†This is an improved version of an earlier result obtained by Einstein alone [E70].

without awareness of numerous earlier contributions to this subject by others [E72]. A second paper dealt with asymmetric connections (see Chapter 17) [E73]. In 1948 Straus received his PhD at Columbia University. He is now professor of mathematics at UCLA.

30. John Kemeny. b. 1926, Budapest. Assistant to Einstein 1948–9. Kemeny wrote to me, 'When Straus left for the West Coast [in 1948], Einstein was searching for a new assistant. I was introduced to him by mutual friends. . . . He was at that time in the final stages of publishing unified field theory. He had narrowed down the search to about three alternative versions of the theory and was trying to choose amongst them. The year's work resulted in choosing one of the versions, which he did publish the following year. After he had settled on a particular theory, the next problem clearly was to try to solve the partial differential equations. That is about as far from my specialty in mathematics as you can get! Therefore I strongly recommended to Einstein that he not reappoint me but that he get a specialist' [K6].*

In 1949 Kemeny obtained his PhD in mathematics at Princeton University, where he was appointed assistant professor of philosophy in 1951. Since 1970 he has been president of Dartmouth College.

31. Robert Harry Kraichnan. b. 1928, Philadelphia. PhD in 1949 at MIT with H. Feschbach. Assistant to Einstein in 1949–50. At present, an independent consultant.

32. Bruria Kaufman. b. 1928, New York City. PhD in 1947 at Columbia University. Assistant to J. von Neumann at The Institute for Advanced Study, 1947–8. Assistant to Einstein from 1950 until Einstein's death in April 1955. (In March 1955, Einstein had recommended an extension of her assistantship to June, 1956 [E74].)

Kaufman was Einstein's last collaborator. She and Einstein wrote two joint papers, both dealing with asymmetric connections [E75, E76]. The last collaborative effort in Einstein's life was completed in January 1955. After Einstein's death, Kaufman and Kurt Gödel put in order the scientific papers in Einstein's office, Room 115 in Fuld Hall. At the Bern conference, later in 1955, Kaufman gave the final progress report on Einstein's unified field theory program [K8].

Bruria now lives in Kibbutz Mishmar ha'Emek.

References

B1. C. Burstin, letter to A. Einstein, April 20, 1933.

C1. N. Chinitz, letter to A. Einstein, March 29, 1953.

D1. A. Duschek and W. Mayer, *Lehrbuch der Differentialgeometrie* (2 vols.). Teubner, Leipzig, 1930.

*For other recollections of Kemeny, see [K7].

D2. H. H. Denman, *Physics Today,* March 1967, p. 141.

D3. H. Dukas and B. Hoffmann, *Albert Einstein, the Human Side: New Glimpses From His Archives.* Princeton University Press, Princeton, N.J., 1979.

E1. A. Einstein and J. J. Laub, *AdP* **26,** 532 (1908); corrections in **27,** 232 (1908) and **28,** 445 (1908).

E2. —— and ——, *AdP* **26,** 541 (1908).

E3. ——, *AdP* **22,** 569 (1907).

E4. ——, letter to C. Habicht, December 24, 1907.

E5. ——, *Phys. Zeitschr.* **9,** 216 (1908).

E6. ——, letter to J. Stark, December 14, 1908. Reprinted in A. Hermann, *Sudhoffs Archiv* **50,** 267 (1966).

E7. ——, letter to M. Besso, December 12, 1911; *EB,* p. 40.

E8. ——, letter to M. Besso, February 4, 1912; *EB,* p. 45.

E9. ——, letter to C. Habicht, August 15, 1948.

E10. —— and L. Hopf, *AdP* **33,** 1096 (1910).

E11. —— and ——, *AdP* **33,** 1105 (1910).

E12. ——, letter to F. R. Schwarz, February 7, 1946.

E13. —— and O. Stern, *AdP* **40,** 551 (1913).

E14. —— in *Helle Zeit, dunkle Zeit* (C. Seelig, Ed.). Europa Verlag, Zürich, 1956.

E15. —— and A. D. Fokker, *AdP* **44,** 321 (1914).

E16. ——, statement prepared for N. Chinitz, April 7, 1953.

E17. ——, *PAW,* 1917, p. 146.

E18. —— and J. Grommer, *Scripta Jerusalem Univ.* **1,** No. 7 (1923).

E19. ——, *PAW,* 1923, p. 359.

E20. ——, *PAW,* 1925, p. 419.

E21. —— and J. Grommer, *PAW,* 1927, p. 2.

E22. ——, *PAW,* 1929, p. 7.

E23. —— and P. Ehrenfest, *Z. Phys.* **11,** 31 (1922).

E24. —— and ——, *Z. Phys.* **19,** 301 (1923).

E25. ——, *Out of My Later Years* (3rd edn.), p. 236. Citadel Press, Secaucus, N.J., 1977.

E26. —— and H. Mühsam, *Deutsch. Medizin Wochenschr.,*1012 (1923).

E27. ——, letter to H. Mühsam, undated, summer 1942. Quoted in Se, p. 412.

E28. ——, letter to L. Szilard, September 12, 1927.

E29. ——, letter to M. Jäger, April 13, 1934.

E30. ——, letter to E. Madelung, September 29, 1928.

E31. ——, *PAW,* 1929, p. 156.

E32. ——, letter to H. Müntz, July 1928.

E33. ——, *PAW,* 1929, p. 156.

E34. —— and W. Mayer, *PAW,* 1930, p. 110.

E35. ——, letter to L. Bieberbach, June 19, 1930.

E36. —— and W. Mayer, *PAW,* 1931, p. 541.

E37. —— and ——, *PAW,* 1932, p. 130.

E38. —— and ——, *PAW,* 1932, p. 522.

E39. ——, letter to A. Flexner, July 30, 1932.

E40. —— and W. Mayer, *Proc. K. Ak. Amsterdam* **36,** 497 (1933).

E41. —— and ——, *Proc. K. Ak. Amsterdam* **36,** 615 (1933).

E42. ——, letter to A. Flexner, March 24, 1933.

E43. ——, letter to A. Flexner, April 13,1933.

E44. ——, letter to A. Flexner, August 4, 1933.

E45. —— and W. Mayer, *Ann. Math.* **35,** 104 (1934).

E46. P. Ehrenfest, R. C. Tolman, and B. Podolsky, *Phys. Rev.* **37,** 602 (1931).

E47. A. Einstein, R. C. Tolman, and B. Podolsky, *Phys. Rev.* **37,** 780 (1931).

E48. —— and W. de Sitter, *Proc. Nat. Ac. Sci.* **18,** 213 (1932).

E49. ——, B. Podolsky, and N. Rosen, *Phys. Rev.* **47,** 777 (1935).

E50. —— and N. Rosen, *Phys. Rev.* **48,** 73 (1935).

E51. —— and ——, *Phys. Rev.* **49,** 404 (1936).

E52. —— and ——, *J. Franklin Inst.* **223,** 43 (1937).

E53. ——, letter to J. T. Tate, July 27, 1936.

E54. ——, *Phys. Rev.* **89,** 321 (1953).

E55. ——, letter to V. Molotov, March 23, 1936.

E56. ——, letter to V. Molotov, July 4, 1936.

E57. ——in L. Infeld, *The World of Modern Science,* p. 5. V. Gollancz, London, 1934.

E58. ——, L. Infeld, and B. Hoffmann, *Ann. Math.* **39,** 65 (1938).

E59. —— and L. Infeld, *Ann Math.* **41,** 455 (1940).

E60. —— and ——, *Can J. Math.* **3,** 209 (1941).

E61. —— and ——, *The Evolution of Physics.* Published simultaneously by Cambridge University Press, Cambridge; Sythoff's, Amsterdam; and Simon and Schuster, New York; 1938.

E62. ——, letter to L. Infeld, undated, probably April 1941

E63. —— and P. Bergmann, *Ann. Math.* **39,** 65 (1938).

E64. ——, V. Bargmann, and P. Bergmann in *Th. von Kármán Anniversary Volume,* p. 212. California Institute of Technology, Pasadena, 1941.

E65. —— in P. Bergmann, *Introduction to the Theory of Relativity,* p. v. Prentice-Hall, New York, 1942.

E66. —— and V. Bargmann, *Ann. Math.* **45,** 1 (1944).

E67. ——, *Ann. Math.* **45,** 15 (1944).

E68. ——, *Naturw.* **10,** 184 (1922).

E69. —— and W. Pauli, *Ann. Math.* **44,** 131 (1943).

E70. ——, *Rev. Univ. Nac. de Tucuman,* **2,** 11, (1941).

E71. C. P. Enz in J. Mehra, *The Physicists' Conception of Nature,* p. 766. Reidel, Boston, 1973.

E72. A. Einstein and E. Straus, *Rev. Mod. Phys.* **17,** 120 (1945); correction in **18,** 148 (1946).

E73. —— and ——, *Ann. Math.* **47,** 731 (1946).

E74. ——, letter to J. R. Oppenheimer, March 31, 1955.

E75. —— and B. Kaufman, *Ann. Math.* **59,** 230 (1954).

E76. —— and ——, *Ann. Math.* **62,** 128 (1955).

F1. F. Fuchs and L. Hopf, *Aerodynamik.* R. C. Schmidt, Berlin, 1922.

F2. P. Frank, *Einstein, His Life and Times,* p. 82. A. Knopf, New York, 1953.

F3. See A. D. Fokker, *Phys. Zeitschr.* **15,** 96 (1914).

F4. B. T. Feld and G. Weiss-Szilard (Eds.). *The Collected Works of Leo Szilard,* Vol. 1, p. 527. MIT Press, Cambridge, Mass., 1972.

F5. M. Flückiger, *Einstein in Bern,* p. 148. Paul Haupt, Bern, 1974.

G1. J. Grommer, letter to A. Einstein, 1929, undated.

H1. M. Habicht, *Verh. Schw. Naturf. Ges.,* 1959, p. 405.

H2. C. Habicht and P. Habicht, *Phys. Zeitschr.* **11,** 532 (1910).

H3. L. Hopf, *Handbuch der Physik,* Vol. 7, p. 91. Springer, Berlin, 1927.

H4. B. Hoffmann, *Albert Einstein, Creator and Rebel.* Viking Press, New York, 1972.

I1. L. Infeld, *Quest,* pp. 261–70. Doubleday, New York, 1941.

K1. L. Kollros, *Verh. Schw. Naturf. Ges.* **118,** 325 (1937).

K2. C. Kirsten and H. J. Treder, *Albert Einstein in Berlin,* Vol. 1, p. 154. Akademie, Berlin, 1979.

K3. —— and ——, [K2], Vol. 2, p. 290.

K3. —— and ——, [K2], Vol. 2, p. 290.

K4. —— and ——, [K2], Vol. 1, pp. 36, 137.

K6. J. G. Kemeny, letter to A. Pais, November 27, 1979.

K7. —— in *Einstein, a Centenary Volume* (A. P. French, Ed.), p. 34. Heinemann, London, 1979.

K8. B. Kaufman, *Helv. Phys. Acta Suppl.* **IV,** 227 (1956).

L1. J. J. Laub, *AdP* **23,** 738 (1907).

L2. ——, letter to A. Einstein, February 2, 1908.

L3. ——, *Jahrb. Rad. Elektr.* **7,** 405 (1910).

L4. C. Lanczos, letter to A. Einstein, October 6, 1928.

L5. ——, *Erg Ex. Naturw.* **10,** 97 (1931).

L6. ——, *Albert Einstein and the Cosmic World Order.* Interscience, New York, 1965.

L7. ——, *Space Through the Ages.* Academic Press, New York, 1970.

L8. ——, *The Einstein Decade, 1905–1915.* Academic Press, New York, 1974.

M1. M. Mühsam, letter to C. Seelig, July 10, 1955.

M2. ——, letter to C. Seelig, May 3, 1956.

M3. ——, letter to C. Seelig, September 10, 1959.

M4. H. Melcher, *Spektrum, Monatszeit. für Wiss. Akad. der Wiss. DDR,* September 1978, p. 23.

M5. ——, *Der Neuerer,* May/June 1979, p. 202.

M6. H. Müntz, letter to A. Einstein, March 14, 1938.

M7. ——, letter to A. Einstein, November 25, 1937.

M8. R. von Mises, letter to A. Einstein, December 17, 1929.

N1. Y. Nohel, letter to A. Pais, January 1, 1980.

P1. L. Pyenson, *Hist. St. Phys. Sci.* **7,** 83 (1976).

P2. W. Pauli, *Encyklopädie der Mathematischen Wissenchaften,* Vol. 5, Part 2, p. 539. Teubner, Leipzig, 1921. In English: *Theory of Relativity* (G. Field, Tran.). Pergamon Press, London, 1958.

R1. W. Ritz and A. Einstein, *Phys. Zeitschr.* **10,** 323 (1909).

R2. M. Russenberger, *Mitt. Naturf. Ges. Schaffhausen* **23,** 301 (1949).

R3. Rosenblueth, letter to the University Committee, c/o Zionist Executive, London, March 25, 1925.

S1. Se, p. 181.

S2. Se, pp. 215–6.

S3. W. Saxer, *Viertelj. Schrift Naturf. Ges. Zürich* **81,** 322, (1936).

S4. Se, p. 412.

S5. Se, p. 15.

S6. Se, p. 16.

S7. L. Szilard, letter to A. Einstein, October 12, 1929.

T1. R. C. Tolman, *The Theory of the Relativity of Motion.* University of California Press, Berkeley, 1917.

T2. ——, *Relativity, Thermodynamics and Cosmology.* Oxford University Press Oxford, 1934.

T3. J. T. Tate, letter to A. Einstein, July 30, 1936.

W1. H. Woolf (Ed.), *Some Strangeness in the Proportion,* p. 459. Addison-Wesley, Reading, Mass., 1979.

W2. E. P. Wigner, *Biogr. Mem. Nat. Ac. Sci.* **40,** 337 (1964).

30

How Einstein
got the Nobel Prize

The procedure of the Royal Swedish Academy of Sciences for awarding the Nobel prize in physics is in outline as follows. Invitations to nominate are sent out by a five-member Nobel Committee (hereinafter called the Committee) elected from the membership. This Committee studies the proposals and supporting material, draws up a protocol of its deliberations, and decides by majority vote on a recommendation to the Academy. The recommendation is then transmitted in the form of a report (hereinafter called the Report) that summarizes the merits of the proposals handed to the Committee and gives the reasons for its decision. The recommendation is voted on first by the Academy Klass (section) of physics. Then follows the decisive vote by the Academy *in pleno* (not just the physicists). These votes need not agree with the Committee's recommendation. For example, in 1908 the Committee unanimously proposed Planck. The Klass vote was also in support of Planck. But the Academy chose Lippmann.

The case of Planck sheds additional light on the controversial nature of the quantum theory in its early days. 'This suggestion [Planck] got a rough treatment in the Academy. . . . After the defeat in 1908, the Committee had gotten "cold feet" as far as Planck was concerned. Also, of course, the importance but also the contradictions of quantum theory came more into focus from around 1910 on, [and] so the award to Planck was postponed in the hope that the difficulties of the quantum theory could be sorted out' [N1].

It was my privilege to be given access to Committee Reports and letters of proposal bearing on Einstein's Nobel prize. Once more, I thank all those in authority for entrusting me with this material, especially Professor Bengt Nagel, who was kind enough to answer additional questions.

The Academy's decisions have nearly always been well received by the community of physicists. To be sure, eyebrows (including my own) are raised on occasion. That, however, is not only inevitable but also irrelevant to the account about to be given. My sole focus will be upon matters of great historical interest: the scientific judgments of leading physicists who made the proposals and the judgment of a highly responsible, rather conservative body of great prestige, the Committee. The story has neither heroes nor culprits.

On November 10, 1922, a telegram was delivered to the Einstein residence in Berlin. It read, 'Nobelpreis für Physik ihnen zuerkannt näheres brieflich [signed] Aurivillius.'* On that same day, a telegram with the identical text must have been received by Bohr in Copenhagen. Also on that day, Professor Christopher Aurivillius, secretary of the Swedish Academy of Sciences, wrote to Einstein: 'As I have already informed you by telegram, in its meeting held yesterday the Royal Academy of Sciences decided to award you last year's [1921] Nobel prize for physics, in consideration of your work on theoretical physics and in particular for your discovery of the law of the photoelectric effect, but without taking into account the value which will be accorded your relativity and gravitation theories after these are confirmed in the future' [A1]. Bohr had been awarded the physics prize for 1922.

Einstein was not home to receive the telegram or the letter. He and Elsa were on their way to Japan. In September, von Laue had written to him, 'According to information I received yesterday and which is certain, events may occur in November which might make it desirable for you to be present in Europe in December. Consider whether you will nevertheless go to Japan' [L1]. Einstein left anyway and would not be back in Berlin until March 1923. Recall that the previous three years had been a hectic period in his life.** In January 1919, he and Mileva divorced. At that time, he promised that he would give her the money he was to receive when his Nobel prize came. In 1923 the entire 121 572 Kronor and 54 Øre (about $32 000 or SF 180 000 in 1923 money) was indeed transmitted to her.† In June 1919, he married Elsa; in November there was the excitement about the bending of light. In 1920 his integrity and his work came under attack from some German quarters. In 1921 he traveled to the United States and England. Early in 1922 he visited France. Rathenau was murdered just a few months before Einstein set out for Japan, glad to absent himself for a while from a potentially dangerous situation. The news of the award must have reached him while he was en route. I do not know, however, when and where he received word. The travel diary he kept during that journey makes no mention of this event.

On December 10, 1922, Rudolf Nadolny, the German ambassador to Sweden, accepted the Nobel prize in Einstein's name and, in a toast offered at the banquet held in Stockholm that evening, expressed 'the joy of my people that once again one of them has been able to achieve something for all mankind.' To this he added

*N.p. for physics awarded to you more by letter.

**See Chapter 16.

†Helen Dukas, private communication.

'the hope that also Switzerland, which during many years provided the scholar a home and opportunities to work, will participate in this joy' [L2].

Nadolny's report to the Foreign Office in Berlin, sent two days later, shows that he had conscientiously coped with a problem in international relations. In November he had been asked by the Swedish Academy to represent Einstein. Next the Swiss ambassador had asked for clarification since, to his knowledge, Einstein was a Swiss citizen. On December 1, Nadolny cabled the University of Berlin for information. On December 4 he received a telegram from the Prussian Academy: 'Antwort: Einstein ist Reichsdeutscher.' On December 11 the Foreign Office informed him that Einstein was Swiss. On January 13, 1923, the Prussian Academy informed the Kultusministerium in Berlin that on May 4, 1920, Einstein had taken the oath as a state official and was therefore German, since only Germans can be state officials. The protocol of the Prussian Academy of January 18 quotes the legal opinion that Einstein was a German citizen but that his Swiss citizenship was not thereby invalidated. On February 15 the Prussian Academy informed Einstein of this ruling. On March 24 Einstein wrote to the Prussian Academy that he had made no change in citizenship status as a condition for his position in Berlin. On June 19 Einstein called in person on Ministerialrat Rottenburg and reiterated his position, noting that he traveled on a Swiss passport. A note on this visit, prepared by Einstein on February 7, 1924, for inclusion in the *Acta* of the Prussian Academy reads in part, '[R.] was of the decided opinion that my appointment to the Akademie implies that I have acquired Prussian citizenship, since the opposite opinion cannot be maintained on the basis of the *Acta*. I have no objections to this view.'* Meanwhile, on April 6, 1923 Ilse Einstein had written to the Nobel Foundation in Stockholm that Professsor Einstein would appreciate it if the medal and diploma could be sent to him in Berlin, adding that if this were to be done via diplomatic channels 'The Swiss Embassy should be considered, since Professor Einstein is a Swiss citizen' [E1]. The end of the affair came when Baron Ramel, the Swedish ambassador to Germany, called on Einstein in Berlin and handed him his insignia.

In March 1923 Svante Arrhenius, one of the Committee members, wrote to Einstein suggesting that the latter not wait until December for his visit to Sweden but that he come in July. He could then attend a meeting of the Scandinavian Society of Science in Göteborg on the occasion of the 300th anniversary of the founding of that city. Arrhenius left to Einstein the choice of topic for a general lecture, 'but it is certain that one would be most grateful for a lecture about your relativity theory' [A2]. Einstein replied that he was agreeable to this suggestion, though he would have preferred to speak on unified field theory [E2]. On a very hot day in July, Einstein, dressed in black redingote, addressed an audience of about two thousand in the Jubilee Hall in Göteborg on 'basic ideas and problems of the theory of relativity' [E3]. King Gustav V, who was present, had a pleasant

---

*All official documents pertaining to this affair are reproduced in [K1].

chat with Einstein afterward [H1]. Einstein later gave a second, more technical lecture at Chalmers Technical Institute for about fifty members of the Science Society.

I turn next to the labors of the Committee.

The records of the Committee show that Einstein received nominations for the physics prize for each of the years 1910 through 1922 except for 1911 and 1915. In order to facilitate its task, the Committee often divides the nominees into more specialized categories, the purpose being to identify the leading candidate for each category and then to compare these leading candidates only. For each year in the following synopsis, I give the name of the category that Einstein was included in, the company joining him in that category, and, in parentheses, the winner of the year.

1910. Investigations of a theoretical or mathematical-physical character. Gullstrand, Planck, Poincaré; (Van der Waals).

(Poincaré had been nominated on several earlier occasions. The exceptionally high number (thirty-four) of signatories to letters nominating Poincaré in 1910 was the result of a campaign mounted by Mittag Leffler. Some physicists also signed: M. Brillouin, M. Curie, Lorentz, Michelson, and Zeeman. In its Report, the Committee noted that neither Poincaré's brilliant mathematical contributions nor his mathematical-philosophical essays (especially mentioned by many nominators) could be designated discoveries or inventions within physics 'unless one gives these concepts an especially broad interpretation')

1911. Einstein is not nominated; (Wien).

1912. Theoretical physics. Heaviside, Lorentz, Mach, Planck; (Dalén). (Lorentz, who shared the 1902 prize with Zeeman, was nominated by Wien for a prize to be shared with Einstein. Mach was nominated by Ferdinand Braun, who shared the 1909 prize with Marconi for his practical contributions to wireless telegraphy. Poincaré, now in another category, was nominated only by Darboux.)

1913. Theoretical physics. Lorentz, Nernst, Planck; (Kamerlingh Onnes). (Count Zeppelin and the Wright brothers were nominated in other categories.)

1914. Work of a more speculative nature, theoretical physics. Eötvös, Mach, Planck; (von Laue).

(Mach was nominated by Ostwald.)

1915. Einstein is not nominated; (father and son Bragg share the prize).

1916. Molecular physics. Debye, Knudsen, Lehmann, Nernst. The 1916 physics prize was never awarded.

1917. Investigations connected with Planck's extremely fruitful researches concerning the quantum hypothesis. Bohr, Debye, Nernst, Planck, Sommerfeld; (prize deferred).

(Bohr appears for the first time, nominated by Chwolson from Petrograd for a prize to be shared with Knudsen.)

1918. Quantum physics. Bohr, Paschen, Planck, Sommerfeld; (prize deferred; 1917 prize goes to Barkla).

1919. Theoretical physics. Knudsen, Lehmann, Planck; (Stark; also, 1918 prize goes to Planck).

1920. Mathematical physics. Bohr, Sommerfeld; (Guillaume).

1921. Same as 1920; (prize deferred).

1922. Einstein is not categorized. On November 9 Einstein is awarded the 1921 prize, Bohr the 1922 prize.

Who nominated Einstein? On what grounds? How did the Committee respond?

The first to propose Einstein was the physical chemist Wilhelm Ostwald, to whom Einstein had unsuccessfully applied for an assistantship in the spring of 1901 (see Chapter 3). Ostwald, winner of the chemistry prize for 1909, the only one to propose Einstein for 1910, repeated his nominations for the 1912 and 1913 awards. In all three instances, his sole motivation was relativity (until further notice, relativity shall refer to the special theory). In 1910 he wrote that relativity was the most far-reaching new concept since the discovery of the energy principle [O1]. In his second nomination, he stressed that relativity frees man from bonds many thousands of years old [O2]. On the third occasion, he emphasized that the issues were of physical rather than of philosophical principle (as others had suggested) and likened Einstein's contributions to the work of Copernicus and Darwin [O3]. For the 1912 Einstein nomination, Ostwald was joined by E. Pringsheim, C. Schaefer, and W. Wien; for 1913 again by Wien and by Bernhard Naunyn, a German professor of medicine. All these nominations were for relativity only, though Naunyn added a remark on the quantum theory. Pringsheim wrote, 'I believe that the Nobel Committee will rarely have the opportunity of awarding a prize for works of similar significance' [P1].

Wien's two nominations were actually for a prize to be shared by Einstein and Lorentz (and Schaefer proposed either Einstein or else a sharing between Einstein and Lorentz). It is important to quote again* from Wien's second letter of nomination. 'Concerning the new experiments on cathode rays and beta rays, I would not consider them to have decisive power of proof. The experiments are very subtle, and one cannot be sure whether all sources of error have been excluded' [W1]. At issue was the verification of Einstein's relation between the rest mass, the energy, and the velocity of a free electron. As was discussed in Chapter 7, by 1908 some experimentalists were already claiming confirmation of the Einstein relation. Doubts remained, however, as Wien's letter shows; these were not dispelled until about 1915. Thus, one important confirmation of relativity became noncontroversial only after the 1912 nominations had been made. Sommerfeld's theory of the fine structure of spectral lines, in which essentially the same Einstein relation is used, also came later, in 1916. By then, the momentous new development of general relativity had drastically changed the situation.

---

*I mentioned these same phrases in Section 7e.

Before turning in more detail to the later nominations, I first note the reactions of the Committee to the earlier ones. In the Report for 1910, it was suggested that one should wait for further experimental verification 'before one can accept the [relativity] principle and in particular award it a Nobel prize. This [need for further confirmation] is presumably the reason why *only now* [my italics] Einstein was proposed, though the principle in question was put forward in 1905 and caused the liveliest stir.' The Committee also noted that Einstein's work on Brownian motion had gained him great recognition. The comments on relativity in the Report for 1912 are similar to those in the Report for 1910. 'Lorentz was undoubtedly more cautious with his hypotheses than Einstein,' it is noted. In the Report for 1913 is found a remark that relativity is on its way to becoming a serious candidate for the award even though (the Committee notes) there may be considerable doubt about likening Einstein to Copernicus or Darwin. I leave my own comments on this period until later except for registering my lack of surprise at not finding Lorentz among those who nominated Einstein for special relativity.

During the next few years, there was an inevitable lull. Einstein was deeply immersed in the struggle with general relativity and was confusing everybody, including himself, with his hybrid theory in which everything was covariant except the gravitational field equations. In 1914 he was nominated by Naunyn (relativity, diffusion, gravitation) and by Chwolson (contributions to several domains in theoretical physics). The Report for 1914 notes vaguely that it may take a long time before the last word is said about Einstein's theory of relativity and his other work. He was not nominated for the 1915 prize. For 1916 there was only one letter. Ehrenhaft proposed him for Brownian motion and for special and general relativity. It is observed in the Report that this last work is not yet complete.

The upswing started, slowly, with the nominations for 1917. A. Haas proposed Einstein for the new theory of gravitation, quoting the explanation of the perihelion precession of Mercury. E. Warburg nominated him for his work in quantum theory, relativity theory, and gravitation. The third and last letter that year, by Pierre Weiss from Zürich, is the finest nomination for Einstein ever written [W2]. For the first time we find an appreciation of the whole Einstein, whose work represents 'un effort vers la conquête de l'inconnu.' The letter first describes Einstein's work in statistical mechanics centering on Boltzmann's principle, then the two axioms of special relativity, next the light-quantum postulate and the photoelectric effect, then the work on specific heats. It concludes by noting Einstein's experimental efforts. The Report for 1917 refers to 'the famous theoretical physicist Einstein,' speaks highly of his work, but concludes with a new experimental snag: The measurements of C. E. St John at Mount Wilson had not found the red shift predicted by general relativity. 'It appears that Einstein's relativity theory, whatever its merits in other respects may be, does not deserve a Nobel prize.'

1918. Warburg and Ehrenhaft repeat their earlier nomination; Wien and von Laue independently propose a shared prize for Lorentz and Einstein for relativity; Edgar Meyer from Zürich cites Brownian motion, specific heats, and gravitation;

Stefan Meyer from Vienna cites relativity (from now on, relativity refers to the special *and* the general theory). The Report is in essence identical with that of the year before.

1919.   Warburg, von Laue, and E. Meyer repeat their earlier nomination. Planck nominates Einstein for general relativity since '[he] made the first step beyond Newton' [P2]. Arrhenius nominates Einstein for Brownian motion. Perrin, Svedberg, and Gouy, all of them major contributors to experiments on Brownian motion, are also put in nomination. The Report goes in detail into statistical problems, including Einstein's PhD thesis and its correction as well as his work on critical opalescence. However, it is noted, Einstein's statistical papers are not of as high a caliber as his work on relativity and quantum physics. 'It would undoubtedly appear peculiar to the learned world if Einstein were to receive the prize for [statistical physics] . . . and not for his other major papers.' It is suggested that one should wait for clarification of the red shift problem—and for the solar eclipse of May 29!

1920.   Warburg repeats his earlier nomination; Waldeyer-Hartz from Berlin and L. S. Ornstein from Utrecht cite general relativity. A letter dated January 24, 1920, signed by Lorentz, Julius, Zeeman, and Kamerlingh Onnes stresses the theory of gravitation. The successes of the perihelion motion *and* the bending of light are emphasized. It is suggested that the red shift experiments are so delicate that no firm conclusions should be drawn yet. Einstein 'has placed himself in the first rank of physicists of all time.' Lorentz was deeply impressed by the results of the 1919 eclipse expeditions. A few months earlier, he had described these to Ehrenfest as 'one of the most brilliant confirmations of a theory ever achieved' [L3].

Bohr adds his voice, too, citing Brownian motion, the photoelectric effect, and the theory of specific heats, but 'first and foremost' relativity. 'One faces here an advance of decisive significance for the development of physical research' [B1].

Appended to the Report for 1920 is a statement by Arrhenius, prepared at the request of the Committee, on the consequences of general relativity. Arrhenius noted that the red shift experiments still disagreed with the theory and that criticism had been leveled from various sides against the bending of light results of the 1919 eclipse expeditions. Some of these objections were indeed sensible (for details and references, see [W3]). Less fortunate was Arrhenius's reference to an alleged explanation of the perihelion effect based on an alternative theory.* The Committee concluded that for the time being relativity could not be the basis for the award.

1921.   In a brief, forceful note Planck repeats his nomination of Einstein.

---

*This was in reference to work by E. Gehrcke, one of the leaders of the 'Arbeitsgemeinschaft Deutscher Naturforscher' (Chapter 16). As early as 1917 Einstein had pointed out that Gehrcke's theory is based on contradictory assumptions [E4]. In 1921 Lenard proposed Gehrcke for the Nobel prize.

Haas and Warburg are also back. General relativity is cited in letters by W. Däl-
lenbach (Baden), Eddington (Cambridge), G. Jaffe and E. Marx (Leipzig), G.
Nordström (Helsingfors), W. Walcott (Washington), and O. Wiener (Leipzig).
J. Hadamard (Paris) proposes either Einstein or Perrin. T. Lyman (Harvard)
cites Einstein's contributions to mathematical physics. Eddington writes, 'Einstein
stands above his contemporaries even as Newton did' [E5].

Professor Carl Wilhelm Oseen from the University of Uppsala proposes Einstein for the photoelectric effect.

At this point, the Committee requests that its member Allvar Gullstrand prepare an account of the theory of relativity and that its member Arrhenius do the
same for the photoeffect.

Gullstrand, professor of ophthalmology at the University of Uppsala since
1894, was a scientist of very high distinction. He obtained his medical doctor's
degree in 1890 and became the world's leading figure in the study of the eye as
an optical instrument. In 1960 it was written of him: 'The ophthalmologists consider him to be the man who, next to Helmholtz, contributed more than anyone
else to a mathematical understanding of the human eye as an optical system. . . .
While making these investigations, he discovered a number of widespread misconceptions about optical image formation, and, being a fighter, he devoted many of
his later papers to an attempt to destroy these misconceptions' [I12]. In 1910 and
again in 1911, he was proposed for the Nobel prize in physics. 'In 1911 the original suggestion from the Committee was that the prize should be given to Professor
A. Gullstrand, Uppsala, "for his work in geometrical optics." Gullstrand had
become a member of the Committee the same year. . . . However, it turned out
that the Committee for Physiology and Medicine had had the same good idea,
giving Gullstrand their prize "for his work on the dioptrics of the eye." So Gullstrand declined the prize in physics, and the Committee wrote an extra report
(now including Gullstrand among the signers) suggesting Wien for the prize'
[N1]. Gullstrand was a member of the Committee for physics from 1911 to 1929,
its chairman from 1923 to 1929.

Gullstrand's report, highly critical of relativity, was not a good piece of work.
I quote from its summary, found in the Report for 1921. Concerning the special
theory: 'The effects that are measurable with physical means are, however, so
small that in general they lie below the limits of experimental error.' Also beside
the mark is his finding about the general theory: 'As Gullstrand has shown, the
situation is that it remains unknown until further notice whether the Einstein
theory can at all be brought into agreement with the perihelion experiment [!] of
Le Verrier.' Gullstrand had fallen into the trap (he was not the only one) of
believing that he had shown that the answer for the perihelion effect is coordinate-
dependent. He also expressed the opinion (more reasonable though not very
weighty) that other, long-known deviations from the pure two-body Newtonian
law should be re-evaluated with general relativistic methods before there could be
even an attempt to identify the residual effect to be explained. On May 25, 1921,

he had presented a paper on these considerations, a reprint of which was appended to his report [G1].*

The main points of Arrhenius's report were first, that a prize for quantum theory had just been given (Planck, 1918) and second, that it would be preferable to give an award to experimentalists if the photoeffect were to be honored.

No prize for physics was given that year.

1922. The list of signatories keeps growing. Ehrenhaft, Hadamard, von Laue, E. and S. Meyer, Naunyn, Nordström, and Warburg are back. There is a beautiful letter from Sommerfeld. M. Brillouin writes, 'Imagine for a moment what the general opinion will be fifty years from now if the name Einstein does not appear on the list of Nobel laureates' [B2]. There are also letters from T. de Donder (Brussels), R. Emden and E. Wagner (Munich), P. Langevin (Paris), and E. Poulton (Oxford).

Planck proposes to give the prizes for 1921 and 1922 to Einstein and Bohr, respectively.

Oseen repeats his nomination for the photoeffect.

The Committee asks Gullstrand for an additional report on relativity and Oseen for a report on the photoeffect.

Gullstrand sticks to his guns. His paper of the previous year [G1] having been criticized by Erich Kretschmann, Privatdozent in Königsberg [K2], Gullstrand published a rebuttal, a reprint of which he appended to his new statement [G2].

Oseen, the theoretical physicist, gives an excellent analysis of Einstein's paper of 1905 on the light-quantum as well as of his work in 1909 on energy fluctuations in blackbody radiation.

The Committee proposes Einstein for the 1921 prize. The Academy votes accordingly.

That is how Einstein got the Nobel prize 'for his services to theoretical physics and especially for his discovery of the law of the photoelectric effect.' That is also why Aurivillius wrote Einstein on November 10, 1922, that his award was not based on relativity.

In his presentation speech on December 10, 1922, Arrhenius said, 'Most discussion [of Einstein's oeuvre] centers on his theory of relativity. This pertains to epistemology and has therefore been the subject of lively debate in philosophical circles. It will be no secret that the famous philosopher Bergson in Paris has challenged this theory, while other philosophers have acclaimed it wholeheartedly.'

Bergson's collected works appeared in 1970 [B3]. The editors did not include his book *Durée et Simultanéité: A Propos de la Théorie d'Einstein.* Einstein came to know, like, and respect Bergson. Of Bergson's philosophy he used to say, 'Gott verzeih ihm,' God forgive him.

---

*Gullstrand had never published on relativity before that time. It is not more than my guess that he might have become intrigued with general relativity because of one feature that he had contributed to in a quite different context: the bending of light.

A further exchange between Gullstrand and Kretschmann settled their differences to mutual satisfaction [K3].

Why did Einstein not get the Nobel prize for relativity? Largely, I believe, because the Academy was under so much pressure to award him. The many letters sent in his behalf were never the result of any campaign. Leading physicists had recognized him for what he was. It is understandable that the Academy was in no hurry to award relativity before experimental issues were clarified, first in special relativity, later in general relativity. It was the Academy's bad fortune not to have anyone among its members who could competently evaluate the content of relativity theory in those early years. Oseen's proposal to give the award for the photoeffect must have come as a relief of conflicting pressures.

Was the photoeffect worth a Nobel prize? Without a doubt. Einstein's paper on that subject was the first application of quantum theory to systems other than pure radiation. That paper showed true genius. The order of awards for quantum physics was perfect: first Planck, then Einstein, then Bohr. It is a touching twist of history that the Committee, conservative by inclination, would honor Einstein for the most revolutionary contribution he ever made to physics.

References*

A1. C. Aurivillius, letter to A. Einstein, November 10, 1922.
A2. S. Arrhenius, letter to A. Einstein, March 17, 1923.
B1. N. Bohr, letter to SAS, January 30, 1920.
B2. M. Brillouin, letter to SAS, November 12, 1921.
B3. H. L. Bergson, *Oeuvres* (A. Robinet, Ed.). Presses Univ. de France, Paris, 1970.
E1. Ilse Einstein, letter to Prof. Sederholm, April 6, 1923.
E2. A. Einstein, letter to S. Arrhenius, March 23, 1923.
E3. ——, *Grundgedanken und Probleme der Relativitätstheorie*. Imprimerie Royale, Stockholm, 1923.
E4. ——, *Verh. Deutsch. Phys. Ges.* **20,** 261 (1917).
E5. A. S. Eddington, letter to SAS, January 1, 1921.
G1. A. Gullstrand, *Ark. Mat. Astr. Fys.* **16,** No. 8 (1921).
G2. ——, *Ark. Mat. Astr. Fys.* **17,** No. 3 (1922).
H1. J. A. Hedvall, letter to H. Dukas, November 19, 1971.
H2. M. Herzberger, *Opt. Acta* **7,** 237 (1960).
K1. C. Kirsten and H. J. Treder, *Albert Einstein in Berlin,* Vol. 1, pp. 113–18. Akademie Verlag, Berlin, 1979.
K2. E. Kretschmann, *Ark. Mat. Astr. Fys.* **17,** No. 2 (1922).
K3. ——, *Ark. Mat. Ast. Fys.* **17,** No. 25 (1923); with an added comment by Gullstrand.
L1. M. von Laue, letter to A. Einstein, September 18, 1922.

*In these references, SAS stands for Royal Swedish Academy of Sciences.

L2. *Les Prix Nobel,* pp. 101–2. Imprimerie Royale, Stockholm, 1923.

L3. H. A. Lorentz, letter to P. Ehrenfest, September 22, 1919.

N1. B. Nagel, letter to A. Pais, May 7, 1981; see also B. Nagel in *Science, Technology and Society in the Time of Alfred Nobel*, Nobel Symposium, Karlskoga, 1981, to be published.

O1. W. Ostwald, letter to SAS, October 2, 1909.

O2. ——, letter to SAS, December 21, 1911.

O3. ——, letter to SAS, December 30, 1912.

P1. E. Pringsheim, letter to SAS, January 12, 1912.

P2. M. Planck, letter to SAS, January 19, 1919.

W1. W. Wien, letter to SAS, early January, 1912.

W2. P. Weiss, letter to SAS, January 21, 1917.

W3. L. Witten (Ed.), *Gravitation*. Wiley, New York, 1962.

31

Einstein's Proposals
for the Nobel Prize

Einstein's Nobel prize proposals enable us to catch glimpses of what, in his judgment, were and were not important issues in his time. In what follows, the reader will find neither a dissertation on the virtues, follies, and harm of prizes and awards, nor a gossip column about personalities.

Nine of the following entries refer to physics proposals. Unless noted otherwise, they are all addressed to the Nobel Committee in Stockholm in the form of letters. There are also seven proposals for the peace prize directed to the Storting in Oslo. One entry deals with correspondence about a Nobel prize in medicine for Sigmund Freud, another concerns a literature prize for Hermann Broch.

1. Fall 1918. In September 1918 Einstein received a request from Stockholm for a nomination in physics for the year 1919. In his response,* he proposes Planck for his achievements on the subject of heat radiation and especially for the two papers "On the law of the energy distribution in the normal spectrum" and "On the elementary quanta of matter and electricity." 'Because of this work, the author has not only given a first exact determination of the absolute size of atoms but especially [he has] also laid the foundations for the quantum theory, the fertility of which for all of physics has become manifest in recent years.'** Einstein stresses that Bohr's theory of spectra is also based on Planck's work.

On November 13, 1919, Planck is awarded the physics prize for 1918.

2. January 19, 1921. Einstein endorses the proposal of the Czech parliament to give the peace prize to Tomáš Garrigue Masaryk, the first president (from 1918 to 1935) of the young nation of Czechoslovakia. In his letter, Einstein lauds Masaryk for his role in protecting oppressed minorities, especially the Czechs and the Jews, and adds, 'I am convinced that awarding him the Nobel prize would represent a beautiful victory for international reconciliation. . . .'†

3. October 26, 1923. In response to another request for a nomination in physics, Einstein writes that he finds it difficult to make one definite proposal. 'In order

*Undated but no doubt written in the fall of 1918.

**The references given in [P1] and [P2] occur explicitly in Einstein's letters.

†See further [N1].

to ease my conscience,' he notes the following 'approximately equivalent possibilities:

[J.] Franck and [G.] Hertz, for their investigations of light excitation by collisions with electrons

[P.] Langevin and [P.] Weiss, for the statistical theory of magnetism

[O.] Stern and [W.] Gerlach, for the experimental proof of orientation of atoms in a magnetic field required by the quantum theory

[A.] Sommerfeld, for his contributions to quantum mechanics

A. H. Compton, for the discovery of the quantum scattering of Roentgen radiation

C. T. R. Wilson, for the *Nebelmethode* as [a method of] proof of the ionization generated by corpuscular rays

P. Debye, for his contributions to our knowledge of molecular forces.'

In 1925 the physics prize is awarded to Franck and Hertz.

4. *May 22, 1925.* Einstein proposes the famous Brazilian explorer Marshal Cândido Mariano da Silva Rondon for the peace prize. 'I take the liberty to draw your attention to the activities of General Rondon from Rio de Janeiro, since, during my visit to Brazil, I have gained the impression that this man is highly worthy of receiving the Nobel Peace Prize. His work consists of adjusting Indian tribes to the civilized world without the use of weapons or coercion.'

5. *September 28, 1927.* In a brief note, Einstein again proposes Compton 'for the discovery of the Compton effect, named after him, which is a milestone in our knowledge about the nature of radiation.'

In 1927 the physics prize is awarded to Compton and Wilson. Compton's citation reads, 'For his discovery of the effect named after him.'

6. *February 15, 1928.* Dr Heinrich Meng from Stuttgart, editor of *Zeitschrift fur Psychoanalytische Pädagogik,* and author Stefan Zweig (then in Salzburg) have written to a number of prominent figures urging them to support the nomination of Freud for the Nobel prize. On February 15, 1928, Einstein replies to Meng, 'With all [my] admiration for the genius of Freud's achievement, I cannot decide to intervene in the present case. About the extent of truth [Wahrheitsgehalt] of Freud's teachings, I cannot come to a conviction for myself, much less [can I] make a judgment that would also be authoritative to others. I would further suggest to you that it is questionable whether the achievement of a psychologist like Freud falls within the domain of the Nobel prize for medicine, which is presumably the only one that should be considered.'

Upon receiving a reply from Meng, Einstein reiterates the same views in a letter of October 26, 1928, adding that 'the unique difficulty of the material definitely requires that this judgment be left to experienced professionals.'

Far more fascinating than this award issue are the relations between two men who each in his own way transformed his own and later times. Their jointly authored booklet *Why War?* gives only minor indications of the personal sentiments of one in regard to the other [E1]. Much more revealing information is found in the excellent Freud biography by Ernest Jones [J1]. I mention here one additional comment by Einstein on Freud, contained in a letter written in 1949: 'The old one had . . . a sharp vision; no illusion lulled him asleep except for an often exaggerated faith in his own ideas'* [E2]. I leave, of course, to myself and to my readers all attempts to analyse what this statement reveals about Freud and about Einstein.

7. *September 25, 1928.* This is the first of three letters in which Einstein focuses attention on the founding of quantum mechanics. 'In my opinion, the most important and not yet rewarded achievement in physics is the insight into the wave nature of mechanical processes.' He makes several suggestions. First, that one half of an award should go to de Broglie, the other half to be shared by 'Davison [*sic*] und ein Mitarbeiter' (C. J. Davisson and L. H. Germer). He finds it 'a difficult case since de Broglie is the decisive initiator without having exhausted the issue [because he] has not thought of the possibility of an experimental proof' of the existence of matter waves. (This is not quite correct. De Boglie did mention the possibility of matter diffraction in his PhD thesis.) Einstein continues: 'Equivalently, the theoreticians Heisenberg and Schroedinger (one shared Nobel prize) should be considered (for 1930?). With respect to achievement, each one of these investigators deserves a full Nobel prize although their theories in the main coincide in regard to reality content. However, in my opinion, de Broglie should take precedence, especially because [his] idea is *certainly* correct, while it still seems problematic how much will ultimately survive of the grandiosely conceived theories of the two last-named investigators.'

As further alternatives, Einstein mentions one prize to be shared by de Broglie and Schroedinger, another by Heisenberg, Born, and Jordan. He does not consider this quite ideal since Heisenberg is relatively the strongest case of the three. Nor does he feel comfortable giving the award for quantum mechanics to theoreticians only.

The Dirac equation was published early in 1928. It is significant that neither in 1928 nor at any subsequent time does Einstein ever propose Dirac.

In 1929 the physics prize is awarded to de Broglie 'for his discovery of the wave nature of the electron.' In 1937, Davisson shares the prize with G. P. Thomson 'for their experimental discoveries of the diffraction of electrons by crystals.'

8. *September 20, 1931.* Einstein is now convinced that quantum mechanics will survive.** He proposes 'the founders of the wave, or quantum, mechanics, Professor E. Schroedinger from Berlin and Professor W. Heisenberg from Leipzig. In my opinion, this theory contains without doubt a piece of the ultimate truth. The achievements of both men are independent of each other and so significant that it would not be appropriate to divide a Nobel prize between them.

*Der Alte hat aber scharf gesehen; er hat sich durch keine Illusion einlullen lassen ausser manchmal durch ein übertriebenes Vertrauen in die eigenen Einfälle.

**See Section 25a.

'The question of who should get the prize first is hard to answer. Personally, I assess Schroedinger's achievement as the greater one, since I have the impression that the concepts created by him will carry further than those of Heisenberg. [Here Einstein adds a footnote: This, however, is only my own opinion, which may be wrong.] On the other hand, the first important publication by Heisenberg precedes the one by Schroedinger. If I had to decide, I would give the prize first to Schroedinger.'

Einstein's judgment of the relative scientific merits of Schroedinger's and Heisenberg's work was indeed wrong. This may not have helped the deliberations in Stockholm. No physics prize is awarded in 1931.

9. January 1932.   Einstein writes in support of the peace prize for the Englishman Herbert Runham Brown.* (At about the same time, a similar proposal is also made by twenty-five members of the British parliament.) Of Brown, honorary secretary of War Resisters' International, Einstein writes, 'Mr Runham Brown is, in my opinion, the most meritorious active fighter in the service of pacificism, who has indefatigably served this important cause with great courage. . . .'

10. September 29, 1932.   'Again this year I propose Professor E. Schroedinger from Berlin. I am of the opinion that our understanding of the quantum phenomena has been furthered most by his work in connection with the work of de Broglie.' The distinction between Schroedinger and Heisenberg is still present.

The Nobel committee for physics decides to drop the 1931 prize altogether and to postpone the 1932 award until 1933. In 1933 they award the 1932 prize to Heisenberg and the 1933 prize jointly to Schroedinger and Dirac.

11. October 27, 1935.   Einstein has written twice before in support of others' peace prize proposals. This time he makes his own suggestion. 'Formally speaking, I have no right to propose a candidate for the Nobel peace prize,' but, he adds, his conscience demands that he write anyway. He then proposes Carl von Ossietzky, 'a man who, by his actions and his suffering, is more deserving of it than any other living person.' Such an award, Einstein continues, would be 'a historic act that would suit to a high degree the solution of the peace problem.'**

Von Ossietzky was chief editor of *Die Weltbühne,* a pacifist political weekly in Berlin, when on March 12, 1929, an article appeared in its columns in which it was revealed that much of the research and development for German civil aviation was secretly directed toward military purposes. Both the author of the article and von Ossietzky were accused of treason and sentenced to eighteen months in jail. He received amnesty in December 1932. In February 1933, very soon after the Nazis came to power, he was sent to a concentration camp. Efforts to nominate

---

*For the circumstances surrounding this action, see [N2]

**See [N3] for an account of the delicate problems arising from this proposal by Einstein and by others. See [G1] for a detailed biography of Ossietzky.

him for the peace prize, initiated in 1934, grew into an international campaign. In January 1936, more than 500 members of the parliaments of Czechoslovakia, England, France, Holland, Norway, Sweden, and Switzerland signed petitions nominating him for the peace prize. He stayed in the concentration camp until May 1936, when he was moved to a prison hospital with a severe case of tuberculosis. In the fall of 1936, Goering offered him freedom in exchange for a declaration that he would refuse the peace prize if it were awarded to him. Von Ossietzky refused. In November 1936 he was awarded the peace prize for 1935. On January 30, 1937, Hitler decreed that no German was henceforth permitted to receive Nobel prizes of any kind. The Nobel committee nevertheless awarded to Germans the chemistry prize in 1938 and the medicine prize in 1939. Both awards were declined. Von Ossietzky stayed in a prison hospital until, in May 1938, he died of tuberculosis.

12. January 17, 1940. Einstein writes to Mrs de Haas-Lorentz: 'Together with some local colleagues, I have proposed Otto Stern and [I. I.] Rabi for the invention of new methods for the measurement of molecular magnetic moments.' In 1944 the prize for 1943 is awarded to Stern, the one for 1944 to Rabi.

13. January 1945. Einstein sends the following telegram: 'Nominate Wolfgang Pauli for physics prize stop his contributions to modern quantum theory consisting in so-called Pauli or exclusion principle became fundamental part of modern quantum physics being independent from the other basic axioms of that theory stop Albert Einstein.' In 1945 Pauli receives the physics prize 'for the discovery of the exclusion principle, also called the Pauli principle.'

14. November 18, 1947. Einstein writes to Guy von Dardel, 'I would find it quite justified that Raoul Wallenberg should receive the Nobel prize [for peace] and I am gladly permitting you to mention this expression of my opinion to any person.'* On December 10, 1947, three members of the Swedish Riksdag formally propose Wallenberg to the Storting.

In 1944 Wallenberg, born in 1912 in Stockholm, was appointed third secretary to the Swedish legation in Budapest, with the task of organizing a large-scale action of relief from Nazi terror. He and his staff managed to bring about 20 000 people under the direct protection of the Swedish legation. His name soon became legendary. Several times the Nazis unsuccessfully tried to entrap and kill him. Early in 1945 Wallenberg fell into the hands of the Soviet army, which was occupying Budapest. He vanished. It is certain that at the turn of 1946-7 he was in cell No. 151 of the Lubianka prison in Moscow. It is believed by some that he may still be alive today. In 1947 Einstein wrote to Stalin, 'As an old Jew, I appeal to you to find and send back to his country Raoul Wallenberg ... [who], risking

---

*I learned much about this case from Wallenberg's half-brother, my friend Guy von Dardel, and from a paper on Wallenberg by G. B. Freed, from which I have quoted liberally [F1].

his own life, worked to rescue thousands of my unhappy Jewish people' [E3]. In reply, an underling stated that he had been authorized by Stalin to say that a search for Wallenberg had been unsuccessful [T1].

15. March 5, 1951.   Einstein writes to Dr Alvin Johnson, president emeritus of The New School for Social Research in New York City. The letter appears to be in response to an earlier letter by Johnson concerning the possibility of a Nobel prize for literature for Hermann Broch. Einstein writes that he has no insight and understanding concerning modern literature. However, from having read parts of Broch's oeuvre, 'I believe that it would probably be quite justified' to propose Broch.

(Broch was born in Vienna in 1886. He emigrated to the United States in 1938. He and Einstein became friends soon thereafter. Einstein had read his main book, *The Death of Virgil,* and admired it [B1]. Broch died in New Haven in 1951.)

16. Sometime in 1951.   Einstein proposes Friedrich Wilhelm Förster for the peace prize: 'It might be difficult to find people who have actually been successful in their efforts to secure peace.' Nevertheless, he adds, Förster belongs to the group of leading personalities who have worked solidly with great dedication for this cause, especially by exposing the dangers of 'Prussian-German militarism' by his writings, first in Germany, then in Switzerland, and finally in the United States.

Förster, a major figure in pedagogy, was a lifelong opponent of German militarism, which he attacked in numerous books, thereby incurring the hostility of Germany's ruling groups from the Second and Third Reichs. In 1895 he was imprisoned for three months on charges of libel against the Kaiser and in 1926 was called a traitor when he published accounts of secret rearmament efforts in Germany. He came to the United States in 1940 and became a citizen. He died in 1966 in a sanitarium near Zürich. For more on Förster, see [F2] and [N4].

17. January 12, 1954.   Einstein writes in support of a proposal by von Laue to award the physics prize to Bothe. In his letter, Einstein refers to the Bothe–Geiger experiment as Bothe's principal contribution.

In 1954 Bothe and Born share the physics prize.

18. March 3, 1954.   By telegram, Einstein sends his last proposal: 'I have the honor of recommending for your consideration for the forthcoming award of the Nobel peace prize the international organization known as Youth Alijah, through which children from 72 countries have been rescued and rehabilitated in Israel.'

The peace prize for 1954 is awarded to the office of the U.N. high commissioner for refugees.

It has recently come to my notice that on 19 December 1925 Einstein wrote to Stockholm proposing A. H. Compton.

References

B1. H. Broch, *The Death of Virgil.* Grosset and Dunlop, New York, 1965.
E1. A. Einstein and S. Freud, *Why War?* First published in German in 1933; English translation by Institute of Intellectual Cooperation, League of Nations, Paris, 1933.

E2. ——, letter to A. Bachrach, July 25, 1949.

E3. ——, letter to J. Stalin, November 17, 1947.

F1. G. B. Freed, *Papers of the Michigan Ac. Sci. Arts and Letters* **46,** 503 (1961).

F2. F. W. Förster, *Erlebte Weltgeschichte.* Glock und Lutz, Nürnberg, 1953.

G1. K. R. Grossmann, *Ossietzky.* Kindler Verlag, Munich, 1963.

J1. E. Jones, *The Life and Work of Sigmund Freud,* Vol. 3. Basic Books, New York, 1957.

N1. O. Nathan and H. Norden, *Einstein on Peace,* p. 41. Simon and Schuster, New York, 1960.

N2. —— and ——, [N1], p. 162.

N3. —— and ——, [N1], p. 266.

N4. *New York Times,* January 22, 1966.

P1. M. Planck, *AdP* **4,** 553 (1901). Reprinted in M. Planck, *Physikalische Abhandlungen und Vorträge (PAV)* (M. von Laue, Ed.), Vol. I, p. 717. Vieweg, Braunschweig, 1958.

P2. ——, *AdP* **4,** 564 (1901); *PAV,* Vol. I, p. 728.

T1. S. K. Tsarapkin, letter to A. Einstein, December 18, 1947.

32

An Einstein Chronology

1876   August 8. Hermann Einstein (b. 1847) and Pauline Koch (b. 1852) are married in Cannstatt.

1879   March 14, 11:30 a.m. Albert, their first child, is born in the Einstein residence, Bahnhofstrasse 135, Ulm.

1880   June 21. The Einsteins register as residents of Munich.

1881   November 18. E.'s sister Maria (Maja) is born.

~1884*   The first miracle: E.'s enchantment with a pocket campass. First instruction, by a private teacher.

~1885   E. starts taking violin lessons (and continues to do so to age thirteen).

~1886   E. attends public school in Munich. In order to comply with legal requirements for religious instruction, he is taught the elements of Judaism at home.

1888   E. enters the Luitpold Gymnasium.** The religious education continues, at school this time, where Oberlehrer Heinrich Friedmann instructs E. until he is prepared for the bar mitzvah.

1889   First encounter with Max Talmud (who later changed his name to Talmey), then a 21-year-old medical student, who introduces E. to Bernstein's *Popular Books on Physical Science,* Büchner's *Force and Matter,* Kant's *Kritik der reinen Vernunft,* and other books. Talmud becomes a regular visitor to the Einstein home until 1894. During this period, he and E. discuss scientific and philosophical topics.

~1890   E.'s religious phase, lasting about one year.

~1891   The second miracle: E. reads the 'holy geometry book.'

~1891–5   E. familiarizes himself with the elements of higher mathematics, including differential and integral calculus.

---

*The symbol ~ means that the date is accurate to within one year.

**This school, situated at Müllerstrasse 33, was destroyed during the Second World War. It was rebuilt at another location and renamed Albert Einstein Gymnasium.

1892   No bar mitzvah for E.

1894   The family moves to Italy, first to Milan, then to Pavia, then back to Milan. E. stays in Munich in order to finish school.

1894 or 95*   E. sends an essay entitled 'An investigation of the state of the aether in a magnetic field' to his uncle Caesar Koch in Belgium.

1895   Spring. E. leaves the Luitpold Gymnasium without completing his schooling. He rejoins his family in Pavia.

Fall. E. fails entrance examination for the ETH,** although he does very well in mathematics and physics.

October 28–early fall 1896. E. attends the Gewerbeabteilung of the cantonal school in Aarau. He lives in the home of 'Papa' Jost Winteler, one of his teachers. In this period, he writes a French essay, 'Mes projets d'avenir.'

1896   January 28. Upon payment of three mark, E. receives a document which certifies that he is no longer a German (more precisely, a Württemberger) citizen. He remains stateless for the next five years.

Fall. E. obtains his diploma from Aarau,† which entitles him to enroll at the ETH. He takes up residence in Zürich on October 29. Among his fellow students are Marcel Grossmann and Mileva Marič (or Marity). He starts his studies for the diploma, which will entitle him to teach in high schools.

~1897   E.'s meeting in Zürich with Michele Angelo Besso marks the beginning of a lifelong friendship.

1899   October 19. E. makes formal application for Swiss citizenship.

1900   July 27. A board of examiners requests that the diploma be granted to, among others, the candidates Grossmann and Einstein. The request is granted on July 28. E.'s marks are 5 for theoretical physics, experimental physics, astronomy; 5.5 for theory of functions; 4.5 for a diploma paper (out of a maximum 6).

Fall. E. is unsuccessful in his efforts to obtain a position as assistant at the ETH.

December 13. From Zürich, E. sends his first paper to the *Annalen der Physik*.

1901   February 21. E. becomes a Swiss citizen. On March 13 he is declared unfit for Swiss military service because of flat feet and varicose veins.

March–April. Seeking employment, E. applies without success to Ostwald in Leipzig and to Kamerlingh Onnes in Leiden.

May 17. E. gives notice of departure from Zürich.

May 19–July 15. Temporary teaching position in mathematics at the technical high school in Winterthur, where E. stays until October 14.

---

*So dated by Einstein in 1950.

**ETH = Eidgenössische Technische Hochschule, The Federal Institute of Technology in Zürich.

†His final grades were 6 for history, algebra, geometry, descriptive geometry, physics; 5 for German, Italian, chemistry, natural history; 4 for geography, drawing (art), drawing (technical), out of a maximum 6.

October 20–January 1902. Temporary teaching position in Schaffhausen.

December 18. E. applies for a position at the patent office in Bern.

1902   February 21. E. arrives in Bern. At first his only means of support are a small allowance from the family and fees from tutoring in mathematics and physics.

June 16. The Swiss federal council appoints E. on a trial basis as technical expert third class at the patent office in Bern, at an annual salary of SF 3500. E. starts work there on June 23.

October 10. E.'s father dies in Milan.

1903   January 6. E. marries Mileva Marič.

Conrad Habicht, Maurice Solovine, and E. found the 'Akademie Olympia.'

December 5. E. presents a paper, 'Theory of Electromagnetic Waves,' before the Naturforschende Gesellschaft in Bern.

1904   May 14. Birth of E.'s first son, Hans Albert (d. 1973 in Berkeley, California).

September 16. The trial appointment at the patent office is changed to a permanent appointment.

1905   March 17. E. completes the paper on the light-quantum hypothesis.

April 30. E. completes his PhD thesis, 'On a new determination of molecular dimensions.' The thesis, printed in Bern and submitted to the University of Zürich, is accepted in July. It is dedicated to 'meinem Freunde Herrn Dr M. Grossmann.'

May 11. The paper on Brownian motion is received.*

June 30. The first paper on special relativity is received.*

September 27. The second paper on special relativity theory is received.* It contains the relation $E = mc^2$.

December 19. A second paper on Brownian motion is received.*

1906   April 1. E. is promoted to technical expert second class. His salary is raised to SF 4500/annum.

November. E. completes a paper on the specific heats of solids, the first paper ever written on the quantum theory of the solid state.

1907   'The happiest thought of my life': E. discovers the principle of equivalence for uniformly accelerated mechanical systems. He extends the principle to electromagnetic phenomena, gives the correct expression for the red shift, and notes that this extension also leads to a bending of light which passes a massive body, but believes that this last effect is too small to be detectable.

June 17. E. applies for a position as Privatdozent at the University of Bern. The application is rejected since it is not accompanied by the obligatory Habilitationsschrift.

1908   February 28. Upon second application, E. is admitted at Bern as Privatdozent. His unpublished Habilitationsschrift is entitled 'Consequences for the constitution of radiation following from the energy distribution law of black bodies.'

---

* the *Annalen der Physik*.

Early in the year, J J. Laub becomes E.'s first scientific collaborator. They publish two joint papers.

December 21. Maja receives the PhD degree in Romance languages magna cum laude from the University of Bern.

1909   March and October. E. completes two papers, each of which contains a conjecture on the theory of blackbody radiation. In modern terms, these two conjectures are complementarity, and the correspondence principle. The October paper is presented at a conference in Salzburg, the first physics conference E. attended.

July 6. E. submits his resignation (effective October 15) to the patent office. He also resigns from his Privatdozent position.

July 8. E. receives his first doctorate *honoris causa*, at the University of Geneva.*

October 15. E. starts work as associate professor at the University of Zürich with a beginning salary of SF 4500/annum.

1910   March. Maja marries Paul Winteler, son of Jost Winteler.

July 28. Birth of E.'s second son, Eduard ('Tede' or 'Tedel,' d. 1965 in psychiatric hospital Burghölzli).

October. E. completes a paper on critical opalescence, his last major work in classical statistical physics.

1911   Emperor Franz Joseph signs a decree appointing E. full professor at the Karl Ferdinand University in Prague, effective April 1.

March. E. moves to Prague.

June. E. recognizes that the bending of light should be experimentally detectable during a total solar eclipse. He predicts an effect of $0''.83$ for the deflection of a light ray passing the sun (half the correct answer).

October 30–November 3: the first Solvay Conference. E. gives the concluding address, 'The Current Status of the Problem of Specific Heats.'

1912   Early February. E. is appointed professor at the ETH.

August. E. moves back to Zürich.

1912–13   E. collaborates with Grossmann (now professor of mathematics at the ETH) on the foundations of the general theory of relativity. Gravitation is described for the first time by the metric tensor. They believe that they have shown that the equations of the gravitational field cannot be generally covariant.

1913   Spring. Planck and Nernst visit E. in Zürich to sound him out about coming to Berlin. The offer consists of a research position under the aegis of the Prussian Academy of Sciences, a professorship without teaching obligations at the University of Berlin, and the directorship of the (yet to be established) Kaiser Wilhelm Institute for Physics.

June 12. Planck, Nernst, Rubens, and Warburg formally propose E. for membership in the Prussian Academy in Berlin.

---

*In later years, Einstein also received honorary degrees from Zürich, Rostock, Madrid, Brussels, Buenos Aires, the Sorbonne, London, Oxford, Cambridge, Glasgow, Leeds, Manchester, Harvard, Princeton, New York State at Albany, and Yeshiva. This list is most probably incomplete.

July 3. This proposal is accepted by a vote of twenty-one to one (and approved by Emperor Wilhelm II on November 12).

December 7. E. accepts the position in Berlin.

1914   April 6. E. moves to Berlin with wife and children. Soon after, the Einsteins separate. Mileva and the boys return to Zürich. Albert moves into a bachelor apartment at Wittelsbacherstrasse 13.

April 26. E.'s first newspaper article appears, in *Die Vossische Zeitung*, a Berlin daily. It deals with relativity theory.

July 2. E. gives his inaugural address at the Prussian Academy.

August 1. Outbreak of World War I.

1915   Early in the year. E. holds a visiting appointment at the Physikalisch Technische Reichsanstalt in Berlin, where he and de Haas perform gyromagnetic experiments.

E. cosigns a 'Manifesto to Europeans' in which all those who cherish the culture of Europe are urged to join in a League of Europeans, probably the first political document to which he lends his name.

Late June–early July. E. gives six lectures in Goettingen on general relativity theory. 'To my great joy, I completely succeeded in convincing Hilbert and [Felix] Klein.'

November 4. E. returns to the requirement of general covariance in general relativity, constrained, however, by the condition that only unimodular transformations are allowed.

November 11. E. replaces the unimodular constraint by the even stronger one that $(-\det g_{\mu\nu})^{\frac{1}{2}} = 1$.

November 18. The first post-Newtonian results. E. obtains 43" per century for the precession of the perihelion of Mercury. He also finds that the bending of light is twice as large as he thought it was in 1911.

November 20. David Hilbert submits a paper to the Goettingen Gesellschaft der Wissenschaften containing the final form of the gravitational field equations (along with an unnecessary assumption on the structure of the energy–momentum tensor).

November 25. Completion of the logical structure of general relativity. E. finds that he can and should dispense with the constraints introduced on November 4 and 11.

1916   March 20. 'Die Grundlage der allgemeinen Relativitätstheorie,' the first systematic exposé of general relativity is received by the *Annalen der Physik* and later, in 1916, published as E.'s first book.

May 5. E. succeeds Planck as president of the Deutsche Physikalische Gesellschaft.

June. E.'s first paper on gravitational waves. He discovers that (in modern language) a graviton has only two states of polarization.

July. E. returns to the quantum theory. During the next eight months, he publishes three overlapping papers on the subject, containing the coefficients of spontaneous and induced emission and absorption, a new derivation of Planck's law, and the first statement in print by E. that a light-quantum with energy $h\nu$ carries a momentum $h\nu/c$. First discomfort about 'chance' in quantum physics.

December. E. completes *Über die Spezielle and die Allgemeine Relativi-tätstheorie, Gemeinverständlich,* his most widely known book. It is later translated into many languages.

December. The emperor authorizes the appointment of E. to the board of governors of the Physikalisch Technische Reichsanstalt. E. holds this position from 1917 until 1933.

1917   February. E. writes his first paper on cosmology and introduces the cosmological term.

E. suffers successively from a liver ailment, a stomach ulcer, jaundice, and general weakness. His cousin Elsa takes care of him. He does not fully recover until 1920.

October 1. The Kaiser Wilhelm Institute begins its activities (both experimental and theoretical) under E.'s directorship.

1918   February. E.'s second paper on gravitational waves. It contains the quadrupole formula.

November. E. declines a joint offer from the University of Zürich and the ETH.

1919   January–June. E. spends most of this period in Zürich, where he gives a series of lectures at the university.

February 14. E. and Mileva are divorced.

May 29. A total solar eclipse affords opportunities for measuring the bending of light. This is done under Eddington on the island of Principe and under Crommelin in northern Brazil.

June 2. E. marries his divorced cousin Elsa Einstein Löwenthal* (b. 1874). Her two daughters, Ilse (b. 1897) and Margot (b. 1899), had earlier taken the name Einstein by legal decree. The family moves into an apartment on Haberlandstrasse 5.

September 22. E. receives a telegram from Lorentz informing him that preliminary analysis of the May eclipse data indicates that the bending of light lies between the 'Newton' value (0″.86) and the 'Einstein' value (1″.73).

November 6. At a joint meeting of the Royal Society and the Royal Astronomical Society in London, it is announced that the May observations confirm Einstein's predictions.

November 7. Headlines in the London *Times;* 'Revolution in science/ New theory of the Universe/Newtonian ideas overthrown'.

November 10. Headlines in *The New York Times:* 'Lights all askew in the heavens/Einstein theory triumphs.' Press announcements such as these mark the beginning of the perception by the general public of Einstein as a world figure.

December. Einstein receives his only German honorary degree: doctor of medicine at the University of Rostock.

Discussions about Zionism with Kurt Blumenfeld.

---

*Elsa's father was Rudolf E., a cousin of E.'s father, Hermann. Her mother was née Fanny Koch, a sister of E.'s mother, Pauline, so that Elsa was a cousin of E. from both his parents' sides.

1920 February 12. Disturbances occur during a lecture given by E. at the University of Berlin. E. states in the press that expressions of anti-Semitism as such did not occur although the disturbances could be so interpreted.

March. E.'s mother dies in E.'s home.

June. E. lectures in Norway and Denmark.

E. and Bohr meet for the first time, in Berlin.

August 24. Mass meeting against general relativity theory in Berlin. E. attends the meeting.

August 27. E. publishes a bitter retort in the *Berliner Tageblatt*. German newspapers report that E. plans to leave Germany. Laue, Nernst, and Rubens, as well as the minister of culture Konrad Haenisch, express their solidarity with E. in statements to the press.

September 8. In a letter to Haenisch, E. states that Berlin is the place with which he feels most closely connected by human and scientific relations. He adds that he would only respond to a call from abroad if external circumstances forced him to do so.

September 23. Confrontation with Philipp Lenard at the Bad Nauheim meeting.

October 27. E. gives an inaugural address in Leiden as a special visiting professor. This position will bring him there a few weeks per year.*

From 1920 on, E. begins to publish nonscientific articles.

December 31. E. is elected to the Ordre pour le Mérite.

1921 April 2–May 30. First visit to the United States, with Chaim Weizmann, for the purpose of raising funds for the planned Hebrew University in Jerusalem. At Columbia University, E. receives the Barnard medal. He is received at the White House by President Harding. Visits to Chicago, Boston, and Princeton, where he gives four lectures on relativity theory.

On his return trip, E. stops in London, where he visits Newton's tomb.

1922 January. E. completes his first paper on unified field theory.

March–April. E.'s visit to Paris contributes to the normalization of Franco-German relations.

E. accepts an invitation to membership of the League of Nations' Committee on Intellectual Cooperation (CIC), four years before Germany's admission to the League.

June 24. Assassination of Walther Rathenau, German Foreign Minister, an acquaintance of E.'s.

October 8. E. and Elsa board the S.S. *Kitano Maru* in Marseille, bound for Japan. On the way, they visit Colombo, Singapore, Hong Kong, and Shanghai.

November 9. The Nobel prize for physics for 1921 is awarded to E. while he is en route to Japan.

November 17–December 29. E. visits Japan.

December 10. At the Nobel prize festivities E. is represented by the Ger-

---

*Einstein again visited Leiden in November 1921, May 1922, May 1923, October 1924, February 1925, and April 1930. His visiting professorship was officially terminated on September 23, 1952.

man envoy, Rudolf Nadolny.* His citation reads, 'To A. E. for his services to theoretical physics and especially for his discovery of the law of the photoelectric effect.'

1923   February 2. On his way back from Japan, E. arrives in Palestine for a twelve-day visit. On February 8 he is named the first honorary citizen of Tel Aviv. On his way from Palestine to Germany, he visits Spain.

March. Disillusioned with the effectiveness but not with the purposes of the League of Nations, E. resigns from the CIC.

June–July. E. helps found the Association of Friends of the New Russia and becomes a member of its executive committee.**

July. E. gives a lecture on relativity in Göteborg in acknowledgment of his Nobel prize.

The discovery of the Compton effect ends the long-standing resistance to the photon concept.

December. For the first time in a scientific article, E. presents his conjecture that quantum effects may arise from overconstrained general relativistic field equations.

1924   As an act of solidarity, E. joins the Berlin Jewish community as a dues-paying member.

E. edits the first collection of scientific papers of the Physics Department of the Hebrew University.

The 'Einstein-Institute' in Potsdam, housed in the 'Einstein-Tower,' starts its activities. Its main instrument is the 'Einstein-Telescope.'

Ilse E. marries Rudolf Kayser.

June. E. reconsiders and rejoins the CIC.

June 7. E. states that he does not object to the opinion of the German Ministry of Culture that his appointment to the Prussian Academy implies that he has acquired Prussian citizenship. (He retains his Swiss citizenship.)

December. E.'s last major discovery: from the analysis of statistical fluctuations he arrives at an independent argument for the association of waves with matter. Bose–E. condensation is also discovered by him at that time.

1925   May–June. Journey to South America. Visits to Buenos Aires, Rio de Janeiro, and Montevideo.

E. signs (with Gandhi and others) a manifesto against obligatory military service.

E. receives the Copley medal.

E. serves on the Board of Governors of the Hebrew University (until June 1928).

1926   E. receives the gold medal of the Royal Astronomical Society

1927   May 7. Hans Albert E. marries Frida Knecht in Dortmund.

October. The fifth Solvay Conference. Beginning of the dialogue between E. and Bohr on the foundations of quantum mechanics.

---

*The prize was brought to E.'s home by the Swedish Ambassador after E. returned from Japan.

**E. never visited the Soviet Union. The association was disbanded in 1933.

1928   February or March. E. suffers a temporary physical collapse brought about
       by physical overexertion. An enlargement of the heart is diagnosed. He has
       to stay in bed for four months and must keep a salt-free diet. He fully recu-
       perates but remains weak for almost a year.
             Friday, the thirteenth of April. Helen Dukas starts to work for E.
1929   First visit with the Belgian royal family. Friendship with Queen Elizabeth,
       with whom he corresponds until the end of his life.
             June 28. Planck receives the first, E. the second Planck medal. On this
       occasion E. declares that he is 'ashamed' to receive such a high honor since
       all he has contributed to quantum physics are 'occasional insights' which
       arose in the course of 'fruitless struggles with the main problem.'
1930   Birth of Bernhard Caesar ('Hardi'), son of Hans Albert and Frida E., E.'s
       first grandchild.*
             May. E. signs the manifesto for world disarmament of the Women's
       International League for Peace and Freedom.
             November 29. Margot E. marries Dimitri Marianoff. (This marriage
       ended in divorce.)
             December 11–March 4, 1931. E.'s second stay in the United States,
       mainly at CalTech.
             December 13. Mayor Jimmy Walker presents the key to the city of New
       York to E.
             December 19–20. E. visits Cuba.
1931   April. E. rejects the cosmological term as unnecessary and unjustified.
             December 30–March 4, 1932. E.'s third stay in the United States, again
       mainly at CalTech.
1932   February. From Pasadena E. protests against the conviction for treason of
       the German pacifist Carl von Ossietzky.
             April. E. resigns for good from the CIC.
             October. E. is appointed to a professorship at The Institute for Advanced
       Study in Princeton, New Jersey. The original intent is that he divide his
       time about evenly between Princeton and Berlin.
             December 10. E. and his wife depart from Germany for the United
       States. This stay was again planned to be a visit. However, they never set
       foot in Germany again.
1933   January 30. The Nazis come to power.
             March 20. In his absence, Nazis raid E.'s summer home in Caputh to
       look for weapons allegedly hidden there by the Communist party.
             March 28. On his return to Europe, E. sends his resignation to the Prus-
       sian Academy. He and his wife settle temporarily in the villa Savoyarde in
       Le Coq sur Mer, on the Belgian coast, where two Belgian security guards
       are assigned to them for protection. They are joined by Ilse, Margot, Helen
       Dukas, and Walther Mayer, E.'s assistant. During the next few months, E.
       makes brief trips to England and also to Switzerland, where he sees his son
       Eduard for the last time. Rudolf Kayser sees to it that E.'s papers in Berlin
       are saved and are sent to the Quai d'Orsay by French diplomatic pouch.

---

*A second grandson died at age six. By adoption, E. also had a granddaughter named Evelyn.

April 21. E. resigns from the Bavarian Academy of Sciences.

An exchange of letters between E. and Freud is published as a slim volume entitled *Why War?*

June 10. E. gives the Herbert Spencer lecture in Oxford.

September 9. E. leaves the European continent for good and goes to England.

October 17. Carrying visitors visas, E., his wife, Helen Dukas, and Mayer arrive in the United States and proceed to Princeton that same day. A few days later the first three move to 2 Library Place.

Ilse and Margot stay in Europe.

1934   Death of Ilse Kayser-Einstein in Paris. Soon thereafter, Margot and her husband join the family in Princeton.

1935   May. E. makes a brief trip to Bermuda. From there he makes formal application for permanent residency in the United States. It is the last time that he leaves the United States.

Autumn. The family and Helen Dukas move to 112 Mercer Street in Princeton.

E. receives the Franklin medal.

1936   September 7. Death of Marcel Grossmann.

December 20. Death of Elsa E.

Hans Albert E. receives a Ph.D in Technical Sciences from the ETH.

1939   Maja joins her brother at Mercer Street, which remains her home for the rest of her life.

August 2. E. signs a letter to F. D. Roosevelt in which he draws the latter's attention to the military implications of atomic energy.

1940   October 1. In Trenton, Judge Phillip Forman inducts Margot, Helen Dukas, and E. as citizens of the United States. E. also retains his Swiss citizenship.

1943   May 31. E. signs a consultant's contract (eventually extended until June 30, 1946) with the Research and Development Division of the U.S. Navy Bureau of Ordnance, section Ammunition and Explosives, subsection 'High Explosives and Propellants.' His consultant's fee is $25 per day.

1944   A copy of E.'s 1905 paper on special relativity, handwritten by him for this purpose, is auctioned for six million dollars in Kansas City, as a contribution to the war effort (manuscript now in Library of Congress).

1945   December 10. E. delivers an address in New York, 'The War is Won but Peace is Not.'

1946   Maja has a stroke and remains bedridden.

E. agrees to serve as chairman of the Emergency Committee for Atomic Scientists.

October. E. writes an open letter to the general assembly of the United Nations, urging the formation of a world government.

1947   Hans Albert E. is appointed professor of engineering at the University of California, Berkeley.

1948   August 4. Death of Mileva in Zürich.

December. An exploratory laparotomy on E. discloses a large intact aneurysm of the abdominal aorta.

1949   January 13. E. leaves the hospital.

Publication of the 'necrology,' written by E., a largely scientific review entitled *Autobiographisches*.

1950   March 18. E. signs and seals his last will and testament. Dr Otto Nathan is named as sole executor. Dr Nathan and Helen Dukas are named jointly as trustees of his estate. The Hebrew University is named as the ultimate repository of his letters and manuscripts. Among other stipulations, his violin is bequeathed to his grandson Bernhard Caesar.

1951   June. Death of Maja in Princeton.

1952   July. Death of Paul Winteler at the home of his brother-in-law, Besso, in Geneva.

November. E. is offered and declines the presidency of Israel.

1954   April 14. The press carries a statement of support by E. for J. R. Oppenheimer on the occasion of allegations brought against the latter by the U.S. Government.

Last meeting of E. and Bohr (in Princeton).

E. develops hemolytic anaemia.

1955   March 15. Death of Besso.

April 11. E.'s last signed letter (to Bertrand Russell), in which he agrees to sign a manifesto urging all nations to renounce nuclear weapons. That same week, E. writes his final phrase, in an unfinished manuscript: 'Political passions, aroused everywhere, demand their victims.'

April 13. Rupture of the aortic aneurysm.

April 15. E. enters Princeton Hospital.

April 16. Hans Albert E. arrives in Princeton from Berkeley.

April 17. E. telephones Helen Dukas: he wants writing material and the sheets with his most recent calculations.

April 18, 1:15 a.m. E. dies. The body is cremated in Trenton at 4 p.m. that same day. The ashes are scattered* at an undisclosed place.

November 21. Thomas Martin, son of Bernhard Caesar, son of Hans Albert, is born in Bern, the first of the great-grandchildren of Albert Einstein.

*By Otto Nathan and Paul Oppenheim.

Name Index

Note: An asterisk (*) after a name indicates that it receives a fuller treatment in the Subject Index.

Subject Index

539